Roberta McCreary

## About the Author

Steve Hodel was born and brought up in Los Angeles. Now a private investigator, he spent almost twenty-four years with the LAPD, most of them as a homicide detective-supervisor. During his tenure, he worked on more than three hundred murder cases, and had one of the highest "solve rates" on the force. He currently resides in the Los Angeles area. Visit his website at www.blackdahliaavenger.com.

## Praise for *Black Dahlia Avenger*

"The most haunting murder mystery in Los Angeles County during the twentieth century has finally been solved in the twenty-first century."
—L.A. County Head Deputy District Attorney Stephen R. Kay

"Crime was rampant as musicals in Los Angeles in the postwar years—this is the age of Bugsy Siegel, the founding of Las Vegas, Mickey Cohen and gun battles on Sunset Boulevard . . . and it's the age of film noir. . . . George Hodel, I think, is fit company for some of noir's most civilized villains—like Waldo Lydecker in *Laura*, Harry Lime in *The Third Man*, or even Noah Cross in *Chinatown*."     —David Thomson, *New York Times Book Review*

"[Hodel] has written an intensely readable account. . . . So what's the final verdict on *Black Dahlia Avenger*? Its accounts of cover-ups and civic corruption are all too believable, and much of the circumstantial evidence it presents against George Hodel is persuasive. . . . Has Steve Hodel solved the case? I think so."     —Jon L. Breen, *The Weekly Standard*

"A must-read."     —*New York Post*

"The book has been described as 'Hannibal Lecter meets *L.A. Confidential* meets *Chinatown*,' but even that Hollywood characterization doesn't do it justice. Former Los Angeles police detective Steve Hodel has written one of the most compelling true-crime books of all time."
—*Seattle Weekly*

"An ex–L.A. cop uncovers a painful answer to the notorious 1947 Black Dahlia slaying. Hodel appears to have solved one of the most sensational murders in the history of Los Angeles."     —*People*

"[Hodel] makes a strong case that the Black Dahlia was part of a larger series of ritual murders that went on for years. This unsparing, chilling account of the actions of a perfect psychopath grips to the end."
—*Toronto Globe and Mail*

"Hodel tells the story well and with incredible objectivity. A real-life tale of a Dr. Jekyll and Mr. Hyde." —*Richmond Times-Dispatch*

"This remarkable book will keep readers riveted from the first page to the very last." —*Tuscon Citizen*

"In this 2003 case study, Hodel declares the case is solved. He offers irrefutable evidence piled fact upon fact as only the mind of a professional detective can present. *Black Dahlia Avenger* is packaged as neatly as a court deposition." —*St. Augustine Record*

"*Black Dahlia Avenger* is a fascinating and horrifying tale of 1940s Los Angeles—as Steve Hodel says, a real-life *L.A. Confidential*." —*San Jose Mercury News*

"The story boasts all the glamour and sinister mystique of film noir." —*The Daily Telegraph* (London)

"Readers must hang on tightly as Hodel hurtles along on his compelling parallel journeys of discovery—a return to the melodramatic days of old Hollywood and a simultaneous plunge into the dark roots of his own family tree." —*London Free Press*

"The best nonfiction book about L.A. crime I have ever read." —Gerald Petievich, author of *The Sentinel* and *To Live and Die in L.A.*

"Los Angeles is the construct of its mythologies good and bad, fact and fiction. The legend of Elizabeth Short is one of the most enduring. Hodel's investigation is thoroughly and completely convincing. So too is this book. As far as I am concerned, this case is closed." —Michael Connelly, author of the *New York Times* bestseller *The Narrows*

# BLACK
# DAHLIA
# AVENGER

# BLACK DAHLIA AVENGER

## *A Genius for Murder*

# STEVE HODEL

HARPER

NEW YORK • LONDON • TORONTO • SYDNEY

HARPER

HarperCollins books may be purchased for educational, business, or sales promotional use. For information please write: Special Markets Department, HarperCollins Publishers, 10 East 53rd Street, New York, NY 10022.

First Perennial edition published 2004.
First Harper paperback revised edition published 2006.

*Designed by API*

Library of Congress Cataloguing-in-Publication Data

Hodel, Steve.
    Black Dahlia avenger : a genius for murder / Steve Hodel.—Rev. ed.
        p.   cm.
    First published in April 2003.
    Includes bibliographical references and index.
    ISBN-10: 0-06-113961-0
    ISBN-13: 978-0-06-113961-1
        1. Short, Elizabeth, 1924–1947. 2. Hodel, George. 3. Murder—California
    —Los Angeles—Case studies. 4. Murder—Investigation—California—Los
    Angeles—Case studies. I. Title.

    HV6534.L7H63 2006
    364.152'30979494—dc22                                      2005059055

06 07 08 09 10 ❖/RRD 10 9 8 7 6 5 4 3

For the victims, living and dead

When I despair, I remember that all through history the way of Truth and Love has always won. There have been tyrants and murderers and for a time they can seem invincible, but in the end they always fall. Think of it, always.

—Mahatma Gandhi

# Contents

# Illustration Acknowledgments

The author would like to gratefully acknowledge the kind assistance he has received from the UCLA Special Collections Department, the Los Angeles Public Library, the Man Ray Trust, and Artists Rights Society.

## UCLA Special Collections files

All UCLA images courtesy of the Department of Special Collections, Charles E. Young Research Library, UCLA
Photograph of Grant Terry/Roger Gardner, page 298
Photograph of Jeanette Walser, page 299

## Man Ray Trust/Artists Rights Society

All Man Ray images copyright © 2003 Man Ray Trust / Artists Rights Society (ARS), NY / ADAGP, Paris
Man Ray, Portrait of Dorothy Hodel, 1944 page 38
Man Ray, George Hodel, 1946 page 79
Man Ray, *Self-Portrait*, page 88
Man Ray, *The Minotaur*, page 241
Man Ray, *Les Amoureux*, pages 241 and 244
Man Ray, *Juliet*, page 242
Man Ray, *The Riddle, or The Enigma of Isidore Ducasse*, page 251
Man Ray, George Hodel and Yamantaka, pages 253 and 265
Man Ray, Dorothy Hodel, Hollywood, 1944, page 299

## Los Angeles Public Library

All LAPL images courtesy of the Herald Examiner Collection / Los Angeles Public Library
Photograph of "Beth Short" telegram, page 156
Photograph of envelope mailed to District Attorney, page 170
Photograph of note sent to *Herald Express*, page 171
Photograph of note sent to *Herald Express*, page 175
Photograph of note sent to *Herald Express*, page 177
Photographs of post cards sent to *Herald Express*, page 178
Photograph of Armand Robles, page 179
Photographs of notes sent to *Herald Express*, page 180
Photograph of note sent to *Herald Express*, page 181
Photograph of envelope addressed to *Herald Express*, page 285
Photograph of LAPD Chiefs Thad Brown and William Parker, page 365

Every effort has been made to contact copyright holders, but if any have been inadvertantly overlooked, the author would be happy to hear from them.

# Foreword

She beckons us.

She's Elizabeth Short. She's a ghost and a blank page to record our fears and desires. She was a flighty child-woman, a roamer, a sweet kid, and a liar. Her iconic noir status shrouds a key truth:

She was her own blank page. She died before she grew up. Her life was her death transmogrified as a riddle. The *real* her only served to fuel speculation: What did she do to attract such devastation?

Elizabeth Short: 7/29/24–1/15/47.

Canonized, damned, and doomed to spark lurid fantasy. A dubious siren and goddess. A postwar Mona Lisa. An L.A. quintessential. A newspaper concoction. A body in a vacant lot and an apparition called "the Black Dahlia."

*After the first death, there is no other.*

That's a Dylan Thomas line. It's Betty Short's murder as metaphor. There are no public deaths as clinically dissected—because there are no public deaths as horrible. There are few public deaths as scrutinized—because the butchery demands that we know who and why. There are few public deaths as singularly misogynistic. There are few public deaths as richly symbolic—this pathetic girl-child as all women.

We can only glimpse who Betty Short was—but now we know who killed her, and why.

The "who" and "why" circumscribe a fifty-seven-year journey. It started on a cold L.A. morning. The crime scene looked like this:

Leimert Park: 39th and Norton. Weed-covered lots north-to-south. The body on the west side, mid-block.

Two inches off the sidewalk, nude, surgically bisected. Marks of protracted torture. The corners of the mouth slashed ear to ear.

The investigation kicks in. The victim is ID'd. The newspapers go wild behind the "Werewolf" savagery. The victim's character is immediately distorted. The signature L.A. murder case assumes lunatic form. Betty Short's death attracts a fifty-seven-year confluence of headline chasers, psycho confessors, voyeurs, and amateur sleuths. Theories are promulgated, theories fizzle behind applied logic. Writers isolate the death and portray it as richly emblematic. Two questions cut through the drama: How could one woman constellate such hatred, and who could perpetrate it?

Now we know.

Betty Short and I go back. My mother was murdered on 6/22/58. I was ten years old then. The crime remains unsolved. My father got me a book for my eleventh birthday. It was called *The Badge*. Actorauteur Jack Webb wrote it. The book detailed the Black Dahlia case. I got obsessed. Betty Short and my mother merged. I entered a world of vivisected women. My 1987 novel, *The Black Dahlia*, attempted to answer the two questions. Fictional embellishment supplied verisimilitude. Another man gave me the hard truth sixteen years later.

Now *I* know.

Steve Hodel grew up in L.A., as I did. He's eight years older. He did not form a childhood bond with Betty Short. He grew up and joined the LAPD. My childhood was bereft and impoverished. His childhood was bereft and baroque. I went at violent death onceremoved, as a writer. He went at it full-bore, as a homicide cop.

We connected in a shared world of Oedipus Rex. We're survivors with dark curiosity. I was the question man. He was the answer man. I was the skeptic. He was the evidence procurer.

Steve Hodel convinced me. His knowledge is conclusively cataloged in this book. I began the book unimpressed, and came away converted. *Black Dahlia Avenger* is a densely packed evidence exhibit and a treatise on the aesthetic of evil. It's a rich story of late-'40s L.A. and an indictment of official negligence and obfuscation. Madness runs equal with redemption. A son addresses his paternal birthright and finds horror.

Unsolved crimes work imaginative magic. Auspicious murders mandate detailed explication. Our need to know runs concurrent with the impact of the death. Motive. Symbology. The victim-killer nexus. Passion, controlled and chaotic. Fluctuating levels of psychic impairment. The parasitic quality of our need to know why.

Steve Hodel transcends the needs of the curiosity seeker and the professional detective. This is the story of a tabloid death and its ramifications up to now and beyond. It's a crusader's notebook. It's a summary report on deaths previously unconnected. It's a narrative that encircles two gifts.

There's the multi-point indictment. It's a purposeful accretion of fact, circumstance, and speculation. There's the portrait of Elizabeth Short—free of innuendo and mythic distortion. This book costs Steve Hodel a father. This book gains him a daughter a generation his senior.

*She lives.*

Sad Betty. Soft Betty. Betty with the urge to move on. Betty—quixotic and outright foolish. Betty—hooked on romance and junk movie-land illusion. Betty and her restless urge to love.

A TV magazine show did a piece on Steve Hodel and his quest. A researcher found a stunning stretch of archival footage. It's L.A. on VJ Day—August '45. Revelers pour down Hollywood Boulevard. It's one long traffic jam. It's Technicolor glare and soaring spirits.

Girls lean out of cars and ride flatbed trucks. Soldiers and sailors run up and grab kisses. There's a pretty, dark-haired girl caught in close-up. It's most likely Betty Short.

I've screened the clip fifty times. I've chosen to believe it's her. Every viewing convinces me more.

There's Betty alive and unmarked by mystification. It's a gift to the man who wrote this brilliant and passionate book. It's a consolation prize for the man who destroyed his patriarchal bond. It's the loving gift of a daughter.

There's Betty. She's young. She's vibrant. *She lives.*

—James Ellroy
1/23/04

# Introduction

For almost twenty-four years, from 1963 to 1986, I was a police officer, and later a detective-supervisor, with the Los Angeles Police Department, a period generally considered to be LAPD's "golden years." I was one of Chief William H. Parker's "new breed," part of his "thin blue line."

My first years were in uniformed patrol. My initial assignment was to West Los Angeles Division, where as a young and aggressive rookie, I was, as Chief Parker had demanded of all his men, "proactive," excelling in making felony arrests by stopping "anything that moved" on the early-morning streets and alleys of Los Angeles. Over the next five years, as a street cop, I worked in three divisions: Wilshire, Van Nuys, and finally Hollywood.

In 1969, I applied for and was accepted into the detective bureau at Hollywood. I was assigned to and worked all of the "tables": Juvenile, Auto Theft, Sex Crimes, Crimes against Persons, Burglary, and Robbery.

My ratings within the detective bureau remained "upper ten," and as the years flew by I was assigned to the more difficult and complex investigations, in charge of coordinating the various task force operations, which in some instances required the supervision and coordination of as many as seventy-five to one hundred field officers and plainclothes detectives in an effort to capture a particularly clever (or lucky) serial rapist or residential cat burglar working the Hollywood Hills.

Finally, I was selected to work what most detectives consider to be the elite table: Homicide. I did well on written exams and with my top ratings made detective I on the first exam ever given by LAPD in

1970. Several years later I was promoted to detective II, and finally, in 1983, I competed for and was promoted to detective III.

During my career I conducted thousands of criminal investigations and was personally assigned to over three hundred separate murders. My career solve rate on those homicides was exceptionally high. I was privileged to work with some of the best patrol officers and detectives that LAPD has ever known. We believed in the department and we believed in ourselves. "To Protect and to Serve" was not just a motto, it was our credo. We were Jack Webb's "Sergeant Joe Friday" and Joseph Wambaugh's "New Centurions" rolled into one. The blood that pumped through our veins was blue, and in those decades, those "golden years," we believed in our heart of hearts that LAPD was what the nation and the world thought it to be: "proud, professional, incorruptible, and without question the finest police department in the world."

I was a real-life hero, born out of the imagination of Hollywood. When I stepped out of my black-and-white, in uniform with gun drawn, as I cautiously approached the front of a bank on a robbery-in-progress call, the citizens saw me exactly as they knew me from television: tall, trim, and handsome, with spit-shined shoes and a gleaming badge over my left breast. There was no difference between me and my actor-cop counterpart on Jack Webb's *Dragnet* or *Adam-12*. What they saw and what they believed — and what I believed in those early years — were one and the same. Fact and fiction morphed into "faction." Neither I nor the citizenry could distinguish one from the other.

When I retired in July of 1986, then chief of police Daryl Gates noted in his letter to me of September 4:

> Over twenty-three years with the Department is no small investment, Steve. However, twenty-three years of superb, loyal and diligent service is priceless. Please know that you have my personal thanks for all that you have done over the years and for the many important investigations you directed. As I am reminded daily, the fine reputation that this Department enjoys throughout the world is based totally on the cumulative accomplishments of individuals like you.

During my years with LAPD, many high-profile crimes became legendary investigations within the department, and ultimately household names across the nation. Many of the men I worked with as partners, and some I trained as new detectives, went on to become part of world-renowned cases: the Tate–La Bianca–Manson Family murders; the Robert Kennedy assassination; the Hillside Stranglers; the Skid Row Slasher; the Night Stalker; and, in recent years, perhaps the most high-profile case of all, the O.J. Simpson murder trial.

Before these "modern" crimes, there were other Los Angeles murders that in their day were equally publicized. Many of them were Hollywood crimes connected with scandals involving early film studios, cases such as the Fatty Arbuckle death investigation, the William Desmond Taylor murder, the Winnie Judd trunk murder, the Bugsy Siegel murder, and the "Red Light Bandit," Caryl Chessman. But in those dust-covered crime annals and page-worn homicide books of the past, one crime stands out above all others. Los Angeles's most notorious unsolved murder occurred well over half a century ago, in January 1947. The case was, and remains known as, the Black Dahlia.

As a rookie cop in the police academy, I had heard of this famous case. Later, as a fledgling detective, I learned that some of LAPD's top cops had worked on it, including legendary detective Harry Hansen. After he retired, all the "big boys" at downtown Robbery-Homicide took over. Famed LAPD detectives such as Danny Galindo, Pierce Brooks, and old Badge Number 1, John "Jigsaw" St. John, took their "at-bats," all to no avail. The Black Dahlia murder remained stubbornly unsolved.

Like most other detectives, I knew little about the facts of the case, already sixteen years cold when I joined the force. Unlike many other "unsolveds," where rumors flowed like rivers, the Black Dahlia always seemed surrounded by an aura of mystery, even for us on the inside. For some reason, whatever leads there may have been remained tightly locked and secure within the files. No leaks existed. Nothing was ever discussed.

In 1975, a made-for-television movie, entitled *Who Is the Black Dahlia?* and starring Efrem Zimbalist Jr. as Sergeant Harry Hansen and Lucie Arnaz as the "Dahlia," was aired. It told the tragic story of a beautiful young woman who came to Hollywood during World War II to find fame and fortune. In 1947 she was abducted and murdered by a madman, her nude body cut in half and dumped in a vacant lot in a residential section, where a horrified neighbor discovered her and called the police. A statewide dragnet ensued, but her killer was never caught. This was all I and my fellow detectives knew about the crime. Fragments of a cold case, fictionalized in a TV movie.

On several occasions during my long tour of duty at Hollywood Homicide, I would answer the phone and someone would say, "I have information on a suspect in the Black Dahlia murder case." Most of the callers were psychos, living in the past and caught up in the sensationalism of decades gone by. I would patiently refer them downtown to the Robbery-Homicide detail and advise them to report their information to the detective currently assigned to the case.

Despite the near-legendary status of the Black Dahlia, neither I nor any detective I knew ever spent much time discussing the case. It had not occurred on our watch. It belonged to the past; we belonged to the present and the future.

Law enforcement has learned a lot since the 1960s, when the first serious attempts were made to identify the phenomena known as serial killers. Earlier, with the exception of a few forward-thinking investigators scattered throughout the country, most cases were characterized in the files of their local police departments as separate, unrelated homicides, especially if they happened to cross jurisdictional and territorial boundaries between city and county. For example, a murder on the north side of famed Sunset Boulevard would be handled by LAPD, but if the body had fallen ten feet to the south it would become the responsibility of the Los Angeles Sheriff's Department. As recently as the 1980s, these two departments rarely if ever shared information, modus operandi, or even notes on their unsolved homicides.

Today, experts in the fields of criminology and psychology are light-years ahead of their counterparts of even a decade ago in dealing with serial killers. Law enforcement officials have become much more aware and effective in their ability to connect serial crimes. Advances in education, training, communication, and technology, particularly in forensics and computerization, have made today's criminal investigator much more aware of crime-scene potentials. He has "gone to school" on the Ted Bundys, Jeffrey Dahmers, and Kenneth Bianchis of the world. Through their independent analysis, joint studies and pooling of data, through interviews and observations, recognized experts in this highly specialized field have fine-tuned what we thought we knew, and have expanded on the old ideas.

Modus operandi, once recognized as only the most general of patterns, has now been broken down into specialized subgroups. Sexually sadistic murderers are categorized as "signature killers," and that category in turn has several subtypes, depending on the specific act or acts of violence.

These experts have assigned new names to old passions that are crime-specific, and have attempted to identify individual psychotic behavior and link it to actions found at the scenes of multiple homicides. Connections are made by identifying conscious or unconscious actions performed by the killer. These actions are so specific that they reveal him or her to be the author, or "writer," of the crimes. Hence the term "signature."

Today, many more crimes are being connected and solved as police and sheriff's departments across the nation open their doors and minds to the information and training made available.

That there exists a mental-physical connection to the commission of crimes is neither startling nor new. Every investigator is familiar with the old maxim of "MOM," the three theoretical elements required to solve a murder case: motive, opportunity, and means. There are numerous exceptions to this rule, especially with today's apparent alarming increase in acts of random violence, such as drive-by shootings. Nonetheless, motive remains an integral part of the crime of murder.

Most murders are not solved by brilliant deduction, à la Sherlock Holmes. The vast majority are solved by basic "gumshoeing," walking the streets, knocking on doors, locating and interviewing witnesses, friends, and business associates of the victim. In most cases, one of these sources will come up with a piece of information that will point to a possible suspect with a potential motive: a jealous ex-lover, financial gain, revenge for a real or imagined wrong. There are as many motives for the crime of murder as there are thoughts to think them.

Our thoughts connect us to one another and to our actions. Our thought patterns determine what we do each day, each hour, each minute. While our actions may appear simple, routine, and automatic, they really are not. Behind and within each of our thoughts is an aim, an intent, a motive.

The motive within each thought is unique. In all of our actions, each of us leaves behind traces of our self. Like our fingerprints, these traces are identifiable. I call them *thoughtprints*. They are the ridges, loops, and whorls of our mind. Like the individual "points" that a criminalist examines in a fingerprint, they mean little by themselves and remain meaningless, unconnected shapes in a jigsaw puzzle until they are pieced together to reveal a clear picture.

Most people have no reason to conceal their thoughtprints. We are, most if not all of the time, open and honest in our acts: our motives are clear, we have nothing to hide. There are other times, however, when we become covert, closeted in our actions: a secret love affair, a shady business deal, a hidden bank account, or the commission of a crime. If we are careful and clever in committing our crime, we may remember to wear gloves and not leave any fingerprints behind. But rarely are we clever enough to mask our motives, and we will almost certainly leave behind our thoughtprints. A collective of our motives, a paradigm constructed from our individual thoughts, these illusive prints construct the signature that will connect or link us to a specific time, place, crime, or victim.

Solving Los Angeles's most notorious homicide of the twentieth century, the murder of a young woman known to the world as the Black Dahlia, as well as the other sadistic murders discussed in this book, is the result of finding and piecing together hundreds of separate thoughtprints. Together with the traditional evidence, these thoughtprints make our case more than fifty years after the event, and establish beyond a reasonable doubt the identity of her killer, the man who called himself the "Black Dahlia Avenger."

# 1

# The Biltmore

**January 9, 1947**

IT WAS MID-WEEK, Thursday evening at 6:30 P.M. There were only a handful of people milling around the Biltmore Hotel lobby, scanning for the bellhops to take them up in the elevators. Few noticed when the strikingly beautiful young woman with swirling jet-black hair was escorted into the lobby by a nervous young red-haired man, who stayed for a while, then said goodbye and left her there. Maybe one or two guests observed the woman as she went up to the front desk, where she begged for attention from a young desk clerk who avoided her stare until she spoke up. She stood there, shifting her weight from one foot to the other, watching the clerk riffle through a stack of messages below the counter. He shook his head, and the young woman made her way silently across the deep red carpet to the phone booth, as if she'd been through the place a hundred times before. A couple of people turned to look at her when she hung up the receiver with a loud click.

Now, as she stood outside the phone booth, she seemed crest-fallen, almost desperate. Or maybe it was fear.

Again she walked over to the desk, then back to the phone booth, endlessly fidgeting with her handbag and looking around as if she were waiting for someone. A date? More people began to notice her. Perhaps she was a newly discovered actress or just another wannabe scratching at the door of fame to get herself in. She didn't look L.A. Maybe she was from San Francisco. She looked more like Northern California — well dressed, buttoned up, edgy, her fingers twitching nervously inside her snow-white gloves.

Increasingly, people in the lobby couldn't keep their eyes off her, this woman in the black collarless suit accented by a white fluffy blouse that seemed to caress her long, pale white neck. A striking presence, she looked a lot taller than most of the people in the lobby that night, probably because of the black suede high-heeled shoes she was wearing. She was carrying a warm full-length beige coat, a portent of the approaching January chill that creeps along Wilshire Boulevard from the ocean every night at the leading edge of the raw, swirling fog.

As the lobby began to fill, each man who passed her, seeing her standing alone with a look of expectation on her face, was sure she was waiting for someone special. Her eyes seemed to widen a bit every time a new guy in a suit came through the door. And each man probably wished in his heart of hearts that he was the Prince Charming she was waiting for that night, probably for a late dinner or dancing at one of the Hollywood clubs.

As time passed, the young woman became increasingly anxious. Where was he? She sat down. She stood up. She paced the lobby. The woman with no name walked over to the check-in clerk at the front desk and had him change her dollar bill to nickels. Again she went into the phone booth and dialed a number, this time more frantically than before as she snapped the rotor with a loud click between each digit. She slammed down the receiver. Still no answer. Where *was* he? She slumped into one of the lobby easy chairs and nervously thumbed through a magazine without reading. Every ten minutes or so she once again went over and made a phone call. What kind of man could keep such a beauty waiting?

One hour turned into two. If you were watching her face from across the lobby, you would have seen her jaw tighten, her anxiety turn to anger. He was always like that, late when you wanted him to be on time, early when you wanted him to be late. It was all his way. She thought about that afternoon in early December, just a month ago, when he'd told her — ordered her was more like it — to meet him at the Ambassador Hotel, Los Angeles's grand dame, west of downtown on Wilshire Boulevard. "Meet me for a drink at five," he had said.

That time he had forced her to suffer through a three-hour wait at the bar. She had sat there spinning on her red barstool, playing with swizzle sticks, nursing her ginger ales and Cokes, and batting away the advances of seven men, from the twenty-three-year-old

bartender to the wealthy real estate broker in his seventies with a
Palm Springs tan that made his face look like leather. The remaining
five guys had thought she was a high-class hooker or possibly a bored
housewife, all dressed up and looking for a little fun. She had suffered a sugar high that night, she complained, after all those sodas
she had drunk at the bar just waiting for him. When he finally
showed, it was without apology. "I was delayed." Arrogant and
simple, just like that. And she took it, too.

That was then. She said to herself she wouldn't take it again. It
was late now, pitch-black outside. The bright lights inside the Biltmore lobby sparkled as if they were still greeting the New Year. The
beautiful young woman thought about the past eight months. She
had expected them to be great when she came back to L.A. from
Massachusetts. She'd marry Lieutenant Right and raise a family. But
it didn't happen that way.

Then things got worse and she was becoming afraid. Maybe the
New Year would bring her better luck.

She dropped another nickel into the payphone and redialed the
office number just a few short blocks from where she stood. Finally
he picked up. "Yes, I'm here," she said with a show of irritation. "At
the Biltmore. I've been waiting well over two hours. Yes, all right,
I'm on my way." She hung up, and her demeanor immediately
changed. She was radiant.

She walked east through the lobby, stopping first at the concierge
desk to look at the large calendar, next at the front desk where she'd
checked for messages when she came in, and then down the interior
steps toward the Olive Street entrance. The doorman held open the
large, ornately designed glass doors for her, and she stepped out into
the chill darkness of a California midwinter's night. She turned back
one last time toward the hotel, noticed her reflection in the glass
door, and straightened the large flower that shone like a white diamond pinned atop her thick black swept-back hair. She paused
briefly to straighten it, smiled at the onlookers who stared at her
from inside the glass divide, and then turned south, walking toward
6th Street into the deepening fog that curled around her like smoke,
making it seem as if she were disappearing into the night. The darkness had a life of its own, folding her into itself.

# 2

# Jane Doe Number 1

*Dahlia: From the family Asteraceae, bred as an ornamental flower whose leaves are often segmented, toothed, or cut.*

THE MORNING OF JANUARY 15, 1947, was especially cool and overcast for Los Angeles. At about 10:30 A.M., a woman walking with her young daughter caught a glimpse of white flesh through a clump of brown grass in a vacant lot. She turned and saw what she figured was a body lying right there in the dirt, just a few inches from the sidewalk's edge. She ran to a nearby home and called the University Division police station.

Even though the communications officer on the other end of the line tried to get her name, in her excitement the woman never gave it, so dispatch assigned the call to a patrol unit as a "possible 390 down in the lot at 39th and Norton Avenue." A 390 is a stuporous drunk. Nobody knew yet that they were dealing with a corpse. The lot in question was in the Leimert Park section of Los Angeles, a middle-class, residential neighborhood west of downtown in LAPD's University Division. The glamour world of Hollywood lay just five miles to the north, a short ten-minute drive away.

When the call went out, it wasn't just to the patrol unit ordered to respond, it was also to a whole cadre of newspaper reporters cruising their beats, with police radios in their cars crackling out cryptic messages to LAPD patrol units. In 1947 it was as common for the newspaper reporters to monitor the police and fire radio bands on receivers hanging under the dashboards in their private cars as it is for today's reporters to carry handheld digital scanners on their belt clips. If you were a reporter working an L.A. beat in the 1940s you bought the most powerful police radio you could find and the longest whip antenna for your car, in the hope of being the first at a crime, fire, disaster, or any other newsworthy event. Even reporters working for the same paper raced one another to a location at the mere scent of a possible story, because a byline for a reporter meant ownership. And that, too, hasn't changed since the 1940s.

*Los Angeles Examiner* reporter Will Fowler, son of the famous writer Gene Fowler, and his photographer partner Felix Paegel caught the call from University Division dispatch just as it was broadcast over the police radio and were the first to arrive at the scene. Before any police officers pulled up and posted men to guard the crime scene, Fowler and Paegel were standing there, two eyewitnesses gaping not at a drunken man but at a naked corpse lying spread-eagled in the grass. Fowler later described what he had seen that morning in his book *Reporters: Memoirs of a Young Newspaperman:*

> Then an ivory-white thing caught my eye. "There she is," I said. "It's a body all right."
>
> There's something about a dead body you couldn't mistake. I approached it like I half-expected it to jump up and run after me.
>
> As I got closer, I called back to Paegel, who was pulling his Speed Graphic from the car trunk: "Jesus, Felix, this woman's cut in half!"
>
> It's difficult to describe two parts of a body as being one. However, both halves were facing upward. Her arms were extended above her head. Her translucent blue eyes were only half-opened so I closed her eyelids.

As Fowler knelt over the dead woman in the moments before the police arrived, he could see that her fingernails had been poorly cared for, and her chestnut hair, as it appeared from the roots, had been dyed jet black. He also could see that the woman's lower thoracic vertebrae had been neatly severed — not sawed — because he could see no evidence of bone granules at the separation.

Paegel began documenting the crime scene itself, taking a shot of the body in the barren field and another of Fowler, all alone, stooping beside the body. The photos, which would be published later that same day in the *Los Angeles Examiner*, were retouched by the photo artist, because the editors wanted to spare their readers the shock of the grisly brutality of the victim's condition. The photo artist covered up the lower part of the woman's body with an airbrushed blanket. He also concealed the gruesome facial wounds the victim displayed by removing the deep slashes on either side of her mouth.

While Paegel was shooting his photographs, the first black-and-white arrived at the scene. The two uniformed officers approached Fowler, not knowing at first who he was, until he showed them his police ID. One of the cops had already pulled out his gun. As more units arrived, Fowler left the scene for a phone booth to call in the story to his city editor, James Richardson. When Richardson heard the victim had been cut in half, he ordered Fowler back to the office right away with the negatives. The photo was quickly processed, and Richardson made the decision to beat the other afternoon papers with an "extra" that he got out onto the street even as Fowler returned to the crime scene for a follow-up.

By now the scene was alive with other reporters, more police units, and detectives who had positioned the uniformed cops and some of the reporters into a human strip of crime-scene tape. Word had spread over the police radios that a woman had been murdered, cut in half, and dumped. That brought an onslaught of reporters, elbowing their way past one another for a closer look at the body. By the time the two crack homicide detectives Harry Hansen and Finis Brown, who had been assigned to the case by Captain Jack Donahoe, arrived at the scene, not only did they have to contend with the groups of reporters and photographers, but also with uniformed officers from the divisions adjacent to the University Division in whose jurisdiction the responsibility for the case belonged.

The crime scene remained open to the press, with photographers free to roam at will for the best shots. Today a crime-scene investigator would never permit the press to trample on what might be evidence and photograph a murder victim lying in the open. But conditions were very different in 1947 Los Angeles. Police and press were interdependent, and in a sense were very real partners. Most reporters carried police badges and often impersonated detectives to get the real stories any way they could. The press needed the power and the doors that were opened by carrying a badge, and the police needed the press to make them look and sound good, even when they screwed up. Before the days of access journalism and a hostile media, reporters and the police in 1947 Los Angeles formed a mutual admiration society.

Whenever investigating detectives asked the press to hold back certain information they didn't want made public, editors and reporters would almost always comply. When a well-connected reporter asked for certain confidential information from the police on a person for a story he or she was working on, the reporter would usually get it. In such a quid pro quo world you broke the rules at your own peril. In this case, the crime-scene photographs of the butchered body would be held back from the public by the press for almost four decades until, it seemed, nobody cared anymore, and the graphic untouched images of the victim's body finally found their way into print. The first public display of these photographs of which I'm aware was in Kenneth Anger's book *Hollywood Babylon II*, published in 1985. More followed, six years later, in Will Fowler's *Reporters*, showing the body at different angles and with longer perspectives.

The photographs from both these books verified for the first time that the body was lying supine, cleanly bisected at the waist. Carefully examining the photographs: the two separated halves lie in close proximity, although the upper torso appears to have been placed asymmetrically, approximately twelve inches above the lower portion and offset to the left by approximately six inches. Both of the victim's arms are raised above the head, the right arm at a forty-five-degree angle away from the body, then bent at the elbow to form a ninety-degree angle. The left arm extends at a similar angle away from the body, and then bends again to form a second ninety-degree angle that parallels the body. This was no normal "dumping" of a victim to get rid of a corpse quickly. In fact, the body had been carefully posed, just six inches from the sidewalk, at a location where the victim was certain to be discovered, to create a shocking scene.

This kind of cold and conscious act was exceptionally rare in 1947. According to criminal researchers, it occurs in less than one percent of all homicides even today. Most veteran homicide investigators, even those who've been involved with hundreds of murder cases, never see an instance where the body is posed the way the victim was that January morning.

As reporters arrived and left and more police units reported in, detectives and forensic crews continued to collect whatever physical evidence they could find. Among the pieces of evidence they retrieved was a paper cement bag with small traces of what appeared to be water-diluted blood on it. This bag, clearly visible in the photographs, was lying just six inches above the victim's outstretched right hand, and one detective speculated that it had been used to carry the two sections of the body from a parked car at sidewalk's edge to the grassy lot.

Police noted a vehicle's tire prints at the curb's edge, close to the body. There was also a bloody heel print from what was believed to be a man's shoe. Later newspaper reports revealed that these two important pieces of evidence were not secured or photographed by the on-scene detectives.

Detectives Hansen and Brown quickly determined that, due to the absence of any blood at the scene, the killer had committed the crime elsewhere, then transported both halves of the body to the empty lot on Norton. No identification was found at the location and the victim was initially listed as "Jane Doe Number 1."

The Los Angeles newspapers were already running wild with the story when, the following morning, Dr. Frederic Newbarr, then chief autopsy surgeon for the County of Los Angeles, performed the autopsy. His findings showed the cause of death to be "hemorrhage and shock from a concussion of the brain and lacerations of her face." He determined further that "the trauma to the head and face were the result of multiple blows using a blunt instrument."

It was clear to the medical examiner that not only had her body been neatly and cleanly bisected, but that a sharp, thin-bladed instrument, consistent with a surgeon's scalpel, had been used to perform the operation. The incision was performed through the abdomen, and then through the intervertebral disk between the second and third lumbar vertebrae. The bisection had been carried out with such precision that it was apparent it was the work of a professional, someone trained in surgical procedures. Police criminologist Ray Pinker confirmed the medical examiner's opinion, and later his findings were confirmed after a study he made with Dr. LeMoyne Snyder of the Michigan State Police.

Dr. Newbarr's preliminary estimate set the time of death within a twenty-four-hour period prior to the discovery of the body, thus establishing the time of the murder as sometime after 10:00 A.M. on January 14.

But who was the victim?

On January 16, 1947, the *Los Angeles Examiner* offered this questionnaire:

## Description of Dead Girl Given

Do you know a missing girl who chewed her
    fingernails?
If so she may be the victim of yesterday's
    mutilation slaying.
The dead girl's description:
Age — Between 15 and 16 years.
Weight — 118 pounds.
Eyes — Gray-blue or gray-green.
Nose — Small turned up.
Ears — Small lobes.
Eyelashes — Virtually colorless.
Hair — Hennaed, but original dark brown grow-
    ing out.
Foot size — 6-1/2.
Toenails — Enameled pink.
Scars — 3-1/2 inch operational scar on right
    side of back: 1-1/2 inch scar on right
    abdomen, possible appendectomy; vaccina-
    tion scar, left thigh; small scar on left
    knee and another above the knee.
Moles — Six small moles on back of neck below
    collar line; another in small of back.
General description — Rather well developed,
    small bones with trim legs.

Scrambling for any piece of the puzzle that would allow the winner of the who-is-Jane-Doe-Number-1 contest to emblazon the victim's name in a full-page headline, the city editor of the *Los Angeles Examiner* suddenly had an idea. In a meeting with LAPD detectives, he made an offer that was immediately accepted — to transmit the fingerprints of Jane Doe Number 1 via an early photo facsimile machine called a "Soundex" through their proprietary communications network to their Washington, D.C., bureau. Reporters in the D.C. office had FBI agents standing by to transport the fingerprints immediately to their records section for identification. That the city editor's motive was to be the first one on the street to carry her identity didn't matter, for the detectives were as hungry for information as the press.

A memo to J. Edgar Hoover, dated June 24, 1947, and now available to the public under the Freedom of Information Act, identifying Jane Doe Number 1, speaks for itself:

FBI MEMO
I. I #590

June 24, 1947

## SOUND-PHOTO TRANSMISSION OF FINGERPRINTS LEADS TO IDENTITY OF ELIZABETH SHORT

During January, 1947, the police in a Southern California city were not only confronted with the problem of solving mad butcher murders of women, but in the first instance were many times unable to determine the identity of the victims.

When the body of a young woman, severed at the waist and mutilated in other ways, was found in a vacant lot in Southwestern Los Angeles on the morning of January 15, 1947, they were again confronted with this problem. It appeared she had been dead about ten hours and the body had been placed in full view only a few feet from the sidewalk. The authorities were practically at a standstill in their investigation until the deceased victim could be identified.

The fingerprints of the body were taken by the police, who then sought the cooperation of the

*Los Angeles Examiner* newspaper to transmit the fingerprints by wire photo to the FBI Identification Division in Washington, D.C. Eliciting the aid of the International News Service, the newspaper transmitted the prints to its Washington headquarters. At 11 a.m. on January 16 the pictures were received by the Identification Division. Within 56 minutes an identification was established with two fingerprint cards previously on file bearing the name of Elizabeth Short.

Despite the fact that two of the impressions were missing entirely and three others were badly blurred, FBI fingerprint technicians were able to make an identification by searching all possible fingerprint combinations. At this time there were approximately 104,000,000 fingerprint cards on file.

One of the fingerprint cards submitted and identified as that of Elizabeth Short indicated that Miss Short was an applicant for a position as a clerk in the Post Exchange of Camp Cooke, California, on January 30, 1943. The other set was submitted by the Santa Barbara, California, Police Department reflecting her arrest on September 23, 1943, on charges of violating juvenile court laws, after which she was released to the probation department.

The successful use of scientific communications equipment in this case was referred to by the Director of the FBI as follows: "The action of the *Los Angeles Examiner* in transmitting to the FBI the fingerprints of the unidentified murder victim is an excellent illustration of the cooperation of the press with law enforcement, and it is such cooperation that aids law enforcement in curbing the increase in crime."

As the FBI memo indicates, within hours of the transmission the victim's prints were connected to an arrest in Santa Barbara, a coastal community some ninety miles north of Los Angeles, where three years earlier in September 1943 the victim had been detained as a minor for being present with adults where alcohol was being served.

That arrest report provided Los Angeles police with the necessary information about her identity and background.

Her name was Elizabeth Short. The Santa Barbara police report from 1943 described her as a female, Caucasian, born July 29, 1924. Her mother, Mrs. Phoebe Short, resided in Medford, Massachusetts. As a result of the records the LAPD assembled, detectives were able to establish a background and history on the victim prior to her arrival in California.

They learned that Elizabeth was born in Hyde Park, a suburb of Boston, and grew up in nearby Medford. Her mother was the sole provider for Elizabeth and her four sisters after their father, Cleo Short, abandoned the family in 1930 and eventually wound up working and living in Southern California. Elizabeth was exceptionally attractive and well liked at Medford High School, but she dropped out in her sophomore year and in 1942 moved to Miami Beach, Florida, where she got a job as a waitress.

It was in Miami, on her own for probably the first time, that she met a Flying Tigers pilot named Major Matt Gordon Jr., who was stationed there. He was shortly sent overseas, and Elizabeth began to correspond with him, reportedly sending him twenty-seven letters in eleven days.

In January 1943, Elizabeth traveled to Santa Barbara, California, where she applied for and was hired at the post exchange at the Camp Cooke military base. Her employment there was brief, after which she left to seek her father, who, she discovered, was living close by, in Vallejo, California. She stayed with her father briefly, but both were uncomfortable with the living arrangements, and she returned to Santa Barbara in September 1943.

Elizabeth liked servicemen and wanted to be around them. Her attraction to men in uniform was clear both from her relationship with Major Gordon and her desire to attend nightspots and clubs frequented by military personnel. It was in such a nightspot that she was arrested on September 23, 1943, because alcohol was being served there and she was only nineteen, in violation of California's liquor law. When she agreed to return home rather than face charges in California, Santa Barbara County probation authorities provided her with a ticket to return home to Medford.

During the rest of the war years, Elizabeth continued to write Major Matt Gordon, and in April 1945 he reportedly proposed marriage. Elizabeth accepted, but before Gordon could return home he was killed in a plane crash in India. Elizabeth Short's marriage plans, and hopes for any future she might have had as an officer's wife, went down in flames with Major Gordon's plane.

During the winter of 1945, Elizabeth remained on the East Coast, and again traveled to Florida, where she took a job as a waitress in Miami Beach. In February 1946, she returned home to Medford and worked as a cashier at a local movie theater, but on April 17, 1946, returned to California, this time to Hollywood. During the nine-month period preceding her death, Elizabeth was known to have lived as a transient at various boardinghouses and with a variety of roommates. She stayed at a hotel in Long Beach for several weeks during the summer months and then returned to Hollywood, where she first shared a room in a private residence, then lived in an apartment with seven other young women. She also shared rooms at several hotels in Hollywood for brief periods. In December she left for San Diego and returned to Los Angeles on January 9, 1947. That was the night she disappeared into the fog after leaving the Olive Street entrance of the Biltmore Hotel.

Subsequent to the discovery of the victim's body, and after many of the descriptive details from the autopsy findings were leaked to the press, not only Los Angeles but the entire country became obsessed with Elizabeth Short's murder. Before the age of the Internet, twenty-four-hour-cable news networks, or television, much of the interest in a mysterious, beautiful murder victim was driven by page-one newspaper headlines and radio announcers. Feeding the public's intoxication with the victim was her sobriquet "the Black Dahlia," which reporters claimed was given her by the men and sailors who saw the attractive black-haired young woman frequent their favorite pharmacy soda fountain in Long Beach.* Along with this name the

---

*It was later speculated that the original source for this name was *The Blue Dahlia*, a Raymond Chandler–penned murder mystery, starring Alan Ladd and Veronica Lake, released and screened in L.A. in the summer of 1946.

newspapers printed blown-up high-school photos of the exotic young woman. This, combined with the horrific details of sadistic torture, bisection, and mutilation, fed the macabre imaginations of newspaper readers from coast to coast.

The ongoing murder investigation remained on page one of the Los Angeles newspapers for a record thirty-one successive days. The January 16 first-day edition sold more newspapers than any other edition in the history of the *Los Angeles Examiner*, with the sole exception of VE Day. This Los Angeles frenzy was also driven by the fierce competition among the six newspapers in the city, as the Hearst syndicate, which owned the *Examiner* and the *Los Angeles Evening Herald and Express*, vied with the Chandler empire, publisher of the *Los Angeles Times* and its tabloid the *Los Angeles Mirror*. Most rounds went to the *Los Angeles Examiner*, whose night city editor had sent the victim's fingerprints to the FBI for quick identification, thus gaining initial favor with LAPD and the investigating detectives.

In truth, the crime reporters were usually way ahead of the detectives, especially when it came to locating and interviewing witnesses. They didn't punch the time clock at five o'clock, but kept on working until they had the story. Reporters also worked for newspaper owners who had deep pockets and paid whatever it took to get a big story on the streets first. If it meant paying cash to help out a witness who was going through a rough patch, a reporter could always get the money. Then, after he'd called in the story, he'd turn over what he had learned to his friendly detective on the force. Thus both the police and the press had the power to get things done for each other. For the most part they tried to share their findings, but ultimately it was an uneasy partnership.

All of these factors were at work in the Black Dahlia case, to such an extent that the reporting of and publicity about her murder were unparalleled in Los Angeles history. Even the Lindbergh kidnapping or the Leopold and Loeb murder trials had not taken up as much local media space. The public was so voracious for any news that reporters spread out across the nation for background on Elizabeth Short. They located and interviewed her family, close friends and acquaintances, roommates and classmates, ex-lovers, and military men. With few exceptions, almost every detail these crime reporters discovered through their independent investigations, no matter how ir-relevant, turned up in print the next day and helped keep the public's seemingly insatiable appetite fed.

After a full month of daily headlines, the Dahlia homicide had found its place as the most notorious unsolved murder of the century.

# 3

# A Death in the Family

**May 17, 1999, Bellingham, Washington**

WHEN THE PHONE RINGS at one in the morning, you hope it's a wrong number. If it's not, it's usually bad news. And that's what it was for me on Monday, May 17, 1999: a hard ring, an insistent ring that wouldn't go away because my answering machine was off, and it woke me from a deep sleep. June, my father's wife, was hysterical on the other end, screaming into her receiver at their penthouse suite in San Francisco. "Steve," she said, trying to regain some composure, "your father. He's dead!" Between her sobs I could pick up snippets of what had happened. "Heart attack. Paramedics still here. Your brother Duncan and his wife are here with me. Come down. Please come down now. I could have saved him, Steven. I should have done something more. I am all alone now."

When I was an LAPD homicide detective, I taught myself how to wake up instantly in the middle of the night when we had to roll out to a call. It was a skill I'd lost over the years since I retired, but it came back to me as June kept talking. I tried to reassure her that we would take care of things, offering her whatever comfort I could over the phone. "I'll be there on the first flight I can get, June." It was the best I could do. I made coffee and got on the phone to find a seat on the first flight to San Francisco from Seattle, some ninety miles south of my home in Bellingham, where I had been living for the past twelve years.

Eight hours later I was boarding the plane at SeaTac airport, looking forward to two hours of time alone to ruminate upon the passing of "the Great Man." The grief and the loss that I felt, that all sons feel at the death of their father, was mixed with the satisfaction

I had from knowing that his life had been long and remarkable. His life, as much as I knew of it, had been unique, much larger than that of most people I knew. George Hill Hodel, M.D., who seemed to have lived four lifetimes, had been held in awe by all of his children from all four of his families. And now he was gone.

As the plane lifted through the cloud cover and carried me toward the passage that almost all sons must inevitably make (the burial of their fathers), I felt oddly grateful that I had been granted the opportunity to repair a relationship with a father I had never really known. There were only snatches and pieces of memory from my childhood in our mysterious Hollywood house, and then, after he had left, nothing.

Now I was fifty-seven. But my relationship with my father had really begun only eight years earlier. Before that the two of us had been strangers, sharing a hello once in a while over the phone or a handshake now and then when I visited him in Asia or when he was passing through L.A. on business. For thirty-five years there had been brief encounters in hotel lobbies, but ours had never been a real father-son relationship.

What we had had were business meetings, where his stiff and formal demeanor was as offputting to me as it was to all his children. To us, he was the "doctor" — clinical, cold, and remote. It struck me as passing strange that my father, with his brilliant mind and extensive training as a psychiatrist, was so obviously uncomfortable among his children. In lectures, using his vocabulary and wit, he was able to charm and hypnotize whole audiences with his charismatic personality and as a leader in his field. Yet in the role of father he was painfully awkward and inept. This paradoxical disconnect, however, actually gave life and body to the eccentricities that made him a distant legend to all of his children. And I was no exception, having lived in the same house with my father in Hollywood in the late 1940s and then twenty-five years later spending time with him in the Philippines when he wanted to woo me away from LAPD Homicide and groom me to take over his business. But that was more than twenty years ago.

Over the ensuing decades, after my retirement and a subsequent career as a P.I. specializing in criminal cases, I had begun to make a breakthrough into the mystery of my father. Slowly, gradually, since his return to the United States in 1991 after a forty-year absence, I had established the beginnings of a relationship with him. I was almost fifty and he was eighty-four.

I believe my change of career had helped us in some ways. I knew that he had on occasion worried about my personal safety. But now I was no longer the metropolitan homicide detective waiting for the midnight callout to a Hollywood murder. No more six o'clock news interviews with the L.A. press reporters who wanted to be assured that "an arrest is imminent." Those glory days were behind me now. I liked retirement. I liked my new work as a P.I. I liked the fairness of it all. It had been twenty-four years for the prosecution and almost fourteen years for the defense. A recent major victory for an innocent client was still reverberating through my psyche. My life was moving toward a natural homeostatic balance. And now, seeing my face reflected in the airplane window at 35,000 feet against a cloudscape so thick you were sure you could walk on it, that balance was upset and all I could feel was a hole where the past had been. I kept picturing my father over the years: the young 1920s crime reporter, the bohemian artist, the silky-voiced radio announcer, the meticulous surgeon, the austere but dominating psychiatrist, and finally the entrepreneurial marketing genius who had moved to Asia in 1950, abandoning all of us.

My father and I couldn't have been more different. My job as a street detective in the Hollywood Homicide Division had taught me how to size up and read a person's character. I was good at it, and most of the time I was right about people. I made lots of mistakes about other things in life, but rarely was I wrong about people. My judgment was intuitive and accurate, partly developed, partly inherent.

Where Dad was rock, I was water. My father was clinical, almost bloodless in his dealings with people. If he was intuitive, it was so far below the surface you wouldn't even know it was there. He was a hard and cold individual with a huge ego whose demeanor bordered on the tyrannical. "King George," friends called him in jest, but it was true. Perhaps his demeanor was the result of his many years of living in the Orient, in Manila, where there are just two classes — the very rich and the very poor. But I think not. I think it was always there, always a part of him. He was a man I had not liked even when he telephoned me out of the blue with what he said could be the offer of a lifetime.

In 1973, he had asked me to come to Manila and take a look at his business. He had said, "Come over and take a look at what I have built in Asia. Come over and consider the possibility of working for me, Steven." By then he had built market research offices in Manila, Hong Kong, Tokyo, and Singapore, and his offer was tempting. I was single again and, at thirty-two, with no children, I was free to remake my life. Visions of exotically beautiful women, along with palatial living quarters, danced like sugarplum fairies in my head at night. So I took six weeks' leave of absence from my work at Hollywood Homicide. I wanted to get as clear a picture of the operation as possible.

By then I had been promoted to detective. It would have been a huge decision if I had chosen to leave LAPD and give up my pension when I was already halfway around the track. Here I would not be my usual impulsive self. Not on something so important that it would affect the rest of my life. So I took a leave to explore my father's world and a life that was waiting for me if I chose to embrace it.

The six weeks in the Orient were totally indulgent. This boss's son was spoiled rotten and catered to beyond his dreams. But beneath the excitement, the fun, and the entertainment of it all, I knew it could not be. I simply could not work for such a man. His over-sized business cards with his near-imperial title said it all: "Doctor George Hill Hodel, Director General." He was a control freak, and I would not subordinate myself to him. I felt like a player in a big-stakes poker game, holding only a pair of sevens and knowing there was a much stronger hand in the game. I folded.

But by the 1990s, all that had changed. He was no longer the megalomaniac of old. He became the prodigal father returning to his native soil, changed and reformed. Now at eighty-three, his fires still burned strong, but not with the white heat of twenty-five years earlier. He was different now, settled into a final long-term marriage with June, whom he had married in 1969. With her encouragement he had exchanged much of his robber-baron lifestyle for a slower, more comfortable existence, more in keeping with his advancing years. By the time he returned to the United States from his expatriate years in Asia, he was more forgiving and accepting. And so was I.

Our attempts at a new relationship were gradual, tentative, and laborious at first, typically expressed through faxes and notes. It was the start of communications between us that would grow stronger as

the trust built. As the years followed I would make increasingly regular trips to visit Dad and June in San Francisco, and they, in turn,
would make occasional trips north to Bellingham to visit me and to
explore the beauty of the San Juan Islands in Puget Sound.

For the first time in our adult lives together, quality father-and-
son time would go beyond the formalities of a business meeting and
take on the aspect of something social and even human. Now our
gatherings would even contain some laughter, and I would be permitted brief glimpses at the man who had always walked through life
behind an iron mask. It would only be a peek, though, and the occasions were rare, but it was enough. I could see that my father, after so
many years of being a stranger to his son, was beginning to mellow. I
had made a breakthrough with him. Though he still felt awkward
and uncomfortable talking about feelings and things of the heart, I
knew I could finally begin to broach some personal and honest top-
ics with him so as to touch on what to me was the only truly important thing in life as far as I was concerned — communication and
relationships. But it was too little too late.

Just a week before my father's passing, I was concerned about his
health. I had heard nothing by fax from him or June for quite a while.
I'd invited them to come up during the summer, stay with me for a
week or so, and we could make the short drive to Vancouver, Canada,
for sightseeing and day trips.

Sensing that his health was failing or something else was amiss, I
faxed them and asked him directly about his physical condition. On
May 9, 1999, I received the following fax:

May 9, 1999

Dear Steve:

Thanks for your fax of yesterday May 8. Your photos also arrived yesterday and are great depictions of your beautiful new
home, and we do wish that we could see it with you.

There is a reason why you haven't heard much from us for the
past few months. We certainly miss seeing you for prolonged periods such as this.

The fact of the matter is that I have been going through a particularly difficult situation in regard to my overall health. We have not wanted to expose to you or to anyone else the full extent of my present debility and overall weakness and general helplessness. This would be humiliating, and could leave a much tarnished image in your minds.

I am now wheelchair-bound, and cannot get around without a great deal of help from June, plus the wheelchair and rolling walker. On the rare occasions when I must go out to see a doctor we also need the help of a hired limo with a strongly built driver.

None of this comes as an actual surprise to me. The overall clinical picture is just about what we would normally expect in a patient who has moved on into the final terminal phase of congestive heart failure. The clinical fact is that I have simply lived a few years too long.

Let me assure you that this thought does not frighten me in the least. For example, I am going into the hospital tomorrow, Monday, for a procedure, which is called cardiac retroversion. This consists of applying two strong electric shocks to the heart, in an attempt to change its present arrhythmia (disturbance of heart rhythm), which in my case is known as "heart flutter" into a more normal rhythm.

But if this and other corrective procedures fail, I shall not be saddened. I have been fortunate enough to lead a very full and interesting life and to know some truly wonderful women and to have some very fine children of whom I am truly proud. The most recent few years have been among the happiest in a long life, thanks to the remarkable help given by June, who is indeed an angel.

In the meantime, June and I send you our love.

                                        George and June

In light of that fax, and intuiting that the end could possibly be near, even for this man considered by all of his children to be an immortal, I felt an urgency to speak from my heart, and mailed a letter to him the following morning.

May 9, 1999

Dear Father:

Thank you for giving me an honest and accurate picture of your current health condition. I very much appreciate it, and know how difficult and naturally reluctant you are to do that, for many valid reasons. Your communication, of course, will always remain confidential. Personally, I appreciate knowing things as they are as opposed to how others or I may wish them to be.

I want you to know that for me, likewise, the past six or seven years have been the happiest. While I have gone through many difficult personal life-changes, emotional adjustments regarding Marsha and the boys, yet I have been extremely happy and content.

The reason for that happiness was the development of our relationship as father and son. Our relationship, yours and mine, has grown and developed and become *real* to me. It was not always so. For many reasons beyond both of our control, we did not have the opportunity to share our thoughts. This was neither your fault nor mine. It simply was *what was*.

But in these past years, thanks to your openness, acceptance, and encouragement it became something real. It was like a reverse of the normal course of a father-and-son relationship. Ours was in my youth, distant, and now has become close. I thank you for that.

And I thank you, Father, for your support and patience in me and of me. I thank you for your wise guidance and advice over the past years. Your positive promptings for me to improve my health in many ways. (I think your encouragement in getting me to quit smoking has probably added ten or fifteen years to my natural life and health.)

Mostly, I thank you for your time. Some wise man said that "Time is our most priceless possession." And of that you have given me much in these recent years. I look on my computer over the past six years and see hundreds and hundreds of faxes and communications from you. Each one requiring your time and your thought.

The memories I have of visits here and there are warm reminders of these years, and will be with me while I breathe and think. Thank you for those, dear Father. I don't want this to sound like a goodbye. But if fate should make it so, then mostly I want you to know how much I love you and how grateful I am to you for the gift of life and for the time we have shared together.

You are truly a great man, and I am very proud that you are my father.

ALL MY LOVE
Steven Kent

My father read this on the final day of his life. And now, just twenty-four hours later, the flight attendant was motioning to me to raise my table to the upright position in the minutes before we made our final approach to San Francisco airport.

The uniformed driver met my arrival at gate 33 with a sincere, "I'm so sorry about your father. He was a special man. Very few like him in the world." I nodded in the polite acknowledgment of his condolences. We drove in silence to downtown San Francisco to their condo, some forty floors above the financial district in the heart of the city.

June was in tears when she met me at the door, and we embraced in our sorrow. I held her as she spoke softly in my ear, "I'm all alone now. I'm so afraid. He didn't have to die, Steven. I thought we would be together for another ten or more years. He died in my arms. I tried to save him but I couldn't." She was shaking and looked near death herself, pale and thin as if his death had drained her of life. I could feel her tremendous grief mixed with the fear of having to go it on her own from now on, after having been under George Hodel's protection and absolute control for thirty years. The apartment seemed woefully empty. No radiant voice, no great intellect, nothing. And that nothingness shouted out the absence of the man. Her man.

The two of them had been inseparable for the thirty years they had been together. During all of that time they had never been apart for more than a day or two, and that mostly for business purposes. Together they had shared 11,000 sunrises, and now, with him gone, the sun would never rise again for her in the same way.

June Hodel, my stepmother, was younger than I by about four years. She had been graduated *ichiban*, at the top of her college class in Japan. Bright, eager, and beautiful, she had answered an advertisement Dad had placed in the Tokyo newspaper for a personal secretary and girl Friday. June had beaten out hundreds of competing applicants for the job working directly for my father.

Getting the job wasn't easy, because Dad personally administered the battery of tests to her, as he had all the other applicants. The tests measured her personality, intelligence, and familiarity with English. At the conclusion of the tests she was told she "would be contacted sometime in the future." A week later the phone call came. And again, as she had been in college, she was *ichiban* — number one.

She took the job and moved from her southern province of Japan to the Tokyo office, away from her home and family for the first time. From that point on, from age twenty-three, she and my sixty-three-year-old father would remain inseparable, working and traveling throughout the world together. They would reside in Manila, Tokyo, and Hong Kong. They would travel to dozens of foreign countries throughout Asia and Europe, and ultimately move to San Francisco, where they remained inseparable. Then, finally, a few minutes before midnight in mid-May, he would gasp for air, collapse in her arms, and die.

Now June would be alone for the first time in her fifty-four years. It was a terrible feeling for her. And in those hours after my father's death when I was holding her there in a sorrowful embrace, I could feel the totality of her loneliness. And I feared for her.

We spent that afternoon and late into the evening talking about "the Great Man" and what a remarkable life he had lived. And despite my previous eight years of conversations with him to reestablish our relationship, I realized I actually knew very little about him — as did the rest of his children. Like the Wizard of Oz, he had been the all-powerful figurehead behind the curtain. But in reality, who was he?

My father's father, George Sr., was born in Odessa, Ukraine, and fled to Paris near the turn of the century. There he met Esther Leov, a dentist, and they married. Like most immigrants, they came through Ellis Island. Then they traveled west to California.

Dad was born in Los Angeles in 1907. I knew that he was a musical prodigy, that he had played his own piano compositions at age seven or eight in the Shrine auditorium, had a genius IQ — one point above Einstein's, I was told — and later went to medical school in San Francisco. He returned to Los Angeles, opened a successful

medical practice, married my mother, had children, and moved us all
to the historic Lloyd Wright Sowden House, on Franklin Avenue in
the heart of Hollywood.

After a family scandal, my father divorced my mother and moved
to Hawaii, where he became a psychiatrist. Then he moved to the
Far East and married a wealthy Filipina woman with whom he had
four children. Ultimately he became a famous market researcher and
respected social scientist with offices throughout Asia.

This was virtually all I knew — just fragments. When my father
and I got to know each other during the last years of his life, much of
his past, particularly as it related to me and my brothers, still remained a mystery. His children from other marriages probably knew
less than I, but that was his way — secret and private — and I respected it. I figured his business was his business and if he chose not
to share it with others, even his family, that was his choice.

Even when he had begun to open up with me during his final
years, what he said about his life was still very general, but it had
taken a new direction. I took it to be more of an attitudinal change
than specific information. Our time together was slower, softer, and
gentler, in stark contrast to the brisk lunch meetings of earlier years,
where my two brothers and I would receive a last-minute summons
to meet him for lunch near L.A. airport, "between flights," where he
would give each of us five minutes to "update him on our lives."

During those last years, when I tried to share my thoughts, feelings, and reflections on life with both my father and June, they
seemed to appreciate my openness, but it was never fully recipro-
cated. Weren't Renaissance men like that — guardians of their secrets? At least that's what I thought. Now I guessed that probably no
one ever knew the real George Hodel, not even his widow.

After consoling June, I returned to my San Francisco hotel room
late that evening filled with an increased sense of loss. For most of
the afternoon I'd been a homicide detective, dealing with someone
else's grief. Now my own feelings moved to the forefront as I finally
realized my father was gone. Whatever wars would have to be fought
between father and son, whatever unresolved issues still lingered in
the air, would remain. From this point forward I'd have to deal only
with his memory and the unanswered questions in his life that would
remain the province of ghosts. At that moment, I too felt the great

sense of aloneness that I knew June was feeling. And as I stretched out on the bed in my hotel room, I was overcome with a melancholy sense of the passage of time, of lost opportunities, and above all the loss of my father.

All of us have our own special days in life, days that relate directly to the core of our being and have the same sign hanging on them, saying, "Private, Keep Out." We usually see such days only in retrospect; only later do we recognize them as turning points in life. May 18, 1999, would be just such a day for me.

On that day I returned to Dad and June's penthouse suite early in the morning, remarking to myself how beautiful the morning sun could be in San Francisco with its promise of a complete renewal. Standing there in the living room, looking eastward, I could see both the Oakland Bay and Golden Gate Bridges, appearing as if by magic through the early-morning fog hanging low over the bay as it was dissipated by the sun. It was a sight that for a moment dissipated our own sadness. But June's sobs as she went through my father's personal effects broke into my reverie.

She was still in a state of shock and emotional trauma. She still blamed herself, believing she could have done something to save him, torturing herself by asking, "What if I had checked on him sooner? What if I had taken him in for a checkup? What if he hadn't gone to have the arrhythmic procedure done? What if the paramedics had arrived sooner?" I had no words to console her. "It was his time, June," I repeated. "He lived a long and wonderful life. Ninety-one years filled with adventure and travel is much more than most men have. The thirty years you shared with him were much more than you could have expected. And they were only possible through your love and care."

But I saw my words gave her no comfort. She wasn't functioning, and I realized I would have to make all the arrangements. My first priority was to notify the rest of his children, my sibling and half-siblings. Father had had ten children from four marriages. Seven of his children were still living. His eldest son, Duncan, now seventy and semi-retired, lived a short distance away in a San Francisco suburb. His second-born was a daughter, Tamar, who was now living in Hawaii. Then there were the four children from my mother. Michael, my older full brother, had died in 1986. I was a twin, and my brother

John had died a few weeks after he was born, his death ascribed to "failure to thrive." Kelvin, eleven months my junior, was living in Los Angeles. Then there were Dad's children from his marriage in the Philippines: Teresa, Diane, Ramon, and Mark. Ramon had died of AIDS at age forty, just four years earlier.

Each child was duly notified; still to be decided were the precise funeral arrangements. I asked June if my father had left any instructions; I found it hard to believe he had not. She looked at me blankly, then without saying a word handed me a paper she had pulled from her files. I read from the formally typed page on his attorney's letterhead:

### FUNERAL AND BURIAL INSTRUCTIONS

TO WHOM IT MAY CONCERN:

I do not wish to have funeral services of any kind. There is to be no meeting or speeches or music and no gravestone or tablet.

I direct that my physical remains be cremated and that my ashes be scattered over the ocean. There are several crematories in San Francisco which provide these services.

If I die in a foreign country, cremation and scattering of my ashes may be carried out in that country, or the ashes may be shipped to San Francisco for disposition, with the choice to be made by my wife JUNE, or if she is unavailable, as the executor of my will shall decide.

/s/ George Hill Hodel

DATED: June 16, 1993

"Well, June, there is certainly nothing vague about that," I said. "No funeral services of any kind, no meeting, no speeches or music, no gravestone or tablet." That said it all. My father and I had never discussed religion or philosophical matters, so I asked June, "Was Dad an atheist?" She didn't answer.

Dad's body had been transported to the mortuary, and his personal physician had already signed a death certificate indicating that the cause of death was "congestive heart failure due to ischemic cardiomyopathy." The cremation was scheduled for a few days later.

"I'll tell my brothers and sisters of his stated wishes," I said to June. "And there will be no funeral of any kind. I guess each of us can in our own way and in our own time say our goodbye to Father." Again June didn't answer. It was almost as if she had become a robot, running on some computer program. As I read his words, a shiver had gone down my spine: I swear I felt Dad's presence in the room. I thought to myself that, even after death, he was dictating and controlling the situation. His will be done.

Next on my list was to notify the various businesses: the banks, credit card companies, the Social Security Administration — all a part of the ritual of one's passing from this world. It didn't take me long to complete the notifications, at which point I turned to June again and asked, "What about notifying his personal friends? I will be happy to make those calls for you. I know you're not up to speaking to anyone right now." Her face remained blank as if, again, my words had not registered. "What personal friends need to be called?" I repeated.

She shook her head. There were none. Not one. They had no personal friends. Oh, there were business associates, many of them over the years, who would be sorry to hear the sad news. But personal friends, social friends: none. While June did not seem to be upset by this, the news pained me deeply. The man had lived a long and remarkable life. After a distinguished medical career, he had also been publicly recognized as one of the world's leading experts in his field of market research. If I was to believe June, there was not one personal friend to notify.

This was a revelation, underscoring the finality of the man's death. I realized that there would be no monument to his existence, no celebration of his life. No funeral, no family, no words, no gravestone, no shared remembrances, and no friends to give voice to the impact my father had had on their lives. Not even his children, separated by his serial marriages, by thousands of miles and a score of years, would ever share a moment of silence to respect the life of their father. Other than June, who had been all things to him — lover, friend, confidante, and caregiver — Dad had completely isolated himself from the world of human affection and emotion.

In life, George Hill Hodel had been raised to mythic proportions by all of his children. Therefore it stood to reason that there was a common, if unvoiced, speculation about his wealth. Perhaps it ranged from a low of several million, to vast amounts of monies secreted in offshore accounts and hidden holdings. While I had indulged in my own speculative accounting based on my observations of their lifestyle during my father's last years, I still didn't know the truth of their financial state. Then June handed me a copy of the will. I had overestimated. His worth would not exceed a million. Comfortable, but, alas, a secret coffer of treasure from his lifetime's work, bulging with bags of gold and jewels from the ancient Orient, did not exist. Father had left a small amount of inheritance to each of his living children in equal shares, and the rest of his estate was to go to June. Probate would be simple, handled by Dad's longtime San Francisco lawyer, who had been named executor. His office was just minutes away and I scheduled an appointment to meet him the following afternoon.

That evening was spent reminiscing. June's tears would not, could not, subside, as if they were cleansing a pain that would not leave her. As we talked, I was amazed at how hungry I was for information about Father, anything that would tell me more about the man as opposed to the myth. I realized that June was my only source. She alone knew the truth or truths. She alone could help me bridge the gap to intimacy with him

I felt our friendship, and our mutual need for emotional support, could possibly open the door that had been locked for over five decades. I knew that only June had the key to his heart, and I wanted it. Badly.

June was cautious. As we spoke about him and their shared lives over the decades, I could sense how tentative she was, as if she were trying to avoid a real conversation. I knew this wasn't her nature. I could feel she wanted to open up, share her innermost feelings. But the reluctance, foreign as it was to her personality, remained dominant, and I quickly got the impression that her responses to me were conditioned. As if she had been programmed not to speak about things personal and private. As she spoke, I could feel Dad's presence coming through her. She was hesitant, secret, aloof, and cautious with me. Was this an Asian cultural response to dealing with grief that kept mourners from sharing emotions? I'd never seen it before, particularly when as a P.I. I worked with my Japanese colleagues on criminal cases. Maybe it was only specific to widows. I didn't know, but I also sensed there was something deeper — and it didn't have anything to do with grief.

I walked to the corner of the living room with its wall of glass. It was almost midnight now, and the evening was clear and in sharp focus. The tall buildings below us shone, even with just a few of the many offices still lit. Behind the buildings the dark bay reflected the lights on the broad spans of the suspension bridges, and headlights still moved across them, hundreds of people going on with their lives as I tried to figure out what to ask June next.

I turned back to the room at the sound of June's footsteps across the carpet as she approached and handed me a small object I had not seen before. It was a tiny, palm-sized wood-bound photo album, with twelve golden fleurs-de-lys imprinted on the front. It appeared quite old; my guess was at least nineteenth-century. I hefted it, thinking how much heavier it was than it looked. The little book in my hand had a power to it, almost like a talisman. I took it over to a coffee table where I sat down and opened it and paused as my eyes fell upon a picture of Father and me. June saw me smile and looked away, allowing me a moment of privacy.

### *Exhibit 1*

*George Hodel's private photo album*

I was looking at a picture I had never seen before. I was two years old, sitting on my father's knee. The photograph would have been taken in Hollywood sometime in 1943 and had been cut from a larger photo to fit the small size of the page in the album. Across from it was another picture of my two brothers, Michael and Kelvin. It was the other half of the photograph of Father and me, and both Michael and Kelvin were sitting on our half-brother Duncan's knee. Duncan was a strikingly handsome young man of about seventeen then. He must have been down visiting us from San Francisco, where he was living with his mother and stepfather.

### *Exhibit 2*

*Steven, Father, and Kelvin . . . Kelvin, Duncan, and Michael*

The next page held a portrait photo of my mother, strikingly beautiful and exotic. Yet one could see the sadness in her face. It had always been there. Rarely had I seen a photo of her that did not capture that terrible sadness, her soul crying out from within her, as her eyes revealed the truth of her unhappiness.

*Exhibit 3*

*Dorothy Hodel*

I paused and wondered; was it the unhappiness within her that had made her into the alcoholic she became, or was it her alcoholism that made her eyes so sad? She too was dead, and it grieved me to think about the shipwreck of her life, wasted as it was, all its enormous potential cast away. I turned the page.

The next picture was of my grandfather, George Hill Hodel Sr., who died in Los Angeles sometime in the early 1950s, after our father had left for Asia. Years later, Mother described his funeral. She said she was amazed that so many strangers and people she did not know had come to pay their last respects. "It was as if a movie star or some celebrity had died, except he was not a celebrity." She hadn't known any of these people nor why they had come.

*Exhibit 4*

**George Hodel Sr.**

When I turned the page again, I froze, gazing at two photographs of a very young Eurasian woman. In one she was wearing what looked like Native American clothing. These two pictures were of my ex-wife, Kiyo, taken when she was barely out of her teens, years before she met me at a Hollywood party. Mother, who had introduced me to Kiyo, had mentioned that they had known Kiyo during the war, but why would my father include her pictures here?

*Exhibit 5*

**Kiyo**

Two more women. Another Asian woman, a Filipina, also taken in her youth. The picture resembled his ex-wife, Hortensia — whom I'd met in Manila in the early '60s. This must have been a photograph taken at an earlier time, perhaps when they lived in Hawaii, in the early 1950s.

The facing page showed a young woman and her dog.

*Exhibit 6*

It seemed as if time itself was out of place in this photo album. There were photos of my mother, looking exotically Eurasian in her setup for the picture, then a photo of Kiyo, who was Eurasian, dressed as a Native American. What was my ex-wife doing among these family photos? I had no idea, but I found it disturbing. And then I turned the page.

Here were two photographs, both of a vividly beautiful dark-haired woman. She was as young and vivacious, her presence reaching out to you across the years, making you believe for a moment that you could step through the frame and be there with her. The right-hand photo was apparently a nude, artistically taken, from her shoulders up. Her eyes were closed as if in a delicate sleep, a sleep of light dreams. In the other photo she was standing next to a Chinese statue of a horse, her eyes also closed, but now she was fully clothed. How exquisite she looked, with two large white flowers in her swept-back black hair and wearing a collarless black dress. I couldn't take my eyes off her. As if she were calling out to me from a moment in time most likely at the end of World War II. I could almost hear the music of a big band. Maybe I could ask her to dance, and she would say yes.

*Exhibit* 7

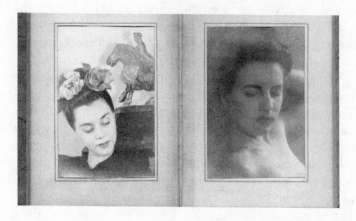

I turned the open album around to June's eyes and asked, "Who is this?" She glanced at the photograph. "I don't know. Someone your father knew. Someone your father knew from a long time ago." June rose from the table, hands shaking, reached for the box on the glass table, and withdrew several white tissues. She turned and walked out of the living room back toward her bedroom. "I'll see you in the morning, Steven," she said. "Goodnight, and thank you for being here."

I was gripping the small album as tightly as I could, not wanting to let it out of my sight. I hadn't figured out how or why, but the album had opened a door into some strange past, almost like a parallel world that had mingled with my own. I felt like a voyeur, as if I were looking directly into another man's heart. In these pages Father had clearly assembled those who were most dear to him. His father, my brothers, myself, two of his four wives, and Duncan his firstborn. But who were these other women? What were my ex-wife Kiyo and this unknown woman's photographs doing here?

As I walked the slow mile back to my hotel through the early-morning fog that covered San Francisco, I tried to understand but could not.

The feelings that were beginning to take shape in my mind were of an old familiar nature. I had felt them hundreds of times in the past. They were very real and very strong and they spoke to me directly. They were my intuitions, and I knew by their strength and power that they were centered in reality. I couldn't identify what reality. But I knew I was only feeling what had already been perceived and understood by some other mind. We were in touch, maybe even across the boundary of death, linked by the photos in my father's secret album. My mind refocused on those two posed photographs of the beautiful dark-haired young woman.

The Sir Francis Drake Hotel loomed up over me out of the fog and darkness. What was it about those pictures? Now she was almost a remembrance. Her hair, the flowers, her dress and style from the forties — all were aspects of someone I strained to remember. But nothing came. But I felt I did know her and had seen her somewhere in the past. Where?

As if in a dream, I walked through the empty lobby of the hotel to the elevators. I entered the waiting car as the doors closed behind me and I felt no motion and heard no sound until the bell rang for the eighteenth floor.

I unlocked the door and a shaft of light from the hall illuminated a cobalt vase of freshly arranged white flowers on my bedside table. A sweet smell of lavender filled the room. I stared at the white flowers caught in the shaft of light, white flowers against the black of night.

I tried to fight the meaning that was trying to break through to tell me what my father's photographs meant. My cop's mind grabbed onto it like a bulldog and wouldn't let go. Were these photographs of her — the one with her stylized black dress and white flowers, and the other one nude — taken by my father? Why had he kept them all these years in his private album?

Then, quietly, softly, as if a breeze were carrying an image from long ago, I remembered the white flowers against the jet-black hair, white flowers set off against a black dress. These were dahlias.

And like a bouquet of flowers overpowering the confines of a narrow room, the realization suddenly filled my conscious mind: it was she, the Dahlia. The Black Dahlia.

# 4

# A Voice from Beyond the Grave

I HAD TO LEAVE SAN FRANCISCO because of my upcoming testimony in court for a case that I was working on as a private investigator. There was nothing more I could do in California, because Father had been specific about how he wanted his remains to be handled, and his wishes, bizarre as they seemed, would be respected. The Neptune Society would take his ashes to sea on their next scheduled burial, and his final wish would be satisfied. All that remained of him would be dispersed, as if he thought that would erase all marks of his presence on earth.

I said my final goodbye to June and promised her I would return within the month to help her get through what for her was a catastrophe. I had seen death visit many lives, but I'd never seen anyone so alone and lost as June.

As I waited for Father's regular limo driver to take me to the airport, June handed me a piece of white paper that contained a full page of Father's handwriting. "This was written by your father about the time of his last birthday," she said. "They are his notes to me. Last October he believed his heart was about to quit and he prepared these notes. They were for a talk he was going to have with me but never did, because his health improved. I found them in his desk. Some I understand, others I do not. You're a good detective, maybe you can help me decipher them. It is important that I know everything he wanted to say to me."

I assured her I would do my best. I would review the notes and call her in a few days. Just then the driver arrived, and with a tearful *sayonara* I was out the door and headed home for what I hoped would be relief from the overpowering sorrow that permeated everything about June and my father's condo.

By being strong and supportive with June, I was also working my way through my own mixed feelings. Just as I was beginning to develop a relationship with him, my father was gone. For the second time in my life, events beyond my control had snatched him away. I felt anger and frustration at the lost opportunity, but I also believed that something had been accomplished in our awkward attempts to close the fifty-year gap in our lives.

Back in Washington, I took a few days off, to let the impact of Father's death and my dealings with June wash over me. I allowed myself to enjoy the solitude of my house on the lake, using the free time from appointments to prepare my case for trial. Then I turned to my father's photo album and the materials June had given me on my final day in San Francisco.

First on the agenda was the picture. Was it really the woman known as the Black Dahlia? I ran a quick search of the photos on the Internet and found what I was looking for almost at once. There she was, a complete digital photo album in itself, accessible by just a few

*Exhibit 7 (enlarged)*

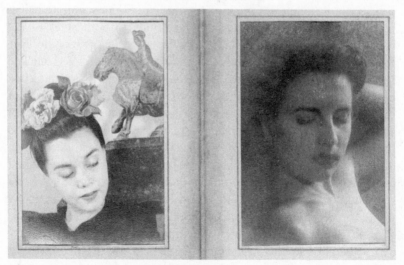

*Elizabeth Short*

keystrokes. I studied the face on the screen: high cheekbones, up-turned nose, jet-black hair with its distinct hairline above the high forehead, her unusual diamond-shaped face. No question: it was she.

On page 45, Elizabeth's photographs are enlarged from Father's album. In the right photograph she appears to be nude, eyes closed. In the left, again eyes closed, she is wearing a collarless black dress with white flowers in her hair. Judging from the background Chinese statuary, these were most likely taken in our Franklin Avenue home.

After this identification, I immersed myself in the history. I backgrounded myself to make sure that I was up to speed with the thousands of Black Dahlia "fans" who, I was surprised to learn, were still contributing information to the different websites. The main Dahlia website (www.bethshort.com) had been established by a writer and journalist, Ms. Pamela Hazelton. It was there that I began my research on the murder. The website provided a mixed bag of information quoting so-called Dahlia experts.

Ms. Hazelton's website also had photo links to the crime and various photos that had been taken by the police or newspaper photographers at the Norton Avenue site. First there was a close-up photograph depicting the victim's body, neatly bisected, the torso placed just a foot or so to the left of and above the lower half. In other photos I could see the incisions and mutilations on both halves of the body as well as extensive lacerations to both sides of the mouth. It looked as if the killer had carved a hideous grin on her face for some reason, which only he could understand. As I clicked through the different photos, I tried to understand how a detective could have leaked or sold these photos to the public or press. But there they were: detailed shots of the brutalized, desecrated body of a twenty-two-year-old woman, on display for the world to view. I was outraged, even though I realized that these photos had been taken over fifty years ago, long before the Internet, long before digital computers, even a year before the transistor was invented.

But my rage was short-lived, quickly overtaken by the enormity of what I had discovered in my father's photo album. First, those two photographs of Elizabeth Short appeared to be more or less contemporary with other photos of her just prior to her disappearance and murder. In both pictures her eyes were downcast and closed. It was clear that she had agreed to be posed this way. But why had Father kept these two photographs for more than fifty-two years in an album, where Elizabeth Short held a place of honor with the rest of those he loved?

Fragments of memory started to fit together. I remembered his overwhelming need to dominate and assert control, especially when it came to the many women in his life. He had left each of them in turn: first Emilia, then Dorothy Anthony, then my mother, whom he nicknamed "Dorero," and then his wife in the Philippines, before he finally settled down with June. He had obviously controlled June, who now seemed completely incapable of taking care of herself.

I knew there might be, and doubtless were, perfectly innocent answers to all of my questions. He could have known Elizabeth Short in the weeks or months before her murder and even taken the photographs of her. Maybe they had even been lovers, which Father had never revealed after she was murdered because he was afraid of becoming a suspect for a crime he didn't commit. There were, I was sure, rational answers to all my questions, and I determined to be objective in resolving them. I could not allow my emotions to come into play.

What would I do as a private investigator if a client came to me with a similar set of circumstances? How would I proceed? The obvious answer: handle it just like I had all of the other homicide investigations I had conducted during my career. It would require a simultaneous, two-pronged strategy: a thorough background check into all available information on the possible suspect, and a parallel check on the victim. There was a lot I didn't know. First, what was Father's real background? I knew generalities, but few specifics. What could I discover about his activities over fifty years ago? Who was left to tell the story? Could I find witnesses and records? What was still available?

I needed to figure out just how much June knew about her husband. I remembered her response when I asked her who the woman was in the two pictures. "Just someone your father knew from a long time ago." She only spoke of Father as a loving, compassionate man.

But June surely would have known something about Father's earlier life. He must have shared with her at least some of his experiences in their long years together. She could help me in my background search, help plot a timeline of his life. My questioning of his past would not be a form of interrogation, but would come from my sincere desire to know the man. If she sensed or suspected that I was looking for something more than that, I knew I would get nothing from her. My search must proceed slowly, with great caution.

The second approach was to find out all I could about the real Elizabeth Short, not just the newspaper creation named the Black Dahlia. I had to track her movements through Los Angeles and California as far back as I could, to connect her to the murderer through mutual friends, relatives, or surviving witnesses. Maybe there was still some physical evidence. Maybe I could find fingerprint evidence or even come up with a DNA match.

I began my investigation by reviewing everything that was publicly known and available, including every old newspaper article, magazine, and book. But I was at a disadvantage relative to my other homicide investigations, because I had not been at the crime scene, nor could I review the investigative notes of the officers who had. I also did not have access to the LAPD homicide file, called a "murder book," that is started on every murder in Los Angeles. I was no longer an active detective, simply one of thousands of retired L.A. cops, so I would not benefit from any of the special privileges, free access, or any of the other door-openers that came from carrying a badge and a gun. But I also knew I had a lot going for me on this one. I had a real advantage: a hot lead in the form of two pieces of evidence that quite possibly had never surfaced in the original investigation.

On June 2, 1999, June Hodel carried out her husband's final instructions. Holding in her lap a green urn containing the ashes and sole worldly remains of the man she had loved for thirty years, she cried as the small ocean craft, the *Naiad*, powered through the fog, passing under the Golden Gate Bridge. A mile more and it was finished. Father's ashes cast to sea, his body returned to the elements. She called me in Bellingham early that afternoon to inform me it was accomplished, just as he had instructed her, alone and without ceremony or words.

At the same time June was scattering Father's ashes, I was setting off to see what I could discover about his mysterious past. I was confident that if I looked long and hard enough, I would find answers to the many questions that were nagging me.

My initial search for information about Elizabeth Short on the

Internet would eventually be expanded to include personal interviews with some of Dad's friends and acquaintances from that time,
along with my own family members, some of whom I had not spoken
to in many years. I would read published statements of credible witnesses who claimed to have actually seen Elizabeth Short in the week
she had been presumed missing. Additional interviews with witnesses in Los Angeles would provide me with some actual physical
evidence, which, I believe, relates to the crime. Eventually, I would
review hundreds of archival microfilm articles from all the major
newspapers of that time and request and receive FOIA material, including the complete dossier on Elizabeth Short, which included
FBI interviews of 1947 witnesses and her associates.

In order to put the case in a historical context, I read the three
most relevant published books on the Dahlia case: *Severed*, by John
Gilmore (1994), *Daddy Was the Black Dahlia Killer*, by Janice Knowlton
and Michael Newton (1995), and *Childhood Shadows*, by Mary Pacios
(1999). I later read James Ellroy's *The Black Dahlia*, even though it is
a work of fiction, because Ellroy based it on fact, using some real
names. I felt it was important to review each of these authors' theories and evidence, to determine if any of them had a real suspect.

After carefully reviewing the contents of each book I can say with
authority that none of the three nonfiction works provide any hard
evidence pointing to a viable suspect. The authors' conjectures and
efforts at building circumstantial cases against their three separate
suspects are exceptionally weak, devoid of any physical evidence linking them to the murder. Mary Pacios's book was the most helpful to
me as I began my investigation, because her extensive documentation of sources and references permitted me to check and recheck
many of the facts I had discovered through my own investigation.

Perhaps the most frustrating aspect of the Black Dahlia case is
the many distortions of fact that have surrounded the few kernels of
truth from the very beginning of the 1947 investigation.

The LAPD's official position on the murder of Elizabeth Short is
that the case remains "open." Though it may be a cold case — one in
which there has been no activity for decades — it remains on the
books and is handed off to one of the division's newest transferees
into Robbery-Homicide. As far as the public is concerned, the LAPD,
after interviewing hundreds of witnesses and spending thousands of

man-hours, is no closer now to identifying any suspect(s) than it was
after the first few months of intensive searching, which back in 1947
involved a thousand Southern California lawmen.

Harry Hansen remained on the investigation from January 15,
1947, until his retirement twenty-three years later. In March 1971
Hansen granted an interview, which was published in the *Los Angeles
Times*, entitled "Farewell, My Black Dahlia," in which he confided
that over the decades he eliminated hundreds of potential suspects
and false confessors by asking a "key question." Hansen was convinced the suspect might be a male with medical training.

> It was a clean, definitely professional job. You have to know exactly
> how and where or you just can't do it. When I asked medical au-
> thorities what kind of person could have performed that bisection,
> they said "someone with medical finesse."
>
> The killing seemed to be based on unbelievable anger. I sup-
> pose sex was the motive, or at least the fact that the killer was de-
> nied sex.

Insofar as the victim was concerned, Hansen made these surprising and professionally uncharacteristic observations:

> She didn't seem to have any goals or standards . . . she never had a
> job all the time she lived in Los Angeles. She had an obviously low
> IQ, lived hand to mouth, day to day. She was a man-crazy tramp,
> but she wasn't a prostitute. There were all kinds of men in her life,
> but we were only able to find three that had any sexual experience
> with her. She was a tease. She gave a bad time to quite a few guys.
> There wasn't very much to like about her.

Regarding his failure to solve the crime he admitted the Black Dahlia
case was his biggest disappointment:

> Being objective didn't mean that we didn't want that killer. I never
> wanted anything more. Every now and then there'd be some new
> development, a lead would pop out of nowhere and we'd think, here
> it is, this is it! But it never really was. Looking at it in perspective

right now, the killer did his thing and got away with it. Most homicides, I think the figure is 97 percent, are solved. A very few aren't. This is the biggest one I ever knew of. You really can't win them all.

Asked why this crime had such a tremendous impact on the public and whether that impact might have been attributed to its savagery or to the youth and beauty of the victim, Hansen said:

> There were crimes that same year that were at least as heinous and victims at least as pretty and none of them got anywhere near the same attention. It was that name "Black Dahlia" that set this one off . . . just those words strung together in that order turned Elizabeth Short's murder into a coast-to-coast sensation. Black is night, mysterious, forbidding even; the dahlia is an exotic and mysterious flower. There could not have been a more intriguing title. Any other name wouldn't have been anywhere near the same.

After Hansen's retirement, the case was inherited by a chain of senior homicide detectives in Robbery-Homicide Division, each one passing the baton upon his retirement to the next senior detective in line. Initially Chief Thad Brown assigned the case to detective Danny Galindo, who had assisted with the case in 1947. Then it went to Pierce Brooks, who was the lead detective assigned to the "Onion Field" case, later immortalized by Joseph Wambaugh, after which John "Jigsaw John" St. John and his partner Kirk Mellecker took over. Mellecker had been my partner more than a decade earlier at Hollywood Homicide.

The truth is, the case only remained active because of its legendary status. By the 1980s there was no real investigation being conducted, with the exception of an occasional writer wanting to sell his or her book as a whodunit based on some pet theory. Detectives would provide information that might, for a few weeks, speculatively stir the pot, but these were only theories. The writer could then go to the newspapers with the speculations, hoping to generate publicity for a book or article. Often, particularly around the anniversary of the murder, the press itself would initiate its own articles on the case. Every five or ten years, again around the anniversary of Elizabeth's death, the press would run a feature story, reviewing the case and interviewing the currently assigned detective for some new information.

Despite the case's open status, little if anything has been done in the way of active investigation for the past fifty-plus years. What is done is solely reactive in nature, in response to a letter that may have been mailed to the department by someone who had a dream or experienced recovered memories of being present while the murder was committed.

The case has also become something of a joke, particularly when the on-call detective at Robbery-Homicide receives a phone call from a would-be informant with a tip. The detective taking the call will put his hand over the mouthpiece as he bellows to his partner, "Hey, Charlie, I've got a witness on the line who says he can solve the Black Dahlia murder for us." His partner will usually respond, "Okay, let's roll!" at which point the detectives in the squad room roar with laughter.

Today, most of the detectives in LAPD's Robbery-Homicide Division hadn't even been born when the crime occurred. Just the mention of the name "Black Dahlia" makes detectives grimace. It serves as an irritating reminder that the department's biggest murder investigation, assigned to LAPD's best detectives, remains unsolved.

Three days after my return from San Francisco, I opened my briefcase and pulled out the notes June had asked me to help her analyze. I readily recognized Father's unique handwriting, block print instead of script, even when signing his name. His handwritten notes appeared a bit more frail and spidery than usual; he had written this just a few days after his ninety-first birthday. June had attached the following typed note to my copy:

I was looking through his pending papers and found the attached. His notes for an intended talk with me, which never occurred. I understand most of them but some are like riddles.

Over the years I was able to sense what he was thinking, when he would speak, and what he needed even before he opened his mouth. So I knew that he was preparing for the worst by collecting various kinds of sleeping pills. But from that October day he gained back energy and strength.

He was working on a proposal and artwork marketing plan this year, through April. He never initiated this "intended conversation" with me. He was not supposed to go that night.

He did talk about the patients with congestive heart failure he saw as an intern at Laguna Honda. Maybe you can help me by figuring out some items in the list?

June

Here is a facsimile of the note my father wrote to June on October 15, 1998:

### Exhibit 8

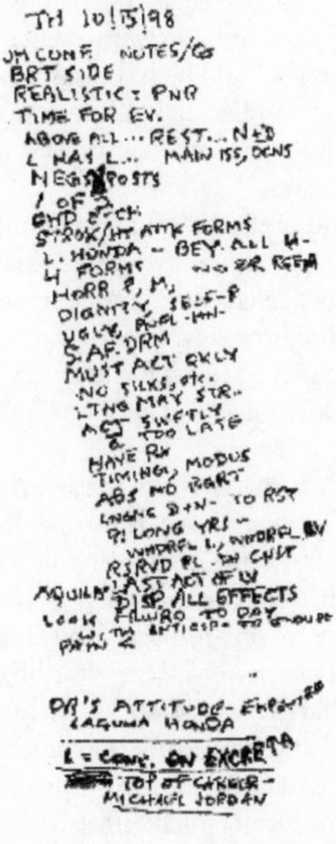

TH 10/15/98

JM CONF  NOTES/CS
BRT SIDE
REALISTIC = PNR
TIME FOR EV.
ABOVE ALL ... REST ... NED
L HAS L... MAIN ISS, DCNS
NEG & POSTS
1 OF 5
CHD & CH
STROK/HT ATTK FORMS
L. HONDA - BEY. ALL H-
4 FORMS    NO ER RGFA
HORR P, M,
DIGNITY, SELF-P
UGLY  PRSL-IM-
S. AF. DRM
MUST ACT QKLY
NO SILKS, etc.
LTNG MAY STR..
ACT SWFTLY
& TOO LATE
HAVE RX
TIMING, MODUS
ABS NO RGRT
LNGNC DIN- TO RST
PI LONG YRS -
WNDRFL L, WNDRFL BY
RSRVD PL IN CHST
AQUILA FAST ACT OF W
DISP ALL EFFECTS
LOOK FRWRD TO DAY
WITH ANTICIP - TO GROUP
PAIN &

DR'S ATTITUDE - EMPWRD
LAGUNA HONDA

L = CONC. ON EXCRETA
TOP OF CANCER -
MICHAEL JORDAN

I began deciphering the note and most of the message was clear to me. He was planning to take his own life, using the sleeping pills he had saved from prescriptions he had written for his wife. He had also decided that he "must act quickly, lightning may strike, act swiftly before it's too late." He indicated he had "absolutely no regrets." He had lived "91 long years," and had had a "wonderful life and wonderful love."

Most of his wording appeared to be a justification for his intended suicide. But also included were two rather curious notations, the first of which was capitalized as if to emphasize its importance and underscored further by his dramatic use of the shorthand words. He wrote to June, "As your last act of love for me you must dispose of all my effects." Then he scribbled an even stranger message in a bolder hand: "L = conc. on excreta." He had used the letter "L" earlier in his notes to refer to "life," so by inference I assumed he meant, "Life= conc. on excreta." Could he have meant, "Life is a concentration of excrement," or, in plain talk, "Life is nothing but shit"? But this hardly seems in line or character or tone with the rest of what he said.

Further, why would Father ask June so dramatically to destroy all of his personal effects by equating the request to her "last act of love"? Obviously, he expected that such a demand would compel her to do what he said. But June never carried out his instructions, because, as she had told me, Father's health took a turn for the better and he decided he had no need to have a final talk with her, as he had planned.

Seven months after he had written these instructions, Father had, as he had anticipated, suffered a severe stroke. It did not incapacitate him, as he had feared, but came to him as a blessing that took his life. There would be no suffering, no infirmity, no prolonged hospitalization, no loss of dignity or self-respect. Now, however, with the discovery of his notes, fate would insure that his private final wishes were revealed, and that he would speak to June from beyond the grave. She would find the note while looking through his pending papers, a final order, an act of control — proffered in the name of love — to destroy all of his personal effects.

In my career as a homicide detective, I have seen the worst of men's and women's passions unleashed as desperate acts against each other. In crime scene after crime scene I have witnessed the aftermath of this violence. But even with the experiences of six thousand nights as a homicide detective behind me, I was unprepared for what would be revealed to me over the course of my investigation. What I would uncover were horrors far beyond what I could even have imagined. What I would ultimately discover would take me to places I had never dreamed of, or expected to go: deep inside my own psyche, to my private heart of darkness.

# 5

# Dr. George Hill Hodel Jr.,
# 1907–1999

DAD'S FATHER, GEORGE HODEL SR., whose family name was Goldgefter, was born in 1873 in Odessa on the Black Sea, the son of Eli Goldgefter, an accountant and a German scholar. In 1894, at age twenty-one, George Sr., facing mandatory conscription into the czar's oppressive military, where Jews were treated only slightly better than slaves, prepared a plan to escape Russia. Using a fictitious name and a forged passport, my grandfather somehow succeeded in obtaining a pass, claiming he was going to visit his sick mother in Vienna. Once across the Polish frontier, he boarded a train to Vienna and freedom, just barely escaping the interest of the suspicious officer who interrogated him. But my grandfather's first-class ticket and expensive luggage convinced the officer he was legitimate, and he was able to cross the border. From Vienna he traveled to Paris, where he assumed the name Hodel (a fairly common Swiss surname) and began a new life.

In Paris he met Esther Leov, a Russian emigrant from Kiev who was a practicing dentist, a very unusual accomplishment for a woman in 1900. I don't have much information on either of my grandparents, except that it was rumored that Esther Leov's family were the direct descendants of French aristocracy, many of whom fled from Paris to Russia during the French Revolution and returned to France in the nineteenth century. George Sr. and Esther married in France on May 5, 1901, and entered the United States through Ellis Island on May 31, twenty-five days later. The two of them migrated west to California from New York, settling in the desert suburb of South

Pasadena, ten miles northeast of the emerging new capital of the silent motion-picture industry, Los Angeles.

My father, their only child, was born on October 10, 1907, at the Clara Barton Hospital at the corner of 5th Street and Grand Avenue in downtown Los Angeles. On the birth certificate George Sr. listed his occupation as "banker" and Esther listed herself as "dentist."

My father grew up speaking French as his primary language, in a completely French-speaking home. At age five, because his parents believed he had exceptional mental abilities that required special development, he was sent to Paris, where he was enrolled in the Montessori school, run by Madame Montessori herself. During this time, George lived with a Count and Countess Troubetzkoy, either relatives or close friends of his mother, in their penthouse suite in the Champ de Mars district of Paris, close to the Eiffel Tower. George's schooling in Paris lasted only a year or two, after which he returned home to begin his public schooling in South Pasadena. His mother, ever mindful of his cultural development, retained the services of a noted piano instructor, Vernon Spencer, to teach her son music. Spencer instantly identified him as a musical prodigy, and within a remarkably short time George had become not only an accomplished pianist but was even writing his own compositions.

By the age of nine, George had become recognized throughout Southern California as a future concert pianist; his teacher predicted a great musical career for him. An old family photograph captures the image of the Russian composer Rachmaninoff visiting the Hodel home in South Pasadena, where he, accompanied by the Russian minister of culture and his wife, attended a private recital given by Father when he was only nine.

My father's fame as a prodigy spread, and soon the newspapers were writing articles about him. On July 14, 1917, for example, the *Los Angles Evening Herald*, alongside a photo of my father, wrote:

## BOY OF NINE CHIEF SOLOIST
## AT SHRINE HOLIDAY EXERCISES

A little boy, 9 years old, has been chosen by the French committee to play before the Belgian mission at the French celebration at Shrine auditorium today.

The lad thus chosen above scores of adult musicians is George Hodel, son of Mr. and Mrs. George Hodel of 6440 Walnut Hill Avenue. He is a pupil of Vernon Spencer and is regarded in the world of music as a genius.

Though a mere youngster, he has studied music for years and he was selected as a piano soloist by the French committee entirely because of his great talent.

While he has composed several musical works, he will play Massenet and Chaminade selections when he appears before the Belgian mission.

The Hodels had erected a handsome estate in South Pasadena, located on Monterey Road, designed by the famous Russian architect Alexander Zelenko. It was built in the style of a Swiss chalet, a ten-room residence complete with a detached guesthouse, which would later become their son's private retreat in which he was allowed to pursue his intellectual creations in complete privacy. Thus, even from his earliest years, George Jr.'s parents treated him as if he were beyond special, indulging him, nurturing what they were convinced was his unique talent, raising him as if he were a child of European aristocracy, with all the privileges of a superior class. But in truth he was an American child growing up in California in the twentieth century, nothing more. And therein, I believe, were sown the seeds of his later problems.

In addition to his musical genius, George also tested exceptionally high intellectually, with an IQ score of 186, which apparently placed him one point above Albert Einstein. This "genius mentality" rapidly advanced him through primary and secondary schools, and he graduated from South Pasadena High School at the ripe young age of fourteen.

In 1923, when he was only fifteen, George began attending college at the California Institute of Technology in Pasadena, intent on pursuing a career as a chemical engineer. Even then, Cal Tech was one of the most important engineering schools in the country, the home of early-twentieth-century experiments in electronics research, magnetic propulsion, and even anti-gravity wave propagation. However, George either dropped out or was expelled from Cal Tech after completing only one year, for reasons that still remain unclear. There are two versions of the story of his expulsion. In the first, he left college because he had a sexual liaison with a faculty member's wife, who became pregnant as a result and was divorced by her husband. In the second version, he was kicked out for playing poker, because gambling was prohibited on campus. In any event, by the time he was seventeen he had left engineering school and was working at a variety of jobs.

In 1924, mostly as a result of his performance on IQ tests required by the California public school system during his early teens, the noted Stanford psychologist Dr. Lewis Terman selected him to become a member of a tracking group known as "Terman's Termites." This was one of the first long-running experiments in developmental psychology, in which Professor Terman, credited with originating the terms "IQ" and "gifted," conducted a survey of more than a thousand intellectually endowed students. Beginning in 1924 with a group of specially selected children, Terman's study began to collect data and follow them as they grew older, to see how their intellectual gifts manifested themselves in their lives and careers. In the seven decades since Dr. Terman's groundbreaking studies began, five books have been published analyzing the data provided from these original students.

Over the years, Father continued to return the extensive research questionnaires; clearly he saw his selection by Dr. Terman as a validation of his own belief that he was special. His scrupulous return of the questionnaires and his adherence to what the study required of him doubtless reinforced in him the elitist feeling instilled in him by his parents. I also believe the fact that his 186 IQ placed him in Terman's highest category of the gifted students to be studied was a vital component of his extraordinary self-esteem that stood him in good stead during his toughest times and into his final years.

From 1924 through 1928, my father worked in various professions in the Los Angeles area normally reserved for much older and more experienced people. In his first job, he worked as a crime reporter at the *Los Angeles Record* during the most violent years of Prohibition. His particular beat was the LAPD Vice Squad, where he rode shotgun on their raids of downtown nightclubs and local speakeasies. Extracts from an article he wrote on August 20, 1924, when he was only sixteen, provide insight not only into what was happening in L.A. during Prohibition but also into my father's thoughts and activities.

# LIFE CAFÉ

## WHERE LIQUOR IS HARD

### A Raid on the Humming Bird Café

Outside the brilliantly lit Humming Bird café, 1243 East 12th street, officers are waiting, watch in hand, ready to swoop down on the place, on the stroke of 12 Saturday night.

All possible exits are guarded, all avenues of escape are watched. They are determined that this raid should not fail — that they should clean up the wettest hole on Central Avenue.

It lacks five minutes of midnight.

Inside, a motley crowd is reveling unaware of what developments are about to take place.

The atmosphere is saturated with the odor of intoxicants. The spirit of the men and women inside is changing from one of tipsy fun to that of licentious debauchery. Strong liquor is doing its work . . .

Three minutes of midnight.

The Negro orchestra strikes up a tune, assertively synchopative. The players sway their bodies in rhythm with the music, deftly juggling their instruments . . .

Abandonment, unreserved and unblushing, is permeating the café. A loud knock at the door. Four men stride in, officers of the prohibition enforcement and vice squads.

They walk rapidly about from table to table, seizing bottles and collaring men. The proprietor calls excitedly to waiters, who dash about warning the men and women. Dozens of glasses are overturned, dozens of bottles are emptied or smashed.

The noise of broken glass fills the room.

The floor is soaked with alcohol.

The four officers have taken five men, sixteen officers could have arrested four times that number.

The siren of the police patrol dies off in the distance.

The music starts up lurchingly.

Bottles are lifted from the floor. Glasses are refilled.

A woman looks sorrowfully at the broken neck of a smashed whisky flask. She breaks out into a loud high-pitched sob, gasping drunkenly . . .

### Arrest Men for Booze

While white women careened drunkenly in the Arms of Negro escorts, in the Humming Bird café, 1243 East Twelfth street, early Wednesday morning, vice squad officers swooped down on the place and arrested several prominent citizens for illegal possession of liquor, marking the third raid carried out on the café in as many days . . .

According to the officers the Hummingbird has been a nightlife rendezvous, where whites dine, dance and drink with members of the city's Negro colony. A bevy of showgirls from a downtown burlesque theater were on the scene, enjoying the festivities.

Many complaints have been received by police authorities against the Hummingbird and it is said that the wildest sort of orgies are carried on there nightly. White women of the underworld make the place a headquarters, according to the officers, and ply their vocation there.

George isn't just reporting on the raid; he is describing a lifestyle and sexual fantasies that had fully engaged him even as a teenager. He actually recreates an atmosphere of forbidden sexual promiscuity that violates even the taboos of the 1920s. Father's writing was so colorful that he was quickly promoted from cub reporter to his own crime beat. Now he was working with the city's top cops on the LAPD's homicide squad. In a front-page *Record* story from 1924 about a murder scene he covered with homicide detectives, where the victim, Peggy Donovan, had been kicked to death, he wrote:

*Los Angeles Record*

June 3, 1924                                            Two Cents

# THE MORNING AFTER A PARTY

The splashes of red about the rooms are beginning to change into brown . . .

Lying in the dust of the floor and bestrewn with the fallen ashes and stubs of innumerable cigarettes are scraps, scraps of paper — rubbish. There are letters — diaries of forgotten years — prayer books — playing cards — . . .

Lying face up on the floor is a card — the ace of diamonds. Over it has fallen a large drop of blood that converts the printed figure of the red diamond to a shapeless and blurred blotch of red.

### Sheets Bloody

Blood-smeared sheets lie crumpled and torn on the littered floor of the bungalow.

A pair of dice have fallen from the smashed dressing table. One of the cubes has on it a splashed red stain.

Rising above the unmistakable odor of spilled and drying blood are mingling those of liquor, of Jamaica gin, of tobacco.

### Forgotten Advice

"Give up every friend that is sinful and learn the 'Truth that makes . . .'"

Hopeful, pathetically hopeful, words written last December, one day before Christmas, to Margaret Donovan — cabaret girl who was killed in a drunken brawl . . .

"Give up every friend that is sinful . . ."

"Find the Truth."

"I confess to Thee, O Lord Jesus Christ, all the sins that I have committed even unto this hour. May the Almighty Lord grant to me pardon, absolution and remission of all my sins. Amen."

These words are underlined in a little blue book of "Prayers for

Daily Use" "Read this some time for Mother's sake," is inscribed on the title page . . .

Wisps of dark brown hair — long and silken — are strewn about the floor. They are blood-clotted, torn.

Torn stockings of sheer silk.

### Detectives Aghast

In the adjoining room detectives are muttering. "Good God, Archie, those ——— kicked her to death about three in the morning and then went and slept till nine!"

Between the pillow and pillow-slip of the overturned cot in which Peggy Donovan was found dead was an age-yellowed newspaper clipping, its sentences underlined:

"In the GARDEN OF LIFE WOMEN are the FLOWERS, some are gorgeous, gay and yet Have NO PERFUME."

A few months later, in another crime-scene story in the *Record*, George turns the description into a literary piece by punning in Latin on the last name of victim Teresa Mors. Mors — her name means "death" in Latin — was shot and killed by her jealous lover, the famous welterweight boxing champ Norman "Kid McCoy" Selby, who was immortalized by the sobriquet "the Real McCoy" when he decked with a single punch a drunk who had challenged his identity in a downtown L.A. bar. Legendary criminal attorney Jerry Giesler would jump-start his career with this famous early Los Angeles murder case by obtaining a manslaughter verdict for his client rather than the death sentence the state wanted.

In his description of the murder scene George Hodel writes:

*Los Angeles Record*
Thursday, August 14, 1924                    Two Cents

## WORDS OF DEATH

Death.

Mors, mortis, morti — glibly the schoolboy declines it. Thought-lessly.

Like a cage in which the canary has been stifled, this apartment on the second floor of the Nottingham — the tall, expensive build-ing with a front of blazing white tiles.

While the yellow bird was alive — flitting and singing —

The cage seemed a pretty thing. Now with the canary dead it is a dirty cage, tawdry and crusted with birdlime.

The canary is dead on the floor of this soft room that seems so close — impinging with walls and ceiling — close like a cage . . .

She lies dead in an unpleasant disarray that is not art but death. And the two batiks of Larry Darwin, monsters of the new niode, bulge with immensity just as the ordered vision of Rubens shrinks into insignificance before the monstrosity on the floor. Larry Dar-win's nudes are phantasms — succubi. One smokes a cigarette, perched cross-legged on the devil's head. The other, with stuffed limbs, prances through a garden of exotic lotus flowers. Both leer at the figure on the floor.

The figure on the floor. Hair waved and hennaed, perhaps. Redly, dankly — plume for a face disfigured by a bullet hole. Eyes purpled. Blood on the bare white arms. And this photograph — of "the Kid." Clasped like a rosary to the breast, flat now, and hard; retreated as a woman's breast retreats when she is on her back.

The Kid placed the photograph in the white hand.

A gesture of drama, a futile touch of the romantic school that heightens the grotesquerie; that causes the naked batik succubi to leer the more it seems.

Pull it away — the picture. The newspapermen would photo-graph it, too. Yes, it's a picture of the kid.

Bloodstains on the glass. The Kid stands up young and proud.

The clutching fingernails scratch and rattle across the back. Ugh! Put it back in the hand. Let her hold it . . .

On their pedestal the nymph and satyr of Perl's have never eased the tension of their eternal embrace . . .

Death.

Mors, mortis, morti — what gender is death?

Feminine of course. It is of that declension. Yes, death is feminine.

Later in 1924, George decided to give up reporting and become a publisher. The following month, he and a friend decided to create a literary magazine. Now living in his own detached studio on his parents' South Pasadena property, he published a magazine with his own printing press and named it *Fantasia*. In his January 1925 introduction to the first issue, he made the following editorial statement:

### A Dedication

To the portrayal of bizarre beauty in the arts, to the delineation of the stranger harmonies and the rarer fragrances, do we dedicate this, our magazine.

Such beauty we may find in a poem, a sketch, or a medley of colors; in the music of prayer-bells in some far-off minaret, or the noises of a city street; in a temple or a brothel or a gaol; in prayer or perversity or sin.

And ever shall we attempt in our pages the vivid expression of such art, wherever or however we may find it — ever shall we consecrate our magazine to the depiction of beauty anomalous, fantasial.

George Hodel wanted to explore bizarre, off-the-edge fantasies, mostly having to do with forbidden sex and violence. His magazine survived two issues; its only notable piece was my father's review of the newly published book by the then relatively unknown author Ben Hecht, entitled *The Kingdom of Evil*. This was a sequel to Hecht's first book, *Fantazius Mallare: A Mysterious Oath*, a journal narrated by the fictional reclusive artist-genius Mallare, which describes the author's visions of decadence, insanity, and, ultimately, murder. Mallare creates a beautiful mistress, Rita, who becomes his phantom or hallucinatory lover. In this twisted story delusion becomes reality and reality dissolves to dreams until, at the story's end, Mallare has transformed himself into an insanely jealous avenger who beats Rita to death because of her flagrant, wanton seduction, in Mallare's own presence, of his Caliban-like manservant, Goliath. The reader never really knows whether Rita is real or a twisted fantasy spun out of Mallare's psychotic torment.

The novel's highly erotic pen-and-ink drawings were created by Wallace Smith, who like Hecht had been a journalist, artist, and author in Chicago. Smith was arrested and prosecuted for what the government considered pornography, and because the book was judged obscene, was jailed for a brief period. Both authors would later come to Hollywood to write screenplays, where Hecht would eventually become one of the highest-paid screenwriters in the industry.

My father's review of *The Kingdom of Evil*, in which he's completely absorbed into Hecht's belief system, is the most accurate picture of his psychology. He writes, in part, "Macabre forms, more dank and putrescently phantasmal than any of Hecht's former imagining, grope blindly and crazedly in the poisonous fog out of which loom the rotting fancies that people his 'Kingdom of Evil.'"

My father's magazine went out of existence in the spring of 1925. A few months later he applied for a job as a cab driver. Lying about his age, which was seventeen, he managed to pass himself off as twenty-one in order to obtain his chauffeur's license (City badge no. 1976, State badge no. 34879) from the city's Board of Public Utilities, permitting him to drive a taxi within the city limits. That he was just over six feet and a solid 148 pounds, with black hair and dark brown eyes, made him look older than he was. Dad's route took him mostly downtown, where he shuttled fares among the various hotels, including the Biltmore, and out to Hollywood. Ironically, one of Father's fellow cab drivers out of the same station, and likely his early acquaintance, was a young man studying for his law degree, who twenty-five years later was destined to become LAPD's most famous chief of police, William H. Parker.

Toward the end of 1925, another story about Father appeared in print, this time by Ted Le Berthon, the drama critic for the *Los Angeles Evening Herald*, who wrote the following unusual and highly illuminating article about Father. In it, Le Berthon changes Dad's last name from Hodel to "Morel" and the name of his magazine from *Fantasia* to *Whirlpools*.

This article reveals another side to my father. Besides being a pampered mama's boy, intellectual elitist, poet, and pianist, he was also a fighter who at the slightest provocation would be eager and ready to trade punches.

*Los Angeles Evening Herald*      December 9, 1925

# THE MERRY-GO-ROUND

## By TED LE BERTHON

### The Clouded Past of a Poet

GEORGE MOREL is tall, olive-skinned with wavy black hair and a strong bold nose. His eyes are large, brown, somnolent. A romantic, hawklike fellow, a pianist, a poet, and editor of Whirlpools, a bizarre, darkly poetical quarterly.

"George is a nice boy but —"

How often did one hear that!

What his friends hinted was that George, being young, was inclined to write of melancholy things.

Of course, George could have pointed to Keats, Rupert Brooke or Stephen Crane for precedent, but — "It's not George's gloom, his preference for Huysmanns, De Gourmont, Poe, Baudelaire, Verlaine and Hecht that pains us," these "friends" would parry, "but his stilted elegance, his meticulous speech!"

George drowned himself at times in an ocean of deep dreams. Only part of him seemed present.

He would muse standing before one in a black, flowered dressing gown lined with scarlet silk, oblivious to one's presence.

Suddenly, though, his eyes would flare up like signal lights and he would say, "The formless fastidiousness of perfumes in a seventeenth century boudoir is comparable to my mind in the presence of twilight."

One might have answered "What of it?" — but one just didn't.

As one of George's "friends" put it: "He's young. He'll get over it. What he needs is contact with harsh realities. At present his writing is tenuous, dreamy, monotonous — and he is like his writing."

## A Future Realistic Novelist

I HADN'T seen George for about a year —

And last night, strolling up Spring street in a sort of Morelian reverie myself, I was startled by hearing a familiar voice. The next moment I saw a tall young fellow in a taxi driver's uniform seize a burly, argumentative man by the coat lapels and growl menacingly:

"Come across with that taxi fare or I'll smack you in the nose, right here and now!"

The speaker was GEORGE MOREL.

By the end of 1925, George had switched his schedule to driving on the night shift while he took jobs as a copywriter, first for a local Army & Navy store and then for the Southern California Gas Company. It was through SoCal Gas that he got his first taste of managing publicity, advertising, and marketing, and landed himself another job as a radio announcer, in which he hosted a live show, introducing the public to classical music during the early-evening hours. SoCal Gas sponsored an hour-long program in the early days of radio. Dad, a gas company employee in advertising, possessed the perfect qualities for the job: a musical prodigy with an encyclopedic knowledge of the classics, he also had a beautiful speaking voice. His uniquely meticulous speech patterns, his ability to use just the right words and diction expressed with perfect intonation, rhyme, and meter, would remain his calling card for the rest of his life. George Hodel's voice was as unique and distinct as his fingerprints. However, after shutting off the radio mike for the evening, Dad put on his cab driver's hat and began looking for fares waiting outside the Biltmore.

Though not yet twenty, Father had already accumulated the life experiences of much older men and had led several lives: boy genius, musical prodigy, crime reporter, advertising writer, public relations officer, public radio announcer, editor of a self-published literary magazine, poet, intellectual elitist, and cab driver.

# 6

# George and Dorero

**Summer 1927**

My MOTHER'S FIRST LOVE, and perhaps her only true love, was John Huston, the son of actor Walter Huston and later one of America's most celebrated film directors. They met in Los Angeles as teenagers, fell in love, married, and then set off on a joint artistic adventure to Greenwich Village, where John painted and boxed and my mother wrote poetry. They both drank. Then they came back to Hollywood, where both would become contract screenwriters at the studios, socializing with the talented and beautiful people of the 1920s Los Angeles entertainment community. They lived in a bubble of all-night parties, all-night drinking, and all-night arguments.

By the 1930s, they'd become a pair of fighters in a ring with no timekeeper, no referee, and no bell to end the rounds. The alcohol and infidelities took their toll, and after an extended trip to England, Mother decided to quit the fight game for good. Huston would go on to many more fights with many more women, and he would win them all. After Mother's death, I found in her personal effects the following three paragraphs she had typewritten on a single lonely page, about John Huston:

> All his life he was fascinated by boxers. He also loved bullfighters even before he read Hemingway. He had a brief enthusiasm for six-day bicycle racers and even looked into dance marathons and flagpole sitters. But boxers were the best specimens he felt that the race of man had produced.
>
> The first time he tried to tell me about all this, he was 19 years old. I was 19, too, and we were at a party where this shocking thing had just

happened. I mean, it was shocking to me, but it left John in an exalted and unusually talkative mood. There was blood all over the floor and on some of the furniture, and my face was green and I was trying not to be sick.

"You're missing the whole point," John said. He pulled me to my feet and steered me to the front porch. With the sweet sick smell blowing away and everything outdoors swinging slowly back in focus again, I said weakly, "I am?"

My mother had known my father, George Hill Hodel, for a long time. They had met in 1920s Los Angeles, before Mother married John Huston. In fact, my father and John Huston were very good friends in their youth and they frequently double-dated. At the time, John was dating Emilia, an attractive young woman who worked at the then brand-new downtown public library, and George was dating my mother. Then they switched, and George became enamored of Emilia and John of Dorothy. After John and Dorothy married and ran off to New York, George and Emilia continued their romance, and together they opened a rare books shop in downtown Los Angeles.

Father had always had a strong love of photography. During the mid-1920s he spent much of his free time photographing people and places around Los Angeles. He had his own darkroom at home, where he would process his film. In 1925 he was asked to select the best of these photographs, and a Pasadena art gallery gave him a one-man show.

Another close friend of both my father and Huston during this period was a young Italian artist poet, Fred Sexton, who socialized and partied with both of them. Sexton also drove a taxi in those early days and made money by running a floating crap game. Fifteen years later, in 1941, Huston would put his friend Fred Sexton's artistic talents to work by having him create the sculpture prop "the Black Bird" for his film *The Maltese Falcon*. Fred Sexton and my father would remain close friends until Dad left Los Angeles in 1950.

By the summer of '27, Emilia was pregnant with my half-brother Duncan, who was born in March of 1928. Duncan visited us only on rare occasions through the decades, and was a relative stranger to me when I saw him again in San Francisco in the days following Father's death.

With their infant son Duncan, George and Emilia moved north to San Francisco, where George enrolled in the pre-med program at the University of California at Berkeley. During his undergraduate years he got a job as a longshoreman and again drove a cab and learned the city streets and its night people and their secret haunts.

In the spring of '32, George returned to writing, when the *San Francisco Chronicle* hired both him and Emilia as joint columnists. Together they wrote a weekly feature column entitled "Abroad in San Francisco," a review and travelogue of the goings-on in the city. Their reviews became popular because of their photo displays and colorful descriptions of the various sections and cultures of San Francisco.

By June 1932, George had graduated from Berkeley pre-med and immediately enrolled in medical school at the University of California San Francisco. At the same time, though living with Emilia and raising Duncan, he became enamored of another woman, Dorothy Anthony. Not wanting to give up Emilia, he convinced her — a testament to his enormous powers of persuasion — that it would be best if they formed a romantic alliance and shared their home with Dorothy Anthony. This arrangement quickly resulted in another pregnancy, and Dorothy, in the spring of 1935, bore George a daughter, Tamar.

George Hodel's exceptional eye-hand coordination made him a natural as a surgeon, and his professors vied with one another to obtain his services as their assistant in many of their operations. It seemed that my father had found his *métier* at last, and in June 1936 he graduated from the University of California Medical School, now known as University of California San Francisco.

As per tradition at the graduation ceremonies of all physicians, on that balmy summer day in June 1936, George Hill Hodel, a tall, handsome man of twenty-eight, stood on the campus of UCSF, raised his right hand, and, with his classmates, took the Hippocratic oath. In those years, doctors took the original oath, longer than the one administered today, which included:

> I will abstain from whatever is deleterious and mischievous. I will give no deadly medicine to anyone if asked, nor suggest any such counsel; and in like manner I will not give to a woman an abortive remedy. With purity and with holiness I will pass my life and practise my Art.

I will not cut persons labouring under the stone, but will leave this to be done by such men as are practitioners of this work. Into whatever houses I enter, I will go into them for the benefit of the sick, and will abstain from every voluntary act of mischief and corruption; and, further, from the seduction of females or males, of freemen and slaves.

While I continue to keep this Oath unviolated, may it be granted to me to enjoy life and practice of the Art, respected by all men, in all times. But should I trespass and violate this Oath, may the reverse be my lot.

George's life was now dedicated to preserving and healing human life. It would be his duty forthwith to alleviate pain and suffering.

Still not yet thirty, my father was now an M.D. with a residency in surgery, having added many more lifetimes to his biography: longshoreman, artist/photographer, weekly travel columnist for the *San Francisco Chronicle*, and father of two children by two different women with whom he was living at the same time.

In 1936, Dad completed his internship at San Francisco General Hospital and accepted a position with the New Mexico State Department of Public Health as a district health officer. With Emilia and seven-year-old Duncan, he moved to a small town near Prescott, Arizona, where he served as the lone doctor at a logging camp. Then he became a public health officer to the Indian reservations and pueblos near Gallup, New Mexico, where he befriended Tom Dodge, chief of the Navajo Indians.

Probably because George had convinced her that he wanted more freedom, Emilia and Duncan returned without him to San Francisco, where she would soon marry a popular local artist/painter, Franz Bergmann. Emilia took a job as a columnist, this time with the *San Francisco News*, and enjoyed a long and successful career as that newspaper's senior drama critic. Soon after Emilia left George, Dorothy Anthony and Tamar joined him in New Mexico, where the three of them lived briefly together near Taos.

Again, however, Father apparently felt too confined, and convinced Dorothy to return with their daughter to San Francisco without him.

In 1938, Dad was offered a job with the Los Angeles County

Health Department as a social hygiene physician. He accepted the position and moved back to L.A., where he initially moved into his old guesthouse at his father's residence in South Pasadena. That same year he took a post-graduate course in venereal disease control at University of California Medical School in San Francisco, and was certified as a specialist in the field.

In 1939, he was promoted to head of the division in the L.A. County Health Department and then appointed venereal disease control officer for the whole department. At the same time, he opened his own private practice in downtown Los Angeles and became medical director and chief of staff of his own office, the First Street Medical Clinic, for which he hired a staff of physicians. Its main focus was the treatment of venereal disease, which at that time, before the introduction of penicillin, had reached near-epidemic numbers in Los Angeles County.

In Los Angeles, George was reunited with my mother, Dorothy Harvey Huston, who by then had divorced John Huston. My parents had a whirlwind romance and my older brother Michael was born the following July. George renamed Dorothy "Dorero" — a combination of two Greek words: *dor*, meaning "gift," and *Eros*, the god of sexual desire — in order to avoid confusion with his earlier girlfriend and the mother of Tamar, Dorothy Anthony.

George purchased a home on Valentine Street in the Elysian Park district of Los Angeles, a ten-minute drive from his downtown office, and my mother and infant brother moved in with him. There was a rumor in the family that John Huston, not my dad, might have fathered Michael. In any case, immediately after Michael's birth both John and his father, Walter, who at that time badly wanted but was still without a grandchild, visited the house daily. As Mother told me later, "Both John and Walter would sit and stare at Michael in his crib for long periods of time, trying to discern whether or not a likeness between John and Michael existed." Mother said that it finally became so embarrassing that she had to order both of them out of the house with a firm "Forget it John, he's not your son." Michael would grow up to be one of the more celebrated FM radio announcers in Los Angeles on station KPFK, and a writer and editor of detective stories and science fiction.

Dorero, at age thirty-three, though intellectually a full-blown bohemian, was also a mother who wanted her young son to have a name as well as a stake in his father's growing fortune. She was territorial about her own house. Mother pushed George to marriage, and during a weekend trip to Sonora, Mexico, George and Dorero were married. My twin, John Dion, and I were born the following November, and Kelvin, the youngest of Mother's four sons, followed just eleven months later.

On May 18, 1942, six months after the United States entered the war, my father received a commission as a surgeon in the U.S. Public Health Service as a reserve officer. Because he wanted to join the active military service like his friend John Huston, however, Dad resigned his commission from Public Health. But, because of a chronic heart condition, he failed his physical and remained in Los Angeles during the war years, practicing medicine, primarily as chief of the Division of Social Hygiene for the Los Angeles County Health Department. He also maintained his private practice at the First Street Medical Clinic and was hired as medical director of the Ruth Home and Hospital in El Monte, where he treated young women with venereal disease.

During the war years my parents' marriage fell apart. Upset and unhappy, Mother began drinking heavily, and Father stayed away from the house most of the time. After their four-year marriage, they separated in September 1944, and Mother filed a complaint for divorce, alleging "extreme cruelty."

During the next three years we lived apart from Father, and from December 1944 through March 1946, on three occasions, the police were called out to arrest Mother for drunk-and-disorderly complaints and child neglect. On two of those occasions, we were released back to the custody of our father, and on the third we were placed in protective custody at MacLaren Hall, a facility for dependent children. Ultimately we were returned to Mother.

Dr. Hodel's chance to enter the international public health service as a military officer did come, after the war ended, when Congress funded UNRRA, the United Nations Relief and Rehabilitation Administration — created to distribute health and human services to war-ravaged populations — and began soliciting applications for service. He filed an application for employment with UNRRA, submitted on August 3, 1945, in which he provided a wealth of personal information past and present that bears upon my investigation into the Black Dahlia and related cases. In addition, I found separate documents containing his personnel service record while employed with UNRRA, which provided details relating to his service history and termination.

In his typed application requesting employment with UNRRA, Dad lists his current private medical practice and business office at the Roosevelt Building, 727 West 7th Street Suite 1242, in downtown Los Angeles — near the corner of Flower Street — and said he had been at this same location since 1939. He also listed himself as medical director and chief of staff of the First Street Medical Clinic, 369 East 1st Street, also located in downtown Los Angeles, and the medical director for the Ruth Home and Hospital, community chest agency for the treatment and rehabilitation of girls and young women with venereal disease, at 831 North Gilman Road, in El Monte. Dad listed his current net annual income as $21,000, and he requested employment "outside the United States, preferably in the Far East."

Dad gave his physical description as "6', 168 pounds," and said he was "married, son, age 17 years, in Merchant Marines (Duncan), daughter, age 10 (Tamar), and three younger sons, ages 6 (Michael), 4 (Steven), and 2 (Kelvin)." Under "Languages," he indicated he was fluent in French and could "speak, read, and write it, and lived in Paris as a child." Further, he stated, "Am currently studying the Chinese language, but have not yet acquired any proficiency."

My father's application was accepted and he was hired by UNRRA, effective December 3, 1945, with a position listed as chief regional medical officer for China and a home station listed as Washington, D.C. His official overseas station was the UNRRA regional headquarters office in Hankow, China, and he was granted an annual salary of $7,375.

President Truman had said that China presented the "largest of all the relief responsibilities," and thus it was to China that my father was dispatched in early 1946 with the honorary rank of lieutenant general, complete with a United Nations quasi-military-style uniform.

Although no records exist to establish his exact date of departure to China, I believe he left sometime in early 1946. From a memorandum he wrote that I found in his file, I can establish that he had traveled to and was in his home station of Washington, D.C., between late 1945 and early 1946, before departing for China. During his absence, Dad maintained his downtown medical office at the same address.

As chief regional medical officer in Hankow, Father was provided with a military jeep complete with a three-star flag, a driver, his own personal cook, and two administrative aides to comprise his staff. Exhibits 9 and 10 are photographs taken of Father during his assignment in China in 1946:

*Exhibits 9 and 10*

*Above: Dr. George Hodel, second from right, with Chinese military, 1946*
*Below: Dr. George Hodel, UNRRA China, 1946*

Exhibit 9 (top) is captioned "arbitrator," which meant that my father's diagnosis and opinion regarding a Communist prisoner's medical condition literally meant life or death. If the prisoner was confirmed as sick he passed through Nationalist lines to safety; if he was not, he remained with his captors; which was probably a death warrant. According to the UNRRA rules of engagement regarding my father's duties, UNRRA and my father were responsible for the following:

## UNRRA Arbitrates:

At the request of peace team #9 (Hankow), UNRRA acted as referee on eligibility for transport of sick and wounded Communist soldiers through the Nationalist lines. Following an agreement by the peace team, 618 disabled Communist soldiers, along with 120 wives and children, were moved by special train from Kuangshui in Northern Hupeh to Anyang in Northern Honan, where better hospital facilities exist.

Nationalist medical officers challenged medical eligibility of 75. These doubtful cases were reviewed by an American physician, Dr. G. Hill Hodel, chief medical officer for UNRRA-Hankow. Dr. Hodel upheld the challenge in 26 cases, overruled it in 49.

Father worked with both the Chinese Nationalist and Communist generals in 1946. His position in the center as "peacekeeper" (exhibit 10) between the two powers is significant and demonstrates why it was important for UNRRA to have granted him the rank of three-star general, so that he would be considered by both sides an equal rather than a subordinate in his role as medical arbitrator.

The review of Dad's UNRRA file also contained a fourteen-page typed memorandum, dated March 20, 1946, in response to a Dr. Victor Sutter, who had obviously requested a summary analysis from Dad of the then current problem of venereal disease control in China.

In one of his summary paragraph headings under "Prostitution and V.D.," Dad included the following observations that reveal what I believe to be his personal feelings about women, venereal disease, prostitution, and the attempts made by government to regulate moral behavior:

> For 9 years, as health officer and as administrator of an official venereal disease control program, I have observed the workings of "regulation" and of repression. It is my opinion that prostitution is an evil which cannot be caused to cease by legislative or police action, but which can only be deflected into other channels . . .
>
> I have learned, however, from my American experience, that for corrupt policemen to chase loose women from one end of town to another contributes neither to the peace, health, nor morals of a community.

My father's personal "American experience" of "regulation," "repression," and "corrupt policemen," most certainly referred to what he had witnessed in Los Angeles, and especially the corruption he had seen in the LAPD.

Dr. Hodel resigned suddenly and unexpectedly from UNRRA on September 19, 1946. His personnel record cites the reason for his termination as "personal," even though the real cause might have been medical. I have reason to believe that while in China Dad suffered a sudden — and severe — heart attack and was sent back to L.A. for hospitalization. I believe that this heart attack required him to remain hospitalized in Los Angeles for up to a month or more before being allowed to return to the Franklin House sometime in October or November 1946.

It is clear that Dad thoroughly enjoyed the prerogatives of his rank, because once he returned to Los Angeles in 1946 he immediately purchased a military-style Willys Army jeep identical to the one in which he had been chauffeured about in China. These surplus jeeps were first offered to civilians for purchase only after the war, in late 1945 or 1946. But the jeep was only part of Dad's lingering romanticized attachment to the military.

In 1946, Father posed for several formal photographs taken by his close friend the celebrated surrealist artist and photographer Man Ray. In these photographs, Dad chose to wear his UNRRA overcoat, complete with epaulets, which gave him the bearing of a military officer. I have reason to believe that during and after the war years —

*Exhibit 11*

*George Hodel, 1946*

perhaps up through 1949 — George Hodel assumed the persona of an Air Force lieutenant in his romantic overtures to the many women he pursued. It is also likely that his camouflaged identity was either unknown to these women or that there was a mutual agreement that this was a cover story to conceal his real identity because of his marital status.

Dad had become fascinated with Asia, and during his tour of duty in China had bought a large number of rare art objects, available at what amounted to liquidation prices in Shanghai if one had American cash. He invested heavily in Asian antique artworks: rare paintings, antique silk tapestries, and bronze statutes of Chinese deities.

Shortly before he left for Asia, Father had made another investment: in 1945 he bought the Lloyd Wright Sowden House on Franklin

Avenue, to which, while he was overseas, he had all of his purchases in
Asia shipped. Upon his return from China, Dad also tried to reconcile
with Mother, and the four of us moved into the Franklin House on his
return in '46. Although my brothers and I believed we had become a
family again, we were actually only there as Dad's guests, unaware of
our parents' divorce and of our probationary status.

Our old home remains today on the Los Angeles historic regis-
trar, as one of Hollywood's most unusual architectural landmarks.
We simply called it "the Franklin House" because of its Franklin Avenue address, but it is officially known as "the Sowden House."

Named for the man who commissioned it, the Sowden House is
an architectural wonder designed and built by Lloyd Wright,* who
was living in the shadow of his famous father, Frank Lloyd Wright.
With its brooding stone archways, long corridors, wide central
courtyard and pool, and hidden rooms, it is like a Hollywood set out
of a 1930s five-reeler: foreign and exotic. Cars driving by would stop
and stare at it in astonishment. Passersby could not believe they were
looking at what was a recreation of a 3,000-year-old Mayan temple
built of giant concrete blocks. It had no visible windows. It was a
high-walled fortress, private and impenetrable, right in the center of
Hollywood's residential district, only fifteen minutes from Father's
downtown medical clinic.

From the busy Franklin Avenue street frontage, heavy stone steps
led steeply up to our house's entrance, which was guarded by an im-
posing iron gate decorated with iron flowers. Once through the gate
you turned immediately to your right and continued up a dark pas-
sageway, then made another right turn to the front door. It was like
entering a cave with secret stone tunnels, within which only the initiated could feel comfortable. All others proceeded with great caution, not knowing which way to turn. Growing up in that house, my
brothers and I saw it as a place of magic that we were convinced
could easily have greeted the uninvited with pits of fire, poison darts,
deadly snakes, or even a giant sword-bearing turbaned bodyguard at
the door. Right out of *The Arabian Nights.*

*After building the Sowden home in 1926, Lloyd Wright's next architectural en-
deavor (1927–28) would be to design the prototype shells for what has become one of
Los Angeles's most recognizable icons, the Hollywood Bowl. This magnificent am-
phitheater is located only two miles west of the Franklin House.

## Exhibit 12

*The Franklin House, Hollywood, California*

Once inside the temple, there was a blaze of light that came at you from all directions, because all the rooms opened onto a central open-air courtyard. The massive stone blocks were laid out in a giant rectangular shape from the front of the street to the alley at the back. There existed no yard exterior to the home, only the open interior atrium surrounded by the four corridors of the house. The high-ceilinged foyer greeted you at first entrance. Beyond and to the west was the living room, with its ornate fireplace and floor-to-ceiling bookcases that concealed a secret room, accessible only to those who knew how to open the hidden door. The west wing contained the dining room, kitchen, maid's quarters, and guest rooms.

The east wing held the master bedroom and master bath, along with four more bedrooms laid out one after the other, until finally at the north wing there was a huge room, which Sowden had constructed as an entertainment hall or large stage for performances. From any room one could step into a central courtyard full of exotic foliage and beautiful giant cactus plants reaching straight into the sky. Once inside this remarkable house one found oneself in absolute privacy, invisible to the outside world.

This was a storybook time for me and my brothers, who played the Three Musketeers in service to our father, who played the king. Our father was dashing and confident. At six foot one, with his dark hair, trim mustache, immaculate dress, and the formal bearing befitting a highly respected physician, he cut an exceptionally handsome figure. It seemed as if he walked with the imperial air of an aristocrat, the type of man one might meet only once but would never forget. There was a charisma and a power to his presence that commanded attention. When he spoke, his voice had a resonance and power of authority that confirmed that one was in the presence of a man of destiny. His bearing and demeanor conveyed his ability and confidence to accomplish anything. If he was the king, we, his children, were the court.

I was four when we moved into the Franklin House, and we lived there until I was nine. My memories of that time are only fragmentary, and it was only through my rediscovery of my father later on that I was able to verify some of the truths behind those memories. But, like shadows, these shards of memory have followed me through life, and only now am I beginning to understand their import.

I remember how much I loved Father's Army jeep, a real World War II surplus model with an engine that growled and gears that clashed. I loved sitting in the front seat when he drove it out from the rear alleyway, across the vacant dirt lot that abutted our property, then over the curb into the busy intersection of Normandie and Franklin. Kelvin and I would take turns riding with Father in the jeep as he made his house calls. Sitting in the front of the open vehicle, I would look over as Dad navigated through the Hollywood traffic, his wondrous big black medical bag on the seat between us. On several occasions when the opportunity permitted, I looked inside this bag without Dad's knowledge. At that young age, I didn't recognize the objects, nor could I pronounce the names of the things there, and only later, as a Navy corpsman, would I learn what they were, but my child's mind knew they were Father's tools and were important. Cold to the touch and mysterious to the eye, his instruments fascinated me. There were his stethoscope, a tightly wound roll of ace bandage, a hemostat, the strange-looking sphygmomanometer, and a tourniquet. There were also labeled vials with names I couldn't understand, such as penicillin, Benadryl, and morphine. But mostly, I recall how I loved the smells that came from inside that bag, the smells of all things medicinal: clean, sharp, antiseptic.

I remember sitting in the jeep outside private homes while Father attended to his patients. After an hour, or maybe two, he would walk outside with a woman, whom I guessed had been his patient, seeing him off. It seemed as if all his patients said the same words, and those words always made me afraid. "Oh, so this is your son. He's darling. Can I keep him here with me?" I would look up as Father stood by the side of the jeep, holding my breath, not knowing what his answer would be until his slow, hesitant response would finally come: "Not this time, perhaps another, we shall see." The woman would touch his arm — they always touched his arm — and would smile at us and say, as he climbed into the jeep, "Thank you, Doctor. I feel so much better after your visit." He would smile, start the engine, and off we would go. Michael was nine, and he never went on these house calls with Dad, nor did Dad ever offer to take him. I never understood why.

Another warm memory from the Franklin years is of Fern Dell Park. My brothers and I spent whole summers there, all day every day. Father would drive us the short distance from the Franklin House to the entrance of the park, just a half-mile from our front door. He would drop us in the mornings with a stern, "Boys, I will pick you up here at 4:00 P.M. Do not make me wait." We hiked and played and scoured the park. We knew every turn, every tree, every hidden cave. Fern Dell had a creek that ran for miles north to south, and we would search for crayfish and bullfrogs, pretend we were explorers, finding and claiming new lands.

Michael, never without his beloved books, would read to us under the shade of a tall oak at the creek's edge. In the summer of '49, he was Robin Hood, Kelvin was Friar Tuck, and I, being larger and taller than either of my brothers, was Little John. Fern Dell became our Sherwood Forest. We laughed at the ferocity of Father's stern commands and rigid dictates: "Be at the entrance at four and do not make me wait." And in our make-believe we transformed our father into the evil Sheriff of Nottingham.

I also remember lots of people — grown-ups, men, and women — laughing late into the night at the Franklin House. Some of the faces and people I remember, most I have forgotten. Sometimes there were angry words with Father yelling, Mother yelling, then Mother crying. But mostly I remember the laughing. I remember Duncan, tall and twenty then, in his sailor's uniform, having come down from San Francisco with his friends to see his father and his three younger half-brothers. Even now I can see him standing in the courtyard, laughing and playing with the grown-ups, having fun with Father and his friends. Duncan would stay only a day or two, then back he would go to San Francisco.

Tamar, our half-sister, also came down from San Francisco to be with us that summer of 1949. She was fourteen, blonde with pretty blue eyes, and seemed to me almost like a grown-up. She was beautiful, and I loved it when she came to play and live with us. She was our secret and trusted friend, and she knew much more about grown-ups than we did. She was smart, and would tell us stories, most of which I no longer remember.

But there was one incident with Tamar that I shall never forget. It was early afternoon on a hot summer day in August 1949. Tamar and I were sitting on the steps at the front of the Franklin House. I can still feel the soft breeze that came from the west and the smell of the eucalyptus trees that helped guard the entrance. Tamar and I were sitting side by side and she was smoking a cigarette like real grown-ups did. She asked me, "Do you want to try?" I did. She handed the lit Lucky Strike to me, and I held it for a moment, then put it to my mouth. And as I started to suck on it, I looked up and there was Father. He approached us with his black bag in hand, and he was not three feet away. There I was, holding the cigarette in my hand, frozen with fear. He looked down at us both, nodded his head, and simply said, "Steven, Tamar," and walked by. He had not seen me holding the cigarette. We both sat, stock-still and silent, as if making any sound would change our luck. When he was safely out of sight we looked at each other and burst out laughing at our good fortune. I threw down the cigarette, stomped on it, and we ran off to play.

Formal dinners were common for our family. We had a live-in maid and cook, and that night when Dad returned from his office we sat in a formal arrangement at the large table: Dad at the south end, the head of the table; Mother at the north; I to Dad's immediate right; my brothers across from me; and Tamar to my right. That night, we had just finished dessert, after the large four-course meal, when Father said, addressing us with his accustomed formality, "I have an announcement to make." He paused until all our heads were turned his way and the attention was undivided.

"It seems that Steven, who is not quite eight, has decided he wants to smoke," he continued. I looked anxiously at Tamar, realizing Father had indeed seen me holding her cigarette. Dad reached inside his jacket pocket and withdrew a cigar. "So," he said, "we are all going to sit here while Steven smokes this." He slowly and ceremoniously unwrapped the large Havana that he usually enjoyed after dinners, cut off the end, carefully lit it so that the tip was a bright orange glow, and handed it to me in a cloud of exhaled smoke. All eyes at the table were locked on me as I took it from him and held it in my hand. He continued in a firm, hard tone, "Go ahead, Steven, smoke it." I fought back the tears as I looked at him, my hands now shaking, as his voice descended into a menacing, controlled anger: "Smoke it!"

I drew on the cigar and coughed loudly. Mother attempted to intervene: "George, I don't think —" He shot back at her, "No, we are all going to sit right here, all of us, until Steven finishes that cigar." There was silence around the table as I was made to take more drags of smoke. I was sick, turning green, and I was afraid of Father, but I tried to hide it. Dad, believing he had made his point, finally said to me, "Well, Steven, what do you think of smoking now?"

I tried to look directly at his face, but could not quite manage it as I responded, "That was good, Dad. Can I have another?" My brothers and sister laughed, he stared hard at me, then looked at them. "You are all excused from the table. Steven, I will see you in the basement in five minutes."

My brothers and I hated the basement. It was a place we never explored and kept out of our minds, because it was a place of punishment. The basement meant the razor strap, and the razor strap meant a searing pain until Father decided we'd had enough.

As noted, among my parents' closest friends during the war years and after were Man Ray and his wife, Juliet. Man Ray, born Emmanuel Radnitsky in Philadelphia in 1890, was one of the world's leading surrealists. In his early twenties, influenced by the nineteenth-century avant-garde French poets Charles Baudelaire and Arthur Rimbaud, he began drawing and painting. Also while still in his twenties, he became acquainted with the American poet William Carlos Williams, as well as artists Marcel Duchamp and Francis Picabia and the burgeoning New York Dada movement. He had a number of one-man shows in New York and became associated with American modernist painters.

In 1921 he went to France, where Marcel Duchamp introduced him to a number of Dadaists. In Paris, he began his photographic work, establishing himself as a portrait artist, photographing such important literary figures as the expatriate American writer Gertrude Stein, as well as James Joyce, Ezra Pound, and Jean Cocteau. Cocteau summoned his friend Man Ray to the deathbed of Marcel Proust, to photograph and immortalize Proust's passing. His fame steadily increased and soon he was an established artist in the surrealist and Dada movements, each of which has its own relevance in the relationship between Man Ray and my father.

Surrealism, for example, stressed the subconscious and nonrational, principally through its representation of unexpected juxtapositions that defy reality. The Dadaists also stressed the incongruity of artistic representation, while at the same time challenging convention and traditional morality.

Along with their mutual passion for France, its people and language, my father shared with Man Ray an interest in the life and work of the Marquis de Sade. During the mid-1930s, Man Ray devoted six or eight paintings and sculptures to the notorious French writer and debauchee, whom he called his "inspiration." During his twenty years in Paris, Man Ray read and studied all of Sade's erotic writings, and through his personal interpretation of the man, the artist represented him as an example of "one of the world's freest of thinkers." Man Ray worshiped what he believed was Sade's complete freedom from convention, from the morals society imposes, and even from the constraints of literary taste. It is believed that while in Paris in the early 1920s, Man Ray was asked to photograph, for preservation purposes, a rare original handwritten manuscript by Sade entitled *The 120 Days of Sodom*, which had been discovered in the French government's archives at the turn of the century.

Man Ray's fame increased as his camera lens continued to capture many of the world's rich and famous personalities, including Virginia Woolf, Henri Matisse, Coco Chanel, Henry Miller, Salvador

Dalí, and Pablo Picasso. Portraits, however, while a nice source of income, were not really what Man Ray claimed to be about. He was an artist, a very special artist. But now, with the shadow of war lengthening across Europe, he felt it was time to go home.

After his successful one-man show in Los Angeles in 1935, Man Ray decided to settle in L.A. Perhaps he was also attracted to the home of the film industry because he had experimented in filmmaking in Paris. He arrived in Hollywood in November 1940. His artistic return was not auspicious. In 1941, he had a museum show in L.A. that was not well received. The *Los Angeles Times*'s art critic, H. Millier, in a review of Man Ray's painting entitled *Imaginary Portrait of D.A.F. de Sade* in the April edition of *Art Digest*, equated the subject matter to "crime and torture magazines."

Man Ray's reverence for Sade is documented again and again throughout his works. A 1933 silver-print photograph entitled *Monument à D.A.F. de Sade* depicts a woman's buttock framed within an inverted cross, an obvious reference to Sade's preference for sodomy and his utter disdain for the church.

To say that Man Ray was a devoted sadist, both aesthetically and philosophically, is an understatement. He never made any attempt to conceal his beliefs regarding the subjugation and humiliation of women. On the contrary, he revelled in depicting them as objects and playthings for the true sensualist because, like Sade, he believed women exist for man's pleasure, which is only enhanced through the humiliation, degradation, and infliction of pain upon them.

Exactly where and how Man Ray and Juliet met Mother and Father I do not know. Most likely they met shortly after his arrival from France, although one unconfirmed report has it that Father originally met Man Ray in New York when he was living and visiting Mother and John Huston in the Village in 1928.

That these four — Man Ray, Juliet, George, and Dorero — would meet was almost inevitable. They were all sensualists; their own likes and strong desires must have drawn them as moths to the same single flame of passion. To Father life itself was surreal, a dream in which each man made up and lived by his own rules and within his own world. Like the sinister Aleister Crowley's "Black Magician" from the turn of the twentieth century, my father conducted his life according to the dictum "Do what thou wilt shall be the whole of the law."

The first of our family photographs by Man Ray that I am aware of were taken in 1944, when we lived on Valentine Street in Elysian Park, the neighborhood where Dodger Stadium stands today, just a hardball throw from downtown. From 1945 until the fall of 1949, both Man Ray and Juliet were regular partygoers at the Franklin House, where Dad's guests could relax and indulge themselves in cocktails, a courtesan, or plenty of cocaine.

During these years, Man Ray took a number of photographs at the Franklin House and several formally posed portraits of my mother at his residence-studio on Vine Street, just a few blocks away and directly across the street from the landmark Hollywood Ranch Market. In some of these photographs Mother was alone; in others, she posed with Juliet. In 1946, Man Ray gave Mother and Dad a self-portrait as a gift, which he would later use as the cover for his auto-biography, *Self Portrait*, published in 1963.

*Exhibit 13*

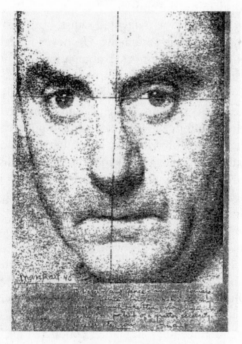

*Man Ray, 1946*

His inscription to my parents on the photograph reads:

> To Dorero and George — and my homage as I am pleased
> when I am asked for my phiz — so much more than when I am
> asked for a portrait of a greater celebrity. I celebrate you.
>
> Man

In 1947, just a few months after the murder of Elizabeth Short and while the investigation was at its most heated, Man Ray left Hollywood for Paris. He later returned and remained in Hollywood through 1950, when both he and Juliet returned to Paris and established permanent residence there until his death in November 1976.

The influence of Man Ray on George Hodel cannot be underestimated. Already an amateur photographer of some note, my father admired and looked up to the world-famous Man Ray. Despite his plethora of professions and accomplishments, in his heart of hearts, George Hodel aspired to be an artist.

# 7

# The Hollywood Scandal

DESPITE HER FOURTEEN YEARS, our half-sister Tamar could have doubled for the young Marilyn Monroe, who the following year would launch her career in John Huston's *The Asphalt Jungle*.

What was most striking about Tamar was her physical maturity. She easily passed for someone in her early twenties. And that's exactly how she acted. Bright and strong-willed, she hungered for attention and affection. Her mother, still living in San Francisco, and now re-married, sent Tamar down to spend the summer of 1949 with her father and her half-brothers. By the end of 1949, life, as we had known and enjoyed it, was over.

The floating sounds of people partying across the courtyard from my room at the Franklin House grew louder night after night during the summer of 1949. So did the sound of my parents fighting: their raised voices would echo through the corridors at night.

Then suddenly, on October 1, 1949, Tamar ran away from the Franklin House and disappeared. Dad tried to search for her pri-vately at first, contacting her friends and schoolmates to see if anyone had seen her. But after coming up empty, Dad was forced to notify the police. A formal missing persons report was filed and two days later she was found hiding at a girlfriend's home.

Tamar was taken into custody by LAPD Juvenile detectives, who, before returning her home, asked her why she had run away.

By the time the questioning was over, she had implicated not only Father but Fred Sexton and two other adult women in engaging her in sexual activities and intercourse. The Juvenile officers were stunned at the revelations and quickly moved to file charges.

Tamar was detained at Juvenile Hall, and five days later Father

*Municipal Court document showing Dr. George Hill Hodel's arrest for incest which establishes his "cash bailout" and release from custody on October 6, 1949 at 10:15 A.M.*

was one of the first to be arrested. He immediately posted $5,000 bail and was released from custody on Thursday, October 6, 1949, at 10:15 A.M. But by then the scandal had already reached the newspapers. The *Los Angeles Times* of October 7, 1949, ran the following article, accompanied by a photo of Dad standing with his attorney after his release on bail:

# DOCTOR FACES ACCUSATION IN MORALS CASE

## *DAUGHTER'S STORY CREDITED ALSO IN ARREST OF 13 BOYS*

Wild parties in which a Hollywood physician and his 14-year-old daughter assertedly participated yesterday led to the arrest of the doctor and 13 boys.

The father, Dr. George Hill Hodel, 38, of 5121 Franklin Ave. was booked in Hollywood Jail on District Attorney's charges of two morals offenses.

### Fellow Students

Det. Sgt. L. A. Bell and Detective Shirley Maxwell said his daughter implicated him and 19 other persons. Some of these are fellow students with her at Hollywood High School.

Dep. Dist. Atty. William L. Ritzi said the daughter ran away from home last Friday because her "home life was too depressing" but she was found Sunday at the home of a friend. She is now held in Juvenile Hall.

Both men and women figured in the series of bizarre parties, Ritzi said. Hodel is a photography enthusiast and said they seized many questionable photographs and pornographic art objects at his home.

The article went on to say that the doctor told Ritzi that he was "delving into the mystery of love and the universe," and that the acts of which he was accused were "unclear, like a dream . . . I can't figure out whether someone is hypnotizing me or I am hypnotizing someone." Dr. Hodel's preliminary hearing was set for October 14.

In a related article in the *Los Angeles Evening Herald and Express* on October 7, under the headline "Doctor Nabbed on Hollywood Incest Charge," the reporter added several important facts to the story:

> The 14-year-old daughter told officers that her father had molested her since she was 11 years old.
>
> Dr. Hodel, a medical officer of the United Nations mission to China, questioned by Deputy District Attorneys Ritzi and S. Ernest Roll admitted, "These things must have happened." He said he wanted to consult his psychiatrist.

Still in juvenile detention and "protective custody," Tamar was reinterviewed by Juvenile detectives, to whom she revealed that her father had also arranged and paid for an abortion performed on her in a Beverly Hills doctor's office. Accordingly, four days after George Hodel's arrest police arrested Beverly Hills physician Dr. Francis C. Ballard, age thirty-six, and his "associate" Charles Smith, also thirty-six, for performing an abortion on Tamar. In the complaint, the abortion was alleged to have occurred in September 1949, a month before Tamar ran away.

Several days after Father's arrest, Juvenile detectives conducted a search of the Franklin House. The search resulted in the seizure of various items deemed "pornographic" in nature, which would have included books, photographs, and several statues of nymphs and satyrs "frolicking" together. During the search, detectives found the statues in a secret storage room behind the living room bookcase, whose existence Tamar had revealed to the Juvenile detectives.

Since it contained all the ingredients of a big juicy Hollywood scandal, the story generated a huge amount of local public interest: a wealthy and prominent, dapper Hollywood physician, his Marilyn Monroe lookalike underage daughter, orgiastic parties, reams of pornographic material and art, some of which was stashed in secret rooms, more than a dozen Hollywood High School teenagers named in a sex ring, a secret abortion, and, just in time for the trial, the showmen defense attorneys of their day, Jerry "Get Me" Giesler and his ringmaster partner Robert Neeb.

A preliminary hearing was held in municipal court a week after the arrest, and based on the testimony of Tamar, who remained under Juvenile Hall detention, and other witnesses present in the bedroom at the time the acts occurred, Dad was bound over to the Superior Court for trial on two felony counts: incest and oral copulation. On December 8, 1949, a jury of eight women and four men were selected and the Superior Court trial of *State of California vs. Dr. George Hill Hodel* began.

The prosecution was confident because they felt they had an unusually strong case. Normally, in a charge of incest you rarely have more than the one complaining victim/witness. Parents generally do not have sex with their children in front of or with other people. Prosecutor Ritzi had three adult witnesses present in Father's bedroom, two of whom allegedly had participated in the sexual acts. Ritzi also had damning statements and admissions made by the defendant that he was "delving into the mystery of love and the universe" and that "these things must have happened." Also, the DA had Dad's statements — a potential "dream defense" — where he told detectives the whole thing was "unclear, like a dream. I can't figure out whether someone is hypnotizing me or I am hypnotizing someone." Ritzi also had the detectives' "loot" from the search of the Franklin House.

The first witness called to testify was Tamar. Because of her age, newspaper photographs of her were not permitted, but the attending press were overly colorful in their verbal descriptions of the young victim, characterizing Tamar in separate articles as "sultry," "blonde, blue-eyed, and loquacious," "precocious," and "gesturing dramatically and frequently to the jurors."

Tamar, questioned by prosecutor William Ritzi on direct examination, testified that on the evening of July 1, 1949, she returned home, changed her clothes, and went into her father's bedroom wearing a green smock, blue jeans, gold slippers, and a brassiere. Present in her father's bedroom were her father, his friend Fred Sexton, and two adult women, Barbara Sherman, age twenty-two, and Mrs. Corrine Tarin, age twenty-seven. Tamar drank a tumbler full of sherry, and then Fred Sexton undressed her and committed an act of oral copulation. She testified that her father then performed both oral sex and an act of intercourse and was followed by Barbara Sherman, who orally copulated with her.

Tamar's direct testimony was followed by what the newspapers described as "two blistering days of cross examination by Giesler's partner, attorney Robert A. Neeb." On the second day, with Tamar just about to leave the witness stand, Neeb begged, "Just one more question, Your Honor." He stepped in close to the young teenager on the stand, turned and looked into the eyes of the jurors, paused for dramatic effect, and then demanded of the witness:

Tamar, do you recall a conversation you had with a roommate at the Franklin House by the name of Joe Barrett? And do you recall, in that conversation, making the following statement to him: "This house has secret passages. My father is the murderer of the Black Dahlia. My father is going to kill me and all the rest of the members of this household because he has a lust for blood. He is insane"?

*Exhibit 14*

*Tamar, age 17 (1952)*

The courtroom was shocked into silence as all eyes focused on the witness, awaiting her response. Trembling and fearful with her eyes downcast, she could not speak. Ordered by the judge to answer, she simply stated, "I don't remember saying that to Joe."

The following morning, December 17, the *Daily News* reported the dramatic testimony: "Girl Accused of Trying to Pin Dahlia Murder on Dad." The *Los Angeles Mirror's* article of the same day declared, "Girl's Story Is 'Fantasy,' Court Hears." The article read, in part:

> The 14-year-old daughter of a prominent Hollywood physician "plotted his downfall" with fantastic stories, including one that he killed Elizabeth (Black Dahlia) Short, his attorney, Robert A. Neeb Jr., sought to prove today.
>
> Neeb hammered at the "fantasies" of blonde Tamar Hodel in her cross-examination at the morals trial of Dr. George Hill Hodel, 38.
>
> Dr. Hodel, who has denied the charges, will seek to show that his daughter is a known "pathological liar" in matters dealing with her alleged relations with men.

Over the next few days the court saw more prosecution witnesses take the stand. Corrine Tarin testified to being present in the bedroom, but denied she had participated in any way. She told the jurors that she saw Tamar kiss Fred Sexton "very passionately," and then Sexton, in the presence of herself and George Hodel, undressed Tamar, orally copulated with her, and then had sexual intercourse with her. She admitted that after Sexton completed the act, Doctor Hodel pulled him off Tamar, they had heated, angry words, and he ordered Sexton out of the bedroom. Tarin remained in the bedroom while Hodel performed cunnilingus on his daughter and began an act of sexual intercourse. She completed her testimony by saying, "I am the mother of two daughters, and at that point, I became very disturbed, and I walked out of the bedroom."

Fred Sexton was called and reluctantly testified that the four of them were in the bedroom, that Tamar was undressed, and he "kissed her and attempted to have sex with her, but did not complete the act."

The third adult present in the bedroom, twenty-two-year-old Barbara Sherman, was called but refused to testify before the jury. Sherman recanted her earlier statements to the police as well as the sworn testimony she had provided at the October 14 preliminary hearing. Prosecutor Ritzi threatened her with arrest if she refused to tell the truth, but still Sherman would not cooperate. She was immediately arrested in the courthouse and charged with perjury and morals violations based on the fact that she had previously provided sworn testimony to having performed sexual acts with Tamar and to having witnessed the sexual acts on Tamar performed by both her father and Sexton. Juvenile officer M. H. Brimson was then called to testify to "finding the pornographic literature and lewd statuary in the mansion at 5121 Franklin Avenue."

After the prosecution had rested its case, the defense called fourteen witnesses, each of whom testified that Tamar was a "pathological liar" and was not to be believed. The first three witnesses were all family members: her grandmother, her own mother, and her half-brother Duncan, who all hammered home the point that whatever Tamar swore to under oath should not be believed. All of this was exhilarating fodder for the dailies chronicling the testimony with headlines such as "Grandma Calls Tamar Hodel 'Untruthful'" and "Tamar's Ma Calls Her an Awful Liar." Each of them in turn admonished the jury not to believe anything Tamar said.

December 21, the shortest day of the year, was the longest of Dad's life, because on that day the wealthy Hollywood doctor at the center of the media frenzy was called to testify in his own defense. Calm and dignified as he unfolded his version of the events that led to his arrest, he held the jury spellbound with the story of how he was "demonstrating hypnosis to the four adults in his bedroom." Barbara Sherman was the subject, and Sexton and Corrine Tarin watched as he ordered Sherman to raise her hands, suggesting to her they were "bars of steel." He told the jury that when he "turned to the others to have them note the experiment," he saw that Tarin's arms were likewise extended, and then he saw his daughter and Sexton sprawled on the bed. He claimed that Tamar "had her blouse and brassiere off and Sexton was fully clothed." He immediately "pulled Sexton off of her, and ordered him out of the bedroom." After Sexton left he ordered Tarin out of the bedroom and sent Tamar to her room.

He related to the jury that Tamar was mistaken on her dates, and the hypnosis session was not July 1, but rather June 18, the same night she had come down from San Francisco to live at the house.

He informed the jurors how he had asked her mother, Dorothy Anthony Barbe, not to send her down because he had recently suffered
a heart attack and was in no position to give his daughter the close
supervision that she needed. He concluded his testimony by informing the jury that Tamar's account was "nonsense, and was the fantasy
of a vengeful and incorrigible child."

It was my father's word against Tamar's and the other witnesses',
particularly Corrine Tarin and Fred Sexton, as well as against the
boxes of evidence retrieved from the Franklin House, all of which
pointed to my father's deep interest in sexual fantasy, clearly focusing
on the perverse. Despite the attacks on Tamar's credibility by her
mother and grandmother, Corrine Tarin's and Fred Sexton's testimony corroborated Tamar's testimony as to the sexual nature of the
events that evening and the fact that she had been molested by an
adult. It would be up to the defense to get my father off the hook in
the face of very damning evidence. If Dad's defense attorneys could
not find a way through the maze, my father would go to jail, lose his
medical license, and his career would be over.

In his summation, Neeb directly attacked the testimony of the
adult witnesses present in the bedroom by not only assaulting the
credibility of the witnesses themselves, but arguing that the jury
couldn't even consider their testimony:

> You are instructed that even if you did believe that there was suffi-
> cient evidence to convince you beyond a reasonable doubt as to this
> particular offense, you still cannot convict the defendant upon the
> testimony of Tamar Hodel, who would be, under the circum-
> stances, if they were true, an accomplice, and you cannot convict
> any person upon the uncorroborated testimony of an accomplice.
>
> You are further instructed that the witness Corrine Tarin, be-
> cause of her conduct, would also be an accomplice, and one accom-
> plice cannot corroborate another, and the same rule applies to the
> testimony of Fred Sexton.

In his next summary argument, Neeb told the jury:

> According to the testimony in this case, the witness Fred Sexton
> has by his testimony admitted that he attempted to have inter-

course with Tamar Hodel, who is under the age of eighteen years, and as a result the witness Fred Sexton could be charged with an attempted rape, a felony, and you may consider, in determining the weight and credibility to be given to the witness Fred Sexton, the question of whether he has been arrested or charged with an attempted rape as it may bear upon the question of his state of mind while testifying, or any hope which he may have of immunity from prosecution as a result of his testifying for the prosecution and against the defendant in this case.

And finally:

You are instructed that if a person aids and abets and encourages another person in the commission of any offense, the person who aids, abets or encourages may be guilty of the same offense of the person who actually commits the act and in this regard you may consider the question of whether or not the witness Corrine Tarin would or would not be in a position of one who was aiding, abetting or encouraging the witness Fred Sexton in an attempted rape, a felony, upon Tamar Hodel, and if said Corrine Tarin is found by you to be in such a position, you are instructed that she would then be an accomplice of the said Fred Sexton, and as such could be subject to prosecution as a principal in the offense of attempted rape, a felony; and you may consider this together with the fact that the said Corrine Tarin has not been arrested or charged as an accomplice with the said Fred Sexton in the commission of an attempted rape as such situation may bear upon her credibility and her state of mind while testifying, and any hope of immunity from prosecution that she may have as a result of her testifying for the prosecution in this case.

Neeb's defense was powerful, instructing the jury that because Tamar Hodel was a partner in the crimes his client was being charged with, the jury couldn't use Tamar's testimony without other corroborating evidence. Therefore, the jury, by law, had to disregard Tamar's testimony. Neeb also argued that the jury should not convict Dr. Hodel on the testimony of either Fred Sexton or Corrine Tarin, because they were both admitted accomplices to felony sex offenses, and both had presumably made deals with the police to tell them what they wanted to hear in exchange for not being charged with crimes and not going to prison.

In his closing argument to the jury, defense attorney Robert Neeb hammered at the fact that Tamar, a "psychopathic liar," should never have been allowed to testify. "She should be in a hospital under treatment as a psychopath," he declared, reminding the panel of eight women and four men of the long parade of defense witnesses who had testified to Tamar's inability to tell the truth.

After final instructions by Superior Judge Thomas L. Ambrose, the case was given to the jury late in the afternoon of December 24, 1949. After less than four hours of deliberation, the jury returned an acquittal verdict on both felony counts. The morning *Mirror* headline read, "Jury Declares Dr. Hodel Innocent of Sex Charges," and continued:

> The prominent Hollywood doctor wept when the jury announced its verdict . . .
>
> Tamar, whose lurid account of a lustful predawn sex circus in her father's bedroom brought the scandal, was not present. She is in Juvenile Hall . . .
>
> In his closing arguments, Neeb pleaded that Tamar be given psychiatric treatment. It was not learned immediately what disposition would be made of the girl.

On January 12, 1950, some three weeks after my father's acquittal, Superior Court judge Thomas Ambrose entered an order directing that certain items be released to the district attorney's office investigators. Those items were the pornographic books, the satyr, centaur-piece statue, and the fifteen or more "photographs."*

Five weeks later, on February 1, 1950, a small article appeared in the *Los Angeles Times*, under the headline "Probation Given in Morals Case":

---

*This seemingly innocuous notation in the court records became a blinking red light for me. Why were investigators from the district attorney's office requesting that the judge release court evidence from an LAPD case to them? Procedurally this was highly unorthodox. Normally only the primary investigators — in this case LAPD Juvenile detectives — would be permitted physical custody of the evidence. It would be many months more before I would learn the answer.

Barbara Shearman, 21, [*sic*] a central figure in the morals trial of
Dr. George Hill Hodel, yesterday was placed on three years' probation after she pleaded guilty to contributing to the delinquency
of a minor.

Judge Ambrose sentenced Miss Sherman to one year in jail, then
suspended the sentence and placed her on probation, ordering her to
refrain from any further association with Dr. Hodel or any of his
friends.

The trial was over. My father was acquitted. Tamar was gone.
And the late-night parties at the house had stopped. But just when I
thought that life for the family would get back to what we had had
before the arrest and trial, my brothers and I, without any explanation from our parents, were enrolled in Page Academy, a highly reg-
imented military school in Los Angeles. We had been banished from
the castle to a place that was little more than a prison. Worse, Father
was gone. Without a word, he simply seemed to have disappeared.
Not even our mother, who would occasionally visit us on weekends,
would talk about where he had gone. All we knew was that he was
selling — or had already sold — Franklin House and was moving
away. Out of the country. After a long silence, I later learned that he
had moved to Hawaii, where he had remarried.

In retrospect, I was too young to know what was really going on during the Franklin House years, other than a child's awareness of lots of
people, noise, music, laughter, and my mother's mix of joy and sadness. Knowing what I now know about both my parents, I realize she
was walking a high wire with no net. The fact was, Mother was living
there at his pleasure. They were divorced, so Father's womanizing
could and did go unchecked. Her drinking, and most likely drug use,
was excessive, and she was dependent upon him for supplying all of
her and our material needs. In addition, I know that Mother was bi-
sexual and hedonistic by nature, and I am certain she took a willing
and active part with the other adult partygoers. I also know that, unlike Father, she had her limits, which most certainly would not have
included sex with Tamar or other minor children. I now see Father's
role as panderer — using Mother's weaknesses and addictions to sex,
drugs, and alcohol for his own and others' benefit. He controlled her

like most pimps control their women, through intimidation and threats. Father's arrest and trial for incest was a last straw, which likely forced Mother to break and run with her cubs. There was no turning back. I expect she and most other family friends and intimates fully anticipated that Father would be convicted and sent to prison.

I make no moral judgments of my mother. I loved and love her as most sons do — unconditionally. She had great strengths and great weaknesses, but above all she protected and raised her three sons as best she knew how, under the most difficult circumstances.

A few months after our arrival at Page Academy, Mother visited us with a friend we knew from the Franklin House, screenwriter and director Rowland Brown, a large gray-haired man who looked like a grandfather. Mother told us that she and Father had divorced and my brothers and I were going to live with her in the desert far from Hollywood, near Rowland Brown and his family. While we were still recovering from the dual shock of our sudden release and the news that our father and mother had divorced, we were told to put our belongings into a large truck that Rowland had parked outside the school. Mother was crying, even as she tried to tell us how wonderful life was going to be without Father, and that made the rest of us cry as well. We knew it was a lie, but there was nothing we could do about it except climb inside the back of Rowland's truck and ride out of the city and into the isolation of the California desert and a place we had never seen called Rancho Mirage.

It was there, Mother kept promising us through her tears, that we would have a whole new life.

# 8

# Gypsies

IF THE LIVES WE LED in the fairy-tale beauty of the Franklin House, with Father holding court every night, were rich and magical, our lives with Mother, until I left the family to join the Navy, were marked by starkly desperate periods of privation and transiency. At first we settled in the harsh California desert, in a small dusty town forty minutes from Palm Springs inhabited by sidewinder snakes and scorpions.

We liked the desert because it was different. The night sky was a spread of a million bright stars against a chorus of howling coyotes somewhere in the distance beyond the scrub and chaparral. During the day the hot winds would blow, sending tumbleweeds like an advancing phalanx before them. But amidst all the fragments of memory of those first few months in Rancho Mirage that I can bring to mind — Mom in the real estate office, Mom and our neighbors, Mom in a stupor on the couch as the duties of carrying the empties out to the garbage fell to us — what stands out the most is the brief, few-hour visit from Dad. He came from Hawaii and brought us as a gift a dog named Aloha.

We loved her, but she quickly ran away and was lost to the desert, where she might have been eaten by a puma. And Dad too had left, returning to his new family and his new life.

We didn't stay in the desert very long, moving back to Los Angeles in less than a year. We had also discovered Mother's secret drinking problem, only it wasn't a secret anymore. Her binges would last sometimes for days, and after the second or third day she could not work, cook, clean, iron our clothes for school, help us with homework, or even stand up and walk. Although we were only nine, ten, and eleven, the three of us had to figure out how to run a household around our semi-comatose mother. We couldn't even bring anyone home, because we couldn't let anyone see her lying on the couch, unable to get up, unable to do anything. We made a pact to protect her and just make do, all the while hoping that we would be rescued, that this bad dream would end, and we'd be back inside the castle. But it was not to be.

By 1951 we had become gypsies, always on the move, because every time our mother went on binges she would lose her job, fall behind in the rent, and wind up with an eviction notice pasted on the door. Fortunately, when she did work it was for real estate offices, where she would jump on the rental listings before they became public. That gave her an inside advantage when cheap apartments came up. So we bounced around from town to town throughout Los Angeles County, moving on an average of every three months. In the early 1950s Mother was arrested several times for child neglect, when neighbors would discover her passed out after she was well into one of her two-week binges. On several occasions, the three of us were taken away from her by social services and placed in county homes, but somehow she would get us back. At which point we would move to another area, another town, and start over again.

Our nomadic existence lasted for two years before we finally wound up in Pasadena, where Mother managed to stay sober long enough to save some money and rent a large home on Los Robles Avenue on the west side of town. Just as we were allowing ourselves to relax and enjoy our new place, she started drinking again, and before long she lost her job and another "pay or quit" notice was stapled to our door. Desperate for money, having tapped out all her usual sources from her friends, and already having been advanced a month's salary from her real estate manager, Mother chanced to see an article in the newspaper about John Huston's return to Los Angeles for the Academy Awards.

She may have been drunk most of the time, but if there was an opportunity, Mother knew how to seize it and make her move. She called us into her room, where she dressed us up in wrinkled but clean shirts and pants, then quickly brushed and leashed our boxer dog, Koko. She hurriedly scribbled a note, folded it into an envelope, and pinned it to my shirt. She spoke to us in her accustomed slur, as she dialed for a taxicab: "Now, boys, I want you to be on your best behavior. You're going to see John. Steven, you will give him this note from me, then after your visit come straight home."

The cab arrived and the driver looked at Mother. "I can't take the dog, lady," he said. She opened the back door of the taxi and motioned for all of us to get inside. "Yes you can. It's all right, take them to the Beverly Hills Hotel, and wait for them, then bring them back here." The cabbie's eyes lit up and he smiled, knowing that it was a twenty-five-mile drive each way.

The Beverly Hills Hotel, a stately pink-and-green landmark at the intersection of Sunset Boulevard and Beverly Drive, is more like an elegant golf or country club than a hotel. In the middle 1950s, it was still one of the last bastions of the old Hollywood aristocracy. It was into this gentlemen's club lobby that I and my two brothers walked, feeling all eyes in the hotel staring at us, making our way to the front desk and holding Koko tightly on her leash. The dog, whose grandsire had been national champion and judged "Best of Show," knew how to perform on a leash. "Koko, sit," I ordered her once we reached the desk. And the dog obeyed. The desk clerk smiled. "Can I help you gentlemen?" I tried to hide my nervousness. "We would like to see John," I said. He suddenly became more guarded and looked down at me with peering eyes. He asked, "Who?"

My older brother Michael responded, "Mr. Huston. We are here to see John Huston." The clerk became more guarded now. "Who might I say is calling?" Michael answered again: "Tell him that it's the Hodels, Michael, Steven, and Kelvin. And Koko." Upon hearing her name the dog began wagging her tail furiously. The desk clerk placed a quick call on the house phone, looked surprised, nodded, and we were escorted to the elevator, which took us up to the penthouse suite. The elevator door opened and in we went.

We hadn't seen John Huston in over two years. We knew him from the Franklin House, where he and his father, Walter, had been regular social guests at many of the parties. Standing there now in the Beverly Hills Hotel, thin and tall, he looked to me to be a seven-foot tower as his booming voice greeted us. "Hello, boys. And who might this be?" Kelvin answered first: "She's our dog, Koko, she's a boxer." John instantly caught the nuance in her name and laughed loudly. "Koko — is that for a double knockout? K.O.-K.O.?" Michael, who had named her, was impressed. "Yes, that's right. You're the only person that has ever figured it out. We always have to tell other people." John laughed even harder.

Excited by hearing her name called out so many times, Koko ran to the center of the suite, squatted on the plush white carpet as if it were high brush on a vacant lot, and took a dump. The three of us stood watching in disbelief, then a loud voice, roaring with laughter from the couch behind us, said, "I'll get it." The tall handsome dark-haired man, obviously in even better spirits than John, staggered to a bathroom and came back with a large roll of toilet paper. He dropped to his knees near where Koko had squatted and started to clean up the mess. John Huston said, "Boys, I want you to meet Greg Peck. When he's not cleaning up dogshit, he acts," and both roared with laughter. John took the envelope from my shirt, read its contents, walked over to a desk, wrote out a check and a note, placed them both back in the envelope, and returned it to me.

"Here, Steven, give this to your mother," he said. The big man with the big voice walked us back down to the lobby and out to the waiting taxi. Huston handed the driver some bills. "Here, cabbie, take them home." And in less than an hour we were standing before our mother, who had come out to meet us at the front door when she saw the taxi pull up. Before I could get out of the taxi, she grabbed the envelope from my hand, opened it, and smiled. "Five hundred dollars. We can pay the rent and we can get some food. You boys can go to the movies and I can buy a new coat." For us, this meant we could stay in Pasadena and not have to flee the sheriff in the middle of the night.

Over the next few months, Mother's drinking became even heavier, and her binges seemed to last longer. Instead of five-day drunks, they would extend to ten, but we had friends now and stayed overnight at their houses as much as we could. Our schoolmates' parents seemed to understand and often fed and housed us for a few days as family when they noticed we hadn't changed our clothes and hadn't eaten. But even that didn't help, because John Huston's money quickly ran out and we had to move again.

It was late one warm summer night in 1954, about midnight, when I entered our newly rented home on Lake Street. Mother had told us that her gypsy spirit demanded a change in houses, but we knew it was because the previous landlord had given her notice after three months' late rent payments. Mother had found a *new* friend of hers to move us, someone we had never seen before. A big man with an old truck, he had large greasy hands and dressed in blue overalls like the picture of Farmer John on a package of sausages. The move took us two days of back-and-forth, but we finally got all our stuff to the new house.

The electricity still hadn't been turned on that midnight as I felt my way cautiously through the maze of boxes in the living room. The house was silent. "Mother," I called out. But there was no answer. I yelled louder, "Mother, are you here?" I could hear muffled sounds in the bedroom and made my way to the door. I opened it. "Mother?" I could barely make out both figures on the bed. "Mother, are you all right?"

I ran to her through the darkness. The large ugly man who had moved us was on top of her, his clothes in a pile on the floor. "Get off, leave her alone!" I grabbed the nearest object — a lamp — and began hitting him on the back with it. He turned and slapped me open-handed, knocking me across the room. "Get the fuck out of here, boy, before I really hurt you." Then I heard Mother's voice, slurred and sloppy: "How dare you touch my son! Get out, get out of this house!" They were both drunk. "I'll get out," the man hollered, "but don't you ever ask for money or help from me again. You and your high airs and fancy clothes, you ain't nothing but a whore, lady, and not even a good one."

I watched in fear and silence as the dark figure fumbled with his clothes, dressed, and staggered toward the door. He stopped, turned toward me, his voice filled with rage: "Just so you know, boy, your mother — she's a lousy fuck!" He left. Mother pulled the blanket over herself, lit a cigarette, and said, "He's a bad man, Steven. He's a terrible man. I should have never let him move us."

I looked at her lying there drunk, barely able to hold her cigarette as she struggled to sit up. Then she collapsed in a heap, cigarette and all. I was filled with hatred. "He's right, Mother!" I screamed. "You are a whore. You are a drunk and a whore! I don't want you for my mother. I hate you. I never want to see you again. Ever! I want to go live with my father. I want to go to the Philippines and live with him. If you don't let me, I'll run away and never come back!" Her voice got louder now, and she began to yell back at me. "You don't know! You don't know! Your father! Your father is a monster! He is a terrible man and he's done terrible things!"

Her voice cracked from the intensity of her screaming. "Your father pretends to be a doctor and a healer, but he's really insane! If you really knew the truth you'd hate your father!"

"You're just saying that because he left you," I cried. "Because he hated you too, like I do. He hated your drinking and your lies."

I ran, not as much from the house as from her words, and for four days stayed with a friend. I returned only when I had made a promise to myself to leave the family as soon as I could figure out a way to get to my father. And when I did return, I found Mother weak, shaky, but at least sober. In front of all three sons she promised that she was quitting drinking, that she would never "touch another drop." We'd heard that a hundred times before, but we were gullible and believed her each time.

When we were alone later that night, I asked her what she meant when she said those things about Father. She looked at me and said, "What things?" I told her what she had said. Her already pale face turned ashen as she said, "I never said those things." I stared at her in disbelief. "You did, Mother, you called him a monster and said he was insane. Those were your exact words."

Now there was real fear in her voice. "Steven," she said, "sometimes I say things when I've been drinking that are fantasies, make-believe. They are made up things, like bad dreams that come to people when they are drunk. Have you heard the word DT? It stands for delirium tremens, and it comes to people when they drink a lot. People see and say imaginary things. Maybe that's what it was, but whatever I said is not true. Your father is a brilliant doctor, a good man, and maybe I was just upset because we have no money and because you said you hated me."

She put her arms around me and held me tight. "I want you to forget about such things. They are ugly and unreal. What is real is that I love you, and I promise you I will never drink again and everything will be back to normal." I looked at her pale face, her shaking hands and sad eyes filled with tears, which I took to be tears of remorse. And in that moment I believed that what she had told me about Father she had said because she was drunk. If it was because of what she called the DTs, then that's what it had to be. And if she would truly quit drinking, then maybe we would be like other families. Maybe we too could be normal. The thought of her quitting drinking forever was all I wanted and needed. It was the only thing that my brothers and I cared about, and now it was going to happen. "I love you too, Mother," I said.

Of course it didn't happen, and we were soon evicted again. In fact, we moved so much during the middle 1950s that we learned not to unpack the boxes because we knew we wouldn't be there very long. From Pasadena we moved to Santa Monica. Next came the San Fernando Valley and Van Nuys High for me for two semesters, and then Glendale. Suddenly I was sixteen and again Dad stopped by to see us out of the blue. He must have discovered it was my birthday, because he brought me a gift. I unwrapped the white tissue paper and discovered a Tinkertoy set. Dad hadn't the faintest notion I was now sixteen.

And then it was November 1958, my seventeenth birthday. I finally felt free. I couldn't wait to leave. Even though Mother urged me to wait until my graduation the following June, I couldn't. I wanted out. I convinced my mother to sign the authorization papers allowing me to leave high school. Three weeks later I joined the Navy. Now that I was grown up, I promised myself I would find some way to see Father. I didn't know how I would pull it off, but joining the Navy seemed as good a way as any.

# 9

# Subic Bay

In January 1959, I started Navy boot camp in San Diego, and after basic training was transferred a few miles north to hospital corpsman school for six months' medical training at Balboa Hospital. I told myself I wanted to pursue medicine and become a doctor like my father when I was discharged, and figured this could give me a solid foundation before entering pre-med. As a doctor, maybe I could finally establish a relationship with my father, complete a part of myself that had been short-circuited by the trial and divorce.

I knew very little about Father's new life. I knew that while in Hawaii he had studied to become a psychiatrist and had taught at the territorial university, then he had gone on to Manila to a new life with his new Filipino wife. Although Mother spent most of her time drunk and bitter, she felt justified in complaining that Dad, who rarely sent any money to support us, was now rumored to have married a very wealthy and well-connected woman. "Her family owns a large sugar plantation," Mother told us. "She belongs to a family that is supposedly close to the political bigwigs of the Philippines."

At the end of 1958, Father and his wife were living in Manila and had four children: two sons and two daughters, half-siblings whom I had never met. Mother told us that Father was "president of a large market research company, and is now very wealthy and living like a raja, emperor, or king."

To be sure, Mother's descriptions of Father's lifestyle had made me hate him all the more for abandoning us. She had nothing, and he had everything. She lived from week to week in squalor and poverty; he lived in comfort in some great palace with servants and cooks, who, in my mind's eye, sounded great exotic brass gongs at dinner-time. Father had sent almost nothing in the way of money or support as we were growing up. After Mother's third or fourth plea when things were critical, he would occasionally wire some "emergency funds" to "tide us over." But there was nothing on a regular basis, nothing of his own volition, nothing from his heart to her or us. No note that said, "Here, Dorero, this is for you and the children. Tell them I love them." There was only the Tinkertoy set when I was sixteen. And now, by way of the U.S. Navy, I was setting out to find him.

My first billet after corpsman school, as I'd hoped and expected the fates would arrange it, was a two-year assignment to a small hospital just outside Subic Bay Naval Base in the Philippines. This posting was not something I had arranged, or would have even been able to arrange, but I had thrown myself into the currents of life, hoping that they would bring me and my father together. Now that it was about to happen, I had mixed emotions. But I told myself that this was nothing I had consciously arranged. I was only a seaman apprentice who wasn't really qualified to ask questions, or, for that matter, to think any thoughts. A sailor's job was to go and do.

Once I was in the Navy and on my own, I soon discovered that if there is a gene predisposing you to boozing, my introduction to life in the military turned it on like a light switch. It took less than a month in the small Navy town of Olongapo, just outside the huge U.S. military installation at Subic Bay, for me to water that gene. Three dollars U.S. bought me twelve scotches, and five dollars U.S. bought me Toni, a nineteen-year-old Filipina beauty. I got drunk and I got laid for cash. The dances with her at the Club Oro to Johnny Mathis's "Misty" were free.

And now it was time for Dad. He was fifty-two when I first arrived to meet him after so many years. We were strangers and I didn't know how I really felt about my own father. Did I love him or hate him? Both, I guessed. Mother's propaganda over the past ten years had given me mixed messages. She had glorified his intellect and doctoring skills, telling me that few knew his true genius as a doctor, which was as a diagnostician. At the same time she had vilified him for abandoning his children. Our first reunion took place a month after I arrived in the Philippines. It was a Saturday luncheon at the

Army-Navy Club on Manila Bay. I wore my Navy blues, he wore a white sharkskin suit, and while I was wilting in the tropics, he sat there, cool and collected, not a hair on his head out of place. Father's appearance surpassed the legends and visions I had woven around him in my mind. Though at six foot one he was an inch shorter than me, he seemed to tower over me, physically as well as in his demeanor. He was strikingly handsome and as strong as if he were in his twenties, and he behaved as if he wielded the power of the universe with his fingertips. Immaculately dressed, he immediately conveyed to one and all that he was not only a man of wealth, but a commanding presence. But it was more than that: it was the force *behind* his words that completely dominated and controlled every situation down to the smallest detail. Whether he was making a major financial decision for his company that would involve millions of pesos, or was simply ordering a glass of iced tea, it was the same.

Dad's arrogance, I soon came to see, put him at the center of his own universe and demanded his listener's complete attention. Women loved him for that power and presence. Men respected and feared him for it. As for me, I was intimidated but not fearful like the others, whom I watched kowtow to him, no matter how outrageous his demands. My relationship with him was cautious, polite, but not obsequious. In the two years I spent in the Philippines and in my father's presence, I saw how he dismissed most people out of hand with an arrogant "Leave us." But he treated me differently. He and I were strangers, but I was blood, and maybe that made the difference.

I also got to meet the children from Dad's new life, my young half-brothers and sisters who at that time were about five, six, seven, and eight years old. All four of them were very beautiful and at the sight of the tall American sailor whom Dad introduced as their brother they laughed and giggled, murmuring in both Tagalog and English.

I also discovered that Dad and his wife, my stepmother,* were living in separate residences. She and the children lived in a large home in a Beverly Hills–type neighborhood in the suburbs of Manila. Dad

---

*Hortensia Laguda Hodel Starke in the early 1960s obtained a divorce from Father through papal dispensation, remarried, and in the 1980s would be elected to the Philippine Congress, representing the people of Negros Occidental (in the southern Philippines), where she owned and operated a 450-acre sugar plantation.

was living and had his offices at the Admiral Apartments on Manila Bay in an impressive five-room layout that had been General Douglas McArthur's headquarters after his return to the Philippines. If it was good enough for the general it was good enough for the emperor. The operation ran smoothly and efficiently, with the help of an omnipresent "manager" named Diana, a beautiful Chinese woman who appeared to be in her late twenties and spoke as if she had been educated at one of the Seven Sisters schools.

Throughout my stint at the Navy hospital, Dad remained aloof and private, completely absorbed in his own world. Hortensia, whom I later discovered had originally met my father at a 1948 party at the Franklin House, was ever the gracious hostess, welcoming me into her home as family. During this period, Father spent most of his time building his market research company, traveling throughout Asia and Europe on business, and our brief encounters were perfunctory, emotionally shallow, revealing none of the intimate details about him that I was looking for. Besides having verified through my own personal observation that my father was a successful, wealthy, politically connected, charming, multitalented, charismatic womanizer, who was also an overbearing, arrogant, egotistical control freak, I discovered very little about the inner man. What was truly troubling, however, and most confusing to me, had little to do with his personality, because, whatever his strengths and shortcomings, I could accept them.

It was his internal blindness that troubled me, his obliviousness to the needs and concerns of anyone around him. He was a psychiatrist, trained to probe the needs of his patients. Yet he was emotionally inaccessible to his family, a fortified castle unto himself, with a moat around his heart.

As a young man and his son, I respected his power, his authority, and his accomplishments. I took great pride when I was in his presence, glory by association. But when I wasn't with him, away from his world, I could sense his sadness, his solitude, his emotional pain, and knew it was dark and ran very deep. I also believed that he would never speak or share that secret pain with anyone, personally or professionally, and that was the saddest reality of all for me. When I left him a year and a half after my arrival, I was less certain about the man than when I had first arrived.

As the end of my enlistment was approaching, I was assigned to

the Mobile Construction Battalion of Seabees stationed out of Port
Hueneme in Ventura, California. I had become my mother's son
rather than my father's. Maybe it was the thirsty Irish genes that had
played themselves out during her long binges while I was growing
up, or maybe I simply learned to drink by example. But drink I did,
and lots of it. "Johnnie Walker" became my new best friend.

Through alcohol, I had come to understand my mother better. It
was as if I had met the enemy and she was me. So I joined her. With
money in my pockets, I stood the two of us our daily ration of booze:
"I'll have a fifth of Johnnie Walker, Black Label, Mom, and here, get
yourself a bottle of whatever."

This was a new twist to the family relationship. With her son
drinking, Mother actually became more relaxed and downright tem-
perate for a short period. Now it was I, not Mother, who was out of
control and excessive. Older brother Michael didn't drink, just shook
his head at me, and kept on reading his beloved books. Michael
Hodel would one day become one of the stalwart radio announcers
on L.A.'s KPFK-FM, with his own sci-fi program, *Hour-25*, as well as
a science fiction editor and writer. Michael's *Enter the Lion: A Posthumous Memoir of Mycroft Holmes* is still considered a detective-fiction
cult classic among Conan Doyle fans.

During my thirty-day leave, Mother, in good spirits one afternoon, turned to me and said, "Steven, let's go to a real Hollywood
party tonight. I haven't been to one in years. It will be like the old
days. I have a friend who called and invited us. It's at her home in the
hills. She's an actress and knows a lot of the Hollywood people from
the studios. It should be fun."

I was in a good mood myself that afternoon, and up for some fun,
so I needed no convincing. What I found at that home that night was
far more than I bargained for. In fact, it would change my life.

# 10

## Kiyo

I HAVE VERY FEW MEMORIES of what went on at the party in the Hollywood Hills that afternoon, because whoever I met and whatever I saw was erased by the presence of Amilda Kiyoko Tachibana McIntyre, known to her friends as Kiyo. Kiyo was a beautiful Eurasian. With her round face, onyx eyes, and straight jet-black hair that flowed like a waterfall to just below her tight buttocks, she was irresistible magic to a sailor newly home on leave.

Kiyo had been a singer and a dancer and had performed in several feature films. She also taught piano and, in the years before the dawning of the Age of Aquarius, was an astrologer to many entertainers and other show-business personalities. She was thirty, sophisticated, smart, eloquent, and she knew from the moment I walked through her front door and our eyes met that I was a goner. We engaged in small talk as she deftly fended off the attentions of other guests. Then, as the afternoon wore on and guests began to leave, we found ourselves touching one another and finding excuses to cross one another's paths in parts of her house where no one else would disturb us. Maybe there were others looking at us, but it seemed as if Kiyo and I had been transported to a world of our own. My mother left the party, but I remained behind, transfixed by Kiyo's beauty and apparent interest in me and determined to find out more about her. She was the most enchanting person I had ever met.

I stayed with her that night, and through the weekend. I couldn't get enough of her. For the first time in my life I was in love. Sunday morning she served hot tea, fresh fruit, and homemade pastries, and her eyes shone as she spoke. "I did your chart last night," she said as

she poured the tea. "You are a Scorpio and Taurus is your rising sign."
I smiled back at her. "No," I answered. "*You* are my rising sign."

She laughed. "Yes, well, there's that, too. But seriously, Steven,
you have an amazing chart. You will make lots of money in real estate
and you will —" She paused as I touched her arm. "Kiyo, I don't
know anything about that stuff," I said. "And, to be honest, I don't
care about it. All I care about is you and me. I've never known anyone like you, and I love the way I feel when I'm with you." Her voice
turned serious. "You must not tell anyone about us, not your mother,
not your brothers, no one. Understand?"

I shook my head. "Why?" I asked, without really wanting to
know the truth. "Are you married or something?"

"No," she said. "It's just that you must promise me you will not
say anything to anyone about us. Promise me that. Give me your
word of honor." I gave her my word.

While I agonized over the slow passing of the final months before my military discharge, I also discovered that Kiyo was a very as-
sertive person. She had an in-your-face attitude that had begun to set
off my warning bells. But I ignored them, because I told myself that
I was in love. Unbeknownst to me, Kiyo had driven up to the Navy
base, demanded to see my C.O., told him we were getting married,
and asked him if it would be possible for me to get an early discharge
in July. She said she wanted me to start college in late August. "You
said *what* to him?" I asked her in disbelief. "Why would you say such
a thing?"

"Oh," she answered. "It's just my Leo way. I have six planets in
Leo, so sometimes I get a bit pushy, but it's not really me."

But it really was. The following weekend, at her insistence, we
drove to the nearest state where we could marry without parental
consent because I was still a minor: I wouldn't be twenty-one for another four months. I hadn't told my mother about Kiyo, nor had I
made any contact with my brothers. I had simply dropped out of
sight to be with Kiyo. I ignored my instincts, which kept shouting,
"Careful! Wait!" I also ignored my emotions when I found myself
eyeing lasciviously the person who was performing our one-witness
marriage ceremony — Miss Idaho of 1954. She had gone on from
winning her state's beauty pageant to become a justice of the peace
in Twin Falls, Idaho. On our drive back we stopped overnight at

Yosemite National Park and stood out near the edge of the high ridge, embracing each other, looking exactly like newlyweds should.

An old man watching us, who looked as if he'd been prospecting in the surrounding mountains since the Gold Rush of 1849, said to me, "You be careful, son. In another two years, she'll be pushing you off the edge of that cliff." Kiyo and I turned around as he walked silently away. I looked at her and teased, "Nice guy. He must be a pushy Leo."

Had I been even a little knowledgeable about astrological combinations I would have known that Scorpios and Leos don't make for an easy relationship. Kiyo was fire and I was water, and the ensuing three years of our marriage generated a lot of steam as each of us tried to force the other to adjust. Kiyo knew a lot of Hollywood people and some of them, like Jane Russell, attended her astrology classes, respected her knowledge, and were genuinely interested in what she was teaching. And Kiyo's relationships with her clients got us on the guest list of lots of Hollywood personalities, particularly with Jane Russell and her husband, Bob Waterfield, the great former quarterback for the Los Angeles Rams.

I was slightly disconcerted that most of Kiyo's friends seemed much older than she. And, of course, since I was ten years younger than Kiyo, I felt awkward and uncomfortable with many of them. They would invariably remark, "Steven, you look so young. How old are you?" They always seemed surprised at my answer, "I *am* young; I'm twenty-one." I began to feel that talking about age around Kiyo and her friends was taboo.

One Sunday morning, about three months after we had married, Kiyo threw the classified section of the *Los Angeles Times* at me and said, "Look, the Los Angeles Police Department is hiring. The starting salary is a hundred dollars a month, more than you're making now." I read the ad out loud:

## LAPD WANTS YOU!

Are you one of the four in a hundred applicants that will make it through the process to our police academy training? Would you like an exciting and rewarding career in law enforcement and retire in twenty years? Apply at City Hall now!

I was working at the time as an orderly at Kaiser Hospital in Hollywood, emptying bedpans, moving patients, making sure that whatever slop came out of a patient was cleaned up before the next patient was brought in. It was a job I hated, certainly not my idea of an "exciting and rewarding" career. I looked back at Kiyo, who had been staring at me in silence, and asked, "What does a policeman do? Write tickets? Direct traffic?" A cop? I knew nothing about it, and cared less. Maybe I could be a detective, I thought, just like Joe Friday on *Dragnet*. After another week of Kiyo's prodding and her wily offhand comments of, "I think guys in uniform are very sexy," and her prompting, "We could sure use the extra money," I'd had enough. I applied at city hall for both LAPD and the sheriff's department.

Two weeks after I had passed both entrance exams and had been rejected by the sheriff's department at the in-person interview for being too young, I was called in for my oral at LAPD. That went better. I fit their job description as if I'd come right out of central casting. I was a young, trim, tall WASP who racked up strong written scores on the exam, was married, and had four years of military training. At that time, the department was trying to rid itself of the old image of the fat sloppy cop stealing an apple. They were looking for young, idealistic men that they could mold into professionals. I was what my interviewers said was the "new breed."

I took the psych test, convincing the department psychological evaluator that, even though my father was a psychiatrist, I wasn't neurotic, or worse. Then I underwent the background check in which the department's investigators checked out every movement I had made on this planet from birth, including personal interviews with out-of-state Navy buddies and neighbors from old addresses ten years back. The only smudge on my background check was a drunken brawl I had been involved in while on Guam, where I punched out a fellow sailor in a bar and got arrested by the MPs. Actually, I think the investigators liked that tidbit: it gave me just enough macho credibility.

But when a few months passed following my original application and exams without any word from the department, I began to get worried. I believed I had made good impressions in person, on paper, and in the difficult physical agility tests. And during the process I had evolved from an emotionally blasé, take-it-or-leave-it attitude to a strong feeling that I really wanted this job. Finally, on a Friday afternoon in mid-January 1963, I received a phone call from a secretary in LAPD's personnel division, informing me that I was scheduled to report to their office the following Monday, January 14, at 9:00 A.M., to meet with the captain.

I was a half-hour early and very nervous as I sat on the long bench outside of room 311 at the police administration building. I knew from other applicants that the civil service standard operating procedure for acceptance or rejection to the police academy was by mail. Why then was I being called in personally to speak with the captain? At which point a heavyset man in his fifties walked down the hall, stood in front of the locked door, turned to look down at me, frowned, and asked, "Hodel?" I stood up, answering, "Yes, sir." He put his key in the lock and turned it decisively. "I'm Captain Sansing," he said over the loud clack of the deadbolt snapping back into the door lock. "You're early — come on in, we might as well get this over with before the others arrive."

I knew from his tone and the way he said "over with" that I was finished, hadn't made it. But why? What had I done? The burly captain opened the door, and I followed him to the rear, where we entered his private office. He shut the door behind me.

I stood at full attention in front of his desk, glancing at the silver nameplate, "Captain Earle Sansing, Commander, Personnel Division." He sat down in the large leather chair and said, "I'm not going to mince words, son. I am not going to certify you for acceptance to the police academy. You have no business being a police officer. I *know* all about your family and your father. It would be a waste of the taxpayers' money to let you go to the academy. It would be a total waste of their time, your time, and my time. I am going to reject your certification."

Standing there in disbelief and intimidated by this man who held the final word, I responded with a mixture of controlled anger and passion. I spoke with real emotion, and before I realized it, I was making a formal plea.

"Captain, sir," I began. "I have spent the last five months preparing for this moment. During that time I have tried to focus my heart and my mind toward one purpose, one goal, making it to the academy. I have finally done that. I have proven myself to be of fit character, mentally, physically, and morally. I don't know what you mean about knowing my father. I can only assume you are referring to his trial back in 1949. I know nothing of it other than he was found innocent of some charges that my half-sister Tamar made against him. He left us right after the trial, and my mother never spoke about it. I do know that I am not my father. I am myself. I also know that it is I, not my father, who wants to become a policeman. It is I, not my father, who has worked and sweated and struggled through each separate test toward this opportunity. Please, sir, do not take away this chance from me now. Let me prove myself in the academy. All I am asking from you is the chance for me to prove myself."

The veteran captain never took his eyes off of me, studying every inch of me, as if he were looking at an X-ray, sizing me up as if he were doing long division in his head. I also got the impression that he was trying to use his street smarts and intuition, which any experienced cop develops over the years on the job. It's what enables him to trust his gut feelings and not second-guess himself when he has to make a shoot/no shoot decision. Captain Sansing was taking a mental photograph of me that morning, looking for something in me that he could compute and confirm a decision he was trying to reach. A full minute passed, but it seemed like an eternal silence. Then he blinked, and I thought I saw his hardness change to a twinkle.

"Hodel," he said, "I am going to certify you to the academy. I shouldn't, and I know I shouldn't, but I am. I say again, it's a waste of time and money. You will start the academy three weeks from today. Now get the fuck out of my office!" Thus began my career with LAPD.

Now, with a steady and secure civil service job and a hundred-dollar-a-month increase in her purse, Kiyo decided we should buy a new home, and almost immediately one came our way. A good friend of hers, who was married to the old-time cowboy-in-black hero Lash LaRue (whose black whip was as fast as his gun), had recently put her Laurel Canyon home up for sale. At the top of a hundred concrete steps, it was more like an estate and it had a Hansel-and-Gretel roof.

Veteran movie director Tay Garnett, it was rumored, had built the home for a beautiful young actress he had fallen in love with, at a cost of more than $100,000, several fortunes in the days of the early studios. Then, just as the final bricks were being put into place, the fairy tale ended when the young starlet ran off to Malibu with a handsome young actor. Heartbroken, Garnett sold the house and ultimately Lash and his wife bought the place.

I especially liked Laurel Canyon, a community of homes high in the Hollywood Hills. The area was filled with actors, writers, artists, bohemians about to be reborn as hippies, lots of right-brain people. And I liked their energy. Kiyo offered Lash and his wife $37,500, which was the amount of money they had paid for the home fifteen years earlier. They happily accepted, figuring they did well to get their money back, and Kiyo and I moved in a few months later. I didn't know how we would ever pay the mortgage, but Kiyo simply told me to hand over my paycheck every two weeks and she'd take care of the rest.

After a year I'd completed my probation both on the LAPD and in my marriage. I'd followed all of Kiyo's rules, my training officer's rules, and the rules of any patrol sergeant who happened to be sitting at a desk in the divisions where I worked. I had kept my promise to Kiyo: neither my brothers nor my mother knew we were living together, much less married. As far as my family was concerned, I had ceased to exist. However, I did write a short message to my father in Manila simply telling him I had married "a Japanese woman" but provided no additional information. I don't remember if he answered my note.

If I had any doubts about my marriage with Kiyo or the growing differences between us, they were obliterated by the Watts riots that took over all our lives in the summer of 1965. Overnight the city became a third-world capital, aflame with massive rioting and running gun battles. I and five or six other uniformed officers were assigned to ride around the streets of South Central, jammed tightly into a single black-and-white, each of us armed with a shotgun. That was our sole function — a "show of force" — moving targets driving around in circles for twelve hours a day, never firing a shot, never making an arrest, and never getting out of the car except to grab a coffee or take a leak. We just drove in circles as a "perimeter control," more afraid of ourselves and the loaded shotguns we carried than of any rioters. The city would require full armored military occupation before order could be restored, and the myth of LAPD's invincibility vanished.

The riots had barely ended when, in October, my father sent a message that he would be in town for two days and asked me to call him at the Biltmore Hotel so he could meet with me and my "new bride." Upon hearing the news, Kiyo seemed oddly excited and urged me to call him immediately and schedule it. We arranged to meet the following afternoon in the lobby of the Biltmore at 6:00 P.M. and have dinner together.

That whole afternoon Kiyo acted rather bizarre. She had bought a new red dress for the occasion and had spent three hours on her hair and makeup, as if she were going to audition for a leading role. She was stunning, and all heads followed her as we walked through the Olive Street entrance into the lobby at 5:50 P.M. We waited in the lobby bar, she with her chardonnay and me with my double scotch, for Dad to make his appearance on the double stairway leading from the elevators to the main lobby. Father, as was his custom, was fifteen minutes late as he approached us with the beautiful Diana on his arm. I blinked as I looked up at them because Diana and Kiyo seemed to resemble each other. They didn't actually look alike, but they carried themselves in the same way. I could almost see sparks flying between them.

As Dad and Diana came within four feet of us, Kiyo looked directly at him, smiled broadly, and said with more intimacy than any stranger would have dared, "Hello, George!" Father looked at my wife, at first blankly, then, as he remembered, his eyes slowly changed from surprise to shock. Uncharacteristically, his speech faltered, and his voice broke as he replied, "Hello, Kiyo."

Diana and I looked at each other, both aware that something very strange had just occurred between the two of them. I said, "Hello, Diana, it's been five years, good to see you. This is my wife, Kiyo." Diana extended her hand, but Kiyo ignored her and kept staring at my father and smiling. I said, trying to paint over the awkwardness of the moment with some small talk, "Dad, I understand you two knew each other when Kiyo was quite young." He had recovered his composure now, and there was fire in his eyes as he replied, "Yes, we did. She was quite young, quite young indeed. Steven, I tried calling you before you left your home to inform you that, unfortunately, we won't be able to have dinner after all. Some very urgent business matters have come up unexpectedly, and we are on our way now to try and put out some fires and deal with them. We're off tomorrow for New York, so perhaps the next time through town we can have more time."

He reached for Diana's arm, and began walking back to the steps that led to the elevators. In a tone that carried finality and total dismissal, without turning around, he said, "Goodbye, Kiyo." I turned toward Kiyo, confused, trying to comprehend what had just occurred in the past ninety seconds. She had tears in her eyes. I walked her over to a bar table, sat her down, ordered us each another drink, and, trying to be compassionate but failing utterly, said, "What the fuck was that all about? What the hell is going on, Kiyo?" I could detect both disgust and defeat in her reply: "Not here. Not now. Let's go home first."

I had never seen my father out of control and at a loss for words. That was a first. He had clearly been shaken just seeing Kiyo. After we got back to Laurel Canyon, I demanded some answers.

"You are still such a child, Steven," she began. "You know nothing of life or love or feelings. Yes, I knew your mother and father when I was young. I met your father for the first time at a bus bench in Hollywood. I was sitting there alone and he stopped his car, got out, and walked up to me. He was immaculately dressed in a brown suit, with a cashmere overcoat, the handsomest man I had ever seen. He handed me his business card and said, 'Excuse me, miss, but I am a physician and I am also a professional photographer. You are the most beautiful young lady I have ever seen. I would like to photograph you, and will of course pay you for your time.' His charm was irresistible. He gave me a ride home and we became friends. I was very young and impressionable and quickly developed a crush on your father back then. That's all."

Somehow, I didn't think that was all. I was determined to find out the truth. I was taking courses at Los Angeles City College three nights a week at that time, and the following night as usual left home, headed for my sociology class. But I didn't feel like going to class; I felt like having a drink. I pulled my car into the local tavern at the bottom of the canyon near Sunset Boulevard where I'd decided I'd drink instead of think that night. It took four double scotches before

I had the courage to drive back up the hill and get the rest of the story from Kiyo. I parked the car and took the hundred steps that led to our oversized front door three steps at a time. As I approached the door, I could see through the window that she had lit a fire in the fireplace.

My second glance froze me in place. I saw two figures lying in front of the fire. Kiyo was naked; her companion had his shirt off and was lying prone against her body, kissing her. I slipped my key into the door lock and entered as Kiyo grabbed for her robe on the couch. The young man grabbed for his shirt on the hearth. Kiyo stood up defiantly as she tied her robe. "It's not what you think. Tom is an actor. He has a love scene in a film. We were . . ." Tom paled at the sight of the gun holstered on my left hip, clearly visible under my open sport coat. He stumbled for words: "It's true. I have this part. I have the script at home. . . . I can show you."

The young man standing in front of me with trembling hands as he tried to button his shirt was almost a mirror of myself in stature and age. I moved my hand toward my gun and I actually weighed the options in front of me. I wanted to draw and fire. I wanted to take every bit of the hatred that was coursing through me at that moment and force it through the nozzle of my off-duty revolver. Just the sight of his bare chest was compelling me to blow huge holes in it. But even filled with liquor, I knew he wasn't worth prison, and neither was she. I fought the urge.

"If you're not out of my house in five seconds," I said in a low growl that I'd never heard myself make before, "I will blow your fucking head off. And if you ever call or see my wife again, as God is my witness, I will kill you."

The young man bolted for the door and took the hundred steps down six at a time. My hatred now turned back full force to Kiyo. "You fucking bitch! How many others have you fucked behind my back? How many other cocks have you sucked while I was sitting in class at night? Tell me! Answer me!" Kiyo turned and walked toward the dining room. "You're so immature, Steven," she said. "You're not my husband — you're my child."

My hands were shaking as I fought to control the anger and hatred I felt for this woman. I knew I had to get out of the house and away before I lost control. My job had shown me what happened when men and women lost control, and I was now part of the job. I kept my weapon in its holster and walked out of the house.

The following afternoon, I had my partner return with me to the house and we parked the black-and-white in front of the steps. Moving day. I knew she was gone to teach piano. All I wanted from the house were a few personal papers and my clothes. Within an hour we had all of my personal effects loaded into the back of the car. I went to the study to look for my passport, birth certificate, and other personal papers. I riffled through her desk, but they were nowhere to be found, but there was a bank savings account with her name on it, "Kiyo Hodel."

I opened the passbook and stared at the balance: $4,500. Jesus Christ! Where did that money come from? I was proud of our joint savings account, into which we'd managed to stash $400, but this was like finding another set of business books. What was going on? The next folder I saw in her desk was labeled "Astrological Charts." I thought to myself, "Screw her, she's not keeping mine in here." I opened the folder and my chart was on top. I pulled it from the stack and looked at the second horoscope with its circle and symbols and read the name "Amilda Kiyoko Tachibana, born in Boston, Massachusetts, August 2, 1920." I stared at the year: "1920." That meant she wasn't thirty-three, as I believed, but forty-five! Could it be?

I dropped my partner off at Van Nuys police station, where I was then assigned, took the rest of the afternoon off, and drove to my mother's apartment in North Hollywood. I told her everything. After Mother got over the shock of seeing me, she sat in horror as I told her of my elopement and secret marriage to Kiyo, and of Kiyo's insistence and my sworn oath not to tell anyone, especially my family, of our marriage. I told Mother of our recent meeting with Father, and his strange reaction, and then my returning home unexpectedly two nights ago and finding Kiyo in the embrace of another man. Finally, I related the discovery of the chart showing her birth date was 1920. Was it true? Was she really forty-five? What did she know about Kiyo?

Mother sat in silence for several minutes, and then she cried as she told me the true story of Kiyo and my father. "I had no idea when

I said, 'Let's go to a party at Kiyo's house' that any of this could have happened. I can't believe it has." She lit a cigarette while she searched for the right words to continue her story:

"Yes, Kiyo *is* forty-five," she continued. "Your father brought her home one night after seeing her standing waiting for a bus or taxi, something like that. I'm not sure exactly how they met; it's been so long. She was a student at the Chouinard Art Institute, and the war was on. They were arresting all the Japanese off the streets and in their houses, and she lived with us on Valentine Street. She was very young and very beautiful, and he felt sorry for her, and was afraid she'd be interned like the others. Then she moved out and away and we lost track of her. After the war, we heard she had married, and she and her husband Brook used to come to the Franklin House to our parties. They later divorced, and she married again. Before that party I took you to, I hadn't seen her in years."

I called a lawyer and filed for divorce that same week. It became final a year later. Kiyo and I never spoke again, and I heard from Rumor Central that she had remarried, or was living with a man even younger than me. She continued to teach astrology classes and found her fifteen minutes of fame, which included her picture and a small article in *Time* magazine as a recognized "astrologer to the Hollywood stars." She died from cancer while she was still in her mid-fifties, about ten years after our divorce.

My only explanation for Kiyo's interest in me was her private moment of truth in those brief minutes in the lobby at the Biltmore Hotel when I introduced her to my father as my wife. To her, it was all worth it for the "Hello, George."

In that single moment, Kiyo had exacted her revenge for the grudge she held against him. Twenty years earlier, in her youth and innocence, she had loved him and succumbed to his seduction. His conquest complete, Father had cast her aside and quickly moved on to other women and other loves. It was a slow road for her to travel, but she would be avenged. Her moment came in the lobby of the Biltmore, as she was introduced as Kiyo Hodel, his son's wife. Standing there, ignorant of the drama, I was hoping and praying that Dad would be impressed with my choice of a wife. He wasn't the only Hodel who knew how to pick beautiful and sophisticated women!

In the following days, after the discovery of Kiyo's infidelity, her lies about her age, and Mother's explanations about her true relationship with Father during the war years, I was shaken to my core, filled with the rage and hatred that only youth can know. However, it would not be for another thirty-four years, until I saw Kiyo's picture in my father's album after his death, that the full impact of Dad and Kiyo would begin to dawn on me. Then only gradually did I come to know the truth. His love for her was no weekend romance. Her picture was there, hidden with the rest. Carried for fifty years in his sanctum sanctorum. He had loved her!

# 11

# The Dahlia Witnesses

**Mid-July, 1999. Bellingham, Washington**

I HAD ALREADY REVIEWED ENOUGH MATERIAL on the condition of Elizabeth Short's body to recognize that what her killer did to her was no mere butcher job. The only person who could have performed a bisection so perfectly had to be a doctor, a skilled doctor. I was also impressed by the indications that the killer had performed a postmortem hysterectomy. Not only did he know the female anatomy, but he clearly possessed a level of surgical skill far beyond that of the average medical student or, as some had speculated at the time, mortician or nurse. The killer or killers were also brutally sadistic: they had tortured and humiliated Elizabeth before putting her to death.

Assuming for the moment that there was only one killer, the amount of time he had and the rage he felt toward his victim indicated to me that he doubtless knew her intimately. Everything about the crime pointed to an act of rage-driven revenge. What, specifically, was the relationship between victim and killer that would result in an explosion of such violence and brutality that even the police at the crime scene could not remember ever having seen anything so degrading and horrifying?

The answers lie in the dynamic of their relationship, and in their lives before they crossed each other's path. The records of those lives are still with us, because neither the victim nor the crime could simply disappear. Considering this, I was convinced that, somewhere buried within the official case records, the interviews with witnesses, and the newspaper coverage, or the memories of people associated with Elizabeth Short, there had to be some answers. That's where I would begin my search: to try and build a composite of Elizabeth Short from scratch — something, I believed, the police had not adequately done back in 1947. I began my search for clues to the real nature of the victim, starting with a complete and thorough review of all known witnesses.

The first group of witnesses would be those people who knew her when she was alive, who could help me reconstruct a chronology of her movements until the day of her murder. They would cover the period from 1943 until January 9, 1947. These people included her family, those who knew her before she came to Los Angeles, and those whom she met during her years in Los Angeles looking for work and a place to live.

## Phoebe May Short

Phoebe Short, the victim's mother, learned that her daughter was found dead and mutilated in a vacant lot when two reporters from the *L.A. Examiner* called her in Medford, Massachusetts, after the paper had learned, from its Soundex transmission of fingerprints to the FBI, that the victim's name was Elizabeth Short. It was a gruesome phone call, because the reporters, in their effort to gain as much information as possible, initially told Mrs. Short that her daughter had won a beauty contest and they needed background information on her for a story. Excited and jubilant, Phoebe began to gush about her daughter, talking about her beauty, her hopes, her dreams, until the reporter finally revealed the awful truth. Crushed and distraught, Phoebe nonetheless answered the rest of their questions, and the reporters had their exclusive.

Information from the reporters' interview of Phoebe Short, and from Mrs. Short's testimony later at the coroner's inquest, revealed that on January 2, 1947, Mrs. Short received a letter from her daughter in which Elizabeth told her mother she "was living in San Diego, California, with a girlfriend, Vera French, and was working at the Naval Hospital." Mrs. Short said that her daughter "was kind of movie struck, and that everyone in Medford had told her how beautiful she was." Her daughter had left high school in her junior year.

"Elizabeth had asthma," Mrs. Short told the reporters, "and every winter Betty would go south, to Florida, and work as a waitress, then she would return home in the summers." While she was living in Los Angeles, Elizabeth told her mother through letters, she had "worked in some films in Hollywood as an extra and had played in some minor roles." With the exception of Elizabeth's engagement to Matt Gordon, Phoebe Short was unaware of any serious relationships her daughter had had with men. "Major Gordon," Phoebe told police, "was engaged to my daughter, but he was killed flying home after the war."

At the coroner's inquest, held in Los Angeles on January 22, 1947, seven days after the discovery of her daughter's body, Mrs. Short identified Elizabeth at the coroner's office and testified that she "was twenty-two years of age, a waitress by occupation, and to her knowledge had never been married." Mrs. Short had last seen Elizabeth when she left home in Medford, Massachusetts, on April 19, 1946, for California. She told the inquest that while her daughter was at home with her, she never spoke of having any enemies, and said she was in love with a man named Gordon Fickling. She added that her daughter always wrote her on a weekly basis while she lived away from home.

### Inez Keeling

Mrs. Keeling met Elizabeth Short in Santa Barbara during the war when she was manager at the post exchange at the Camp Cooke Army base in Santa Barbara, where Elizabeth, then eighteen, was employed in early 1943. Mrs. Keeling said, "Elizabeth told me that she had come out to California because of her health. She told me that the doctors in the East were concerned she might contract tuberculosis if she remained in a colder climate, and that is why her parents allowed her to come to California alone. I was immediately won over by Elizabeth's charm and beauty. She was one of the loveliest girls I have ever seen and one of the most shy." Mrs. Keeling told newspapers that Elizabeth "never visited with the men over the counter at work, and she didn't date the men. She was a model employee; she didn't smoke and only occasionally took a drink." Keeling last saw Elizabeth when she left the base early in 1943.

## Cleo Short

The police discovered that Cleo Short, Elizabeth's fifty-three-year-old father, was living in Los Angeles, working as a refrigerator repairman. LAPD characterized him in its reports to the press as "uncooperative." Short explained that he wanted no contact with his daughter, who had traveled to California to live with him, and said he had paid for her bus fare back to her mother in Massachusetts. In 1930, according to Mrs. Short, Cleo had abandoned her and his five young daughters in Massachusetts, and simply "disappeared." Mrs. Short had raised the children on her own and had no desire to see or speak with Cleo at the time of the inquest.

Both police investigators and reporters interviewed Cleo Short at his Los Angeles apartment at 1020 South Kingsley Drive, only three miles from the vacant lot where his daughter's body had been discovered. Short told them that he couldn't provide any current information about his daughter or her activities. "I last saw my daughter Elizabeth three years ago, in Vallejo, California. I gave her two hundred dollars and she came out from Massachusetts. She came to live with me in Vallejo, but she spent all her time running around when she was supposed to be keeping house for me, so I made her leave. I didn't want anything to do with her or any of the rest of the family then. I was through with all of them." Cleo made it clear to the police that since he had no information about his daughter, he wanted nothing to do with the investigation of her death.

The interviews with Phoebe Short and her ex-husband, Cleo, revealed to police a mother who could not control her daughter's wanderlust, as innocent as that may have been, and a father who had abandoned his family and had no desire to be further involved with it. The interviews also revealed that Elizabeth was probably looking for a father figure, someone in authority, probably someone in uniform, who would stabilize her life. She thought she had found it in Matt Gordon, but his death had dashed her hopes and set her on a path to find a replacement. Whether she still lived in the fantasy of her engagement to Major Gordon during her stays in Hollywood and San Diego or was simply in denial about her own reality, she would drift from relationship to relationship until she met her killer.

When she met Arthur Curtis James in 1944, three years before her death, and agreed to model for him, she was already dancing very close to the edge.

## Arthur Curtis James Jr. (aka Charles Smith)

Arthur James was a fifty-six-year-old artist and ex-convict, awaiting sentencing in a pending forgery charge, who first met Elizabeth in a Hollywood cocktail lounge in August 1944. "She showed an interest in my drawings," he told police, who interviewed him in 1947 after they discovered that James had known Elizabeth Short. James told police that he was in a bar drawing sketches and she was seated nearby. After she said she liked what James had sketched, he revealed to police, the two of them became friends. "She modeled for me, and I made several pictures of her," he explained. He corroborated his statements by giving police the names of the current owners of his artwork. "One, a large oil painting, I later turned over to a man named Frank Armand, who lived in Artesia." The second one he identified as "a sketch of Elizabeth, which I turned over to a Mrs. Hazel Milman, Star Route 1, Box 24, Rodeo Grounds, in the Santa Monica, Palisades district." James then told police that his contact with Elizabeth ended abruptly three months later in November 1944 after he was arrested in Tucson, Arizona, for violation of the Mann Act, while he was using the alias of Charles Smith. The press later established that the federal charges against him, involving the "transporting of girls across a state line for immoral purposes," did not involve and were totally unrelated to the Elizabeth Short homicide.

As a result of those charges James was convicted and served two years in Leavenworth prison. After his release in 1946, he ran into Elizabeth in Hollywood that November, when he bought her several pieces of luggage. James quickly ran afoul of the law again, because the check he wrote for the luggage bounced and he was arrested. At the time of his interview with reporters in January 1947 he was awaiting sentencing on those charges.

## Mrs. Matt Gordon Sr.

The press interviewed Mrs. Gordon, fiancé Matt Gordon Jr.'s mother, over the phone at her home in Pueblo, Colorado, after a telegram she'd sent to Elizabeth was found in Elizabeth's luggage stored in the downtown Los Angeles bus depot. Mrs. Gordon denied rumors that Elizabeth and her son were ever actually married, but confirmed that her son had first met Elizabeth in Miami, Florida, in 1944, where he was stationed after his return from China. She also confirmed that the two did correspond after he left the United States for India, adding that she was proud that "my son had been awarded the Air Medal with fifteen oak clusters, the Distinguished Flying Cross, and the silver and bronze stars."

Upon being notified by the War Department that Matt had been killed in an airplane crash in India in August of 1945, Mrs. Gordon sent a telegram to Elizabeth: "Received word War Department Matt killed in crash. Our deepest sympathy is with you. Letter follows. Pray it isn't true. Love." In her telephone interview with reporters four days after Elizabeth's body was discovered, she said, "My heart goes out in sympathy to that girl and to her mother."

## Anne Toth

Elizabeth Short's former roommate Anne Toth was a twenty-four-year-old film actress and extra who had had bit parts in several movies. She'd briefly shared lodging with Elizabeth at the private residence of Mark Hansen, part owner of the Florentine Gardens, a popular nightclub in Hollywood, which featured what newspapers called a "Girlie Revue." It was common practice for Hansen to rent rooms at his Hollywood residence at 6024 Carlos Avenue, Toth said, to "girls trying to break into the business."

Toth first met Elizabeth in July or August of 1946, when Elizabeth moved in. "She lived at the house for several months, then went away for about three weeks, then came back." Toth did not know where Elizabeth had gone during that three-week period, but indicated that "Elizabeth's girlfriend, Marjorie Graham, had left for

Boston, but that Elizabeth said she hadn't gone with her and she would rather die than bear the cold of the East."

"About three weeks before Christmas," Toth said to the press, "Elizabeth told me she was going to go to Berkeley, to visit her sister, but instead went to San Diego. I don't know why she went there." Toth received a telegram from Elizabeth during the Christmas holidays saying that she was low on funds. "She was asking me for twenty dollars," Toth said. "Three weeks later I got a second telegram saying she was coming back and a letter would follow." That was Elizabeth's last communication; Toth never received the promised letter.

"She was friendly with several men while she stayed at the house on Carlos Avenue with me," Toth said. "I remember three of the men. One was an Air Force officer from Texas, another a radio announcer named Maurice, and the third was a language teacher. He was about thirty-five years old, 5'-6", medium build, and he drove a black Ford or Chevrolet. I remember he had promised to set Betty up in an apartment in Beverly Hills if she left our place on Carlos." Toth added, "We used to think the world of that kid. She was always well behaved and sweet."

## "Sergeant John Doe" (unidentified U.S. Army man)

Elizabeth Short's FBI file, obtained under a FOIA request, contains a memo dated March 27, 1947, of a lengthy interview by special agents of the FBI's Pittsburgh office with a soldier in the U.S. Army whose name, rank, and home base were blacked out, as were the names of other identified individuals. The interview, which provides important information about Elizabeth's background and movements, and insights into her overall character, describes a twenty-four-hour relationship between the soldier and Elizabeth in downtown Los Angeles on September 20–21, 1946.

The interviewee told the FBI agents that after being granted special leave for four days in Los Angeles he went downtown to 6th Street and Olive, arriving at that corner at approximately 2:00 P.M. wearing his full Army uniform with campaign ribbons and shoulder patches identifying his "outfit." He told agents that two women approached him, one of whom he identified from photographs as Elizabeth Short.

Noticing his shoulder patch, Elizabeth asked him whether he knew a certain soldier, whose name was stricken from the transcript. The interviewee replied that the two of them had served overseas together in the same outfit. Elizabeth told him that she and ——— had been "childhood sweethearts" in her hometown of Medford, Massachusetts. She added that she had heard he had reenlisted, but didn't know where he was stationed.

The interviewee told the agents he'd asked Elizabeth for a date that night and she'd agreed, introducing herself as "Betty Short." She had also introduced her girlfriend, but the interviewee could not recall her name. The interviewee and the two women walked the short distance to the Figueroa Hotel, where Elizabeth was registered, and the three of them stayed in the hotel lobby and talked for a while until Elizabeth excused herself and went upstairs. According to their memo, the sergeant told the FBI agents, "He is positive that the name that Betty was registered under at the hotel was [blacked out]."

The second woman remained in the lobby with the sergeant while Elizabeth was upstairs and informed him that she "had been married, was separated, then divorced," adding that she had been employed in Hollywood, though her employer's identity was stricken from the transcript. Elizabeth was currently unemployed, she said, and she had to loan her money from time to time. The sergeant then asked Elizabeth's friend if she knew where he could get a hotel room for the night. She told him she thought it would be extremely difficult but that "Elizabeth had twin beds in her room and might allow me to sleep there." The sergeant wanted her to "ask Betty if it would be agreeable with her if I stayed in her room." The girlfriend then left him in the lobby and went upstairs.

Both women rejoined the FBI's unidentified witness in the lobby of the hotel a little later in the afternoon and walked a short distance from the hotel, then caught a bus to Hollywood. Sergeant John Doe was seated next to Elizabeth's girlfriend, and Elizabeth sat in a vacant seat next to a Marine, with whom she immediately struck up a conversation. Noting this, the sergeant told the FBI agents that Elizabeth was "the type of girl who was very friendly and would talk to anyone." During the bus ride to Hollywood, he said, Elizabeth's girlfriend said she had asked her about his staying in her room, and Elizabeth had agreed he could. When the bus stopped in Hollywood,

Elizabeth's girlfriend said goodnight to Elizabeth and the soldier and went off on her own.

Elizabeth and Sergeant Doe went to a live Tony Martin broadcast at the CBS radio studio and from there to Tom Breneman's restaurant at the corner of Hollywood and Vine. The interviewee told the FBI agents that when he and Elizabeth got there they saw a long line of people waiting for tables, but upon seeing Elizabeth the headwaiter immediately whisked the two of them inside and got them a table. The soldier could see, he told the FBI, that "Elizabeth was a regular customer, as all the waiters were on friendly terms with her and all recognized her."

During dinner Elizabeth talked more about her childhood sweetheart back in Medford, remarking that he "had been quite jealous when they were young, and had told me not to have any other boyfriends," which she found "quite amusing." The soldier mentioned to Elizabeth that he had known her friend only under combat conditions and "really did not know him very well."

Throughout their dinner, the soldier noticed that many of the patrons kept eyeing Elizabeth, noticing how well dressed she was, and constantly making whispered comments, as if "they recognized her as an actress from RKO or some other film studio." The two of them finished dinner and left the restaurant in the early-morning hours of September 21, 1946.

They caught a trolley back to downtown Los Angeles and got off about five blocks from the Figueroa. As they were walking, a black car drove up beside them. Inside, the soldier said, he could see five men, "all appearing dark complexioned, possibly all Mexicans." Three of these men jumped out of the car and yelled, "There she is!" The soldier said he turned to Elizabeth and suggested he "beat the men up." "No," Elizabeth told him, "it would be better to run" — which they did.

As they reached the hotel, Elizabeth asked the soldier "to wait outside for about 20 minutes" while she went to her room first, because, she said, "the hotel has strict regulations." The soldier waited about half an hour, then went up and knocked on the door. "She opened it wearing a flimsy negligee." He made love to Elizabeth that night. In fact, he stated he "had relations with her numerous times during the night," adding that "at no time during the night was Elizabeth in a passionate mood."

On the morning of September 21, Elizabeth's girlfriend returned to the hotel and the three of them agreed to double-date, the soldier promising to fix Elizabeth's girlfriend up with an Army buddy. They agreed to meet at the drugstore across the street from the Figueroa between 2:00 and 3:00 P.M., which they did. As they were leaving the drugstore, however, Elizabeth suggested that they play a little joke on ———: she and the soldier would write a postcard to ——— saying they were "happily married and living in Hollywood." The soldier bought several postcards and stamps at the drugstore, wrote the messages, and addressed them to ——— at his home address in Medford, Massachusetts.

The foursome went to what the soldier described as a "nearby beer garden." Then the soldier and his Army buddy, whose name was stricken from the record, suggested to Elizabeth and her friend that they head back to the hotel. But Elizabeth and her girlfriend turned them down, saying they "had dates with other men later that night." Elizabeth said that her date that evening was "with a man with a car" who was taking her to some specific place that he could not recall. After the soldier realized he would not have another date with Elizabeth, he asked if he could correspond with her, and see her again. He gave her his address, which, he told the FBI, "was noted down by her girlfriend in a small notebook."

After walking the girls back to the Figueroa, the two soldiers left them there at about 7:00 P.M. As Elizabeth started to enter the hotel the soldier noticed that she ran into someone she apparently knew and was having a heated argument with him: "a short, chunky, well-dressed man who appeared to be 40–45 years of age."

Sergeant Doe told the FBI agents that he never saw, heard from, or corresponded with Elizabeth after that day, returning to the East Coast the following day, September 22. When four months later he read about her murder in the newspaper he immediately wrote the LAPD about his date with Elizabeth. He said he "was fearful that my name would be discovered in the victim's girlfriend's address book, and that was the reason I contacted LAPD as soon as I heard about her murder." He never heard back from the police. But since he

wasn't in California from January 9 through 15, he could not have
been a suspect.

In closing the interview, the agents asked Sergeant Doe if he
could recall any additional conversations he had had with Elizabeth
during their thirty hours together. The soldier made these additional
observations, which the agents included in their casefile memo:

Elizabeth had told him "she was afraid to be alone on the streets
of Los Angeles at night." In the hotel lobby, he said, "Elizabeth had
shown me a newspaper that recounted the number of murders and
rapes that had occurred in Los Angeles over a short period." Elizabeth also told him she was going out with a man "she did not like
very much, but she did not want to hurt his feelings by stopping relations." The soldier could not recall this man's name.

Sergeant Doe assured both agents that he had never really been
married to Elizabeth Short and "the postcards were only a joke to
her former boyfriend."


## Marjorie Graham

A friend of Elizabeth's from Massachusetts, Marjorie Graham had
originally met Elizabeth in Cambridge, where they had both worked
together as waitresses in a restaurant near the Harvard campus. The
Los Angeles press contacted Marjorie Graham back in Massachusetts on January 17, and in the telephone interview she provided the
following information:

Marjorie had come out to Hollywood to visit Elizabeth in October 1946 and shared a room with her. She told reporters that "Elizabeth had told me her boyfriend was an Army Air Force lieutenant,
currently in the hospital in Los Angeles," adding that "she was worried about him and she hoped that he would get well and out of the
hospital in time for a wedding they planned for November 1."

Marjorie said that she (Graham) had "returned to Cambridge,
Massachusetts, on October 23, 1946," adding, "I received one letter
from Elizabeth since my return to Massachusetts, but in it Betty did
not tell me whether the wedding had taken place or not." Nor, said
Marjorie, had Betty "included the name of her prospective husband
in the letter."

## Lynn Martin (real name: Norma Lee Myer)

Lynn Martin was a fifteen-year-old runaway from Long Beach, California, who, according to most accounts, looked as if she were a woman in her early twenties. By the time she met Elizabeth, Martin had already spent a year at the El Retiro School for Girls, a correctional institution. Describing herself as "an orphan," the already street-smart Martin admitted to a juvenile record of eight prior arrests in Los Angeles and Long Beach when she was arrested by police and told them she was one of the seven women who had shared room 501 at the Chancellor Hotel on North Cherokee Avenue in Hollywood with Elizabeth. Martin also briefly shared a room with Elizabeth and Marjorie Graham at the Hawthorne Hotel at 1611 North Orange Drive, also in Hollywood.

Because her guardians in Long Beach had filed a missing persons report on her, Martin was afraid of being arrested as a runaway and attempted to elude the police for the first several days after the murder. Almost a week after the murder, she was located by the police in a motel at 10822 Ventura Boulevard in North Hollywood and was arrested and detained at Juvenile Hall, where she was interviewed by LAPD Juvenile detectives.

Martin told the police that she knew Elizabeth "only casually." Martin said that Elizabeth's friend Marjorie Graham had come out from Massachusetts, and Elizabeth persuaded Graham to share a room with her and Martin at the Hawthorne Hotel. The three women lived together for a short time until, "after a brief argument" with Martin, "Short and Graham moved out of that room and took another room in the same hotel." Martin told police that she "learned of the murder on January 17, when a friend stopped me on the street in Hollywood and showed me my picture in the newspaper."


## Joseph Gordon Fickling

Pilot Joseph Gordon Fickling was an Army Air Force lieutenant, honorably discharged at the end of the war, who flew for a commercial airline in Charlotte, North Carolina. Because of letters LAPD detectives found in Elizabeth Short's luggage on January 17 between the two, they contacted Fickling in January 1947 and had detectives from the Charlotte Police Department interview him.

The letters reveal a long-distance romance, more in Elizabeth's mind than in Fickling's. According to their notes, he said he had first met Elizabeth in Southern California in 1944, before he had gone overseas, and while he had corresponded with her he "denied ever being engaged or contemplating marriage to Elizabeth Short."

In a letter found in Elizabeth's trunk, Fickling wrote to Elizabeth on April 24, 1946:

> You say in your letter you want to be good friends, but from your wire you seem to want more than that. Are you really sure just what you want? Why not pause and consider just what your coming out here to me would amount to? In your letter you mentioned a ring from Matt. You gave no further explanation. I really don't understand. I wouldn't want to interfere.

In a second letter, also found in her trunk, Fickling wrote:

> I get awfully lonesome sometimes and wonder if we really haven't been very childish and foolish about the whole affair. Have we?

He wrote that an engagement or marriage to her was out of the question:

> My plans are very indefinite and uncertain. There's nothing for me in the army and there doesn't seem to be much outside. Don't think I think any less of you by acting this way, because it won't be true.

Fickling told the Charlotte detectives he had received a final letter from Elizabeth dated January 8, 1947, in which she told him not to write her anymore at her address in San Diego because her plan was to relocate to Chicago.

## Five unidentified youths

Immediately after LAPD detectives identified their "Jane Doe Number 1" as Elizabeth Short, they located three young men and two women who knew her and had been in Hollywood in December 1946. Detectives interviewed them but refused to divulge their names to the press. The interview notes and witness statements that would have been entered into the LAPD murder book case file have never been made public and may no longer exist. Similarly, the whereabouts of the investigators' summaries of their interviews are unknown. All that exists is a brief but very important collective statement, made by the five to the police and released to the newspapers the day after the discovery of Elizabeth Short's body. In that statement, published in the *L.A. Times*, the LAPD is quoted as saying, "These five witnesses recognized the victim as Betty Short. They had seen her in Hollywood in December of 1946, and the five had visited a nightclub in Hollywood with her earlier in the fall. These acquaintances of Elizabeth Short described her as 'very classy,' and they said that Elizabeth Short told them that 'she planned to marry George, an army pilot from Texas.'"

## Juanita Ringo

Juanita Ringo was the apartment manager at the Chancellor Hotel in Hollywood, at 1842 North Cherokee Avenue, where Elizabeth shared room number 501 with seven other girls, each of them paying a dollar a day for rent. In interviews with reporters following the identification of Elizabeth Short's body, Juanita Ringo stated, "Elizabeth came to the apartment building on November 13, 1946," adding, "she wasn't sociable like the other girls who lived there with her. She was more the sophisticated type."

On December 5, 1946, Mrs. Ringo said she attempted to collect the rent from Elizabeth, who told her she did not have the money. So, Ringo said, she "held her luggage as collateral." Elizabeth then asked one of her roommates to accompany her to a Crescent Drive apartment in Beverly Hills, where, she told them, "A man would pay the rent." Elizabeth went there, obtained the money that evening, paid her landlady the following day, and moved out. Mrs. Ringo told the papers, "I felt sorry for her even when she got behind on the rent. She looked tired and worried."

## Linda Rohr

Twenty-two-year-old Linda Rohr, who worked in "The Rouge Room" at Max Factor's in Hollywood, was one of Elizabeth's seven roommates at the Chancellor Apartments. During interviews three days after Elizabeth's body was discovered, she told the newspapers, "Elizabeth was odd. She had pretty blue eyes, but sometimes I think she overdid it with makeup an inch thick. Elizabeth dyed her brown hair black, then red again." Rohr said that Elizabeth dated men frequently. "She went out almost every night and received numerous telephone calls at the apartment from different men."

Specifically recalling December 6, 1946, the day Elizabeth moved out, Linda Rohr said, "Elizabeth was very anxious the morning she left. She told me, 'I've got to hurry. He's waiting for me.' None of us ever found out who 'he' was." It was Rohr's impression, she told reporters, that "Elizabeth was going to leave and go visit her sister in Berkeley."

## Vera and Dorothy French

Elizabeth Short's last known address before she was driven back to Los Angeles on January 9, 1947, and into the arms of her killer, was in San Diego at the home of Elvera (Vera) French, whose daughter, Dorothy, had befriended Elizabeth after she met her at a local movie theater. When she learned that Elizabeth had no money or a place to stay, Dorothy invited her to stay temporarily with her and her mother, because she felt sorry for her. Reporters learned about Vera and Dorothy from the victim's mother, Phoebe Short, and quickly drove the three hours south from L.A. to interview them.

Vera French described Elizabeth as "a shy and somewhat mysterious" person "my daughter, Dorothy, brought home one night as a friendly act because she was down and out." Elizabeth told the

Frenches that she "had been married to a major in the Army who had been killed in action," adding that she had "borne him a child, but the child had died."

Elizabeth also mentioned to the Frenches "her friendship with a Hollywood celebrity, who helped her out," but never revealed a name. Mrs. French told reporters, and also later the LAPD, that during the month Elizabeth had stayed at her home in December 1946 she had "dated a different man each night after December 21 through the New Year." During her stay, both Frenches noted, "Elizabeth colored her black hair with henna-blond streaks."

Mrs. French also recalled that "Elizabeth had received a one-hundred-dollar money order from a friend, a Lieutenant Fickling from North Carolina," which Fickling mailed to her at the French residence in December of 1946. Mrs. French also gave detectives a black hat that Elizabeth had left behind at the house, which, she had told Vera, she'd received because "she had modeled for a Los Angeles milliner and he gave her the hat as payment."

The last time Vera French saw Elizabeth was on January 8, 1947, when she left her home in the company of a man named "Red," who, Elizabeth had told her, was an "airline employee." Elizabeth had received a telegram from Red on January 7, the day before he arrived to pick her up. She packed her two suitcases and they left together in his car. The next time they heard about Elizabeth was over a week later when she was identified as the mutilated murder victim who'd made headlines in all the California papers.

Both French women recalled having met Red, or "Bob," as he sometimes referred to himself, at their house in December, shortly after Dorothy had brought Elizabeth home. They described him as a handsome, well-dressed man about twenty-five years old, who had taken Elizabeth out on a date in December after she had introduced him when he came to pick her up at the house. He seemed well-spoken and had been kind enough to drive Elizabeth back to Los Angeles on January 8, 1947.

During her stay, Elizabeth "frequently spoke of an ex-boyfriend from whom she was hiding out of fear," but gave no reason why she was so afraid.

After police identified "Red" as Robert Manley, whose identity had been corroborated by the Frenches, they were interviewed again by LAPD detectives at University Division police station, after which Lieutenant Jess Haskins told reporters that the women verified what Manley had told the police. Both he and the Frenches repeatedly said that Elizabeth "was living in fear of a jealous boyfriend." Mrs. French described to the police an "alarming" incident that had taken place the night before Elizabeth's departure. It had been witnessed by Mrs. French's neighbor, who remains to this day unidentified.

The neighbor told Mrs. French that at a very late hour on the night of January 7, 1946, she observed "three individuals, two men and a woman, drive up, park a car, then walk to the front door of the French residence and knock." Possibly because it was so late, the neighbor kept watching. "The three waited for a few minutes, then all three of them ran to the parked car and drove off." The following morning, after her neighbor told her what she had seen, Mrs. French asked Elizabeth what she thought. Elizabeth said she too had seen the nighttime visitors: she had peeped through the window when the three had come to the door, but she had made no move to answer the door or acknowledge her presence.

Mrs. French described Elizabeth's alarm over the incident to detectives, telling Lieutenant Haskins that "Elizabeth was constantly in fear of someone, and was very frightened when anyone came to the door." Mrs. French tried to find out what or who Elizabeth was afraid of, but was unable to, simply saying, "Elizabeth was very evasive and would not talk to me about the people, so finally I just gave up asking."

## Glen Chanslor

Even though Elizabeth Short had lived at Vera French's house in San Diego from December 12, 1946, to January 8, 1947, she had, according to the statements of other witnesses, gone back to L.A. for a few nights around Christmas. One witness was Glen Chanslor, who identified the woman he drove to a hotel in downtown Los Angeles on December 29 as Elizabeth Short. Chanslor, a taxi-stand manager with an office at 115 North Garfield Avenue in East Los Angeles, described an incident that occurred on December 29 at approximately

7:30 P.M., when Elizabeth Short came running up to his taxi stand seeking help from a man who had just assaulted her.

The woman, whom Chanslor positively identified as Elizabeth, ran to his stand "wild eyed and hysterical, bleeding from her knees." He said her "clothing was torn and her shoes were missing." He remembered her saying that she had just gotten a ride from some strangers who dropped her off at his cab stand. She said that "a well-dressed man she knew and worked with had offered to take her to Long Beach so she could cash her weekly paycheck." But instead "the man drove her to a lonely road south of Garvey Boulevard, near Garfield Avenue, parked his car, and tried to attack her."

Chanslor calmed Elizabeth down, then drove her to a hotel where she was staying in downtown Los Angeles, at 512 South Wall Street. He waited at the hotel while she went to her room and then she returned "all dolled up, but didn't have the cab fare." Chanslor figured he "wouldn't get the money from her, and just wrote it off." Chanslor was positive that the individual was Elizabeth Short, who told him "she was a waitress."

Chanslor said he could not remember whether "she was cut or bruised or scratched elsewhere on her body," as he just saw her bleeding from her knees.

## Robert "Red" Manley

One of the most important witnesses police were able to identify and question was Robert Manley, who had met Elizabeth in San Diego and spent an evening with her in a hotel, had driven her back to Los Angeles the day she disappeared, and, police thought at first, might have been the last person to see her alive. The twenty-five-year-old salesman from Huntington Park, California, initially became the LAPD's prime suspect, but after days of intense questioning and repeated polygraph examinations administered by LAPD criminalist Ray Pinker, he was cleared of any involvement in the case.

Police at the Hollenbeck Station allowed *Herald Express* chief crime reporter and veteran newswoman Agness Underwood a chance to soften up Manley in an initial interview in the hope he might open up to a woman. Initiating her conversation with a smile, a cigarette, and a warm handshake, Underwood got the full story, complete with photograph, within the hour, just in time for the evening edition, published as a four-page *Herald Express* exclusive feature under the headline "Red Tells Own Story of Romance with Dahlia." The other dailies were quick to follow, summarizing Manley's statements to police and press.

Manley began his statement with a complete denial of any involvement in the murder of Elizabeth Short and provided a chronological account of his contact with the victim from the day he first met her in mid-December until he left her in the lobby of the Biltmore Hotel on the late afternoon of January 9, 1947. Manley said he "drove to San Diego about ten days before Christmas in December of 1946" because his employer had sent him to San Diego to make business sales calls. "After hitting all of my sales spots," he said, "I saw Elizabeth Short standing on a corner, across the street from Western Airlines in San Diego."

Manley admitted he was interested in the strikingly beautiful woman, saying that, although he was married, "my wife had just had a baby and she and I were going through an adjustment period." He explained that there was a method to his madness. "I decided to see if I could pick her up, make a test for myself, see if I loved my wife or not." So he approached Elizabeth at the street corner and asked her whether she wanted a ride.

Elizabeth ignored him, turned away, and "refused to look at me," but Manley persisted and, he said to the police, he told her "who he was and continued attempting to talk with her." Elizabeth turned around to him and responded, "Don't you think it's wrong to ask a girl on a corner to get in your car?" He agreed that he thought it might be wrong, but he "just wanted to give her a ride to her home." Manley said she finally climbed into his car and directed him to Pacific Beach, where "she was living with some friends."

Manley invited her out to dinner that evening and she accepted, but, he explained to the detectives, "she was worried what she would tell the two women at the residence where she was temporarily staying." She decided to introduce Manley to the two women as "a friend who worked at Western Airlines." Elizabeth had told him that she worked at Western Airlines. Then, as agreed, Manley dropped Elizabeth off at the Frenches' and found a motel room nearby. He acknowledged that he "was nervous about stepping out on my wife, that this was the first time, and that I and my wife had only been married since November of 1945."

Manley returned to the French residence at 7:00 P.M., was introduced to Elvera and Dorothy, and left with Elizabeth on their date. They had drinks and dinner, then returned to the French residence, where they sat in front of the house in his car and talked for some time. Manley admitted kissing Elizabeth, but "found her non-responsive, and kind of cold." He told her he was married, and Elizabeth said that "she had been married to a major, but he had been killed." Manley walked her to the front door and then asked whether he could wire her if he was returning to San Diego in the near future. She replied, "Yes, but I might not be here. I don't like San Diego very much." He returned to Los Angeles after that one date.

When he learned that he would be returning to San Diego on business on January 8, 1947, he wired Elizabeth at the French residence and asked if he could see her again.

Believing she worked at the Western Airlines office, Manley drove there at about 5:00 P.M. and waited for her to leave the building. Since she didn't really work there, she never appeared, so he drove over to the Frenches'. Elizabeth greeted him at the front door and asked, he later told police, if he could take her to make a telephone call. As they were driving to make the call, she changed her mind and asked him if he could drive her up to Los Angeles. He agreed, but not until the following day, because he had business to attend to in San Diego. They returned together to the French residence, where Elizabeth said her goodbyes to Vera and Dorothy, packed her suitcases, and left with Manley.

Manley found a motel room, checked in, and the two of them went downtown for drinks and dancing. Elizabeth raised the possibility of taking a bus back to Los Angeles that night, but they decided instead "to get some hamburgers and return to the motel." She told him that "she was cold," and he lit a fire in the motel fireplace. She complained of "chills and not feeling well," and the two of them went to sleep without any attempt at lovemaking.

The following morning Manley made his business calls, returned to the motel at 12:30, picked up Elizabeth, and drove her back to Los Angeles, stopping along the way at a restaurant for sandwiches, and again for gasoline in Redondo Beach. As they drove, Elizabeth asked if she could write to him. "Of course," he said, and gave her his address, which she noted in her address book. She told him she was "going to Los Angeles to meet her sister, Adrian West." Manley asked, "Where's the meeting, the Biltmore?" "Yes," she said, "the Biltmore."

When they arrived in downtown Los Angeles, Elizabeth asked Manley to drive her first to the Greyhound bus depot, so she could check her luggage. Manley carried her bags inside, she checked them, and he drove her to the Biltmore just four blocks away. They both entered the lobby of the hotel and Elizabeth asked Manley to "check the front desk to see if her sister had checked in, while she went to the restroom." Manley did as she had bid, was told no Mrs. West had checked in, so he "asked a couple of women who were standing in the lobby if either one might be Mrs. West." They both said no. After waiting with her for a few more minutes, Manley left Elizabeth in the lobby of the Biltmore. It was the last time he saw her, he told the detectives.

Red Manley swore he was telling the truth, repeating the same story over and over to his interrogators, who grilled him hard to try to find any weak spots. The more intense the questioning, the more firm Manley became, finally offering to take a lie detector test, even truth serum, to prove his innocence.

When the police asked him if there was anything else he could remember from any of his conversations with Elizabeth, he said that on the evening of January 8 at the motel, he remembered seeing "bad scratches on both of Elizabeth's arms on the outside, above the elbows." He also reported that Elizabeth had told him that "she had a boyfriend who was intensely jealous," describing him as "an Italian, with dark hair, who lived in San Diego."

He also recalled that "Elizabeth made a long distance telephone call to a man in Los Angeles on January 8 from a payphone in a café at Pacific Highway and Balboa Drive, just outside San Diego." Manley overhead just enough of the call to know that she was arranging to meet her caller — a man — in downtown Los Angeles the following evening, January 9. Manley did not hear her mention the man's name, but suspected it was actually this man, not her sister, whom Elizabeth was planning to meet. Finally, Manley said he learned of the murder and the discovery of her body from the newspapers during a business trip he made to San Francisco in mid-January.

On January 25, 1947, detectives recontacted Manley and took him to the University Division station to see if he could identify a purse and high-heeled shoes possibly belonging to Elizabeth Short. He was shown a pile of some two dozen shoes and ten different purses, and positively identified both the shoes and purse as hers: she had been wearing the shoes and carrying the purse when he had left her in the lobby of the Biltmore. Asked by police how he could be sure about the shoes, since there were several similar pairs, Manley stated, "These shoes have double heel taps on them, and I remember that she asked me to take her to a San Diego shoe repair shop to have the extra taps put on her shoes." Manley also identified the "faint traces of perfume inside the purse as the same as the perfume she wore."

In my review of these initial twenty-one witnesses originally interviewed by the press and police, I found that only a very few of them had played a public role in the investigation. Apparently the police had ignored most of the other witnesses, which obviously concerned me. Especially disconcerting were references to the Army, or Army Air Force, lieutenant from Texas named "George," who had been hospitalized in Los Angeles and whom she said she hoped to marry in November.

The police had also seemed to have ignored the independent — and crucial — information provided by the taxi-stand owner, Glen Chanslor, about the incident the night of December 29, 1946: the vicious assault on her by a well-dressed man, the friend who had offered her a ride. Chanslor's statements were consistent in all respects with what Manley would later tell the police when he described the deep scratches he saw on her arms just eleven days later, which Elizabeth said had come from an earlier assault by her jealous boyfriend.

Rather than providing answers, the information seemed to raise further questions. On the surface, it would appear that LAPD detectives had either dropped the ball or deliberately kept important witness information from the public. Why?

Perhaps the answer to these and other troubling procedural questions, I told myself, could be found through a day-by-day reconstruction of the joint police and press investigations, beginning with the discovery of the body on January 15, 1947.

# 12

## The LAPD and the Press:
## The Joint Investigation

LOS ANGELES WAS USED TO BIZARRE CRIMES, and, although this crime went beyond brutality, into the world of pure evil, the LAPD command tried to take it as much in stride as possible. But even in 1947, Los Angeles, like New York, was a media capital, with a corps of crime reporters who knew well how the scent of blood sold extra editions of papers and could make a crime reporter's career. Therefore, even in the earliest hours of the investigation into the death of Elizabeth Short, as the sensational nature of the case began to overtake the gumshoe routine of LAPD Robbery-Homicide, the crime reporters themselves quickly got involved. Over the next few weeks it would be the reporters who were calling the shots as they tracked down leads, witnesses, and suspects for the police in exchange for exclusives. The police knew that once they arrested the "Black Dahlia Avenger," as he had called himself in a taunting note to investigators, their case would have to stand up to the scrutiny of a clever defense attorney. Thus they began to worry about disclosing too much sensitive information. Sloppy police work, either at the investigation or arrest stage, could result in an acquittal, no matter how compelling the evidence. The police brass had seen it before and did not want to walk around with mud on their faces as some clever defense attorney like Jerry Giesler took his client by the arm and walked him out of court a free man. This time it would have to be different, because this person was more than a killer: he was a "fiend," a "sex-crazed torture killer," as the papers were calling him.

The LAPD needed to rely on the newspapers if they wanted to

keep up with fast-moving crime reporters, but they also knew they had to keep some cards face down on the table.

To see what aspects of the investigation actually made it into the light of day, it was necessary for me to document how the case actually unfolded, which witnesses were brought in, what they said. I needed to discover what was consistent and what was not.

I have therefore laid out a chronology of the early months of the investigation, not only to see how the police proceeded in the Dahlia case during its first stages, but to establish a timeline enabling me to set the Dahlia murder in the context of the disconcertingly high number of other murders of lone women taking place in L.A. during the same period.

## Wednesday, January 15, 1947:
## LAPD's 1947 Investigation Begins

The detectives who responded to the crime scene in Leimert Park, some five miles south of Hollywood, probably knew that the location where the body was found was a vacant lot that had been characterized by police as a "lovers' lane." They therefore knew that whoever had placed the body must have been familiar enough with the location to have felt secure that he, or they, would not be seen. Investigators were also quick to note that the victim's body had been deliberately and carefully placed just inches from the sidewalk, as if posed for maximum effect.

While the surrounding grass near the body was dry, the grass under the two sections was wet, leading them to conclude that the body had been placed there after dark, once dew had formed on the ground.* Police canvassed the neighborhood for any potential witnesses. Within days, people started to come forward.

---

*Investigator's note: An alternative theory, which LAPD hadn't seemed to consider, is that the killer, who we know had washed the body clean, could have placed it at the location *while it was still wet*, which could explain their observations yet still account for a later — 6:30 or 7:00 A.M. — placement of the body, which would be consistent with a sighting of a possible suspect vehicle parked near the body at that time.

## Betty Bersinger

Housewife Betty Bersinger, a resident of the Leimert Park area, discovered the body of "Jane Doe Number 1" while walking along Norton Avenue with her three-year-old daughter, Anne. Mrs. Bersinger, who did not give her name when she called the police on the morning of January 15, finally contacted police on January 24 after learning through the press that they were trying to locate her and thought "she might be a suspect."

Mrs. Bersinger said that when she saw the body she grabbed her daughter and ran to the nearest house, which she described as "being the second house on Norton Avenue from 39th Street, and that it belonged to a doctor." She phoned the police but "the police didn't ask me for my name and I was too upset myself to think of giving it to them. I do recall that the policeman asked me for the telephone number I was calling from, and I looked at the number on the dial and gave that to him."

Embarrassed LAPD detectives later admitted to the press that the original officer receiving the call from Mrs. Bersinger not only neglected to take her name but lost the number she had given him. In an audit of their own records, the University Division station officers, ten days after the call-in, on January 25, located the ticket on Betty Bersinger's call, which documented that she had originally notified the police of her discovery of the victim's body at 10:54 A.M. on January 15, 1947.

## Robert Meyer

Leimert Park resident Bob Meyer, interviewed on the morning of January 15 by both police and press, said that between 6:30 and 7:00 A.M. that morning he saw a "1936 or 1937 Ford, sedan, black in color" pull up to the curbside near where the body was found. The car was there for "an estimated four minutes, and then left the location." Mr. Meyer was unable to get a clear view of the driver because weeds were blocking his view.

## Sherryl Maylond

Sherryl Maylond, one of the seven girls sharing room 501 with Elizabeth Short in Hollywood, also worked in Hollywood as "a bar girl"
at an unidentified bar. She told the police and press that on Wednesday, January 15, 1947, a man, who gave his name as "Clement," came
into the bar and asked the night bartender if he could "speak with
Sherryl." The bartender told him it was Sherryl's night off, whereupon the man left. He returned the following evening, and again
asked for Sherryl Maylond, who was working that night and agreed
to talk to him. Clement, "a slight, dapper, olive-skinned man, with
hair graying at the temples," told Sherryl he wanted to talk to her
about Betty Short. Despite his repeated requests, she refused, until
he finally left.

## Thursday, January 16, 1947

Once the identity of the victim had been established, the investigation intensified. For a city with more than its share of bloody
homicides, including the violent sexual murders of women, the characterization of the Elizabeth Short murder by LAPD as the city's
"most brutal killing ever" made the local press corps even more frantic, desperate for every scrap of news, even if they had to create it
themselves.

Gradually, as the LAPD crime laboratory developed more information, the police, under increasing pressure to feed a crime-hungry
public, released information that the victim "was killed elsewhere."
She was murdered by a sadistic killer and then driven to the crime
scene, where the suspect's vehicle "hurriedly stopped as evidenced by
tire tracks in the gutter."

The same day the police released information about the tire
tracks, detectives brought in policewoman Myrl McBride to question her about the woman she had reported seeing near the downtown bus depot. Officer McBride positively identified the victim in
the photograph as the same woman who had come to her "sobbing in
terror" on January 14 and whom she later saw leaving a downtown

bar in the company of two men and a woman. At that point, the police had, via a reliable witness, Officer McBride, a description of the three people who were with the victim only hours before she was murdered.

The group of witnesses referred to in LAPD press releases as "five unidentified youths" told detectives that they had been with the victim at various Hollywood nightspots both in December 1946, and also a few months earlier, when she had told them about her plans "to marry George, an army pilot from Texas." Also on January 16, the police interviewed in Hollywood two of Elizabeth's former roommates, Anne Toth and Linda Rohr, as well as Inez Keeling, the former manager of the Camp Cooke PX.

## Friday, January 17, 1947

The consulting psychiatrist for the Los Angeles Police Department at the time of the murder, Dr. Paul De River, said in the *Los Angeles Evening Herald Express* two days after the murder that whoever the suspect was, he "hates womankind," a "sadistic fiend." The killer was unlike a typical killer the LAPD might face because, said, Dr. De River, "In his act, the murderer was manifesting a sadistic component of a sado-masochist complex. He evidently was following the law of analytic retaliation, 'What has been done to me, I will do to you.' These types of killers," he continued, "are usually highly perverted, and resort to various forms of perversion and means of torture to satisfy their lusts."

The psychiatrist further noted, "This type of suspect above all seeks the physical and moral pain and the disgraceful humiliation and maltreatment of his victims," adding, "These sadists have a super-abundance of curiosity and are liable to spend much time with their victims after the spark of life has flickered and died." Moreover, he said, "The suspect may even be a studious type who delighted in feeling himself into the humiliation of his victim. He was the experimenter and analyst in the most brutal forms of torture."

## Saturday, January 18, 1947

By the weekend, the investigation had widened its circle of witnesses
to include Dorothy and Elvera French in San Diego, California,
whom reporters from the *Examiner* newspaper had been able to locate from the return address on a letter Elizabeth had sent to her
mother in early January. The Frenches told reporters that Elizabeth
had stored a trunk at the Railway Express station in Los Angeles.
The reporters quickly located the trunk and *Examiner* city editor
Richardson cut a deal with Captain Donahoe to reveal the location of
Elizabeth's luggage in exchange for an *Examiner* exclusive on its contents. Captain Jack didn't like the condition that he had to open the
trunk at the *Examiner* offices, but getting his hands on the trunk was
more important than butting heads with a hungry city editor, so he
reluctantly agreed.

The detectives and reporters who opened the trunk found many
photographs of Elizabeth posed with a variety of men, most in uniform, from enlisted men to a three-star general. They also found
love letters from Elizabeth to a Major Matt Gordon and a Lieutenant Joseph Fickling, along with telegrams sent to her by a number
of people.

One of these telegrams — undated — was sent to "Beth Short
220 21st Street, Miami Beach, Florida," presumably from an unknown suitor in Washington, D.C., who gave no name and no return
address. The telegram simply read:

*Exhibit 15*

A promise is a promise to a person of the world=Yours.

LAPD sent investigators to Miami Beach, but whatever they found was not released to the public. As curious as the telegram may seem today, it's obvious the sender knew that Elizabeth would know who it was from. The telegram was too familiar, too confident in tone, to have been a prank or a joke. This was a real message from someone in an ongoing relationship with Elizabeth, someone who felt he or she had been crossed because Elizabeth had gone back on her word. Given Elizabeth's oft-related fears about a jealous boyfriend, and Myrl McBride's report to her superiors of spotting Elizabeth in downtown L.A. too afraid to go back into a bar to retrieve her purse, there is no doubt Elizabeth was very afraid of someone not just during the second week in January but much earlier.

The police also interviewed Mrs. Matt Gordon Sr. by phone in Colorado about a separate telegram she had sent the victim notifying her of her son's death, which was also found in the victim's luggage while detectives in Charlotte, North Carolina, were interviewing Joseph Fickling. The Fickling interview was important because it revealed that Elizabeth, evidently believing she was about to escape from whoever was pursuing her, had written that since she "would soon be leaving for Chicago, not to write her in California."

That same Saturday also saw some crack investigative work by crime reporters from the *Examiner*, who interviewed the Frenches in San Diego about a man named Red Manley. They obtained a description of his car from Vera and Dorothy, searched the surrounding area, found the motel where Manley had signed for a room, got his license number from the registry, and called it in to city editor James Richardson. From the California DMV, Richardson got Manley's home address in the L.A. suburb of Huntington Park and sent reporters to stake out the location. When on January 18 Manley returned from a business trip to San Francisco, the reporters were there to greet him, along with the cops, who took him in for questioning. He was grilled at the station house for the next twelve hours without a lawyer and without being charged. He adamantly stuck to his guns that he knew nothing about the murder, and begged the detectives to administer a polygraph or shoot him up with sodium pentathol to satisfy themselves that he was telling the truth.

## Sunday, January 19, 1947

Manley, still in police custody, took an initial polygraph, which according to LAPD was "inconclusive." He continued to deny any involvement with the murder, but the police remained unconvinced and had a second polygraph test administered by criminalist Ray Pinker, during which Manley fell asleep. He was awakened and pressured further, but eventually Pinker had to admit that Manley had passed the test, removing him, at least temporarily, as a suspect.

At the request of the police, *Herald Express* crime reporter Agness Underwood subsequently interviewed Manley at the police station to see if she could find out anything the police had overlooked. In the course of her interview she learned of a phone call Elizabeth had made to an unknown man from the San Diego restaurant where she and Manley had stopped. During this call Elizabeth had made arrangements to meet someone on the evening of January 9, in downtown Los Angeles.*

## Monday, January 20, 1947

In what might have been the first real solid eyewitness lead, East Washington Boulevard Hotel owners and managers Mr. and Mrs. William Johnson told the police and reporters that Elizabeth Short and a man claiming to be her husband had registered for a room as "Mr. and Mrs. Barnes" on Sunday, January 12, 1947, only two days before the murder. The Johnsons described what they termed the man's "bizarre behavior," particularly his nervousness and agitation after his return to the hotel on January 15. When "Mr. Barnes" showed up in the hotel lobby on January 15, Mr. Johnson joked that because he and his wife had disappeared for three days, he thought the couple was "dead," at which Mr. Barnes, visibly shaken, turned and walked out of the hotel.

---

*LAPD in the following weeks would send detectives to San Diego to pursue this lead and search the paper trail of phone records.

After detectives showed the Johnsons separate photographs re-trieved from Elizabeth Short's luggage, the Johnsons positively iden-tified both the victim and the man who had checked in as Mr. and Mrs. Barnes. This photo identification was a vital clue for detectives, because it was the first time someone had actually put the person calling himself Elizabeth Short's husband together with the victim at the same place only two days before the murder. Then, when "Mr. Barnes" had returned alone, his behavior had been so bizarre that Mr. Johnson remembered it clearly. As of January 20, 1947, LAPD detectives therefore had in their files a photograph of someone who should have been their prime suspect in the Black Dahlia case, a man identified by two eyewitnesses as being with the victim alone in a ho-tel room just forty-eight hours before her murder. Who was this man? Where is that photograph today?

In addition to the Johnsons' interviews, a new search of the crime scene by fifty LAPD officers combing the area in a human grid turned up a man's military-type wristwatch lying in the vacant lot close to where the victim's body was originally discovered. The watch was taken into custody and, according to the newspaper re-ports, "Police chemists were checking ownership of the military watch," which was described as a "17-jewel 'Croton' with a leather-bound, steel snap band. Engraved on it are the words 'Swiss made, water proof, brevet, stainless steel back.'"

## Wednesday, January 22, 1947

At division roll calls that morning, homicide detectives circulated the following Los Angeles special police bulletin (exhibit 16) containing a photograph of Elizabeth Short and a detailed description of her clothing, and provided copies to uniformed officers working the var-ious foot beats throughout the divisions. The bulletin requested of-ficers to try to locate anyone with knowledge of the victim in the week preceding her murder. This special bulletin was posted in bus and cab terminals to enlist the public's help.

## Exhibit 16

### SPECIAL

Issued Daily
Except Saturday
Sunday & Holidays by Police
Printing Bureau

# Daily Police Bulletin

For Circulation
Among Police
Officers
Exclusively

**OFFICIAL PUBLICATION OF POLICE DEPARTMENT, CITY OF LOS ANGELES, CALIFORNIA**

CHIEF'S OFFICE, City Hall (Phone Michigan 5211—Connecting all Stations and Depts.)    C. B. HORRALL, Chief of Police

| Vol. 40 | Tuesday, January 21, 1947 | No. 14 |
|---|---|---|

## WANTED INFORMATION ON ELIZABETH SHORT
### Between Dates January 9 and 15, 1947

Description: Female, American, 22 years, 5 ft. 6 in., 118 lbs., black hair, green eyes, very attractive, bad lower teeth, finger nails chewed to quick. This subject found brutally murdered, body severed and mutilated January 15, 1947, at 39th and Norton.

Subject on whom information wanted last seen January 9, 1947 when she got out of car at Biltmore Hotel. At that time she was wearing black suit, no collar on coat. probably Cardigan style, white fluffy blouse, black suede high-heeled shoes, nylon stockings, white gloves full-length beige coat, carried black plastic handbag (2 handles) 12 x 8, in which she had black address book. Subject readily makes friends with both sexes and frequented cocktail bars and night spots. On leaving car she went into lobby of the Biltmore, and was last seen there.

Inquiry should be made at all hotels, motels, apartment houses, cocktail bars and lounges, night clubs to ascertain whereabouts of victim between dates mentioned. In conversations subject readily identified herself as Elizabeth or "Beth" Short.

Attention Officers H. H. Hansen and F. A. Brown, Homicide Detail.

KINDLY NOTIFY C. B. HORRALL. CHIEF OF POLICE, LOS ANGELES, CALIFORNIA

*LAPD Special Bulletin, January 1947*

There was also a brief statement released to local newspapers concerning fingerprints that were lifted from a wine bottle found in the room at the East Washington Boulevard Hotel where Elizabeth and her "husband" had stayed. The paper quoted two unnamed detectives, believed to have been from the Gangster Squad, assisting in the investigation, as having said they "were satisfied that it was perhaps a case of mistaken identity" since "the fingerprints did not belong to the victim, Elizabeth Short."*

An LAPD organizational explanation is here called for. The "Gangster Squad" no longer exists as an entity within the LAPD. In 1947, however, it was a separate squad of a dozen or so detectives, within the Homicide Division. The detectives assigned to this squad were supervised by their own lieutenant. Under his leadership, they were responsible for gathering intelligence and surveillance of "known gangsters," as well as for conducting city-wide investigations to identify and prosecute abortionists. The Gangster Squad detectives were the first officers to be loaned to assist regular homicide squad detectives in their manpower needs for any high-profile investigations. Historically, an uneasy relationship always existed between these interdepartment units and squads, each acting almost as its own fiefdom, with a lieutenant as lord. This was especially true in the 1940s when LAPD was rife with corruption, with many officers on the take. Anyone outside the separate squads, including "brother officers," were not to be trusted. After Chief Parker's selection as chief of police in 1950, the Gangster Squad was eventually split to become OCID (Organized Crime Intelligence Division) and PDID (Public Disorder Intelligence Division).

## Thursday, January 23, 1947

Others conducting the investigation obviously took the Johnsons seriously, as newspapers reported that all LAPD officers had been instructed to "be on the lookout for a man who might have registered with Miss Short as 'man and wife' at a hotel located at 300 E.

---

*Investigator's note: This official public statement was of immediate and grave concern to me when I first read it. A seasoned homicide detective would *never* make such a statement. The absence of the victim's prints on the bottle indicated absolutely nothing. Neither did these detectives address or comment on the possibility that the unidentified prints could have belonged to the suspect, "Mr. Barnes." By making this statement it seemed as if they were attempting to publicly discredit Mr. and Mrs. Johnson's identification and statements. Why?

Washington Blvd., on January 12." A detailed description of "Mr. Barnes," positively identified by the Johnsons as checking in with the victim, was given to officers, but his description was not released to the general public.

Police also re-canvassed the Leimert Park neighborhood near 39th and Norton for a third time, conducting a door-to-door search for possible witnesses to the crime in yet another effort to identify somebody who might have seen anything on the morning of January 15. As part of this follow-up investigation, officers asked citizens in the immediate neighborhood the following two questions:

1) "Do you know anyone in the neighborhood who is mentally un-balanced?"
2) "Do you know of any medical students?"

But the re-canvass turned up no new eyewitnesses whose names police could release to the newspapers, whose coverage had already begun to turn against the police and their apparent lack of progress. On January 23, Agness Underwood wrote, in the *Herald Express*, a story under the headline "Will 'Dahlia' Slaying Join Album of Un-solved Murders?" in which she included the names and photographs of Ora Murray, Georgette Bauerdorf, and Gertrude Evelyn Landon, three earlier Los Angeles–area unsolved murder victims. The story suggested there might well be a connection between these previous unsolved homicides and that of Elizabeth Short.

*Los Angeles Herald Express, January 23, 1947*

Underwood's article began:

WEREWOLVES LEAVE TRAIL OF WOMEN MURDERS IN L.A.

In the gory album of unsolved murders, kidnappings and crimes against women in general, Los Angeles police may have to insert a new page — "The Mystery of the Sadistic Slaying of Elizabeth Short — the Black Dahlia." So far all clues have failed. This latest murder mystery which has provoked the greatest mobilization of crime detection experts in the city's history, is the latest in a long series. The finding of her dismembered body was preceded by other gruesome discoveries of women victims slain for lust, for revenge, for reasons unknown.

Underwood's article provided the names and details of seven recent L.A. lone female victims of unsolved sex-related murders.

On the afternoon of January 23, *Los Angeles Examiner* city editor James Richardson received a phone call from a man identifying himself as the Black Dahlia killer. In Richardson's autobiography, *For the Life of Me: Memoirs of a City Editor,* he describes the eerie call and the killer's follow-up. Richardson explained that he never published the story in the paper at the time because he wanted to keep the evidence confidential, even though there was a feeding frenzy among crime reporters for any stray piece of information on the case. His revelation of the phone call became an important piece of evidence for me, primarily because of his verbatim description of his brief conversation with the killer and his impressions of the suspect. That this call came from the real killer is not in doubt. During their conversation he promised Richardson to send him "a few of her [Elizabeth's] belongings." As Richardson described the conversation:

> The story dwindled to a few paragraphs and was about to fade out altogether when one day I answered the phone and heard the voice I'll never forget.
> "Is this the city editor?" it asked.
> "Yes."

"What is your name, please?"

"Richardson."

"Well, Mr. Richardson, I must congratulate you on what the *Examiner* has done in the Black Dahlia case."

"Thank you," I said, and there was a slight pause before the voice spoke again.

"You seem to have run out of material," it said.

"That's right."

A soft laugh sounded in the earpiece.

"Maybe I can be of some assistance," the voice said.

There was something in the way he said it that sent a shiver up my spine.

"We need it," I said and there was that soft laugh again.

"I'll tell you what I'll do," the voice said. "I'll send you some of the things she had with her when she, shall we say, disappeared?"

It was difficult for me to control my voice. I began scribbling on a sheet of paper the words: "Trace this call."

"What kind of things?" I asked as I tossed the paper to my assistant on the desk. I could see him read and start jiggling the receiver arm on his phone to get the attention of the switchboard girl.

"Oh say, her address book and her birth certificate and a few other things she had in her handbag."

"When will I get them?" I asked, and I could hear my assistant telling Mae Northern the switchboard girl to trace my call.

"Oh, within the next day or so. See how far you can get with them. And now I must say goodbye. You may be trying to trace this call."

"Wait a minute," I said but I heard the click and the phone was dead.

Richardson concluded his book with some observations and reflections about the caller/killer he had spoken with seven years earlier. He was, Richardson was convinced, an egomaniac who planned the murder to show the world he was a superman, someone who could "outwit and outthink the whole world." He also stated — and again he was right — that the killer had placed the body where it would be quickly found, and mutilated it so horribly to attract the greatest attention on the part of the police and public. "He would be one against the world," he wrote, "the perpetrator of the perfect crime."

Richardson was also certain the killer would strike again, and in the same manner, but that ultimately he would make a mistake that would result in his capture. Richardson hoped that the Dahlia killer would again pick up the phone, dial the city desk, and ask for him. He revealed that his switchboard operators had developed a sixth sense and screened the "nuts and crackpots," but every now and then did put through a call to him, which invariably was important. He said he still believed that one day he would pick up the receiver and "again hear that soft, sly voice."

## Friday, January 24, 1947

Police claimed a major break in the case when they learned that the suspect originally had left Elizabeth Short's purse and shoes atop an open trashcan in front of a restaurant and motel located at 1136 South Crenshaw Boulevard, approximately twenty blocks north of 39th and Norton. Robert Hyman, the manager of a café at 1136 South Crenshaw, the witness who found the purse and shoes, said he observed a pair of women's shoes inside a black handbag just as the garbage truck was picking up the trash in front of his café. Hyman described the purse as "large and oblong, and the shoes as black with very high heels."

Hyman spoke to the trash collector and suggested that "perhaps the purse and shoes should be turned over to the police."

"Oh, we find lots of things like this, and they never amount to anything," the city employee responded. The man then dumped the purse and shoes in his truck along with the other trash and drove away.

Hyman called LAPD, and officers were dispatched to the city dump, where, after an extensive search, the purse and shoes were found. An LAPD unit brought them to University Division police station, where, as noted, Red Manley identified them.

# 13

# The LAPD and the Press:
# The Avenger Mailings

**Saturday, January 25, 1947**

THE *LOS ANGELES EXAMINER* REPORTED that someone, presumably the killer, had sent a package containing some of the contents of the victim's purse to the paper by mail, postmarked January 24, 1947, at 6:30 P.M. from downtown Los Angeles. The killer included Elizabeth Short's identification, an address book, her birth certificate, and her social security card. Along with the victim's personal effects, the sender had assembled a note pasted out of various-size letters taken from the *Los Angeles Examiner* and other L.A. papers. It read:

*Exhibit 17*

Here is Dahlia's belongings. Letter to follow

The package was opened in the presence of LAPD detectives and postal inspectors who had intercepted it before it was delivered to the newspaper office. The detectives found fingerprints on the package, which were sent to the FBI office for examination and possible identification.

The address book was of particular interest to detectives, because it contained over seventy-five names. Also of note, the name "Mark Hansen" was embossed in gold lettering on the cover. One page of the book had been torn out. Police theorized that the murderer himself may well have torn it out before mailing the address book to the newspaper.

That same day, in response to questions from reporters, Captain Donahoe said of the widening investigation, "This is the big push. Our men are fanning out now to bring in the killer. We will bring in all sorts of people for questioning, and eliminate them so long as they can eliminate themselves."

## Mark Hansen

Mark Hansen was a part owner of the Florentine Gardens, a well-known Hollywood landmark and popular nightspot that featured a popular burlesque show for patrons, who included some of the city's powerful politicians, underworld figures, and many of the rich and famous in the entertainment industry. Hansen was also Anne Toth's boyfriend at the time of the murder. Toth was one of a number of attractive young women Hansen employed at the club, Hollywood's answer to New York's nightlife and chorus lines. Hansen's manager and master of ceremonies was Nils Thor Granlund, known as "N.T.G.," a familiar personality in the world of Hollywood clubs. Many of Hansen's Hollywood chorus girls were trying to break into the movies and, like Toth, were struggling to pay their rent. Some of them, like Yvonne De Carlo, Marie "the Body" McDonald, Jean Wallace, Gwen Verdon, and Lili St. Cyr, would graduate from the Florentine Gardens stage to become familiar names on the screen and the New York musical stage. Mark Hansen would have been exactly the kind of person Elizabeth was looking for when she said she had aspirations of meeting "the right Hollywood people," who could possibly help her "break into the business."

Hansen was one of the first people contacted by LAPD detectives after they opened the killer's package. In his formal statement, Hansen explained to the police and reporters that the address book had been stolen from his residence sometime during the period when Elizabeth had lived there in the summer of 1946. It was now clear it was she who had taken it.

Hansen said that he owned and lived at 6024 Carlos Avenue, in Hollywood, just behind his club. Hansen often rented out single rooms to girls, especially those who wanted to work for him or were trying to break into the business. He admitted having rented a room to Elizabeth for about a month during the summer of 1946 but, almost in the same sentence, adamantly denied ever being intimately involved with her or even ever having dated her. He added that he was aware that Elizabeth had dated many different men while she was living there, including "a language teacher I know, and many other persons, mostly hoodlums whom I wouldn't even let in my house."

Anne Toth, also present at his interview, took offense at his comment that Elizabeth had dated "hoodlums." "She was a nice girl," Toth said. "She was quiet, she didn't drink and she didn't smoke, and we ought to look on the good side of people."

Hansen identified the brown leather address book as his, saying it had been "sent to me from Denmark, my native country." He believed it had been taken from his desk; he hadn't known where it had gone until he had seen it pictured in the newspaper. As for the names in the book, "There were no entries in the book," Hansen said, "no names of any individuals when I last saw it."

He thought Elizabeth Short had stolen the address book, along with an item he described as a "memorandum and calendar book," which had also disappeared from his desk at roughly the same time that Short had moved out. In defining his relationship with the victim as simply that of landlord/tenant, he said that reports in the papers that he had dated Short were erroneous. Further, he claimed no knowledge of the crime either before or after the fact, telling reporters, "The last time I saw Elizabeth Short was last Christmas, three weeks before she was murdered."

## Monday, January 27, 1947

In a second postcard mailed to the *Examiner* from downtown Los Angeles on January 26, the suspect wrote:

*Exhibit 18*

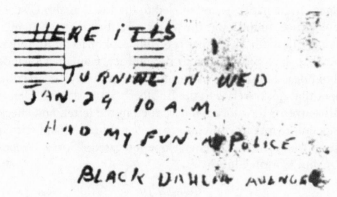

Here it is
Turning in Wed
Jan. 29 10 A.M.
Had my fun at police
Black Dahlia Avenger

In his public statement about the note, Captain Donahoe said he believed that the postcard was "legitimate" and might well be the "message to follow" that the killer had promised to send in his original pasted-up note. "The fact that the postcard was printed rather than lettered with words cut out of newspapers," Donahoe said, "also supports the theory that the killer intends to turn himself in to the police, and no longer needs to take pains to conceal his identity." By the killer's signature line, "Black Dahlia Avenger," he surmised, "he is indicating that he murdered Elizabeth Short for some avenged wrong, either real or imagined. So far we haven't seen any evidence of that, but we hope that the killer who is writing these notes keeps his promise to turn himself in on Wednesday." In a public message, Donahoe promised the killer, "If you want to surrender as indicated by the postcard now in our hands, I will meet you at any public location at any time or at the homicide detail office in the City Hall. Communicate immediately by telephoning MI 5211 extension 2521, or by mail."

That same day, police were reviewing a separate typed message they believed was written by a woman — because there were lipstick smudges on the paper — and mailed to the Los Angeles District Attorney's Office. In the letter the writer described in detail an incident involving Elizabeth Short that probably took place at a Hollywood nightclub a day or two prior to the murder. Captain Donahoe refused to release any details of the letter except to say, "it described an incident that might relate to the Elizabeth Short slaying. Detectives will also investigate a location described in the letter, and check out other details before its contents are made public." A handwritten notation on the outside of the envelope indicated, "Sorry, Greenwich Village, not Cotton Club."

### *Exhibit 19*

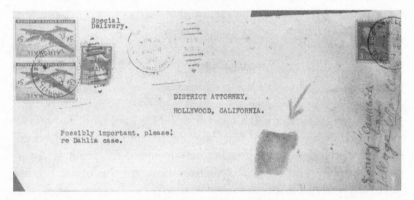

*Typed letter mailed to DA*

The details of this letter were kept strictly confidential in a meeting between LAPD's Captain Jack Donahoe and then district attorney Simpson.

That same day, the police also released this public statement: "A complete roundup of the 75 names in the Mark Hansen address book was completed yesterday without adding anything to the sorry story that is already known."

## Tuesday, January 28, 1947

The analysis of the printed postcard in which the suspect had promised to turn himself in revealed that he had used a "new ballpoint pen" when he wrote the address of the *L.A. Examiner*. For the police, this was important, because ballpoint pens were a rarity in 1947. While they had been provided to officers in the military during the war, commercial distribution to the general public only began on Christmas 1945, and at a heady cost of $12.50 (approximately $125 today). They were used primarily by professionals, such as doctors, lawyers, and business executives.

## Wednesday, January 29, 1947

The newspapers and police received two additional notes, purportedly from the suspect, that were published on the front page of the dailies. Note #3 was again assembled out of pasted letters cut from newspapers, and said:

*Exhibit 20*

Dahlia's Killer Cracking,
Wants Terms

Note #4 was assembled the same way and promised:

### *Exhibit 21*

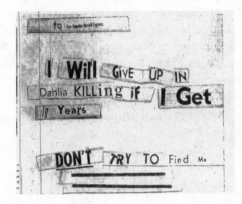

To *Los Angeles Herald Express*
I will give up in
Dahlia killing if I get
10 years
Don't try to find me

The night edition of the *Herald Express* included a front-page photograph of the latter note, and in a front-page headline revealed:

# 'DAHLIA' KILLER NOTES WORK OF SAME MAN, TESTS SHOW

The LAPD crime lab analysis had quickly connected the envelopes and paper used and indicated that the same suspect who sent the original packet containing the victim's identification and address book also sent the subsequent offers to surrender in exchange for a ten-year sentence. Additional important evidence found on these notes by the crime lab were that several dark hairs had been imbedded in the Scotch tape used to paste on the words. Upon comparison, the hairs were found not to be those of the victim, but nonetheless became an important clue, to be matched to the hair of future suspects.

Publicly, LAPD detectives stated, "We are dealing with a homicidal maniac who craves attention for his crime and may come forward in a bold and spectacular manner for his curtain call after he has wrung out the last drop of drama from his deed."

Federal inspectors at the Terminal Annex Post Office in downtown Los Angeles received a fifth note on Wednesday that they characterized as a "semi-illiterate death threat," reported to have been "scribbled on glossy paper, torn from a note tablet." Though not reproduced in the newspaper, the message read:

A certain girl is going to get same as E.S. got if she squeals on us.
We're going to Mexico City — catch us if you can.
2K's

On the reverse of the mailed envelope someone, presumably the sender, wrote:

E. Short got it. Caral Marshall is next.

The *Examiner* engaged questioned-document expert Clark Sellers, considered by most to be one of the nation's leading forensic handwriting experts of the day, to review and analyze the handprinting on the postcards it had received from the purported suspect. Sellers had gained public notoriety as one of the chief forensic experts who testified for the prosecution in the Lindbergh baby kidnapping trial, in which he connected handwriting samples from the suspect, Bruno Richard Hauptmann, to the ransom note and helped the state win a conviction.

In his expert analysis, Sellers told the *Examiner*, "It was evident the writer took great pains to disguise his or her personality by printing instead of writing the message and by endeavoring to appear illiterate. But the style and formation of the printed letters betrayed the writer as an educated person." The *Examiner* also revealed that Sellers had conducted "microscopic tests" on the Black Dahlia message and made "several important discoveries the nature of which is being withheld."

A second questioned-document expert, Henry Silver, was also contacted to analyze the original note the killer had sent with the victim's belongings, as well as some of the later postcards received by the press. Silver said:

The sender is an egomaniac and possibly a musician. The fluctuating base line of the writing reveals the writer to be affected by extreme fluctuations of mood, dropping to melancholy. The writer suffers from mental conflict growing out of resentment or hatred due to frustration of sex urge. Because the last letters of many words are larger, it reveals extreme frankness. The writer is telling the truth. Furthermore, he can't keep his secret and feeds his ego by telling. There is a fine sense of rhythm present, showing the penman to be either a musician or possibly a dancer. He is calculating and methodical.

## Thursday, January 30, 1947

A day after he had promised to surrender, the killer sent a new pasted note addressed to Captain Donahoe that read:

*Exhibit 22*

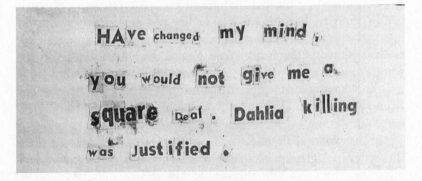

Have changed my mind.
You would not give me a
square deal. Dahlia killing
was justified.

That same day, Daniel S. Voorhees, a thirty-three-year-old restaurant porter, called police to ask them to meet him at 4th and Hill Streets, downtown, where he confessed to killing Elizabeth

Short. Voorhees was quickly eliminated when his handwriting was compared to that in the killer's note. Mentally and emotionally unstable, Voorhees was one of the first of a long list of what the police would term "confessing Sams," people seeking five minutes of "fame" by attempting to link themselves to the sensational murder.

### Friday, January 31, 1947

The *Herald Express* published photographic copies of six additional messages, all purported to have been by the Dahlia killer. The first, in letters pasted from a newspaper, read:

*Exhibit 23*

'Go Slow'
Man Killer Says
Black Dahlia Case

The next read:

*Exhibit 24*

I have decided not to
surrender Too much
fun fooling police
Black Dahlia Avenger

Another note, also pasted together from cut-out newspaper type, was sent in. This contained a photograph of a young male with a stocking mask drawn in covering his face to conceal his identity. Pasted words glued to the note read:

### Exhibit 25

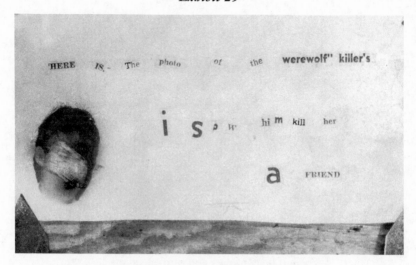

Here is the photo of the werewolf killer's
I saw him kill her
a friend

The *Herald Express* also published photographic copies of three additional "crudely" hand-printed notes, each written and mailed to them on a separate postcard. The first two apparently referred to the surrender and confession of Daniel Voorhees:

### Exhibits 26 & 27

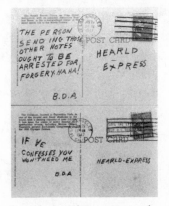

26) The person sending those other notes ought to be arrested for
forgery. Ha Ha!
B.D.A.
27) If he confesses you won't need me
B.D.A.

The third read:

### Exhibit 28

Ask news man at 5 + Hill for clue.
Why not let that nut go
I spoke to said man
B.D.A.

*Exhibit 29*

*Armand Robles, age 17*

Accompanying their article on page one, the *Herald Express* also ran a photograph of a young man with the following request addressed to its readers:

> A "poison pen" is using a picture of this young person in the "Dahlia" case letters. If this person will call at the *Evening Herald and Express* office, a line may be obtained on the "poison pen" author of letters which send police on "wild goose" chases.

The following day, seventeen-year-old Armand Robles and his mother, Florence Robles, contacted the newspaper and were interviewed by reporters for a story that ran the next day in which Armand explained that the photographs printed in the newspaper the previous days were of him and had been stolen about three weeks before by a strange assailant. He had been walking in the vicinity of the 4300 block of Eagle Street in Los Angeles on or about January 10, young Robles said, and "he was about to approach a footpad,"* when

*A 1940s term for a dirt path.

he was "knocked down by a man, who then took his wallet." The photographs sent to the *Examiner*, which Robles had taken "about 3 months ago at a shooting gallery on Main Street in downtown Los Angeles," had been in the wallet. He described his assailant as, "well dressed, tall," and "driving a newer model car."

In a later mail, the *Herald Express* received a new pasted-up note, which read:

### *Exhibit 30*

yes or no?

## Saturday, February 1, 1947

In response to Armand Robles's going public with his information, another "poison pen" pasted-up note arrived at the *Herald Express* with a different photograph of Robles. This time the sender had hand-drawn an arrow pointing to Robles's picture, with the word "next" above his head. The pasted message itself read:

*Exhibit 31*

"that young! I'll do him like I did the
'Black Dahlia'
"Black Dahlia Avenger"

That same day, in a statement to the press about where the crime had occurred, Captain Donahoe speculated:

It appears impossible the Short girl was murdered in the city. We are forced to this conclusion by the failure of anyone to report a possible place where she was killed within the city limits. If she was slain in a house or a room or motel in the city it seems impossible that some trace has not been reported or found. This leads us to the conclusion that she was killed outside the city. The killer could not have emerged from the place in clothing worn when the murder was committed and the body drained of blood. He could have been too easily detected and stains would have attracted attention.

Donahoe also suggested, "The killer used a thick bristled brush of coconut fiber to scrub the body clean before he removed the body from the murder den."

The foregoing exhibits are photographs published in the various newspapers in 1947, and show the separate communications, pasted and handwritten notes, sent in by the Black Dahlia Avenger. Excluding the D.C. telegram and the typed letter to the district attorney's office, the suspect has, incredibly, within a two-week period posted a total of *thirteen* separate taunting notes to the press and police.*

## Monday, February 3, 1947

With newspapers desperate for feature copy about the murder to attract readers, a number of editors asked some of the city's best-known mystery and scriptwriters for their take on the Black Dahlia. Ben Hecht, Craig Rice, David Goodis, Leslie Charteris, Steve Fisher, and others were asked to profile the character traits and personality of the killer for the public. Ben Hecht, whom we recall from his bizarre 1924 murder mystery *Fantazius Mallare*, which was reviewed and praised by the then young editor of *Fantasia* magazine, George Hodel, now some two decades later had become Hollywood's highest-paid screenwriter of mysteries. Hecht's brief but serious profile of the Dahlia killer was the most bizarre: "a dyke lesbian with a hyper-thyroid problem."

Novelist-turned-screenwriter Steve Fisher was very much on target in his character analysis for the *Herald Express*. Fisher — who wrote *I Wake Up Screaming*, *Destination Tokyo*, *Song of the Thin Man*, and *Winter Kill* for MGM and a screenplay based on Raymond Chandler's *Lady in the Lake* — not only evaluated the Dahlia case as

*I don't pretend to be an expert on London's notorious nineteenth-century serial killer, "Jack the Ripper." However, on the surface, it would appear that the Dahlia killer had more than a passing knowledge of the famous case, and demonstrated that knowledge after his murder of Elizabeth Short. Like their modern-day counterparts, the newspapers of the 1880s published the handwritten, taunting Ripper letters, which included *very similar wording, phrases, and drawings used by the 1947 Avenger*. Jack the Ripper wrote, "Catch me when you can." In many of his letters he included the taunting phrase, "Ha ha!" and drew childlike drawings of a knife blade. In addition, the Ripper mailed items connected to his victims, such as a partial kidney, to the police, leading some authorities to suspect the killer might well have been a surgeon.

it stood, but suggested what the fictional character Nick Charles would have done to force the suspect to turn himself in. Here are some extracts from his extensive "profile" that appeared in the *Herald Express* on February 3, 1947, under the headline "Noted Film Scenarist Predicts 'Dahlia' Killer Will Soon Be in Toils":

> By following the case in the *Evening Herald* I think I know who the killer is, and think the police do also, and in a very short time will have his name. When the killer's name is published I think a lot of his friends will be very surprised and terrified. I think he is still in Los Angeles. When arrested his attorneys will plead insanity, but the killer will be his own worst enemy. He will not want people to think he is crazy. He is an egomaniac . . .
>
> I believe that the killer believed that the Dahlia had wronged him, and because of his punctured ego, she had to be exposed. People had to know it. Vengeance had to complete itself. That is why he tortured her and chopped her up in ways so gruesome that many of the revolting details have not been revealed, even with all that has been printed about the Dahlia.

Fisher went on to conjecture that the killer wanted "recognition," and reveled in the publicity: It was his ego that impelled him to write to the police. (He was convinced the notes and cards sent to the authorities were authentic.) Presciently, Fisher also theorized that the killer must have been furious about all the "nuts" who kept confessing to *his* murder, but comforted by the thought that, one by one, the police dismissed them. But, added Fisher, if "a 'legitimate' suspect made a 'confession' . . . and the police announced the case solved," the real killer would be so frustrated and upset that he would "be driven at some point to come in and give the lie to the phony suspect's confession . . . But, I believe the police right now have a definite 'line' on the real killer, and that kind of 'staging' won't be necessary. Look for a thriller finish to this case."

That day the *Express* also ran a report about a forcible rape, including a photograph of the attractive victim, a Mrs. Sylvia Horan, who was described as "30 years old, honey-haired and shapely." At first glance, the crime appeared to be an unrelated and isolated sexual attack, though the paper noted that it had occurred "near the

Dahlia murder spot." Sylvia Horan might have been an important living witness to detectives in the Black Dahlia investigation if law enforcement had linked the Horan crime to the Short case.

Although the rape had occurred within the city limits, Mrs. Horan lived in the county and reported the crime to the sheriff after having been thrown out of the suspect's car in the sheriff's jurisdiction. She told deputies who took a "courtesy report" for LAPD that she was an ex-WAC and married, but that her husband was in New York on business. She had gone alone to downtown Los Angeles to see a show. Afterward she was standing on the corner of 7th Street and Broadway when a "suave stranger, driving a black coupe, drove up to her and offered to drive her home." "I accepted the ride," she said, "due to the late hour." The stranger, who identified himself only as "Bob," drove her to a lonely spot on Stocker Boulevard between Crenshaw and La Brea Avenues, only eight blocks from where the body of Elizabeth Short had been found, and forcibly raped her.

Mrs. Horan reported, "He grabbed me in his arms . . . we were parked in his car on a very dark street . . . I was paralyzed with fright . . . I had a vision of the Black Dahlia, her body cut in half . . . I was in a situation . . . so I submitted to his advances. I knew we were near the place where the Black Dahlia's body had been found, and I was terrified. All I could think of was to escape and get home alive."

Mrs. Horan told the deputies that after the attack the man drove her to the Inglewood area and "rudely pushed her from his automobile and fled. I was so afraid I forgot to get the license plate of his car." The case was reported in the *Examiner*, but according to the public record of the Black Dahlia investigation, it was never incorporated into the Elizabeth Short case file and remained an isolated sexual assault.

### Tuesday, February 4, 1947

Police reported to the press that they were on the lookout in San Diego for a "sleek-haired Latin type, one of the most favored of the host of admirers attracted by the Dahlia's flashing beauty." LAPD detectives told reporters they were "working with San Diego authorities to run down clues to the handsome Latin's identity, and that they were also checking some new leads."

In a separate statement the same day, detectives reported that,

"Due to the surgical neatness of the severed body, they were checking the possibility that she could have possibly been slain in a mortuary."

## Wednesday, February 5, 1947

Famed mystery writer Leslie Charteris, creator of the fictional amateur sleuth "the Saint," was called in to analyze the Dahlia murder for the *Herald Express*. His profile described a "lone wolf" type, possibly suffering from impotence. Here is a brief excerpt from his long article:

> Whether the murderer's impotence was or was not due to alcohol, and whether his resulting rage was or was not inflamed by the same thing, I can see him saying something like "So you think you can laugh at me, do you? I'll keep that laugh on your face for good" — and he slashes her cheeks from the corners of her mouth to her ears, in the ghastly grin which is preserved on the morgue photos . . .
>
> I am practically certain that the man will be caught and I base this on a rather gruesome reason. My reason is that even if he should get away with this murder, it is almost certain that he will repeat it, and the next time he does it he has another chance to make a slip.

## Thursday, February 6, 1947

Not to be outdone by their morning competitor, the *Evening Herald Express* brought in their own hired gun, the popular mystery writer David Goodis, who had recently written the bestseller *Dark Passage*, which, at the time of the Dahlia murder, was in production at Warner Brothers Studios. The now classic noir film would be released a few months after his article appeared, and paired film legend Humphrey Bogart with sultry Lauren Bacall. Goodis's lengthy "profile" of the killer speculated that he met her in a bar:

> The man — and I am certain it was a man — met her on the street or in a bar. They talked. They found each other interesting. Somewhere along the path of their conversation they fell into the channel of an erotic subject. This was the initial spark. It grew. Within

the mind of the man it expanded and formed a chain between the conscious and the subconscious.

Suddenly, he was insane — completely. But Elizabeth Short did not notice this. She was intrigued by the man. There was something about him that magnetized her particular personality. When he invited her to his "place," she offered no argument.

As if writing a fictional ending to his story, Goodis concocted a strange scenario in which LAPD would try to lure the killer using a Dahlia lookalike as bait. She could be "wired," and the police could pounce on the killer just as he was about to strike.

That day, the *Evening Herald Express* ran a front-page story on a new suspect in the murder, a twenty-nine-year-old Army corporal named Joseph Dumais, who was purportedly in police custody at Fort Dix, New Jersey. Over the next four days, as more and more revelations were reported in the papers, particularly Corporal Dumais's own confessions, he became an even stronger suspect in the eyes of the public. Los Angeles readers were riveted by the unfolding story of the Dumais confessions that played across each day's newspaper editions like a serialized novel.

February 6, *Herald Express*:

## GRILL G.I. ON L.A. DAHLIA DATE IN TRY TO SOLVE LOST WEEK

February 6, *Examiner*:

## SUSPECT IN DAHLIA SLAYING JAILED BY ARMY AT FORT DIX

February 8, *Daily News*:

## "BLACKOUT" MURDER OF BETH SHORT CONFESSED SOLDIER ADMITS CRIME BUT HOLDS BACK HORROR DETAILS CORPORAL DUMAIS SIGNS 50 PAGE CONFESSION

February 8, *Herald Express*, in four-inch bold headlines:

# CORPORAL DUMAIS IS BLACK DAHLIA KILLER

## Identifies Marks on Girl's Body in Long Confession

February 9, *Examiner*:

## MILITARY CAPTAIN CONVINCED THEY HAVE THE DAHLIA KILLER

February 9, *Examiner*:

## NEW DAHLIA CONFESSION

**Monday, February 10, 1947**

After all the week's stories about Dumais, whom newspapers now dubbed "the real Dahlia killer," since he had confessed to the crime, readers were jolted on February 10 by a sudden and startling turn of events. Dumais, it was revealed, was not the killer! The story was a complete hoax, a ruse foisted on the Black Dahlia Avenger by the newspapers, in which they "manufactured" a suspect to confess to the crime, a tactic not unlike Steve Fisher's suggestion that the police trick the real murderer by "rigging a phony killer" to bring the real culprit in. Here, however, it wasn't the police putting out a false story, but the media.

Despite the Dumais "confessions," the public was never told, either by the police or the press, that LAPD detectives were almost certain from the outset that Dumais was not the Black Dahlia Avenger: four of his Army buddies had testified he was at Fort Dix, New Jersey, on January 15. The newspapers knew this too, but played up the story in the hope that, if Fisher was correct in his psychological assessment of the Black Dahlia Avenger, the killer's ego would force him to turn himself in to police, if only to expose Dumais as a false confessor. Unfortunately, the newspapers' hoax did entice the killer to make himself known — not by turning himself in but by striking again.

# 14

# The "Red Lipstick" Murder

A SCANT TWO DAYS AFTER the *Herald Express* announced that the Black Dahlia killer, Corporal Joseph Dumais, had confessed and the Black Dahlia case was solved, the *Herald Express* put out a special edition on Monday, February 10, 1947, with the headline:

## WEREWOLF STRIKES AGAIN! KILLS L.A. WOMAN, WRITES "B.D." ON BODY

This time the victim's nude body was found in an isolated vacant lot, on a direct parallel line some seven miles west of where Elizabeth Short's body had been found three weeks earlier. According to crime-scene descriptions, the victim had been "kicked and stomped to death." Like the Black Dahlia, her mouth had also been slashed, and the killer had used lipstick from her purse to write obscenities on the naked body, signing his now infamous initials, "B.D.," to let the police know — or think — he was the same person who had sent the notes in the Dahlia case. The local press quickly dubbed this second crime with two names: "Jeanne French: The Flying Nurse" and "the Red Lipstick murder."

In the early 1930s, Jeanne French had gained a measure of fame and notoriety in the Los Angeles area as a socialite and starlet. She had worked as a studio-contract actress under the name Jeanne Thomas, had become a registered nurse, and had gotten her license as one of America's first female airplane pilots. The papers loved her and had nicknamed her "the Flying Nurse." Said to be one of the most promising candidates for screen fame in the early days of talking pictures, but dogged by a host of suitors, she finally married and gave up her career.

Jeanne French had also been well-known in European social circles as the nurse and traveling companion of Millicent Rogers, the famed oil heiress of the 1920s. French was also the nurse of Marion Wilson, known to the public as "the Woman in Black," who for many years after the death of Rudolph Valentino returned on the anniversary of his death as the mysterious veiled woman seen placing flowers on his grave.

Just after eight in the morning on Monday, February 10, 1947 — less than four weeks after the murder of Elizabeth Short — construction worker Hugh Shelby discovered Jeanne French's nude, bludgeoned, and lacerated body in a vacant lot in the 3200 block of Grandview Avenue.

Detectives who examined the victim's body at the crime scene discovered that the killer had written an obscenity on her torso with red lipstick — an obscenity the police never disclosed — and then signed "B.D." The worn-out lipstick stub was found close to the body, as was the victim's empty purse.

Foot and heel marks were clearly visible on the victim's face, breasts, and hands, indicating that she had been brutally stomped by a maddened assailant. Captain Donahoe told the press that the victim had been savagely beaten with "a heavy weapon, probably a tire iron or a wrench, as she crouched naked on the highway."

The victim's stockings and underclothing were missing. However, the killer had ceremoniously draped her blue coat trimmed with red fox-fur cuffs and her red dress over the body before leaving the scene. A man's white handkerchief was also found near the body. There was also a wine bottle that search-team detectives found nearby that was taken to the crime lab in the hope of obtaining fingerprints.

Police obtained photographs of the handwriting on the body and plaster castings of the clearly defined footprints found at the scene. Handwriting experts were called to the crime scene to study the macabre note on her torso before her body was taken to the morgue. Other letters were observed on the nude body below the "B.D." that were difficult to decipher but possibly read "Tex" and "O" or "D" or possibly "Andy D," leading to police speculation that possibly two men might have been involved in the murder.

The police criminalists recovered important physical evidence in the form of black hair follicles found under the victim's fingernails, which indicated that she had put up a violent struggle before being slain. In their reconstruction of the crime, homicide detectives speculated to the press that the victim "was stripped naked in the parked car and then beaten."

Detectives also concluded that because a large pool of blood was found in the highway near the crime scene, the killer must have dragged the victim from the highway to the lot, where he wrote the message on her body, then draped the clothing over her. As a last act, he had carefully arranged her shoes on either side of her head at an equal distance of approximately ten feet, then fled.

The coroner's physician, Dr. Newbarr, conducted the autopsy and found the cause of death to be "ribs shattered by heavy blows, one of the broken ribs having pierced the heart creating hemorrhage and death." Dr. Newbarr stated that the victim had "dined on chop suey within an hour of her death." Newbarr determined that the victim was murdered the same day her body was found, sometime between midnight and 4:00 A.M. Results of a blood alcohol examination by the chemist returned a level of .30, twice what was then considered legally drunk, and more than three times the level by today's standards in California.

Police described the Lipstick crime scene as a "sort of lovers lane area" — the same phrase that had been used to characterize the vacant lot where Elizabeth Short was found. They also put out an all points bulletin to law enforcement agencies, including the FBI, notifying them that "the killer would have blood on his shoes and pants, and possibly in his vehicle."

In tracing Jeanne French's movements in the hours before her death, the police and witness statements established that at 7:30 P.M. Sunday, February 9, 1947, she had gone into the Plantation Café, 10984 Washington Boulevard in Los Angeles, in the company of two men, one of whom was described by waitress Christine Studnicka as having "dark hair and a small mustache." In its coverage, the *Los Angeles Examiner* also reported that the description matched that of a dark-haired man the victim had had dinner with five hours later. Studnicka also observed that "the two men entered a booth and ordered food, while the victim went to a pay telephone in the restaurant." The victim's phone call to the unknown person lasted approximately ten minutes.

During the phone call, Studnicka said people nearby could hear French bark into the receiver in a very loud voice, "Don't bring a bottle, the landlady doesn't allow it." While still on the phone, the victim yelled to the two men in her booth, "Don't put any liquor in the car" and "Don't take any liquor." Studnicka observed that the two men appeared "to be arguing between themselves," and it was her impression that they were "arguing over which one was going to accompany the victim."

After they had eaten, the two men left the restaurant, followed shortly by Jeanne French. Studnicka did not know whether the three met up outside the restaurant, nor could she provide a further description of the second man who accompanied the "dark-haired man."

Later that Sunday evening, at 9:30 P.M., witnesses saw Jeanne French driving away from her home at the wheel of her 1928 Ford Roadster. Half an hour later, restaurant owner Ray Fecher saw her inside his Turkey Bowl restaurant at 11925 Santa Monica Boulevard, Los Angeles, where he told police, "She was intoxicated, making loud remarks, while drinking a cup of coffee."

At 10:30 P.M., French was identified as the person inside a bar at 10421 Venice Boulevard on the west side of Los Angeles, where she told bartender Earl Holmes she was going to "commit her husband to a psycho ward at the Sawtelle Veteran's Hospital the following morning." Police later verified the accuracy of this statement, because Jeanne French's husband, whom she was planning to divorce, had slapped her a week before, and as a result she had forced him to move out.

At 10:45 P.M., Santa Monica PD officers Chapman and Aikens received a radio call in their patrol car reporting "a drunk driver, driving an automobile described as a 1928 Ford Roadster." They searched the vicinity and located an empty car of that description parked curbside at Stanford and Colorado Boulevards. But because they were unable to locate the driver, they left.

What the officers did not know was that French was in an upstairs apartment at 1547 Stanford Avenue visiting her estranged husband, Frank. She told him to "meet her at her attorney's office the next day at 11:00 A.M., as she was filing for divorce and wanted to commit him to the hospital as a psycho." The drunken woman argued with her husband for approximately the next thirty minutes, then drove away, arriving at the Piccadilly drive-in restaurant, at 3932 Sepulveda Boulevard in Los Angeles, shortly after midnight.

Between 12:10 and 1:00 A.M. Monday, February 10, Toni Manalatos, a carhop at the Piccadilly, served the victim what would turn out to be her last meal. She told police she saw Jeanne French in the company of a "dark-haired man with a small mustache."

French's Ford Roadster was later found, still parked in the Piccadilly's parking lot, at 2:00 A.M. by Mr. Anzione, a cleanup man coming to work at the restaurant. Doubtless she had left her car at the Picadilly and driven away with the dark-haired man. Her body was found only fifteen blocks away, and, given the medical examiner's estimated time of her death, that man was probably the last person to have seen her alive. Based on time of death and the murder's proximity to the restaurant, he was also probably the killer.

After detectives identified the victim and learned that she had filed for divorce, the initial thrust of their investigation focused on Jeanne's husband, Frank, as the likeliest suspect. Within several days of the murder, Captain Donahoe ruled him out: Frank French could not and did not drive a car, his shoe size was different from those found at the crime scene, and handwriting samples compared to those found on the body did not match. The police didn't report it, but it is assumed that the other physical evidence — hair samples and possible fingerprints found at the scene — also helped to eliminate Frank as the suspect.

After they had initially linked the Lipstick murder to the Dahlia murder, police detectives theorized that whoever killed Elizabeth Short may have been infuriated by Corporal Joseph Dumais's "confession" and murdered Jeanne French to disprove his claim. This, police told the press, would also account for the "taunting obscene phrase written on her chest." One police official was quoted as saying, "For two days before Mrs. French was kicked to death, the newspapers had been full of Dumais' confessions that it was he who had killed Beth Short. We know that the killer is egotistical, and it's possible that the real killer resented the claims of Dumais and wanted to show that the real killer was still here." Thus, in a tragic and unintended way, Steve Fisher's strategy of smoking out the Black Dahlia Avenger with a false confession had proved to be chillingly effective.

On February 12, 1947, the *Herald Express* ran a story under the headline, "Quiz Mystery Man Sharing P.O. Box of 'Lipstick' Victim," in which the reporter said that an unidentified male had shared a secret post office box with Jeanne French and was being questioned by detectives. No further details about his identity or his relationship to Jeanne French were ever released, nor have I found any information that would indicate that LAPD said anything more to the press about him in the weeks or months that followed.

In the course of my investigation, I came across a reference to a book, *Death Scenes: A Homicide Detective's Scrapbook*, edited by Sean Tejaratchi, containing over a hundred photographs of unsolved crimes in the L.A. area during the years of LAPD homicide detective Jack Huddleston's service, from 1921 to 1950.

The scrapbook was a compilation of Detective Huddleston's own photo collection of suicides, murders, and accidental deaths, clearly his own personal macabre fetish. Its pages contained pictures of tattooed men, nude drag queens, child homicides, murdered prostitutes, and even a decapitation caused by a train wreck, all packaged into an album of horrors. Next to many of the photographs the detective had written his personal observations and locker-room dark humor.

In her introduction to the book, Katherine Dunn says that the collection of photographs, found at an estate sale after Huddleston's death, was eventually made into a video called *Death Scenes*. Although essentially a revelation of one person's fascination with the brutality of homicide, *Death Scenes* contains three photographs next to which Huddleston had typed the following information:

## "THE RED LIPSTICK MURDER."

Mrs. Jeanne Axford French Age 40. (Nurse) of 3535 Military Ave, Sawtelle L.A. Killed by ???? Her body was found in a field near Grand View Ave, & National Blvd. L.A.

> She was stomped to death by a fiend who crudely printed an obscene phrase (FUCK YOU) on her chest.

The three photographs were obviously from the 1947 LAPD investigation. One of them, a close-up, showed the victim lying supine in the vacant lot, completely nude, with the lettering clearly visible on her body. In large block printed lettering, the killer had written in red lipstick the following words across the midsection of her body: "FUCK YOU, B.D." What the LAPD had not revealed to the press, Detective Huddleston unintentionally revealed to the public through the bits and pieces of his own obsession years after his death.

*Exhibit 32*

*Jeanne French, "Red Lipstick" murder, February 10, 1947*

Simultaneous and parallel to the "Red Lipstick" murder, the Dahlia investigation remained ongoing, as Captain Donahoe told the public that in his opinion the Dahlia and Lipstick murders were likely connected. In the month of February 1947, leads and additional evidence continued to pour in.

## Tuesday, February 11, 1947

Imagine the surprise of downtown Los Angeles cab driver Charles Schneider when he discovered a mysterious note in his cab, possibly written by the Black Dahlia Avenger. Schneider told police and reporters that he had gone to a restaurant in the 500 block of Columbia Street — ten blocks from the Biltmore — and when he returned to his parked cab he found a note in the glove compartment. Addressed to the *Examiner*, but not released to the public, the note, with a crude illustration of a knife and a pistol on it, read:

> Take it to Examiner at once. I've got the number of your cab.
> $20,000 and I'll give B.D. up. Is it a go?
>                         B.D.

Police quickly lifted fingerprints from the glove compartment of Schneider's cab, which did not belong to him. They also checked similarities between the letter and the original envelope sent to the *Examiner* with Elizabeth Short's belongings and immediately eliminated Schneider's fingerprints from both the prints on the glove box and the original note. Those fingerprints remain unidentified to this date.

## Wednesday, February 12, 1947

Ica Mabel M'Grew, a twenty-seven-year-old resident of Los Angeles, reported a kidnapping and forcible rape that occurred in the early-morning hours of February 12 as she was leaving a South Main Street café in downtown Los Angeles. She reported that two men had forced her into their car and driven her to an isolated spot on East Road in Los Angeles, where both had raped her. After the attack one of the assailants had warned, "Don't tell the police, or I'll do to you the same as I did to the Black Dahlia." They then drove her close to her home in Culver City, only three miles away from where Jeanne French had been murdered. The only descriptions of the assailants released in the news article were "two swarthy men."

## Sunday, February 16, 1947

By the middle of February, the LAPD said that it had "hit a stone wall" in its investigation of the murders of both Elizabeth Short and

Jeanne French, announcing that the one remaining lead, a key to the two mysterious homicides, was their search for a dark haired man with a small mustache, who was known to have had dinner with Jeanne French just two hours before she was murdered.

Police indicated they had a close watch on their important witness, Mrs. Antonia Manalatos, the waitress who had seen the dark-haired suspect dining with the victim.

That same day, Otto Parzyjegla, a thirty-six-year-old linotype operator at a Los Angeles printing shop, was arrested for the bludgeoning murder of his seventy-year-old employer, Swedish newspaper publisher Alfred Haij. After confessing to police that he had "hacked the torso into six pieces and then crammed them into three boxes at the rear of the print shop," Parzyjegla told authorities that "the whole thing was like a dream," insisting to his interrogators that "he must be dreaming and was waiting to wake up."

Captain Donahoe quickly entered the case, believing that Parzyjegla might possibly be the suspect in the Black Dahlia and Lipstick cases. Donahoe theorized that the violence that Parzyjegla had displayed in killing and mutilating his employer could well link all three murders. Donahoe informed reporters that Parzyjegla worked in a print shop, adding, "one of the letters received by the Black Dahlia suspect bore evidence of having been mailed by someone working in a printing establishment." After his preliminary investigation, Donahoe said, "Parzyjegla is the hottest suspect yet in the 'Black Dahlia' killing."

### Tuesday, February 18, 1947

Captain Donahoe organized a live "show-up" of suspect Parzyjegla for 2:00 P.M. for Toni Manalatos. He wanted her to "attend the show-up of Parzyjegla," along with those witnesses "claiming to have seen Elizabeth Short with various men during the last six days of her life." Donahoe wanted to give Parzyjegla the largest exposure possible in front of the broadest array of witnesses, in the hope that someone who had seen either Elizabeth or Jeanne French in the company of a man would identify Parzyjegla as the person who had been with one or both of the victims. The description given for Parzyjegla was "a tall 36-year-old male, of light complexion, with darkish blonde hair and powerful hands." Parzyjegla, however, while he readily admitted to slaying his employer, "vehemently denied any connection with the slayings of the two women," according to press reports.

At the same time Donahoe was organizing his witnesses to see Parzyjegla, the LAPD crime lab began conducting an examination of possible physical evidence that could potentially connect him to the other murders. LAPD police chemist Ray Pinker conducted an examination of "proof-sheet" paper taken from Haij's printing office, because, according to Captain Donahoe, "at least one of the notes sent in by the Dahlia killer in that case, used proof-sheet paper, of a type commonly found in printing shops." Donahoe was hoping the print shop would be the key that could link the three murders to the suspect, someone who would have had access to the blank proof sheets.

### Thursday, February 20, 1947

Suspect Otto Parzyjegla was formally charged with his self-described "dream murder" of his employer, and the case was closed. At a police show-up conducted at the Wilshire Division station on February 19, the six women victims of attempted attacks, as well as other witnesses from the French and Dahlia investigations, eliminated Parzyjegla as a suspect.

With Parzyjegla out of the picture, the search for the person(s) responsible for the Black Dahlia and the Red Lipstick murders turned back to San Diego, where apparently a new clue was discovered. Four detectives were assigned to San Diego, but LAPD and San Diego detectives kept secret, even from reporters, what that new clue might be.

As indicated, initially Captain Donahoe publicly confirmed LAPD'S belief that the Dahlia and the French cases *were* connected. Within days of that announcement a strange and never-explained series of events occurred, all related to the investigation.

First, Captain Donahoe was personally removed, by Chief of Detectives Thad Brown, as officer-in-charge of both investigations, and was summarily transferred from his position as commander of the

Homicide Division and placed in charge of Robbery Division, then a separate entity. This effectively terminated his personal involvement in both murder cases. What was it about this case that made the LAPD brass nervous enough to remove the one commander who could have solved it? Was Donahoe getting too close to the truth?

Next, as I saw it, there appeared to be a simultaneous lockdown of information in two separate and critical fronts of the investigation. First, the "San Diego connection" sounded as if LAPD had successfully traced Elizabeth Short's January 8 phone call to a man in Los Angeles. Second, relative to the recent newspaper reports of the "mystery man" who was sharing Jeanne French's P.O. box, again LAPD acknowledged they had identified, interviewed, and "eliminated" him. However, his identity, unlike other "non-involved" witnesses, was kept secret, and to this day remains a mystery.

In addition, the police high command made another startling revelation. Immediately after Donahoe's removal from the case, LAPD revised their assessment of the Jeanne French murder. They no longer saw it as a second homicide by the same suspect, but rather as a "copycat murder." Within less than a year, the Lipstick murder became totally disassociated from the Dahlia case and quickly fell into obscurity. Now the official LAPD line was that the murder of Elizabeth Short was a standalone, unconnected to any other crimes of murdered, sexually assaulted, and bludgeoned women. That remains the official LAPD position to this day: Elizabeth Short's murderer never killed anyone before or after that brutal murder. Why did LAPD take such a hard line on this? Why was it that, immediately after Donahoe's transfer out of Homicide, the link between the two murders was officially severed? All of this was not a coincidence but, as will ultimately become clear, part of an organized conspiracy within the LAPD to protect the identity of the self-described Black Dahlia Avenger. In doing so, the conspirators were covering up one of the biggest corruption scandals in the history of the Los Angeles Police Department. These overt and deliberate actions by LAPD's highest-ranking officers would ultimately transform them from respected law enforcers to criminal co-conspirators, accomplices to murder after the fact.

# 15

# Tamar, Joe Barrett, and Duncan Hodel

MAYBE IT WAS MY OWN DESIGN and not simply the passage of time that kept the true story of Tamar and the family scandal a dark mystery to me for many years. Even in my adult mind, Tamar was the image of the adolescent temptress Lolita. She would go on to blaze a trail from the folk era of the middle 1950s to the civil rights movement of the late '60s, and then become a mother to the flower children of the 1970s.

Tamar was described by singer Michelle Phillips in her book *California Dreamin': The True Story of the Mamas and the Papas* as her "very best friend, who got me interested in folk music, or at least into folk music people." Michelle's description of Tamar is a snapshot of the young girl who, a decade earlier, unwittingly had come within a hair of playing a critical role in the Black Dahlia investigation. Phillips writes:

> So, off we went to Tamar's. As soon as I set eyes on her, I thought she was the most fabulous, glamorous girl I had ever met. She had a wonderful lavender colored room, with lavender pillows and curtains, lavender lead-glass ashtrays, all of that. I thought it was just great. She had just acquired a new pink and lavender Rambler, buying it on time.
>
> She hung out with a very hip Bohemian crowd — Josh White, Dick Gregory, Odetta, Bud and Travis. Tamar was incredible. She gave me my first fake ID, my first amphetamines ("uppers" to help me stay awake in class after late nights). This was a girl after my own heart, and we became very close . . . and now she was my idol.

But everything Tamar Hodel would become by the 1960s, she already was during those few months in the summer of 1949 when, as a teenager, she moved into my life and set into motion a series of events that would result in the breakup of the only family life I had ever really known.

In court, during my father's incest trial, she was in the eyes of the prosecutors an innocent minor debauched by her sexually depraved father. In Robert Neeb's brilliant cross-examination she was portrayed as a pathological and sinister liar, capable of twisting the truth to satisfy and manipulate the adults around her. After Dad's acquittal, she grew up with the stigma of being just such a liar.

I think that, other than her own children, I was the only one who believed she was the victim. My mother, of course, knew the truth of what had happened that night but could not reveal what she knew to the police and ultimately took it with her to her grave. I know now that Mother lived in daily terror of what my father could do when he was crossed. So while Mother could never be a support, I could, once I knew the broad strokes of the scandal. And as we grew older I let Tamar know that I believed her, while at the same time I let Father think I believed him. The scandal was never discussed, never mentioned. It just hung there over the years like a cloud of unknowing, enveloping all of us, palpable, real, yet ignored because no one wanted to acknowledge it.

"Tamar the Liar" became Father's established party line to all of us in his immediate family, all in the extended family, and to all of his women, past and present. "The scandal" was almost never talked about, but Father's position was clear: he had been wrongfully accused by his fourteen-year-old, disturbed, deceitful, and sexually promiscuous daughter, who had lied to the police, lied to the prosecutors, and lied on the witness stand. Even though he had been acquitted, he made it clear to all of his children that our sister had tarnished his good reputation and high moral character. With most family members, her name did not even invoke pity, only disgust. Dad had made it an edict that Tamar was a pariah, our family's bad seed, whose punishment for her crimes of lying and disloyalty was ostracism and banishment.

Following Father's death, in my efforts to gain a deeper understanding of who he was and obtain more details about his life, I turned to Tamar for help because I believed that she knew more about him than any of us. More importantly, in light of the investigation I had undertaken, I asked her to tell me all that she could remember about the Franklin House years, the incest trial — which we'd never actually talked about — and any other incidents in her past that involved Father and her relationship with him.

I found that even though she had just turned sixty-six, her memory of those early years was remarkably clear and strong, and though the big picture, which I was beginning to see, completely eluded her, her ability to recall isolated, anecdotally significant events painted an incredible picture of our father. The composite picture of his demeanor, personality, and psychology blended with elements of my clandestine criminal investigation and the powerful thoughtprints that became signposts along the trail to my stunning conclusion.

What Tamar told me were simply stories, communications between older sister and younger brother about a man we'd both held in awe but who had demanded nothing less than fear and worship from his children.

Tamar did not know, of course, that I was actively conducting a criminal investigation of those years. I provided her with no information, and any references to the "Black Dahlia" came only from her. As far as she was concerned, I was simply a listener.

Tamar first came down to Los Angeles from San Francisco when she was eleven, but she returned to her mother, only to come down again when she was fourteen. It was about that second visit that she told me, "The only time I ever slept with George was on that one occasion. I thought that it was going to be this big romantic wonderful thing cause he promised me that when I was sixteen I would get to be a woman and he would make love to me."

But my father had not counted on his fourteen-year-old daughter's getting pregnant.

"George said he was going to send me away to an unwed mothers' home," Tamar told me. "The fact that I was going to be sent away was horrible to me. I was scared to death. My girlfriend Sonia told me, 'Oh, you have to have an abortion.' I didn't even know what an abortion was. Then I talked to a few more friends my age and they all said, 'You have to have an abortion.' So I went back to George and put the pressure on him, told him I had to have an abortion. He arranged it with a doctor. It was horrible. They didn't give me any anesthetic, nothing. In the middle of it I was screaming, 'Stop, stop!' But you can't stop in the middle. It was awful, the worst physical experience of my life. I was throwing up and in shock. This very strange man who was a friend of Dad's drove me back to the house on Franklin."

Tamar told my mother about the abortion, the pain and her fear, and Dad's friend who drove her back to the house when the procedure was over. When she heard the story, Mother exploded.

Tamar then related to me a most incredible story told her by my mother, who was Tamar's true and trusted friend and, for that brief period of time, her surrogate mother. The story involved a young woman who had worked, possibly as a nurse, for Father at his First Street Medical Clinic. She never learned the woman's name, but as told by Dorero, "the girl was in love with George." They had had an intimate relationship, and then Father, as was his nature, had moved on to other women. Soon after their breakup, the girl began to write a book, an "exposé" which would reveal hidden secrets about George, his life, and his activities. Mother told Tamar that late one night she received a telephone call from George. He ordered her to come immediately to the girl's apartment, where George informed Dorero that the girl had "overdosed on pills." Mother told Tamar it was clear that "the girl was breathing and still alive." Father handed Dorero the secret books the girl had written and ordered her to "burn them." Mother did as she was told, left the apartment, and destroyed the writings. According to Mother's narrative to Tamar, George could have saved her but let his young ex-paramour die. Dorero's story was later independently confirmed by the police, who, after taking Tamar into custody on the runaway charges, told her they "found the death suspicious, suspected George Hodel was involved in her overdose, but couldn't prove anything." Tamar never learned the girl's name or any other information about her.

When Tamar was eleven, shortly after the Black Dahlia murder, she recalled, she was living at the Franklin House and her mother sent her a doll that had curly hair. Tamar took it to Father to have him name her because he had a knack for picking great names. "He told me to call her 'Elizabeth Anne,'" she told me. "I thought that was really strange because he never picked names like that, he always picked unusual names. He did it kind of laughing, like it was a joke. So I called the doll Elizabeth Anne. Years and years later, I told a friend the story and she brought me a magazine, and I opened it and there was a very pretty face with this name, Elizabeth Anne Short. I went 'Oh, my God.' I never knew that was her name. I just heard it as the Black Dahlia."

Tamar also revealed that Man Ray had taken portraits of my parents and was a frequent guest at Father's wild parties. He and Father shared the same hedonistic tendencies, indulging themselves in their pleasures in clear defiance of the society in which they lived. Man Ray was living in Hollywood, just a mile from the Franklin House, when the incest scandal broke, but, according to Tamar, "He and his wife left the country at the time of the trial. He was afraid he was going to be investigated."* Tamar also said that Man Ray had taken some nude photographs of her when she was thirteen.

Although my sister appreciated Man Ray as an artist, she admitted that personally she disliked him. "He was another dirty old man." Nor did she like my father's good friend and my mother's first husband, John Huston. "I don't care how great John was, when I was eleven he tried to rape me. It was your mother, Dorero, who pulled him off of me. He was a big man. He had straddled me in the bathroom at the Franklin House, and he was very drunk. But your mother came in and pulled him off of me and saved me. The next time I saw him he was playing that man in *Chinatown.*"

Tamar remembered Kiyo as our father's beautifully exotic young girlfriend, and recalled that the Franklin House was filled with women: "George had all of these women at the house just waiting to see him. They were literally standing in line at his bedroom. I felt lucky if I could get in to see him. He was a perfect example of an ego gone wild. I think Huston did sex stuff with Dad and Fred Sexton and all the women. I know for sure Huston filmed stuff at the house."

She had this to say about Dad's physical violence: "George was so terrible when it came to punishing you three boys. He was very cruel. Michael got it the worst. It broke my heart to see how he treated you

*Tamar's source regarding Man Ray was Joe Barrett, a young painter who in the mid-1940s rented a room in the Franklin House.

three. Especially how he was with Mike. And he was so cruel with Dorero. I remember before Franklin, visiting you at the Valentine Street house, where I would see Dad pull her around the driveway by her hair."

What was most important to me about Tamar's memories of 1949 and the trial wasn't the trial itself, which was a matter of public record, but the attitude of the prosecutors who interviewed her two years after the murder of Elizabeth Short. Here Tamar was, at the very center of one of the most scandalous news stories in Holly-wood — a story that could well have wound up involving Man Ray and John Huston — and firmly under the control of prosecutors, who now believed they could nail my father for crimes they suspected him of having committed but couldn't prove. Tamar was the key to getting George Hodel behind bars.

When she told my mother about the abortion — which, in 1949, was illegal — my mother realized that Tamar was a walking piece of evidence and believed Tamar's life was in danger. My mother lived in deathly fear of George and knew that getting Tamar out of the house would probably save her life. So Tamar fled.

"I ran away," Tamar told me. "And I was found because Dorero had called my mom and told her, 'Tamar has run away and you had better come down here and help her.' So my mom came down unannounced, and George just couldn't say, 'I don't know where she is.' So George put out a missing report. I wasn't adept at running away because I had never done it before. I had just gone to friends' houses."

The parents of Tamar's friend in whose house she was hiding were away in Europe, but her friends were living there with the servants. It seemed to be a safe haven. Tamar knew the police were looking for her, which frightened her, because she'd never had any dealings with the law. So her friends protected her. "This little gang of my friends took me from place to place, hiding me out. That's how all this came about with all the boys. All the guys helped me out, hiding me from place to place."

In talking with the various teenagers, the police found her hiding out with a girlfriend, and Tamar, taken to the police station as a "runaway," was questioned, and quickly began to talk. "The police took me in and, because I had just had the abortion, I thought that they could tell that I had had an abortion. So I told them. Then one question led to another."

Soon the entire story of the incest and the goings-on at the Franklin House were out in the open, and the prosecutors had their case. But they still needed Tamar to testify against her father. They needed her trust. As Tamar remembers it, a husband-and-wife team from the DA's office brought her to court every day and promised her that they would protect her and take care of her. Tamar told me, "They said that I had never been loved and I didn't know what love was and that when this trial was all over that they were going to adopt me. I guess that was just their way of handling it to get me to say everything. I really believed them when they told me they would adopt me and give me love."

Adding political urgency to the incest trial and the prosecution of George Hodel was the fact that William Ritzi, the state's lead trial attorney, was also running for the Los Angeles County District Attorney's Office. And apparently Ritzi thought he knew more about my father than what was simply in the case he was prosecuting. As Tamar remembers it, "He told me that Dad might be a suspect in the Black Dahlia case. 'We know all about your father and you,' he said. That's how they got me to talk to them.

"I know that the police did talk to George back in 1947 because George said, 'We have to be careful about doing our nude sunbathing because the police are watching the place.' I'm pretty sure it was the year the Black Dahlia was killed when the police came out to the house. George never mentioned anything to me about that case. My gut feeling is that he knew and had met the Black Dahlia, but I really can't say for sure."

Dad's statutory rape of Tamar notwithstanding, he was still cautious about how he treated her at the house. Tamar confirmed that the testimony at the incest trial, about what had happened on the night of July 1, 1949, was all true. She remembered it clearly. Even the witnesses Corrine and Barbara had told the truth to the police investigators and the prosecutors, but Dad's sharp defense attorneys were still able to make it seem as if the entire event was a figment of Tamar's imagination.

In my conversations with her it became obvious to me that Tamar has no current memory of the questions she was asked by attorney Robert Neeb relating to her accusing Dad of being the killer of the Black Dahlia and having a lust for blood. Nor did she remember telling anyone of her being afraid that, in her words fifty-two years ago, "My father is going to kill me and all the rest of the members of this household." Moreover, because she had been detained in Juvenile Hall during the entire trial, she had had no access to newspapers, and so to this day remains unaware of what Neeb said about her in the courtroom after his cross-examination of her. I do believe that the "lust for blood" statement and the Black Dahlia original accusations attributed to Tamar by Neeb and Giesler had originally been told to her by Dorero, because those are the identical references, "blood-lust" and "insanity," that Mother said to me in her drunken state when we lived in Pasadena.

It is probable that Mother, while intoxicated, told Tamar about her fears or suspicions that Dad had killed Elizabeth Short after Tamar made her initial disclosure to Mother about Dad's having had sex with her. Mother was clearly fearful that if George discovered that Tamar had told anyone about their incestuous relationship, he would most likely have murdered his daughter before she could have an opportunity to reveal it to the authorities. Mother knew that Dad was capable of killing anyone, including a family member who might reveal his deepest secrets. Genuinely fearful for Tamar's safety, Mother told her of her suspicions, and may well have encouraged her to run away, to get her away from the house. That set into motion the search for the missing Tamar, the arrest of Father, the trial, and Dad's flight from Los Angeles after his acquittal.


## Tamar, Dad, Michelle Phillips, and the Mamas and the Papas

Tamar remembered a night in 1967 when Dad visited her in San Francisco at the same time Michelle Phillips and the Mamas and the Papas were coming into town to perform their first live concert at the Pan Pacific. Tamar took George and the two beautiful Asian women he had brought with him to the St. Francis Hotel where Michelle was staying. "I introduced them to her," she told me, "and she almost fainted, and her eyes rolled back in her head and she curtsied and said to George, 'I feel like I've really known you since I was twelve.' It was because of all the things I had told Michelle about him."

Father took over like an impresario, Tamar said. After discovering they had ordered a large dinner to be brought up by room service before the scheduled concert, Father stepped in and took control, informing them that they "shouldn't eat a large meal before a big concert." She added, "Dad had the waiters take everything back and changed it all to just appetizers, like pupu and stuff. They all began smoking hash, and Dad passed it around, but he didn't smoke it."

Afterward, Tamar remembers, "I met Dad and his two girlfriends and we went out to Enrico's for dinner. George got quite drunk and I was supporting him as we walked up the hill. That's when he said to me, 'Why did you do it?' I was so stupid. I didn't know what he was talking about because I always loved him. I thought he meant why had I always pursued and loved him. So I said, 'I always loved you, that's why.' Which, of course, was a very strange answer to someone who is really asking me, 'Why did you tell on me?' He was so drunk; we never really understood each other."

Later on, Tamar asked one of the Asian women whom Dad had brought along why he hadn't smoked the hash pipe. Tamar told her he'd always smoked it in the past, that's why his refusal was so strange. And the woman said, "Oh no, he doesn't do that anymore." She explained, "Before when he smoked hash, he made me lock him in his bathroom. He always made me lock him in there and told me not to let him out. George said to me that when he smokes it sometimes he does terrible things. He would make me lock him in the bathroom and he would cry and stay there all night."

"It made my hair stand on end," Tamar said. "I was so afraid of him because I do believe he has done so many terrible dark things."

## The Los Angeles Hotel, 1969

About two years after the Mamas and the Papas concert, Dad saw Tamar again in Los Angeles when he was making one of his business trips through town from Manila. Tamar was pregnant when Dad took her to lunch at one of the Beverly Hills hotels. As they were walking through the lobby, George suddenly stopped and pointed to a design on the carpet. He asked Tamar, "What does that remind you of?" She looked at the carpet and said, "I don't know, some kind of flower or something. Maybe rhododendrons?" George said, "No," and pointed around the edges with his finger. Then he said, "No, look again, it's a vagina and lips." He said, "They are nether lips." Then he stomped hard on the design and he said, "Did that hurt?" "God," Tamar told me, "I couldn't believe it. It sent chills down my spine. 'Nether lips'. He never used that word before."

The next day, George took out Tamar's daughter, Deborah, who was then thirteen. Deborah is Tamar's second daughter, born from her marriage to folk singer Stan Wilson.

Deborah kept secret for many years what happened that night, only telling her mother about it after she had become an adult. At dinner, Deborah suddenly became groggy, attempted to stand up, and almost collapsed on the floor. As she described it to Tamar, both the waiter and George rushed to her side, Dad catching her before she fell. Dismissing the waiter, he then helped her walk out of the dining room. The next thing Deborah recalled was waking up in a hotel. She was lying on a bed, completely nude, having been undressed while she was unconscious. Her legs had been spread open, and George was taking pictures of her with a camera. Deborah was convinced she had been drugged.

Tamar was stunned at hearing her daughter's disclosure. Now, she thought, with Deborah's supportive testimony, maybe Tamar's mother would believe her. But it was not to be. "Well, she didn't believe either one of us, and said she never wanted to see either of us again. She refused to believe her granddaughter just as she refused to believe her daughter." To this day, Deborah told her mother, she "still hopes that the truth about what happened to her in that hotel room with her grandfather would be believed." As for Tamar, since her truth has been buried for more than fifty years, I suspect she has by now given up all hope of ever being vindicated.

## Joe Barrett and the Franklin Years

In early 1948, a year after the murder of Elizabeth Short, a talented twenty-year-old artist named Joe Barrett rented the studio at the north end of the Franklin House, became friends with my father, and lived in the studio through the entire incest trial. Even after the family broke up when Dad left the country, Joe remained a good friend to my mother and kept in touch with her through the years, whenever he could find our gypsy encampment in L.A. He and my mother remained good friends until her death in 1982.

Joe and I saw each other only a few times during my years in the LAPD and we lost touch after I retired and moved to Washington State. But he had kept in occasional contact with my brother Kelvin in Los Angeles. And when the time came for me to talk to him about the past, it was through Kelvin that I was able to reach him in 1999, shortly after my father's death and at the early stages of my investigation.

Joe was an important window to the past. He was a young adult living there right at the time of the rape and the trial, the DA's investigation into my father's behavior, and the comings and goings of Man Ray. In the same way that I approached my interviews with Tamar, I did not tell him I was conducting an investigation. I merely talked with him in the hope of gaining deeper understanding about a father I had just lost and wanted to know more about. I told him I wanted to get an accurate picture of my father as he really was, as Joe knew him from the Franklin years.

Barrett's insights were astonishing, because in addition to providing me with detailed descriptions of Dad, he also informed me, long before I discovered it through my own independent sources and research, that he himself was officially solicited by the Los Angeles District Attorney's Office to assist them in their investigation of my father as "the prime suspect in the Black Dahlia murder." I would discover through my interviews with Joe Barrett that in early 1950, Barrett was picked up by the DA's detectives, taken to their office, and actively solicited to be their mole inside the Franklin House — "to be their eyes and ears there" was how they put it — in their effort to establish that Dr. Hodel was indeed the Black Dahlia Avenger.

## The Trial

Joe's was an intimate view of the activities at the Franklin House for almost two years, from 1948 to 1950. He told me that Father was gifted with a perfect photographic memory that permitted him to absorb ideas from other people and make them sound as if they were his own. He was super intelligent, but not particularly original.

Joe was not an invitee to my father's parties, but he saw a lot of human traffic going through the house and lots of heads bobbing around in that large middle room between the living room and Dad's bedroom. These were parties, he said, where there was a great deal of intense sexuality and there were lots of people in attendance. Joe reminded me that my father's venereal disease clinic on First Street downtown was also frequented by lots of important people. These were the days before modern drugs, when venereal disease was rampant and those who could afford private treatment were very dependent on the doctors who could provide it. My father was one of those doctors.

Barrett told me that he also knew Man Ray, who was often at the Franklin House. Joe saw him there the last day Man Ray was in Hollywood. He came to visit Dad, and he also visited Joe in the studio, where they talked for an hour or so. Joe said, "Man Ray was leaving town that day, probably going back to Europe, after the shit hit the fan, at the end of '49 or maybe it was into 1950. He and Juliet were living over by the Hollywood Ranch Market." The trial had just concluded, and though Dad had been acquitted everyone in his circle had fallen under the scrutiny of the district attorney. Man Ray's reputation was already such that he did not want to be caught in the web. He must also have been doubly concerned that Tamar might reveal that he had taken nude photographs of her at the Franklin House, or that the prints had been discovered by the police.

Another of Dad's acquaintances, and Man Ray's as well, was the novelist Henry Miller, whom Joe remembered seeing talking to Father in his library. The Franklin House had become, in those days, almost like a salon, where artists flouting convention and social mores gathered around my father, who had the means to entertain them.

Joe told me, "Tamar had named so many names to the district attorney that lots of people got arrested." Even my father's close friend Fred Sexton was offered a deal by the DA if he would testify against George and his relationship with Tamar. But, Joe told me, "Man Ray was somehow kept off the list of witnesses." Joe said that Dad's defense attorneys, Giesler and Neeb, had cost him a fortune, and that to raise the needed money he had to sell all of his rare and imported art objects. "I remember that a well-known jockey of the time named Pearson bought most of George's artwork," he told me.*

## The Black Dahlia Murder

Joe Barrett remembered that a Dr. Ballard was arrested for performing the abortion on Tamar. He was acquitted, partly because of my father's acquittal and because of the credibility of Tamar's testimony. Out of the blue Barrett also said, "Did you know that your dad was a suspect in the Black Dahlia case? I know that for a fact. She had been murdered a year or so before I moved into the Franklin house. From what I heard, your dad had apparently known her."

After the trial, when Joe was picked up by the DA investigators and taken to their office downtown, "they were really pissed," he remembered. "'God damn it, he got away with it!' they exclaimed, referring to the Tamar trial, adding 'We want this son of a bitch. We think he killed the Black Dahlia.' I'm sure it was investigators from the district attorney's office and not LAPD. They wanted me to spy on George for them. I remember one of the DA investigators was a man named Walter Sullivan. I think these investigators also tried to get a couple of gals that George knew to spy on him and report back to them."

Joe was also present when the police served a search warrant on Dad at the Franklin House after he was arrested for incest. "Thad Brown was out there standing around at the house with these DA investigators. I remember him from the newspapers. He was a police big shot back then."

*Billy Pearson was a prominent jockey in the 1940s, who was an art connoisseur and also a close friend of John Huston's. In Lawrence Grobel's biography *The Hustons*, the author writes that Pearson, one of the first contestants to win the grand prize on the infamous 1950s quiz show *The $64,000 Question*, helped Huston smuggle rare pre-Columbian art pieces out of Mexico.

## Duncan Hodel's Memories of the Franklin House

I was stunned by my conversations with Tamar and Joe Barrett. Their incredible revelations about what went on at the Franklin House around the time of Elizabeth Short's murder, and in the following two years, filled in many of the blank spots in my own life during that period.

Encouraged by what I had gained from Tamar and Joe Barrett, I decided to pursue a third source.

My eldest half-brother, Duncan, now seventy-one years old, had been another actual living witness at the Franklin House through the late 1940s, and he had testified at the Tamar trial.

In an October 1999 meeting in San Francisco, Duncan provided me with many details of our father's early life, before I was born.

Duncan had made regular visits to the Franklin House in the years preceding Dad's arrest and was twenty-one when the scandal broke. To this day, Duncan believes that Tamar invented the incest charges in an attempt to ruin Father's life. Although he apparently never questioned that Tamar might have been telling the truth, his interview would provide a damning revelation about another murder that took place shortly after Elizabeth Short's body was discovered. Duncan provided me with a thoughtprint so powerful that, had there been a murder trial in the Jeanne French "Red Lipstick" murder, he would doubtless have been called by the prosecution to testify against Father. In our conversation, Duncan linked him to a critical element in the crime:

> Dad had some very wild parties at the Franklin House. After Dad bought the house, I used to go down with my buddies from San Francisco and stay there, and Dad would fix my friends and me up with women. It was funny, when I was there Dad told me to tell all the women I was his brother. When women were around us at the Franklin House, he didn't want them to know he was old enough to have a son my age. I was twenty then.
>
> I remember one party where everybody was laughing and having a good time and Dad got this red lipstick and wrote on one of the women's breasts with the lipstick. She had these big beautiful breasts, and Dad took the lipstick and wrote these big targets round

each one, and we all laughed and had a good time. I remember meeting Hortensia, his future wife from the Philippines at the Franklin House. She was visiting the U.S. and came to Dad's parties at the house. I guess that's where he first met her. Then after the trial they got married.

I asked Duncan if he remembered or was acquainted with any of Dad's girlfriends from that time, and after pausing for reflection, he noted:

I remember one of his girlfriends was murdered. Her name was Lillian Lenorak. She was a dancer and artist. But the murder didn't happen until many years after she broke up with Dad. I think her young boyfriend killed her in Palm Springs or something.

I recognized her name from the court records of the trial and knew she had been on the prosecution's witness list. I then asked Duncan if he remembered any other names. He answered, "I remember after Dad stopped seeing Kiyo in 1942 or so, he started dating this other woman. I think her name was Jean Hewett. Jean was this drop-dead beautiful young actress. She really looked like a movie star. I don't know whatever happened to her."

## The Trial

Duncan testified briefly at the trial as a defense character witness for Dad, or, he thinks, to talk about Tamar's promiscuity. But after the trial was over, he recalled, Dad told him something strange.

Dad told me that the district attorney had said to him, "They were going to get me." They were out to get him, and so I think that is why Dad left the country right away and went to Hawaii. That is what he told me at the time, just before he left the U.S.

Tamar's, Joe Barrett's, and Duncan's independent knowledge of Father's activities corroborated that Dad was suspected at the time not only of committing incest with his daughter but also of murdering Elizabeth Short. Both Tamar and Joe Barrett stated that the police believed Dad killed the Black Dahlia. Duncan, while apparently unaware of any Dahlia connections, had unintentionally and inadvertently become a witness linking our father to the Jeanne French murder.

These interviews were shattering. Till now I had proceeded cautiously, as I had hundreds of times before. Conducting my investigation as an objective and impartial homicide detective, amassing facts and evidence, I slowly and carefully built my case. But now a terrible, undeniable truth was hitting deep within me: my father, the man I had looked up to, admired, and feared, this pillar of the community, this genius, was a cold-blooded, sadistic killer. Probably a serial killer.

Having come to this horrific conclusion, I suddenly wished I had never begun the journey. Part of me wanted to close Father's tiny album, destroy the photographs, and run from the truth. I felt fear and omnipotence. A few simple, undiscoverable acts by the son, and the father's sins would be destroyed — like him, reduced to ashes. The Hodel name and reputation would remain intact. A few simple acts, and his crimes would never be known. I could cheat infamy. A cover-up for the good of the family. I could easily do what the LAPD command had done, only better. This time the cover-up would be permanent. But the other part of me knew I could not, and would not, run or hide the truth.

# 16

# Fred Sexton: "Suspect Number 2"

FROM THE MANY WITNESS SIGHTINGS and descriptions relative to both the Elizabeth Short and Jeanne French murders and the separate kidnappings and sexual assaults of Sylvia Horan by "the Dahlia suspect" and Ica M'Grew by "two swarthy men," both within days of the French murder, it seemed apparent there were two men committing these crimes, and I suspected the two were operating together and separately, at their whim. If George Hodel was Suspect Number 1, who was his accomplice? Based on his overall physical description, his close friendship with my father going back to 1924, and the fact that he had, in his own words, admitted to being my father's accomplice in the 1949 statutory rape of Tamar, Fred Sexton was, obviously and logically, the most likely candidate for Suspect Number 2.

Realizing I could no longer conduct a long-distance investigation, and needed to talk face to face with whatever witnesses I could find, I moved back to L.A. in June 2001. Joe Barrett, due to his personal familiarity with Sexton, was at the top of my list of people to question. Once I settled into my new Hollywood apartment, I called, made the short drive north to Ventura, and we met for lunch.

I asked his impressions of Sexton from the Franklin years, telling him the truth, which was that I hardly remembered the man. From Joe's description, though they were fellow artists, they were not kindred spirits. Joe did not like Sexton, and he said so. Here is the picture he gave me:

> Fred was tall and thin, like your dad. He had a dark complexion. I
> think he was Italian. He was good friends with your dad and spent
> a lot of time at the Franklin House. Sexton and I actually worked

together for a short time, at the Herb Jepson Art School, downtown at 7th and Hoover Streets. Sexton lasted there only about two
months. He had a bad attitude. He was hitting on all the young
girls in class. Half or more of them actually left his class because of
it. He had many complaints from the kids in class, and so many
dropped out because of him that Herb Jepson fired him.

When Sexton refused to leave the art school, Jepson and a couple
of his "big friends" forcibly evicted him from the premises. Barrett
concluded:

> I ran into Fred a year or two after that in downtown L.A. He was
> living in a second-story apartment on Main Street. He tried to
> avoid talking to me, probably feeling sheepish because he had tes-
> tified as a witness for the prosecution in your dad's trial. That day
> was the last time I ever saw or heard from him.

Joe's knowledge of Fred Sexton and his association with him
were limited, although he corroborated Sexton's predatory sexual
habits and the "swarthy" description so often connected with the
crimes. Public information about Sexton was also limited, but I discovered that he was born in the small mining town of Goldfield,
Nevada, on June 3, 1907, just four months before my father. He was
the second child born to Jeremiah A. Sexton and Pauline Magdalena
Jaffe, who had two other sons and three daughters. Fred Sexton married his first wife, Gwain Harriette Noot, on June 13, 1932, in Santa
Monica, California.

Sexton made an application to the Social Security Administration
on May 23, 1939, listing his place of employment as "Columbia Pictures Corp., 1438 N. Gower Street, Hollywood, California," and at
that time he gave his residence as White Knoll Drive in the Elysian
Park district of Los Angeles, just a mile from downtown. The house
is still owned by his surviving first wife.

Sexton died at eighty-eight, on September 11, 1995, in Guadalajara, Mexico. All I knew about the man was what I had been told by
Tamar and Joe Barrett. Now it was time to see what Sexton's own
surviving relatives could tell me.

I spoke to Sexton's daughter in two separate meetings, the first of which took place in Los Angeles in October 1999. At that time I was in no position to confront her with any suspicions I harbored about her father and his possible criminal involvement with mine. In the spring of 2000, five months after our initial meeting, Sexton's daughter mailed me two photographs of Fred, which she told me had been taken in Los Angeles in the mid-1940s. In this mailing, she also included pictures of herself shown playing with an eight- or nine-year-old Tamar. She was three years older than Tamar, and they were friends from the early 1940s until Tamar's arrest and detention in 1949. She had known Kiyo during the time Dad was having an affair with her, and the pictures she sent me were, ironically, taken shortly after their "breakup," and showed the two children playing in front of Kiyo's beachside home in Venice.

I contacted her again in August 2001, informed her I was now living in Los Angeles, and scheduled a second interview to meet her at her home, telling her I had some important information to discuss. At this meeting, realizing that what I was about to tell her would be very similar in effect to the many death notifications I had made to family members during my long career in Homicide, and knowing she would need some emotional support, I requested that her husband be present, and she agreed. I opened our conversation with the shocking revelation that, based on my two-year investigation, it was my professional opinion that our fathers had been crime partners and had committed a series of abductions and murders of lone women in Los Angeles during the mid- to late 1940s. I informed her that all of my research and investigation was well documented, that the full story would be revealed in a book I was writing. I did not provide her with the names of any victims and was circumspect in my references to the crimes. Specifically, I did not indicate that the case focused on Elizabeth Short, the Black Dahlia.

Understandably, Sexton's daughter was profoundly shocked by my news. She found it difficult to believe that her father could ever have been involved in such violent crimes. She doubted my assertion that he, like my father, was a practicing sadist. Even though she acknowledged that he was a controlling person, she felt he was incapable of physically harming women to that extent.

In this interview, she disclosed a wealth of information. She was specific and provided much deeper insight into her father's personality and character, underscoring and increasing the probability that he was in fact the partner-in-crime of his close friend George Hodel.

## Mary Moe

"Mary Moe," which is the name I have given Sexton's daughter to protect her identity, was sixty-five at the time of our first conversation. She had known our family since before I was born, and in another incredible twist of fate, as an eight-year-old girl had come with her father to the hospital to visit my mother on the day my twin brother John and I were born.

Fred Sexton was of Irish, Jewish, and Italian descent. When he was about thirteen years old, the police arrested his father on Christmas Eve and dragged him out of the house, an incident that instilled in Fred a lifelong hatred of the police. The family was then living in California, but his dad had been bootlegging in Nevada during the '20s and '30s.

Sexton had been John Huston's close friend at high school in L.A., and they remained friends through the years. As a child, Mary remembered Huston as a kind of "godfather" who would suddenly appear with extravagant presents for her, then vanish. Mary also thought her father had been acquainted with the notorious gambler Tony Cornero, but was not absolutely sure. She did know that Fred's father had been a gambler and bootlegger like Cornero.

I learned that, like my father, Sexton had a secret and mysterious past and had concealed important early truths from his daughter. For instance, from her mother Mary discovered that her father had had an affair with a married newspaper reporter in San Francisco in the 1920s. The newswoman became pregnant and gave birth to a son. Growing up, Mary was shown pictures of a small, dark-complexioned boy, and was told these were pictures of her father. Only as an adult did she learn the truth: the pictures were not of her father but her half-brother! To this day she knows nothing further about him, has never met him, does not know if he is living or dead, nor does she even know his name.

She remembered that her father ran a "floating crap game" in Los Angeles, where he reportedly "made very good money." Like my

Father, Fred drove taxis during his youth, both in Los Angeles and in San Francisco.

Regarding Sexton and his women, Mary told me, "My dad had lots of different girlfriends when I was young. He was very much like your father when it came to women. He had so many women, one after the other."

In the early 1930s, Sexton went to Europe for a year or two, then returned to Los Angeles, married Gwain, and Mary was born. He pursued his artwork, gained some notoriety, and reportedly had several one-man shows, which received excellent reviews from L.A. art critics.

Mary recalled that in 1938 George Hodel moved into the house next door to theirs. "We were neighbors on White Knoll for about a year," she recalled. It was at that time, Mary said, that the two Dorothys were living together with George. "Both Tamar's mother, Dorothy Anthony, and your mom were living with him next to us. Then, after about a year, the three of them moved not far away, to Valentine Street."

During the war years Sexton, like my father, remained in Los Angeles:

> My dad was working at all the movie studios and he worked at the shipyards, then he drove a cab again in '43 and '44. My dad wasn't in the war because he had to take care of my mom, who was bedridden for many years. Your dad, who had known my mom and was a good friend for so long, also treated her and was her doctor.

Fred Sexton had an art studio in a downtown building, at 2nd and Spring Streets. I learned from Mary that my father had an apartment on the top floor of the same building, where they could go upstairs onto the roof of a German beer-hall. According to her, this apartment was where George would "rendezvous" with all his girlfriends. Mary had been inside George's "apartment" with her father on one occasion around 1948, and remembered that the interior was beautiful and, in her words, had a "very fancy decor."

I asked if she had any information or remembered an incident related to a woman, possibly a girlfriend of my father's, who had committed suicide during those years. Her response was:

I think that the person you are talking about was your dad's office manager at the First Street Clinic. I'm not sure of her name, but it might have been Ruth Dennis. What I heard was that she didn't come to work one morning at the clinic, and your dad went to her apartment and found her dead. As I recall, it was a suicide, an overdose.

Then Mary related a telling incident, which again involved both of our fathers.

In the late '40s there was a woman named Trudy Spence, who at that time was my dad's girlfriend. Her husband found out about the affair and came after Fred at his Spring Street art studio, intending to kill him. To escape, Dad had to jump off the roof and landed in the parking lot. He tore up his leg really bad and was laid up for months. Your dad brought him a gun, which he kept hidden in a cigar box under his bed, because he thought the husband might arrive. The whole thing made me very nervous.

Though Mary told me she did not know the details of the incest scandal, she did say there was no doubt in her mind that Tamar had told the truth. Her next revelation caught me completely off guard:

I, like Tamar, was also a victim of incest. My own father sexually molested me from age eight to eleven. I know firsthand exactly what Tamar went through. When I was sixteen, a year before the trial, I had a bad argument with my father, because he tried again to have sex with me. I told him that if he didn't leave the house, I would. He left and went to live with John Huston and Paulette Goddard in West Hollywood. The next year, the Tamar thing happened. It took a long time, but Dad finally admitted the incest with me to my mom.

"Tamar was an incorrigible teenager," Mary said, "and seemed obsessed with sex all the time." But Mary, without reservations, believed the story Tamar told the police about having had sex with Fred, Barbara Sherman, and my father.

"When I was around your father," Mary admitted, "my dad never took his eyes off me. He was going to make sure that George never touched me. Dad was very protective of me around your father."

She learned most of the facts about the scandal from her father, who had told her that Man Ray was also involved. "The police talked with Man Ray," her father had told her, "who would have been arrested and charged along with them, except he got a letter from his doctor saying that he couldn't have done anything to Tamar, because he was impotent." Mary noted that "Man Ray had lots of clout. I think my dad was a terrific artist and Huston was a terrific director, but they both were rotten people."

After separating from his wife, Gwain, in the 1950s, Sexton traveled back and forth to Mexico. In the early 1960s, he remarried and lived in Palos Verdes for a short period, then divorced again. Sexton returned to Mexico in 1969, and in 1971, at age sixty-three, married his third wife, who was only a teenager. The two of them lived in Guadalajara until his death in 1995. Mary informed me that on his death, "his wife destroyed all of his papers." Mary said her father passed for either Spanish or Italian, and spoke both languages.

Before his final return to Mexico, Fred gave his daughter a list of various bank accounts; he had used different names on different accounts. She said, "On his passport, he put the name of his brother Robert, who was dead. He also used another alias, 'Sigfried Raphael Sexton.' "

In an attempt to further establish that my father and Sexton were lifelong friends, I showed Mary Moe a photograph of a young, dark-complexioned man that had been given to me by June after Father's death. It was one of a collection of photographs taken by my father in 1925. Though it was of poor quality, I believed it bore a resemblance to Sexton, who would have then been about eighteen. I initially e-mailed a copy of the photo to Mary, and then showed her the actual photograph during our second meeting. She said:

> I can't say for sure or not if it is a photo of my father. It's really hard to tell. It certainly could be, because the mouth and lips resemble his, but I'm unsure. Dad had the same dark complexion as in the picture. I know they knew each other back then, because it was the strangest thing. Guess who did an art review of my dad's work — it was your dad's ex-wife, Emilia Hodel! I came across this review

from a San Francisco paper where she gave him this terrible review as an artist. Everyone else gave him great reviews, but Emilia wrote him this really bad review. I'll try and find a copy for you.

Mary Moe's candor revealed a man chillingly similar to my own father. The two men had been practically inseparable for thirty years, from boyhood until my father's departure in 1950. Except during Father's medical training years, both had lived within a few miles of each other and both had offices in downtown Los Angeles. When trouble came stalking Sexton, my father unhesitatingly provided him with medical aid and a gun. They shared sexual favors with women, and in the case of my father, he even shared his teenage daughter. Clearly these men held each other in the closest confidence, and one protected the other.

With my own investigative insights, Joe Barrett's brief but telling story of Sexton's sexual obsession with the young female art students, coupled with the biography I had learned from Mary Moe, I was now focused on Fred Sexton as Suspect Number 2.

Most of the crimes I researched involved two mysterious and unidentified suspects. The primary suspect was a suave and polished, tall, thin, well-dressed man who had been seen with the victims just before they were either killed or disappeared. The second man, of similar physical build, was more often referred to simply as "swarthy complexioned."

I believe it's important to see exactly how these two men appeared in the mid- to late 1940s, to compare them to the victim and witness descriptions we have already heard and those yet to come. Following are photos of each man as he looked in the late 1940s, along with his overall physical description, and character traits:

*Exhibit 33*

*George Hodel, circa 1952*

In 1947, Dr. George Hill Hodel was thirty-nine years old, tall at six foot one, trim at about 165 pounds, with black curly hair, an olive complexion, and a well-trimmed mustache that made him look Mediterranean or Middle Eastern. He had a soft, educated, and deeply resonant voice that was partially the result of his training and experience as an announcer on public radio.

A meticulous and stylish dresser, he was very aware of how he looked and how important his looks were as a method of control. His physical demeanor demanded respect. He sought a position of dominance in all situations; he sought to exercise control, and he was an intellectual, sophisticated, and charismatic personality. He was also an experienced, accomplished, and self-professed womanizer.

*Exhibit 34*

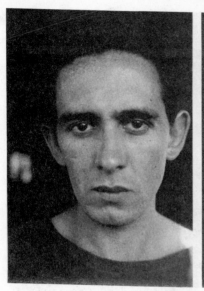

*Fred Sexton, circa 1947*

Fred Sexton's swarthy looks would easily have allowed someone to take him for an Hispanic, Italian, or Portuguese. A self-educated and intelligent bohemian, Sexton had penetrating eyes and a menacing cold stare.

We have been told he was fluent in both Italian and Spanish. With his smoldering good looks and brooding demeanor, he looked a lot like one of the stars of the silent movie era. At thirty-nine years old, six foot one, 180 pounds, and with sleek, slicked-back hair, Sexton, who also wore a mustache and a goatee from time to time, was as much of a womanizer as my father.

# 17

# LAPD Secrets and the
# Marquis de Sade

*Crime is the soul of lust. What would be pleasure if it were not ac-
companied by crime? It is not the object of debauchery that excites us,
rather the idea of evil.*
— Marquis de Sade

RELATING TO THE BLACK DAHLIA INVESTIGATION, the LAPD possessed and was actually able to keep some "key questions" confidential, away from the press and public, for forty years, until they were
finally leaked. Some of these secrets were learned from the unaltered
photographs of Elizabeth Short's body. Others came from police and
coroner's files, and were alleged to be "hand copied reproductions of
originals."* All of this "secret information" related to the autopsy
findings, the horrific details that fully described exactly where and
how the sadistic killer(s) tortured the victim.

Once I learned of these atrocities, I was shaken to my core. A
hardened veteran who personally attended hundreds of post-
mortems, I thought I had seen everything. But I was wholly unprepared for what I learned. I believe for the sake of truth, accuracy, and
above all, *relevance*, that the details, however gruesome, of the autopsy findings need to be disclosed.

Dr. Newbarr's autopsy report describes a victim who endured a

---

*The actual protocol (coroner's formal report) to my knowledge has never been
published, therefore I am unable to confirm the validity of some of the findings alleged
in the "hand copied" versions. However, most of what is here reported is consistent with
photographs that were released in the 1980s showing trauma to the body.

horrific and painful death at the hands of a suspect or suspects who took the infliction of physical punishment to the extreme. The young woman was trussed and bound by her hands and feet, was tortured initially by the killer's inflicting minor cuts to her body and to her private parts, then cutting away her pubic hairs, which he would later insert into her vagina. She was then beaten about her entire body. She was forced to endure the overwhelming humiliation of being made to eat either her own or their fecal excrement. Finally, she was beaten to death, and her face and body were viciously lacerated and defiled. The killer(s) cut large pieces of flesh from her body, which they inserted into her vagina and/or her rectum. Her killer sliced her mouth from ear to ear into a bloody grin, lacerated her breasts, and cleanly and surgically bisected her body. To a trained forensic pathologist, of even greater significance was the four-inch gaping laceration cut into the victim's lower torso from her umbilicus down to the suprapubic region, a spot right above her pubic area, with numerous crisscross lacerations cut into that region as well. This incision in length, description, and location is consistent in every respect with that made by a skilled surgeon performing a hysterectomy. After the operation was performed, the body was drained of blood — exsanguinated — and her hair and skin were washed clean. Dr. Newbarr found fibers on the body that he believed to have originated from a scrub brush, and later told one of the newspapers, "From the nature of the knife cuts the girl was probably in a semi-recumbent position in a bathtub."

These were not random acts of violence and torture but were part of a discrete set of procedures carried out to gratify the killer's (or killers') enjoyment of the suffering of their victim. They reduced their victim, through such specific and defined stages as degradation, humiliation, terror, torture, and defilement, to a state of complete and abject surrender of her humanity. Then they killed her and began a new round of postmortem procedures.

These actions, unique in their execution, clearly demonstrated an intellectual familiarity with the philosophies and practices of a classical sadist.

Finally, by posing the body for discovery, the killer(s) intended to sustain themselves through the ensuing investigation and public horror over the discovery. At least one of the killers was not only possessed of surgical skill and a psychotic ability to enjoy the pain of others, but was also someone who might have known exactly how the police investigation would play out and how the newspapers would handle the story. What did the killer know?

For anyone experienced in homicide investigations or in the literature about homicide investigations, one thing is clear: this was not a random or one-time-only crime. This was a whole different category of homicide, far removed from the vast majority of homicides that are the result of uncontrolled passions, random acts of violence deriving from another felony, or deliberate murders in which the killer wants the crime hidden from the police and the public. Both violent sexual and physical assaults upon the victims are not unusual in these types of homicides. What is unusual here is that what the killer did far outstrips any normal pattern of abuse. These were ritualistic, systematic, specifically defined, and volitional acts of torture, all of which indicate the pure focus of a highly sophisticated, skilled, and practicing sadist.

A powerful influence on my father, as well as on Man Ray, was the Marquis de Sade, a man whose life and writings are important to this case because of the tremendous influence his philosophy of the violent subjugation of others held over the four people I see at the center of the events that took place at the Franklin House: my father, Man Ray, John Huston, and Fred Sexton. Most people have a general understanding of who Sade was and what "sadism" means. But it's not until one reads some of Sade's actual material that one can truly understand the nature of the psychosexual deviancy that characterizes his thinking. This is a form of sexual nihilism that redefines the borders of deviant human behavior.

The Marquis de Sade's published writings and descriptions of his violence-driven, sexually psychopathic visions are unparalleled in literature, as are his vivid descriptions of the specific forms and types of sexual depravity and torture he advocates inflicting upon his victims. His images of sexual delights, which he calls "pleasures," are so dark and malignant that they surely were meant to disgust and outrage his contemporaries, a blueprint for evil.

A quick comparison of Sade's manuscript *The 120 Days of Sodom* with the coroner's findings of Elizabeth Short's death goes a long way toward explaining what her killer was doing: he was following Sade's details of sexual atrocities as closely as he could. I submit as evidence Sade's entry on January 15 — the date of Elizabeth's murder — from which one recognizes that what Sade prescribed — including blood-letting — the killer(s) executed. (Another Sadean entry of that same date — "He writes letters and words upon her breasts" — was inflicted upon his subsequent victim Jeanne French.)*

It's clear from even a cursory review of Sade's manuscript that he was the source of inspiration to my father, Man Ray, and their friends. Even the description of the castle as an enclosed fortress opening onto an inner courtyard is an exact description of the Franklin House and might even have been the reason, consciously or not, that George Hodel bought the property. That Father, like Man Ray, read and studied all of Sade's writings seems clear. And Father, being endowed with what roomer Joe Barrett described as "his perfect photographic memory," no doubt retained each and every one of those six hundred savage images in his mind.

Even my father's funeral instructions in his last will and testament echo Sade's own last will:

> I do not wish to have funeral services of any kind. There is to be no meeting or speeches or music and no gravestone or tablet.

> I direct that my physical remains be cremated and that my ashes be scattered over the ocean.

Sade's written funeral instructions:

> Finally, I absolutely forbid that my body be opened upon any pretext whatsoever.

> I would have it laid to rest, without ceremony of any kind.

Dad's friends John Huston and Fred Sexton were also in the circle of friends under the intellectual influence of Sade. Huston's love for Sade is well-known and well documented. He enjoyed Sade's

*The 120 Days of Sodom and Other Writings, Grove Press, 1967, p. 610.

writings and he indulged himself in living his legend as "a genius and a monster." The lightly veiled characterization of John Huston as sadistic egotist in Peter Viertel's novel *White Hunter, Black Heart* is one indication. Describing Huston's personality and, for our purposes, his fondness for sadism, Lawrence Grobel, in his book *The Hustons*, referring to a conversation between Huston and screenwriter John Milius (*Apocalypse Now*), who had written the script for Huston's movie *Judge Roy Bean*, recounted:

> When Milius asked him what was the best part of being a director, John answered in one word: "Sadism." He recommended that Milius read the Marquis de Sade at night and Jim Corbett during the day. "If you read Corbett at night," he warned, "it will scare the holy shit out of you. De Sade you can read anytime."
>
> When Milius asked John about women, John's advice was, "Be anything they want. Mold to their caresses. Tell them anything. Just fuck 'em! Fuck 'em all!" (p. 641)

Fred Sexton, we know, was a close friend of Father's, so close in fact that the two of them frequently shared sexual experiences, experiments, and fantasies with their women at the Franklin House. Sexton was also a longtime school chum and friend of Huston's, and sold him some of his artworks. Sexton's friendship with Man Ray derived from their shared passion as artists and their relationships with my father. From the perspective of such eyewitnesses as my sister, I can represent with absolute certainty that this "gang of four" socialized with one another, partied together, and, in the case of my father, Fred, and John, even shared women.

With a sense of what my father's background was, his predilections, the violence-driven sexual deviancy that colored his relationships with just about everybody, and the group of friends with whom he shared an artistic fascination with sadistic sexual perversions, some of the aspects of the Black Dahlia murder come into clearer focus. However — and this to my mind is crucial — *no sexual offender who inflicts the levels of violence inflicted on Elizabeth Short can be a one-time killer.* These killers are serial offenders, who, as Dr. Joel Norris has said in *Serial Killers: A Growing Menace*, engage in "episodic violence," reenacting the same kind of psychodrama from crime to crime. They taunt police to prolong their sexual thrill after each murder, and not only troll for victims, but live within their victim pool as predators lying in wait for their next opportunity.

Accordingly, if my father fits any part of this psychological profile, there should be ample evidence of a series of crimes he committed, probably upon the same type of victims and probably within a circumscribed geographical area and timeframe. In other words, thirty years before Ted Bundy, the Hillside Stranglers, the Son of Sam, and even the Green River Killer, my father, most likely some of the time with Fred Sexton, was a long-term, serial sexual killer of defenseless women in the areas of Hollywood, Beverly Hills, and downtown Los Angeles.

Amazingly, these serial murders not only remain unsolved today, but the LAPD does not even acknowledge the possibility that the killings were connected or related to each other. As the evidence will soon reveal, however, the relationships among the killings are so strong they cry out for resolution even within their dust-covered LAPD murder books shelved into cold storage a half century ago.

# 18

# Elizabeth Short's "Missing Week"

IN THE OFFICIAL STATEMENTS the police released to the public regarding the activities of Elizabeth Short in the period leading up to her death, detectives said the last time any witness saw her was the night of January 9, 1947, when she left the Biltmore Hotel through the Olive Street entrance. The Dahlia's "missing week," originally established and promoted by detectives Finis Brown and Harry Hansen, has become legendary, and remains with today's LAPD as unquestioned fact. As we will see, this was crucial to the 1947 cover-up.

My own investigation and research reveal quite a different story. In reviewing the newspaper accounts of the day to see what other witnesses turned up to give statements to the police, I discovered a number who positively identified Elizabeth Short during the LAPD's "missing week." My review of what those witnesses told police shows that Elizabeth Short spent a very active week in Hollywood, the San Fernando Valley, and downtown between January 9 and January 14 and was seen not only by strangers who later identified her, but by numerous acquaintances and a policewoman to whom she complained that she was in fear for her life. In truth, LAPD knew there never was a "missing week."

Iris Menuay, an acquaintance of Elizabeth Short at the Chancellor Hotel at 1842 North Cherokee Avenue, Hollywood, was one of the first people to run into Elizabeth after the victim got back to L.A. on January 9. Menuay reported to the police that she had seen Elizabeth Short sitting in the lobby of the Chancellor Hotel on January 9 or 10, at approximately 8:30 P.M. At that time, Menuay told police, she observed Elizabeth "embracing a man dressed like a gas station attendant." It was unclear whether Menuay actually meant that Elizabeth was embracing a gas station attendant or just somebody in a uniform she couldn't otherwise identify.

The next person to recognize Elizabeth was bartender Buddy La Gore at the Four Star Grill, at 6818 Hollywood Boulevard, where she was one of the semi-regulars. He told the police and press that she had come to the bar on January 10, 1947, during the late-evening hours in the company of two other women. Elizabeth Short didn't drink hard liquor, La Gore explained. Though in the past she had spent long hours at his bar, "It was her custom to order soft drinks." "She always dressed immaculately," he told the cops, "and her clothing, makeup, and hair were perfect."

On the evening of January 10, however, La Gore noticed, her appearance and demeanor were drastically different. "When she came in on January 10, she looked like she had slept in her clothes for days," he told police. "Her black sheer dress was stained, soiled, and otherwise crumpled." La Gore said he was surprised at the difference. "I'd seen her many times before and always she wore the best nylons, but this time she had no stockings on."

But it was more than just her clothing, he said. "Her hair was straggly and some lipstick had been smeared hit-and-miss on her lips. The powder on her face was caked." He also described a dramatic change in her demeanor. "She was cowed instead of being gay and excited, the way I'd seen her before. Also, she was friendly and nice to me this time. The other times I saw her she acted like the 'grand lady' and was bossy." La Gore told the police that he'd seen the women who accompanied Elizabeth Short on January 10 on other occasions as well, but always with Elizabeth.

That same day, Elizabeth was spotted by an unnamed witness whom Donahoe dubbed "John Doe Number 1." John Doe Number 1 told the detectives he'd seen Elizabeth Short, accompanied by two other women, drive up to the curb in a "a black coupe" along the 7200 block of Sunset Boulevard on the Sunset Strip. The witness overheard them say they were "staying in a motel on Ventura Boulevard, and were on their way to the Flamingo Club on La Brea Avenue."

He also provided the following description of the other two women: "One was 27 years old, 5'6", 125 pounds, with long black hair. The second one was a female who appeared to be in her 20s with light brown hair, combed up." During the police interview, the witness readily identified Elizabeth Short from her photographs.

Mrs. Christenia Salisbury was another acquaintance who recognized Elizabeth when she was in Los Angeles during the week of January 9. Salisbury had known Elizabeth since 1945 when Elizabeth had waited tables in her Miami Beach restaurant, where the two women became friends. Salisbury, a Native American and vaudeville performer, had played several seasons with the Ziegfield Follies as a featured dancer named "Princess Whitewing." After she retired from show business, she bought the café in Miami Beach that she operated until just a few days before Christmas, 1946, when for health reasons she moved to Los Angeles in early January 1947.

In the offices of the *Los Angeles Examiner* on January 28, 1947, Salisbury told reporters that on January 10, at around 10:00 P.M., she "ran into Elizabeth as she and two other women were coming out of the Tabu Club on the Sunset Strip in Hollywood." She described one of them as "a very tall blonde, 30 years of age, weighing about 160 pounds," and the other "about 27 years old, with very black hair, and very heavy makeup." Salisbury and Elizabeth began to talk while the other two women walked to a parked car. Salisbury was aware that the blonde was "very intoxicated, and got behind the driver's wheel."

She and Elizabeth continued their conversation for ten minutes or so on the sidewalk while her two friends waited. Elizabeth "appeared happy and cheerful," Salisbury told reporters. She asked her for her phone number, to which Elizabeth replied, "I'm living with these two girls in a motel in San Fernando Valley. We don't have a telephone. Give me your phone and I'll call you." Salisbury gave Elizabeth her number, after which Elizabeth hurried to the car.

Paul Simone was a painting contractor living in Hollywood who had been employed by and was working at the Chancellor Hotel on Saturday, January 11, 1947, the same hotel where Elizabeth Short had shared room 501 with seven women the previous December. While working at the building on January 11, he told police he heard "loud arguing" coming from the rear of the hotel. Checking to see what the commotion was, he saw Elizabeth Short and another woman involved in what he described as "a bitter argument." The second woman was "cursing loudly at Elizabeth," according to his statement, and Simone feared the two women were on the verge of physically fighting. The second woman saw Simone approach, looked at him, and yelled, "Oh, nuts to you!" then turned and walked out of the hotel. When she was gone, Elizabeth asked Simone, "Is there a rear exit to the hotel?" He said there wasn't and walked Elizabeth to the front door, where she got into a waiting taxi.

I. A. Jorgenson was a Los Angeles cab driver who provided evidence to police of another sighting of Elizabeth Short, this time on the night of January 11, 1947. Jorgenson told the detectives his cab was parked outside of the Rosslyn Hotel, at 6th and Main Streets in downtown Los Angeles, when a man and a woman he positively identified as Elizabeth Short got in. The man told him to drive them to a motel in Hollywood. Police sources would not provide the press with the description of the man or the name of the motel, telling reporters "they would first conduct a follow-up and interview employees of the motel in Hollywood."

"John Doe Number 2," another secret witness police kept under wraps from reporters, was a gas station attendant working at the Beverly Hills Hotel who saw Elizabeth Short in the Beverly Hills area in the early-morning hours of January 11. The witness told detectives that around 2:30 A.M. he saw a vehicle, which he described as "a 1942 tan Chrysler coupe," stopped at the service station for gas. He positively identified Elizabeth Short from police photos as the same woman he saw in the backseat of the car. "She seemed very upset and frightened," he noted. He also saw a second woman in the car, whom he described only as "wearing dark clothing." He described the male driver as "about thirty years of age, six foot one, 190 pounds."

As reported earlier in the LAPD investigative chronology chapter, Mr. and Mrs. William Johnson, owners and on-site managers of a hotel located at 300 East Washington Boulevard in downtown Los Angeles, are the two most important witnesses police never brought forward to the public, because on January 12 they saw Elizabeth in the company of the man who most likely killed her. They saw this prime suspect again on January 15, after Elizabeth's body had been discovered. They told police that on Sunday, January 12, 1947, at approximately 10:00 A.M., they were working at their hotel when a man, whom they described as "25 to 35 years of age, medium complexion, medium height," came to the desk and "asked for a room."

An hour later, a woman they positively identified as Elizabeth Short came to the hotel and joined the man who had booked the room. Mrs. Johnson provided the following description: "She had on beige or pink slacks, a full-length beige coat, white blouse and white bandanna over her head, and she was carrying a plastic purse with two handles."

Mr. Johnson told police that "the man refused to sign the registration, when he checked in, and told me to put down Barnes and wife." The man told Mr. Johnson they had just moved out of Hollywood. The Johnsons watched the man and Elizabeth go to their room, and that was the last time either of them saw Elizabeth Short.

LAPD detectives showed both Mr. and Mrs. Johnson photographs found in Elizabeth Short's luggage, and after viewing the many separate photographs the Johnsons positively identified the victim, Elizabeth Short, and her male companion who checked into the hotel with her as "Mr. Barnes." The police did not release the identity of "Mr. Barnes."

C. G. Williams, a bartender at the Dugout Café at 634 South Main Street in downtown Los Angeles, told police and reporters that when he was working at the bar on the afternoon of January 12, 1947, he saw a woman, whom he positively identified as Elizabeth Short, walk into the bar accompanied by "an attractive blonde." Elizabeth was a regular customer well-known to him. The bartender clearly remembered Elizabeth's visit that day, as "a fracas occurred," along with shouting, after two men tried to pick up the ladies and were rejected.

Former jockey John Jiroudek had known Elizabeth Short when she worked at the Camp Cooke PX during the time he was a G.I. stationed there. He remembered her in particular, he told police, because he was there when she was chosen as the Camp Cooke "Cutie of the Week." He told detectives he saw her again in a brief encounter on January 13, 1947, when they crossed paths at the corner of Hollywood Boulevard and Highland Avenue. She was a passenger in a 1937 Ford sedan. A blonde female was driving the car. He spoke briefly with Elizabeth at the intersection, and the two women drove off.

As also referred to earlier in the LAPD investigative chronology, policewoman Myrl McBride, walking a beat in downtown Los Angeles, was probably one of the last people to have seen Elizabeth Short alive. She came forward to her bosses in the department after seeing photographs of the Jane Doe Number 1 who had just been identified from FBI records as Elizabeth Short. Myrl McBride positively identified her to superiors as the same woman who had come running up to her at the downtown bus depot, in fear for her life.

McBride reported that on the afternoon of January 14, 1947, while she was on her beat at the bus depot in downtown Los Angeles, Elizabeth Short ran up to her "sobbing in terror" and told her, "Someone wants to kill me." Short said that she had come from a bar up the street and had just run into an ex-boyfriend. Officer McBride said that Short told her she "lives in terror" of a former serviceman whom she had just met in a bar up the street. McBride added, "She told me the suitor had threatened to kill her if he found her with another man."

McBride said she walked the victim back into the Main Street bar, where she recovered her purse. A short time later, McBride again observed the victim "reenter the bar, and then emerge with two men and a woman." At that time McBride had a brief second conversation with Elizabeth Short, who told her that she "was going to meet her parents at the bus station later in the evening."

On January 16, the day the body was identified and photographs obtained, Officer McBride provided an unequivocal positive identification of Elizabeth Short as the same person who ran to her "in terror, fearful of being killed." A day or two following that positive identification, her statement was then "modified by detectives to being uncertain." My initial evaluation of McBride's statement from positive to uncertain was that LAPD detective-supervisors wanted the officer to, in police terminology, "CYA" (cover your ass). They couldn't allow the public to think that one of their own basically took no action and allowed the victim to walk into the hands of her killers just hours before she was murdered. Better to have her modify her statement and let the public think that maybe the woman McBride had contact with was not Elizabeth. (Sadly, this was not the case.) LAPD's need to minimize or reverse McBride's positive identification pointed to a much more sinister intent.

From the various witnesses who saw Elizabeth Short between January 9 and January 14, 1947, it's clear there was no "missing week" in Elizabeth's life. That week was crisscrossed with sightings by both

complete strangers and acquaintances, most of whom spoke unequivocally about Elizabeth's moods and movements in the days and
hours before her murder, and all of whom saw her within a twelve-
mile radius of downtown Los Angeles. These twelve witnesses, culled
from reports of other sightings that are less than reliable, are sound.

Officer McBride's sighting of Elizabeth just twenty hours before
the discovery of her body, and a mere eight hours before Dr. Newbarr's forensic estimation of the time of her murder, must focus anyone's attention and suspicions on the three individuals in whose
company she was seen. Who were these two men and the woman
with Elizabeth? What were the descriptions of them provided by Officer McBride but not released to the public? Was one of these two
men the person that Elizabeth told Officer McBride about in the bus
depot, while "sobbing in terror"? Was he the same man whom Elizabeth just a short time earlier had fled from in the Main Street bar,
the same "jealous suitor who had threatened to kill her"?

There is one interesting aspect to Elizabeth Short's "missing
week" that may not have been apparent to the LAPD at the time but is
now. In the statement made by Linda Rohr, a roommate of Elizabeth's
at the Chancellor Hotel in Hollywood, she said that she last saw Elizabeth on December 6, 1946, confirming landlady Juanita Ringo's
statements. Linda also said that when Elizabeth was packing to leave,
she was very upset. She quoted Elizabeth as saying, "He's waiting for
me," but added, "None of us ever found out who 'he' was."

The next known sighting of Elizabeth was on December 12,
when she met Dorothy French at the San Diego moviehouse and was
offered a place to stay at her home. So from December 6 to December 12 there is indeed a missing week for Elizabeth, but it is *before* she
goes to San Diego and not after she leaves the Biltmore.

Since at the beginning of that week in early December we know
Elizabeth was hurrying to meet her mysterious boyfriend, who that
day was "waiting" for her, we can fairly assume she spent part if not
all of the missing week with him. It was here that she disappeared off
the radar screen. Who was this man? Where did they stay? What
happened to her? Five days later Elizabeth resurfaced in San Diego,
huddling for warmth in an all-night moviehouse, lonely, destitute,
and afraid.

# 19

# The Final Connections:
# Man Ray Thoughtprints

THROUGHOUT THE COURSE OF MY INVESTIGATION, the more I researched, the more I became aware of how important Man Ray was to George Hodel, who clearly considered him a kindred spirit. However, it was some time before I realized just how close and influential that relationship had been. Did that profound influence, I wondered, have anything to do with the Black Dahlia?

It was the "Black Dahlia Avenger" who told police that he'd murdered Elizabeth Short and, through his notes, that his sadistic torture and murder was justified. Perhaps, like the "Ballad of Frankie and Johnny," in which Frankie kills her lover "cause he done her wrong," in his mind Elizabeth had wronged him. I suspect he and Elizabeth were lovers and were going to be married. I also believe Elizabeth had made a promise to him — "a promise is a promise to a person of the world," the anonymous 1945 telegram from Washington, D.C., had said — but Elizabeth broke that promise. In breaking her word she "done him wrong," and like Johnny she would pay for it with her life.

Essential to the nature of a true "avenger," the killer had to inflict pain on the person, but it differs in that the acts were seen by the avenger as retribution and were, in the avenger's mind, therefore morally justified. The avenger likened himself to a state-sanctioned executioner, who takes the life of a prisoner in the name of the people, exacting retribution for a capital offense. As his pasted message to the press announced, "Dahlia killing was justified."

What distinguishes the crime of Elizabeth Short from the murder of many other lone women in L.A. in the 1940s is the manner of her execution, the horrible mutilation of her body, and the posing of her corpse.

Through the years, one of the most intriguing and frustrating questions the police had never been able to answer was: why had the killer gone to such extraordinary lengths to "pose" his victim? Surely this was a thoughtprint, a message for the world to read, if only it could. It was surreal, fiendishly surreal ... There was clearly a method to the killer's madness, a reason he posed the body the way he did. In his game of cat and mouse with the police and public, the "avenger" was, by that bizarre pose, leaving a message, as if he was challenging police to pick it up — a riddle, a test of wits, with himself as the master criminal.

Given George Hodel's relationship to and love of Man Ray's work, I examined hundreds of photographs in all of Man Ray's books. Just as I was about to give up, I found what I was looking for: a painting, *Les Amoureux (The Lovers)* (1933–34), and a photograph, *The Minotaur* (1936), two of his most celebrated pieces. The former portrays a pair of lips as two bodies entwine and stretch across the horizon from end to end, the latter shows a victim of the mythological monster, which had the head of a bull and the body of a man. The Minotaur was kept imprisoned in the labyrinth on the island of Crete, where it was fed young maidens to satisfy it and keep it alive.

In Man Ray's *Minotaur*, we see a woman's naked body with her arms raised over her head, the right arm placed at a forty-five-degree angle away from the body and then bent at the elbow to form a ninety-degree angle. The left arm is similarly bent at the elbow to form a second ninety-degree angle. This positioning recreates the horns of the bull-headed beast. The body is bisected at the waist so that only the upper torso is in frame. One can easily imagine the two breasts as a creature's ghoulish eyes and the shadow above the stomach as the creature's mouth, as if the face of the carnivorous beast is superimposed on the body of its victim.

I pulled from my file the crime-scene photo of Elizabeth Short as she was discovered by police on the morning of January 15, 1947, in the vacant lot on Norton. The positioning of Elizabeth's arms precisely duplicates the position of the subject's arms in Man Ray's photograph! In this precise posing of the arms, the killer had replicated the horns just as Man Ray intended them in his original photograph. But there's more. The excised piece of flesh below Elizabeth's left breast imitates the shadow below the victim's breasts in the Man Ray photograph. I offer as evidence exhibits 35a and 35b.

*Exhibits 35a and 35b*

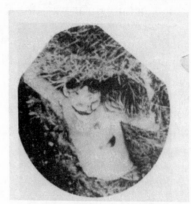
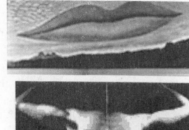

*a) Elizabeth Short crime scene b) Man Ray's* Les Amoureux *and* Minotaur

From the view in exhibit 35a we cannot see whether Elizabeth's right side was also excised in similar fashion. Perhaps most tellingly, the laceration the killer cut into Elizabeth's face extends her mouth from ear to ear, and her lips appear grotesquely identical to the lover's lips extending across the horizon in Man Ray's *Les Amoureux*.

The killer had to make her death extraordinary both in planning and execution. In his role as a surreal artist, he determined that his work would be a masterpiece of the macabre, a crime so shocking and horrible it would endure, be immortalized through the annals of crime lore. As avenger, he would use her body as his canvas, and his surgeon's scalpel as his paintbrush!

Much as I wanted to deny it to myself or to look for other possible explanations, I now realized the facts were undeniable: George Hodel, through the homage he consciously paid to Man Ray, was provocatively revealing himself to be the murderer of Elizabeth Short. Her body, and the way she was posed, was Dr. George signature — both artistic and psychological — on his own surreal masterpiece, in which he *juxtaposed the unexpected* in a "still death" tribute to his master, *using human body parts!* The premeditated and deliberate use of these two photographs — one symbolizing my father and Elizabeth as the lovers in *Les Amoureux*, and another my father as the avenger, the Minotaur himself, the bull-headed beast consuming and destroying the young maiden, Elizabeth, in sacrifice — is my father's grisly message of his and Man Ray's shared vision of violent sexual fantasy. Given George Hodel's megalomaniacal ego, it was also a dash of one-upmanship.

Another instance of the morbid influence of Man Ray's photographs on my father is exhibit 36: Man Ray's 1945 photograph of his wife, Juliet, beneath a silk stocking mask. I maintain that photo was the inspiration for Father's altering the photograph of his assault victim, seventeen-year-old Armand Robles (exhibit 36):

### Exhibit 36

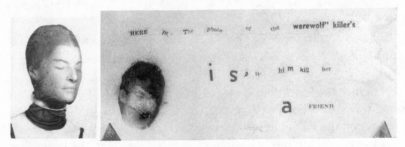

**Juliet Man Ray**               **Armand Robles (exhibit 25)**

In the early 1970s, after having lived and practiced in Manila for twenty years, George Hodel attended a one-man show at the Philippines Cultural Center called the *Erotic and Non-Erotic Drawings of Modesto*, where he discovered the promising young artist Fernando Modesto. Father was instantly drawn to the twenty-two-year-old artist's erotic works and to what he would later term "the brilliant style of the artist's approach." From that first showing until his return to the United States from Asia in 1990, Father would be Modesto's patron, buying virtually everything he created. And Modesto was prolific. By 1990 Father had amassed a personal collection of over 1,600 Modesto works, 95 percent of which would have to be considered erotica.

In the months prior to his death, George Hodel was preparing to market his private collection to the public, which required that he develop a strategy and promotion campaign. His first step would be to tell the world something about the artist, who by that time had developed a reputation in Europe and Asia but was less known in the States. Included in this marketing program would be a description of the artist and his developing vision, which had evolved over his twenty-year career through various stages. A sampling of the works from Modesto's different periods of development were included in Father's brochure, along with relevant catalog descriptions. This catalog copy was not comprised of Modesto's interpretations of his own art, but rather those of his patron, a pioneer in marketing, a businessman, and a psychiatrist.

## FERNANDO MODESTO
### by Dr. George Hodel

Page 2, 1976 — (Examples 17–21)
They seem to have several levels of meaning. One level appears to reflect the artist's views on the universality of the erotic drive, which impels all creatures and unites them in a cosmic identity.

Page 3, 1982 — (Examples 35–36)
Homage to Man Ray. Modesto has always greatly admired, and has been inspired by, the work of Man Ray. He has collected many books on Man Ray, and often looks at these photos, paintings, and sculptures.

From Father's private collection of these artworks, there is only one piece that specifically relates to the investigation of the murder of Elizabeth Short. I call it *Modesto's Lovers* (exhibit 37). It is displayed here in comparison to its inspiration, Man Ray's 1934 *Les Amoureux*. I came across it only after Father's death while I was helping June photograph and catalog the entire collection.

*Exhibit 37*

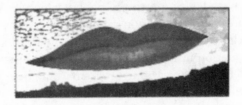

*Top: Man Ray's* Les Amoureux; *Bottom:* Modesto's Lovers

June told me that she and George had traveled to Paris in 1986 or 1987, where Father had presented an identical work to Juliet Man Ray.

Did George Hodel specifically commission this drawing and provide the artist with all of the details to be included, or did Modesto merely use his own creative energies and imagination, independent of his patron? The answer may be hidden in the work itself and what it appears to represent. First, the work is a form of flattery: it's an imitation of Man Ray's "lovers' lips" that extend across the horizon. However, unlike the Man Ray work, the lips in the Modesto are not full red, and the bottom lip is only partially covered. Also, the irregularity of the bottom line in the Modesto suggests dripping blood rather than lipstick. And directly above the lips are three human phalluses. To the left of the lips is a blue canal the shape of a vagina, above which a squadron of nine yellow and ten blue oval-shaped objects seems to be flying, each with its own trailing spermlike tail. Do the two different colors represent George Hodel and Fred Sexton? These were some of the questions I asked myself when I looked at this painting again in the context of what I had just discovered. I am also convinced that my father's trip to Paris was no simple visit but a pilgrimage, a formal presentation of *Modesto's Lovers* to Juliet Man Ray to honor the memory of her late husband and Father's friendship with him.

In and of itself, the Modesto painting is at best tangential to the case I'm building. But, *Modesto's Lovers* actually becomes an integral part of the suspect/psychiatrist's own Rorschach blot, revealing his personality and emotions in the context of Father's using lipstick at a Franklin House party, writing in lipstick on the body of Jeanne French at her crime scene, cutting Elizabeth Short's lips, and interpreting a pattern on a hotel floor as a pair of lips that need to be stomped out. In that context, the violent erotica expressed in *Modesto's Lovers* is a variation on a theme that ran throughout George Hodel's life and becomes important and relevant evidence in evaluating his culpability in the Elizabeth Short and Jeanne French murder cases.

In former Los Angeles crime reporter Will Fowler's 1991 book *Reporters: Memoirs of a Young Newspaperman*, the author closes his chapter on the Black Dahlia by saying:

> Intense interest lingers regarding this murder mystery simply because it remains a mystery. And by this fascination, it has earned its niche in the annals of crime history as being the most notorious unsolved murder of the twentieth century.
>
> Elizabeth Short's slaying might be solved in the distant future, but I sincerely hope not. It's like an unopened present. The present always remains a wondrous thing, as long as it remains unopened.
>
> The Black Dahlia murder still remains "a riddle wrapped in a mystery inside an enigma."

I take strong exception to Fowler's comparing the unsolved torture-murder of a young woman to "an unopened present" and "a wondrous thing." It is his statement, however, that "the Black Dahlia murder still remains 'a riddle wrapped in a mystery inside an enigma'" that has become almost a signature quote for the entire Black Dahlia murder investigation. Most people think the quote originated with Winston Churchill, who in a 1939 radio broadcast used the phrase to describe Russia. When I first read the quote in Fowler's book during my early research on the case, I knew I'd heard it before but couldn't recall where. The next time I read it, I was able to pinpoint the source and put together a pattern of thoughtprints that led me directly back to my father and Man Ray.

The memory link for the "riddle wrapped in a mystery" quote dates back to the winter of 1980, when I became the senior field homicide detective at Hollywood Division. Only months away from turning forty, I had mellowed and I could see my father on a gray scale instead of a stark black and white. I reached out to him.

On January 27, 1980, I mailed a highly personal letter to him in the Philippines. In it, I communicated my current thoughts and reflections in many areas of my life, and how in maturity I had come to realize, despite our physical separation, how much I loved and respected him. I enclosed an article and photographs from the *Hollywood Independent* that mentioned me and my then partner Rick Papke after we'd been chosen to receive the "Inspector Clouseau" Award for solving a Hollywood murder case in which veteran film actor Charles Wagenheim, age eighty-three, had been murdered at his residence.

Roughly four months later, in June of that year, I received the following reply. This was the only time Father ever communicated with me on such a personal level.

Dear Steve:

It was good to get your last letter with its long perspectives. To communicate is such a mysterious process, at any level. And to truly communicate is rare. I am glad that you made the effort, and that you succeeded. That you succeeded in beginning to make a breakthrough. One of these days, if time permits, let's try together, to push through further.

It is not easy to explain what I mean. But let me give you an example. A parable. But a true example. When you visit here in Manila again I'll show you the birds, and the glass, and the watchers (we), and we can try together to unlock the secrets of the three. Or is it four?

Safely hidden away from harm, in the overhead roof rafters of my penthouse in the Excelsior, are a tribe of small birds. Perhaps they are sparrows, house sparrows. They

build their nests there, slip between the curves of the galva-
nized roofing into their separate havens, mate there, and
raise their young.

Each season a generation of brave new little birds
squeeze out through the curves of the roofing, and survey
their cosmos. They practice hopping about, and pecking at
each other, and winging along the balcony. They even discover a tiny swing which I have put up for them (birds love
to play, you know) and they jump from the window frames
to the metal swing, push back and forward, and hop back
delightedly to their take-off place.

And then, somewhere along the line, and usually pretty
soon, they make a discovery. A discovery based on advanced technology. A discovery which is totally incomprehensible, but which fills them with joy, and hope, and high
excitement.

In Manila, as you may remember, my penthouse apartment faces out toward the west, onto Manila Bay. All
through the afternoon, and until the sun sets behind the
mountains of Bataan and the island of Corregidor, the sun's
rays beat relentlessly on the glass west wall of my apartment. Air conditioners find it hard to compete with this
heavenly barrage.

Therefore, in self-defense, we put up synthetic plastic
coating--a mirror film--on all the western windows, to reflect the sun's rays and help to cool the rooms. It works quite
well, and cuts down on heat and glare. Through the glass,
we look out on the bay and the mountains and the sunset
with slightly bluishly tinted glasses. And they look fine; they
look all the better for this bit of blueness.

But to anyone on the outside (and we come back now
to our brave young sparrows) the plastic-coated glass is a
mirror. It is meant to be a mirror so as to turn away light
and heat. It was not designed to deceive little birds. But they
are deceived, and aroused, and delighted.

What do they see in the tinted mirror? They see beautiful young birds, amazingly like themselves, hopping about
like they do, and full of life, and curiosity. Above all else,

our little sparrows yearn to join their companions, and to sport with them, fly with them, even mate with them and continue their flight through eternities of love and time.

But there is a barrier to all these hopes. They do not know and cannot believe that the barrier, the wall of glass, can never be surmounted. There must be a way, they say, to break through somehow, into this paradise of beautiful young birds who await them, who tempt them, and who respond dancer-like to their every movement. How to enter this paradise which is right here, right at hand? How, they ask? Surely there must be a way, if they only persist. Surely they will somehow prevail, they say. Paradise will be theirs. Paradise awaits the brave, the strong, the pure in heart, they say.

And so, for hours on end, our little birds dash against the silent glass. Foray after foray, swooping from a vantage point (the Chinese lanterns near the roof) the little birds strike against the glass. The braver and more patient ones may go on all day, in their assault. The tinted glass is flecked with a thousand marks where little beaks have crashed against it, hour after hour after hour.

And then there is the third partner in this mystery. Ourselves. The tireless birds, the silent glass, and we. We stand wonderingly behind the glass, and contemplate the battle. We are like the gods, watching all and knowing all, knowing that the battle is fore-ordained. But how can we communicate our knowledge to the brave battalions of the birds? How can we warn them, console them? Send them off on other more hopeful missions?

Sadly, as we contemplate the glass and the determined little birds we must settle with the truth. And the truth is that we cannot warn them, cannot tell them, and can only feel for them, and love them for their courage.

But are there only three of us? The birds, the glass, and we? Or is there a fourth? Who is standing behind our glass, invisible to us, incommunicable to us, gravely watching our brave attacks against the walls we cannot see? Is there a fifth presence, watching all the others? And a sixth, and others, hidden in mysteries beyond our dreams?

When you visit in Manila, I'll show the countless marks on the glass to you. If you come at the right season, you'll see the brave little birds themselves, and their efforts to break through.

There are other ways, too, in which life's secrets are shadowed forth. Have you ever watched the insect who flies back and forth in the jetliner, seeking a tiny crumb or wanting out? How can I inform him that he is flying from Amsterdam to Tokyo, and that his life is joined with the lives of us who see beyond the crumb. But not too far beyond. We know as little about our real voyage as the insect knows about the trans-polar flight.

It is good to know that you love me, for this is not easy to achieve, for you, for many reasons. Some of the reasons you have stated, and it is fine that you are able to begin to understand and overcome them. Some of the other reasons, for our love, may be harder to understand, for they may be shrouded in mysteries, like those of the birds and the glass.

I too love you, and this is easier, because you are the very by-product and testimonial of my love. There is an old Irish saying that "Ah, I knew you, me boy, when you were only a gleam in your father's eye."

It is also easy (indeed, it is mandatory) for me to love you because I remember things that you do not. I remember the happy, well-controlled, serious, beautiful little boy whom we loved so much. And now love equally, but differently. Only a little difference.

I am enclosing a check for Dorero, for the six-month period from July through December. Wish it could be more. Try to find ways to give to her--a bit of money, a bit of time, and love, much love. Remember--it was she who responded to the gleam. If she had not . . .

Dorero asked me to send her another enlargement (I brought one to her before in 1974) of her wonderful photo

by Man Ray. I have had this copied, and will send it soon.
If you want a print, I'll make one for you too. And for Mike
and Kelv, if they do not have them and want them.

Congratulations on your work in the case of Charles
Wagenheim and Stephanie Boone. There must be an
enigma inside a mystery there, too.

Hope to be out your way one of these days soon. I am
interested to know what you plan to do after three years.
Your life may just be beginning then.

Give my love to all!

Always,

Dad

There it was. Latent in a twenty-year-old letter was hidden Father's automatic and unconscious response to my reference to the
Wagenheim investigation, which involved my informing him, briefly,
about a man, a woman, and a murder in Hollywood. In the letter,
from within the context of my investigation, I could see how his
mind unconsciously responded to its unique and individual program-
ming after I filtered the keywords "enigma inside a mystery." "Congratulations," he'd written, "on your work in the case of Charles
Wagenheim and Stephanie Boone. There must be an enigma inside a
mystery there, *too* [my emphasis]."

Father's response had no significance to me then, other than the
obvious reference to unraveling a murder mystery, but with what I
have since discovered, the "too" took on a great significance. What
other case might my father have been comparing the Wagenheim
murder to? I believe he was making an unconscious reference to the
Black Dahlia case, not because Will Fowler would use that same
quote ten years later, but because the Black Dahlia case had remained
a mystery over the years and was still in my father's mind. I think he
gave himself away, but I had no way to appreciate that reference.
Now I do.

In July 2001, I discovered what I believe to be the actual linkage
and original source of Father's riddle-and-enigma quote, and again
the path led directly back to Man Ray. The source for the quote

actually predated Churchill's use by some nineteen years and related to a controversial and provocative 1929 photograph created by Man Ray entitled *The Riddle, or The Enigma of Isidore Ducasse* (exhibit 38).

*Exhibit 38*

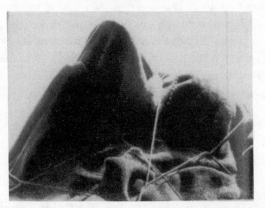

**The Riddle, or The Enigma of Isidore Ducasse**

The photo depicts an object or objects wrapped in a carpet and tied with rope. After photographing the unknown subjects, Man Ray left it up to the beholder to figure out what the blanket concealed. Is it a human body, or perhaps something less sinister? Some believe that Man Ray provided a clue to what was hidden inside his "riddle or enigma." Man Ray's biographer writes:

At this time, Man Ray was developing an interest in vanguard French literature. The work that perhaps best exemplifies this new influence — and reveals his reliance on the very sources that had been an important literary precedent to dada — is *The Riddle, or The Enigma of Isidore Ducasse*, a photograph of an unidentified object, or objects, wrapped in the folds of a thick carpet, which in turn is tied with rope. Although the entire assemblage was discarded after the photograph was taken, Man Ray wanted the viewer to believe that two rather commonplace objects were hidden under the carpet. The only way a viewer could know what they were, though — and thus solve the riddle — was to have been familiar with the writings of the obscure, though extremely influential,

French author Isidore Ducasse, whose pseudonym was the Comte de Lautréamont . . .

By 1920, at least two statements by the French author had attained near legendary status: his observation that, "Poetry must be made by all, not by one." And his oft-quoted "Lovely as the fortuitous encounter on a dissecting table of a sewing machine and an umbrella." It was of course, this bizarre, though visually provocative, exemplar of beauty that Man Ray illustrated in *The Riddle*. "When I read Lautréamont," he later explained, "I was fascinated by the juxtaposition of unusual objects and works." Even more important, he was drawn to the count's "world of complete freedom."*

Man Ray never revealed to anyone the actual objects inside his photograph, leaving it to the viewer to judge these obscure references to a dissecting table, a sewing machine, and an umbrella. With respect to the Dahlia investigation, it is enough to understand this further linkage to Man Ray's use of the quote in the light of Father's statement to me in response to my solving the Wagenheim murder, with his "there must be an enigma inside a mystery there, too."

Man Ray's 1920 photograph *The Riddle, or The Enigma*, which to many people would represent a human body, or body parts, wrapped and bound with rope, becomes the fourth compelling photograph informing the influence Man Ray had on my father and his actions in the Black Dahlia case. Along with Man Ray's other three works of art mentioned above — *Les Amoureux*, *The Minotaur*, and *Juliet in Silk-Stocking* — they reveal the vivid images that will later turn up throughout the Black Dahlia case. In fact, the Man Ray images themselves help to unwrap the mystery of the case, which has been my father's riddle-and-enigma to the world for over fifty years.

For my purposes, one of the most telling portraits Man Ray photographed was the one of my father and a statue of the deity Yamantaka (exhibit 39), which probably sums up their relationship to each other and to their private sexual fantasies.†

---

*Foresta, Merry, et. al. *Perpetual Motif: The Art of Man Ray*. Abbeville Press, New York, 1988, p. 80.

†Uncertain of the deity's identity, I consulted Dr. Momi Naughton, professor of Asian art at Western Washington University, who confirmed it to me.

*Exhibit 39*

*George Hodel and Yamantaka*

Man Ray took this photograph of my father in 1946, in his UNRRA "lieutenant general" topcoat. Knowing that Father rarely took any action that did not hold a symbolic meaning, I was sure this Man Ray photograph contained some hidden intent. It is important because it represents a collaboration between Man Ray and George Hodel to create what Man Ray believed all his photos would become — works of art. Therefore, the object that my father is embracing in the photograph takes on a great significance both to him and to Man Ray.

A Tibetan deity and one of the most complex divinities of the Lamaistic pantheon, Yamantaka is a powerful nine-headed god whose primary head is that of a bull. Yamantaka's manifestation is purportedly so terrible that he is said to have overpowered Yama, god of death, roughly equivalent to Satan or the ruler of the underworld. In this particular statue, Yamantaka is shown in what is termed the "yab-yum" position, performing sexual intercourse with his consort.

In the photograph, Father, in what appears to be a state of worshipful reverence, looks as if he's transfixed by Yamantaka. Like Yamantaka, George Hodel believed he was omnipotent and, as a doctor, could overthrow death. He also believed he was sexually omnipotent, and inflicted this belief upon all the women he met, including his own daughter; thus the choice of Yamantaka in the act of sexual intercourse. For Man Ray, the fascination of Yamantaka is the bull-headed deity itself, the Lamaistic counterpart to Man Ray's own destroyer of maidens, the *Minotaur*.

In this portrait of my father embracing Yamantaka, both Man Ray and my father juxtapose their own representations of omnipotence, sexuality, and dominance over death itself. But the portrait goes beyond juxtaposition; it is an objectification of all the elements that define their relationship to each other and to the visions they shared.

There is, in addition, a secondary deviant psychology that I believe also explains the way Elizabeth's body was posed. The Black Dahlia crime scene was a kind of flowering in my father's mind of the kinds of scenes he had written about as a young crime reporter in the 1920s, when, I believe, the early seeds of his violent sexual visions were first sown.

Further, Father worshiped and identified with Charles Baudelaire, whom he read and studied in the original French. It is likely that Father read these words, from Baudelaire's *Journal*, took them to heart, and would later translate and apply them as part of his own surgical crime:

> *Squibs.* I believe I have already set down in my notes that Love greatly resembles an application of torture or a surgical operation. But this idea can be developed, and in the most ironic manner. For even when two lovers love passionately and are full of mutual desire, one of the two will always be cooler or less self-abandoned than the other. He or she is the surgeon or executioner; the other, the patient or victim.*

Finally, there is exhibit 40 in comparison with Father's original two photographs of Elizabeth (exhibit 7). I call it "The Dream." Taken in 1929, the photo portrays a gathering of the major surrealists in Paris, including André Breton, René Magritte, Max Ernst, and Salvador Dalí. Each member of the group has formally posed for his portrait with his eyes closed, affirming his support and preference for the subjective dream state in defiance of the conscious and rational.

---

*\**Writers in Revolt: An Anthology* (Frederic Fell Inc., New York, 1963), p. 50.

*Exhibit 40*

*The surrealists, 1929*

In the 1920s, André Breton became the spokesman for surrealism and wrote the movement's first manifesto in 1924. His stated philosophy relating to the importance of dreams and the state of sleep is described in that original manifesto:

> The mind of the man who dreams is fully satisfied by what happens to him. The agonizing question of possibility is no longer pertinent. Kill, fly faster, love to your heart's content. And if you should die, are you not certain of reawaking among the dead? Let yourself be carried along, events will not tolerate your interference. You are nameless. The ease of everything is priceless . . .
>
> I believe in the future resolution of these two states, dream and reality, which are seemingly so contradictory, into a kind of absolute reality, a *surreality*, if one may so speak.*

My father's most revealing thoughtprints are those two damning photos of Elizabeth Short, as seen on page 41 as exhibit 7. Here again the artist/photographer has signed his work, only this one was private and was meant to remain so.

*\*Manifestos of Surrealism* (University of Michigan Press, Ann Arbor, 1972), pp. 13–14.

In these photographs of his lover, George Hodel reveals his eso-teric "marriage" to Elizabeth Short by personally initiating her into his world. After carefully posing her in both photographs, Father in-structs Elizabeth to close her eyes, as if she is asleep or in a dream state. With his lens, he then captures the dream, transporting her to his world, the world of the surreal, where dreams are reality, where the rational and the conscious are only backgrounds and are reversed to become the shadows of unreality.

True to his philosophy, George Hodel remained the absolute surrealist throughout his life, the young poet of seventeen, described in the newspaper of his day:

> George drowned himself at times in an ocean of deep dreams. Only part of him seemed present. He would muse standing before one in a black, flowered dressing gown lined with scarlet silk, oblivious to one's presence.

Add to that his published statement to the police at the time of his 1949 arrest for incest that he was "delving into the mystery of love and the universe," and that the acts of which he was then ac-cused were "unclear, like a dream. I can't figure out whether some-one is hypnotizing me or I am hypnotizing someone."

And finally, Father's "Parable of the Sparrows" letter of 1980, with its mystical questioning:

> But are there only three of us? The birds, the glass, and we? Or is there a fourth? Who is standing behind our glass, invisible to us, incommunicable to us, gravely watching our brave attacks against the walls we cannot see? Is there a fifth presence, watching all the others? And a sixth, and others, hidden in mysteries beyond our dreams?

These two photographs of Elizabeth Short taken by her then lover, most probably at the Franklin House in the month preceding the crime, are unique and macabre in the extreme, premortem por-tent of the horrors about to befall her. They are the ultimate surreal irony, where the artist has captured both of their pasts and futures as mistress-victim and lover-avenger.

# 20

# The Franklin House Revisited

I BEGAN MY INVESTIGATION on the premise that the photographs of Elizabeth Short in Father's album were the innocent mementos of his wanton youth, about which I had always known and because of which my mother had suffered so greatly. Elizabeth Short, I assumed, was probably just one of dozens of women in his life who were nothing more to him than a "three-month fling."

As I went deeper and deeper into both my father's mysterious past and that of Elizabeth Short, however, fitting many scattered biographical jigsaw pieces of their separate lives into time and place, I was slowly moved to the inescapable conclusion: my father was in fact guilty of her murder. Alone, or with an accomplice.

In the pages and chapters that follow, I offer the accumulated evidence, along with the relevant photographs, that will prove beyond any reasonable doubt that Dr. George Hill Hodel was the Black Dahlia Avenger.

In October 1999, during the initial stages of my investigation, I contacted the owners of the Franklin House, whom I had met thirty years earlier while working Hollywood Division. The owner's father had purchased the house through my father's attorneys in 1950, after the Tamar incest trial.

"Bill Buck" (an assumed name to protect his anonymity) and his wife had moved into Franklin House in the early 1970s and begun restoring it. While working Hollywood Division in 1973, I chanced to meet the owners while they were gardening in front of the residence. After learning of my connection they graciously offered me a tour. In 1999, after my father's death, I learned that both Bill Buck and his wife were still living there and made an appointment to visit them again. We spent several hours discussing the history of the house, its construction, and its former owners, me sharing with them some memories of my Franklin years. As they had done so many years before, they took me on another tour, during which I took a number of photographs of both the interior and exterior. Included in the tour was a trip to the basement, which for the most part had remained untouched since the original sale some fifty years before.

During a cursory search of the dust-covered past deep in the basement, I found two items of interest, the first of which was a wooden crate, sent from China and addressed to "Dr. George Hill Hodel, 5121 Franklin Avenue, Los Angeles, California."

Inside the crate I discovered a bill of lading, dated October 16, 1946, which inventoried eight packages.

### Exhibit 41

*Franklin House bill of lading*

This document established that the various art treasures purchased and shipped by Father from China had arrived at the Franklin House in the fall of 1946. Whether the crate followed his departure either by sea freight from China or via a reasonably fast military air transport, the receipt date supports my suspicion that George Hodel had arrived back in Los Angeles sometime in September 1946, discharged for what his UNRRA record cited as "personal" reasons. Father's stay in a hospital corresponds to what Elizabeth Short's

Massachusetts girlfriend Marjorie Graham told reporters in her telephone interview with them on January 17, 1947:

> Elizabeth had told me her boyfriend was an Army Air Force lieutenant, currently in the hospital in Los Angeles. Elizabeth told me that she was worried about him and she hoped that he would get well and out of the hospital in time for a wedding they planned for November 1.

Bill Buck mentioned that my father had left some old magazines in the basement, but he thought they had been disposed of over the years. During my brief tour of the basement, which for me still held painful memories of leather straps and spankings, I came across a cobweb-covered box of old medical magazines dating from the mid-1940s. Examining the contents, I discovered a medical calendar book for the year 1943 that had belonged to Father. I asked Bill Buck if I could take it and he said, "Of course."

*Exhibit 42*

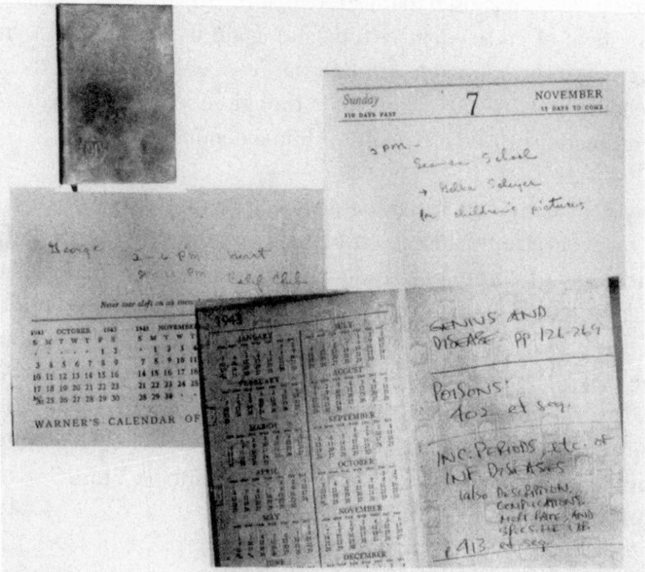

*George Hodel's 1943 medical calendar*

The book was titled *Warner's Calendar of Medical History, for the use of the Medical Profession, 1943.* A later careful examination of each page of the book provided some interesting discoveries, including samples of my father's handwriting on the inside cover, as well as other entries in my mother's hand. Printed in George Hodel's handwriting on the front inside cover of the book were the following notations: "Genius and Disease: pp 126–269." Page 126 was earmarked and said:

## GENIUS & DISEASE

Many attempts have been made to define genius. Some believe it to be no more than "an infinite capacity for taking pains"; others, like Lombroso, aver that it borders on insanity or is a matter of heredity. The fascination of the subject lies in the fact that any approach to it leads to interesting, if futile, speculations. Of course, not all great men have been of unstable nature, but the fact remains that all too frequently geniuses have had to contend with physical, nervous, or mental anomalies of one kind or another. The sketches following have been chosen to illustrate that the superlatively talented in any field of endeavor may time and again be held in check by seemingly insurmountable physical burdens, only to find in them the challenge to greater efforts, even though in some cases the burden ultimately proved too great for human endurance.

Each day following this introduction, beginning with April 24, featured a brief biographical sketch of historical geniuses listed alphabetically, many of whom suffered either physical or mental maladies, including frequent listings of insanity. The list of geniuses included most of the literary heroes from my father's youth. A partial naming from the calendar: Baudelaire, Dostoyevsky, Flaubert, Guy de Maupassant, Napoleon Bonaparte, Nero, Nietzsche, Peter I (the Great), Poe, Richard Porson, Rousseau, Schopenhauer, A. C. Swinburne, Tchaikovsky, van Gogh, Paul Verlaine, and François Villon.

Handprinted by my father was the entry:

Poisons: 402 et seq.

This page read:

## Symptoms and Treatments of Poisoning

Unless otherwise stated, oral poisoning is to be understood.
The *lethal* dose — taken in a single dose — is of course an indefinite figure. It is to be understood that smaller doses have been taken with lethal effect, while larger quantities have not proved fatal.

The following pages provided a chart of most of the known poisons, listing each one's lethal dosage, symptoms, and treatment.

All the following were dated entries in my mother's handwriting:

November 7, 1943 — Seaman School. Gelka Scheyer for Children's pictures.
November 8, 1943 — George 10–11 am 727 [Presumably this notation refers to Father's downtown office address, which was 727 W. 7th St.]
November 9, 1943 — George 7–10:30 pm Eye lecture Gen. Hosp
November 11, 1943 — George 2–6 pm Heart [Presumably four hours set aside for testing and examination by specialist relating to George's heart condition.]
November 11, 1943 — 8–11pm Calif Club
November 12, 1943 — 12–2 Committee Meeting Chamber of Commerce
November 13, 1943 — KFI–Syphilis Show

Two of the last three entries are important because they reveal that Father was associated with both the prestigious California Club, originally established by the Chandler dynasty, and its offshoot, the L.A. Chamber of Commerce. The back-to-back meetings are of particular interest, because they show Father's close connection to some of the most influential men in Los Angeles at the time, the men who were running the city.

As for the final entry, KFI was the NBC outlet in Los Angeles. Mother, in conjunction with Bob Purcell, David Eli Janison, Karl Schlichter, and producer Jack Edwards, wrote a series of radio dramas called *13 Against Syphilis: The Unseen Enemy*, which were sponsored by city, county, and state public health departments in an effort to "disperse the fog of ignorance" surrounding venereal disease. Because of his position as the Los Angeles County Health Department's venereal disease control officer, Father served as technical adviser to the show.

I believe both the bill of lading and the 1943 calendar I discovered in the basement of the Franklin House in 1999 are valuable pieces of evidence. The former establishes that Dad's Chinese artifacts, his spoils of postwar Hankow, arrived in mid-October 1946. The latter establishes Dad's 1943 interest in the lethal dosage of numerous poisons. It also demonstrates his fascination with genius and his need to satisfy himself that many men of genius led troubled and dysfunctional lives and tortured themselves emotionally, often to the point of violence either upon themselves or others. There is also independent verification of Father's serious heart condition.

When I moved back to Los Angeles in July 2001, I saw an article in the Sunday, July 8 edition of the *Los Angeles Times*, featuring the Franklin House as the "Home of the Week," on sale for $1.5 million. The house was on the market. So I made another appointment with Bill Buck for a final conversation and some more photographs.

When we met, I explained to Buck that I was writing a book about my father that dealt with his mysterious past, adding that my research over the past two years had connected him to some Hollywood underworld figures from the 1920s through the 1940s.

Although Buck had no information regarding the connections of previous owners of the house to any underworld crime cartels in Los Angeles, I did get a chance to take photographs of the secret room, the light fixture in the den, and Father's shipping crate from China, which was still in the basement.

Buck also told me that our fathers had known each other, at least professionally, because both were prominent medical doctors in Los Angeles. They had met at the Franklin House back in the 1940s when Dad called a meeting of a group of six physicians in connection with the L.A. County Department of Community Health. Buck said, "As my father described it to me, after the meeting was over, your father clapped his hands loudly and out came these two geisha girls dressed in full regalia. I guess it was 'party time' or whatever. My father nervously looked at his watch, thanked your dad, and promptly left. I guess some of the other physicians stayed."

Buck said that after his father bought Franklin House from my father, he found some pornography and pictures of naked women hidden there. "It was about a year after he had moved into the place," Buck said, which would have made it 1951 or 1952. "He was changing some light bulbs over that glass fixture above the fireplace and discovered a box wedged and hidden in a far corner. He brought it down and it contained what he called 'kinky pictures.' I'm pretty sure he destroyed them."

Another strange incident: Buck told me about the appearance of a "bag lady" who came to the door back in the 1970s or early '80s. "She looked quite old," he said, "but with street people it's hard to tell." I spoke with her and she said, 'This house is a place of evil.' " He said that normally he would have simply dismissed her, but then she continued to describe the interior of the house. "It was very scary," he said. "She obviously had been inside this place before we owned it. She described in detail to me: the great stone fireplace, and your father's gold bedroom, and the all-red kitchen that your father had painted. No question that she was very familiar with the house when your dad had lived here. She looked at me and said again, 'This is a house of evil.' God knows what connection she had with this place. She left, and I never saw or heard from her again."

Based on a conversation I had with former tenant Joe Barrett, it is my belief that the person Buck described as a "bag lady" was most probably our former maid, Ellen Taylor, Father's live-in house-maid/girlfriend, who lived at Franklin House from 1945 to 1950. In later years, Joe Barrett had run into Ellen on the street in downtown Los Angeles and discovered that she had been in and out of mental hospitals. Joe Barrett described her as "living on the fringe, delusional, claiming she had had affairs with a number of prominent and locally famous personages." (Knowing what we now know, perhaps Ellen was not as delusional as Barrett thought.)

Bill Buck also told me that another man who had visited the house on three different occasions over the years was a photographer named Edmund Teske, "a local photographer and sort of a fixture here in old Hollywood. He had a home just down the street on Hollywood Boulevard. He visited here three separate times over the years and told me he was a good friend of both your father and Man Ray."*

The overhead fixture where Dad's photographs had been hidden and obviously not discovered during LAPD Juvenile detectives' 1949 search of the house after Father's arrest but only a year or two after his departure would most likely have included Man Ray's nude studies of my then thirteen-year-old sister Tamar as well as other damning photographic evidence.

I thanked Bill Buck for his openness and many courtesies over the years and left the Franklin House in what I fully expect was my final visit. I exited the massive stone structure and paused near the top of the steps in the same spot where I had, as a naive and innocent boy of eight, smoked my first cigarette with Tamar and been caught by Father. I turned and gazed one last time at this Mayan temple, which for me had now been transformed into a haunted house of horror, and in a final reflection paused to wonder how many other unsolved mysteries would forever remain buried in the belly of this beast.

*Teske would in later years become a highly acclaimed L.A. photographer. He was dubbed a romantic surrealist, and some of his works are currently on display locally, in the J. Paul Getty Museum.

# 21

# The Watch, the Proof-Sheet Papers, the FBI Files, and the Voice

## The Dahlia Military Watch

*Exhibits 43a and 43b*

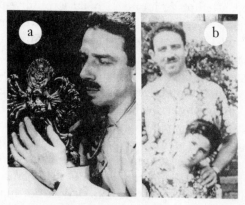

*George Hodel watches, (a) 1946 and (b) 1947*

The 1946 Man Ray photograph of my father embracing Yamantaka (exhibit 43a) reveals what appears to be a black-face military watch, commonly worn by officers during the war years, on Father's left wrist. As we know, George Hodel loved to portray himself as a military officer, displaying the power and prestige associated with his three-star rank. His officer's watch was another accessory of his former status, and he treasured it. We know that this photograph was taken by Man Ray, after father's return from China, most likely after his Yamantaka statue arrived in mid-October 1946. This means he was wearing the military watch just weeks before Elizabeth's murder.

In 43b, Father is posing in a family picture probably in the spring or summer of 1947, but in any event shortly *after* the Elizabeth Short murder. On his left hand, resting on my brother Kelvin's shoulder, he is wearing a different wristwatch, this one with a white face.

We know that "50 LAPD recruits" in their re-canvass and search of the 39th and Norton crime scene on January 19, 1947, found a "man's military-type wristwatch on the vacant lot close to where the victim's body was originally discovered." The watch discovered at the crime scene was "a military-style 17-jewel 'Croton' with a leather-bound, steel snap band. Engraved on it are the words 'Swiss made, water proof, brevet, stainless steel back.'" There was no further mention in the press concerning police efforts to locate the owner of the watch.

To date, my attempts to locate a similar Croton watch for comparison to the one described in the article have proved futile. In 1946 the Croton Watch Company was located on 48th Street in New York City, but apparently the company is no longer in business. Other than the one newspaper article referring to the police finding the watch, I have found no other references. This would be considered extremely important physical evidence in the crime, and normal police procedure would be to photograph the item, contact the manufacturer, and attempt to identify and trace the item through potential witnesses. That no further information or follow-up were forthcoming is of serious concern. Apparently LAPD made no public appeal for assistance in helping identify the item. It does not appear that any special police bulletin was prepared or circulated within the confines of the local law enforcement agencies throughout Southern California.

Based on Father's apparent loss of his military-style watch matching the description of the Dahlia watch found at the crime scene, and his simultaneous documented wearing of a new watch, there is a strong possibility that it was Father's watch found near the body.

Moreover, the watch in the Man Ray photograph did not turn up among my father's possessions after his death. It simply disappeared, possibly at the 39th and Norton Black Dahlia crime scene. Does this watch still remain hidden in a secure LAPD evidence vault, awaiting inspection and identification?

## The Proof-Sheet Papers

We know that LAPD's chief criminalist, Ray Pinker, forensically examined "proof-sheet paper" in the murder case of Otto Parzyjegla and compared them to the proof-sheet paper sent to the newspapers by the Black Dahlia Avenger. Parzyjegla's papers were eliminated as not being the same.

In January 1947, my father did have a printing press in the basement of the Franklin House. It was the same press he had had since his teens when he printed the first edition of *Fantasia* in January 1925. He also had proof-sheet paper of a size and type similar to those mailed in by the Dahlia suspect in January 1947, a sample of which I possess because he returned to me my original childhood drawings in 1995. Specifically, exhibit 44, the "Chinese Chicken" I drew and Father subsequently inscribed "Steven April 1949," was from that stock.

*Exhibit 44*

*"Chinese Chicken–Mountains–Sun"*

A second sample of this proof-sheet paper came into my possession from an original sales brochure Father designed and printed in late 1949 or early 1950, in connection with his marketing of the Franklin House.

Both samples should be considered potential physical evidence, and while the possibility exists, because two years had elapsed between the Dahlia murder and my father's writing on my drawing and his sales brochure, that they may not be from the same stock as the Dahlia proof sheets, a chemical and spectrographic analysis and comparison of my original copies could verify whether the stock is identical or similar. The state of the art is much advanced, and I believe the comparison would be conclusive. I suspect the pasted evidence notes retained in police custody are identical to Father's proof stock and could possibly match the Avenger notes in size, shape, and fiber content. LAPD booked into evidence these original notes mailed to the papers by the Black Dahlia Avenger. Those original proof-sheet notes correspond to our exhibit numbers 20, 21, 22, 24, 25, 30, and 31. These original pasted notes should still exist in police custody in the evidence lockers, because any destruction of physical evidence known to have been connected to the LAPD's most notorious unsolved murder case would have to have been deliberate. The destruction or "accidental loss" of evidence would tend to further substantiate a cover-up to protect the perpetrator(s) of the Dahlia and French murders.

## The FBI Files

As I had for Elizabeth Short, I requested via the Freedom of Information Act any and all available information on my father. It was a slow process, but eventually I received the following information from the FBI.

No investigation has been conducted by the FBI concerning the captioned individual (George Hill Hodel) or his father. However, our files reflect the following information, which possibly relates to captioned individual.

I. A confidential informant of unknown reliability advised in October, 1924, that [redacted] . . . was a member of The Severance Club. The informant described The Severance Club as being composed of the leading "Parlor Bolsheviks" and "Pinks" of Pasadena, Los Angeles, and Hollywood, California, and its membership was limited in the club members' own language to "The Cream of the Intellectual Radicals."

II. During May, 1947, one George Hodel, 5121 Franklin Avenue, Hollywood, California, was in contact with the Soviet Embassy, Washington, D.C., concerning the "Information Bulletin" of the U.S.S.R.

The FBI further indicated that they were withholding from release two additional pages that related to an inquiry dated October 8, 1956, from an unnamed agency related to George Hodel.

Based on the timing of the 1956 inquiry, I suspect it may have simply been a routine background check from the Manila office of the Department of Defense or possibly the United States Information Agency, both of whom Father had contracted with to perform market research. Of primary interest, however, is Father's timely and clandestine inquiry to the Soviet Union, shortly after the murder of Elizabeth Short.

Though the killers' taunting note to the press on January 29, 1947, stated that they were leaving the country for Mexico, it is possible that Father was also considering seeking a safe haven in the country of his family's beginnings — Russia.

The Department of Justice FBI file on "Elizabeth Ann Short, The Black Dahlia" contains almost two hundred pages of previously classified material. Included in these files is the important interview their agents conducted with "Sergeant Doe," who dated and dined with Elizabeth Short in late September 1946 and then spent the night with her at the Figueroa Hotel.

Her dossier contains other important and hitherto unknown investigative facts:

People were led to believe from local newspaper reports and police statements in the days immediately following Short's murder that no fingerprints of the suspect existed because (a) the suspect in mailing

Elizabeth Short's personal effects to the press "soaked the materials in gasoline," and (b) while fingerprints were found on the notes, "they belonged to postal inspectors who touched the materials."

The FOIA documents I received clearly establish that the FBI possessed four readable fingerprints, obtained from one or more of the suspect notes, and that they were actively comparing these original prints to potential suspects as late as 1949. Due to redaction of individual suspect(s) they cannot be identified by name. Regarding the suspect fingerprints, Special Agent Hood of the FBI's Los Angeles office said in a letter to the Bureau's Fingerprint Section in Washington, D.C.:

January 31, 1947

Director, FBI

Re: Elizabeth Short

Dear Sir:

There are enclosed herewith three photographs of fingerprints removed from an anonymous letter addressed to the Los Angeles Police Department concerning the mutilation murder of ELIZABETH SHORT. It is requested that these prints be checked through the single Fingerprint Section and if an identification is made that this office be notified by teletype immediately. In the event an identification is not made from these prints, it is requested that same be retained in the Single Fingerprint Section for possible future identification.

> Very Truly yours,
> P. B. Hood (Special Agent, Los Angeles)

The Bureau's Washington Fingerprint Section responded to Agent Hood in Los Angeles on February 15, 1947.

Reference is made to your letter of January 31, 1947, submitting three photographs of latent fingerprints for examination in connection with the above entitled matter, your file #62-2928. You are

*Left:* Esther Leov Hodel, George Hodel's mother and the author's grandmother, circa 1912.

*Below:* This Hodel family photograph was taken circa 1917 at the Hodel residence in South Pasadena. It depicts composer Sergei Rachmaninov seated between the Russian minister of culture and his wife (possibly the Zelenkos).

BOY OF NINE CHIEF
SOLOIST AT SHRINE
HOLIDAY EXERCISES

George Hodel, young musician who will perform at Fall of Bastile celebration

George Hodel, age nine. Photograph from the *Los Angeles Evening Herald* of July 17, 1917. George, a musical prodigy, was selected to play a piano concert at the L.A. Shrine Auditorium in honor of Bastille Day.

Dorothy Harvey Huston and John Huston arriving in Los Angeles, circa 1926, shortly after their marriage. They are being met at the train by John's father, Walter Huston *(left)*.

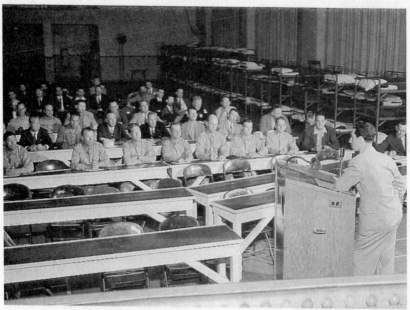

This remarkable photograph, dated July 29, 1942, was discovered by the author in 2002. Dr. George Hill Hodel lectures police recruits and vice detectives at the Los Angeles Police Academy on the newly enacted "May Act," which temporarily established prostitution as a federal offense. Though his son was an LAPD officer for nearly twenty-four years, Dr. Hodel never mentioned the fact that he had once lectured to police officers, obviously at the request and invitation of the department brass.
*(Photograph courtesy of the Department of Special Collections, Charles E. Young Research Library, UCLA)*

Dorothy Harvey Hodel, circa 1943, in front of the Valentine Street home, with her two sons, Steven *(left)* and Kelvin.

Dorothy Hodel, in the courtyard of the Franklin House, circa 1946–47.

"The Three Musketeers," Franklin House, circa 1948.
*From left to right:* Steven, Michael, and Kelvin.

Dr. George Hill Hodel in the living room of the Franklin House,
in early 1950, just months before he left the United States.

Joe Barrett, U.S. Navy, circa 1945. From 1948 to 1950, he was a boarder in the Franklin House, and privy to many of its secrets.

The author, age 18.
Photograph taken in Manila, Philippines, while he was visiting his father from his naval base in Subic Bay.

Rookie LAPD officer Steve Hodel and Chief Thad Brown, 1966. Why would the chief insist on having his picture taken with the raw rookie? This photograph would later prove to be an important clue in the Black Dahlia investigation.

LAPD Detective II Steve
Hodel, Hollywood
Division, 1983.

Tamar Hodel, the author's half-sister, circa 2000. Her
information would unwittingly play a major role in
helping the author solve the Black Dahlia and
other Los Angeles area murders.

Los Angeles County Head Deputy District Attorney Stephen R. Kay. Kay has prosecuted many of Los Angeles's most notorious murderers, most notably Charles Manson and the rest of the Manson Family.
*(Photograph courtesy of David Fairchild Studio)*

Silhouette of George and June Hodel, taken by the author in 1998 from their 38th-floor, penthouse suite in downtown San Francisco.

advised that the four latent fingerprints appearing in the photographs were searched through the single fingerprint file, but no identifications were effected. The photographs are being retained for any future comparisons, which might be desired.

Documents reveal that fingerprint comparisons were being conducted as late as January 19, 1949, which means that these unidentified prints were not those of the postal inspectors, whose prints would already have been on file. Whether these were actual suspect prints or not and whether they yet remain in existence for comparison is not known.

The file also contains extensive memorandums between LAPD and the FBI verifying that they were in fact looking for a suspect with surgical knowledge. LAPD obtained the names of three hundred students from the University of Southern California Medical School, and requested they all be compared by the FBI against the lifts obtained from Avenger notes. LAPD further advised the Bureau that their own experts were in the process of conducting handwriting comparisons of some of these students to Avenger notes. Additional memorandums from J. Edgar Hoover show that he was attempting to utilize the high-profile status of the Black Dahlia case as a means of accessing Social Security Administration files on private citizens. His request to SSA to obtain information on Elizabeth Short's associates was denied. The director of SSA reminded Hoover that the files on private citizens were sacrosanct, the only exception being wartime, where the national security was at risk.

## The Voice

*Los Angeles Examiner* city editor James Richardson was the only person ever to hear the voice of the person who identified himself as Elizabeth Short's killer. He described the voice as that "of an egomaniac, that had a soft sly sound I will never forget."

After the intense interest in the Dahlia case had faded away, Richardson said it was still his dream and hope that one day the Dahlia killer would pick up the telephone, dial his city desk number, and again ask for him.

That never happened, but from the description of other people who heard a voice that matched Richardson's description, I believe it is one that I know very well — my father's educated and professionally trained voice.

Various witnesses in separate crimes have described the killer's voice as "suave and cultured." Even in his youth, his colleagues and friends had mentioned the distinctiveness of his voice when they were describing him to the drama critic Ted Le Berthon, who wrote the 1925 "Clouded Past of a Poet" article in the *Evening Herald*. What had they told Le Berthon?

"It's not George's gloom, his preference for Huysmanns, De Gourmont, Poe, Baudelaire, Verlaine, and Hecht that pains us," these friends said, "but his stilted elegance, his meticulous speech!" Le Berthon himself commented on "the voice" later in the same article, a voice that due to its distinctiveness, allowed him to recognize the speaker even before he turned and saw Father in his taxi uniform.

Knowing my father's voice, from its resonance at the Franklin House dinner table, from his authoritative manner in his executive offices in Manila, and even during his final years in San Francisco, I can recognize both Le Berthon's and Richardson's descriptions as being more than just reminiscent of how my father sounded. They and I heard the same voice.

# 22

# Handwriting Analysis

DURING THE COURSE OF MY INVESTIGATION I recognized my father's unique handwriting on two separate occasions, the first being on the promise-to-surrender note. The original note mailed to the press from downtown Los Angeles on January 26, 1947, by the Black Dahlia Avenger (as seen on page 169 as exhibit 18) was confirmed by LAPD as having been written using a new, expensive, and at the time, relatively uncommon writing instrument, a ballpoint pen. In that note, the suspect promised he would surrender to the police three days later.

I recognized this undisguised handwriting as my father's unique style of printing, and I here formally and unequivocally identify that printing as his.

Unlike some of the other notes mailed to the police and the press, in this note the killer made no attempt to distort or conceal his handwriting. I suspect that, at the time he wrote it, he fully intended to turn himself in, until at the last moment he reversed his decision. In the later notes, where he attempted to barter and "make a deal" with the police, he disguised his handwriting.

Returning to his early days as a journalist, he sent several headline-like messages to the papers such as: "Dahlia's Killer Cracking, Wants Terms."

The second time I recognized Father's handwriting was when I saw it written in lipstick across the naked body of Jeanne French, in a photo published for the first time in LAPD homicide detective Huddleston's morbid collection, *Death Scenes*. Although I was sure it was my father's handwriting in both instances, I still needed independent

corroboration — solid physical evidence clearly connecting Father
to both the killings.

As an associate member of the Washington Association of Criminal Defense Lawyers in Seattle, I contacted them for a referral to a
handwriting expert. They recommended Ms. Hannah McFarland, a
member of both the National Association of Document Examiners
and the American Handwriting Analysis Foundation. I learned she
was highly skilled in both questioned-document examination relating to authenticity and authorship, and graphology relating to
personality evaluation. Her experience included the analysis of hundreds of handwriting documents, and she had testified and was an accepted, certified expert before Washington state courts.

In engaging Ms. McFarland, I did not reveal to her, nor did she
know, the connections between, or the names of, any victims. Nor
did she know the name of the suspect or his connection to me. All
she knew was that the crime had occurred during the mid-1940s
somewhere in California and that it involved the suspect writing on
the body of the victim using lipstick. I did not inform her that the
samples were from two separate crimes. I did not tell her that some
of the documents had been previously analyzed by questioned-
document experts at the time of the crimes. I wanted her opinions to
stand alone.

I asked Ms. McFarland to compare and analyze some known
handwriting documents to the questioned documents. These included
several of the notes mailed to the press, as well as a portion of the
death-scene photograph showing the printed letters on the body:
"FUCK YOU, B.D."

In the samples I submitted to her, all the "Black Dahlia Avenger"
signatures were excluded, to avoid identifying the specific crime.
There were enough writing samples on the many notes to make a
comparison to known samples without having to identify the actual
cases. The known samples came from a range of Father's handwrit-
ing/handprinting spanning almost seventy-five years, including
examples from the years 1924, 1943, 1949, 1953, 1974, 1997, and
1998. I also asked Ms. McFarland to simplify the terminology of her
technical analysis and present her information and findings in layman's language.

I presented her with nine "knowns" (K) and nine "questioned

documents" (Q), all of which she examined and microscopically compared. The questioned documents were first compared to each other in an attempt to determine if the same writer wrote them. Then they were cross-compared to all the known documents. Sample K-10 is also included, and will be discussed after the analysis is presented.

## The Knowns

K-1  Handwritten notes prepared by George Hodel 10/15/98 for "conference" with his wife, "JH," in preparation for his contemplated suicide. The "conference" never took place; however, the note was found with his personal papers after his death.

K-2  "DAD," printed signature, signed and mailed to me in 1997.

K-3  "Love To Dorero, December, 1974."

K-4  "Love and Aloha To Father and Alice, Honolulu, 9/25/53."

K-5  "Chinese Chicken" drawing, handwriting by George Hodel, April 1949.

K-6  Handwriting of George Hodel written in 1943, medical calendar book: "Genius and Disease," "Poisons," etc.

K-7  Handwriting of George Hodel written in 1924 on the back of a self-portrait photograph, "portrait of a chap suddenly aware of the words of Sigmund Freud."

K-8  Handwriting of George Hodel written in 1924 on the back of a self-portrait photograph, "Merlin gazes at cracked mirrors."

K-9  Enlargement of sample K-5, focusing on Father's writing of the name "STEVEN" (1949).

## The Questioned Documents (all samples are from the year 1947)

Q-1  Postcard mailed to *Los Angeles Examiner* (reverse — addressed side of Q-5).

Q-2  Postcard mailed to *Herald Express*.

Q-3     Postcard mailed to *Herald Express* (reverse-addressed side of
        Q-2).
Q-4     Postcard mailed to *Herald Express*.
Q-5     Postcard mailed to *Los Angeles Examiner* promising to sur-
        render on Jan. 29.
Q-6     Postcard mailed to L.A. press.
Q-7     Postcard mailed to *Herald Express*.
Q-8     "FUCK YOU, B.D." written in lipstick on body of victim
        Jeanne French.
Q-9     Postcard addressed to *Herald Express*.

In her letter of April 6, 2000, Hannah McFarland detailed the comparisons.

### RE: Handwriting Examination

Dear Mr. Hodel:

You have advised me that the printing on nine scanned computer
prints is under investigation regarding authorship. You informed
me that all of these printing samples hereinafter referred to as Q1
through Q9, were originally printed on paper, except for Q8 which
was printed on a human body using lipstick. These printing samples
were represented to me as having been authored in 1947.

### Exemplars (Knowns)
For the purpose of comparison, I have examined eight printing
samples on scanned computer prints, which were represented to
me as being of known authorship. These exemplars are hereinafter
referred to as K1 through K8. The dates of these exemplars range
from 1924 to 1998.

### Assignment
You have requested an evaluation of Q1 through Q8 in an attempt
to determine if they had been printed by the same printer of K1
through K8.

## Findings from Examination

After careful detailed study I have formed opinions regarding the printing in question. My opinion is expressed without bias or liability in so far as legal action is concerned.

The unique printing features in the following questioned printing samples are compellingly present in the known printing. I identified 4 individual characteristics that are present in the Known and Questioned samples. Individual characteristics are evident in the letters B, O, D, S, E & P. There are no unexplainable differences between the Known and Questioned samples. Therefore, it is my opinion that it is highly probable that the printer of Q8 (the printing on the body) also authored the printing of K1 through K8. Also, I think it is highly probable that the printer of Q2, Q4, Q7, and Q9 printed K1 through K8.

There is an indication that the printer of Q3 & Q6 could have authored the known printing, but the evidence falls far short of a stronger opinion. My opinion regarding authorship of Q1 and Q5 is inconclusive due to a lack of identifying characteristics in these samples.

Please contact me if you need additional information regarding my conclusions.

Sincerely,
Hannah McFarland

Simply put, after carefully comparing all of the known and questioned handwriting samples, Ms. McFarland arrived at the expert opinion that it is highly probable the same person who wrote at least four of the postcards in the Black Dahlia case also wrote the lipstick message "FUCK YOU B.D." on the body of Jeanne French, and that person is the same person who wrote all ten of the known handwriting samples submitted. Her analysis, independent and confidential from my own identification of my father's handwriting, forensically substantiates that Dr. George Hill Hodel in fact wrote the messages mailed to the press in the murder of Elizabeth Short and also the taunting message on the body of Jeanne French.

In making her authorship identification, Ms. McFarland used the term "highly probable" because, she explained, "absent the examination

of the actual original documents, due to having to work with photo-
copies and scans, which would allow for the possibility of cut and paste,
and alterations, it is standard practice that a positive opinion cannot be
given." Her "highly probable" finding, she said, is the same as her being "virtually certain that the questioned and known writings were
written by the same person." Her opinion was based on my assurance
to her that the submitted samples represented accurate copies of the
originals, and that none of the documents presented for comparison
were altered, cross-scanned, or tampered with in any fashion.

Here are the document samples and examples that Ms. McFarland prepared for her examination along with her written explanation of the separate documents. I believe it proves to a legal standard
the specific points of identification and unique characteristics that
identify George Hodel as the author of the writings, calling himself
the "Black Dahlia Avenger."

As requested, Hannah McFarland provided me with the following summarized verbatim report of her analysis in lay language:

Handwriting identification (or in this case printing) is done by
identifying the unique features in a sample of writing or printing,
and then seeing if the individual characteristics appear in both
known and questioned printing. If the same individual characteristics are seen in both known and questioned printing, and there are
no unexplainable differences, then it is likely that they were executed by the same person.

Below is a reproduction enlargement of Q8, the questioned
printing sample written on a human body in 1947. It reads, "FU . .
YOU BD." Two letters in the first word are not readable. There are
3 individual characteristics in this printing sample:

1) The letter "O" in "YOU" slants dramatically to the left,
   whereas, the other letters are vertical or slant slightly to the left.
2) The letter "B" is open at the bottom.
3) The letter "D" has unusually long horizontal strokes that start
   and end far to the left.

Below are two enlarged samples of printing known to be
printed by the murder suspect. K5 was a sample written by the

suspect in 1949, and K6 was a sample written by him in 1943. It is preferable, when possible, to compare known and questioned printing (such as these) that were printed within a few years of each other. Both known printing samples (K5 & K6) show the unusual "O" that slants to the left.

### Exhibit 45

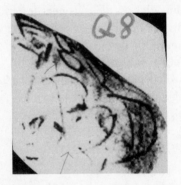

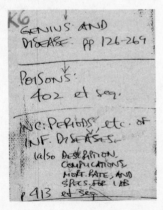

A person's handwriting can change over time. This is why it is best to compare known samples of writing that are current with the questioned handwriting.

The known samples below were printed 50 + years *after* the questioned printing samples. In spite of the passage of time, all 3 individual characteristics shown in the questioned printing are seen in K1. The shaky strokes of the printing are due to age, or possibly infirmity, as I am told the printer was 91 years old when he wrote K1.

In spite of time, the loss of his manual dexterity, all 3 individual characteristics are seen in this sample and are relevant in identifying him as the author of the questioned printing.

The K2 sample was printed only one year prior to the K1 sample, and clearly demonstrates his use of the unusual "D." The author still had good motor control as seen in the smooth strokes.

### Exhibit 46

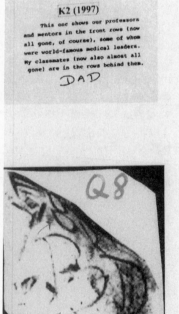

After having formed the opinion that it was highly probable that the printing on the body, referred to as Q8, was printed by the suspect, who is known to have printed K1, K2, K5, and K6, I was then asked to investigate if any of the other Questioned printing samples related to the murder investigation had been printed by the suspect. Because I had concluded that Q8 was most likely printed by the suspect, I could then use Q8 as additional material for comparison, along with the Known printing, to determine if other Questioned printing had been printed by the suspect.

Below is a Questioned printing sample hereinafter referred to as Q2. I concluded that it was highly probable that the same person who printed Q8, K1, K2,& K5, printed Q2. The "B" at the end of Q2 is open on the bottom as is the case with the "B" in Q8 and on the second and eleventh lines of K1.

Microscopic examination and enlargement of the "O" in "NOT" from the third line of Q2 revealed that the letter slants to the left. This matches the "O" in "YOU" in Q8. The similarity of the "O" in Q2 to the highly unusual "O" in Q8 is very significant. This "O" is also seen in K1, K5, and K6. (K1 is shown below. K5 & K6 may be seen in the following illustrations.)

Another individual characteristic, though not as significant as the "B" or "O," is the "S" in "SAID" in the sixth line of Q2. The middle portion of the letter is straight, forming an angle on each end of the straight stroke. This "S" is also seen in K1, K5, K6, as well as Q7 and Q9, which follow.

Due to the presence of the unusual "O" and "B" present in both the Questioned and Known samples, and the "S" I concluded that it was highly probable that Q2 was printed by the same writer as Q8 and the printer of the Known samples, who is the suspect.

The use of the initials "B.D." that Q2 and Q8 have in common would be significant for identification purposes, except that the initials had been publicized. Due to the possibility of a copycat, the common initials are not significant in this comparison.

*Exhibit 47*

The printing on Q7 was most likely printed by the same person who printed Q8 and the known printing samples. The letter "P" in "Express" from Q7 has long horizontal strokes that start and end to the left of the body of the letter.

The letter "D" in "BD" on Q8 has the same long horizontal strokes. This unusual "D" (that is similar to the "P") is also present in K1 & K2, which were shown in the previous illustrations.

Of secondary significance in identifying the author of Q7, are the two "S's" at the end of "Express." The middle portion of the two "S's" is straight and thus forms a soft angle at each end of the straight line. This is also seen in the samples of the letter "S" in K1, K5, K6 (below), Q2, (shown previously) and Q9 (which will be shown next).

### Exhibit 48

I formed the opinion that the printing sample referred to as Q9 was most likely printed by the same person who printed Q8, Q7, Q2, and the Known printing samples.

The "O" in "Los Angeles" in Q9 slants to the left which matches the "O" on Q8, Q2, and the Known printing as well (shown in previous illustrations).

The "S's" in Q9 tend to be straight in the middle portion of the letter, forming angles (some of them soft) at one or both ends of the straight stroke. This is similar to the "s's" seen in Q7 as well as Q2 and the Known printing samples (shown in previous illustrations). The final stroke of the letter "s" is extra long in Q9 & Q7, making for a stronger identification between these two printing samples.

The "E" in "Express" in Q9 has unusual horizontal strokes. The top horizontal stroke is far to the left, the middle horizontal stroke is slightly to the left of the downstroke. The same pattern is reflected on the right side of the "E" as well. This unusual pattern in the "E" on Q9 is also seen in "Express" in Q7. Because Q7 has been linked (by different handwriting indications) to Q8 and the Known printing, the connections ("S's" and "E" in "Express") between K7 and K9 provide an indirect, yet significant additional link between Q9 and the Known printing.

The overall appearance of the printing in Q2, Q7 and Q9 looks disguised. Handwriting that is natural (undisguised) usually has a smooth, spontaneous flow, which reflects the unconscious nature of normal handwriting. The printing in Q2, Q7 and Q9 is slowly drawn because the writer is carefully thinking of how to make each letter. Other additional attempts at disguise are evident in Q2 by the poor sentence construction and misspelling of the word "Hearld." The wavy baseline may also be an attempt at disguise in these Questioned samples.

The presence of the individual identifying characteristics shown in these samples in spite of the author's attempt at disguise, vividly illustrates the unconscious nature of handwriting and printing.

Another interesting feature about this case is the presence of the individual characteristics evident over a long period of time. A person's handwriting can change over time. But this writer, the suspect, in this case retained his identifying traits over a period of fifty years.

## Exhibit 49

## Exhibit 50

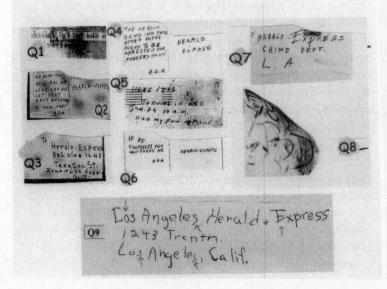

*Questioned document samples Q1–Q9*

After independently verifying that the handwriting in both murders did originate from my father, I asked Ms. McFarland to evaluate the character and personality of the writer.

As before, she was provided no background or personal information of any kind relating to the author of the samples.

## HANDWRITING CHARACTER ANALYSIS FOR STEVE HODEL
### APRIL 25, 2000

The printing samples I examined, dated from 1924 to 1998, indicate that this printer is highly intelligent. With lightning speed, this printer zeros in on the essentials of a matter. Digesting new information comes easily for him. New information does not need to be explained in detail to this printer, since he does well and prefers to figure things out on his own. He excels at problem solving and derives considerable satisfaction from using his mind. His mind is so fast and agile that he readily anticipates several moves ahead. He is a shrewd strategist. This printer is adept at juggling several different projects at once and adjusts easily to changing conditions.

This printer is impatient for results and is therefore not one to stand back waiting for things to develop. He prefers fast action and does not waste time in reaching his goals. I expect that he understands the importance of details but does not like to get bogged down in them due to being eager to move on to the next step.

There are indications that this printer has highly developed tastes and is visually sophisticated.

In dealing with people, this printer can easily be all things to all people if it suits his purpose. Though if someone is slow to catch on and is not essential for his success, then this printer is inclined to be short and dismissive with another person. He does not suffer fools gladly, nor does he like to be told what to do.

I expect that this printer's mother or mother figure was emotionally distant due to neglect, stress, illness, accident, or death. The nurturing he received lacked warmth, so that he was not able to properly bond with his mother or main caretaker. This disturbance in the original mother-child bond has resulted in him currently having considerable difficulty in developing close relationships with other people, even though he may function well in casual social settings. He is always aware of the amount of distance between himself and other people.

This printer knows he has superior intelligence and taste. Consequently, he has a desire to leave his mark. Beneath this exterior of sophistication though, he is not nearly as secure or invulnerable. He takes things more personally than he lets on about. He comes off as cool and objective but is more sensitive than he appears.

Because I had not had an occasion to use graphology as an investigative tool during my career as a homicide detective, I sent the following reply:

April 27, 2000

Dear Hannah:

Thanks for the report on the character analysis, which I received yesterday.

Forgive my ignorance on the subject, as this is the first time I have ever required a character analysis from handwriting. Can you tell me if these analyses are readily accepted in the main?

I guess my question really relates and attempts to address the question for potential subjective analysis through what is written, versus how it is written.

By example, in your analysis, is the "high intelligence" revealed through his manner of writing or through what is written? Such as the known sample that reads "portrait of a chap suddenly aware of the words of Sigmund Freud." I would not expect that sentence to be written by a plumber in Sedro Woolley, although one never really knows!

Guess my real question is: Is the source of this analysis strictly coming from the actual mechanics of the writer as opposed to any extraneous outside knowledge or information that might be gleaned from the wording and text of the sample?

Regards,
Steve Hodel
Hodel Investigations

To which she responded:

To: Steve Hodel
From: Hannah McFarland
Date: May 6, 2000

Dear Steve:

Following is my response to your questions.

You want to know if these analyses (personality assessments) are readily "accepted" in the main. That is a thorny question. If you talk with academic psychologists, they will tend to be skeptical of handwriting analysis. Even though handwriting analysis was developed in the psychology departments at universities in Europe and the U.S., few psychologists are aware of this. Also, most psychologists know nothing about handwriting analysis, so are thus speaking out of ignorance, when they criticize it.

The general public has an entirely different view of handwriting analysis. Many people are quite receptive to it, and many people are very interested in it. High profile cases (such as the Jon Benet Ramsey case) involving handwriting have been in the news lately, which has brought much more exposure and awareness about handwriting.

Even though personality assessment via handwriting (HW) also known as graphology is a different discipline from questioned document examination (determining authorship) the public does not differentiate between the two. So, even though the Ramsey case is primarily about who wrote the "ransom" letter, it has also stimulated considerable interest in graphology (personality assessment).

6,000 U.S. businesses are using graphology as part of the hiring process, according to Inc. magazine. In spite of the lack of conventional psychology's blessing, corporate America has found it to be accurate.

One reason why graphology has yet to achieve mainstream acceptance, is that there is not a standard licensing available. Anyone can claim to be an "expert" graphologist. Thus there are plenty of amateur types promoting themselves as professional. Their work is inferior as a result and does not improve the reputation of graphology.

I hope the above makes sense to you, Steve. It's a complicated topic! Your next question was about the source of the analysis. My report was based on the HW only. Knowing that the printer had committed murder, I could have been inclined to write that he was prone to violence. I did not see a lot of signs of propensity toward violence in the printing, so did not report that. The intelligence is seen in the printing, not the content of what is written.

If you desire, I could also write an explanation of how I arrived at the personality assessment conclusions.

Sincerely,<br>
Hannah McFarland

Ms. McFarland noted an extremely unusual characteristic in the suspect's writing that, to my mind, demonstrates a bridge connecting the psychological orientation of graphology to what I consider the more empirical science of questioned-document analysis.

Graphological analysis falls within the area of psychological profiling, which has tremendous potential value in possible screening and detection to be used as an investigative tool. However, due to the subjective and highly complex nature of the human mind, its evidentiary value must be viewed with healthy skepticism. In this case, knowing what we do about the writer, we find that the expert was highly accurate in her personality assessment/analysis.

This bridge between these two branches of handwriting analysis specifically relates to the "Chinese Chicken" sample, K-5, and the printing Father wrote on the drawing in 1949.

In the sample below, I have enlarged my name, "STEVEN." During her character analysis of the known writing, Ms. McFarland noted a handwriting phenomenon so exceptionally rare that in her examination of documents over many years she had never come across it. This rarity related to the manner in which the three letters "TEV" in "STEVEN" were written.

As Ms. McFarland explained:

It appears that all three letters were highly connected. The T bar connects directly to the top of the E. Most people lift the pen at this point to complete the E. But instead, this printer keeps going in order to form the V, and then goes back to complete the E.

She advised me that to find two connected letters was not particularly rare, but three connected was unheard of, and would indicate the type of exceptionally high intelligence and forethought that might be found in a master chess champion such as a Boris Spassky or a Bobby Fischer. Confirmation of her observation was possible because I possessed the original drawing and was therefore able to verify the three unbroken letters. Thus, in this particular instance, because we were able to view the original document, her analysis of the three connected letters was "positive" instead of highly probable.

*Exhibit 51*

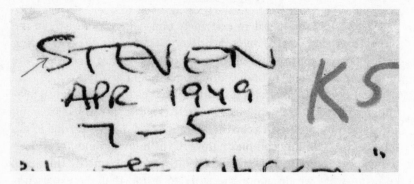

Above is the sample K-5, with an enlargement of the name "STEVEN" demonstrating the printed "TEV" connected and unbroken.

Here, also, is one final sample (K-10), although it was not used as a submitted known sample to the expert. K-10 is copied from a portion of a contract document and was written and dated by George Hodel on January 11, 1999, just four months before his death. I include it because it demonstrates his consistency in the use of a specific characteristic. Within this limited sample of his printing, where he has printed only five sentences, we find he has written the open-bottomed letter "B" (circled) seven out of the eight times he used it.

## Exhibit 52

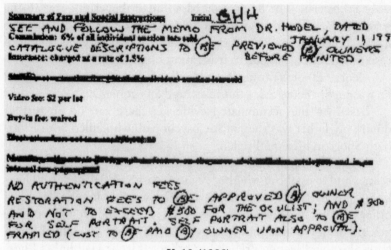

K-10 (1999)

This open "B" is only one of the four unique and individual characteristics of my father's handwriting that identify him as the author of the Black Dahlia Avenger and Jeanne French notes.

Hannah McFarland's opinion was confirmed in large measure by two previous handwriting experts in their separate 1947 analyses. Like their modern-day counterpart, both of these earlier experts were a combination of graphologist and questioned-document examiner. Submitting a character analysis of the suspect, they concluded that an unspecified number of the postcards were handprinted by the same person.

Clark Sellers, the internationally recognized handwriting expert who provided forensic testimony that resulted in the conviction and execution of Bruno Hauptmann for the murder of the Lindbergh baby, was requested to examine the Black Dahlia evidence. He told the police and public that, in his opinion, "It was evident the writer took great pains to disguise his or her personality by printing instead of writing the message and by endeavoring to appear illiterate." But, he added, "The style and formation of the printed letters betrayed the writer as an educated person."

In examining the Black Dahlia documents, handwriting expert

Henry Silver told the police, "The sender is an egomaniac and possibly a musician. The fluctuating base line of the writing reveals the writer to be affected by extreme fluctuations of mood, dropping to melancholy. The writer suffers from mental conflict growing out of resentment or hatred due to frustration of sex urge."

George Hodel's profile includes all three of these characteristics: he was highly educated, a musician, and an egomaniac.

Based on the accumulated evidence, there can be no further doubt: my father was the sadistic psychopath who killed both Elizabeth Short and Jeanne French.

However, it's also important to examine the "why" behind the crimes and to establish whether or not George Hodel, and in all likelihood his partner Fred Sexton, were responsible for the deaths of other lone women during the 1940s and '50s in and around Los Angeles. Was it possible that George Hodel had not only killed Elizabeth Short and Jeanne French but others as well? Had he, as I now began to fear, been a serial killer?

# 23

# More 1940s L.A. Murdered Women Cases

BECAUSE OF THE SENSATIONAL COVERAGE of the Black Dahlia murder in newspapers around the country in the late 1940s, most people who followed the case don't realize that Elizabeth Short's murder was only one of a series of crimes against lone attractive women from 1943 through the end of the decade. These cases bore striking similarities to one another, not only in the victims' profiles but in the nature and proximity of their crime scenes, the types of evidence that turned up, the descriptions of the men last seen with them, and the ways in which the police were taunted after the crimes.

In researching many of these crimes, some of which have already been examined by earlier researchers and authors, I found that law enforcement agencies other than the LAPD, such as the Los Angeles Sheriff's Department, the Long Beach police, and the San Diego police, had also considered the possibility that these crimes were, in the newspapers' words, "Dahlia-related." Because of LAPD's dogged resistance, and in some instances outright refusal, to share information with neighboring law enforcement, nothing came of the connections that to me seem readily apparent.

During a grand jury investigation in 1949, later articles quoted several LAPD officers who testified that when they had attempted to pursue leads possibly connecting the Dahlia case to one in Long Beach, they were summarily removed from the active investigation and transferred to another division. Unless some commander ordered detectives to share information, the rule was, "It's our case," and little or no information was exchanged between agencies, nor was it even distributed to divisional detectives within the department. This LAPD exclusivity and informational lockdown was maintained for over five decades. As it relates to the Elizabeth Short investigation, nothing has changed from day one. That, I firmly believe, is why, despite what I consider some very compelling evidence, the killers of Elizabeth Short and Jeanne French, plus three additional women that I present below — Ora Murray, Georgette Bauerdorf, and Gladys Kern — and probably many more victims, were never caught. As we shall see, it was neither ignorance nor inefficiency that prevented these crimes from being solved, but rather a massive cover-up on the part of the LAPD.

Following are three investigative summaries on victims Ora Murray, Georgette Bauerdorf, and Gladys Kern, the first two crimes occurring before Black Dahlia, the last roughly a year after.

## Ora Murray ( July 27, 1943): The "White Gardenia" Murder

Early on a Tuesday morning, July 27, 1943, the fifteen-year-old son of a golf course greenskeeper discovered the nude body of Ora Elizabeth Murray, age forty-two, lying on the ground near the parking lot of the Fox Hills golf course in West Los Angeles. The victim's dress had been wrapped around her body like a sarong, a white gardenia placed under her right shoulder. She had been severely beaten about her face and body. The wristwatch Ora Murray was wearing had been smashed and broken during the assault, probably as a result of her raising her arms to defend herself against the blows to her head as her assailant repeatedly struck her with a heavy blunt instrument. The destruction of her watch in all likelihood fixed the exact time of her murder, 1:50 A.M., consistent with an early-morning attack just six hours before the body was discovered. At the scene that morning, detectives picked up what was described by the newspapers as "a torn credit card from an oil company, containing a serial number," a potentially important piece of evidence that detectives said they would investigate.

The autopsy performed on the victim revealed that the cause of death was due to "constriction of the larynx by strangulation" along with the contributory factors of "concussion of the brain and subdural hemorrhage." The body was found just outside the Los Angeles city limits, and therefore was in the jurisdiction of the Los Angeles County Sheriff's Department, whose homicide division handled the investigation.

Sheriff's detectives quickly discovered that the victim, who was married to an Army sergeant stationed in Mississippi, had only arrived in Los Angeles the previous Thursday. Mrs. Murray had been visiting her sister, Latona Leinann, and her husband, Oswald, who lived in L.A. and who, at the time Ora Murray's body was discovered, were in the process of filing a missing persons report with the sheriff.

Tracing Ora's movements the night before her murder provided homicide detectives with the following information from Latona:

On Monday night, July 26, 1943, Ora and her sister decided to go dancing at the Zenda Ballroom, at 7th and Figueroa Avenue, in downtown Los Angeles (one block from Father's medical office at 7th and Flower). At the Zenda, Ora and Latona met two men whom the latter described as "Preston," an Army sergeant, and a civilian, "tall, thin, with black hair," named "Paul," whom she characterized as "very suave and a very good dancer." Latona said that Paul was wearing "a dark double-breasted suit and a dark fedora." She also remembered, "Paul told us that he lived in San Francisco and was just down visiting Los Angeles for a few days."

The foursome danced for some time, then Paul offered to show the two women "around Hollywood and go dancing at the Palladium." At that point, Preston took off, leaving the two women with Paul.

Latona reluctantly agreed to go along with her sister and Paul, but only on condition that they drive to her house to pick up her husband. Paul agreed, and drove the women in what Latona told detectives was "a flashy blue convertible coupe" to Latona's house. The *Los Angeles Examiner* quoted Latona as saying, "We went home to get Oswald, but he was sleepy and wouldn't go and finally my sister told the man she would go with him anyway." Latona said she saw her sister leave her residence with the handsome stranger and that was the last she saw of her until she identified the body for sheriff's detectives the following afternoon.

The Los Angeles Sheriff's Department continued its search in an effort to identify Paul, whom they considered their prime suspect. By the following week they took a statement from a witness, thirty-one-year-old secretary Jeanette Walser, who said she had met someone who might be connected to the Murray murder investigation. The man called himself Grant Terry and told her he was a federal attorney from the East Coast. After what Jeanette Walser called a "whirlwind ten-day courtship," they became engaged and were to be married five days later. However, it turned out the man called "Terry" was a con man who bilked Walser out of $700 cash and her diamond ring before he vanished.

The jilted witness told detectives that she had also loaned Grant Terry her blue convertible the day before the murder had occurred, and he had returned it to her the day following the murder. At that time, Terry had told his fiancée that "he had to go to San Diego with a man named *George* [my emphasis] to try a case that had unexpectedly come up, but would return in two days." Grant Terry never came back.

Jeanette Walser also provided detectives with a photograph of Grant Terry, which ran in the *Los Angeles Examiner* on August 5, 1943, alongside the front-page story Walser had told police.

Detectives showed Walser's photograph of "Grant Terry" to Latona, as well as to several other unnamed women who saw "Paul" with the victim the night of her murder. These witnesses, while not making a positive identification, said that the photograph strongly resembled "Paul," but that none of them could remember Paul's having glasses — in the Walser photograph he was wearing glasses.

The case was submitted to the district attorney's office. Based on the circumstances and tentative identifications, Deputy District Attorney Edwin Myers issued a felony fugitive warrant charging "Grant Terry, age 34," with the murder of Ora Elizabeth Murray.

In a related article in the *Los Angeles Examiner* three days later, headlined, "U.S. Joins Hunt for Gardenia Slayer Suspect," the newspaper reported that a U.S. federal warrant had also been issued by the FBI on August 7 charging separate felony counts and naming "Grant Terry" as a fugitive. The felony warrant, based on the information provided by Jeanette Walser, charged Grant Terry with "impersonating an attorney of the lands division of the War Department, in which false capacity he allegedly obtained $700 from Miss Jeanette J. Walser, 8019 South Figueroa Street."

At a coroner's inquest on August 5, Ora Murray's sister provided a hesitant but tentative identification of the photograph of "Grant Terry" provided by the witness Jeannette Walser, stating, "It could very easily be Paul, but I can't say positively." She told the inquest jurors that "while the photograph strongly resembled 'Paul,' that at no time during the evening, either at the dance hall or while driving the convertible did he wear glasses, as seen in the photograph."

A *Los Angeles Examiner* story on August 6 reported that, even though a felony warrant had been issued for a suspect by the name of "Grant W. Terry," the coroner's inquest jury returned a verdict that the death of Ora Murray was "caused by person unidentified to the jury." The jury's ruling was based on the fact that they considered the sister's tentative identification insufficient to name Grant Terry as the murder suspect.

The investigation remained dormant until the arrest of a man named Roger Lewis Gardner, aka "Grant Terry," on the fugitive warrant in New York in March 1944. Gardner was extradited to California, where, after Latona Leinann changed her tentative identification to a "positive," he was formally arraigned for the murder of Ora Murray.

At Gardner's two-week jury murder trial in Los Angeles in October 1944, the defendant took the stand in his own defense and, while he admitted that he had "promised to marry Jeannette Walser and did commit the theft of her ring," adamantly denied knowing or ever seeing Ora Murray or her sister Latona. He stated he had never set foot in the Zenda Ballroom and denied any involvement whatsoever in the murder of Ora Murray.

Gardner testified, and his alibi was confirmed by defense witnesses, that he had been with his "fiancée" Jeanette Walser until 8:15 P.M. on the night of the murder, therefore making it physically impossible for him to be at the downtown dance hall at 8:30 P.M. Further testimony showed that on the night of the murder, just minutes before "Paul" was seen dancing with the victim, Gardner was twenty miles away wearing "sport clothes" rather than the dark suit and fedora known to be worn by "Paul."

On November 11, 1944, the jury was "hopelessly deadlocked," with half of them convinced that it was a case of mistaken identity. Gardner, some of the members of the jury believed, while a self-confessed

con man, lothario, and thief, was nevertheless not the same sophisticated, well-dressed "Paul" who drove Ora Murray away from her sister's house to see Hollywood and later bludgeoned and strangled her
to death at the nearby Fox Hills golf course.

The Walser photograph of "Grant Terry" that appeared in the
newspaper and was later determined to be Roger Lewis Gardner was
of poor quality. In checking records, I found that the photographic
negative from the *Los Angeles Times* article of August 5, 1943, still remained in the file at UCLA. An eight-by-ten print from that negative (shown below as exhibit 53) was a snapshot taken by Walser
during her "whirlwind ten-day courtship" with Gardner in July
1943. While the image was slightly out of focus, it revealed, despite
the wire-rimmed glasses, a striking similarity between Roger Lewis
Gardner and George Hodel and how easy it would have been for
witnesses to mistake one for the other.

### Exhibit 53

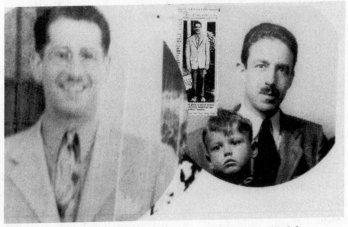

Roger Gardner                          George Hodel

Both of the above photographs were taken in the same year, 1943.
The photo of Father, where I am seated on his knee, was taken in
November 1943, just three months after the Ora Murray murder.

At the Ora Murray crime scene, police also discovered a Native
American bracelet on her wrist, the kind of bracelet my father col-

lected when he was working for the Public Health Service on the Navajo and Hopi reservations. My father had given just such a bracelet to my mother (exhibit 54a), which she was wearing in the photograph taken by Man Ray in Hollywood in 1944. Man Ray's photograph clearly shows the Indian bracelets and Thunder God ring my father had given her at the time of their marriage three years before this photograph was taken. The sheriff's department detectives never released a photograph or a complete description of the Native American jewelry that "Paul" gave Ora Murray on the night they met and danced together; the actual bracelet, or photographs of it, may still be in the unsolved-case file.

### Exhibit 54

 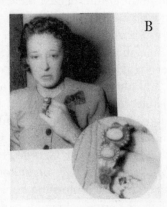

*Dorothy Hodel*                    *Jeanette Walser*

Photograph B shows a Southwest Native American bracelet given to witness Jeanette Walser by con man Roger Gardner, which is also similar to my mother's, and is identical to the type given to the murder victim, Ora Murray, by the suspect.

Some of the available information pertaining to the Ora Murray murder investigation remains confusing and unclear. Without access to the actual case files a number of questions remain unanswered. For example, to whom did the torn credit card found next to the body belong? And did the detectives ever check out this easily trace-able evidence, as they told the press they would? Certainly the card did not belong to their suspect Roger Gardner, because the information was never introduced at his trial. Could the credit card have been exculpatory evidence and thus, the way things were done in 1944, held back from the defense?

From researching the investigation and trial testimony prior to Gardner's release from custody, I found that on the night of the murder Gardner had borrowed Jeanette Walser's blue convertible, which he claimed he drove to the Ambassador Hotel and parked overnight. Upon preparing to return it the following morning, Gardner discovered that it had a flat tire. Gardner also had given Walser an Indian bracelet, similar in appearance to the one found on victim Ora Murray's wrist. Gardner, having completed his con and theft of her jewelry, then told his fiancée — who at this point had become his victim — that something unexpected had come up and "he had to go to San Diego with a man named George, to try a case." Was the mysterious "George" actually George Hodel?

While all of these facts may be an accumulation of coincidences, the very real possibility exists that Gardner and Hodel knew each other and that George Hodel, either with or without Gardner's knowledge, may have "borrowed" the convertible from where Gardner had parked it at the Ambassador Hotel. The cocktail lounge at the Ambassador was one of Father's favorite hangouts. It is possible that after taking the car, George Hodel, calling himself "Paul," drove Ora Murray on her late-night tour of Hollywood, committed the murder in the early-morning hours, and returned the vehicle to the hotel, where Gardner found it parked with a flat tire.

In all likelihood, we will never know the facts surrounding this murder. I strongly suspect, however, that Hodel and Gardner did know each other and that Dr. George Hill Hodel did murder Ora Murray.

Ora Murray did not immediately fade into history after the trial and acquittal. Her name resurfaced two years later on January 23, 1947, when she was mentioned by crime reporter Agness Underwood in her feature article wherein the reporter asked rhetorically in a headline, "Will Dahlia Slaying Join Album of Unsolved Murders?" Underwood raised the possibility that the 1943 Ora Murray, the 1944 Georgette Bauerdorf, the 1946 Gertrude Evelyn Landon, and the 1947 Elizabeth Short murders might all be connected.

## Georgette Bauerdorf (October 12, 1944)

"Oil Heiress Found Dead in Tub Mystery," the *Los Angeles Examiner* headline said on the morning of Friday, October 13, 1944. Twenty-year-old Georgette Bauerdorf was the pretty brunette daughter of wealthy oil magnate George Bauerdorf, a close friend of William Randolph Hearst. She was living alone in an upscale apartment on the west side of Hollywood at 8493 Fountain Avenue, in a complex that lay just a block beyond LAPD's jurisdiction, which meant that this case too fell under the jurisdiction of the Los Angeles County Sheriff's Department.

Georgette's body was discovered by Mr. and Mrs. Charles Atwood, the apartment janitor and his wife, on the morning of October 12. While working with her husband in an adjacent apartment at approximately 10:30 in the morning, Mrs. Atwood heard the sound of running water coming from the Bauerdorf apartment. She knocked at Georgette's front door, which she found was ajar, and when no one answered she called her husband to go inside with her, where they discovered the victim lying submerged in the bathtub, which was overflowing. Georgette Bauerdorf was dead.

The Atwoods, who lived across the hall from the victim, told detectives they had been awakened during the early-morning hours by a "commotion" in the Bauerdorf apartment and a crash of "something metallic," but were unable to pinpoint the exact time.

The crime-scene investigation by West Hollywood detectives and the sheriff's homicide team determined that Georgette Bauerdorf had returned to her apartment the previous evening, fixed herself a snack, changed into her pajamas, and written an entry in her private diary. At some point after that, she was assaulted, beaten, and strangled. Her body was placed in the bathtub and the water turned on. When discovered, the victim was wearing only the top half of her pajamas; the bottom, which had been torn, was found lying near the bed. A gag had been forced into her mouth.

A coroner's inquest determined that the cause of death was "obstruction of upper air passages by inserted cloth" and was ruled a homicide that had probably taken place after midnight on the morning of October 12, 1944. Coroner's examiner Dr. Frank Webb also wrote, "Abrasions on the knuckles of the girl's hands showed she had fought desperately against the attacker. Thumb and finger marks on her face, lips, abdomen, and thighs prove the attacker was powerful with almost ape-like hands." The coroner determined that the victim had not drowned, but had been murdered by forced asphyxiation prior to her body being placed in the bathtub.

Because many of the victim's expensive belongings, including her jewelry, were in plain sight and had not been taken by the assailant, the motive of robbery was ruled out. Her purse was found at the crime scene, but without her car key, which was the only article removed from her residence. The suspect apparently stole the victim's car, which was found several days later at 728½ East 25th Street near the corner of 25th and San Pedro, a mile south of the downtown area. The car was out of gas; the key had been left in the ignition.

Georgette Bauerdorf had graduated from the prestigious Westlake and Marlborough schools for girls. Marlborough, in a wealthy residential section of southern Hollywood, was only a few miles southeast of her apartment. As part of her personal war effort, Georgette had volunteered to serve and entertain servicemen at the Hollywood Canteen, where they came to relax and dance with the pretty girls. Every Wednesday night she served as a junior hostess at the club, where she was well liked, popular, and considered generous and kind to all she met. According to entries found in her diary, Bauerdorf had a boyfriend named Jerry, who was about to graduate from an Army Air Force school in El Paso, Texas. She was planning a surprise flight down to see him graduate.

Georgette was seen on the evening of Wednesday, October 11, at 10:30 p.m. when she left the Hollywood Canteen for home, a short two-mile drive west of Hollywood. Her girlfriends at the canteen told police she had been dancing as usual with different servicemen that night. Georgette's friend, twenty-year-old June Ziegler, who worked with her at the canteen, told Sheriff's Department homicide detectives what she saw on that Wednesday evening:

> She [Georgette] was seated in her car near the canteen when I arrived about 6:30 p.m. She was knitting and appeared quite nervous. I climbed in the car and we talked for about 30 minutes before we

went inside. She told me she was nervous and asked if I would spend the night with her. At the time I did not pay much attention, because I thought she was just nervous about the plane trip, which I knew she had kept secret from everyone but myself.

In his book *Severed,* John Gilmore mentions Agness Underwood's belief that the Dahlia and Bauerdorf murders were connected. Gilmore also refers to an anonymous tip that Underwood received about a week after the Bauerdorf murder, in which the informant indicated that a white male had been seen walking away from Bauerdorf's car at 25th and San Pedro. The man was described as tall and thin, wearing what appeared to be a military uniform but without the Army jacket. Underwood speculated that he might have been impersonating a serviceman to pick up girls at the canteen.

It was also rumored that Bauerdorf may have made some additional entries in her personal diary, recovered at her home by the sheriff's detectives, that related to the friend of a soldier, an older man, with whom she had danced that Wednesday evening. Acquaintances said that Georgette had indicated to others at the canteen that she did not like him because he was aggressive and persisted in dancing with her.

Unidentified latent fingerprints were found in the bathroom near the body, throughout the apartment, and in her recovered vehicle, and detectives were hopeful at the time that they would eventually lead to the identification of the suspect. A latent print obtained from a light bulb in the foyer, believed removed by the suspect, added speculation that he could have been taller than the average male.

Blood spots were also found on clothing at the crime scene, and could have been either the victim's or the suspect's. If the clothing was not disposed of, it could still be of potential value for blood typing or DNA evidence.

In my review of published facts from the investigation, I discovered a most important and unique piece of evidence: the murder weapon. Most accounts simply refer to it as a "gag" or piece of cloth. However, one article in the *Los Angeles Herald Express,* reporting on the autopsy inquest on October 20, 1944, was more precise:

# DEPUTIES TESTIFY

Deputy Sheriffs A. M. Hutchingson and Ray Hopkins told of the routine investigation and failure to find, so far, any clue to the girl's slayer.

Exhibits shown to the jury included the gag, which was stuffed down Miss Bauerdorf's throat. The material in this gag has been identified by medical supply men as elastic cotton knit ace bandage, such as used by athletes to ease sprained muscles and by orthopedic physicians . . .

Deputy Sheriff Howard Achenbach, acting on a hunch, entered the Orthopedic Supply Co. at 309 South Hill St., where the material was identified as bandage. However, it was learned that the material in this 9" size of the gauge had not been sold in this city for 22 years.

The killer brought this most unusual weapon with him to the apartment, and after beating the victim suffocated her by forcing it down her throat. Who, other than a medical professional, would be carrying such a "weapon"?

### *Exhibit 55*

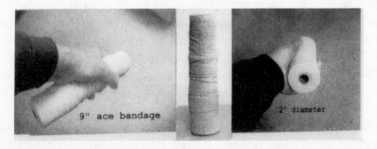

Above is a photograph of my reconstructed version of how the murder weapon must have appeared, based on the sheriff's deputies' description.

The Los Angeles daily papers covered the Bauerdorf investigation for several weeks, but the Hearst papers minimized their coverage, probably because of Hearst's close friendship with, and respect for, the victim's father.

Nearly a year after the murder, an article appeared in the *Examiner* on September 21, 1945, that read almost like an epitaph. The story included a typed note from someone claiming to be her killer. Below the headline the paper ran Georgette's picture, along with the note, in which the killer taunted the police and promised to revisit the Hollywood Canteen within the month. The note, exactly as the self-proclaimed killer typed it, read:

> To the Los Angeles police--
> Almost a year ago Georgette
> Bauerdorf, age 20, Hollywood
> Canteen hostess was murdered
> in her apartment in West Holly-
> wood--
> Between now and Oct. 11--a year
> after her death--the one who
> murdered her will appear at the
> Hollywood Canteen. The murderer
> will be in uniform. He has since
> he committed the murder been in
> action at Okinawa. The murderⓈⓍ
> of Georgette Bauerdorf was Divine
> Retribution--
>
> Let the Los Angeles police arrest
> the murderer if they can--

An eleven-year-old student named Marilyn Silk had found the note on her way home from school. Written on a sheet of personal notepaper and stuffed inside a dirty envelope, the missive was lying on a stone retaining wall near Fairfax High School in Hollywood. The newspaper also dropped a clue that had not been disclosed to the public at the time of the homicide a year earlier when it reported, "There was the suggestion by friends that she [Bauerdorf] was accompanied home by a man in uniform."

What struck me in the Bauerdorf case was its obvious similarity to the later Dahlia killing, in which the suspect also taunted police via notes to the newspaper. The Bauerdorf suspect promised police that he would appear at the Hollywood Canteen in uniform by October 11. (Father's birthday was October 10.) The killer's "Let the Los Angeles police arrest the murderer if they can" echoes the words used two years later in the pasted message to the police in the Dahlia case: "We're going to Mexico City — catch us if you can." The killer's need to seek recognition and publicity for his crimes was a way to exert control both over the police and his victim. Announcing that Georgette's murder was not a crime but his dispensation of "Divine Retribution" also bears an eerie resemblance to what Elizabeth Short's killer would say two years later when he called himself the "Black Dahlia Avenger."

## The Bauerdorf Note

Other similarities in both the Elizabeth Short and Bauerdorf homicides are, in my opinion, striking enough to be considered thoughtprints linking the same suspect to the two crimes.

In both cases, the notes the suspect wrote to the police suggest that he had some experience as a journalist. In the Bauerdorf murder note, the taunting letter opens with a lead paragraph similar in style to the lead paragraph of a morning newspaper in which the "what, when, where, and who" are all answered.

To the Los Angeles police--

*(when)*

Almost a year ago

*(who)*

Georgette Bauerdorf, age 20,

*(What)*

Hollywood Canteen hostess, was murdered

*(where)*

in her apartment in

West Hollywood--

The killer tells us the "why" in his next sentence, where he identifies the crime as an act of retribution, and in so doing identifies himself indirectly as an "avenger."

In the pasted Dahlia notes, the killer again demonstrates journalistic knowledge, this time as a headline writer, in his two separate taunts to police:

### 'GO SLOW'
### MAN KILLER SAYS
### BLACK DAHLIA CASE

Followed in a few days by:

## DAHLIA'S KILLER CRACKING, WANTS TERMS

These are not notes from a streetwise thug, but professional headlines. So professional, in fact, that true-crime author and commentator Joseph Wambaugh told television viewers in the Learning Channel's production *Case Reopened: The Black Dahlia* that:

> Obviously journalists sent the letter. Cutting and pasting newsprint as was done in B-movie clichés of the era. The same cruel and unscrupulous reporters who elicited background information from Mrs. Short, the mother, by claiming her daughter had won a beauty contest. But, at the end of the day, they didn't prevent the case from being solved.

There exists another clue to the identity of the letter writer in his unique method and manner of typing, seen in six different locations in the Bauerdorf note, in which he unconsciously leaves two dashes (--) at the end of some of his sentences. In the Bauerdorf note these double-dashes follow the words: "police--", "Hollywood--", "Oct. 11--", "death--", "Retribution--", and "can--".

In the long letter Father sent me on June 4, 1980, referred to here as "The Parable of the Sparrows," which he typed himself rather than giving it to his secretary or wife to type, there are four separate instances where he used his unique double-dash endings:

Page 2

"plastic coating--"

"mirror film--"

Page 3

"to her--"

"Remember--"

The use of these double-spaced dashes is such a rarity that their appearances in the Bauerdorf note and in my father's letter to me set off a loud alarm.

Exhibit 56 shows how the original note appeared in the September 21, 1945, *Examiner* article along with Georgette's photograph. A separate *Los Angeles Times* article on the same date informed readers that detectives believe red *iodine* stains visible on the typed paper were placed there by the suspect to represent blood.

***Exhibit 56***

**Los Angeles Examiner,** *September 21, 1945*

**Gladys Eugenia Kern (February 14, 1948)**

On February 17, 1948, *Los Angeles Times* headlines again blared news of the city's latest murder:

# WOMAN SLAIN IN HOLLYWOOD MYSTERY; POLICE SEEK ANONYMOUS NOTE WRITER

The victim was fifty-year-old real estate agent Gladys Eugenia Kern, who was stabbed to death while showing a house to a potential buyer. Her body was found two days later at 4217 Cromwell Avenue in the exclusive Los Feliz section of the Hollywood Hills, by another real estate agent who was showing the house to a client.

The murder weapon, left at the crime scene by the killer and found in the kitchen sink wrapped in a man's bloody handkerchief, was described as an eight-inch jungle knife of a type used by soldiers during the war. Police found unidentified fingerprints at the crime scene, which, if not lost or disposed of, presumably remain as potential evidence in the unsolved homicide.

A check of Gladys Kern's movements by LAPD detectives revealed she had last been seen the previous Saturday, Valentine's Day, February 14, meeting with a man at her Hollywood real estate office at 1307 North Vermont Avenue. The manager of a drugstore at the corner of Fountain Street and Vermont Avenue, directly across the street from the victim's office, saw her enter the drugstore at approximately 2:00 P.M. accompanied by a man she described as "having very dark curly hair, and wearing a dark blue suit." The two of them sat at a counter, had a soda, and then left the drugstore together.

Possibly the last person to have seen the victim alive was radar engineer William E. Osborne, whose laboratory was next door to Mrs. Kern's office. Osborne saw the victim talking with a man at her Vermont Avenue office on February 14, 1948, at approximately 4:00 P.M. The witness told police that at that time, "She put her head in the door of my laboratory and told me she was leaving. There was a tall chap in the office with her." Osborne had the impression that she knew him, because, he told police, "They were talking generalities, not business."

He provided the following description of the man, which was

broadcast by the LAPD as an all points bulletin: "Male, approximately 50 years of age, 6' tall, long full face, graying hair, wearing a
business suit with a moderate cut, well dressed and neat, with a New
York appearance in his dress and manner."

After their initial press releases, police told reporters that they had
the names of five additional witnesses who had seen the victim with a
similarly described individual, but the police did not release their names.

Two additional witnesses, Japanese gardeners working across the
street from the murder scene at the hillside mansion, were located by
police and told of seeing "two men coming out of the mansion, and
down the steps," on Saturday afternoon, the day of the murder. The
gardeners saw the two men get into a parked vehicle and drive off,
but the police provided no detailed description of these two suspects
or their vehicle.

During their search of the victim's office, police discovered that a
"clients' book" containing Mrs. Kern's appointments and clients'
names was missing from her desk. During their search of the victim's
desk, police also discovered a small snapshot showing the victim standing with an unidentified man, whom they were attempting to identify.

The strongest lead in the investigation was a bizarre handwritten
note the police received that had been left in a downtown mailbox at
5th and Olive, on Sunday, February 15, the day after the victim's
murder and a day before her body was discovered. The note, written
on "cheap blank paper," was neither addressed nor stamped but had
been folded in half, glued closed, marked "Hurry, give to police," and
deposited in a mailbox in the same city block as the Biltmore Hotel.
Its condition — glued and folded — was strikingly similar to the earlier Dahlia note left in the downtown cab driver's vehicle that said,
"Take to Examiner at once. I've got the number of your cab." In the
Dahlia murder, we recall, the suspect alternately directed his notes to
both police and the press.

The Kern note was found by the mailman and given to police.
The mailbox, only two city blocks from my father's medical office on
7th Street, was on the same block where another 1947 note (exhibit
28) was left by the Black Dahlia Avenger. That Dahlia Avenger note
told police to "Ask news man at 5+ Hill for clue. Why not let that nut
go I spoke to said man B.D.A."

LAPD detectives and forensics experts concluded that the Kern note had most probably been written by the suspect, who, they believed, had altered his handwriting and deliberately used odd phrasing and misspelled words. This note was excerpted, precisely as the writer had spelled and punctuated it, in the *Los Angeles Examiner* on February 17, 1948:

I made acquaintance of man three weeks ago while in Griffith Park he seemed a great sport we got friendly friday night asked me if I wanted to make about $300. He said he wanted to buy a home for his family but he was a racketeer and no real estater would do business with him he suggested I buy a home for him in my name then he would go with person to look at property to make sure he liked and I was to tell real estater that he was lending me the cash so he had to inspect and I waited outside after while I went up to investigate, there I found her lying on floor, him trying to take ring off fingers he pulled gun on me and told me he just knocked her out he knew I carried money so he took my wallet with all my money tied my hands with my belt let lay down on sink and attached belt to faucet.

After he left I got free and tried to revive her I turned her over, I was covered with blood pulled knife out then suddenly I came to I washed my hands and knife then I looked in her bag for her home phone and address then left and ran out while inside I found he put small pocket book in my coat pocket and threw it away, also in my pocket was an old leather strap.

I knew this man as Louis Frazer he has 36 or 37 Pontiac fordor very dark number plates look like 46 plates but with 48 stickers about 5 ft.-10, Jet black curly hair wears blue or tan garbardine suit told me he was a fighter and looks it I won't rest till I find him I know every place we went together I know that man is my only aliby and without him I feel equally guilty.

The *Examiner* article stated that the writer of the note "related that he himself was robbed and bound by the slayer, described as tall, dark and Latin."

On February 17, 1948, an LAPD police artist obtained a composite drawing of the suspect as described by their unnamed witnesses. The sketch (exhibit 57) was published on the front page of the *Daily News* of February 18, 1948.

*Exhibit 57*

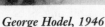

*George Hodel, 1946*      *1948 LAPD*      *George Hodel, 1954*
                         *composite*

The above two photographs of George Hodel were taken in 1946 and 1954. The only alteration made to the Hodel photos was the airbrushing out of the mustache, for comparison to the police composite sketch.

The art of composite drawing in criminal investigations is particularly difficult, as the police artist is required to try and reproduce a physical likeness of the suspect from eyewitnesses' subjective and oftentimes varied verbal descriptions. While these composites frequently take on a generic appearance, in the Kern investigation it is obvious the police artist possessed unusual skill and ability. As can be seen, the overall likeness of the murder suspect bears a strong resemblance to that of Dr. Hodel. Of particular note are: the shape of the face, the nose, and left ear, the Asiatic appearance of the eyes, and the hair highlighting and style.

Five days after the Kern murder, the *Los Angeles Times* reported that a realtor associate of the victim, "A man cloaked in anonymity, a mystery man, possessing vital information, is aiding police in their investigation." The article said the man, who had "intimate details" about the transaction involving the victim and the sale of the house where she was murdered, had agreed to cooperate only if his identity was kept secret. Further, all the documents and papers relating to the sale of the house had disappeared, along with the victim's "client notebook."

In exchange for the details and information, LAPD detectives pledged not to reveal the informant's name to the public.

After what would normally seem to have been many strong potential leads pointing to a suspect — the composite drawing, the unidentified photograph of the man found in her office desk drawer, a confidential informant providing police with the identity of the victim's "secret client," various eyewitnesses providing a detailed physical description of the suspect, and a rambling, handprinted note — the Gladys Kern homicide remains in the LAPD files more than fifty years later as an "open" and unsolved case.

## Kern Physical Evidence: Kern Murder Weapon

As in many homicide investigations, a critical piece of physical evidence would not be discovered until years, if not decades, after the crime. As if by chance, it would surface from an offhand remark made fifty years later, totally unassociated and unconnected to the actual investigation.

In July 2001, I called Joe Barrett and we met for lunch in Santa Barbara, where Joe reminisced about his old friend Rowland Brown and the comings and goings at the Franklin House in the late 1940s when he was rooming there. He told me the following story:

> You know, Steve, that your brother Mike took a knife from my room there at the Franklin House, and I never got it back. Mike was only about eight or nine years old then and he told me that he "lost it." That was too bad because it had sentimental value to me. A good friend of mine had given it to me when we were overseas during the war years. Mike took it from my room, then he said he was playing with it in the vacant lot next door and must have lost it. That would have been in 1948.

His words jarred me and, without trying to sound too anxious or too professional, I asked, "What did the knife look like, Joe?"

"It was a jungle knife," he said. "A Navy buddy of mine, a machinist mate, had made it for me while we were serving together aboard a destroyer, in early 1945."

"Would you recognize it if you saw it?" I asked him. Joe gave me a quizzical look. "Sure I would. There's not another like it in the world." We parted, and I told him I would send him a photograph I had, "just for curiosity's sake."

Recalling the unusual description of the murder weapon used in the Gladys Kern murder in February 1948, I immediately pulled the file and searched for the picture.

It was there! The homicide detective held it in his hands as the press photographer from the *Daily News* photographed it for the morning edition: a jungle knife precisely as Joe Barrett had described it. I cut off all references to the Kern murder and mailed the picture to Joe.

Two days later, he called me back. "It is my knife, Steve. What's this all about?"

"Are you positive, Joe? How do you know it's your knife? Isn't it just like any other jungle knife?"

His response was measured and firm:

I'm sure it's mine because he made it especially for me. If I could see the knife itself I could verify it positively, because he machined the handle. The knife had different-colored washers, which I think he had painted like blue and green and red and yellow and orange. He then put some kind of Plexiglas handle over the colored rings and the paint hadn't dried completely so they were smeared inside, but that was fine with me. I can recognize the knife immediately, even though it's been fifty or more years now. Your picture is black and white and the knife has multicolored inserts, which you can't see in the photo. I will draw you a picture of the knife as I remember it with the colors and everything. But Steve, I'm sure it's my knife. What is this all about? Where is it? Where is the picture from?

Feeling I could no longer keep him in the dark, I told him the knife in the photograph had been used in a murder back in 1948. And though I couldn't provide him with any more information just then, I promised that "all would be made clear in the near future." He reiterated that he would draw as complete a description of the knife as he could, including the colors on the handle, and mail it to me.

Exhibit 58 is the drawing Joe sent, which I received on July 26, 2001.

*Exhibit 58*

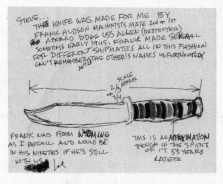

*Joe Barrett drawing*                    *Kern 1948 murder weapon*

Joe Barrett's notations read:

Steve . . .

The knife was made for me by Frank Hudson, machinists mate 2nd or 1st aboard DD66 USS Allen (destroyer) sometime early 1945. Frank made several for different shipmates all in this fashion. Can't remember any of the other's names unfortunately.

Frank was from Wyoming as I recall and would be in his nineties if he's still with us.

This is an approximation though in the spirit of it 53 years later.

Joe

Hopefully, the Kern murder weapon, or a color photograph, remains in police evidence, so that they can be compared to Barrett's artistic rendering.

Even before this latest discovery, we had a strong case connecting

George Hodel to the murder of Gladys Kern: the matching composite, the handkerchief, the witness descriptions, the bizarre letter writing, not to mention that the Franklin house was only a mile from both the crime scene and the place where Gladys Kern was last seen alive. Now here was a witness who, unaware of the crime, positively identified the murder weapon as his own knife, stolen from him, he believed, by my brother Michael, in 1948.

Unlike Joe Barrett, we can speculate what really happened. Father doubtless found his eight-year-old son in possession of Joe's knife, took it from him, and kept it. Just weeks, or perhaps only days later, he used it in the Kern homicide. Confident that the knife could never be linked to him, he simply left it at the crime scene in the sink after washing off the blood with water and wiping it clean of prints with his white handkerchief.

Does the LAPD still have the Kern murder weapon in evidence? They should, inasmuch as it is LAPD's policy that "all unsolved homicides remain open until they are solved." If not still in physical evidence, is there a photograph of the knife in the murder book file? Is there a color picture? If not, the evidence reports should detail the color descriptions on the unique handle, as Joe had drawn them for me. Finally, is the knife in police custody handmade, a "one-of-a-kind" due to the smeared colors? If so, it would be distinct from the thousands of factory-tooled jungle knives issued during the war years.

These are all questions to be answered by LAPD, along with the dozens of others that this investigation has raised. For now, it is enough to know that one witness has corroborated the identity and provided a highly detailed description of what is believed to be the murder weapon. Further, he has traced it to the Franklin House, and linked it to George Hodel.

## The Kern Handkerchief

In the summaries of the crimes in this chapter, we have been forced to rely on what was reported in the newspapers at the time. But there were facts never reported to the newspapers by the police because it was, and still is, routine for the assigned investigators to withhold many findings from the public, because they often use them later in interviewing suspects and witnesses. Police often reserve information so that it can be used in developing key questions that can be used in polygraph examinations to exclude those who come forward and falsely confess to a crime. The Dahlia murder brought out many such people, most of whom were mentally disturbed or simply seeking momentary celebrity.

In both the Jeanne French and the Gladys Kern homicides, white handkerchiefs were found near the bodies, which is highly unusual. In my experience — which includes the investigation of more than three hundred homicides — I have never encountered a case in which a suspect left a handkerchief at the scene of his crime. It is as if this was a "calling card," like dropping an ace of spades on the body. Such information would not normally be released to the public, and if the killer had left his "calling card" at his other crime scenes, it could have been withheld by detectives in many of L.A.'s other unsolved murders.

Of special interest are the comments about the handkerchief found at the Gladys Kern murder scene. According to the *Los Angeles Times* of February 21, 1948:

## HANDKERCHIEF IN MURDER FAILS TO YIELD CLUE

Only one shred of new information was turned up yesterday at the inquest into the murder of Mrs. Gladys Kern — the killer probably is a man whose laundry is done at home. This deduction was made from testimony given by Police Det. A.W. Hubka.

Hubka said that when he and Det. Sgt. C.C. Forbes investigated the slaying in the six-room vacant home at 4217 Cromwell Ave., in the Los Feliz district, a balled-up man's handkerchief was found in the kitchen sink near the body. No laundry marks were on it.

Dr. Hodel did not send his laundry outside to be done because he had a full-time live-in maid, Ellen Taylor, who did all his cleaning and laundering. Like the handkerchief found at the Kern crime scene, and possibly the French and later Newton homicides, his handkerchiefs would be without a laundry mark to aid in any tracing.

The Murray, Kern, and Bauerdorf homicides are only three of the murders that took place during roughly the same period as the Black Dahlia that, in my opinion, are linked by the same suspect behavior and descriptions, as well as by victim profile.

Just as compelling are the murders of Mimi Boomhower and Jean Spangler, which also occurred in Los Angeles during the key Dahlia years. Like the above three, they too bear distinctive, perhaps unique, thoughtprints.

# 24

# The Boomhower–Spangler
# Kidnap-Murders

## Mimi Boomhower (August 18, 1949)

THE STORY OF MIMI BOOMHOWER's disappearance broke on August 24, 1949, in the morning editions of the Los Angeles papers. The Bel Air socialite and "prominent heiress" had apparently vanished from her mansion six days earlier. Mimi, referred to by her friends as "the Merry Widow" because of her fondness for "going out on the town" and partying at various Hollywood nightclubs, had lived alone since the death of her husband in 1943. LAPD police detectives, who responded to the Boomhower home in Bel Air, discovered that all the house lights had been left on, her car was in the garage, the refrigerator was filled with fresh food and produce, and items recently ordered by her from stores had been delivered the day after her disappearance. Deputy Chief of Detectives Thad Brown issued a statement to the press in which he said, "We simply do not know what happened to her."

An unidentified witness found Boomhower's white purse in a telephone booth at a supermarket located at 9331 Wilshire Boulevard in Beverly Hills, with a note written directly onto the purse in large handprinted letters that read:

POLICE DEPT. —
WE FOUND THIS AT BEACH THURSDAY NIGHT

In retracing her movements, the police learned that the last known person to have seen her was her business manager, Carl

Manaugh, who had spoken with her at his Hollywood office on
Thursday afternoon, August 18. Manaugh told the police that Mrs.
Boomhower had informed him "she was meeting a gentleman at 7:00
P.M. at her home," whom he believed may have been a prospective
buyer for the mansion. An article in the *Mirror* revealed, "The police
were discounting rumors that a scar faced gambler was angry at Mrs.
Boomhower for not selling him the place for a gambling palace."

A possible suspect, identified by the newspaper as "Tom E.
Evans, ex-host on Tony Cornero's gambling ship and former dope
peddler, is to be questioned in West Los Angeles today." An ex-
LAPD officer phoned in a tip that several days before her disappear-
ance he saw Evans with the victim having drinks at the bar at the
Roosevelt Hotel in Hollywood.

Tom Evans was a gambler, with a criminal record in Los Angeles
dating back to the early 1920s. He had prior local arrests for bootlegging and robbery and had convictions for "opium running." As the
former associate and employee of Los Angeles vice czar and gambling
ship owner Tony Cornero, Evans was well-known to LAPD, who ran
him out of town after the shooting and wounding of Cornero in Hollywood in 1948. Cornero's assailant was never identified or arrested.

Evans told reporters who questioned him after he was identified
in the paper, "Sure I was in the bar at the hotel last week — I'm there
every day." He was taken to West Los Angeles Division police station
and questioned by detectives, but denied knowing the victim. Detectives told the press they believed that Evans was "in the clear, and that
someone probably just had a grudge against him," adding that they
had been receiving numerous phone calls and tips and had eighty
names of possible suspects. In the course of my investigation, I
learned that Tom Evans was not only Tony Cornero's bodyguard, but
also an acquaintance and associate of my father, dating back to 1925.

After interviewing Mrs. Boomhower's friends and business associates, police learned that only days before her disappearance she had inadvertently acknowledged to her furrier William Marco that she "had
been secretly married." She said she couldn't give Marco an order for
a fur she was contemplating buying, because "I'll have to talk it over
with my present husband." Then Marco said that the victim "checked
herself" and said, "I'll talk it over with my family and come back."

The only public clue of substance was the victim's purse, which the police laboratory determined contained no particles of sand that could have substantiated its having been found at the beach. The police believed that the purse had been left at the phone booth by the suspect himself, because the phone booth was only a few miles from her home and the purse appeared only a few hours after her kidnapping. A citizen who anonymously turned in evidence to police would more likely attach a note to it.

On September 30, 1949, the court declared that Boomhower was dead, but to this day her body has never been recovered and the case remains in LAPD files as another unsolved homicide.

## The Physical Evidence

As indicated, it is highly unusual that a witness would write a note directly on the victim's purse. People who make such finds usually attach a note to the evidence. Los Angeles's three largest newspapers — the *Times*, the *Herald Express*, and the *Examiner* — all simply reported the text of the message on the purse. Only the *Los Angeles Mirror* ran a photograph of the purse itself, in order to display the handwritten message as it physically appeared.

*August 25, 1949*

Earlier, I had sent Hannah McFarland the known and questioned documents relating to the Black Dahlia and Jeanne French cases. At this point in my investigation, in September 2000, I sent her a copy of that photograph, informing her only that the questioned-document sample was written in the year 1949 and that the purse was believed to be made of leather. Below is the photograph as it originally appeared, modified by the arrowed markings that were made by McFarland as part of her analysis.

*Exhibit 59*

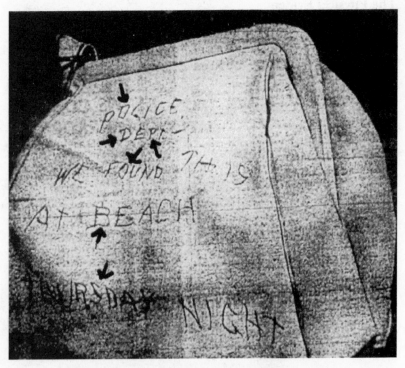

*Boomhower purse — questioned document 10 (Q10)*

Here is her report:

September 28, 2000
RE: Analysis of Q10 — Printing on Purse

Dear Mr. Hodel:

I am informed that Q10 was printed on a leather purse. This sample, from 1949, has three individual characteristics that are also present in the Known and Questioned printing samples:

1)   The O in *police* and *found* on Q10 is slanted to the left. This O is also found in K1, K5, Q2, Q8, and Q9.

2)   Q10 has letters with horizontal strokes that start far to the left of the body of the letter. This is seen in the letters D and P in *dept*, and the letter B in *beach*. This formation is also found in K1, K2, Q7, and Q8.

3)   The letter S in *Thursday* on Q10, has a straight stroke in the middle of the letter that forms an angle on each end. This S is also seen in K1, K5, K6, Q2, Q7, and Q9.

Due to the three individual characteristics that are common between Q10 and the Known and Questioned printing samples, I concluded it was highly probable that Q10 was printed by the same person who printed the Known and Questioned samples.
    The differences between the printing on Q10 and the Known printing samples can be explained by the disguised appearance (irregularity) on Q10.
    The unusual printing conditions presented by printing on a leather purse may also play a role in some of the differences between Q10 and the Known samples.

Hannah McFarland's forensic analysis of the handwriting on Boomhower's purse irrefutably connects George Hodel to the kidnap and murder of Mimi Boomhower, one more victim in the skein of lone women murders that took place in the late 1940s.

One month after Mimi Boomhower disappeared, I believe the Dahlia Avenger struck again.

### The Jean Spangler Kidnap-Murder

On Tuesday morning, October 11, 1949, the *Los Angeles Daily News* headline read:

# FEAR NEW DAHLIA DEATH
# 200 IN ACTRESS HUNT

The victim, a prominent actress, had been kidnapped off the streets of Hollywood, and evidence found in Fern Dell Park sent two hundred LAPD officers on a search for her body.

Jean Elizabeth Spangler was a twenty-seven-year-old actress on her way to becoming a star. She was beautiful, intelligent, filled with vitality and promise, and well liked in the film industry and the brand-new television business, where she had just started working.

After the first headline story in the *Daily News*, early in the week, the other local newspapers picked up the scent. The grisly headlines quickly proliferated: "Spangler Mystery Deepens," "Cryptic Note Clue to Missing Actress Mystery," "Probe Dancer's Secret Date with Death," "Glamour Girl Body Hunted; Parallel to 'Dahlia' Case Seen," "TV Actress Feared Sex Murder Victim."

Under pressure from the growing unrest in the district attorney's office at the unacceptable performance of his detectives, Deputy Chief Thad Brown held a meeting with officers in the Homicide Division, and then told the press, "Death by violence is indicated in her disappearance." He'd sent up the red homicide flag.

Spangler presented an intriguing challenge to detectives, because, as a background check of the victim's activities in the years preceding her disappearance revealed, there were a number of times her path had crossed Elizabeth Short's. In fact, Spangler had once worked as a dancer at Mark Hansen's Florentine Gardens.

Spangler had married Dexter Benner in June 1941, six months before the start of World War II. The couple had one daughter,

Christine, born on April 22, 1944. Shortly after her birth, Benner was inducted into the service and sent to the South Pacific.

Other court documents showed that Jean had asked her husband to initiate formal divorce proceedings in 1943, prior to her pregnancy and the birth of Christine. At that time, Spangler told her attorney she "did not want to appear in court," and revealed her infidelities with a "handsome Air Force first lieutenant," whom she "intended to marry." Jean freely admitted that she'd become involved in an "affair with this pilot," and they "had been living together off-and-on, in a Sunset Boulevard motel." In 1943, a few months after making these revelations, Jean became pregnant, reconciled with her husband, Dexter, and Christine was born the following April. Court papers revealed that after Dexter's assignment overseas, Jean again began seeing "Lt. Scott," and, on her husband's return, informed him of the resumed affair, which caused them to immediately separate and divorce. After their separation, the two became embroiled in a bitter child custody dispute that ended with the court awarding full custody of their daughter Christine to Jean.

Albert Pearlson, Spangler's divorce attorney, told police (after her 1949 kidnapping and disappearance) that "Scott had, during the time of their relationship, beaten her up, blackened her eye, and threatened to kill her if she ever left him." In the same court documents, the Army Air Force lieutenant was described as being "tall, about 5–11, slender build, clean-cut and handsome." Jean Spangler refused to identify and provide the true name of her lover to the court. After her disappearance, her attorney indicated that he "could not recall the officer's name" and that "everyone just called him 'Scottie.'"

Sensing another Dahlia-type murder story in the making, newspapers quickly sent reporters out to pursue their own investigations. Here is my reconstructed timeline of what they reported:

## Wednesday, October 5, 1949

Spangler, while working on a movie set at Columbia Pictures studios with actor Robert Cummings, told Cummings that she "had a happy new romance" and was having the time of her life. She did not tell Cummings her new boyfriend's name.

## Thursday, October 6, 1949

LAPD detective W. E. Brennan, in charge of the investigation, told the press that "Miss Spangler had a date with a man the night before her disappearance." Reporters also learned that a married couple, friends of the victim, had spoken with her briefly in front of the Hollywood Ranch Market. Spangler had been seen sitting with a "clean cut man in his thirties" in a black sedan parked in the Ranch Market parking lot. A short time later, witnesses saw Spangler and her companion standing at a nearby hot dog stand, which was located directly across the street from the studio apartment where Man Ray and his wife, Juliet, were living, approximately one mile from the Franklin House.

## Friday, October 7, 1949; 5:30–7:30 P.M.

Jean Spangler left her apartment at 6216 Colgate Avenue in Hollywood at 5:30 P.M. after telling her sister-in-law Sophie Spangler, who was babysitting Christine, that she would be home that night but expected to be late. Jean called the apartment two hours later at 7:30 P.M. to check on her daughter, spoke briefly with her sister-in-law, and again confirmed she would be home that night.

## Saturday, October 8, 1949; 1:30 A.M.

Witness Terry Taylor, the proprietor of the Cheese Box Restaurant at 8033 Sunset Boulevard in Hollywood, who also knew the victim personally, recalled seeing her seated at a front table with a man he described as, "male, 30–35, brown hair, clean cut, tallish with a medium build." His information was confirmed by a second witness, Joseph Epstein, who sold papers in front of the restaurant, who also identified Spangler as being there at about 2:00 A.M. on Saturday morning.

## 2:00 A.M.

Witness Al "the Sheik" Lazaar, a radio personality who broadcast his show live from the Cheese Box, said he saw Spangler sitting at the restaurant with two men he didn't know. When he approached the threesome at their table to do a radio interview, he saw that Miss Spangler "appeared to be arguing with the two men." When one of the men saw him walk up to the table, he abruptly signaled to him that they did not want to talk to him, and "the Sheik," in his own words, "veered away and did not attempt to conduct the interview."

### 9:00 A.M.

When Jean Spangler failed to return home, her sister-in-law, fearing foul play, contacted LAPD and filed a missing persons report. Dexter Benner picked up his daughter at his ex-wife's apartment and took her home to his place, intending to bring her back the following day.

### Sunday, October 9, 1949

On Sunday morning, October 9, Jean Spangler's purse was found lying ten feet off the roadway at the entrance to Fern Dell Park, the exact location where Father would drop me and my brothers off to play during the summer months of 1949 when he went to his downtown office or made house calls. The park is exactly six-tenths of a mile from the Franklin House. A park employee, Hugh Anger, found the purse and called the police.

The handle on Spangler's purse was torn loose and the purse itself had been ripped, which indicated a struggle. A handwritten note, written in pencil by the victim, was found in the purse:

Kirk,
Can't wait any longer. Going to see Dr. Scott.
Will work best this way while Mother is away.

*Daily News* headlines on October 11, 1949, read, "Fear New Dahlia Death," and speculated that the Spangler disappearance could be connected to other murders.

. . . some of the officers working the case inclined to the belief that she may be the 10th victim of a series of unsolved female mutilation murders. The maniacal slaughter of women began with the famed Black Dahlia case in 1947, when the tortured and gruesomely carved body of black-haired Elizabeth Short was found naked in a weed-grown lot.

As in the Spangler disappearance, also in the Black Dahlia case a purse was featured when some unknown person mailed it to police during the investigation of her baffling fate.

And more recently a purse containing a note was found in the unsolved mystery of the disappearance of Mimi Boomhower, wealthy and flirtatious Bel Air widow.

Jean's mother, Mrs. Florence Spangler, was out of town visiting relatives in Kentucky when she heard of her daughter's disappearance. She immediately returned home and, according to the papers, provided detectives with the name of a man whom she thought was responsible. The *Daily News* headline for the October 12, 1949, story read, "Mother Sure Film Player Murdered," and went on to say:

> The mother of film actress Jean Spangler, who mysteriously disappeared five days ago, said today she is convinced her daughter has been murdered, and gave police the name of the man she thought responsible for the girl's death. "I am sure this man hired somebody to do away with my daughter," said Mrs. Florence Spangler, who arrived here today from a vacation in Kentucky.
>
> Police refused to reveal the name of the man named by Mrs. Spangler but said they had already questioned him at some length.

The intensive two-hundred-man search by LAPD officers of Fern Dell Park, on horseback and on foot, revealed nothing new. The victim's body was never found, and the police never released the name of the man provided by Florence Spangler, whom they had questioned regarding the victim's disappearance. Although no progress was made in the case, Deputy Chief Thad Brown, in what appeared to be more of a public relations move than part of the actual investigation, interviewed actor Kirk Douglas to ascertain whether he might be the "Kirk" mentioned in her note. Douglas in-

dicated he did not personally know the victim and could provide police with no information related to her disappearance.

On October 13, 1949, some six days into the Spangler murder investigation, LAPD homicide detectives again arrested Tom Evans.
Evans was booked on a technical charge of robbery after detectives
found him in possession of a large amount of cash, with, according to
the charges, "no visible means of support."

The newspapers indicated that Evans was being held for suspicion of robbery and would be questioned the following day by Captain Jack Donahoe himself, now head of Robbery Division, in
connection with both the Spangler and Boomhower investigations.
Captain Donahoe told the papers, "We have no evidence linking him
to either case, but he is known to play women to get money." Evans's
photograph was prominently displayed in three local newspapers;
yet, once again, he denied any involvement in either crime. "I didn't
know either one of the women," he said to newspaper reporters.
"Next they will be trying to pin Cock Robin on me. I'm presently involved in promoting a deal in the Philippines involving sugar and
hemp. Now I suppose this current publicity will ruin my Manila
deal." Evans told reporters that a similar roust by LAPD a month
earlier on the Mimi Boomhower investigation had "ruined a Las Vegas deal" he was about to close. Evans blamed his troubles on a "retired LAPD detective, now working as a private investigator."

As Evans had predicted, no charges were filed against him in
connection with the Spangler case, and, even though the press applied relentless pressure on the LAPD to come up with some resolution, the hunt for the perpetrator of the Spangler kidnapping, like
that for the killer in the Dahlia and Lipstick homicides, came up
empty.

There were, however, reports in the papers that a real struggle
was taking place inside the LAPD over the handling of the Spangler
case, notably in the search for the person named Scott to whom
Spangler had referred in her note. A *Los Angeles Times* article of October 12, 1949 stated:

> Yesterday the investigators had a conference with top brass in the
> Police Department to discuss the case. Meeting with Dep. Chief
> Thad Brown were Inspector Hugh Farnum, Capt. Harry Elliott of

the Central homicide squad, Det. Lt. Harry Didion of Wilshire Division and Dets M.E. Turlock and William Brennan, who are handling the case. After the conference, Didion said that investigation has confirmed the existence of a "Scotty" or "Dr. Scott," who was known to Miss Spangler and her coterie of night-clubbing friends. But what is lacking is knowledge of the man's whereabouts, he said.

Detectives from the Gangster Squad, assigned to pursue and attempt to identify "Dr. Scott," later reported that while they had checked out six different "Dr. Scott"s during the investigation, none was the Dr. Scott of Spangler's note and none claimed to know or were connected with her. Similarly, LAPD detectives claimed they were never able to identify any individual or friend of Jean Spangler by the name of "Kirk," to whom she had addressed the original note.

Focusing on the Spangler case, I believe the real "Scottie" — and later "Dr. Scott" — could well have been George Hodel, who closely fits the profile of everything known about this mysterious "Scottie." Jean's Scottie, like Elizabeth Short's fiancé "George" and Georgette Bauerdorf's boyfriend, was an Air Force lieutenant from Texas. "Scottie" had an affair with Jean during the war years while her husband was overseas. They shared a motel room on the Sunset Strip. He was tall and handsome. He assaulted her and was violent and extremely jealous.

Because of her affair and the threats her lover had made to her, Jean Spangler had felt compelled to divulge the facts to her husband, with the results we have seen. In her original interview with detectives, Mrs. Florence Spangler gave the name of her daughter's boyfriend, "Scott," the abusive Army lieutenant who had figured prominently in her divorce. The detectives never released his true name and "doubted there was a connection."

LAPD detectives, working out of separate offices, unknowingly provided conflicting information to the press relating to "Scottie" or Dr. Scott. On the one hand, Homicide Division's Gangster Squad detectives indicated they had checked out all the known "Dr. Scott"s in Los Angeles and were unable to identify any doctor by that name who was connected to Ms. Jean Spangler. On the other hand, Detective

Lieutenant Harry Didion stated, "The investigation has confirmed the existence of a 'Scotty' or 'Dr. Scott,' who was known to Miss Spangler and her coterie of night-clubbing friends. But what is lacking is knowledge of the man's whereabouts."

Which statement was true? Further, what happened to the name of the suspect Jean Spangler's mother provided the LAPD? Was that name George Hodel? Had Jean Spangler been so intimate with Dad and his business that she possessed information and knowledge related to Tamar and the incest trial, which, upon learning of his arrest, she threatened to expose? Were her public argument with the two men and her disappearance minutes later, just hours after Father's arrest and release from custody, related?

Assuming for the moment that my father was "Scottie," what else did Spangler know about him that might have put her in jeopardy? Could Jean Spangler have been the 1944 girlfriend that my half-brother Duncan told me about in our conversations when he said, "I remember after Dad stopped seeing Kiyo in 1942 or so, he started dating this other woman. I think her name was Jean Hewett. Jean was this drop-dead beautiful young actress."

Very reluctantly, I also have to consider whether the elusive "Scottie" might be Christine's real father. Was she the issue of Jean's Hollywood affair with my father? Did Jean Spangler's acknowledged 1943 affair result in a pregnancy? Could Christine be my half-sister and is she still alive somewhere, with only the most fragmented memories of her mother and grandmother?

Or perhaps things are exactly as they appear on the surface, and Jean Spangler, as she represented to actor Robert Cummings, did meet Father only a few days before her kidnap-murder and was "having the time of her life with a new romance." Perhaps the mysterious Lieutenant Scott, whose identity she took great pains to conceal during the war years, was a different lover, with no connection to the events of 1949. Perhaps the anonymous "Lieutenant Scott" and invisible "Dr. Scott" are just coincidences in Spangler's short life. However, the real possibility exists that both men were one and the same and that Jean Spangler, upon learning of Father's arrest on October 6 for incest, met him after he posted bail and threatened to give damning information to the police. Two men — Dad and Sexton —

argued with her at the Hollywood restaurant in the early-morning hours of October 8, and she vanished, never to be seen again.

But, as we will see, her disappearance was not "without a trace," because she left behind in her own note important clues, as if she were telling us from beyond the grave, "Look to 'Kirk' and 'Dr. Scott,' because they will help you find my killer."

# 25

# Sergeant Stoker, LAPD's Gangster Squad, and the Abortion Ring

CAUGHT IN A WEB OF MACHIAVELLIAN INTRIGUE and systemic corruption within the highest ranks of the LAPD that eventually ended his career as a police officer, Sergeant Charles Stoker wound up unwittingly documenting the information that would, fifty years later, become the nexus linking LAPD Gangster Squad detectives and their superiors to a willful and deliberate cover-up of the Black Dahlia investigation and the other sexual serial homicides committed in the 1940s and beyond. Stoker never learned the true extent of his influence or effectiveness as an honest cop trying to fight corruption inside the police department. In his book *Thicker 'n Thieves* he provided a powerful record of his personal investigation that ultimately helped me unravel the mystery surrounding my father's escape from justice. In particular, his chapter "Angel City Abortion Ring" showed me what the motives were for the LAPD's cover-up of the Dahlia case and explained why the department chiefs made their decision to aid and abet the efforts of George Hodel, a known, identified serial killer, to flee the country rather than prosecute him.

Sergeant Stoker was an idealistic, no-nonsense, by-the-book vice squad officer, who believed that the LAPD was the finest police department in the world. However, in the spring and summer of 1949 his naiveté earned him a crash course in realpolitik that not only toppled his beliefs in the efficacy of the system he'd come to rely on, but took away his job and security, permanently tarnished his good name, and left him tragically disillusioned about people and government. He died without ever being publicly vindicated.

Charles Stoker had joined LAPD in May of 1942, worked briefly in uniformed patrol, and was then transferred to administrative vice. Stoker was a smart, perceptive, and honest cop, surrounded by partners with their hands out, reaching for a crooked buck within a system that not only tolerated corruption but fostered it. Stoker kept his hands in his pockets, which was not an easy or a popular position to take in the plainclothes units, especially in vice, where money greased the skids for felons at all economic levels, particularly purveyors of illicit sex operations run by L.A.'s organized crime cartels. While it worried many of his partners that Stoker remained squeaky clean, they treated him as an oddity and were careful not to do or say anything around him that would force him to report any corrupt activity.

What those officers and the rest of LAPD did not know, however, was that Stoker was more than an honest cop: he was a crusader, for whom police work — and specifically LAPD police work — was above politics. His zeal for the job and the organization, coupled with a tenacious personality, quickly put him on a collision course with his corrupt superiors all the way up the chain of command to an assistant chief of police and his counterparts in city hall. Stoker's refusal to back down also made him a target of many of the top-echelon politicians in the mayor's and district attorney's offices.

Stoker's troubles began with the 1949 arrest of Hollywood vice queen Brenda Allen, whom newspapers referred to as "Hollywood Madam" and "the Queen of Hearts." Allen ran a stable of 114 prostitutes and was paying off Hollywood vice officers as well as officers from the centralized Administrative Vice Unit, which conducted city-wide vice investigations. Hollywood Division needed to be paid off, as that was the division in which Allen lived and from which she based her operation. Brenda's monthly income generated plenty of juice for the policeman's fund and her friends at city hall. Corrupt police and city officials had come to rely on a steady stream of income from graft and payoffs.

In addition to Stoker's arrest of Allen, the newspapers revealed that LAPD had surreptitiously — and without a court order — listened in on telephone calls coming from gangster Mickey Cohen's Hollywood residence. So brazen was the LAPD command that in 1948 several officers experienced in audio electronics donned old clothing and, posing as construction workers, installed bugging devices at Cohen's home as it was being constructed. For over a year, LAPD officers maintained audio surveillance on Cohen's operations, tape-recording the comings and goings of his henchmen as well as many of his guests, which included state agents, police officers, and investigators and staff from the district attorney's office. After gathering a year's worth of covert "intelligence," several enterprising LAPD vice officers in 1948 approached Cohen with a shakedown, demanding $20,000 for some "campaign contributions." All of this would be revealed the following year, and that investigation threatened to topple the entire police department.

In May 1949, Stoker testified in secret before a grand jury to everything he had discovered about internal LAPD graft and corruption by high-ranking police officers. He blew the whistle, even though he had been told that it would ruin his career and probably the rest of his life. But he persisted. The newspapers picked up the scent of scandal, and for months he and the story made local headlines. Stoker's testimony resulted in indictments and perjury charges against then chief of police Clemence Horrall, his assistant chief Joe Reed, a lieutenant, and several sergeants. Many more were expected to follow, with the prospect that L.A.'s best-known gangster, Mickey Cohen, was rumored ready to talk to the 1949 grand jury. It was anticipated that Cohen would reveal high-level LAPD police corruption, as well as corruption within the ranks of the DA's office and the Los Angeles Sheriff's Department, which had a shared jurisdiction with the LAPD on Brenda Allen's bordello. Cohen's testimony would confirm all that Stoker had testified to and much more.

Cohen was persuaded to rethink his position about testifying. At 3:00 A.M. on the morning of July 20, 1949, he and his entourage — which included Neddie Herbert, a New York gangster and Cohen's number one man; state attorney general's investigator Harry Cooper, who had been assigned to bodyguard Cohen after rumors circulated of a planned assassination; newspaper columnist Florabel Muir; and actress Dee David — walked out the front door of Sherry's cocktail lounge onto Sunset Boulevard in Hollywood. Sherry's, a notorious meeting place and hangout for local gangsters, was owned and operated by colorful retired New York detective Barney Ruditsky. As the group was saying its goodnights on the sidewalk in front of the bar, shotgun blasts were fired from across the street into the crowd. Cohen, Neddie Herbert, Harry Cooper, and Miss David were all hit. Agent Cooper and the actress, though seriously wounded, survived. Herbert died two days later. Though Cohen received only a minor wound to his right shoulder, it apparently affected his vocal cords. After the attempted hit, the usually forthcoming Cohen refused to make any statements relating to police corruption and provided no information or fuel for the grand jury investigation.

When Cohen backed down, anyone else who might have come forward fell silent as well. And with no one at a high level willing to corroborate the charges the outspoken Stoker had made, he stood alone. Now it was his turn to feel the heat. A policewoman, Stoker's former partner, was quickly brought forward to testify that she had been with him when he committed a burglary of an office building. She alleged he stole back a personal check he had written for some construction work. He was arrested, booked, and charged with a felony count of burglary. Fortunately, Stoker had an airtight alibi for the time the policewoman claimed she had been with him, and a jury speedily found him not guilty.

LAPD regrouped, charging Stoker with "conduct unbecoming a police officer" and secondary allegations of insubordination. The former is an administrative charge so nebulous as to involve almost anything imaginable, a catch-all that permitted the department to get rid of anybody, anytime, for anything — for example, for driving your city car six blocks to your home to share a forty-five-minute lunch with your wife. "Conduct unbecoming" was a ground for dismissal.

The hearing board, comprised of LAPD captains and above — the senior chair being held by Deputy Chief of Detectives Thad Brown — quickly convened, refusing to allow Stoker's case to be continued until after the burglary trial could be heard. The board found him guilty of administrative violations, and the case was then submitted to the newly appointed chief of police, W. A. Worton, who would decide the penalty, which could range anywhere from a one-day suspension in pay to termination. Chief Worton reviewed the case and immediately fired Stoker. After Stoker's acquittal on the false and perjured burglary charge in the criminal case, in which most jury members concluded he had been framed, Stoker attempted to be reappointed as a police officer, but his request was denied.

Immediately before he was fired, and three months prior to my father's arrest for incest, Sergeant Charles Stoker was subpoenaed by the sitting 1949 grand jury to testify about all aspects of police corruption that he had discovered while assigned as a Hollywood vice operator. His revelations included firsthand information that went beyond the Brenda Allen scandal and the wiretapping and attempted extortion of monies from gangster Mickey Cohen.

Sergeant Stoker's secret testimony, some of which was leaked to the press, also included his discovery of an abortion ring within the City of Los Angeles, run by medical doctors who were paying protection money to members of the LAPD Gangster Squad, the specialized unit within the Homicide Division.* Stoker learned that this ring of abortionists included only M.D.s; each member paid regular "dues," which entitled him or her to operate freely and conduct abortions without fear of arrest.

Stoker became aware of the activities of the abortion ring when he was approached by a retired LAPD lieutenant, now an inspector for the California State Medical Board, who informed him he had heard about Stoker's good work and ability, admired his courage, and needed to talk to him. In checking out the inspector's reputation, Stoker learned that he had a solid reputation for honesty and would not connive, play ball, or cut corners.

The investigator told Stoker that he and others in his unit believed that members of LAPD's Gangster Squad, the unit responsible for making the arrests on the referrals from the medical board investigators, were protecting the abortionists, either by informing the medical doctors that they were under investigation, or if an arrest was actually made, smothering it before any charges could be formally filed with the DA. This occurred only in the cases of those doctors suspected of being within the ring of protection of the Gangster Squad detectives. All others — non-M.D.s, midwives, and chiropractors — were arrested and successfully prosecuted.

The inspector told Stoker that the suspected leader of the

---

*The organizational structure of the Gangster Squad and their duties and responsibilities within the Homicide Division have been explained at length in an earlier chapter. This is the same detective unit that had, in January 1947, "assisted" in the investigation of the Black Dahlia murder and had discredited two key witnesses, the Johnsons, and their positive identification of the probable killer, "Mr. Barnes," who had checked into their Washington Boulevard hotel with Elizabeth Short.

abortion ring was a Dr. Audrain, whose office was located in downtown Los Angeles at 6th and St. Paul. The investigators had an informant who had received an abortion from Dr. Audrain, and they wanted Stoker to conduct an undercover operation, using a policewoman as an operative. Stoker was informed that the medical board investigators' supervisor, who was also on the take, was on vacation; with him away, it was unlikely the LAPD Gangster Squad would receive word about the planned investigation and forewarn Dr. Audrain. The medical board inspectors asked Stoker to investigate the doctor in secret, which would circumvent the standard operating procedure of notifying the Gangster Squad detectives.

Stoker went to Lieutenant Ed Blair, his vice-supervisor, told him what he wanted to do, and explained that he had learned that the state investigators had requested his assistance because they suspected the Gangster Squad detectives of taking payoffs and protecting doctors performing illegal abortions. Lieutenant Blair, recognizing that the operation was far afield of Stoker's normal assignment as a vice squad officer, still approved Stoker's request, but ordered him to "take it easy and keep me out of it."

A policewoman posing as a "girl in trouble" made an appointment at Dr. Audrain's office, located at 1052 West 6th Street. She was examined and told by the nurse the "test came back positive for pregnancy."* An appointment was scheduled late the following week. The policewoman was advised to bring $250 in cash and return to the office at 7:30 in the morning the day of the operation. Normal abortionist working hours were from midnight until 9:00 A.M.

The day before the scheduled appointment, Stoker was contacted by the medical board investigators, who were, in Stoker's words, "down in the mouth." They advised him that their supervisor had returned from his scheduled vacation early, and they were left with no choice but to inform him of Stoker's pending investigation. Although their supervisor had told them to go forward with the plan, they were sure he would warn the Gangster Squad, who would in turn warn the doctor.

---

*While a sample was taken, no real test was ever completed, as was standard operating procedure. At $250–$500 for a half-hour's work, it was an excellent financial decision to inform all women they were pregnant.

Ever confident and optimistic, Stoker decided to go ahead with the plan anyway, and the following morning the policewoman, backed up by Stoker and his partner, Officer Ruggles, went to Audrain's office. The state investigators had surmised correctly. The doctor had indeed been tipped off; the office was locked tight and remained closed for a full week following the anticipated arrest. The investigation having ended in failure, Stoker returned to his normal duties, putting the abortion ring concerns out of his mind.

In the spring of 1949, the subject of this protected abortion ring resurfaced. This time, the same medical board inspector approached Stoker with a new case, involving a female M.D. (her name was never revealed by Stoker) believed to be connected with the abortion ring, who was performing abortions to well-recommended customers out of her expensive office in the movie colony district on Ventura Boulevard in Sherman Oaks.

The state investigators had obtained the name of one of the doctor's former clients, which they could use as an entrée and reference. This time they asked Stoker to operate on his own, without involving their office, which would obviate the necessity of their having to inform their supervisor, thus effectively bypassing LAPD Homicide and its Gangster Squad.

Stoker agreed, and the same undercover policewoman who had attempted to obtain the abortion at Dr. Audrain's office again posed as a pregnant woman seeking help. She met the woman doctor at her office, who informed her that "she was not doing abortions as she could not find a dependable assistant." The doctor said she would personally contact another doctor who would perform the abortion. The policewoman was advised to call back the following morning and the doctor would provide the other doctor's name. The following morning, the woman doctor told the undercover policewoman that she had spoken with another doctor, Eric Kirk, who had agreed to perform the abortion. She gave her Kirk's phone number.

Sergeant Stoker immediately contacted the state medical investigator, who told him that while Eric Kirk was a suspected abortionist, he was a chiropractor, therefore not a member of the ring. A decision was made to proceed anyway, to see if an arrest could be made on Kirk.

The policewoman made an appointment, was examined at Kirk's office on Riverside Drive in the North Hollywood area, was again,

per standard operating procedure, found to be pregnant, and was
given an appointment for an abortion for the following Saturday. She
was again advised to bring $250 in cash. I checked the 1949 Los An-
geles telephone directory for a listing of chiropractors and found
Eric Kirk's office listed at that time at 2157 Riverside Drive. In the
same directory, Kirk advertised his specialty as "Obstetrics and Gy-
necology."

On the day of the scheduled appointment, the cash was marked
and the policewoman was driven to Kirk's office by Stoker and Officer Ruggles, where they maintained surveillance a block away. The
policewoman entered the office and within five minutes exited the
front door and was observed to enter a large sedan that had pulled up
in front of the office. Stoker and Ruggles, on foot and out of their
unmarked police car, ran back to it and quickly searched the area for
the sedan, but could not locate it. Now fearful for the policewoman's
safety, they entered the office and found a receptionist inside. Initially, the woman denied any knowledge of the appointment with a
pregnant woman seeking an abortion, but when confronted with arrest as an accessory, she identified herself as Eric Kirk's wife, breaking into tears. "I knew it," she said. "He's done it again. I hope you
catch the son-of-a-bitch and send him to jail for life!"

Stoker contacted his vice unit, reported the police officer missing, and put out a broadcast for all units to be on the lookout for the
vehicle and the missing policewoman. At that point, the policewoman walked into the medical office accompanied by Dr. Eric Kirk,
who, upon learning that his patient was an undercover police officer,
related the following story to Sergeant Stoker, Officer Ruggles, and
the policewoman.

Two days after he had scheduled the appointment with the policewoman, Kirk said, two officers from LAPD Gangster Squad
came to his office and arrested him for soliciting abortions. Stoker
asked Kirk to identify the detectives and he complied. In his book,
Stoker referred to them as "Detectives Joe Small and Bill Ball" —
not their real names.

Since Dr. Kirk had not completed a solicitation for abortion with
Stoker and the policewoman, Stoker lacked enough reasonable cause
to make an arrest and was therefore forced to call the Gangster
Squad detectives and inform them of the circumstances. Stoker

contacted the two detectives and advised them of his own investigation and what had transpired that morning. He was told by them to "keep his nose out of their business and stop conducting unauthorized abortion investigations."

A few months later, the third and final incident involving Stoker, the California state medical investigators, and the Gangster Squad detectives took place. This one involved a nurse who was arranging for abortions for young girls at a cost of $500. The suspected doctor was one of the protected M.D.s, and again the state investigators asked Stoker to operate without the knowledge of their supervisor. This time they added another twist: he would have to obtain the $500 from his own department, in order not to tip off their connection to the investigation. Stoker went to his supervisor, Lieutenant Blair, who again said, "I'll try and get the money for you, but keep me out of it." Blair obtained the $500 from a vice slush fund, Stoker signed for the cash, and all was ready to proceed. The following morning at eight o'clock Stoker's phone rang. It was detective "Joe Small" from Homicide. "What do you think you're doing?" he asked, reminding Stoker that he had "already been told once to stay out of abortion investigations." Small informed Stoker that an officer would be by to pick up the $500 and would give him a signed receipt for the cash. Stoker signed over the cash to this officer: that ended his involvement in the abortion ring investigations. Eric Kirk was convicted of performing abortions and speedily sentenced to prison at San Quentin.

In May 1949, behind closed doors, Sergeant Charles Stoker was called before the grand jury and testified to everything he had learned about the abortion ring and the involvement of Gangster Squad detectives "Joe Small and Bill Ball." As a result of this testimony, the information he provided about the Brenda Allen scandal, and other testimony from LAPD officers, grand jury indictments were secured against Chief Clemence B. Horrall, Assistant Chief Joe Reed, Captain Cecil Wisdom, Lieutenant Rudy Wellport, and Sergeant E. V. Jackson.

After Stoker's testimony, Kirk, who remained behind bars in San Quentin, submitted, through his attorneys, a written affidavit to the Superior Court in an attempt to get a new trial based on the evidence provided by Stoker. In his affidavit, Kirk stated that he had been told by three separate Los Angeles attorneys that "some politicians, or the Los Angeles Police Department, were out to get me, but that they [the attorneys] could not identify the interested parties or give their reasons for wanting me out of the way." In his affidavit, Kirk said that immediately after his initial arrest, a co-defendant by the name of Tulley (no additional information was provided by Stoker) informed him that $2,500 would "square the beef." The Monday following his arrest, Kirk and Tulley, out on bail, met with a seventy-one-year-old man named Dan Bechtel at his office in downtown Los Angeles. Upon receiving $2,500 each from Tulley and Kirk, Bechtel immediately called a man by the name of "Joe," spoke with him, and then told both defendants that the charges "had been quashed by Joe." Both Tulley and Kirk left Bechtel's office, but several days later were contacted and told to return. Both complied, and their monies were returned, whereupon Bechtel explained, "the deal could not go through, as too many people were involved." Bechtel made a final contact with Kirk, where he advised the chiropractor that "he could get the charges dismissed but it would cost Kirk $16,000." Kirk could not raise that amount of money and, after his conviction, was remanded to custody and sent to prison. According to Stoker, in 1950 Dan Bechtel was indicted by the grand jury "for accepting large sums of money from abortionists on the pretense that this money would be utilized in paying off law enforcement officers whose duty it is to arrest and prosecute abortions."

From the moment that Sergeant Charles Stoker walked in and testified before the 1949 grand jury, his fate was sealed. He lost his job, lost his good name, and was publicly ridiculed. Ignoring warnings and threats to his life, he did ultimately publish a book about what had happened to him, which concluded:

> Villains in the story books always get their just desserts, and we — the members of the 1949 county grand jury, and I — can only hope that justice and virtue will triumph in the future. In the words of the poet Young, "Tomorrow is a satire on today, and shows its weakness."

Ironically, on the same day a Superior Court jury was hearing testimony in the incest trial of my father — Wednesday, December 14, 1949 — the following article appeared in the *Los Angeles Evening Herald and Express*:

# OUST STOKER AS LONE VICTIM
# OF VICE PROBE

Charles F. Stoker, former vice squad sergeant, who touched off the lengthy grand jury investigation of police protected vice, wound up today as the only victim of the much-publicized purge.

He was discharged from the police force by Chief W.A. Worton, who approved the recommendation of a police board of rights, which found Stoker guilty of insubordination and conduct unbecoming an officer.

The article went on to note that, although five other police officers, including former Police Chief C. B. Horrall and former Assistant Chief Joe Reed, were also indicted on perjury and bribery charges, all were cleared.

Twenty-five years later, on March 10, 1975, the following article appeared in the back pages of the *Los Angeles Herald Examiner:*

# STOKER, EX-OFFICER, DIES AT 57

Former Los Angeles Police Sgt. Charles Stoker, who was a central figure in a 1949 department scandal, has died of an apparent heart attack.

Stoker, 57, died yesterday morning in Glendale Memorial Hospital, where he was taken after suffering chest pains, while working in the Southern Pacific railroad yards. He was employed as a brakeman.

Stoker played a key role in exposing corruption in the LAPD vice squad, but was later accused of a burglary, which led to his dismissal from the force. Stoker contended that he was framed on the burglary charge.

Dr. Francis C. Ballard, the Beverly Hills physician to whom Father paid $500 for performing Tamar's abortion, was in all likelihood a member of the abortion ring Charles Stoker was trying to expose. As a matter of record, despite the strong case surrounding his October 1949 arrest for the abortion performed on Tamar, criminal charges against him were ultimately dismissed in 1950 after attorneys Giesler and Neeb successfully branded Tamar as "a pathological liar and a young girl in need of psychological treatment, who should be in a hospital, not a court of law."

## Dr. Walter A. Bayley

In January 1997, *Los Angeles Times* staff writer Larry Harnisch, to commemorate the fiftieth anniversary of the Dahlia murder, wrote an article entitled "A Slaying Cloaked in Mystery and Myths," which provided a very good overview of many of the known facts relating to the fifty-year-old unsolved case.

Several years later, his search for a suspect would develop into a lengthy Internet article promoting his theory that the Black Dahlia killer was a Los Angeles physician by the name of Walter A. Bayley.

Harnisch based his theory on several points: first, that Bayley was a prominent surgeon, which was in keeping with LAPD's premise that the murder and bisection of Elizabeth Short had to have been performed by a skilled surgeon; that Bayley's wife — from whom he was separated — lived at 3959 South Norton Avenue, less than a block from the Black Dahlia crime scene; that Bayley's daughter knew Adrian West, Elizabeth Short's sister, and indeed had been a witness at her marriage; and, finally, that Bayley had left his wife for a woman colleague, Dr. Alexandra von Partyka, who worked in the same office with him. Harnisch speculated that she had discovered his "crime" and was blackmailing him.

In fact, Dr. Walter Bayley had no connection whatsoever with Elizabeth Short, or her murder. For one thing he had developed Alzheimer's disease, and had neither the mental nor physical capacity to either commit such a crime or taunt the police about it. No, his legitimate fears that Dr. Partyka would ruin his reputation arose from another source: she was undoubtedly blackmailing him with her knowledge that he was a member of the L.A. abortion ring.

My search of the 1946 Los Angeles–area telephone book showed that Dr. Walter Bayley's private practice was located at 1052 West 6th Street, the same address as that of Dr. Audrain, Stoker's head of the protected abortion ring. It is very likely that the name of the warned abortionist, contacted by the Gangster Squad detectives the night before Stoker's pending arrest, and who closed his office for a week following, was indeed Dr. Walter A. Bayley.

My research revealed a coincidental connection that seems to have gone unnoticed by police and press in the early days of the Dahlia investigation. Mrs. Betty Bersinger, who first discovered Elizabeth Short's body, told reporters that in notifying the police, she "ran to the closest house," which she described as "the second house on Norton Avenue from 39th Street," and said that it belonged to a doctor. It is highly probable that this house was the residence of Dr. Walter Bayley and his wife Ruth, out of which Dr. Bayley had moved the previous year.

I suspect, too, that my father knew Dr. Bayley, and probably Dr. Partyka and Dr. Audrain as well. All had worked for Los Angeles County, and their downtown medical offices were within six blocks of each other. If George Hodel knew or worked with active members of the M.D. abortion ring, which I believe he did, the probability that they were acquainted would be very strong. Although I don't believe George Hodel performed abortions, because he was opposed to them in principle — except in the unusual position of being coerced by his own daughter under an implied threat of disclosure — it is almost certain that he not only associated with the doctors inside the ring but knew they were being protected by the LAPD's Gangster Squad.

As a result of this inside knowledge and the people he could incriminate were he to have been prosecuted for any of the murders he committed, he was himself protected by the very same Gangster Squad that protected and profited from the work of the abortion ring that Charles Stoker sacrificed his career to expose.

## Abortion Ring-Spangler Connections

It is my further contention that the Spangler note,

> Kirk,
> Can't wait any longer. Going to see Dr. Scott.
> Will work best this way while Mother is away.

related to the fact that Jean Spangler needed to obtain an abortion. I believe that "Kirk" is not a first name, as LAPD chief of detectives Thad Brown tried to suggest when he personally interviewed actor Kirk Douglas, but a surname. Kirk, I submit, was Dr. Eric Kirk, Sergeant Stoker's chiropractor, abortionist, and informant. I further submit that Jean Spangler was initially planning to have Kirk perform her abortion. Her note was directed to him! Because he was suddenly and unexpectedly arrested and incarcerated by Detectives "Bill Ball and Joe Small," and because time was of the essence, she was forced to find a replacement for "Kirk," either through or with the help of "Dr. Scott."

On September 17, 1949, just twenty days before Jean Spangler's kidnapping and murder, an article appeared in the *Los Angeles Mirror* over the headline "Wife of L.A. Abortionist in Hiding." The story carried a picture of Dr. Eric H. Kirk, captioned: "He'll testify." The article said that Kirk's wife, Mrs. Marion Kirk, "a key witness in a huge abortion-payoff-ring probe, was in hiding after it was learned that she received numerous telephone threats to 'keep her mouth shut.'" The article indicated that Dr. Kirk would testify to what he knew, with the following caveat: "I'm not going to name other doctors. I'm no stool pigeon. If all the doctors who perform abortions in Los Angeles were cleaned out, there wouldn't be many doctors left."

As a matter of procedure, it's likely that the Gangster Squad detectives involved in the Spangler investigation, in a fox-in-the-hen-house type of scenario, were assigned the task of trying to locate and identify the "Kirk" and "Dr. Scott" in the Spangler note. This would be logical because of their familiarity with abortionists city-wide. It of course permitted them to protect themselves, and their operation, by keeping the identities of both men secret. As we know from newspaper reports, despite these detectives' "exhaustive search," neither "Dr. Scott" nor "Kirk" was ever located or identified.

It is inconceivable to me that the LAPD was unable to make the obvious connection between the abortionist Kirk and Spangler's handwritten note, addressed to him. Kirk's identity should have been obvious to the investigators, because "Bill Ball and Joe Small" arrested him for performing illegal abortions just three weeks prior to the discovery of the Spangler note. Their failure to identify the real Kirk was all part of the abortion ring cover-up. As we will soon discover, these same Gangster Squad detectives were subpoenaed and forced to testify in secret before the 1949 grand jury. Their testimony would be labeled "evasive" and "contradictory" and they would publicly be accused by both the grand jury members and the district attorney's Bureau of Investigation of "covering up" facts and destroying evidence relating to "the Wealthy Hollywood Man" (Dr. George Hodel) named in secret before the grand jury as the prime suspect in both the Black Dahlia and Red Lipstick murders.

Thanks to Sergeant Stoker's detailed explanation of how the L.A. abortion ring operated, we are able to connect the dots not only to Dr. Bayley and his role as an abortionist, but, more importantly, to "Bill Ball and Joe Small." With Stoker's help, we see them as they were: active ringleaders in a LAPD high-stakes money-for-protection racket. By successfully silencing Dr. Eric Kirk, and speedily sending him to prison, the Gangster Squad detectives prevented any linkage between Kirk and Jean Spangler, who had likely sought him out to perform her abortion in the weeks preceding her disappearance. Then with his arrest and incarceration, she wrote the note, which remained undelivered in her purse, and was found only three weeks later, after she was kidnapped and murdered.

It was October 1949. In the previous two years, more than a dozen lone women had been found savagely murdered in the streets of Hollywood and downtown L.A. Two other socially prominent Hollywood women had disappeared and were suspected to have met the same fate. Gangsters were firing away at each other in open gun battles on Sunset Boulevard, wounding government officials and nearly killing a member of the press. An LAPD chief of police, an assistant chief, a lieutenant, and two vice squad officers were under indictment. My father had just been arrested for incest in a sex scandal that was making the front pages of the local papers. Sergeant Stoker, after testifying in secret before the grand jury as a whistle-blower, along with his partner, Officer Ruggles, had been fired. Corruption in the city and throughout its administration was so pervasive that even sexual predators were able to prey on women without fear of arrest.

Who was actually governing the city and why were the police powerless to stop crime?

# 26

# George Hodel: Underworld Roots — The "Hinkies"

"As your last act of love for me you must dispose of all my effects." This was, as noted, Father's order to June after he suffered a stroke in 1998 and planned on taking his life. He did not want June to handle his personal effects either while he was still alive or after his death. There were secrets he wanted buried with his ashes.

Father wanted his photo album destroyed because it contained his only link to Elizabeth Short, and we now know why. But he had said "all my effects." Were there other links to his past that he also wanted erased? I now know that the answer was yes.

Among these personal effects to be destroyed were his early photographs, which June had showed me on a visit to San Francisco some months after Father's death. The photographs, which had been taken in the mid-1920s, had been shown in a Pasadena art gallery as part of his one-man show. There were architectural photos of early L.A. — Long Beach oil derricks, downtown buildings, all artistically composed — plus many portraits: a black man, an oil rigger, construction workers, and others with hard faces, rough men whose visages were etched by years of cunning.

There was also a group of savvy street-smart faces from the 1920s. Who were these men? Friends? Were they people he knew when he was driving a cab in L.A.? His wife didn't know. Perhaps they were nobodies, forgotten people from a distant past. June kept the originals but allowed me to make copies for myself.

Among these photographs were six men I was curious about and wanted to identify. Cops have a term for men with faces like these:

we call them *hinkies*. "Hinky" is a combination of "suspicious," "evasive," "dirty," or just plain up to no good. And these faces were hinky; they had too much experience with what cops normally see — the dark side of life. They had eyes that said, this guy has seen and known hard anger and brutality. These were criminal eyes, gangster eyes, part shifty, part confrontational, mostly desensitized — thoroughly tough. I wanted to know who they were and why they were part of his past.

To date I have not been able to obtain positive identifications on all of these men, but in exhibit 60 I do have tentative identifications for three of them.

### Exhibit 60

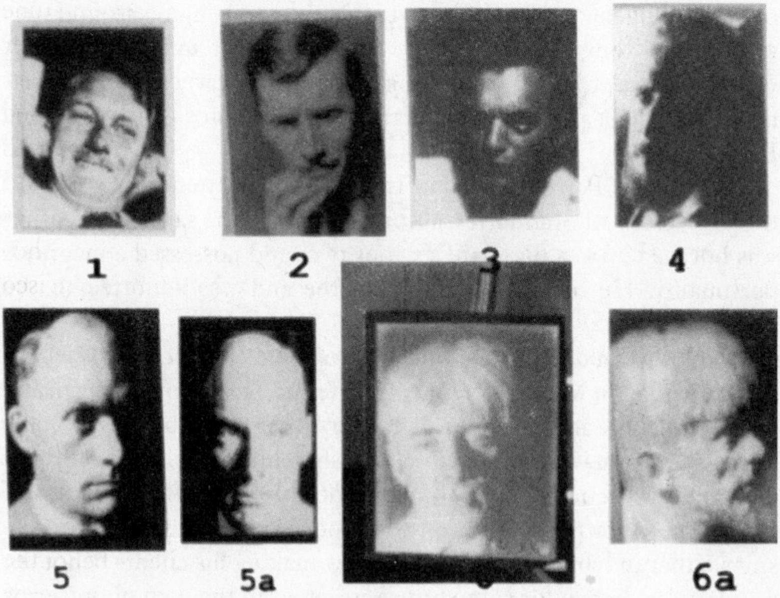

*George Hodel photos taken circa 1925*
*Photograph 1: Kent Kane Parrot, tentative ID*
*Photograph 2: Tom Evans (age approx. 26), tentative ID*
*Photograph 3: Fred Sexton (age approx. 19), tentative ID*
*Photographs 4, 5, 6: Unidentified to date*

Based on the fact that three of the six photograph subjects were connected with L.A.'s underworld, there is a strong probability the remaining three have gangster connections as well. I believe that George Hodel and Fred Sexton were either full-fledged henchmen of an early crime gang, or, at least, remained close friends and associates for the next twenty-five years. To me, these photographs are more dark shadows from George Hodel's past, which might well connect him to notorious gangsters and killers of the time.

Photo 2 is especially compelling: it's of Tom Evans at age twenty-six, the convicted rum-running, drug-smuggling con man we have earlier identified as Tony Cornero's bodyguard, the same man who, in his words, was "rousted" by LAPD in 1949 under suspicion of the kidnappings and murders of both Mimi Boomhower and Jean Spangler. These photographs show that Evans was linked to George Hodel as far back as 1925. What was my father, who prided himself on his intelligence, erudition, and culture, doing hanging around with a thug like Tom Evans? Perhaps the answer lies in photograph 1, which, I suspect, is a much younger picture of early L.A.'s least familiar but most powerful syndicate boss, the notorious Kent Kane Parrot.

Kent Kane Parrot arrived in Los Angeles to attend law school at the University of Southern California in 1907, the same year Father was born. He was a big man, six foot two, and possessed a magnetic personality. He obtained his law degree and was admitted to the state bar.

Parrot was a deal-maker with phenomenal "people skills," whose real talent lay in his ability to bring together people of diametrically opposed beliefs and lifestyles — conservatives and liberals, prohibitionists and rum-runners — to establish some common causes that would allow them to unite. He didn't do this out of the goodness of his heart. A consummate broker, he pocketed handsome commissions either in hard cash or by somehow making his clients beholden to him in exchange for some future payment in the coin of power or influence. Through his ability to forge relationships, Parrot got himself into politics, which he once defined very simply as "people in motion." And that's exactly how he played the game.

By 1924, Kent Parrot had become the power behind the throne in Los Angeles municipal politics. In the 1921 race for mayor, he successfully selected and got elected George Cryer, who became known as "Parrot's Puppet," at which point Parrot quickly aligned himself with Los Angeles's vice lords, including the young bootlegging czar Tony Cornero. Parrot, while publicly discreet in his dealings with the underworld, would entertain its members and broker relationships among them at his private apartment at the city's newest and finest downtown hotel, the Biltmore, about which he once boasted, "Everyone in the state of California has possibly been there in the official line."

As Parrot's influence and power grew, he placed more and more importance in the Los Angeles Police Department. Wielding payoffs, bagmen, and vice-supervisors, Parrot wound up with most of LAPD in his pocket and, though out of the public eye, became the most powerful man in Los Angeles politics from the 1920s through the 1940s. Citizen Kent Kane Parrot's word was law, because he owned the law.

In researching Parrot's early days in Los Angeles, hoping to find an early photograph to compare to the one my father had taken, I contacted his old alma mater. They didn't have one, but they were able to provide me with his classmates' prophetic reference to him in his 1909 law school yearbook, *Stare Decisis*:

> Not all the pumice of our college town
> Can smooth the roughness of this New York clown.

On a personal note, I have only seen my father stumble, falter, and find himself at a loss for words on two occasions. The first was in 1965, when he met my wife, his ex-mistress, Kiyo, in the lobby of the Biltmore. The second occurred some three years before his death, during a weekend visit in San Francisco, at Sunday brunch. Knowing Father always had a reason for choosing specific names, and knowing that my older brother Michael Paul's namesake was chosen from Mother's close friendship with renowned bacteriologist and "microbe hunter" Paul De Kruif, and my younger brother, Kelvin George, was named after Father, I asked him what was the source of my own middle name, Kent. Who had I been named after? It seemed as if he was caught off guard, as he hemmed and hawed nervously and finally came out with a most implausible, "Oh, no reason. It's just a nice-sounding name, that's all." Though surprised, I took his statement at face value. Armed with today's biographical knowledge, the photograph, their twenty-year friendship, and Father's admiration for the man and his influence and power, I submit that Father chose to honor his old friend, Kent Parrot, by making me his namesake.

Tony Cornero, aka Tony Canaris and Tony Cornero Stralla, got his start in California during Prohibition. A San Francisco cab driver in the early 1920s, he began as a rum-runner, overseeing the unloading and distribution of contraband liquor from ships off the California coast. Smaller boats would taxi the precious cargo to deserted beaches, where Cornero would then receive and coordinate the shipments throughout Los Angeles and Southern California.

On March 11, 1925, the *L.A. Record* headlines read, "Jail Rum 'King' with $50,000 Liquor." At the time of his arrest, after a raid in which the authorities seized his high-grade scotch whisky, Canadian bourbon, and French champagne, reporters quoted him as saying, "I've had nothing but misfortune. I've been in the business over three years. I've been hijacked, fined, and robbed of over $500,000. I have paid out more than $100,000 for police protection, which I never got. This present beef means a long stretch for me. It's a bum business." Cornero's girlfriend told the *Record* that Cornero "made $500,000 in 2 years." Cornero, of course, did what he did, paid who he had to, the charges "went away," and by his thirties he became a millionaire, having succeeded in his self-described "off shore drilling."

By 1937, twelve years after his bust, Tony was promoted to "Admiral Cornero" and owned several large gambling ships off the coast of Los Angeles just outside the three-mile limit. From the pier at Santa Monica, customers could take a twenty-five-cent, ten-minute ride and be drinking the best imported liquor and shooting dice or playing blackjack aboard his lush floating casino, which was triple the size of any of those offered in Las Vegas in those early years before Benny (Bugsy) Siegel built the Flamingo. Night after night, Angelenos lined up by the thousands to try their luck against his blackjack dealers or at the shipboard crap tables. While Cornero's offshore investment profits were a tightly guarded secret, they have been estimated at a nightly net of $30,000.

Like many other local successful businessmen, Cornero bought himself a home in Beverly Hills alongside such prominent neighbors as Benny Siegel and Mickey Cohen. Cornero remained a major crime figure in Los Angeles for almost twenty-five years, though he remained strictly local and did not ally himself with the East Coast or Chicago-based Cosa Nostra families. As a result, he always remained an outsider, never able to establish any onshore gambling establishments, because police and sheriffs quickly shut them down as soon as he started them up. Gangsters Jack Dragna, Benny Siegel — an early investor in Cornero's floating casino the *Rex* — and Johnnie Rosselli, together with the help of corrupt mayor Frank Shaw and well-positioned, high-ranking officers within LAPD and LASD, would maintain control of city business, gambling, and prostitution throughout Los Angeles.

In 1938, LAPD captain Earle Kynette headed the department's Intelligence Squad. As part of his intelligence-gathering, he wiretapped Mayor Frank Shaw's opposition candidate, fifty or more prominent Los Angeles citizens, and retired LAPD detective Harry Raymond, at that time employed by the reform candidate to obtain information relating to corruption within the mayor's office and LAPD. Kynette and members of his squad decided that Raymond was getting too close to the truth, so they placed a bomb in his car. When he turned the ignition key the explosion totally demolished the vehicle and blew hundreds of pieces of shrapnel into Raymond's body. He was rushed to the hospital, where, in critical condition and about to succumb from his injuries, he put in a call to the crime-fighting city editor of the *Los Angeles Examiner*, James Richardson, who rushed to Raymond's bedside. Believing he had only minutes to live, Raymond whispered the name of his assailant into Richardson's ear and made him promise he would see to it that Kynette would be prosecuted.

Miraculously, Raymond survived, and, though a cover-up was attempted by then LAPD chief James Davis — who had the gall to put Captain Kynette in charge of the car-bombing investigation — the facts eventually came out. Kynette was charged and convicted of the attempted murder of his brother officer and sentenced to a ten-year prison term. Mayor Frank Shaw, under whose auspice the crime was allegedly carried out, was promptly voted out of office in September 1938, replaced by the reform candidate Fletcher Bowron.

In his recently published *The Dream Endures: California Enters the*

*1940s,* State Librarian Kevin Starr had this to say about city reformers Clifford Clinton and Fletcher Bowron, and their investigation and revelations of the Shaw regime in 1937:

> Los Angeles, Clinton discovered, was supporting an intricate network of brothels, gambling houses, and clip joints, all of it run by well-organized syndicates headed by gambler Guy McAfee and Bob Gans, chief concessionaire of slot machines throughout the city, with attorneys Kent Parrot and Charles Kradick serving as mouthpieces. Obviously, a number of police were on the take for so many operations — an estimated six hundred brothels, three hundred gambling houses, eighteen hundred bookie joints, twenty-three thousand slot machines — to be flourishing. (p.168)

Within his first two months in office, Mayor Bowron forced LAPD police chief James Davis to retire, after the bombing investigation showed that, while Davis's memory was hazy about specific details, "perhaps" he had, after all, ordered Raymond and fifty other city reformers to be placed under surveillance by Kynette's Intelligence Squad. Bowron then met in secret with his good friend James Richardson and asked him to help identify and rid Los Angeles of the corrupt politicians and police officers on the take.

As Richardson wrote in *For the Life of Me,* he simply picked up the telephone, called Tony Cornero at his Beverly Hills home, and set up a meeting to see if Cornero would be willing to help him and the mayor. Cornero, ever the entrepreneur and quick to size up a good deal, agreed to meet with Richardson and Mayor Bowron.

The three met in secret at the mayor's home in the Hollywood Hills, where Cornero told Mayor Bowron that he knew all about corruption within the LAPD. In fact, he said, according to Richardson's account, "'I've got their names all written down on this slip of paper.' And he handed Bowron the paper . . . the mayor read the names of twenty-six of the highest ranking officers in the department."

Bowron hired an ex-FBI agent to investigate all twenty-six, most of whom were the department's most powerful commanders. The mayor's investigator conducted wiretapping and surveillance of all those Cornero had named. One by one they were called before the mayor, who demanded their resignation. If anyone protested or refused to resign, Bowron simply played his tape-recorded conversations. End of story.

According to an official LAPD history of "the Purge" and Mayor Bowron's campaign to reform the LAPD, as written in *Los Angeles Police Department 1869–1984:*

> On the morning of March 3, 1939, the Commissioners struck. Citing Charter Section 181, which authorized the retirement of any officer eligible for pension "for the good of the Police Department," the Mayor, supported by the Police Board, requested the immediate resignation of 23 [sic] high-ranking officers. Included in the "forced retirement" were former Chief (now Deputy Chief) Roy Steckel, Chief of Detectives Joe Taylor, Assistant Chief George Allen, 11 captains and 9 lieutenants. Within the next six months 45 high-ranking officers resigned. (p.82)

After the purge of what by LAPD's reckoning was sixty-eight high-ranking officers, Tony Cornero's own troubles began. The syndicate had been conducting its own surveillance against the reformers by placing its man inside city hall. Unbeknownst to Mayor Bowron, his trusted driver was working as a paid informant for the very crime bosses he was fighting. The driver reported back on the Cornero/Richardson/Bowron secret meeting, and the syndicate leaked the news to the press, claiming that Bowron had "made a deal with Cornero, promising him control of vice and prostitution throughout the city."

Bowron, left with no alternative, and to prove to his constituency that he was not in league with any gangster, was forced to turn on Cornero and promptly ordered law enforcement to shut down his gambling ships as an illegal operation. Richardson reported that Cornero, while he initially came out swinging in defense of his ships' being legal and outside the jurisdiction of the courts, eventually took the whole thing in stride and resigned himself to the political and philosophical ironies, all with relatively good humor.

Like many gangsters of his day, Cornero was romanticized, and fact soon became fiction: in the 1943 movie *Mr. Lucky*, Cary Grant portrayed Cornero as a charming draft-dodging gambler and closet patriot putting the big woo on elegant socialite Laraine Day.

In reality, Cornero was no different than Ben Siegel or Mickey Cohen. Behind the comical Runyonesque slang and purported good humor was a powerfully positioned, politically connected, stone-cold sociopathic killer. Gangsterism was big business in the Los Angeles of the 1930s and 1940s, and each crime boss had his own retinue of lawyers and businessmen through whom they owned the men who ran city hall and the police and sheriff's departments. They had the power and the money to make any investigation vanish, and they and those who worked for them were inoculated against criminal prosecution.

When I looked at my father's photographs of Kent Parrot, Tom Evans, and the young Fred Sexton, I realized that the latter two of them were connected to some of the most powerful bosses in the Los Angeles crime syndicates, maybe even having begun their own criminal careers as young henchmen or drivers during Prohibition. George and Fred likely remained connected to these crime figures for the next three decades. I reflected on what Sexton's daughter "Mary Moe" had told me about her father's youth:

> After Dad's death, I discovered something rather strange. He had all these different bank accounts in different names. I don't know what that was all about . . . He used to make his money when he was young from having a floating crap game. I know he made good money. I think he knew Tony Cornero, but I'm not sure. My father's dad was a bootlegger and gambler. My dad's third wife told me she destroyed all Fred's papers and records after he died.

I suspect my father's relationship with the Los Angeles underworld changed dramatically from his early days as a cab driver hustling downtown for whatever he could make from the high tippers at the Biltmore.

But Father abandoned his role as chauffeur after he left Los Angeles and then returned as a medical doctor and skilled surgeon. No need for street hustling now, no longer any need to threaten a passenger in his hack to "cough up the fare or I'll bust you in the nose." That was all behind him.

By 1939, as head of L.A. County's venereal disease control office, his relationship with the top crime bosses would put him on a far more powerful footing because, as a respected physician and a man of influence in his own right, perhaps even as their *consigliere-medico*, he would be allowed inside the center ring.

In addition, we see his documented association with elite members of the California Club and its spin-off, the L.A. Chamber of Commerce, where he came in contact with millionaire businessmen and shared any professional secrets they cared to impart. Perhaps a little bartering could be conducted between them. The doctor could provide prescriptions for prostitutes and drugs for wives and daughters. The businessmen could provide money and protection and share their information with my father, the kind of information that translated into power and influence.

I suspected another source of privileged information that was independently available to Father was the repository of medical files in his possession at his First Street Medical Clinic. There, at his venereal disease clinic, he discreetly treated the rich, the famous, and the powerful for any complications resulting from their personal and private indiscretions. This sensitive information gave George Hodel a tremendous source of power — leverage for exacting favors, or for downright extortion. These suspicions were again, unexpectedly and dramatically, confirmed by my mother's old friend Joe Barrett. By 2002, after our many talks, I had come to think of Joe affectionately as my "Franklin House mole." I was grateful for the friendship he had shown Mother and her three young sons during those difficult "gypsy" years. Joe spoke of his many conversations with my mother during 1948 and 1949, when he roomed at Franklin House. He recalled her interactions with Walter Huston; her working and writing dialogue for John Huston's soon-to-be-released *The Treasure of Sierra Madre;* the stories of Father's cruelty and his beatings of both her and us three boys. But here let us focus on what is relevant, namely, *why* George Hodel felt himself not only above the law but seemingly impervious to arrest.

"Your Mother, Dorothy, and I would talk for hours at the Franklin House," Joe said:

> in the courtyard, the kitchen, in the living room, and in my studio. Dorothy had an elegant mind. Our talks were almost always when George was away from home. Just the two of us. She talked of

many things. Here is what I recall her telling me about the First Street Clinic. It was a place where primarily the rich and famous were treated for venereal disease. Top people from the movie industry. Directors, producers, actors, and also police officials. She told me it was a very active place, especially in the late thirties and early to mid-forties, before penicillin had been discovered. George had a partner, a Japanese doctor, who had developed a special treatment, which drew celebrities and important people. The socially elite came to be treated, along with their girlfriends and prostitutes. Dorothy said that George kept detailed files on all his patients and that in her words, "The files made for some interesting income." Those were Dorothy's exact words.

Barrett's words verified my suspicions. In 1940s L.A., George Hodel knew too much about too many people in high places. He had all the files and all the names. He knew everything. And now we know from what Mother told Joe Barrett that not only did he possess that highly incriminating information, he was using it to his full advantage. He was actively extorting the rich for cash and the powerfully connected for protection. The medical files under his lock and key were his insurance. Unquestionably, George Hodel made it known to those in power that should anything happen to him, either by way of arrest or personal harm, the knowledge and files he possessed would be made public.*

George Hodel was, in a word, too hot to handle. Knowing this, whatever constraints or concerns he may have felt when he first went on his murder spree must have fallen away. Not only was he a genius, he was untouchable.

---

*Clearly the Tamar arrest in October 1949 was an aberration. The autonomous Juvenile detectives, unaware of Dr. Hodel's Gangster Squad/Homicide protectors, had acted too quickly, but Tamar's disclosures, which involved not just her father but sixteen others, could not be ignored. It was another example of LAPD's right hand not knowing what the left had done. All Dad's LAPD confederates could do was assure him that they would assist from the inside in helping him "beat the rap."

# 27

# Dahliagate: The Double Cover-up

*Sixty years ago Los Angeles politicians had the best police depart-*
*ment that money could buy. LAPD was part of the political machine*
*that ran this city. We must never allow ourselves to return to those*
*days.*

— Bernard Parks, LAPD chief of police
Jonathan Club Breakfast, April 9, 2002

## Deputy Chiefs Thaddeus Finis Brown and William Henry Parker: Their Fight for Power

IT IS IMPORTANT TO HAVE some understanding of the political dynamics at work within the Los Angeles Police Department in the fall
of 1949 through the summer of 1950. While the local press was
blasting away at the LAPD with charges of inefficiency and corruption, the DA's office, as we have just learned, believed that some police officers and detectives were destroying evidence, covering up the
facts, even protecting a prime suspect in the Black Dahlia and Jeanne
French investigations. Also, the DA believed, LAPD commanders
were receiving extensive payoffs in return for protection they were
offering local gangsters.

By February 1950 public opinion about the LAPD was at an all-
time low, worse even than it had been a decade earlier when the
sixty-eight high-ranking officers had "resigned."

As the heirs apparent to the chief's office, LAPD deputy chiefs
Parker and Brown knew that their careers, and indeed the department's collective survival, were at stake. Another major scandal could

put a knife right into the heart of the LAPD. Neither man could allow this to happen, no matter what the cost, no matter what scandals had to be covered up. Both Brown and Parker desperately needed to shepherd the department through its current difficulties, hoping they could implement their own remedies at a later date.

Brown and Parker: it was a toss-up which one would be appointed chief of police. They were two very different men, not unlike the U.S. Army generals Patton and Bradley. Like Patton, Parker was hard-drinking — known to his men as "Whiskey Bill" — arrogant, ambitious, and aggressive. He would certainly not have hesitated to slap around one of his officers if he felt it would do some good. A brilliant strategist, he won every campaign he ever began within the department. LAPD interim chief William Worton favored Parker, who had achieved the highest score on the written examination.

Brown, also a hard drinker, was more the diplomat and, like Omar Bradley, was considered to be the "GI's general" by his foot soldiers. Officers from the rank of lieutenant on down loved him. While Brown did not possess the academic strengths of Parker, he had superior people skills. During his long and distinguished career, he had built a broad base of informants, and could learn virtually anything about anybody with a simple phone call. He was loyal to his men, and would back them and their plays unquestioningly. At that time, many considered Brown to be the best detective in the United States. Throughout his entire career he had been at the center of many prominent and celebrity investigations, and he had a reputation as not only an effective but an honest cop. Most of the local press gave him high marks, and Norman Chandler, owner of the *Los Angeles Times*, wanted Brown as "his chief," referring to him as "the master detective."

Before he joined the LAPD, Parker, like my father, had worked the trenches of 1925 Los Angeles as a downtown-area cab driver, trolling for fares outside the Biltmore Hotel. It was almost certain that they had known each other, working the same job, at the same place, at the same time, since the Yellow Cab Company during those years had only ten cabs and a force of thirty men. They might have even been partners from time to time, working the same cab on different shifts and carrying the same fares from nightspot to nightspot. Reflecting on his early days as a hackie in an *L.A. Herald Examiner* article entitled "Early L.A. Cab Boom: Big Brawls Bump Business in Taxi Heyday," Chief Parker was quoted as saying this about his first job: "Driving back then made a man tough enough for anything. As chief, whenever I could, I gave a cabbie every legal break."

Despite Parker's eminent qualifications, in June 1950 word spread that Thad Brown would be the next chief of police. The police commissioners would vote in early July, and he had the swing in his pocket, which would be just enough to tip the scale in his favor. So assured seemed the outcome of the decision that Chandler's *L.A. Times* printed a story that Thad Brown had actually been appointed chief of police, having received three votes from the police commissioners.

At the last moment, however, fate intervened. The night before the final vote, Thad Brown's anticipated victory was snatched from him through the unexpected death of Police Commissioner Mrs. Curtis Albro, whose crucial swing vote would have guaranteed his appointment. The balance of power was tipped, and in August 1950 William H. Parker was appointed LAPD's new chief of police. Parker would rule the department as an absolute despot for the next sixteen years, and Brown would remain chief of detectives.

Upon Chief Parker's death from a heart attack shortly after the Watts riots, Thad Brown would be appointed interim chief of police in July of 1966. At the same time, a young rookie Hollywood patrol officer named Steve Hodel would be ordered by his watch commander to attend the swearing-in ceremony at the police administration building, which would shortly thereafter be renamed Parker Center. After the ceremony, Chief Thad Brown walked out of the auditorium and approached the young officer with the silver nameplate "Hodel" above his shirt pocket and asked the startled rookie if he would like to have his picture taken with the chief. A photographer at the chief's side walked us outside and snapped a photograph. Apparently, Chief Brown could not resist the temptation to memorialize the irony of the two of us standing together in uniform.

The chief, the rookie patrol officer, and the photographer would quickly go their separate ways from there, never to see each other again. Some weeks later, I received a copy of the photograph through the interdepartment mails as a memento from an unknown sender, which, at the time, was meaningless to me. I threw the photo in my desk, moved it with me in boxes from desk to desk as I advanced up the ranks, and packed it with other memorabilia from the job when I retired. I never looked at it or even wondered about why it was taken in the first place, until I eventually recognized it as a thoughtprint in my own life some thirty-three years later.

Chief Thad Brown retired on January 12, 1968, having served forty-two years on LAPD, his final twenty-one years as a deputy chief. He died only two years later at age sixty-two on the eve of Dr. George Hodel's sixty-first birthday. My father outlived his contemporaries Chief Parker and Chief Brown by some thirty-three and twenty-nine years respectively.

Parker was the department's most respected leader, credited with taking a corrupt and sloppy police force and transforming it into what he said was the world's "number one police department." And my own timing was such that I was a Parker man from the get-go. Parker was a living legend for me and my classmates, who believed he possessed near-divine qualities of leadership, intelligence, integrity, and honesty. Parker had my unquestioning respect and devoted loyalty. There is no doubt he made the LAPD a more professional organization than it ever had been in the past. It's also clear he contributed much to reduce the graft and corruption that ran rampant in the decades before he took over.

There was, however, a dark side to Bill Parker, clearly described by people who had private and personal contact with him. First, in *Thicker 'n Thieves*, Sergeant Charles Stoker reveals that in mid-May 1949 he had a secret meeting with then inspector Bill Parker. (Inspector was a police rank above captain but below deputy chief.) At the meeting, Parker flattered Stoker, reminding him how much they had in common as individuals: both were World War II vets; both Catholic. Parker questioned Stoker about the Brenda Allen scandal and seemed to listen as Stoker filled him in on the entire story. Parker in turn revealed to Stoker several cases of police corruption. Stoker described one case in particular, involving Chief Horrall:

> According to Parker, one source [of police corruption] was controlled by Chief of Police Clemence B. Horrall. Aligned with him as a lieutenant was Sergeant Guy Rudolph, his confidential aide. He then related this story concerning Rudolph, which I have never verified.

For years, while Bowron was in office, Rudolph had controlled the vice pay-offs in Los Angeles, and when Horrall held the chief's job, Rudolph was under his wing. At one time Rudolph had kicked a colored prostitute to death on Central Avenue; and during the investigation of that incident, he and his partner had gone to a local downtown hotel where they engaged in a drunken brawl with two women. Then, while Rudolph was out of the room buying a bottle of whiskey, one of the prostitutes had been killed. (p. 182)

Parker asked Stoker if he had heard the story about Rudolph and the prostitutes, and when Stoker said he hadn't Parker told him he could prove it. Parker further confided to Stoker that Sergeant Rudolph controlled the lottery and numbers rackets operated by Chinese and blacks.

Stoker described in detail Parker's explanations about how corruption operated within the LAPD:

[Parker] had described the two police cabals, which controlled graft under what he termed a "cop setup." By this he meant that no true underworld boss ran the rackets in Los Angeles and that racketeers were controlled and plucked by department members of the two police outfits who, in reality, were themselves racketeers as averred in the forepart of this book. (p. 187)

As for the purpose of this clandestine meeting with the inspector, Stoker explained, Parker wanted to make him a "fair and square proposition." Unaware that Stoker had already testified in secret before the grand jury a week before their meeting, Parker asked him to go to the grand jury, tell all he knew about the Brenda Allen investigation, plus what Parker had just revealed about police corruption. That, he surmised, would force Mayor Bowron to rid the department of both Chief Horrall and Reed and put Parker in a position to take command. Parker candidly informed Stoker that the department was out to get him "one way or another," and that if he, Stoker, played ball with Parker, he would make him his assistant and protect him from harm. As we know, Stoker passed on any "deals" offered by the ambitious inspector, took the road less traveled, and within weeks was drummed from the corps.

In his autobiography, *In My Own Words*, Mickey Cohen also described the dynamics of his relationship with Bill Parker, this time from the perspective of someone on the other side of the law. First, he said, he believed he exercised some control over who would become chief in 1950. He had the swing vote for Brown because Brown, he believed, was in his pocket:

> The one copper who really gave me trouble out here was William Parker, who got into power when he was named chief of police in 1950. See, it was very important for me who was the chief of police at that time. I had gambling joints all over the city, and I needed the police just to make sure they ran efficiently. In L.A. the chief of police is chosen by the Board of Commissioners, *so we had connections on the board who were going to make sure another connection of ours got named.* [my emphasis] At a meeting, we all decided it was best if I left town until the selection was made, just to blow off any stink that could possibly come up.
>
> . . . But, when I get to Chicago, I learn that the guy on the board that we were depending on — the one that had like the nuts, the deciding vote — passes away twenty-four hours before the selection was made. Parker made chief of police, and if it had been my decision, I would have taken anyone but Parker. (pp. 146–147)

In 1957, Cohen, after strong encouragement from TV news magazine commentator Mike Wallace, agreed to be interviewed on his television show, an early version of *60 Minutes*. Cohen flew back east and met with Wallace and his writers for several days before the live telecast and went over the various questions, some of which they would ask him on the air. When Wallace asked Cohen — off the air — what he thought of Police Chief William Parker, Cohen said, "He's a sadistic degenerate cocksucker." The following day, Wallace, now live in front of millions of viewers, decided to ask Cohen the same question. Cohen, an accommodating wiseguy if nothing else, gave Wallace the exact same answer he'd given off camera the day before.

Chief Parker, watching the live interview, immediately picked up the telephone and advised the network that he would be suing the network and Cohen for libel.

Cohen met daily with a crew of ABC attorneys, and describes how, together, they prepared the defense, pointing out his jailhouse knowledge of the law where he states, "The only defense against libel is the truth, and believe me, I had Parker right by the fucking nuts." Cohen had obtained a number of LAPD sworn officers still on active duty who were ready to testify, in Cohen's words, "where William Parker was an absolute bagman for Mayor Frank Shaw's administration."

The threatened libel suit was never heard, because in 1958 ABC settled with Chief Parker out of court for a purported $46,000.

*Exhibit 61*

*Chiefs Thad Brown and William Parker, circa 1950*

## Captain Jack Donahoe

LAPD's Captain Jack Donahoe and the very real part he played in the Dahlia investigation has, for me, become one of the most enigmatic questions of my own investigation. We may never discover his true role. Was he hero or villain? There is no simple answer, and probably, like Chief Parker, he was both.

It's clear from the outset that he controlled the Dahlia investigation, because it was his administrative responsibility as the captain of Homicide Division. In the early weeks, he fully cooperated with the press and provided them with ongoing updates about where the investigation was heading. In my estimation, and certainly by today's standards, he was overly candid and released far too many investigative details that should have been kept secret. The press's ability to stroke one's ego on page one each morning can be a not-so-subtle seduction, and Captain Jack may have simply enjoyed and succumbed to the notoriety. But Donahoe didn't last too long as the supervisor of the Dahlia investigation, because once he went public with his belief that the Elizabeth Short and Jeanne French murders were connected, Chief of Detectives Thad Brown promptly removed him.

It is obvious to me that, at least initially, Donahoe didn't know who committed the murder of Elizabeth Short and was actively and energetically chasing every lead. Had he possessed knowledge of the suspect or been involved in the cover-up, he would not have pursued the investigation so aggressively or released vital information to the press and public in the hope of developing new leads. Donahoe was taken off both investigations by his superiors, presumably by Chief of Detectives Thad Brown, in mid-February 1947.

His years inside the detective bureau and his promotions during the 1930s and '40s would have assured Donahoe of being in the loop within the department. While no one knows what he did or didn't do, whether he was on the take or not, we certainly can be confident that having survived the corrupt years of Mayor Frank Shaw and Chief James Davis and "the Purge," he knew who was dirty and who was not. He was Chief Thad Brown's right-hand man, and in this case the right hand had to know what the left hand was doing.

If Donahoe was not actively involved in corruption, he certainly knew of its existence. His position as captain in charge of the Homicide Division would have placed him in direct supervision of Charles Stoker's "Bill Ball and Joe Small." It is difficult to believe that Donahoe could or would have turned a deaf ear to this large-scale operation without either taking his share of the profits or taking action to eliminate the corruption, which was an immediate threat to his power and authority as Homicide commander. If he did know of the Dahlia-French-Spangler cover-ups, it would make Captain Jack as dark and as sinister a police captain as his fictional counterpart, Captain Dudley Smith, in James Ellroy's novel *L.A. Confidential*.

Donahoe retired fifteen years after the murder of Elizabeth Short and, like the fictional Captain Smith, died a hero to the department and the world. Here are extracts from what the *Los Angeles Herald Examiner* had to say about the man and his career in his obituary of June 20, 1966:*

## 37-YEAR L.A. POLICE VETERAN CAPT. JACK DONAHOE DIES

> Capt. Jack Donahoe, 64, was mourned today by law enforcement officers everywhere.
>
> One of the most noted detectives in the country, Donahoe died yesterday at his Hollywood home after a lengthy illness . . .
>
> After 37 years on the Los Angeles Police Department, the detective better known as "Captain Jack" retired four years ago. He was honored by more than 700 men and women from every walk of life at an official banquet at the Police Academy . . .
>
> The 6-foot-1, more than 200 pound enemy of crime, had been suffering for the past three years from a back injury, and was found dead in his living room chair by his wife, Ann . . .
>
> On Donahoe's retirement, Chief of Detectives Thad Brown said: "I have lost my right hand."

What I, then only a three-year rookie out of the Hollywood Division, and most of the rest of LAPD were never told was that Captain Jack, at 11:21 on the morning of June 18, 1966, while seated in his living room chair, had removed his service revolver, placed it over his heart, and pulled the trigger. His death report, a public record, reads not "after a lengthy illness" but "John Arthur Donahoe,

---

*Three weeks later, Chief Parker would suffer a massive heart attack while giving a public speech and die. Thad Brown would then assume command.

Suicide, Cause of Death — Gunshot Wound of Chest Perforating Heart and Aorta with Massive Hemorrhage."

It is almost certain that we will never know why this senior command officer, the highest-ranking detective assigned to the Black Dahlia murder investigation, took his own life. Was it illness? Depression? Or was it guilt? If he left a suicide note or explanation of any kind, it has long since been destroyed.

Even though we may never discover the entire truth about what actually took place inside the LAPD during the years from 1947 to 1950, it's possible to speculate with confidence about what probably happened as the two candidates for chief, Brown and Parker, vied for power. I firmly believe that both men, possibly thinking they were acting in the department's best interests, actively covered up not only the abortion ring investigation, but the Dahlia, French, Spangler, and other sexual homicides as well. Even the grand jury investigation of 1949 could not pry the full story loose.

It's important to figure out who knew about the cover-up and what exactly they knew. From what Joe Barrett told me, at the time my father was arrested in 1949 the district attorney's office strongly suspected he was involved in the Dahlia case. If the DA thought so, it's clear the police must have suspected him as well but buried what they knew to protect themselves.

Who knew? Most certainly Chiefs William Worton, William Parker, and Thad Brown knew the evidence against George Hodel and Fred Sexton. The primary investigators, Finis Brown, brother of Thad Brown, and his partner, Harry Hansen, had to know as well. Gangster Squad detectives "Bill Ball and Joe Small" were certainly in the loop, because I believe they initiated the cover-up to protect the members of the abortion ring. District Attorney Simpson, his chief of Bureau of Investigation, H. Leo Stanley, and his chief investigator, Lieutenant Frank Jemison, along with his partners who testified before the grand jury and provided them with the name of the prime suspect, all knew. And, as we will see, all eighteen of the grand jury members also heard my father named as the suspect. Therefore, in the closing months of 1949, at least twenty-eight people were informed and given the name of the prime suspect in the murders of both Elizabeth Short and Jeanne French.

But there were doubtless many more; a "secret" like that is quickly passed around within the high-ranking inner circle. If not immediately, then ultimately, Captain Donahoe and Captain Earle Sansing discovered the truth, but were forced to keep it to themselves.* Sansing doubtless wanted to see if I knew the truth about my father when in 1963 he told me bluntly that it would be a waste of time and taxpayers' money for me to enter the L.A. Police Academy. It's also possible that many of today's surviving top brass know this secret, and are expected, like the good soldiers they are, to take it to their graves.

But why was the cover-up allowed to continue? It's clear that "Ball and Small" were only doing what they were paid to do when they wrapped protection around the doctors in the abortion ring. If my father knew the names of the doctors in the ring, it's likely that the Gangster Squad detectives protected him as well. But when the information about the Dahlia murders reached the higher ranks, someone at the very center of power had to make the decision to suppress it.

Now, try to imagine what it must have been like in October 1949, when Deputy Chief William H. Parker and Deputy Chief Thaddeus Finis Brown faced off against each other for the top job in the LAPD. Each man realized that the department and its officers had been under constant fire from the press and the public during the past year. Crime was still rampant. Worse, terror was gripping the city's female population as a result of the dozen or more rape-murders that still had not been solved. A crazed sex killer was on the loose — back in 1949 nobody knew what a serial killer was — and no one could stop him. The stigma of the nation's most horrific and sadistic murder, the Black Dahlia, had been burned into the collective psyche of the L.A. public, and the case remained an open wound that would not heal.

Against this background, either Brown or Parker — or both — in what I suspect was a late-1949 briefing of an Internal Affairs investigation, were told by their subordinates that "there is another problem."† Two years earlier, in the weeks following the murder of

---

*Daryl Gates, in his autobiography, *Chief: My Life in the LAPD*, refers to Sansing as LAPD's "greatest captain of all time."

†LAPD's Internal Affairs Division (IAD) was established in 1949, by then interim chief Worton, who promoted Inspector Parker to the rank of deputy chief and placed him in charge of this newly established unit. IAD detectives were (and are to this day) both feared and hated because of their role of investigating and ferreting out crooked cops.

Elizabeth Short, several detectives working on the Homicide Division's Gangster Squad were assigned to assist in the investigation due to the fact that the crime may have been gangster-related, as a prominent citizen and friend to known hoodlums — also a boyfriend of the victim — was a possible suspect. The two Gangster Squad detectives (known and friendly to this suspect) informed the regular homicide detectives assigned to the Dahlia case that they had checked him out and were able to eliminate him as a suspect. They likely further minimized his 1947 connections to the crime by informing other detectives that it was simply a mix-up, a case of mistaken identity. Chiefs Brown and Parker, in their 1949 briefing, were likely further informed of the following: two years after the Dahlia murder, in October 1949, the suspect/acquaintance of these same two detectives, a prominent and wealthy Hollywood man, a medical doctor, had been arrested and charged by LAPD Juvenile Division detectives with having committed incest with his fourteen-year-old daughter. Now this guy was going to trial.

The candidates received more bad news. An independent investigation by Internal Affairs officers had just turned up evidence that the two Gangster Squad detectives who had originally eliminated this suspect had probably destroyed some bloody clothing that may have connected him to another murder shortly after the Dahlia killing. In fact, according to IAD, these detectives might well have done everything they could to cover the doctor's tracks, so that he would not be discovered. What were their motives? Probably financial, because it's known that this Hollywood doctor was not only tied to known gangsters but also might well have either been involved in payoffs to the police or been tied to the abortion ring Charles Stoker testified about before the grand jury. Perhaps both.

But the worst was yet to come. According to the IAD officers, it was highly likely that many more of the recent murder victims since 1947 were connected to this same man, and he might well have been responsible for a dozen or more sexual homicides over recent years. *This killer, whose identity was known to police, was still on the loose.*

Both Parker and Brown — and it was Brown's own brother who had investigated this suspect — knew that they had everything to lose and nothing to gain by putting this guy away and risking a full disclosure. With the elections eight months away, were the truth to become public, each candidate and everything he'd worked for would be swept away in a tidal wave of scandal. The humiliation sure to follow would not only result in each man's total loss of power within the department, but would probably destroy the department as well. The LAPD would never recover.

Could either Parker or Brown, both of whom were creatures of the system, admit to the public that two of their veteran detectives were running an abortion ring, taking protection money as payoffs, and then covering up Los Angeles's most brutal murder to protect a friend tied to the same gangsters who were paying them off? Finally, as a direct result of their actions, this madman had been allowed to remain free to continue his killing spree for two more years within the city.

Disclosure was not an option. The liability to the city alone from the lawsuits by relatives would almost certainly bankrupt the city. Two corrupt policemen could not be allowed to destroy the careers of the many. Nor could they be allowed to destroy the reputation of the department. There was only one solution: a cover-up of the Gangster Squad detectives' cover-up. For the good of the entire department, for the good of the city, and probably for their own good as well, the two candidates for chief rationalized and justified their actions and put in place a cover-up.

So the orders came down: all Dahlia records were to be sealed, entombed at Homicide Division. It was an informational lockdown. No one was to see the investigation. One detective was to be assigned to the case and even his own partner would be restricted from access to the files. Nothing on the Dahlia case was to be shared with any other jurisdiction, and trusted sentinels were to be posted as gatekeepers to the locked files. Maybe even the files themselves were destroyed in an attempt to remove anything that might shed light on the truth. After all, these women were all alone in the world. And they were dead. Nothing would bring them back. Why destroy the department when it would accomplish nothing? Both Brown and Parker were united in the same conclusion — the department could not look back, only forward. Each man, were he to be made chief, doubtless vowed to put reforms into place that would keep a disaster like this from ever happening again. And when Parker became chief, he began just such a decade of reforms.

These, I believe, were some of the main reasons — and justifications — by a few men in power at the very top to implement a cover-up: to preserve the department, the administration, and the city coffers.

In 1949 Los Angeles it was business as usual.

# 28

## The Grand Jury

*Even truth itself decays, and lo, from truth's sad ashes pain and falsehood grow.*
— Herman Melville

WHILE MUCH OF THE INFORMATION that follows is probative and directly supports the fact that George Hodel, the 1949 grand jury's "wealthy Hollywood man," was the prime suspect in both the Black Dahlia and Red Lipstick murders, we need no further proof. We have reviewed the evidence, seen the proof, and now know he was without question the killer.

But there remains a further truth that needs be addressed. Like myself, many will find this second truth to be as dark as, or darker than, the stark reality of my father's madness.

That truth has to do with proving my allegation that the Los Angeles Police Department did commit a Dahliagate. The department's two highest officers, Thad Brown and William Parker, in a conscious and deliberate obstruction of justice, aided and abetted a cover-up and, along with their subordinates, were directly responsible for knowingly permitting a psychopathic serial killer to remain free until he was finally forced to leave the country in 1950.

I make these allegations with the utmost reluctance and a heavy heart. These two leaders, Parker and Brown, were on the job and in command during my watch. Both were my personal heroes and remain unarguably LAPD's two most important legends. But the facts are undeniable.

Violence was so prevalent on the streets of Los Angeles by 1949 that the public had finally had enough. Each day's headlines featured new stories of kidnapping, rape, and murders of women even in the city's upscale neighborhoods. No one was safe, and the community was outraged over the ineffectiveness of their police department. Worse, the department itself seemed to be no better than the gamblers, hoods, and thugs it was supposed to be getting off the streets.

First, there were the revelations of graft and corruption that came out of the Administrative Vice Division when Sergeant Stoker went public with the story of the Brenda Allen scandal. Hard on the heels of a public airing of LAPD's dirty laundry came the murder of Louise Springer, whose body was found strangled in her car near downtown. Then came what was to be known as "the Battle of Sunset Boulevard," when famed gangster Mickey Cohen and his entourage were gunned down on the streets of Hollywood. Then people began disappearing under mysterious circumstances, one after the other. First was Mimi Boomhower on August 18. Then on September 2 came the turn of Barney Weiner, a fifty-year-old newspaperman and district manager for the *Daily Racing Form*. Frank Niccoli, a close friend and business associate of Mickey Cohen, vanished on the same day. Their respective cars were soon located, but no bodies were found. Actress Jean Spangler disappeared on October 7, and three days later Dave "Little Davey" Ogul, another Cohen henchman, also vanished, and his car, like the others, was found abandoned in West Los Angeles. Cohen was quoted as saying about Niccoli and Ogul, "I'm afraid the guys ain't living. They was swallowed up."

By October, Los Angeles had jokingly become known as "the Port of Missing Persons," but it was no joke and its citizens were not laughing. Not only notorious hoods and gangsters went missing, but ordinary people as well. It was time the district attorney did what he was elected to do and put a stop to it.

In 1949, a grand jury was empaneled. Very quickly, it became proactive and, led by fiery jury foreman Harry Lawson, seemed determined to get some answers. Conducting its own investigations, and using its subpoena powers, it began with the Brenda Allen case and Stoker's charges of a systemic corruption within the LAPD, reaching all the way to the top.

After the Brenda Allen case and Charles Stoker, the next item on the grand jury's agenda was the Black Dahlia murder. Why hadn't the case been solved, and, if a fix had been put in, who was behind it?

Investigators from the district attorney's office, working through their own operatives, interviews with witnesses, and information developed by unnamed private investigators independent of the LAPD, provided dramatic new information to the grand jury.

The actual testimony itself, as with all grand juries, was secret and, because the case is still technically open, remains secret to this day. However, from articles printed in the dailies, it became clear that DA investigators believed that detectives within the LAPD assigned to the Gangster Squad had orchestrated the cover-up. DA investigators testified before the grand jury with respect to their own investigation and findings, which were the results of having assembled and organized all facts related to the Dahlia investigation during the thirty-four-month period since the murder. They suspected that the Gangster Squad detectives were protecting the identity of "a wealthy Hollywood man" who was a prime suspect. The DA investigators gave the grand jury the name of the suspect and his address, saying they had found witnesses who would testify to having seen bloody clothing of the type and size worn by Elizabeth Short, as well as bloody bedsheets, inside the suspect's home.

While it did not release the name and address of the suspected murder residence to the public, an article in the *Herald Express* dated September 13, 1949, under the headline "Black Dahlia Murder Site Found in L.A.," reported on part of the grand jury testimony. The article stated, "It was reported that the room where the murder took place was less than a 15-minute drive and in a bee line from the vacant lot where the nude and bisected body of the girl was discovered January 15, 1947 . . . and the home was on one of Los Angeles' busiest streets."

In secret testimony, DA investigator Lieutenant Frank Jemison identified this "wealthy Hollywood man" as the same person whom Elizabeth Short had phoned from San Diego on January 8, 1947; the same man, who, four days later, on January 12, using the name "Mr. Barnes," checked into the East Washington Boulevard Hotel with Elizabeth Short as "husband and wife." Moreover, the DA investigators testified, the hotel owners had positively identified "Barnes" from a photograph found in the victim's belongings, and the man, according to the testimony, was "connected to a foreign government."*

Because of this dramatic new testimony from the DA investigators, the grand jury subpoenaed LAPD detectives to testify how they had investigated the case and what they had found. The jury called seven members of the Gangster Squad, including the head of the unit, Lieutenant William Burns (could Bill Burns be Stoker's "Bill Ball"?), and a Detective J. Jones ("Joe Small"?). The remaining Gangster Squad detectives called were Sergeants James Ahearne, John O'Mara, and Conwell Keller, and Officers Loren K. Waggoner, Archie Case, and Donald Ward.

Next, the grand jury subpoenaed Deputy Chief Thad Brown, as well as interim police chief William Worton, who had replaced former chief Clemence Horrall. Horrall, one recalls, had resigned shortly after his perjury indictment resulting from Charles Stoker's testimony in the Brenda Allen case. In June 1949, Mayor Bowron had appointed Worton, a retired Marine Corps general, as the LAPD's interim chief. Worton, restricted to one year of service, would remain only until the police commissioners made their final vote between the two top candidates, Brown and Parker.

The grand jury asked Chief Worton about the overall investigation of the Black Dahlia case and about the possibility that the wealthy Hollywood man was being protected by members of his department's Gangster Squad. A December 7 article published by the *Los Angeles Examiner* under the headline "Dahlia Motel Angle Probed by Grand Jury" indicated that Worton had personally investigated both matters related to the Hollywood man's meeting the victim at the downtown motel and being protected by the Gangster Squad and said that "Chief Worton does not believe there is a case against the man on either score on the basis of information presently available."

It was the statement "information presently available" that

*This public comment made by the Johnsons strongly suggests that the photograph originally shown to them in 1947 by LAPD, then again by DA investigators in 1949, was our exhibit 9 or 10, George Hodel's China photos that "connect him to a foreign government." It is believed he mailed these photographs to Elizabeth Short from his overseas assignment in 1946.

red-flagged the chief's statement for me. It meant that Worton had left himself a very convenient back door were the Dahlia case ever to blow up in his face.

After its two-month review of the Dahlia case, the grand jury, whose authority had expired on December 31, 1949, came out with a scathingly critical report of the Los Angeles Police Department and a demand for a complete reinvestigation of the Elizabeth Short murder, as well as of many other unsolved murders of female victims during the previous five-year period. On January 12, 1950, a front-page headline appeared in the *Herald Express*, "Unsolved L.A. Crimes Ripped By Grand Jury," with an article featuring photographs of seven of the victims, including Elizabeth Short, Jeanne French, Louise Springer, Gladys Kern, Laura Trelstad, Dorothy Montgomery, and Evelyn Winters.

*Exhibit 62*

*Herald Express,* **January 12, 1950**

The article published the grand jury's final report, and enumerated its specific findings, which included LAPD officers receiving bribery payoffs for protecting gangsters, and bookmakers, gamblers, and abortionists being allowed to run free without fear of prosecution. Addressing the grand jury's full report, the article noted, "the report was almost reminiscent of Chicago in its heyday of crime, although perhaps on a smaller scale."

Sharply criticizing the Black Dahlia investigation, the grand jury intimated a "cover-up" by certain police officers. Below are excerpts directly from the grand jury's report that was summarized in the *Express* article:

> Testimony given by certain investigation officers working this case was clear and well defined, while other officers showed apparent evasiveness. There was not sufficient time left to the jury to complete this investigation, and this Grand Jury recommends that the 1950 Grand Jury continue the probe.
>
> This jury has observed indications of pay-offs in connection with protection of vice and crime, and gross misconduct on the part of some law enforcement officers.
>
> In some cases jurisdictional disputes and jealousies among law enforcement agencies were indicated. In other cases, especially where one or more departments were involved, there seems to have been manifested a lack of co-operation in presenting evidence to the Grand Jury, and a reluctance to investigate or prosecute.

In addition to its findings and critical report, the 1949 grand jury, in its boldest move, recommended that the Black Dahlia investigation be taken over by the district attorney's office investigators and taken out of the hands of the Los Angeles Police Department. They also requested that those same investigators contact and interview the "wealthy Hollywood man" cited by DA investigator Jemison as a possible prime suspect, regarding his links to the crime.

On April 1, 1950, a few months after the grand jury closed its investigation, the *Los Angeles Times* printed a story under the headline "Murder Cases Reopened by District Attorney; Investigators Start Again on Slaying of Nurse and 'Black Dahlia' Brutality," which revealed that the DA investigators were actively "searching for a man they believed to be a 'hot suspect' in the three-year-old murder cases. Investigators Frank Jemison and Walter Morgan told reporters that their office was co-investigating both the Black Dahlia and Jeanne French murders." Further, the article said, "H. Leo Stanley, chief investigator for District Attorney Simpson, said that his investigators remain unconvinced that a bloody shirt and trousers found in the home of an acquaintance of Mrs. French have been fully eliminated as a clue to the murder." Investigators had refused to name the man they were seeking as a prime suspect but said, "He is the owner of the mysterious bloody clothing that has disappeared from LAPD police evidence lockers." The DA investigators planned to "take lengthy statements from two close women friends of the slain nurse" and had been assigned to investigate the two unsolved murder cases at the request of the 1949 grand jury.

The actual police reports themselves were never released. However, from public disclosures and statements provided by the district attorney's investigators and from my own research, it seems that LAPD had recovered some bloody clothing from the residence of the "wealthy Hollywood man," including pants and a shirt belonging to him, which was booked into evidence and then either "lost" or deliberately disposed of, probably by members of the Gangster Squad. Indications were that investigators believed the clothing possibly related to the Jeanne French murder investigation, since several of French's women friends had identified the wealthy Hollywood man as being acquainted with her.

Next, and separate from the man's bloody clothing evidence, the independent private investigators located a different set of witnesses, who when interviewed by Lieutenant Jemison told of seeing women's bloody clothing of a size and description similar to those worn by Elizabeth Short as well as bloody bedsheets inside the wealthy Hollywood man's residence.

There can be no doubt, therefore, that Lieutenant Jemison's "wealthy Hollywood man" was known and identified by both the Los Angeles district attorney and LAPD as the prime suspect in both those murders.

As noted, the DA's office testified that "the murder site was located on a busy street, 15 minutes from the crime scene." I submit that the murder site was in fact the Franklin House, located on the busy streets of Franklin and Normandie Avenues in what is called the Los Feliz section of Hollywood.

In October 1999 I conducted a time-and-mileage check by driving from 39th and Norton to the Franklin House. In normal Hollywood traffic, the 7.7-mile drive took me seventeen minutes. And the Franklin House garage opens onto a tiny alley. Once inside the closed garage one has direct access to the interior of the residence, where one could easily remove a body from the house in the dead of night and be undetected.

None of the publicly released documents reveal at what time the LAPD detectives found and recovered the bloody clothing believed to be owned by my father. On what date, and in what year, did they remove this clothing from the Franklin House? The two strongest possibilities are (1) either in February or in the weeks or months immediately following the 1947 murder of Jeanne French, or (2) in the days following George Hodel's arrest for incest on October 6, 1949.

For the moment, the questions relating to the two separate sets of bloody clothing that connected George Hodel to both Elizabeth Short and Jeanne French must remain unanswered. What is certain, and has been answered, is that in secret testimony the 1949 grand jury received from district attorney's investigator Lieutenant Frank Jemison two startling facts: (1) LAPD detectives were covering up the Dahlia and Red Lipstick murders, and (2) Dr. George Hodel was the prime suspect in both crimes.

# 29

# The Dahlia Myths

AMONG THE MORE FASCINATING AND DISTURBING aspects of the Black Dahlia murder was the amount of myth that gathered around both victim and assailant as the case aged over the years. Because the case was so much in the headlines in 1947 and in the years since, it has become the subject of a number of books, films, and television movies. Writers and commentators have come up with their own notions of the truth, and all too often their opinions unfortunately become considered fact. Commentators have theorized endlessly about the nature of Elizabeth Short and that of her assailant. In every case, however, the theories about both have been woefully off base. First, there is what I call "the Dahlia myth."

The brief, tragic life of Elizabeth Short stands apart from the other victims in our investigation for two primary reasons. The first is the way she was murdered and her body disposed of. Second is the name "Black Dahlia," which both horrified and fascinated the public and immediately identified her with this beautiful flower, turning the crime into a piece of lore. Although some of the other victims were more beautiful and more exotic than Elizabeth, it was the name that made her crime stand out.

As the beloved *Los Angeles Times* columnist Jack Smith said about her in his book *Jack Smith's L.A.*:

I have always supposed that I was the first one to get "the Black Dahlia" into print, though I didn't make it up. As I remember, one of our reporters picked up a tip that Miss Short had frequented a certain Long Beach drugstore for a time. I looked the number up in the phone book and got the drugstore and talked to the pharmacist.

Yes, he remembered Elizabeth Short. "She used to hang around with the kids at the soda fountain. They called her the *Black Dahlia* — on account of the way she wore her hair." *The Black Dahlia!* It was a rewrite man's dream. The fates were sparing of such gifts. I couldn't wait to get it into type.

From day one, with the birth of that name, her real identity disappeared. Few today can tell you the actual name of the Black Dahlia, but most know her story. Not only was her name forgotten, but also her true character. Truth gave way to fiction almost immediately. Initially, the press was to blame, through insinuation and innuendo.

Her character assassination started out slowly in the dailies, with one-liners scattered here and there: "Elizabeth was seen at a Hollywood bar with a mannish-looking female." "Elizabeth was seen in a vehicle with a large muscular blonde woman." "Unidentified sources indicated Elizabeth preferred the company of women."

To LAPD's credit, no confirmations discrediting her reputation came from any detectives assigned to the investigation, at least in those early years. Unfortunately, that would change in later decades.

But what the cops didn't do, the authors and self-proclaimed "true-crime experts" did quite well. Hank Sterling, in his 1954 book *Ten Perfect Murders*, comments:

It's fair to say that her death was the result of her deplorable way of life. Did she go there [Biltmore Hotel] because she hoped to find a pickup, found one and was lured to her death? If so, we can say that the same thing could have happened to a blameless virgin intrigued by a deceptive personality. In that case her death would have nothing to do with her lurid past. In fact, it can be said that a girl with Beth's experience would have been too wise to be trapped that way.

A few years later Elizabeth Short was mentioned in another book, *The Badge*, by Jack Webb, who portrayed Detective Sergeant Joe Friday on the television show *Dragnet*.

She was a lazy girl and irresponsible; and, when she chose to work, she drifted obscurely from one menial job to another . . . To the sociologist, she is the typical, unfortunate depression child who matured too suddenly in her teens into the easy money, easy living, easy loving of wartime America.

Closing his chapter on the Dahlia, Webb wrote:

All LAPD can say is that its detectives exonerated every man and woman whom they have talked to. Beyond that you are free to speculate. But do him a favor; don't press your deductions on Finis Brown.

By the 1980s, Elizabeth's character had reached rock bottom. In *Fallen Angels: Chronicles of L.A. Crime and Mystery*, by Marvin Wolf and Katherine Mader, we find this description:

She hung around radio stations, went on casting calls — and soon descended into the netherworld of the street hustler where scoring a meal, a drink, a new dress, or a little folding money was as easy as finding a willing guy on Sixth Street. For a few months in 1946, she was a fixture of the Hollywood street scene, a pretty girl not too mindful about where or with whom she slept, a girl pretty and desperate enough to pose nude for sleazy pornographers, a pretty girl descending into a private hell.

She spent a drunken night in a Hollywood hotel with a traveling salesman in return for a bus ticket to San Diego and pocket change.

Three years later, Steven Nickel, in *Torso: The Story of Eliot Ness and the Search for a Psychopathic Killer*, made even more startling claims:

The odyssey of Elizabeth Short was a tragic and progressively sordid story. At age seventeen, she had left her home in Massachusetts and headed west in an attempt to break into motion pictures in Hollywood. But her break never came, and she had drifted among the hustlers and flesh peddlers of Santa Barbara, Long Beach, San Diego, and Los Angeles during the next five years. Her romance with a young pilot ended tragically when he was killed in the war; her lover's death marked a turning point in Elizabeth Short's brief life. For a time, she operated as an expensive call girl with a flashy lifestyle. Some of her clients were Hollywood producers who promised her movie roles, but before long she degenerated into a common street prostitute hooked on alcohol and drugs, posing for nude photos to earn extra cash and occasionally living with a lesbian lover.

. . . Her blouses, her dresses, her hosiery, her shoes, and her undergarments, as the detectives who searched her apartment found, were exclusively black. It was easy to see how Elizabeth Short had come by her nickname. She apparently realized it; there had been a tattoo of the exotic black dahlia on her left thigh that her killer viciously gouged out.

In 1993, the editors of Time-Life Books, in their *True Crime — Unsolved Crimes*, characterized the Black Dahlia as follows:

Short gravitated to Hollywood, hoping to break into the movies, but the closest she got was a job as a movie-house usherette. Her main line of work was prostitution.

Years after his 1971 retirement, LAPD detective Harry Hansen dealt the final blow: "She was a bum and a tease."

From one of the case's lead homicide detectives to the star of television's *Dragnet*, comments about Elizabeth Short proliferated, resulting in a composite of the victim that, in the end, had nothing whatsoever to do with who she really was. These "profilers," as if scripting a Hollywood B-movie, writing more from their own fantasies or prejudice than from the facts in the case, recreated Elizabeth Short as a gutter whore, an unclean and unkempt woman, turning tricks in dark downtown alleyways to support her alcohol and drug addictions. They described her as a user and manipulator of men who, because of her low intelligence and loose morals, was destined to fall prey to the dark forces that fed on wannabe starlets.

But none of this is true. Worse, what people had to say about Elizabeth, from Hansen right through to today's commentators, is actually a blame-the-victim rationale for why the case was never solved. In reality it *was* solved, but then covered up. Elizabeth Short does not deserve to be so maligned. She was, after all, a crime victim, not a perpetrator. If she yearned for the attentions of men or lived in a world of fantasy, that did not make her complicit in her own death. For commentators to make such claims with little or no real knowledge of who Elizabeth Short was and what events drove her to her fateful meeting is, to my mind, the height of unprofessionalism. Writers can say what they want, but for law enforcement people to strike out against a victim is, at the very least, a violation of their ethical responsibility. Whatever she might have been in life, Elizabeth simply did not fit the profile created for her by Hansen, Webb, scores of reporters, and the editors of true-crime anthologies. Those who knew her provide the best evidence about her personality, and it's from them and from Elizabeth's own letters that people should draw their conclusions. We have heard in detail the descriptions of her by those who knew her in life. In their personal composites we find the following: "immaculately dressed," "shy, and sweet," "always well behaved model employee, who didn't smoke or drink," and "good kid."

Elizabeth herself is her own best spokesperson. Her letters abound in naiveté, which I read as a belief in the essential honesty of others. For example, in her letters to her self-described fiancé Major Matt Gordon, written in April and May of 1945 and published in newspapers after Elizabeth's murder, she shares her heart's secrets. In anticipation of Matt's return from overseas and her pending marriage, she wrote:

My Sweetheart:

I love you, I love you, I love you. Sweetheart of all my dreams . . .

Oh, Matt, honestly, I suppose when two people are in love as we are our letters sound out of this world to a censor . . .

Just dreaming and hoping for a letter and now you are going to be mine . . .

It is going to be wonderful darling, when this is all over. You want to slip away and be married. We'll do whatever you wish, darling. Whatever you want, I want. I love you and all I want is you . . .

                                                                    Beth

Or this later letter to Matt:

> My Darling Matt:
>
> I have just received your most recent letter and clippings. And, dar-
> ling, I can't begin to tell you how happy and proud I am . . .
>     I'm so much in love with you, Matt, that I live for your return
> and your beautiful letters so please write when you can and be care-
> ful, Matt for me. I'm so afraid! I love you with all my heart.
>                                                                 Beth

After Matt Gordon's death, Elizabeth dated another officer,
Lieutenant Joseph Gordon Fickling, in the hope of finding a new
love. Fickling discouraged her; in a letter from him to her found in
her luggage he wrote:

> Time and again I've suggested that you forget me as I've believed
> it's the only thing for you to do to be happy.

Discharged from the service in 1946, Fickling returned to Charlotte, North Carolina. Letters addressed to him but *not mailed* were
found in Elizabeth's luggage. On December 13, 1946, Elizabeth, her
hopes for marriage with Fickling all but extinguished, wrote, but
never mailed, the following:

> . . . Frankly, darling, if everyone waited to have everything all
> smooth before they decided to marry, none of them ever would be
> together.
>     I'll never love any man as I do you. And, I should think that you
> would stop and wonder whether or not another woman will love
> you as much.

Another letter found in her luggage, written by a Lieutenant
Stephen Wolak, speaks directly to the issue of Elizabeth's obsessive
desire to marry a military man. Wolak wrote:

> When you mentioned marriage in your letter, Beth, I got to won-
> dering about myself. Seems like you have to be in love with a

person before it's a safe bet. Infatuation is sometimes mistakenly accepted for true love, which can never be.

A letter from a fourth serviceman, identified only as Paul Rosie, was found bound with ribbons with the rest of the letters. He wrote, as a response to what we must assume to be another love letter from Elizabeth:

> Your letter took me completely by surprise. Yes, I've always had the feeling that we had a lot in common and that we could have meant a lot to each other had we only been together more often. It's nice to receive a warm friendly letter such as yours.

These letters, addressed to four separate servicemen and published on the front pages of L.A.'s major newspapers, are all windows into her heart. They were never expected to be read by anyone except the men to whom they were addressed, but they reveal a young woman's desperate need to find love and to marry, her overwhelming joy at finding love, and her ecstatic anticipation of her fiancé's triumphant return. After the tragic news of his sudden death, she goes into a tailspin at having lost the man of her dreams and returns to California in the hope of finding another man to heal her broken heart.

The Dahlia letters themselves have never been previously discussed by the press, the police, or in any of the books written about the investigation, yet to my mind they raise a serious question about Elizabeth's emotional or psychological health. We know from the conflicting stories Elizabeth told friends that she was not only extremely secretive, but prone to distort the truth. On a number of occasions she clearly fantasized or lied. For example:

- She told both Dorothy and Elvera French that she had been married to Matt, had borne him a child, and the child had died.
- In early letters she told her mother she had had some minor roles in films as an "extra." In her last letter to her mother in early January 1947, she told her she was working in San Diego at the hospital at Balboa Park.
- She told Robert "Red" Manley that she had been married to a major and was working at the Western Airlines office in San Diego.

All these fabrications relate directly to her own self-image, her attempts to cast herself in a specific light: she needed to show others she was able to function normally in the world, to form relationships, to marry, to have a child, to hold a steady job.

This raises a question: was she ever really the fiancée of Major Matt Gordon or was that too a fantasy? I believe it was. When Elizabeth was staying with the Frenches in San Diego, she showed them a newspaper clipping announcing the engagement of Matt Gordon. But Elizabeth had crossed out the fiancée's name, explaining, "They had made an error on the name in the paper."

When Matt Gordon's mother was interviewed after Elizabeth's murder, she never confirmed that her son was engaged to marry Elizabeth. All she said was the two had known each other in Miami in 1944 and that she had sent Elizabeth a telegram informing her of her son's death. If Matt Gordon had been engaged to Elizabeth Short, why hadn't he told his mother and why didn't his mother confirm this to the police?

Further, how could Elizabeth still be in possession of the letters she had written and supposedly mailed to Matt overseas? We know she wrote the letter or letters on VE Day, May 8, 1945, and we know Matt was still overseas. There are only two possibilities: (1) the letters were found in his personal effects and returned to his mother, who forwarded them to Elizabeth; (2) far more likely, the letters were written by Elizabeth and, like those found in her suitcase to Lieutenant Fickling, *they were never mailed*. No letters were found in her suitcases *from* Major Matt Gordon. In fact, it's likely that Gordon actually rejected Elizabeth, who, heartbroken, then fantasized a relationship with him. When Elizabeth learned of his engagement to another woman, she was forced to create her own fantasy, writing the letters for herself, changing the story's ending from sorrow to joy, and keeping them wrapped in ribbons. They become unmailed reminders of what might have been. To the world this becomes the true story. She found and married Major Right, and they even had a child, but, unhappily, both father and infant died.

*Examiner* editor James Richardson, whose reporters scoured Medford, Massachusetts, Miami, Los Angeles, and San Diego to provide him with background information on Elizabeth, got it right when he described her in his 1954 memoir:

Elizabeth Short . . . was in search of a good husband and a home and happiness. Not bad. Not good. Just lost and trying to find a way out. Every big city has hundreds just like her.

From her own letters and from those that knew her in life, it is obvious that Elizabeth, at the young age of twenty-two, had several faces. As for myself, I will always think of her as the ingénue with only traces of the soubrette.

# 30

## The Dahlia Investigation, 2001–2002

OVER THE MORE THAN TWO YEARS that I'd been conducting my investigation into the Black Dahlia case, I had come to realize that police administrators have their own agendas, which may or may not coincide with the needs of the people they are supposed to serve. Arriving at that conclusion, I was afraid that, once my disclosures became public, LAPD could well take a predictable and traditional defensive stance, responding with a terse public statement such as:

> Dr. George Hill Hodel was a prime suspect throughout our investigation. His name figures prominently in our files. He was always at the top of our list of suspects. We simply did not have enough evidence to proceed with a complaint, and then he left the country, effectively halting our investigation.

Even as a retired senior homicide detective, with almost twenty-four years of service to LAPD, I knew that the possibility of accessing or directly viewing any of the casefile information was nil. I was not even inclined to make such a request, because I already had all the proof I needed, and had made the case. Still, I had a burning curiosity to see if the Hodel name was somewhere in the official LAPD case file. Were today's Dahlia case detectives aiding and abetting a fifty-year-old cover-up by standing guard over the locked files? One possible course of action might give me that answer, and I decided to pursue it.

. . .

Kirk Mellecker had been my partner at Hollywood Homicide in the mid-1970s. After we had worked together for about a year, he had taken the traditional course and transferred from divisional detectives to downtown Robbery-Homicide Division. I knew that he and John "Jigsaw" St. John had become partners and grown very close, having almost a father-son relationship during the decade or so they worked together until St. John's retirement in the late 1980s. Kirk himself retired in 1991. But because he had been John St. John's partner, Kirk had been assigned to the Dahlia investigation some sixteen years longer than any other detective, with the exception of the original detective, Harry Hansen.

I had not seen or spoken to Mellecker since my retirement in 1986. We had always been friends, and I knew him to be intelligent, dedicated, and hardworking. We had shared some special times and camaraderie at Hollywood. I wrote a letter to his last known retirement address, hoping it would find its way to him, and asked him to call me in Los Angeles. Three weeks later, on July 30, 2001, he called.

Ironically, I learned he was now a major case specialist at NCAVC, the National Center for the Analysis of Violent Crime near Quantico, Virginia. Kirk's current job was to train law enforcement officers nationwide in the use of a national crime computer database and retrieval program called VICAP, which is primarily used for analyzing patterns and potential evidence in serial sexual homicides and identifying possible suspects.

During our conversation, Kirk and I talked about old times, and when he asked what I was up to, I told him I was taking a look at a number of old unsolved Hollywood homicides, particularly the Elizabeth Short–Black Dahlia investigation, and writing a book. I knew he had worked the case with St. John, I told him, and asked if he might be willing to discuss it with me, without betraying any confidences. I specifically told him that I would not ask him to reveal anything he knew to be confidential.

Here is a summary of some salient points of that astonishingly revealing conversation, in which he cleared up for me a number of mysteries.

I was assigned the Elizabeth Short case when I first got to Robbery-Homicide in about 1976. I read the case in detail back then. After reading it, there were a couple of things I wanted to check out, but I quickly realized that it was the department's attitude to, "Well, let's get working on things we got going today, and not worry so much about the old days." John-John [John St. John] and I played with it over the years, but not as much as we would have liked to.

"Kirk, was the name Hodel in the case files?" I asked him.

"What are you talking about?" he said.

"Did you see the name Hodel anywhere in any of the case files?"

When Kirk asked what I was getting at, because he truly didn't understand my question, I finally informed him, "My father's name was George Hodel. There are family rumors that he knew Elizabeth Short. Indeed, she may have been his girlfriend. Did you ever see his name anywhere in any of the reports?"

"Jesus!" he said. "Are you serious? Your *father*? No, his name was not in any reports. The name George Hodel never came up. You're saying your dad might have been a suspect? No, I'm positive that name never came up. Hodel is not that common a name, and you and I were partners at Hollywood for two years or so. Of course I would recognize the name Hodel if I saw it. Yes, I can say positively that the name is not in any of the reports I looked at. I looked at the case in detail during 1976 and 1977 and then we got hit with the Hillside Strangler and everything after that until the late eighties."

Then I turned to the "Red Lipstick" murder and asked, "Do you recall the name Jeanne French, a nurse who was murdered three weeks after Elizabeth Short? Was her name and her case file connected to the Short case?

Kirk gave me a lengthy answer, which solved a bunch of mysteries right away, including the real identity of the lead investigator on the case and why the case was able to be covered up.

No, the name [Jeanne French] doesn't sound familiar. I don't recall any nurse being connected. No reports on that. The case files and investigation that I saw dealt pretty much with Elizabeth Short's background and lifestyle. I think there were about four guys that she was hanging out with at the time. They always treated the Short case as a single case, that's why when you mention the nurse thing, it doesn't ring a bell. But I got to tell you, by today's standards, had I worked

THE DAHLIA INVESTIGATION, 2001–2002393

the case, I would have looked at the possibility that he had done it before. I mean that classic of a style has to make you think serial killer. And if she wasn't his first, it certainly wouldn't have been his last.

No, I never saw the name Sexton come up, as far as I can recall. It's been a long time though. No, there was no mention about any grand jury investigation. I don't know anything about that.

I'm trying to remember the original detective on the case. He had a funny name. No, not Hansen, it was another name. [I provide him with the name of Finis Brown.] Yes, that's it, Finis. He came into the office one day. He was retired and living in Texas. He was the real investigator on the Short case. He was the one that did all the work but Hansen took all the credit. St. John and I were going to talk to Hansen about the case in Palm Springs, but we never got to it, then he passed away. Brown did too, I guess. Really? I didn't know that Finis Brown was related to Thad Brown. [Finis Brown was Chief Brown's brother.]

Well, I would hope they still have the physical evidence on the case. I never pulled any of it, because I never had a need to at the time. I would think it's still there. No, I don't remember anything about anybody finding a watch. Don't remember that in any of the reports, but it's been a long time now. No, I don't think they had any fingerprints on the case. Just a body dump as I recall.

No, there was never any indication that Elizabeth Short was a prostitute. I think Finis Brown did a tremendous job of putting the case together. No, there wasn't ever any hint of any kind of cover-up. No, I never heard any reference to any grand jury investigation, I think if I had I would have remembered that.

Danny Galindo had the case, and so did Pierce Brooks. I don't know who has it now. No, I never heard the name Brian Carr, but I don't know any of the new guys. They are all pretty much gone from the old days. When I first went down and was working the case, I had a lead in Oklahoma or somewhere. Wanted to talk to them. That's when I realized it was merely a token assignment, where they didn't really want anything done. I mean unless there was like a safe-deposit box with a confession inside it . . .

As I hung up, I was dumbfounded. I had just gotten off the phone with a man whom I fully respected, who had personally reviewed and maintained the Dahlia case files for over fifteen years. A highly trained professional, he had been entirely honest and open with me. He had read the file, reviewed all the evidence, and told me that there was nothing there, nothing about my father, nothing about Jeanne French, nothing about the grand jury and what they had found. Where had the information gone?

It was clear verification that the original detectives — Finis Brown and his partner Harry Hansen — had done their duty. It was obvious that Kirk Mellecker, and most likely his predecessors Danny Galindo and Pierce Brooks, had inherited a completely *sanitized* investigation. Incredibly, Kirk Mellecker and John St. John knew practically nothing about the facts of the original investigation.

Mellecker was totally ignorant of the suspected cover-up, nor did he know about the DA's investigation and grand jury recommendations that the case be taken away from LAPD. He was not aware that George Hodel had been a suspect; nothing was in the file about his link to the case as the "wealthy Hollywood man." Further, Mellecker had not known that, early on, Captain Jack Donahoe had provided definite links to the Jeanne French "Red Lipstick" murder. In fact, he had not even heard of that victim's name! He was also unaware that in 1947 alone more than a dozen additional rape-murders and "dumpings" had occurred in and around Los Angeles in the weeks and months preceding and following the murder of Elizabeth Short and had been publicly connected by the press.

He did not know that a man's military-style watch had been found at the crime scene. Kirk had not spoken with Harry Hansen, LAPD's reputed expert on the Dahlia case, and had no idea that the co-investigator, Finis Brown, was the brother of LAPD's most famous and highest-ranking detective, Thaddeus Brown. He did, however, establish definitively that it was Detective Finis Brown, and not Harry Hansen, who was actually in charge of the investigation, in control of the files and running the show during those important early years.

Kirk Mellecker and his predecessors Danny Galindo, Pierce Brooks — made famous in Joseph Wambaugh's *The Onion Field* — and John St. John were all links in a chain that was forged well before they took over the Dahlia case file and, as such, bear no blame for the cover-up. The blame goes to the source, to the original detectives,

Brown and probably Hansen, as well as their bosses, who knew the truth and covered it up.

After my conversation with Mellecker, I realized that what I had suspected — that the LAPD was involved in an ongoing concealment — was inaccurate. The body of the truth was never *buried* within the case files; it had, in all likelihood, been ordered destroyed, so that no linkage could be made. But inasmuch as nothing — absolutely nothing — disappears without a trace, the truth was actually out there, if you knew where to look for it.

The only possible way for any of these detectives to have discovered the truth behind the cover-up would have been to do as I had done — go back in time to 1947–1950 Los Angeles and reconstruct day-by-day the scattered facts from the four separate newspapers and the thousands of separate articles. The truth is buried in what would have to be a three-year, week-by-week, reinvestigative search for the coverage of the events as the bits and pieces of the truth appeared in the press. This is what I did, and my steps are completely retraceable.

As of this writing, the currently assigned LAPD detective on the Elizabeth Short–Black Dahlia investigation is Brian Carr. Presumably, Carr received the baton from John St. John some six or seven years ago. I located two published interviews with Detective Carr, the first dated June 1999, the second in October of that year. Both interviews were brief. The first was conducted by Pamela Hazelton, who had established a Black Dahlia website, www.bethshort.com, as a research center for Dahlia case devotees. For that interview, Hazelton reported on her website, she met personally with Detective Brian Carr at LAPD's Homicide Division at the police administration building, Parker Center.

Ms. Hazelton said that Detective Carr told her that "due to the lack of his emotional involvement in the Black Dahlia murder investigation, and because he was not able to get to know the victim's parents and family, it is difficult for him to slot unlimited time to the case." She quoted Carr as saying, "When I get emotionally involved in a case, that's a really huge motivating factor."

According to Hazelton, Carr also said that he was "doubtful that the case will ever be solved." He revealed, "It's [the Dahlia murder] got signs of serial murder all over it, but again, they never found another murder linked to it." Carr correctly refused to answer any specific questions related to the suspect's modus operandi, but did confirm that "the suspect appeared to have some medical knowledge," and most surprising of all, he told her, "The killer probably knew the victim," but he did not elaorate on how or why he arrived at this conclusion. Carr said that "any possibility of releasing any portion of the case files while he's assigned to the case is non-existent."

The second interview with Carr appeared in an article on the APBnews.com website, under Celebrity News, written by staff writer Valerie Kalfrin, and entitled "Writer Reopens Black Dahlia Murder Case." In the article, Ms. Kalfrin revealed *L.A. Times* writer Larry Harnisch's "new theory" related to his favorite suspect, Dr. Walter Bayley. She also personally contacted Detective Carr, noting that he had been assigned to the Dahlia case since 1994. When she asked if Carr planned to follow up Harnisch's new theory, he said, "I'd be more than happy to check it out if I had the time and resources to do it," adding, "I will probably hand this over to somebody when I retire."

Detective Carr has made it clear that as lead investigator with sole access to the Elizabeth Short files, neither he nor his department has the time or resources to investigate even a single suspect, in this case Dr. Walter Bayley. Though not connected to the murder of Elizabeth Short, Bayley was, as Sergeant Stoker had revealed, a member of the Gangster Squad's abortion ring and possibly one of my father's associates.

In addition to Kirk Mellecker, I discovered a second LAPD officer who had been intimately connected with the Dahlia investigation, retired policewoman Myrl McBride, a critical original witness who, one will recall, had an encounter with Elizabeth Short just hours before she was murdered. McBride, I learned, was living only an hour or so from Los Angeles. I called, introduced myself, and met her for an interview.

While Myrl McBride has little present memory of the facts as she originally reported them to detectives two days after the murder occurred, nevertheless, the facts themselves are not in dispute. My interview with Myrl confirmed two very important points. First, she was never unsure of her original identification of Elizabeth Short as the woman who came up to her and with whom she returned to the Main Street bar. Second, she was never shown any pictures of a potential suspect by detectives in the weeks, months, or years that followed.

Though she cannot today recall the original descriptions of the "two men and a woman" who were with Elizabeth Short as she exited the bar at 5th and Main streets, those descriptions, like McBride's original reporting of the victim's actions, would have been recorded, and unless they, like the George Hodel connections, have been destroyed, they would still be in the case file as an accurate record of her description of the suspects who were known to be with Elizabeth just hours before her murder.

Officer McBride, unlike her civilian counterparts, the downtown motel owners Mr. and Mrs. Johnson, could not be as easily dismissed by the Gangster Squad detectives as "being mistaken" in her identification of Elizabeth Short. The cat was out of the bag and into print on the front pages of the Los Angeles newspapers too quickly.

McBride's original identification of the victim did not stand alone. It was also strongly corroborated by what Elizabeth had told McBride and was later found to be entirely consistent with personal facts of the victim's life. McBride's positive identification of the victim on January 17 was supported by McBride's reporting to police that Elizabeth Short had told her she was terrorized by a jealous suitor who "had threatened to kill her if he saw her with another man." These were the same threats that had caused her to flee to San Diego in fear for her life and the same story she told Robert Manley and the Frenches while she was in hiding at their home.

LAPD detectives could not discredit or refute one of their own. Too much information had already been released to the press. The likely scenario back in January 1947 would have been for the detectives to approach McBride and "suggest" she take a moment to rethink her statement and positive identification of Elizabeth Short, and while she was rethinking it, consider what kind of light she was placing LAPD in with regards to the public! In all likelihood, the detectives asked, "Are you *absolutely* sure the person you released was a terrified Elizabeth Short, who told you she was going to be killed? Might the woman you saw *possibly* have been someone else? Think about it before you answer us." Then, by way of damage control, they told the press in reviewing the case with McBride, "she was no longer absolutely certain that the girl that came running up to her 'in terror' the day before the murder was Elizabeth Short."

After she had become a witness who could place Elizabeth Short with a possible suspect or suspects during her "missing week," Myrl McBride was ultimately transferred to the Harbor Division, where she quietly and inconspicuously finished her career in a "Sleepy Hollow." Fifty-four years later, Myrl McBride reestablished unequivocally that the woman she saw exit the Main Street bar was Elizabeth Short.

This interview with Myrl was the strangest of my career. On the surface, we were sitting together in her home, sharing a cup of coffee, linked as we were, "fellow retired LAPD" discussing the facts of an ice-cold murder case. Below the surface, the link was surreal. The last known witness to see and speak with Elizabeth Short — and that in the presence of her killers — was, five decades later, seated next to that killer's son, now an ex–homicide detective, who was putting the final pieces in place to solve the murder.

Fifty-plus years after the Black Dahlia case was put into cold storage, at least three basic points remain clear.

First, the victim herself has been obscured and vilified over time so that to the uninitiated she has been made to appear complicit in her own death.

Second, profilers, detectives, and writers have relied on the myth of the Black Dahlia, instead of the facts, to come up with their own theories behind the murder. Simply stated: the facts about the case still speak for themselves. Elizabeth consistently reported to anyone who would listen that she was deathly afraid of a certain person. She told that chilling story to the Frenches, to Manley, and to police officer Myrl McBride.

Finally, it's clear that the Black Dahlia file, which was handed down from case manager to case manager, had been sanitized or destroyed, probably by Thad Brown's brother Finis. None of the officers, from Galindo to Carr, probably ever saw the real file or even knew that the DA's investigators had considered my father to be the prime murder suspect.

We know that, after discovering my father's connection to the Elizabeth Short and Jeanne French murders as the "wealthy Hollywood man," the DA's office had launched a separate investigation into LAPD corruption that they presented to the 1949 grand jury, based on their own "codified files" from their own two-year investigation. This meant that a DA case file existed on the case, separate and apart from LAPD's.

Lieutenant Frank Jemison of the L.A. DA's Bureau of Investigation and his detectives knew that George Hodel was a prime suspect for the Black Dahlia and Red Lipstick murders. They had multiple witnesses who had independently connected him to both victims. They probably also suspected him of the brutal stabbing murder of Gladys Kern in 1948.

The DA knew that LAPD had a dozen more kidnappings and lust-murders, most of which had occurred after the Dahlia murder, up until Dr. Hodel's departure to the territory of Hawaii in the spring of 1950, when they suddenly stopped. Many of the bodies were found within sight of the DA's downtown office. From the grand jury revelations, we now know why LAPD was not solving these obviously serial, connected rape-murders, and the DA's investigators also knew why. That is why they took the drastic measure of going around LAPD and submitting their own investigation to the grand jury in secret, in an effort to reveal the cover-up and try to stop the killing.

Desperate to survive, LAPD's top brass orchestrated a cover-up that they hoped would prevent these victims' brutal murders from ever being solved, with the expectation that their own crimes would be buried with them.

# 31

# Forgotten Victims, 1940s:
# The Probables

I HAVE PREVIOUSLY PRESENTED A SERIES of seven killings and one
Dahlia-related assault-robbery. Based on all the evidence from my
investigations, it is my confident belief that George Hodel and Fred
Sexton committed those crimes. Those eight victims are: Ora Mur-
ray, Georgette Bauerdorf, Armand Robles, Elizabeth Short, Jeanne
French, Gladys Kern, Mimi Boomhower, and Jean Spangler.

The more I reviewed and researched the period 1943 to 1950,
the more I became convinced that these two men were serial killers.
I suspect history will ultimately prove them to have far outdone their
counterparts of the late 1970s, Los Angeles's Hillside Stranglers
Kenneth Bianchi and Angelo Buono, who were charged with twelve
murders of Los Angeles–area women. I am not alone in my suspicion; many of the crimes that follow were identified as "suspect" by
the press as possibly being "Dahlia related."

As we have seen, some law enforcement officers of other Southern California localities, including the Los Angeles Sheriff's Department, the Long Beach police, and the San Diego police, also believed
there might well be a connection between Elizabeth Short, Jeanne
French, and their own unsolved murders. In the early months of the
serial killings, even some "renegade" LAPD detectives believed that
the Dahlia and Red Lipstick murders, as well as that of a third victim,
Evelyn Winters, were connected, and went so far as to release their
"11 Points of Similarity" to the press, which printed the speculations
in March 1947. The more I looked at the crimes and the patterns,
the more I found.

As preface to this next grouping of murders I will provide some personal and professional observations as relates to serial killers. First the personal.

I have no desire to add to my father's and Fred Sexton's already horrendous body counts. Nor have I arbitrarily sought out unsolved L.A. murders to throw in "just in case." I'm an old-school homicide detective, trained by much older schoolers. As a rookie detective they told me, "Kid, you're standing in the shoes of the victim. It's your case. If you don't find the killer it's likely nobody ever will. Go get 'em!" I am proud that I was indoctrinated and "programmed" to believe that a detective's highest responsibility is to the victim and his family. That responsibility never stops. It remains as true fifty years after a killing as it did on the first day of the investigation. It is a sacred trust, handed down to the next generation of officers. They too stand in the shoes of the victims. Knowing this, even at the risk of overloading the reader with so many additional crimes, I believe it is my responsibility to make known what I see, what I believe, and what my professional instincts tell me is so.

From a professional standpoint, I would point out that there exist many misconceptions about serial killers and their M.O.s. Often these misconceptions come from in house, from experienced homicide detectives, who are simply wrong! Fixed attitudes, quick judgments, mixed with egos — a dangerous combination. Here are a few examples: "Can't be the same killer, all his victims were white girls." "Nope, he only liked dark-haired girls in their twenties. "Definitely not, he only used a white sash cord to strangle, not a stocking." "He stabbed them in the back, not the front." "He never struck on Saturdays." "That crime is too far away, our guy never went south of 5th Street." Endless reasons for detectives to say, "Not our guy." However, as we have seen so dramatically in the previous cases, one should not disregard or eliminate a suspect *based on differences*. Look at our proven cases and their obvious inconsistencies, yet the suspects were the same! Some completed rapes, some not. Ages varied from twenties to fifties. Inside residences and street abductions. Strangulation, bludgeoning, and stabbing. Acquaintances and complete strangers. Sending notes and not. Posing bodies and not. George Hodel and Fred Sexton were all over the radar screen. They were consistently inconsistent! The point being, a murder investigation must remain objective and inclusionary and consider all the facts, all the possibilities.

Here then, in this chapter and the next, are summaries of an additional nine murders and one attempted murder that I believe need to be examined by law enforcement as attributable to the same two men.

For various reasons, these ten are a rung or two down the evidentiary ladder from the victims cited earlier. Therefore, lacking additional information and documentation, I am classifying them as "probables."

These crimes span the years 1947 to 1959. The victims include: Evelyn Winters, Laura Trelstad, Rosenda Mondragon, Marian Newton, Viola Norton, Louise Springer, Geneva Ellroy, Bobbie Long, Helene Jerome, and a "Jane Doe."

With very few exceptions, these crimes followed similar patterns: abduction; savage, sadistic beatings; occasional mutilation and laceration of the victim's bodies; generally followed by ligature strangulation and dumping of the nude or partially clad bodies in public places, with no attempt at concealment. In many of the crimes, the suspect(s) ceremoniously wrapped or draped the victim's dress, coat, or cape over her body, and in at least one inserted a large tree branch inside the victim's vagina. I interpret all of these actions as a variation of posing, as Father and or Sexton had done in the White Gardenia, Dahlia, and Red Lipstick murders.

## Evelyn Winters (March 12, 1947)

On the morning of March 12, 1947, just fifty-eight days after Elizabeth Short's murder, and thirty-two days after that of Mrs. Jeanne French, another woman's body was found in downtown Los Angeles.

She was quickly identified as Evelyn Winters. Her crime bore strong similarities to both the Jeanne French and Elizabeth Short killings.

Evelyn Winter's nude and severely bludgeoned body was found dumped on a vacant lot at 830 Ducommun Street, near some railroad tracks, just two miles from downtown Los Angeles. The victim's shoes and undergarments were found at Commercial and Center Streets, one block from where the body lay. The victim, who was forty-two, had been struck repeatedly with a club or pipe about the head and face.

Before he — or they — left the scene, the killer wrapped the victim's dress around her neck. Police believed she had been slain elsewhere, then the body dragged from an automobile to the dirt lot. Footprints and tire tracks were visible nearby. The cause of death was due to "blunt force trauma causing a concussion and hemorrhage to the brain."

A check of the victim's background revealed that Evelyn's life had taken a downward spiral, most likely because of alcoholism. From 1929 to 1942 she had been a secretary at Paramount Studios. In 1932 she met and married the head of Paramount's legal department, attorney Sidney Justin. Divorced five years later, Evelyn married a soldier during the war, but they too were divorced within a few years.

The victim's arrest record in recent years showed that she had been booked by police for a number of alcohol-related offenses, all in downtown Los Angeles.

The victim was known to frequent the downtown bars on Hill Street and was last seen on Monday night, March 10, by James Tiernen, a friend, when she left his apartment at 912 West 6th Street.* Tiernen, a thirty-three-year-old bowling-pin setter, was detained and arrested by police but considered "not a good suspect" and promptly released. Tiernen told police he had known Winters for two years and "had run into her in the public library" on Sunday, March 9, where Winters had told him "she had no place to sleep."

He offered to share his hotel room with her and she accepted, staying Sunday night. Tiernen told police, "She was gone all day Monday, then came back about 8:00 P.M. very drunk," imploring him, "Talk to me. I want to talk to someone." Tiernen told her she was "too drunk to talk," at which point she left. That was the last time he had seen her. Her body was found the following morning.

An article in the *Los Angeles Examiner* of March 14, 1947, headlined "Dahlia Case Similarities Checked in Fourth Brutal Death Mystery," offered an eleven-point list of similarities provided by LAPD that detectives believed strongly supported the theory that

---

*912 West 6th Street was only two blocks from George Hodel's medical office on 7th Street.

the murders of Elizabeth Short, Jeanne French, and Evelyn Winters were all related. This was published in the early months of the Dahlia investigation, before the need was fully recognized by LAPD to disconnect and isolate the murders. The article notes:

> Checking similarities between the death of Miss Winters and the Short and French killings, police listed the following:
>
> 1) All three girls frequented cocktail bars and sometimes picked up men in them.
> 2) All three were slugged on the head (although Mrs. French was trampled to death and Miss Short tortured and cut in two.)
> 3) All three were killed elsewhere and taken in cars to the spots where the bodies were found.
> 4) All three were displayed nude or nearly so.
> 5) In no case was an attempt made to conceal the body. On the contrary bodies were left where they were sure to be found.
> 6) Each had been dragged a short distance.
> 7) Each killing was a pathological case, apparently motiveless.
> 8) In each case the killer appears to have taken care not to be seen in company with the victim.
> 9) All three women had good family backgrounds.
> 10) Each was identified by her fingerprints, other evidence of identity having been removed.
> 11) Miss Short and Miss Winters were last seen in the same Hill Street area.

The murder of Evelyn Winters, like the other murders, was never solved. It remains in today's LAPD files as another "whodunit" — with one major distinction. Today's detectives no longer are treating it as possibly, or as we see from the above article, probably, connected to the other crimes. Knowing now that George Hodel did commit the Short and French murders, we must concur with LAPD's *original speculations* that he was doubtless also guilty of the brutal murder of Evelyn Winters, either alone, or with the help of Fred Sexton.

## Laura Elizabeth Trelstad (May 11, 1947)

On May 11, 1947, the body of Laura Elizabeth Trelstad, age thirty-seven, was found in the 3400 block of Locust Avenue near the Signal Hill oil fields of Long Beach. The newspaper reported, "An oil field pumper discovered the body at 5:00 A.M. while coming to work." She had been strangled with "a piece of flowered cotton cloth, believed torn from a man's pajamas or shorts."

Signs of a struggle were visible, and the police found both tire marks and footprints near the body. Detectives told reporters, "Their best evidence and only clue was a plaster casting they obtained of a footprint found close to the victim's body at the crime scene."

Dr. Newbarr determined the cause of death to be "asphyxia due to strangulation, and a skull fracture and hemorrhage and contusion of the brain." The coroner's office indicated the latest victim had been drinking and had been forcibly raped. Long Beach Police Department detectives told the press that the victim had been slain elsewhere and the body dumped in the vacant lot close to the oil rigs.

Detectives discovered she had been drinking and had left a party after a minor argument with her husband, Ingman Trelstad. She told him, "If you won't even take me out on Mother's Day, I'm going to a dance at the Crystal Ball Room [on Long Beach Pike] by myself." In tracing her movements, detectives discovered that a bartender had refused to serve her alcohol at a Long Beach bar after she got into an argument with other patrons. A sailor, who had been drinking with her earlier at this same bar, placed her on a homeward-bound bus.

The sailor was eliminated as a suspect, and police believed the victim had missed the bus stop for her home and continued on to the next stop, where she then got off the bus and began walking back. On May 16, 1947, almost a week after the crime, Long Beach homicide detectives finally located and interviewed the bus driver, Cleve H. Dowdy, who had been vacationing with his wife in Kansas City. The driver clearly recalled the victim being on his bus during his last run on Sunday, May 10, at 11:30 P.M. He told authorities, "She had argued with me, telling me I had passed her stop at 36th Street and American Ave." He recalled that when the victim exited the bus, a stranger, whom he described as "a tall and well-dressed man," followed her off.

The Long Beach homicide was never solved. This is one of the few crimes where the police actually released a confirmation statement that "the victim had been raped." This affirmative statement would suggest that during the autopsy they were able to obtain slides confirming the presence of sperm, which, if not disposed of, could yet prove to be valuable evidence for blood typing and possible DNA linkage. Also, should the plaster casting still exist, it could be compared to the known foot size of George Hodel.

### Rosenda Josephine Mondragon (July 8, 1947)

On July 8, 1947, another victim was found at 129 East Elmyra Street, near downtown city hall.

Rosenda Josephine Mondragon's nude body was found with a silk stocking wrapped around her neck. The twenty-year-old had been strangled, her right breast slashed, and her body thrown from an automobile.

Separated from her husband in April, she had purportedly been driven to his residence by an unknown male, and after a brief argument with her husband, she had served him with divorce papers at about 2:30 A.M. on the morning of her murder. "She was very drunk and mentioned something about having a date," her husband told police. He followed her outside and saw her run over to a waiting vehicle, where she was driven away by an unknown male.

Prior to the early-morning meeting with her husband, the victim had been seen by an operator of an all-night vegetable market at Mission and Main Streets. The merchant told police that she had telephoned for a taxicab from his business between 2:00 and 3:00 A.M., and while she was waiting for the taxi to arrive, a male in a dark-colored coupe drove up and spoke with her. She then canceled her cab and left with the man.

The day after her nude body was found, police located her dress at the corner of 26th and Griffin. Police told reporters, "The dress had been ripped from her body and was undergoing examination at the police lab." Her body was found just one mile from the Winters crime scene, and within two miles of both my father's medical office and Fred Sexton's 1947 address. Mondragon's murder was never solved and remains "open" in LAPD case files.

## Marian Davidson Newton (July 16, 1947)

Marian Newton, age thirty-six, was an attractive divorcée from Vancouver, British Columbia, who was vacationing in San Diego.

On the afternoon of Thursday, July 17, 1947, her body was discovered by a young married couple, Mr. and Mrs. Ward Robbins, who were on an outing to Torrey Pines Mesa just north of San Diego. While hiking in the afternoon, they discovered her body lying at the side of an isolated dirt road near some high brush.

San Diego homicide detectives responded to the crime scene and discovered that Marian Newton had been strangled to death with a thin wire or cord.

Bruises were found on her body, and she had been forcibly raped. Tire tracks were visible nearby, and a coroner's examination estimated the time of death to be between midnight and 4:00 A.M. that day. Two men's handkerchiefs were found nearby the body. One of them had stains, the other did not.*

The victim's purse and identification were later discovered on the sidewalk at University and Albatross Streets, near the downtown area of San Diego. The suspect had apparently thrown her purse out of his vehicle after he had disposed of the body.

Upon checking the last known movements and sightings of the victim, authorities were able to establish a description on the probable suspect and piece together the last hours of her life. Incredibly, her story would mimic — in details, actions, and words — the circumstances of Ora Murray's murder in 1943. From newspaper accounts and public records, here is a summary of what was known of her murder.

On Wednesday, July 16, 1947, the victim, accompanied by Miss Edna Mitchell, whom she had met at the hotel where she was vacationing, decided to go to Sherman's nightclub. Sherman's was a

---

*As referenced in our earlier investigations, this unusual "calling card" evidence corresponds to handkerchiefs also left at the French and Kern crime scenes.

popular military men's club and tourist attraction, famed for having nine different bars and the largest indoor dance floors in the world.

During the evening, the two women met and danced with a number of military men. Miss Mitchell told detectives that at one point a civilian male began dancing with the victim. She described him as "tall, over six foot, thin, possibly in his thirties, with dark hair, wearing a tan sport coat and slacks, and a bright colored tie."

The victim introduced him to Miss Mitchell, who could not recall his name for the detectives. When the suspect left momentarily, Mitchell told Marian Newton that she "didn't like the look of the guy," and warned her "not to get into any car with *any* man she met at the club." Edna left the nightclub at 11:45 P.M. Witnesses there later confirmed that Marian Newton was seen leaving with a man who matched the description provided by Edna Mitchell.

Working in conjunction with San Diego FBI agents, homicide detectives discovered that the description of this suspect closely matched that of someone previously known by them who had been frequenting downtown San Diego dance halls and nightclubs in the weeks and months preceding the murder of Marian Newton. The suspect was believed to be using various names and aliases, including "Michael Vincent Martin." Representing himself at different nightspots both as an FBI agent and as a naval officer, the suspect was known to have used stolen and false identification in San Diego, and had rented a vehicle using fake ID. A Wanted Special Bulletin was circulated within the law enforcement communities requesting information on the suspect.

Authors Janice Knowlton and Michael Newton (no relation to the victim) make reference to an interview, purported to have been conducted by Knowlton, of a retired sheriff's deputy, Thad Stefan, on July 12, 1993, during which Stefan referred to his original field notes dating from 1947. Stefan had documented an unusual incident that had occurred in Hollywood, at the Hub Bar and Café on Santa Monica Boulevard, in the sheriff's department territory. The incident was reported to him on January 26, 1947, and included a statement by a waitress, Dorothy Perfect, who reported that a man identifying himself as "George" came to the café and initially propositioned her, telling her, "I can fix you up with your own apartment on the Sunset Strip."

Ms. Perfect described "George" as "a male Caucasian in his early forties, with wavy hair and glasses." She indicated "that while he did not appear drunk, he may have been under the influence of narcotics." "George" identified himself as "an FBI agent assigned to work the *Black Dahlia* investigation," and informed Perfect that "I can tell you who killed Elizabeth Short." Deputy Stefan's notes included the fact that this same "George" had first come to the Hub Café on January 21, only six days after the discovery of Elizabeth Short's body. At that time he had stayed in the bar area and was very talkative, informing the bartender he was an "FBI agent working on the Dahlia investigation." The bartender asked to see his agent's badge, at which point "George" mumbled something about "not being afraid of guns," and left the bar. Other employees at the Hub confirmed that "George" had returned again on January 25, but left after only a few minutes, then returned one last time, on January 26, and was recognized by Ms. Perfect from the prior contact, and she immediately summoned sheriff's deputies, but "George" left the bar before they arrived.

Initially, San Diego detectives considered the possibility of a connection between their victim and the Los Angeles wave of killings of lone women, including that of Elizabeth Short, but again LAPD discounted and denied any connection.

Though the first known to occur outside of Los Angeles County, this crime is identical in M.O. to the Ora Murray killing. Coupled with physical description of the suspect, it must be included with the rest of George Hodel's suspected serial killings.

## Viola Norton (February 14, 1948)

The headline of the Saturday morning *Herald Express* of February 14, 1948, read, "Woman Beaten Near 'Black Dahlia' Scene; Alhambra Woman Near Death after Beating by 2 Men."

At approximately 1:00 A.M. on Saturday morning, Mrs. Viola Norton, thirty-six, left a cocktail lounge in Alhambra, a community immediately east-southeast of the Los Angeles city limits. "Two men, both appearing to be approximately 40 years of age, approached her in a car and asked her to get in." She informed the two men that "she was walking home."

Both men exited their vehicle, dragged her inside, and drove off. The victim stated she "remembered a tussle, but nothing else."

Viola was beaten savagely about the face and head, her skull was fractured with a tire iron, and the two men left her for dead in an isolated area just four blocks from where the body of Elizabeth Short had been found thirteen months earlier. A neighbor discovered the victim unconscious and summoned an ambulance. The information regarding any follow-up investigation was sketchy, but it is believed the victim, though in critical condition, survived. The Norton kidnapping occurred only six miles east of where the bodies of victims Mondragon and Winters were dumped.

This crime occurred just twelve hours before the two suspects would commit another murder in Hollywood. Their next victim would be the real estate agent Mrs. Gladys Kern, previously summarized.

### Louise Margaret Springer (June 13, 1949)

On June 17, 1949, the *Los Angeles Examiner* morning headlines read:

*Exhibit 63*

Four days earlier, on June 13, twenty-eight-year-old Louise Springer, married with a two-year-old son, had been reported kidnapped. Her frantic husband had called the police minutes after her disappearance.

Louise's husband, Laurence Springer, a hairstylist of wide reputation, worked at a salon on Wilshire Boulevard. His wife worked at a beauty parlor in a department store at Santa Barbara and Crenshaw, just two blocks from where the Black Dahlia's body had been found two and a half years earlier. The couple had been living in Hollywood for a year, after relocating to Los Angeles from the San Francisco Bay area.

On Monday evening, June 13, at 9:05 P.M., Springer had left his wife seated in the passenger seat of their brand-new 1949 green Studebaker convertible in the parking lot while he ran inside to retrieve her eyeglasses, which she had left at work. He returned within ten minutes, but both his wife and their car were missing. Springer desperately searched the parking lot, then summoned LAPD.

After a search of the area by University Division patrol officers, the police reluctantly documented the husband's account on a missing persons report, but told him she probably "just decided to take off and would likely return in a day or two."

On the morning of June 16, Mrs. Lois Harris, a resident of 102 West 38th Street, having observed a new green Studebaker parked across from her home for three days, called the police to report an "abandoned vehicle." Police ran a DMV (Department of Motor Vehicles) check and, discovering the car was registered in the Springers' name, dispatched detectives to the location.

Louise Springer's body was found in the backseat, draped and covered with a white cape-type material, which belonged to the victim and which, as a beautician, she used to cover and protect her customers.

A later autopsy revealed that she had suffered blows to the head, possibly rendering her unconscious, after which she was strangled to death with a white sash cord that, the police said, the suspect had carried with him.

Robbery was not a motive, since the victim's purse and expensive jewelry and money were not taken. The autopsy surgeons and police detectives released two details relating to the condition of the body.

First, the suspect was unusually strong, because the sash cord he had placed around the victim's neck had been constricted so tightly as to leave only a two-and-a-half-inch-diameter space in the knotted noose.

The second piece of information, in the *Los Angeles Examiner* of June 17, read:

## BODY VIOLATED

And with a 14-inch length of finger-thick tree branch, ripped from some small tree, the killer had violated her body in such manner as to stamp this crime at once and indelibly in the same category as the killing of Elizabeth Short, "the *Black Dahlia*."

Police located witnesses in the 38th Street neighborhood, who provided a limited description of the murder suspect and additional information relating to the time he drove to the location and parked the car. The Springer vehicle at 38th and Broadway was only a mile from where Georgette Bauerdorf's vehicle had been found, also abandoned, at 25th and San Pedro.

Four teenagers provided police with further information: on June 13, they were inside a residence at 126 West 38th Street. At approximately 10:00 P.M., hearing a loud squeal of brakes outside, they saw a green Studebaker convertible abruptly turn in and stop at the curb. The driver quickly turned off the car's headlights.

Seconds later, a black-and-white police vehicle stopped their friend Jack Putney, also a teenager, for a traffic violation. The officers exited their police vehicle and talked to Putney for five or ten minutes by their police vehicle, which was parked just three feet away from the Studebaker. Seated behind the driver's wheel, the murder suspect sat motionless in the dark until finally the police drove off. The teens then saw him turn toward the backseat, lean over, and reach for something. Because of the darkness, the only description they could provide police was that he "was a white man with curly hair."

After the police pulled away, the witnesses paid no further attention to the man or the parked car, nor did they see him emerge from the vehicle and leave the area on foot. The Studebaker, they told the police, remained there for the next three days.

On June 18, 1949, the *Los Angeles Examiner* headline read:

"Police Missed Mad Killer, in Auto with Slain Victim, Parked Near Squad Car."

The *Examiner* printed a diagram showing the relative positions of the police, the traffic offender, and the murder suspect on 38th Street.

### Exhibit 64

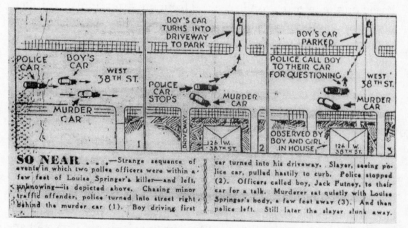

*Los Angeles Examiner, June 18, 1949*

The two LAPD traffic cops were subsequently located and identified as 77th Street Division officers, who admitted being "out of their area," and acknowledged stopping and warning Putney, who appeared to be "driving erratically." Both denied seeing the green Studebaker, but they admitted, "It could have been there."

In the month following Louise Springer's murder, the usual suspects were questioned, none of whom proved to be the killer. On June 21, a newspaper article appeared under the headline: "Mystery Man Hunted in L.A. Sex Murder." It hinted at a possible jealousy motive, indicating that in the weeks preceding the murder the victim's husband, Laurence Springer, had received six suspicious telephone calls from a male caller to a payphone located inside his office. Tabloid-type references were also made to the fact that police were looking into "the husband's relationship with an as yet unidentified girl."

Heartbroken, disillusioned, and bitter at the lack of cooperation from local authorities, Laurence Springer took his two-year-old son and moved out of Hollywood. His wife's kidnapping and murder also remains "open" in the police files at LAPD's Parker Center.


## "Jane Doe" (Unknown date, 1947-49)

Based on the information I received from my sister Tamar, as told to her by my mother and later confirmed in a slightly modified version by Sexton's daughter "Mary Moe," I must include another victim in our list of women believed slain by George Hodel. I have been unable to learn her identity, but if all that Tamar has told is accurate — and I believe it is — then LAPD has already investigated Father as a named murder suspect to the crime, and the victim's name is known to them.

I shall refer to her as "Jane Doe." Her death likely occurred sometime after the murder of Elizabeth Short, although I cannot be certain, since Mother's story to Tamar could have referred to an earlier murder. One recalls that her death was originally listed as a "suicide" from an overdose of pills, and, according to what Mother told Tamar, Father apparently signed her death certificate. Procedurally this would be dubious and highly suspect. Legally, all suicides occurring within Los Angeles County are required to be assigned as a coroner's case, which requires that an autopsy be performed.

Based on the possibility that "Gloria," the dark-haired young woman found in Father's photo album, might be this Jane Doe, girl-friend/employee, I have included an enlargement of that photograph to allow for potential identification. Should "Gloria" not be that employee, then perhaps a reader will recognize her as a relative or acquaintance. On the reverse side of her photograph she had written, "George — the teacher, from Gloria. Too little time — No?"

*Exhibit 65*

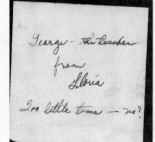

*"Gloria"*

# 32

# Forgotten Victims, 1950s:
# The Probables

In the summer of 1997 I had finished my investigative work on a high-profile, year-long investigation for a local Northwest attorney. The results had been positive and he was grateful for the many hours of hard work I had put in. Along with my final paycheck, he gave me the gift of a book, saying, "You might find it interesting, since it's about a writer and a retired detective working on an old unsolved murder case from Los Angeles." Having spent the past few years working as a defense investigator on a Japanese/Los Angeles murder investigation, I had little interest in and less curiosity about doing any recreational reading on the subject of murder. I glanced at the dustjacket: the title was *My Dark Places*, by an author named James Ellroy. I had no desire to read about other people's dark places. Without opening the present, I tossed it into a box in my garage and forgot about it.

Three years later, the author's name would resurface in connection with my Dahlia investigation, for I learned that he had written a novel entitled *The Black Dahlia*, a fictionalized account of Elizabeth Short's murder. Though tempted to read it, I also had no desire to confuse fact with fiction and fought off the part of me that was naturally curious. I told myself that Ellroy was probably just another sensationalist, wanting to capitalize on Hollywood noir and the brutality of her story. Besides, I wasn't into whodunit novels. I prided myself in wanting to know things as they are, not as they are imagined.

Six months later, having gained a thorough working knowledge of the Dahlia case on my own, I felt more confident and my curiosity won out. I sat down and read *The Black Dahlia*. I found Ellroy's fiction to be simultaneously disgusting and brilliant, profane and prophetic. It was obvious that he had done his homework and knew a great deal about the case. He mixed real names, real dates, and real locations with fictitious ones. I especially respected his street smarts: it was apparent he knew cops inside and out. I admired his ability to walk their walk and talk their talk. He knew their strengths and weaknesses. His "soft time" in L.A. County Jail, his homelessness, his sleeping in the L.A. public parks, and his golf caddying in West Los Angeles for the rich and famous had prepared him well. His novel clearly revealed that he understood people. Like a cop, he knew about their goods, their bads, and their uglies.

Forgetting that I already owned a copy of *My Dark Places* — I hadn't made the connection between Ellroy the novelist and Ellroy the true-crime author — I e-mailed an order for a copy.

I read it nonstop. In 1958, Geneva "Jean" Ellroy, the forty-three-year old mother of then ten-year-old James Ellroy, was raped and murdered in El Monte, a town twelve miles east of downtown Los Angeles. The crime was never solved. Thirty-four years later the victim's son-cum-novelist teamed up with Sergeant Bill Stoner, a retired L.A. Sheriff's Department homicide detective, and in the spring of 1994 the two men became "partners" to try and solve the crime. Because Stoner had worked in LASD's Homicide Unsolved Unit, which had originally investigated the case, and Ellroy was not only the victim's son but a respected author, the two were given carte blanche by the sheriff's brass. All the 1958 police files were opened to them; they were provided copies of the photos, evidence, and original witness statements. Together the two-man team gumshoed the hell out of the case. Their investigation began in the spring of 1994 and it appears they spent almost a year pursuing every possible lead.

The results of their investigation were fully documented in Ellroy's writing. *My Dark Places* served as an impressive homicide progress report, as well as a son's tribute to the memory of his murdered mother. Ellroy and Stoner's thoroughness and hard work may have been successful.

Based on my review of their entire investigation as documented in *My Dark Places*, it is my professional opinion that, like many of the other crimes previously described in my investigative summary, the

rape-murder of Geneva Ellroy in June 1958, and the rape-murder of
Elspeth Long seven months later, in January 1959, may well have
been committed by Fred Sexton. Here is a summary of the original
facts and the subsequent Ellroy/Stoner investigation that provide the
basis for my belief.

## Geneva Hilliker Ellroy (June 22, 1958)

Betty Short became my obsession . . . my symbiotic stand-in for
Geneva Hilliker Ellroy.

—James Ellroy

At 10:00 A.M. June 22, 1958, a woman's body was found near the
playing field of Arroyo High School in El Monte, California. Originally a "Jane Doe," since no purse or identification were found near
the body, she had been assaulted with numerous blows to the head,
which likely rendered her unconscious, and then strangled with two
separate ligatures, one a thin white clothesline-like cord — identical
to that used in the earlier Springer murder — and a second the victim's own nylon stocking, identical to the suspect's action in the earlier Mondragon strangulation.

The killer dumped the body in an isolated location known to be
a "lovers' lane" and placed her dark blue overcoat over the lower portion of her body, just as the killer(s) had done in the Jeanne French
murder. Like French, Geneva Ellroy, known to most of her friends as
Jean, was a nurse by profession. The investigation was handled by
LASD, which in 1958, because of their superior manpower and ex-
pertise, provided "contract service" for the smaller municipalities in
the county, including El Monte.

After hearing a public radio broadcast, a citizen called the police
and the victim was quickly identified as Jean Ellroy, a forty-three-
year-old divorcée. She lived in El Monte with her ten-year-old son,
James, and had not returned home the previous night. Based on later
witnesses statements and coroner information, the time of death was
believed to have been between 3:00 and 5:00 A.M., that is, five to
seven hours before the body was discovered.

An investigation into Jean Ellroy's movements prior to the killing revealed that she had left home in her own car, a 1957 Buick, at approximately 8:30 P.M. the previous night. Two primary witnesses were able to recognize the victim and provide a description of the man she was seen with on three separate occasions at two locations in El Monte just hours before her murder: Stan's Drive-In restaurant and the Desert Inn nightclub, both only three miles from where her body was found.

The first witness, Margie Trawick, age thirty-six, a part-time waitress and regular patron of the Desert Inn, provided detectives with the following information:

On the previous evening, June 21, 1958, she was seated at a table inside the Desert Inn as a customer and observed the victim walk into the establishment at 10:45 P.M., accompanied by another female described as a "dishwater-blonde with a ponytail, heavyset, 40 years of age." They sat down at a table, and almost immediately a man, who appeared to be of Mexican descent, walked over to their table, helped Ellroy off with her coat, and began to dance with her. Trawick had the impression that both women knew the man, whom she described as follows: possible Mexican, age forty to forty-five, five foot eight to six feet tall, dark hair slicked back, receding on both sides, with a noticeable widows' peak, thin-jawed ("you might think he had no teeth until you saw him smile"), swarthy complexion, dark suit, white shirt, open at the collar.

Trawick left the Desert Inn with a male friend at approximately 11:30 P.M. and noted that the Mexican was seated at the table with the two women. When she returned at 12:50 A.M. they had disappeared.

The second witness was Lavonne Chambers, a twenty-nine-year-old carhop waitress employed at Stan's Drive-In, located six blocks from the Desert Inn. Chambers provided sheriff's detectives with a formal statement on June 25, three days after the body was discovered.

She was serving customers on Saturday, June 21, 1958. She first observed the victim at the drive-in at 10:00 P.M. She was seated in the front passenger's seat of what Chambers believed was a 1955 or 1956 Oldsmobile, dark green, possibly two-tone in color, with a dull paint job. The driver, a male, ordered "just coffee," and the victim asked for "the thinnest sandwich you have," to which Chambers responded, "That would be a grilled cheese sandwich," and the victim replied, "Okay." After their brief meal they left the drive-in. The witness provided detectives with the following description of the driver: possibly Greek or Italian descent, thirty-five to forty years of age, thin face, dark complexion, dark receding hair combed straight back and thick on top.

Chambers informed detectives that the same two returned to the drive-in at approximately 2:15 A.M. Sunday morning, shortly after the bar closed. She again served them, the victim ordering "a bowl of chili and coffee" and the male "just coffee." The two finished their food and drink and left.

Chambers positively identified a photograph of the victim and her clothing. She had no doubt that Jean Ellroy was the same woman she had served on June 21 and 22.

Based on the witnesses' statements, a police artist prepared a composite drawing, both witnesses agreeing that the drawing was a good likeness of the suspect.

A third witness at the Desert Inn was interviewed and thought she remembered seeing the suspect with the victim and described him as "swarthy complected." Throughout his book, Ellroy would refer to the killer of his mother as "the Swarthy Man."

## Elspeth "Bobbie" Long (January 22, 1959)

In their ongoing search for the killer, Bill Stoner and James Ellroy discovered a second murder with a similar M.O. Seven months to the day after the murder of Jean Ellroy, another body was found dumped on an isolated gravel road in the adjacent town of La Puente, three miles from El Monte. The distance between the two dump locations was slightly over four miles. This dump location was approximately one mile from the Desert Inn and Stan's Drive-In. The similarities to the Ellroy case were uncomfortably close. Elspeth "Bobbie" Long, fifty-two, had received multiple blows to the head with a crescent-shaped weapon and had been raped and strangled to death, the suspect using Long's nylon stocking as a ligature.

As in the Ellroy murder, the suspect had placed the victim's coat over the lower portion of her body. Her purse, which was found nearby, revealed her address to be 2231½ West 52nd Street, Los Angeles. The purse also contained a bus ticket to the Santa Anita Racetrack, purchased at 6th and Main in downtown Los Angeles the previous day. Acquaintances interviewed later by detectives confirmed that the victim loved to play the horses and was a regular at the local tracks.

An autopsy confirmed multiple skull fractures and, as with Jean Ellroy, slides obtained indicated the presence of semen, confirming sexual intercourse and the probability of rape. Unlike with the Ellroy murder, detectives were unable to locate witnesses who could place anyone with the victim in the hours immediately preceding her death. Some witnesses believed they may have seen her at the Santa Anita track the previous day, but the information was sketchy and unreliable.

Based on the Bobbie Long murder information, Ellroy and Stoner debated the possibility of a serial killer. Stoner believed they were the same suspect; Ellroy had serious doubts. They decided to do a psychological profile on both unsolved homicides and obtained the services of a respected Department of Justice profiler, a retired LASD homicide detective named Carlos Avila. Avila's profiles on both victims were published in Ellroy's book, and I found nothing in them that added to the weight of the other investigative evidence. What was important in the profiler's review was his opinion that the suspect was, most probably, a serial killer.

It has been my experience that at best, these "profiles" should be considered an investigative tool; at worst, they can be dangerously speculative, demographically overweighted, and misleading, and, if given too much credence, can actually misdirect and impair an investigation. Profiles or patterns of predictability, like one's daily horoscope, often make more sense ex post facto. Human beings, especially human beings who murder, and above all those who murder and get away with it, are rarely predictable. Like wild beasts, they are cunning, predatory, and instinctual, and their environment has taught them survival and how best to avoid trappers.

In the Black Dahlia case, for example, John Douglas, former head of the FBI's serial crime division, provided over the past five years several separate published profiles on Elizabeth Short's killer. In virtually everything, his profiles were wide of the mark. He theorized: 1) that the killer was a white man in his late twenties; 2) he had no more than a high school education; 3) he lived alone and made his living working with his hands rather than his brains; and 4) though Douglas had made no review of any of the police files, he stated to a "certainty" that Elizabeth Short's death was the result of a "stranger murder," in other words that she was a victim of opportunity.

Douglas was not the only profiler to be wildly wide of the mark. More recently, in the 2002 Washington, D.C., area serial sniper case, profilers had a field day, theorizing in the media, among other things, that the sniper was white, that he had no children, and that he was from the D.C. area, none of which was true of the alleged perpetrators, John Allen Muhammad and John Malvo

Coming back to the Jean Ellroy and Bobbie Long homicides, there remains the question of composite drawings. Often, police composites are weak or generic; this one is not, and it is evident that it bears a remarkable likeness to Fred Sexton. The physical description of "the Swarthy Man" in all respects matches Sexton's appearance. As we know from numerous other witnesses sightings in 1947–50, many referred to the second man in just those words. I am not privy to a photograph of Sexton from the 1958 time period, so we must use our own imaginations to age him some ten years or more. As can be seen in this photograph, Sexton could pass for Hispanic, Italian, or Greek.

*Exhibit 66*

*1958 LASD composite*    *Fred Sexton, circa 1945–47*

Exhibit 66 is a photograph of Sexton, along with the composite drawing of the Ellroy murder suspect that was published in the newspapers of that time as well as in Ellroy's *My Dark Places*. This, in conjunction with what we know to be Sexton's M.O. throughout the entire decade of the 1940s, qualifies him as an exceptionally strong suspect in these two murders that occurred some eight and nine years later. Future investigation may well connect Sexton to the town of El Monte, and possibly to a car of like description. His close friend and accomplice to many of the rapes and murders, George Hodel, was medical director at the Ruth Home and Hospital in the 1940s, which was located at 831 North Gilman Road in El Monte. This girls' home and hospital was only *one mile* from the Desert Inn, and would most likely have been the closest nightclub for Father's after-work drinks, dancing, and entertainment. As of this writing, I have not conducted any additional research into other unsolved homicides that may have occurred between 1950 and 1957.

## Helene Jerome (August 27, 1958)

On August 28, 1958, the *Los Angeles Examiner* ran the headline "Actress Found Dead in Hollywood." Helene Jerome was a graduate of London's Royal Academy of Arts, and had devoted most of her career to the stage. She had acted with Barbara Stanwyck in Frank Capra's 1933 romantic melodrama *The Bitter Tea of General Yen*, and later with Mae West in the 1936 film *Klondike Annie*, in which she says to West, "Too many girls follow the line of least resistance." Mae answers, in what has become a classic response, "Yeah, but a good line is hard to resist."*

The paper reported that the nude body of the fifty-year-old actress had been found in her apartment at 1738 North Las Palmas. The night clerk at the building, Orio Janes, was the last to see the victim, at approximately 4:00 A.M., when he went to her apartment to

*An article written on August 28, 1958, in the *Los Angeles Examiner*, which I used as source material, incorrectly identified the murder victim as being actress Helene Jerome (Eddy), who starred in over one hundred films. Ms. Jerome actually lived a long, full life, dying of natural causes at the age of ninety-two. Little is known about the actual murder victim, Helen Jerome, other than that she was an actress of the same name.

check on her because her telephone had been "off the hook" for over an hour. At that time the witness saw her in the company of a man; however, his description was not released to the public.

It was learned that roughly six hours before the murder, the victim's estranged husband, Edwin Jerome, had been visiting her at the apartment. During his visit, a man telephoned from the lobby asking for Helene. Mr. Jerome told the caller she was sleeping. "Just tell her *George* [italics mine] called," the caller responded. Police were given a description of "George" by the clerk, but it was not made public. Deputy Chief Thad Brown put Hollywood detective Henry Kerr in charge of the investigation.

Dr. Newbarr performed the autopsy and determined that the cause of death was strangulation. In his words, "The victim was strangled with such force that it fractured the Adam's apple."

Though we have minimal information on this crime, the facts as presented would seem to indicate that the victim could well have known the suspect "George." Like some other victims, Jerome had links to Hollywood and the film industry dating back to the 1930s. Based on his actions, the suspect could well have been Fred Sexton, using the name "George." Sexton's ex-wife's residence, which he was known to visit regularly and stay in for weeks at a time, was only a few miles from the crime scene. This murder occurred two months after the Geneva Ellroy strangulation, and five months prior to that of Bobbie Long.

Though not dumped, the victim was found nude and strangled. In my opinion, while Fred Sexton would appear to be a more likely suspect, my father's involvement cannot be completely ruled out, since he would occasionally "pass through town" on business trips from the Far East.[*]

It is not known if physical evidence (fingerprints or DNA) still exist on the Jerome murder investigation, and to the best of my knowledge this crime also remains as an LAPD unsolved homicide.

---

[*]We recall Tamar's reporting that it was on just such a trip eleven years after this murder (1969) that he drugged and took salacious pictures of his thirteen-year-old granddaughter, Deborah.

A statistical summary of the twenty separate crimes reviewed in this investigation over a two-decade span reveals the following:

1) LAPD crimes — 10 murders (Elizabeth Short, Jeanne French, Gladys Kern, Mimi Boomhower, Jean Spangler, Evelyn Winters, Rosenda Mondragon, Louise Springer, Helene Jerome, and Jane Doe); 2 kidnap-rapes (Sylvia Horan and Ica M'Grew); 1 robbery (Armand Robles)

2) LASD crimes — 4 murders (Ora Murray, Georgette Bauerdorf, Geneva Ellroy, and Bobbie Long).

3) Long Beach PD — 1 murder (Laura Trelstad).

4) San Diego PD — 1 murder (Marian Newton).

5) Alhambra PD — 1 kidnap/attempted murder (Viola Norton).

Since I have no access to the various police files, I acknowledge that some of these crimes may have since been solved. Each law enforcement agency can easily and quickly do their own review to ascertain if the case was cleared or not.

## By the Numbers

One final observation about these serial murders: the numbers themselves. In the *Los Angeles Times* article "Farewell My Black Dahlia," LAPD detective Harry Hansen noted, "Most homicides — I think the figure is 97 percent — are solved. A very few aren't. You can't win them all."

I would argue with Hansen's math. A homicide clearance rate of 97 percent in a major metropolitan city like Los Angeles is all but impossible. A remarkable clearance rate, with lots of hard work and lots of lucky breaks, would run around 80 percent.

A review of the latest California Department of Justice statistics for Los Angeles County during the last ten-year period (1990–2000) shows an alarming drop in the solve rate! A mere 37 percent of all Los Angeles homicides were solved for the year 2000. The highest clearance rate for the decade occurred in 1991: *63 percent*. The decade's average was *57 percent*.

Let's give the department the benefit of the doubt and say that in the mid-1940s they cleared 75 percent of their annual homicides.

Given enough negatives, one may well prove a positive. In the Los Angeles area from 1943 to 1949 I have reviewed eleven "lone woman" homicides, excluding the Jane Doe "suicide" and the Marian Newton San Diego murder. How many of these kidnap-rape-murders did they clear? Assuming for a moment that what LAPD told its citizens was the truth, that these murders were not connected to the Dahlia or to each other — according to Harry Hansen's math, ten of the eleven murders should have been cleared (or, using my more conservative rate, eight). How many were solved? *None.*

I offer these numbers not to belittle LAPD and LASD homicide detectives but rather to make a point. This rash of crimes was not solved because they were most likely committed by the same suspect(s). These attacks and murders were not committed by eleven different sadistic rapists all operating in the same locale. No, it is my sad but firm belief that most of these crimes were committed by George Hodel and Fred Sexton, operating sometimes together, sometimes alone. That is why LAPD and LASD didn't clear any of the crimes. Had they been committed by different suspects, statistically at least *half* of the crimes would have been solved.

For me, as a professional in law enforcement, the most painful reality of all is knowing that the blood of these many victims is on the hands of those officers and commanders within the Los Angeles Police Department who initiated, then perpetuated, the cover-up. Perhaps earlier crimes as well, but certainly at a minimum all the crimes committed and all the lives taken after January 21, 1947, the date George Hodel's photograph was positively identified by the Johnsons at their East Washington Boulevard Hotel, can be attributed to those officers who obstructed justice and aided and abetted in the cover-up.

# 33

# George Hodel–Elizabeth Short: Reconstructed Timeline

IN MY INTRODUCTION I said that solving the murder of Elizabeth Short, as well as the other sadistic murders discussed in this book, "is the result of finding and piecing together hundreds of separate thoughtprints."

In telling this complex story, I have tried first to present all the evidence related to identifying our suspects, then in later chapters to explain the connections to and motivations for LAPD's cover-up.

The evidence linking George Hodel and Fred Sexton to the crimes has been spread across many chapters. We have heard from more than seventy witnesses, and reviewed over sixty separate exhibits. By incorporating many of the "ghost witnesses," those establishing Elizabeth Short's movements during LAPD's so-called "missing week," we now know why they had to be kept silent and discredited. By uniting the fuller knowledge of both Elizabeth Short's and George Hodel's movements during the mid-1940s, we can now reconstruct and distill a more accurate timeline of events, one which is most unique, as we can now walk in the shoes of both the victim and her killer.

## 1944–1945

George and Elizabeth meet and begin a relationship of sorts, platonic or otherwise. George wines and dines her in the finest restaurants. Together they frequent the Biltmore, and downtown and

Hollywood nightclubs. Elizabeth gets financial aid for food and rent from George when needed.

## August 1945

Major Matt Gordon is killed in an airplane crash over India. George Hodel, after learning that Elizabeth's fiancé has been killed, asks her to marry him instead. Heartbroken and despondent over the loss of her fiancé, she agrees, or at least leads him to believe she will think about it.

## October–December 1945

While Elizabeth waits tables at Princess Whitewing's restaurant in Miami Beach, Florida, George Hodel, having joined UNRRA in December, is at the agency's home office in Washington, D.C., studying Chinese. George contacts Elizabeth and asks her to marry him when he returns from China. She expresses second thoughts about marriage. Infuriated at her rejection, he manages to control himself long enough to wire her a restrained telegram from D.C., reminding her that "a promise is a promise to a person of the world" and signing it simply, "Yours."

## April 1946

Stationed in China with the honorary rank of lieutenant general, George sends Elizabeth the photographs showing him both in uniform and civilian clothes as "arbiter."

Elizabeth writes to Lieutenant Gordon Fickling about her desire to return to California to see him. Fickling cautions her, "Why not pause and consider just what your coming out here to me would amount to?" Despite his admonition, she travels to California.

## August 1946

Elizabeth returns to Hollywood and stays at Mark Hansen's Carlos Street residence, where she lives for three weeks with Hansen's girlfriend, Anne Toth. Looking for work wherever she can find it and left to her own devices, Elizabeth, rummaging through a desk, finds Mark Hansen's blank address book with his name embossed on the outside and takes it.

## September 1946

George suffers a heart attack in China and returns to Los Angeles, where he is admitted to a hospital and discharged from UNRRA.

## Late September 1946

Elizabeth leaves Mark Hansen's house before the end of September and moves into the Hawthorne Hotel at 1611 North Orange Drive in Hollywood, where she briefly shares a room with Lynn Martin, then shares a room with her friend from Massachusetts, Marjorie Graham.

## September 20–21, 1946

Elizabeth meets the Army soldier "Sergeant Doe" in downtown Los Angeles, has a dinner date with him, and as they walk back to her hotel they are seen together and chased by a carload of "Hispanics," one of whom, I suspect, is Fred Sexton. Father, still hospitalized, and knowing Elizabeth is in Hollywood, may well have asked his good friend Sexton to hit the streets and see if he could find her. These males clearly recognize her, because Sergeant Doe hears one of them yell out, "There she is!"

Elizabeth and Sergeant Doe spend the night together at the Figueroa Hotel.

## October 1946

Elizabeth is still rooming with Marjorie Graham at the Hawthorne and tells her that her boyfriend is an "Army Air Force lieutenant" in the hospital in Los Angeles. She hopes he gets well soon so that he will get out of the hospital in time for their planned marriage on November 1.

## November 13–December 6, 1946

Elizabeth moves to a room at the Chancellor Hotel, 1842 North Cherokee Avenue in Hollywood, which she shares with seven other women. Broke and unemployed, she is forced to move out.

## December 6, 1946

On the day she leaves, an anxious Elizabeth tells roommate Linda Rohr, "I've got to hurry. He's waiting for me." I submit "he" is Dr. George Hodel.

## December 6–11, 1946

It is likely that during this period of time after she leaves the Chancellor and for the five days that follow, Elizabeth and George are together. She could be staying at the Franklin House, or perhaps George puts her up in a nearby hotel and she just visits him at his home. It is at this time that he photographs her in the nude and adjacent to the Chinese art object. An incident occurs between them, something traumatic and untoward, perhaps a physical assault, which causes Elizabeth to become fearful for her life. What is known is that Elizabeth arrives in San Diego a few days later, alone and without friends, unemployed, with little or no money, and with no place to live. She has fled!

## December 12, 1946

Dorothy French finds Elizabeth in an all-night movie theater, homeless and without prospects, and invites her to stay temporarily with her and her mother, Elvera, at their home in the suburbs of San Diego. The Frenches report to the police that Elizabeth has dated a number of different men during her stay at their house, and that she is especially afraid of "an ex-boyfriend who [is] extremely jealous of her." Dorothy and Elvera French describe Elizabeth's emotional condition as highly agitated and secretive throughout her stay with them and that she becomes "especially frightened when anyone [comes] to the front door." But Elizabeth remains tight-lipped, continually refusing to tell Elvera French the name of the man she fears.

## December 15, 1946

Robert Manley sees Elizabeth at a bus bench across from the Western Airlines office in San Diego and offers to give her a ride home. At the house, he briefly meets Dorothy and Elvera French and returns later in the evening to take Elizabeth out for dinner and dancing.

## Mid-December, 1946

Elizabeth is temporarily back in Los Angeles, where "five unidentified friends" see her at an unnamed nightclub in Hollywood. These same friends tell police that they also saw Elizabeth at a nightclub in Hollywood earlier in the fall, at which time she told them she "planned to marry 'George,' an Army pilot from Texas." These separate witnesses are the first to link George Hodel's first name to the military pilot Elizabeth has told other friends about.

## December 24 or 25, 1946

Mark Hansen sees Elizabeth around Christmas, three weeks before her murder. Hansen, in his later report to police, does not say where or with whom, but it is likely in Hollywood either at a private party or possibly a public holiday gathering or at his nightclub, the Florentine Gardens.

### December 29, 1946, 7:30 P.M.

A terrified and hysterical Elizabeth runs up to a taxi-stand manager at 115 North Garfield Avenue in East Los Angeles. Barefoot and bleeding from her knees, she relates the story of her assault "by a well-dressed man who was her acquaintance." This description matches that of George Hodel, who most likely, after arguing with her, drives her to an isolated area, attacks her in a fit of anger, and may have killed her on the spot had she not escaped.

### January 2, 1947

Phoebe Short, Elizabeth's mother, receives a letter from her daughter, telling her that she is "living in San Diego, with a girlfriend, Vera French." In the letter, Elizabeth lies to her mother, telling her she is "working at the Naval Hospital."

### January 7, 1947

Robert Manley wires Elizabeth at the French residence in San Diego and tells her he has plans to come down the following day and wants to see her.

### January 7, 1947, 11:30 P.M.

That same night, Dorothy French's neighbor sees a car drive up outside of Dorothy's residence just before midnight. The neighbor sees three individuals, two men and a woman, get out of the car and go to the front door, where they knock, then wait for a few minutes. Elizabeth secretly watches them but does not answer the door, and the three hurriedly return to their car and leave. I submit that these two men are George Hodel and Fred Sexton, who somehow have found out where Elizabeth is staying.

## January 8, 1947, 5:30 P.M.

Robert Manley arrives at the French residence to see Elizabeth, who asks for a ride with him back to Los Angeles. He tells her he has business to take care of first but that he will take her with him and they can return to Los Angeles the following day. Manley gets a motel room in San Diego for the night, and, for the first time, as he tells the police after they pick him up for questioning after Elizabeth's murder, he notices deep scratches on her arms. Elizabeth informs him they are from "a jealous dark-haired, Italian man from San Diego." These visible marks and scratches on Elizabeth's arms are completely consistent with the story of her attack that she told the taxi-stand manager ten days earlier. Elizabeth places a phone call from a café at Pacific Highway and Balboa Drive just outside San Diego to a man in Los Angeles. Red Manley, standing nearby, overhears parts of the conversation, enough of it at least to inform police later on that she called a man in Los Angeles and "made arrangements to meet him somewhere in the downtown area, the following evening, January 9." LAPD and DA investigators will later successfully trace the phone records and verify that the person she called was the "wealthy Hollywood man," whose identity has been established as Dr. George Hodel.

## January 9–11, 1947

Over the course of these two days, friends and acquaintances see and speak with Elizabeth in the downtown and Hollywood areas.

Also, between these dates, George Hodel accosts and assaults seventeen-year-old Armand Robles while the young man is approaching a footpad in the downtown area. George will later send the young man's photos to the press, identifying Robles as "the werewolf killer."

## January 12, 1947

George and Elizabeth go to the downtown hotel at 300 East Washington Boulevard, where the hotel owners, Mr. and Mrs. Johnson, see the couple during check-in and, after the murder, make positive identifications of both from photographs.

## January 14, 1947, in the afternoon

A sobbing and fearful Elizabeth runs up to Officer McBride in a downtown bus depot. McBride escorts her back to a Main Street bar to obtain her purse and later sees her exit with two men and a woman. I believe these three are the same trio that came searching for Elizabeth at the Frenches' residence a week earlier, that is, George Hodel, Fred Sexton, and the same unidentified woman.

## January 14, 1947, 3:00–4:00 P.M.

From the downtown bar, George Hodel takes Elizabeth Short to the Franklin House. He gags her mouth, binds her hands and feet with rope, and then begins a prolonged and systematic process in which Elizabeth is beaten and subjected to ritualistic and sadistic torture, is sexually assaulted and then slain.

## January 14–15, 1947

George Hodel removes Elizabeth's body from the Franklin House, drives due south on Normandie Avenue and parks his car at the isolated vacant lot at 39<sup>th</sup> and Norton. Father removes both sections of the body, and carefully poses his "masterpiece." On his drive home he stops halfway and places her purse and shoes on top of a trashcan on Crenshaw Boulevard.

## January 15, 1947

Tying up loose ends, possibly to pay for the hotel room, and still using the identity of "Mr. Barnes," George Hodel returns to the hotel at 300 East Washington Boulevard, where he tells Mr. Johnson he "expects his wife to join him." When Johnson jokingly replies, "You were gone a few days; I thought you might be dead," George becomes agitated, visibly nervous, and immediately leaves.

## January 15, 1947, late evening

George Hodel enters an unidentified Hollywood bar, where he asks the bartender whether "Sherryl" is working that night. After being told it is her night off, he leaves.

## January 16, 1947, late evening

George Hodel returns to the same bar the next night and meets Sherryl Maylond, the ex-roommate of Elizabeth Short's at the Chancellor Hotel, room 501. Identifying himself as "Clement," George Hodel informs Sherryl he wants to talk to her "about Betty Short." But Sherryl refuses to talk to him and he leaves the bar.

## January 21, 25, and 26, 1947

George Hodel enters the Hub Bar and Café on Santa Monica Boulevard in Hollywood, where on three separate nights he identifies himself to women and the bartender as "George, an FBI agent working on the Black Dahlia investigation." On the final day he approaches an attractive waitress named Dorothy Perfect, whom he propositions by promising her, "I can fix you up with your own apartment on the Sunset Strip." He also informs the waitress, "I can tell you who killed Elizabeth Short." Dorothy Perfect, believing the man is under the influence of narcotics, calls the sheriff's department, while George Hodel flees into the night, never to return.

In the days and weeks that follow the discovery of Elizabeth
Short's body, George phones city editor James Richardson, promising to mail him a few of her personal belongings, which he does.
Then, as the Black Dahlia Avenger, he sends a dozen taunting mailings to the press and detectives, makes and then withdraws his promise
to surrender, and continues his ongoing cat-and-mouse game with
the police department.

In rapid succession during the months following the Dahlia
killing, George and Fred kidnap, rape, and murder lone women off
the streets of Los Angeles, most of whom they savagely beat and
strangle. More kidnappings and murders follow in 1948 and 1949.
Even after Father's arrest for incest on October 6, 1949, he and Sexton commit one more crime, the kidnap and murder of actress Jean
Spangler on October 7, the day following his bail out from lockup.

After his acquittal in December, 1949, the DA investigators confront him in early 1950 at the Franklin House, where they inform
him they are aware of his crimes and promise they will arrest him and
bring him to justice. George Hodel, confronted with the probability
of an imminent arrest by the DA investigators, who are outside of his
sphere of LAPD protection, quickly flees the United States and remains outside the country for forty years.

After the incest trial, Sexton eventually flees to Mexico City. Unlike George Hodel, however, Sexton returns to live off-and-on in the
Los Angeles area during the 1950s and '60s, continuing his sporadic
serial killings.

In the mid-to late 1960s, Sexton returns and establishes a permanent residence in Mexico and, at age sixty-two, marries a teenager
who, like June, will remain his wife for the next thirty years. Sexton
dies in Mexico in 1996, his death preceding that of his lifelong friend
and accomplice George Hodel by just four years.

# 34

# Filing My Case with the District Attorney's Office

AT THE TIME I CONCLUDED MY INVESTIGATION, I had no idea whether the district attorney's office had any files from its presentation to the 1949 grand jury. Still, I needed to know whether the material I'd assembled would persuade the district attorney that there was a prosecutable case here. I therefore submitted the results of my investigation to a former colleague, someone I'd worked with and respected during my years as a homicide detective. I presented the material as I would have brought him a case twenty years ago, hopeful that I had assembled enough evidence to convince a prosecutor that there was sufficient probable cause to file charges.

The final stage of all criminal investigations comes with the formal presentation by the detective of his case to the district attorney's office for a filing. General filing policies within the prosecutor's office vary from state to state and county to county. From my experience in L.A. County, the reviewing deputy district attorney needs to be convinced that the suspect(s) did indeed commit the crime, and be strongly confident that he or she will win a conviction in court. Anything less will result in an outright rejection, or a "continued for further investigation," requiring an immediate release of the person arrested. This is how it's supposed to work under our Constitution. All good working detectives know and prepare for this moment of truth.

It had been almost twenty years since I had last walked into the district attorney's office to present my investigation and request a murder filing on a suspect. None of the old guard in the DA's office was around anymore, except one. Fortunately for me and for the public, he was among the best.

In his thirty-fifth year of service in the DA's office, Head Deputy District Attorney Stephen Kay had prosecuted many of Los Angeles's most notorious murderers. His career convictions read like a Who's Who of California killers, including the Manson case, where he was co-counsel with the celebrated prosecutor and author Vincent Bugliosi. He later personally prosecuted the rest of the Manson family members — Tex Watson, Bruce Davis, and Leslie Van Houten. Kay was the first deputy district attorney in California history to attend a lifer parolee's hearing and argue before the parole board for denial based on the merits of the case. To date, Steve Kay has attended a total of fifty-eight parole hearings arguing against the release of the various Manson family members.

Kay prosecuted serial killers Lawrence Bittaker and Roy Norris, who during the commission of their crimes had actually tape-recorded one of their vicious rape-murders. Bittaker and Norris would kidnap and murder four additional victims, ages thirteen to eighteen, before being apprehended, prosecuted, and convicted by Kay.

In 1996 Kay prosecuted and convicted killer Charles Rathbun for the vicious murder of Raiderette and beauty-queen model Linda Sobek, whose body was found in Angeles National Forest.

During my career I had gone to Steve Kay and presented dozens of murder cases for his review and filing of complaints. I had always found him to be highly intelligent, conscientious, and, most importantly, a man of total integrity. Knowing he could be trusted in all matters requiring confidentiality, and knowing that above all he would give me the benefit of objectivity, I decided to submit the Dahlia investigation to him as if I were asking for a criminal filing.

We met for three hours. I gave him an overview of the investigation, informing him of my suspicions relating to the serial killings and my belief, based on my two-year-plus investigation, that my father was not only the killer of Elizabeth Short but also the "wealthy Hollywood man" identified in 1949 by Lieutenant Jemison as the DA's prime suspect. I provided Kay with my entire manuscript and investigation, complete with photographs and exhibits.

Understandably, Steve Kay was shocked and stunned by my disclosures, but he maintained his composure, voiced his confidence and trust in my ability as a homicide investigator, and said he would review the entire case file on his own time, not as an official in the DA's office. He would, he said, review it as if I were actively submitting it to him for a criminal filing. Further, he promised he would use the same rigorous standards he requires of all investigators and would give me his opinion after a careful and considered review.

A month later I received the following letter in the mail.

September 30, 2001
To Whom It May Concern:

The most haunting murder mystery in Los Angeles County during the twentieth century has finally been solved in the twenty-first century. The case of the Black Dahlia murder was solved by one of the Los Angeles Police Department's finest homicide investigators, Steve Hodel. This, however, was anything but a normal LAPD homicide investigation, since Steve retired from the LAPD in 1986 and since the murderer was none other than Steve's father, Dr. George Hill Hodel.

I first met Detective Steve Hodel in 1973 when, after being on the prosecution team in the Tate–La Bianca murders and the Gary Hinman and "Shorty" Shea murders against the Manson Family for three years, I received an assignment to the Central Operations Complaint Division. This Division is the largest felony case filing Division of the Los Angeles District Attorney's Office. I liked Steve from the first time I met him. Not only was he very bright and personable, but the cases he presented for filing were always well prepared and well investigated.

Also, if Steve believed that he did not have sufficient evidence to have a case filed, he would come right out and say so!

Steve was a tenacious detective. If he believed someone was guilty, he would leave no stone unturned in attempting to prove his guilt. On the other hand, if he believed that a suspect was not guilty, he would do everything in his power to establish his innocence. Because of his objectivity and fairness, Steve was able not only to be an outstanding police detective, but in his retirement years he has easily adapted to becoming an excellent criminal defense investigator.

The readers should know that Steve Hodel was not an average

LAPD detective; he was simply one of their best homicide investigators. For many years he was the supervising homicide detective for the Hollywood Division of the Los Angeles Police Department. Steve has investigated over 300 murders and earned an excellent reputation not only among his peers but also among members of the Los Angeles County District Attorney's Office.

If Steve had not found the photographs his father had taken of Elizabeth Short (the Black Dahlia) in his father's cherished photo album, Steve would never have even considered investigating the famous Black Dahlia murder case. Steve is a highly trained and accomplished homicide investigator, and in the Black Dahlia case he is just doing what he has been trained to do, and that is to objectively investigate a murder case. How ironic is it that the son of one of the most brutal murderers in Los Angeles history would become a LAPD Homicide Detective and be the one to establish his father's guilt.

What Steve did not know when he started his investigation was that his father had actually been a major suspect in the Black Dahlia murder. In fact, during the early part of 1950, when the Los Angeles District Attorney's Office was involved in the Black Dahlia investigation with the LAPD, Dr. George Hodel, in my opinion, was the prime suspect. The DA's office finally cleared him because of a lack of evidence. In an interview with Steve, witness Joe Barrett quotes DA Investigator Walter Sullivan and other DA investigators saying, "God damn it, he got away with it. Yeah, talking about the incest trial with Tamar." Then they said, "We want this son of a bitch. We think he killed the Black Dahlia." Dr. Hodel was so worried about the DA's office that he fled the country for the next forty years.

Based on the results of Steve's investigation, I would have no reservations about filing two counts of murder against Dr. George Hodel. Of course, I do not speak for the Los Angeles District Attorney's Office on this subject and all views I express are my own, based on 34 years of experience in the DA's office, including experience prosecuting some of the highest profile murder cases in the history of Los Angeles County. I have personally read all of Steve's written account of his father's life and crimes and I have *no* doubt that his father not only murdered Elizabeth Short (the Black

Dahlia) but also murdered Jeanne French less than one month after the Black Dahlia murder.

## THE BLACK DAHLIA MURDER

Steve makes a compelling case against his father for the murder of Elizabeth Short on January 15, 1947. The evidence against Dr. George Hodel is circumstantial, but I believe that circumstantial evidence cases are often a lot stronger than direct evidence cases, because there is no potential problem of misidentification by an eyewitness. I view each piece of circumstantial evidence like the strands in a rope where each fact pointing to the suspect's guilt is a separate strand.

Eventually if you have enough incriminating facts, you can build a rope that will be strong enough to bind the suspect to justice.

The first thing that Steve does in his investigation is to establish a personal relationship between Elizabeth Short and Dr. George Hodel. This is accomplished by Steve's discovery of two photographs of Elizabeth taken by his father. One was apparently taken in the Franklin house where Dr. Hodel lived. The second photo is a seductive nude photograph of Elizabeth. Both of these photos were found in a section of Dr. Hodel's photo album reserved for family members and "loved ones."

Handwriting analysis points directly at Dr. Hodel as a murderer, not only in the Elizabeth Short murder but also in the Jeanne French murder, which I will discuss in more detail later. It is a common practice in criminal trials to have a family member, a friend, or a co-worker identify someone's handwriting. Steve is very familiar with his father's handwriting and makes some important identifications in both murder cases.

Steve positively identifies his father's hand printing on the note mailed to the *Los Angeles Examiner* from downtown L.A. on January 26, 1947, where the "Black Dahlia Avenger" promises to turn himself in on January 29 at 10 A.M. Steve also identifies his father's hand printing in lipstick on the body of Jeanne French, where the murderer wrote "Fuck You. B.D."

Elizabeth Short was murdered on January 15, 1947, and Jeanne

French was murdered on February 10, 1947. We now have Steve's hand printing identification linking the person who was sending letters and postcards about the Black Dahlia murder to the press with the murder of Jeanne French.

Steve did the right thing with his hand printing evidence. He hired an unbiased handwriting expert, Hannah McFarland from Washington, to review the evidence. Steve did not tell her who the suspect was or that the suspect was his father. He also did not tell her who the victims were.

Hannah McFarland concludes that the same suspect who wrote the message in lipstick (on the body of Jeanne French) also hand printed 4 of the postcards about the Black Dahlia murder that were sent to the *Los Angeles Herald Express*. We learned that the suspect in the Black Dahlia murder liked to have contact with the *Los Angeles Examiner* and the *Los Angeles Herald Express*.

The suspect even called the city editor of the *L.A. Examiner*, then mailed a packet addressed to the "*Examiner* and other newspapers" containing some of Elizabeth Short's personal possessions, including her Social Security card, her birth certificate, and an address book with about 75 names in it (with one page torn out). By sending possessions that the actual murderer would have obtained from Elizabeth's purse on the night of her murder, we know that we have to take contacts with the press as major clues in determining the identity of the murderer.

The fact that the murderer of Jeanne French signed the initials B.D. on her body (Black Dahlia) ties him into the Black Dahlia murder. The fact that his hand printing on Jeanne French's body has been tied by Steve and Hannah McFarland to postcards and letters sent into the *L.A. Examiner* and the *L.A. Herald Express* also ties the murderer of Jeanne French to the Black Dahlia murder. We know from Steve and from Hannah McFarland's analysis that Dr. George Hodel is the printer.

I am not familiar with Hannah McFarland since she practices in Washington State and I prosecute in California. I find her to have an excellent analytical style. When she makes a comparison, I can actually see what she is talking about. That would be very impressive to a jury. Her opinion "highly probable" is strong, considering that she does not have the original writings of the suspect to use for comparison purposes. Hannah McFarland assured Steve that her "highly probable" findings were the same as her being "virtually certain" that the questioned writings (hand printing on Jeanne French's body plus the four hand printed postcards sent to the *L.A. Herald Express*) and the known writings (Steve's submitted printings of his father) were written by the same person.

Analysis by the LAPD crime lab connects the envelopes and the paper used, indicating that the same suspect who sent the original packet containing Elizabeth Short's Social Security card, birth certificate, and address book to the *L.A. Examiner* also sent the subsequent note to the *Examiner*, offering to surrender for a 10 year sentence. LAPD criminalist Ray Pinker determined that at least one of the notes sent by the Dahlia murderer used proof sheet paper of a type commonly found in printing shops. We know from Steve that his father had a printing press in the basement of the Franklin house and had a supply of proof sheet paper such as the one on which Steve made his "Chinese Chicken" drawing.

These are more important pieces of evidence connecting Dr. George Hodel to the Black Dahlia murder — more strands in the rope.

The manner of bisection of Elizabeth Short's body leads me to conclude that a doctor was the murderer. In a letter from Special Agent P. B. Hood of the Los Angeles office to J. Edgar Hoover, he states "the body was cut into around the waist with a very sharp instrument and the cut was very cleanly done — none of the internal organs being touched except to sever the intestines. The cut through the backbone was very cleanly done. There is some speculation that the murderer had some training in the dissection of bodies. The manner in which Elizabeth Short's body was dissected has indicated the possibility that the murderer was a person somewhat experienced in medical work . . ." USC turned over a list of 300 names of their medical students for follow up investigation.

Dr. Frederic Newbarr, the Chief autopsy surgeon for the County of Los Angeles, performed the autopsy on Elizabeth Short on January 16, 1947. He determined that a sharp, thin bladed instrument consistent with a scalpel had been used to perform the bisection. The incision was performed through the abdomen, and then through the intervertebral disk between the second and third vertebra.

BLACK DAHLIA AVENGER

The body had been washed clean and drained of blood. Fibers believed to originate from a scrub brush were found on the body.

In a 1971 *L.A. Times* interview entitled "Farewell My Black Dahlia," the original Black Dahlia homicide investigator, Detective Harry Hansen, upon his retirement stated that his own personal theory was that a man with medical training was the murderer. He stated, "It was a clean definitely professional job. You have to know exactly how and where or you just can't do it. When I asked medical authorities what kind of person could have performed that bisection, they said someone with medical finesse."

We know from Steve's investigation that when attending UC San Francisco medical school that George Hodel had an outstanding reputation as a surgeon. More strands in the rope.

The body of Elizabeth Short had been posed. In all the murder cases I have handled over the years, I have only had one body posed. It is a very rare occurrence. When I prosecuted photographer Charles Rathbun for the murder of model and former Los Angeles Raider cheerleader Linda Sobek, Rathbun posed Linda Sobek in the grave he dug for her before covering her up with dirt.

How was Elizabeth Short's body posed? Both arms were raised above the head, the right arm placed at a 45-degree angle, away from the body, then bent at the elbow to form a 90-degree angle. The left arm was placed at a 45-degree angle away from the body and then bent again to form a second 90-degree angle that paralleled the body. Why was her body posed? To answer this question, Steve cleverly delves into his father's admiration of his close friend and now world famous photographer, Man Ray.

Steve notes that Man Ray's position was that women exist "at man's will and for man's pleasure, and those pleasures are often enhanced and increased through humiliation, degradation and the infliction of pain upon them." This could explain why Elizabeth was tortured before she was killed.

Steve points out that the position of Elizabeth's arms is an exact duplication of Man Ray's photograph entitled *The Minotaur* (the destroyer of young maidens). The excised flesh below Elizabeth Short's breast imitates the shadows seen in the photograph. The lacerations to her face give the appearance of the lips in Man Ray's famous photograph entitled *The Lovers*.

From Dr. Newbarr's autopsy report, we learn that Dr. Hodel inflicted unbelievable pain and degradation on Elizabeth before he killed her. Dr. Newbarr states that Elizabeth was tortured initially by the infliction of minor cuts to her body and private parts where the pubic hairs are cut away. She was then beaten and kicked about her entire body (as was Jeanne French). She was then forced to eat her own or his fecal excrement. Also large pieces of flesh were cut from her body and inserted into her vagina and rectum. Is it just a coincidence that Elizabeth Short's body was posed, and her face and breasts were cut to imitate two of Man Ray's famous photographs? More strands in the rope.

Another piece of evidence I have taken into consideration in forming my opinion that Dr. Hodel murdered Elizabeth Short is the doctor's missing black-faced military watch. In a photo of the doctor by Man Ray in 1946, the doctor can be seen wearing a military style watch with a black face. In an undated photo Steve believes to have been taken in the spring or summer of 1947, the doctor is wearing a watch with a white face. On January 20, 1947, LAPD utilized fifty officers to carefully comb through the vacant lot at 39th and Norton where Elizabeth Short's body was found on January 15, 1947. As a result of this search, a man's military type wristwatch was found in the vacant lot close to where Elizabeth's body was found. Another strand.

The murderer threw Elizabeth's empty purse and her shoes in the trash bin in front of 1136 South Crenshaw. This location is between where Elizabeth's body was found and the Franklin house where Dr. Hodel lived. The purse and shoes were found 3 miles from the body and 4 miles from the Franklin House. The doctor could have easily thrown the evidence away on his way home from where he "posed" the body. Another strand.

From everything Steve has told me about his father, he seems like just the type who would be capable of committing such a horrible crime. The doctor treated women like objects to be used and then thrown away.

Until his last marriage, he went through women at a rapid clip and was obsessed with sex. He was an egomaniac who would not take kindly to anyone disagreeing with him or refusing him. According to Steve's mother, the doctor had a lust for blood. According to a girlfriend, he asked her to lock him in the bathroom after he smoked hashish because "Sometimes I do terrible things." We know he had a relationship with Elizabeth and that she must have done or said something to cause him to torture her in the most brutal ways possible.

## Jeanne French
### (The Red Lipstick Murder)

I strongly believe that Dr. Hodel also murdered Jeanne French. There are many reasons for my opinion, not the least of which I have already discussed, and that is the fact that both Steve and Hannah McFarland identify the doctor's hand printing in lipstick on Jean French's body.

The two murders were very close together in time. Elizabeth Short was murdered on January 15, 1947, and Jeanne French was murdered on February 10, 1947. Both bodies were found in vacant lots. Jeanne French's body was found 7 miles west of Elizabeth Short's body in a direct parallel line.

Jeanne French's nude body had been kicked and stomped, as was Elizabeth Short's body. Foot and heel impressions were visible on Jeanne French's face, breasts and hands. Her mouth had been lacerated in what was described as a "werewolf fashion." Elizabeth Short's mouth had also been lacerated. One side of Jeanne French's mouth was almost cut to the ear.

Captain Donahoe of the LAPD informed the press that the victim had been savagely beaten with a heavy weapon, probably a tire iron or a wrench, as she crouched naked on the highway. A large pool of blood was found in the highway near the crime scene. The body had been dragged from the highway to the lot.

Again, vicious overkill, as with Elizabeth Short. However, Jeanne French was not tortured the way Elizabeth Short was. That could be due to the fact that Dr. Hodel had a more involved personal relationship with Elizabeth Short than he did with Jeanne French.

Nevertheless, it appears that the doctor was the last one seen with Jeanne French before her murder. Witness Toni Manalatos at the Piccadilly Drive-In restaurant located at 3932 Sepulveda Blvd. served the victim her "last meal" between 12 and 1 A.M. This witness tells of seeing the victim accompanied by a "dark-haired man with a small moustache." They left from the restaurant together and Jeanne French's body was found 15 blocks from the restaurant. Dr. Newbarr, who also did the autopsy on Jeanne French, determined that she was murdered between midnight and 4 A.M. on February 10, 1947. The fact that LAPD was looking for suspects who had dark hair, small moustaches and were in the low 6' range in height fits Dr. Hodel to a "T."

Captain Jack Donahoe, the original senior officer in charge of the Black Dahlia investigation, believed that the murders of Elizabeth Short and Jeanne French were connected. He unfortunately was removed from the investigation approximately 10 days after he made that connection. I fail to see why it was so hard to make a connection when the killer prints the initials B.D. on Jeanne French's body.

I have had only three murder cases where the killers have written words in the victim's blood. Susan Atkins wrote the word "PIG" in Sharon Tate's blood on the front door of the Polanski residence. The next night Patricia Krenwinkel wrote the words "rise," "death to pigs," and "Healter (sic) Skelter," all in Leno La Bianca's blood. Krenwinkel also scratched the word "WAR" into Leno La Bianca's abdomen with the tines of a carving fork. Less than two weeks earlier, Manson Family member Robert Beausoleil wrote the words "political Piggy" in the blood of rock musician Gary Hinman.

I have never even heard of a killer writing on the body of a victim in lipstick. With this in mind, I noted with great interest something that Steve's half brother Duncan Hodel said. Duncan said that he visited the Franklin House in 1947, 1948, and 1949. "I remember one party where everybody was laughing and having a good time and Dad got this red lipstick and wrote on one of the woman's breasts with the lipstick. She had these big beautiful breasts and Dad took the lipstick and drew these big targets around each one, and we all laughed and had a good time." Since I consider writing on a woman's body with lipstick unusual (we are not talking about drawing on a little child's face for Halloween), I would definitely try to get Duncan's incident in front of the jury.

Unfortunately, there will be no jury trial or death penalty for Dr. George Hodel. One could easily say that he got away with at least two murders. However, thanks to some great detective work by his courageous son Steve, the name of Dr. George Hodel will live in infamy. I do consider Steve's work exposing his father to be courageous, especially since Steve and his dad had a good relationship at the time Dr. Hodel died at the age of 91.

Sincerely,

Stephen R. Kay

# The Final Thoughtprint

MY INVESTIGATION HAD BEEN COMPLETED for some four months. I was working on the final editing of the manuscript when on April 24, 2002, my phone rang. It was my sister Tamar. "Steven," she said, "I have the most amazing news. Fauna [her eldest daughter] has just spoken with a man named Walter Morgan." (I immediately recognized his name as a district attorney investigator, Lieutenant Jemison's partner from the 1950 investigation, and swallowed hard at hearing his name come from her lips.) "He was a private detective or something back in the 1940s," she said. "He was involved in investigating, guess who: *Dr. George Hodel!* He told Fauna that they put a bug in the Franklin House to listen in on Dad's conversations. Can you call Fauna and find out what this is all about?"

I assured Tamar I would check it out immediately. Contacting Fauna, whom I had not spoken to for ten years, I learned she was working in the San Fernando Valley and had been visited in her place of work by a casual acquaintance, Ethel. In her seventies, Ethel was with her boyfriend, whom she introduced as Walter Morgan. Walter shook Fauna's hand, and said, "'Hodel?' That's an unusual name. I once worked a murder case on a Dr. Hodel. Any relation?" Fauna and Walter compared notes, and quickly learned that Morgan's suspect and Fauna's grandfather were one and the same.

Two days later, on April 26, I called Walter Morgan and told him my name was Steven Hodel, the uncle of Fauna Hodel, and the son of Dr. George Hill Hodel, who had died in 1999 at the age of ninety-one. I also informed him that I had retired from LAPD after working most of my career as a homicide detective in Hollywood Division.

Morgan greeted me warmly, in that unspoken bond that exists cop to cop, and proceeded to reminisce about the Hodel story.

Morgan, now eighty-seven, said he had worked for the sheriff's department from 1939 to 1949 on radio car patrol, in vice, burglary, and in other details. Then he left LASD and became a DA investigator in 1949, where he remained until retirement in 1970. He worked homicide on temporary assignment for a few months back in 1950. He was sent over to help out Lieutenant Frank Jemison, who he said "had picked me to be his sidekick."

Walter Morgan remembered well the day they had installed listening devices at the Franklin House, which he authoritatively informed me "was built by Frank Lloyd Wright."*

Morgan continued:

> We had a good bug man, a guy that could install bugs anywhere and everywhere. He worked in the DA's crime lab. So the chief assigned me to take him over to the house on Franklin, and he was going to install a bug system at the Hodel residence. My chief at the DA's office had me take him over there and we met the LAPD at Dr. Hodel's house. It was during the daytime and nobody was home. I remember there were some ranking LAPD officers outside, and no one could figure out how to get in. I suggested, "Well, have any of you officers tried a card to see if it would open the door?" They laughed, so I pulled out my wallet, and took out some kind of a credit card or whatever card I had, slipped it through, and the front door popped right open! They couldn't believe it. Anyway, our man went in and installed some bugs there. That was our job, to get the bugs installed so we could listen in.

Morgan, though not personally involved in listening to the secret recordings or transcribing conversations, confirmed that they existed. He knew that others had listened in, but didn't know the context, only that they never filed any charges against Dr. Hodel.

Morgan said he had worked, or, in his words "rehashed," the Black Dahlia case with Lieutenant Jemison, and then they had turned

*As we know, the true architect was his son, Lloyd Wright.

their attention to the Jeanne French murder. "But we ran into problems with the investigation," he said. "On the Jeanne French murder, Jemison accused the LAPD of hiding some bloody clothes, or getting rid of some bloody clothes from a locker. They called that the Black Dahlia number two. The accusation made headlines the next day, so the DA just took him right off the case. The DA didn't give a damn if we knew who murdered Jeanne French at that point. We thought we were making some progress, and Jemison thought he had a good suspect, but when he said that about LAPD, that was it."

Morgan remembered that my father had been suspected of "doing away some young girl," as he put it. "A youngster — nineteen, twenty, or twenty-one — something like that."

Morgan recalled that his chief in the DA's Bureau of Investigation back then was H. Leo Stanley. I asked him if he remembered an investigator by the name of Walter Sullivan (the DA investigator who picked up Joe Barrett and took him to their office in the spring of 1950) and Morgan said that of course he did.

Morgan offered that he retired from the DA's office in March 1970, but Lieutenant Jemison remained on the job for some years longer.

Two articles from the spring of 1950 corroborate what Morgan told me, namely that Lieutenant Jemison was about to make an arrest of a prime suspect. From our previous investigative summary we know that the suspect was Jemison's "wealthy Hollywood Man," Dr. George Hill Hodel.

In an April 1 article, the *Los Angeles Times* reported:

## MURDER CASES REOPENED
## BY DISTRICT ATTORNEY

### INVESTIGATORS START AGAIN ON SLAYING
### OF NURSE AND 'BLACK DAHLIA' BRUTALITY

District Attorney's investigators are now searching for a man they believe to be a "hot suspect" in the three-year-old murder of Mrs. Jeanne French.

The investigators, Frank Jemison and Walter Morgan, also

have reopened the notorious Black Dahlia murder case and are completing a list of persons to be interviewed.

H. Leo Stanley, chief investigator for Dist. Atty. Simpson, said that his investigators remain unconvinced that a bloody shirt and trousers found in the home of an acquaintance of Mrs. French have been fully eliminated as a clue to the murder.

### Suspect Not Named

Morgan and Jemison declined to name the man they are seeking as the prime suspect, but indicated that he is the owner of the mysterious bloody clothing which has disappeared from police evidence lockers.

The status of the Black Dahlia murder of twenty-year-old [*sic*] Elizabeth Short, whose nude, bisected body was found Feb. 15, 1947, in a vacant lot on Crenshaw Blvd., remained in the preparatory stage.

Jemison and Morgan were assigned to investigate the unsolved murder cases at the request of the 1949 grand jury.

The grand jury of last year, in its final report, indicated that jury members felt that a complete investigation had not been made by the Police Department and that important clues or evidence may have been overlooked.

A second article, from the *Los Angeles Daily News* of the day before, March 31, 1950, supports the fact that Lieutenant Jemison was "stalking the mutilation killers," implying that there may have been more than one suspect involved in what sounds like an imminent arrest.

# D.A. AIDE STALKS
# MUTILATION KILLERS

Dist. Atty. William E. Simpson said today one of his investigators is making "very good progress" in a renewed investigation of the unsolved mutilation murders of Jeanne French and Elizabeth Short, the Black Dahlia.

Simpson disclosed investigator Frank C. Jemison has been working several months on the cases, independent of the Police department. Jemison was assigned to the task at the request of the 1949 County Grand Jury.

The district attorney added his aide will continue with his inquiry "until he thinks he has sufficient evidence against a party or parties, and then will ask for formal murder complaints."

The bisected body of Elizabeth Short, 22, was found Jan. 15, 1947, in a vacant lot in the southwest sector.

Exactly one month later the body of Mrs. French, 45, obscenely marked with lipstick, was discovered in a field in West Los Angeles.

Chief of Detectives Thad Brown meanwhile discounted reports that vital evidence in the French slaying, in the form of blood-stained clothing, had disappeared from the West Los Angeles detective bureau.

Brown said the clothing, belonging to a short-lived suspect in the case, never was recorded as evidence because its owner was absolved of any connection with the crime two weeks after it occurred.

Hidden in the last sentence of this 1950 article was the answer to a question I had been asking for three years. When was the bloody clothing found? What year? Thad Brown was quoted as saying, "its [pants and shirt] owner was absolved of any connection with the crime two weeks after it occurred." This supports my theory that LAPD had identified George Hodel, possibly as the "mystery man sharing a P.O. Box with Jeanne French," and interviewed him at the Franklin House, in February 1947.

The article clearly establishes Chief Brown's further complicity in the ongoing 1950 cover-up of George Hodel. Brown knew full well that George Hodel had, just two months earlier, finished a three-week incest and sexual molestation trial, was the surgeon boyfriend of Elizabeth Short, and was on intimate terms with Jeanne French, sharing her P.O. box. Brown also knew he had been named by the 1949 grand jury as the prime suspect in both murders; nevertheless, in the days immediately before Dr. Hodel fled the country, Brown informed the press and public that the wealthy Hollywood mystery man "was a short-lived suspect and was absolved two weeks after the Red Lipstick Murder occurred."

Incredibly, in what would normally be an impossible scenario,

Lieutenant Jemison's surviving partner, now eighty-seven years old, has, fifty-two years later, stumbled into the family of the very man his partner was stalking, and given us information not only implicating but naming Dr. George Hodel as the prime suspect in both the Black Dahlia and Jeanne French murders. Moreover, he was present at the Franklin House with a number of "ranking" LAPD officers, and Morgan himself personally "shimmed" the locked door, after which an electronics specialist from the DA's crime lab entered the house and placed listening devices to monitor Dr. Hodel's conversations in the hope of incriminating him.

In 1950, Walter Morgan was a rookie investigator, with only one year on the job. As, in his own words, a "sidekick" to Lieutenant Jemison, he would not have been privy to detailed specifics related to this highly sensitive investigation. But from what he told me we know that both the DA's office and LAPD were conducting a joint investigation and possessed surreptitiously taped conversations of my father from inside our home. Standard operating procedure would have been to make transcripts of these conversations, as well as investigative follow-up reports documenting the findings. *Where are these transcripts? Where are these reports? What do they say?*

What guided Walter Morgan, a hitherto unknown survivor and witness of the truth, to the Hodel doorstep to tell his story, defies all the laws of probability. I neither knew he was alive nor did I seek him out. He came to me! Like so many other witnesses to these crimes, Morgan was unaware of his story's real import. Just another "anecdote." This is what many would call a "coincidence." It was not. There are no "accidents." There are no "coincidences." Like the night watchman discovering the burglars at the Watergate, Walter Morgan brought home the final pieces of the Dahliagate, to help prove that both city and county law enforcement officers were complicit in the cover-up and obstruction of justice.

When Lieutenant Jemison discovered that Dr. George Hodel was the Black Dahlia Avenger and had killed both Elizabeth Short and Jeanne French, and attempted to reveal those facts, he was immediately removed from the case and forced into silence. Morgan's unwitting revelation to me, the son of the killer and the solver of his crimes, closed a circle that had been broken for over fifty years. For the Black Dahlia investigation, it was the final thoughtprint.

# Epilogue

I STAND IN THE PRESENT, and my mind, my intellect, the objective, analytical part of me, looks back through the recent past. Thirty months! So many pieces of the puzzle, so many thoughtprints, have fit into place. Most of the riddles and enigmas relating to this strangest of murder cases have been solved. My role as homicide detective is finished.

But what about the other part of me, the part that *felt?* I entered this bizarre, strange, and, ultimately, horrifying investigation as I have many times in the course of my homicide detective career — strictly as a professional. It was the only way I could pursue this journey. My personal feelings would twist, confuse, and contaminate the evidence.

In 2000, I was still living in Bellingham, Washington, at my house on the lake. It was a cold, rainy night, near midnight. Cedar logs were crackling in the fireplace. Seated on the couch, I had a dozen unopened envelopes before me on the coffee table. They had all arrived that day in the afternoon mail. Inside, I knew, were the death certificates I had ordered six weeks earlier, from the Los Angeles County Recorder, the Vital Statistics section. By then I had identified and was familiar with most of the details of the many specific crimes and had ordered the official documents for comparison with what I had read and researched.

Pen and notebook in hand, I opened the first envelope, and began to read the cold, unfeeling statistics summarizing the cause of death for each of the victims, who, I now believed, had died at the mad sadistic hands of my father and, in several cases, his friend and accomplice Fred Sexton.

Elizabeth Short . . . Georgette Bauerdorf . . . Jeanne French . . .
Ora Murray . . . I paused and looked around. I thought I had heard
someone, or something, in the living room. I could see no one, but I
felt a presence. No, several. It was they, the victims standing silently
next to one another. I was surrounded by pain and sadness, as if they
had been summoned from beyond, invoked by my reading the details
of their deaths. I felt the sorrows of lives cut short, the loss their families and relatives had felt, thought of the long line of generations affected by their murders. They were there, I sensed, to help me find
my way safely through the labyrinth of the Minotaur.

The feelings that came next were overwhelming. For the first
time since I had begun my investigation, I realized that all of this
havoc, all of this pain, all of this misery, had come from one man: my
father! Not from some unknown suspect, like the hundreds I had
pursued during my career. No, this was my *father*, the man who had
given me life, made my bones and sinew! His blood mingled with my
own, pumped through my heart. I felt bitter anger and hatred.

As these feelings were pouring over me, it was as if a light switch
had suddenly been turned on: all the silent visitors had vanished.
Gone! I was back in the rational. Real or imagined, at that moment I
determined to make these silent victims my muses.

What I have learned, what has been made real to me since em-
barking on this, my own personal voyage of discovery, is that there
are no accidents in life. Each step I took was both meaningful and in
sequence: our own thoughtprints can, if pieced together, reveal our
individual puzzles, our destinies, as we move through life.

My mother had named me Steven after her own personal hero in
James Joyce's *Ulysses*, Stephen Dedalus. As if in some self-fulfilling
prophecy, my life had, like his, always been one of half-priest, half-
pagan. My personal heroes were General George S. Patton and Mahatma Gandhi, men who achieved near-impossible goals at opposite
ends of the human spectrum.

But there is more to my personal odyssey. Like Telemachos in
search of his father, I too had found mine. My discovery did not
bring me the heroic Odysseus, come back to Ithaca as hero to his
clansmen. Instead, I uncovered the true identity of a monster, calling
himself an avenger but in truth a psychotic killer. My journey's end
revealed to me a father who was evil incarnate, everything I had

spent my career trying to remove from society. He was the amalga-
mation of selfishness, cruelty, and extreme brutality; a sadistic but
brilliant and controlling megalomaniac who turned his hatred on a
segment of society and tried to eradicate it. In the case of my father —
a misogynist and serial killer — it was women. He tortured, cut, and
bludgeoned his victims, then slowly strangled the life out of them for
the pure lust and pleasure it brought him.

I hated Father. I hated him for all that he had done to us, his family, and for what he had done to my mother, and my brothers
Michael and Kelvin. I despised him for what he had done to Tamar.
Now I would have to be the one to reveal what he had done to our
family name, and I hated him for that as well. Try as I might to convince myself that after all these years I was still a cop, who had to de-
personalize this like any other investigation, my entire being was
filled with loathing for this man.

I wanted him to suffer as greatly as his victims had. And I wanted
to be the one to make him suffer. I would inflict the same slow tortures on him he had inflicted on others. Let me be my father's executioner, in the name of Elizabeth Short, Jeanne French, Georgette
Bauerdorf, Gladys Kern, Mimi Boomhower, Jean Spangler, Ora
Murray, and all those who were never discovered and whose names
will never be known. Let me serve as the hand of retribution, to become the "Black Dahlia Avenger."

Throughout my investigation, as the linkage was made from victim to victim, I asked myself the same question — Why? What was
the trigger?

Then I recalled the story of Folly.

For more than fifty years Folly's existence had been a whispered
family rumor. Mother had told me bits and pieces of the story when
I was in my twenties: a vague reference to Father having had an early
affair as a teenager, which resulted in the birth of a child; somewhere
out there another Hodel, a half-sister, predating Father's acknowledged firstborn son Duncan, born in 1928.

In the summer of 1997, Father and June visited me in Bellingham
for a three-day tour of the San Juan Islands. We had returned from
our ferry crossing, having filled our day with spectacular vistas, and
an early dinner on Orcas Island. The three of us sat in my bay-front
apartment as the sun began to set late in the evening. I had noticed

that Father was especially mellow and the three of us, sated with the beauty around us, felt close and comfortable. He reminisced about how quickly time had passed, remarking that he was just months away from his ninetieth birthday!

It was then I broached the subject of the family rumor and Folly. "Was it true, Father? Is there a Folly out there? A sister I've never met?" He paused, and I could almost see him turn back the pages of time in his mind. "The rumor is true," he said. "I was very young, a boy of fifteen, and very much in love." As I listened intently, Father told the story of Folly.

In Los Angeles, while attending Cal Tech, he had had an affair with a much older married woman. Her husband discovered the infidelity and they separated. She moved to the East Coast and gave birth to the child, a girl whom she christened Folly. "I followed her east," Father continued, "found where she was living in a small town, and told her I wanted to marry her and raise the child. She wouldn't have it. She laughed at me and said, 'You're just a child yourself. Go away, George. This has all been a terrible mistake. Just go away from me. I never want to see you again.'" Father said he remained in the East and tried to convince her that they should be together, but to no avail. In the end he left, returned to Los Angeles, and never again attempted to make contact with mother or daughter.

As follow-up to his story, and by way of demonstrating the new computer software I had recently purchased for searching and locating witnesses and individuals nationwide, I suggested we check to see if Folly was "in the system." He provided me with the mother's last name, and the name of the small town in the East where she was last known to be living, some seven decades past. I input the information and pressed "enter." Incredibly, there she was! First initial "F," same last name, with her address and telephone number. Gazing at the screen in disbelief, Father paled. I suggested that maybe it was now time to make contact. Wouldn't he like to see and meet a daughter he had never met? For the third time in my life, I saw him visibly shaken. In a firm voice that bordered on anger, he said to me, "No! You must destroy this information. She must never know. There must never be any contact. Do you understand?" I didn't, but I said I did. That was the last words ever spoken about Father's "Folly."

Now, some four years later, filled with a knowledge of his serial killings, I wondered: was this the trigger? George Hodel's ardent love for a woman, most likely his "first love." His passionate pursuit east to marry her, only to be laughed at and rejected with a stinging "you're just a child."

Was this why he had become the "Avenger"? In his twisted mind, had his hatred of women begun here, with a proud fifteen-year-old boy insulted for trying to be a man? Would all future women who dared reject him pay the price? Elizabeth Short rejected him and she suffered the most brutal of deaths. Georgette Bauerdorf also rejected him and paid the price. How many others had said no? Certainly "Folly" was a piece of the puzzle. A big piece, I suspected. But there was more.

Clearly Father's own seeds of insanity grew to become his *Flowers of Evil*. Did nurture and nature conspire to unhinge the mind of this child prodigy? Was he also avenging himself for the terrible wrongs he had suffered as a boy, he who was viewed as an "intellectual freak" by his schoolmates? Had he grown to adulthood with the mind and potential of an Einstein, locked inside the emotions of a child? Time and time again, in his crimes, we heard and saw the voice of this emotionally arrested genius. His childish notes and drawings with their misspelled words, mailed to the police and press. Though he was a brilliant professional, and a man of forty, he could not conceal the psychotic child that hid just below the surface: "We're going to Mexico City — catch us if you can." "The person sending those other notes ought to be arrested for forgery! Ha Ha!" Father's childlike arrow pointing to the photo of Armand Robles, saying, "Next." His stocking drawing over the face of Robles: "Here is a picture of the werewolf killer's. I saw him kill her."

As briefly noted earlier, these Avenger Mailings also clearly demonstrate that Father was well versed in Jack the Ripper lore. He used and demonstrated this knowledge not just in the Dahlia murder but in others. The Gladys Kern note, mailed and received by authorities before her body was discovered, uses the same kind of odd words and made-up slang found in some of the 1888 Ripper letters, which were also mailed before the victims' bodies were found.

Further, I submit that George Hodel lifted the term "Avenger" from the 1926 Alfred Hitchcock silent movie *The Lodger*, based on the life of Jack the Ripper. Originally, Hitchcock wanted — and surely George Hodel knew this — to title the film *Avenger*, but was forced to change it before its release. In it, the "Jack the Ripper" character referred to himself as "the Avenger," a term that clearly lodged itself in George Hodel's young, increasingly perverted mind, to surface twenty years later with the Black Dahlia. By then, I suspect, Father saw himself in competition with the world's most infamous serial killer, and in his "mad ego," believing himself, in the words of James Richardson, "a superman incapable of making a mistake," he set out to "out rip" the Ripper.

In the future, the "experts" will weigh in with their varied theories as to why George Hodel was motivated to kill. There is no simple answer, nor can any one reason suffice. There are many. We each view and interpret life and people through our own unique lenses.

As for myself, I see the confluence of a number of causes. First and foremost was his high genius, a mental aberration, accelerating his intellect far beyond the ability of his emotional self to keep pace, and perhaps in some strange way actually causing its arrest at an age of eleven or twelve. Congenital insanity appears obvious.

Next came the disassociation with his peers, and the teasing because he was so "different," forcing him into a world of older men and women, with his attendance at Cal Tech at the young age of fifteen.

Father was clearly sexually precocious, with a satyr-like appetite for women; at age fourteen or fifteen he found himself fathering a child. It was at this precise point that Father asserted himself as an "outsider." His magazine *Fantasia* was born, with its dedication to "the portrayal of bizarre beauty . . . in a temple or a brothel or a gaol; in prayer or perversity or sin." In 1925 (the same year he was rejected by Folly's mother) he reviewed Hecht's *Fantazius Mallare* and praised the story, whose protagonist beats and strangles to death his black-haired mistress Rita, avenging himself for her teasing, rejection, and laughter at him, as she tauntingly seduces his malformed manservant, Goliath, in front of him.

From here Father quickly moved into association with the underworld figures of Los Angeles, ruthless killers and drug smugglers. He himself began using alcohol, hashish, opium, and most likely stronger drugs. Already long recognized throughout Los Angeles and Southern California as a musical prodigy, from his FBI file we learn that he freely associated with the Severance Club, aligned himself with communist and leftist causes, and developed a distinguished reputation as a charismatic ladies' man and bold intellectual. He became a top debater and regular insider frequenting the elite parlors of wealthy Pasadena and South Pasadena's polite and not-so-polite societies.

It was at that time, I believe, that all these separate influences converged, and Father became Fantazius Mallare, with his schoolmate Sexton playing the initial role of Goliath, his omnipresent manservant, who would eventually become semi-independent from his master and learn to kill on his own time, in his own way.

I have been trained to deal with facts and to analyze the known. I have the added insight that comes from being the son of George Hodel. My contact with killers has always been divided by a cell door. On the outside, looking in, cop to suspect, detective to defendant.

Not so with this investigation. I have watched my Father through many eyes. Watched him through the innocent eyes of a child. Watched him with the naiveté of an adolescent about to become a man. In my twenties, we drank, whored, and played high-stakes poker. I watched him charm, manipulate, and control his many women. In my thirties, I sat with him in business interviews, saw him misjudge men and misread their abilities. Finally, as he became old, I saw our relationship change, and as he weakened, he softened. It was evolutional. Only in his eighties did I become the stronger, quicker animal: such was the power of this man.

In all of our years, in our in-and-out existence, broken as it was by decades of time, never once did I glimpse Father's evilness. In a Sexton you could see it. The evil was etched in his face and in his eyes, the windows of his tortured soul. But not in George Hodel. Vanity, megalomania, womanizing, and even the emotional instability — all could be found with relative ease. But never his evil. And that is precisely what made Father so terribly dangerous.

In all my years dealing with the evil that men do, I have never known such a man. From my old Hollywood murder investigations, two separate murderers, two "dead men walking," await their executions on Death Row. Both are terribly evil men, but their crimes pale when compared to my father's psychotic mayhem.

Can it not be argued that to some degree all of us may have a capacity for evil? Does this dark side not lie hidden in us all, held in check by a moral gyroscope and a healthy respect for the law?

My father was a prodigy. A genius. In the chaos that roiled Asia in the years right after the war, he saved many peoples' lives. He also perpetrated one of the most infamous and bloody crimes in the history of Los Angeles, and kept right on killing. I have just returned from the horrors of my father's private hell and now know and am convinced that nothing more than a hair trigger separates the heaven of a Dr. Schweitzer from the hell of a Dr. Hodel.

# The Aftermath

## Background

ON FRIDAY, APRIL 11, 2003, a national press conference was held at the Hollywood Roosevelt Hotel in Los Angeles, where my until then embargoed book *Black Dahlia Avenger: A Genius for Murder* was finally released. At that press conference I announced the findings of my three-year investigation into the murder of Elizabeth Short, known to the world as the Black Dahlia. It was my painful task that day to inform the print and television media that my investigation had led me to the undeniable conclusion that the murderer was none other than my own father, Dr. George Hill Hodel. Further, I believed him to have been a serial killer, responsible for numerous unsolved murders of lone women in Los Angeles during the mid-to-late 1940s.

The weeks and months following that announcement have been some of the most challenging of my life, full of conflict, discovery, and reward. My book has become a coast-to-coast bestseller, and my personal life filled with both acclamation and denigration. I am not surprised. These are the trappings of controversy. I expected there to be heat in the kitchen.

What I did not expect, and was not prepared for, was a total subornation of the truth and investigative facts in the wake of the book's publication. Despite the international coverage of my story as *news*, with major print articles in *Newsweek*, *People* magazine, the Associated Press running the story in most U.S. cities, and massive radio and television coverage including major pieces on *Dateline NBC*, CNN, CBS's *The Early Show*, and ABC's *The View*, neither the LAPD (my LAPD) nor any Los Angeles newspapers have seen fit to conduct any investigative follow-up.

In the days preceding the publication of *Black Dahlia Avenger*, columnist Steve Lopez of the *Los Angeles Times*, armed with the information I provided, conducted his own investigation in the L.A. County District Attorney's Office. Meeting with DA Steve Cooley, Lopez obtained permission to review hitherto unexamined secret Dahlia investigation files that had lain dormant for over fifty years. Following the book's release, Lopez wrote two articles in his weekly column confirming not only that Dr. Hodel was indeed a named, identified suspect in the Black Dahlia murder, but also revealing for the first time that transcripts of covert electronic surveillance recordings still existed from a forty-day wiretap of our Franklin Avenue residence in 1950. These transcripts included statements and admissions by George Hodel implicating himself not only in the Black Dahlia murder but in other crimes as well.

At the same time, the editor of the *Los Angeles Times* requested an assessment by their "in-house Dahlia expert," copy editor Larry Harnisch,* who after a forty-five-minute review of my 500-page investigation opined that it was "preposterous," and was quoted in the first Lopez article equating my conclusions to "seeing Jesus' face in a tortilla."

Despite their own columnist's extraordinary findings and revelations, and despite the statement by Head Deputy District Attorney Stephen Kay that "the Black Dahlia case has been solved," the *L.A. Times* has since then chosen to ignore the story, and has conducted no follow-up investigation.

---

*Harnisch was interviewed for a 1999 documentary, *Case Reopened: The Black Dahlia with Joseph Wambaugh*, in which he presented his own theory. In the documentary Wambaugh concludes that Harnisch's suspect, Dr. Walter Bayley, "could not have committed the crime."

## The LAPD Cold Case Files

Based on my own findings, plus Head Deputy DA Steve Kay's own conclusion that my father was in fact the Dahlia killer, I was confident that LAPD would take swift action. When asked what I thought the department's reaction would be, I remained strongly optimistic, expecting that any day they would announce they were reopening the case. As of this writing, I am still waiting. I am told that LAPD detective Brian Carr, the sole keeper of the LAPD Dahlia files for the past nine years, has neither read my book nor made any effort to examine the DA's Dahlia files. According to my sources, Carr has refused all requests for information regarding the case, indicating that "it is open and the LAPD files are closed." Detective Carr's seemingly arrogant attitude and position are of serious concern.

Steve Lopez's April 13, 2003, article provided new information from LAPD files. He indicated that a confidential source revealed that Dr. Hodel was named in a secret memo as being the suspect in the murder of his secretary. That crime was identified in chapter 31 as a "Jane Doe" murder before Lopez's confirmation of its existence from LAPD records. LAPD authorities have so far refused to release the name of Hodel's murdered secretary or the date of the crime.

It is LAPD's firm position that until the revelation of this secret memo, found during a search of their files in April 2003, today's detectives, including Brian Carr, had no previous knowledge that Dr. George Hodel was a suspect. The department's knee-jerk response to this new information was that they would "check out his fingerprints."

## The L.A. District Attorney Hot Case Files

After almost a full month with no activity or response by LAPD detectives, I requested and was granted permission by District Attorney Steve Cooley to view the Dahlia files myself. To his credit, Cooley kept his word to "whenever possible, grant an open-door policy," a major shift from previous administrations' policies.

In mid-May 2003, I spent a full day at the L.A. County DA's Office reviewing all the Dahlia files. Further, I was permitted to copy those documents, which I am now able to make part of the public record. What I found only confirms, in almost every respect, what I have previously claimed, namely that my father was *the prime suspect* in both the Elizabeth Short murder and that of Jeanne French, known as the "Red Lipstick murder," and was a suspect in numerous other murders of lone women of that time. The Dahlia documents further substantiate, as I alleged, that from 1947 to 1950 LAPD obstructed justice, sanitized LAPD files, and perpetuated a cover-up of the facts — a cover-up that continues to this day.

## DA Investigative Documents

The following documents are only a small part of the entire DA case files from 1949 and 1950. They are not LAPD files but rather represent the DA's separate attempt to reinvestigate what the 1949 grand jury believed was a cover-up by some LAPD officers of the 1947 murders of Elizabeth Short and Jeanne French.

In late 1949, at the specific order of the grand jury, district attorney's investigator Lieutenant Frank Jemison was placed in charge of *reinvestigating* the entire Black Dahlia murder. Certain LAPD homicide detectives, who were familiar with the then almost three-year-old cold case, were assigned to assist Lieutenant Jemison and provide him with intelligence information and brief him on previous (1947–49) investigative findings.

These documents have been locked in a vault at the district attorney's office for over fifty years, where they were secreted in 1951 by Lieutenant Jemison, by order of his Bureau of Investigation chief H. Leo Stanley. It is believed that no one has seen or examined them since, and the first to gain access, open, and peruse them — however cursorily — was Steve Lopez. There are hundreds of documents in that file; only those directly relating to my father as a suspect, or information pertinent to the murders, will be examined here.

## Electronic Surveillance of the Hodel Residence

This district attorney's "Investigator's Progress Report," dated February 27, 1950, provides additional documented evidence that as of mid-February of that year, Dr. George Hodel was the prime suspect in the murder of Elizabeth Short.

### *Exhibit 67*

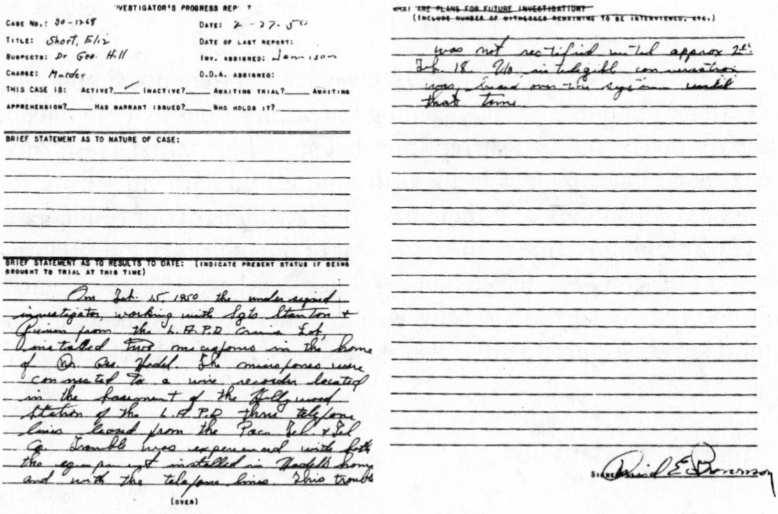

The handwritten report above reads as follows (all spellings and punctuations as they appear in the original):

| | | | |
|---|---|---|---|
| Case No.: | 30-1268 | Date: | 2-27-50 |
| Title: | Short, Eliz | Date of last report: | |
| Suspects: | Dr. Geo. Hill | Inv. Assigned: | Jemison |
| Charge: | Murder | | |
| THIS CASE IS: | Active | | |

BRIEF STATEMENT AS TO RESULTS TO DATE: (indicate present status if being brought to trial at this time)

On Feb. 15, 1950 the undersigned investigator, working with Sgts Stanton & Guinnis from the LAPD crime lab, installed two microfones in the home of Dr. Geo. Hodel. The microfones were connected to a wire recorder located in the basement of the Hollywood Station of the LAPD thru telefone lines leased from the Pac. Tel. & Tel. Co. Trouble was experienced with both the equipment installed in Hodel's home and with the telefone lines. This trouble was not rectified until approx 2:00, Feb. 18. No inteligible conversation was heard over the system until that time.

Signed-- David E. Bronson

This form reveals that the DA investigators were not simply conducting a "phone tap" and listening to conversations in a van outside the residence, but had surreptitiously entered my father's residence, concealed microphones in his bedroom, leased hard-lines from the phone company, and run them from the basement of our residence at 5121 Franklin Avenue to the basement of the police station at Hollywood Division — a distance of 2.4 miles — where DA investigators monitored conversations between my father and his guests for almost six weeks, until Father fled the country in late March 1950.

## The DA "Hodel File"

A thousand hours of surveillance recordings were obtained by DA investigators. The twenty-four-hour surveillance, collected on "41 wire-spools," covers forty days. Only "highlights" of these conversations were summarized in the detectives' log. This log, labeled the "Hodel File" and consisting of 146 typewritten pages, contains only partial, excerpted entries made by the on-duty monitoring detective, along with his notations and admonition to "listen to wire-recording for complete statements."

What follows is a selection of pages from the "Hodel File" as it was prepared in 1950. No alterations or changes have been made to the selected passages. All notes, spellings, and punctuations are as they appear in the original log.

## Exhibit 68

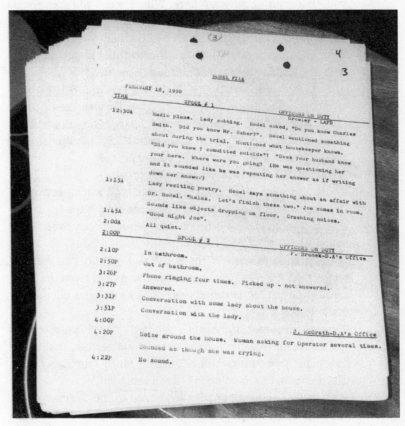

*1950 Hodel residence bugging transcripts (146 pages)*

HODEL FILE

FEBRUARY 18, 1950

| TIME | SPOOL #1 | OFFICERS ON DUTY |
|------|----------|------------------|
|      |          | Crowley – LAPD   |

12:30A Radio plane. Lady sobbing. Hodel asked, "Do you know Charles Smith. Did you know Mr. Usher?". Hodel mentioned something about during the trial. Mentioned what housekeeper knows. "Did you know ? committed suicide"? "Does your husband know your here. Where were you going? (He was questioning her and it sounded like he was repeating her answer as if writing down her answer)

1:15A    Lady reciting poetry. Hodel says something about an affair with Dr. Hodel. "Relax. Let's finish these two." . . .

| 2:00P | Spool #2 | OFFICERS ON DUTY |
|---|---|---|
| | | F. Hronek–D.A.'s Office |
| 4:00P | | J. McGrath – D.A.'s office |

4:20P    Noise around the house. Woman asking for Operator several times. Sounded as though she was crying.

7:35P    Conversation between two men. Recorded.

Hodel and man with a German acent had a long conversation; reception was poor, and conversation hard to understand. The following bits of conversation, however, were overheard.

Hodel to the German – "This is the best pay off I've seen between Law Enforcement Agencies. You do not have the right connection made." Hodel states, "I'd like to get a connection made in the D.A.'s office.".

General conversation between the two – "Any imperfections will be found. They will have to be made perfect. Don't confess ever. Two and two is not four.". Much laughter. "Were just a couple of smart boys". More laughter.

Hodel then – in exact detail – explained to the German about his wife being stopped on Wednesday morning by McGrath and Morgan of the District Attorney's office when they stopped her going up her steps to the house on Franklin. It should be noted that every question asked of Mrs. Hodel was repeated ver-batum by Hodel to this German. He then began to explain to the German about his recent trial – making statements that "Ther'e out to get me. Two men in the D.A.'s officer were transferred and demoted because of my trial." Hodel then explained about his being questioned at the D.A.'s office on Wednesday morning, and told in great detail as to questions perpounded to him at that time. One statement made to the German was as follows: "Supposin' I did kill the

Black Daliah. They couldn't prove it now. They can't talk to my Secretary anymore because she's dead." . . .

One point of the conversation was also "Have you heard from Powers".

8:20P   Sounded as though the two men went down steps and entered the basement and began digging. Something was referred to "Not a trace". It also appeared as though a pipe was being hit.

8:25P   Woman screamed.

8:27P   Woman screamed again. It should be noted that a woman was not heard before the time of screaming since 6:50PM. She was not in any conversation, and not heard of again until the time of letting out these two screams.

NOTE:   Officer Crowley, LAPD, arrived for duty at 7:45 PM while the above mentioned conversation was taking place. His log is as follows:

7:45P   Hodel talking to a man with an acent, possibly German. "Telephone men were here. Operator ? Realize there was nothing I could do put a pillow over her head, and cover her with a blanket. Get a taxi. Call Georgia Street Receiving Hospital right away. Expired at 12:39. They though there was something fishy. Anyway, now they may have figured it out. Killed her. Maybe I did kill my Secretary* . . .

FEBRUARY 19, 1950    (Spool #5)

12:00P                                            Jemison–D.A.'s office.

[N.B.: Officers report a conversation between George Hodel and "Kenneth Rexerall." However, it is generally believed this was in fact Kenneth Rexroth, an acquaintance and friend of both my parents. Rexroth was a poet of some repute associated with San Francisco and the emerging "beat generation." — SKH]

*This insertion of the 7:45 P.M. Officer Crowley log at a later time period, I believe, has resulted in a possible misinterpretation of the facts. It is my opinion that the 7:45 P.M. conversation is more likely a continuing part of my father's 7:35 P.M. story being told to the German male, and may relate to the killing of his secretary, at another date, time, and location. (This however, does not explain the real-time screams of a woman some forty minutes later, or what became of her.)

3:30P   Hodel – "Read thru this, then we can discuss it more intelli-
        gently. Hodel laughs. "It has some coverage. I'm selling my
        art collection Monday and Tuesday, and I'm then taking off
        for Asia."Kenny – I am in process of breaking up with my
        wife of 15 years. No children".

        Hodel – "I have 3 boys. You'll see them later. Dorothy lives
        here a while, and then takes off". . . .

FEBRUARY 22, 1950    (Spool #9)

2:00A                                          Brechel, LAPD on duty

2:10A   Hodel and Ellen enter room. [N.B.: Ellen was our live-in house-
        maid. — SKH]

2:12A   Hodel – "Will you leave that light on there, I'm just a little
        nervous". . . .
        Hodel has conversation with Ellen – asks if something is too
        difficult. Hodel says he is worried.

2:25A   . . . Ellen admires a chinese box. Hodel says a manchurian
        princess gave it to him. He

2:27A   says he is going to sell it. . . .

2:29A   Ellen wants to stay with him, he tells her to go to bed, she
        can stay with him tomorrow.

2:32A   Movements around room. Low conversation unable to make
        out.

2:35A   Deep breathing. Hodel and Ellen probably having inter-
        course.

2:40A   Ellen says she wants to go now. Hodel says she should have
        gone to her room. He is pretty well tired. Sounds indicates
        movements on bed.

2:45A   Deep breathing. Movements on bed.
        Definite sounds of climax of intercourse. Hodel sighs loudly
        and passionately.

2:49A   Hodel and Ellen talking. Ellen wants him to stay with her all
        night. She begs him. He says no, he is tired.

FEBRUARY 22, 1950

10:30A  Put on Spool #10

12:00noon                                          Morgan on duty.

12:35P  Telephone rang – Hodel – "Oh yeah Power – are you in town –
        good – things are sort of busy right now for the next ten

days – we're tapped now again – well there is pretty much going on regarding yourself and me – I was questioned about you and so forth – maybe you can find out – Don't you know
12:35P   someone up there? Maybe you can find out what the hell is going on up there. I would like to see you in person when we get a chance – what's your phone? That's your new phone? (Ends) "OK – so long".

FEBRUARY 24, 1950   (Spool #14)

4:00P   Hronek, D.A.'s office on duty

4:25P   Phone rings – Hodel answered – Ellen took over – still talking about the citizenship, Ellen, didn't I tell you not to tell people things over the telephone. Hodel ordered Ellen not to answer any questions over the telephone. . . . Ellen said something about the FBI investigating us.

FEB. 26, 1950

8:00P   Crowley, LAPD on duty

8:45P   Spool #19

9:20P   Water running in bathroom, and lady says something about bath tub.

9:30P   Hodel–wisecracks. Hodel–a peculiar people, the Persians, the country produces no virgins. They fuck all day in a violent way, and at night they practice sexual perversion.

9:55P   Put on Spool #20

FEBRUARY 27, 1950

12:00A   Door bell rings. Ellen goes to door. Hodel say – Come in. . . .

12:10A   Hodel – You made the headlines today or tomorrow.

12:10A   Man – I made the headlines?

12:11A   Hodel – Like Hitler said.

12:11A   Hodel – your a rich man. Hodel – I can see you beating her up. . . . Man – "(Laughing) Suspicion. Hah. In one place I am a composer of poetry or opera, a hot tempered erratic woman – We've got to get out of here and get some fun for a change.

12:25A   Hodel – Well anyway, she hasn't said she'd committed incest or killed the Black Dahlia. (other man has an accent – talking about this country) . . .

(Spool #21 put on between 12:30A and 12:35A)

1:57A   Brechel, LAPD on duty

4:15A . . . She (Ellen) is helping him to undress. She wants some love tonight, but he refuses her. He wants to sleep alone.

4:22A Hodel tells Ellen not to argue with him while Dorothy is around. Tells her how to act in company of Dorothy as Ellen then goes to her room, she appears to be angry with Hodel because he sent her to her room without allowing to have any love.

FEBRUARY 28, 1950

4:00P Snyder over to McGrath, D.A.'s office

5:40P Changed to spool 24

6:10P Lt. Frank Jaminson phoned, said Hodel moving furniture out – if Bug is found or all furniture moved phone him at CR 14917. His name is pronounced (JAMINSON) any time, day or night.

MARCH 1, 1950 (Spool #25)

8:00A Morgan relieves Brechel

10:30A . . . (This spool #25 and following should be checked with federal income tax man in the future as Hodel's income tax is computed with this man, and it looks like they are about to "take" Uncle for a few bucks.)

10:35A . . . Conversation about auction–something about FBI.
   Hodel "I had an offer in Hawaii" . . .
   conversation about Mrs. Hodel, alimony, support of children . . .

SPOOL 26 11:22A  Wire changed to Spool #26

11:30A Morgan requested Bimson to check cars parked in front of Hodel residence.

12:00P Walter Sullivan relieves Morgan

12:05P . . . (Spools 25 and 26 and 27 will prove very interesting to income tax investigators)

2:30P Start spool #28. . . .

8:00P Meyer, LAPD, on duty.

11:37P Phone rang. Hodel answered – Whoever he was talking to he said, "Don't say anything over the phone – it is tapped – said he had there phone number, and would call tomorrow – said he would have to go out to call – checked but would not repeat number on phone. Said it is WE 1670 and he knew name of Street. Would have phone people check – said if he

said phone number "They" would be out and bother them –
that is what "They" always do. When Hodel hung up, Ellen
asked him how he knew – Hodel said he was just talk-
ing. . . . [N.B.: These comments indicate that even if he believes or
suspects the phones were tapped, he has no inkling that the whole house
is bugged. – SKH]

MARCH 2, 1950

SPOOL 29–12:30P Spool No. 29 put on

3-3-50    (Spool #29)

1:30A    Brechel, LAPD on duty

4:10A    Hodel and Ellen have conversation in Spanish. They are in
bedroom having sex intercourse or something, probably perversion. Sounds like he got another blow-job.

3-3-50

SPOOL 30–12:00P Changing reel – Sullivan, D.A.'s office on duty.

12:00P    Phone rings, Hodel answers, "Let me look and see".

12:07P    Lady talked (recorded) "I owe 4 times 75.00, that's 300.00
(Possibly his wife) "I have to pay my rent or get out".

12:15P    Conversation with woman continues. Relative to her ex-
penses and the childrens.

12:28P    More conversation (recorded) Hodel "I've lost money every
year". Talking about what money she's earned. Hodel dis-
cusses his losses "$6,000,00 in 1946, "I sold the clinic to
pay for the losses of that year. Now, I must sell the house.
Hodel – something about pennitentiary. . . .

1:11P    Started recording. She's talking about the children. . . .
Much racket. Hodel talks about having wife and children
with him again.

3-4-50    (Spool #31)

12:00P    Sullivan Relieves Morgan

1:21P    Phonerings. Hodel answers (recorded) "Your'e talking over
a tapped line. Oh yes, it's been tapped for a long time. I'll be
home for the next hour. Be sure and come.

2:45P    Man still talking (recorded) talking to Hodel about some
woman. Mentions Barbara Sherman. Dorothy Black (?) . . .

2:55P    Spool #31 runs out.

3:26P    Hodel to man "In about 2 or 3 weeks I'll probably be on way
abroad.

3-6-50

12:00noon    Snyder – D.A.'s office on duty

No wire

No recording

3:10P    (. . . Belle and Bimson playing back recordings)

8:00P    Wean, LAPD, on duty.

8:25P    Woman leaves – man enters – talks with Hodel about moral of spanish girls. Hodel tells man he should have seen his Chinese collection which was worth $100,000.

3-10-50 (Meyer, LAPD on duty at 8:00P, 3-9-50. Spool #?)

12:15A    One or two men and about same amount of women– Talking to Hodel. Hard to understand – something about a place in Mexico not too far from Arizona – good roads – something about a Whore House, or sanatarium. One man seems to be a doctor. Talking about she at Camarillo. Hodel – "She was going to shoot me and commit suicide "Tamara" (way it sounded) . . .

8:00A    J. McGrath, D.A.'s office on duty. . . .

12:25P    Sgt Belle – said he has found out the man with the German accent is one Baron Herringer – a supposed ex-German – Baron. The two new girls are Vilma (age 19) and Sonia (age 15) . . .

3-14-50 (Spool #37)

8:00 A    J. McGrath, D.A.'s office on duty

8:15A    Using a pretext – determined Hodel is back from Mexico.

3-17-50 (Spool #37)

7:55P    Meyer, LAPD, on duty. . . .

11:30P    . . . Hodel and man with accent – talking recorded – hard to hear. Hodel says probably they are watching me, talks about selling some of his stuff at an auction – says someone don't know anything to tell. Hodel said something about getting married again – talks about place in Mexico. . . .

3-18-50 (Spool #37)

12:40A    Hodel – "Do you think those "Bastards" will try to bring action because I am renting rooms". Hodel says "Do you think we could hire some girl to find out what they are doing".

1:00A    Man with accent left. . . .

3-21-50 (Spool #38)

8:00A    J. McGrath, D.A.'s office on duty

10:55A  Hodel phones someone about $50.00 a month he paid some
        woman "Said I'm in trouble" . . .

3-22-50 (Spool #38)

12:00P  Sullivan, D.A.'s office on duty

1200P –

4:00P   Bimson, Belle, and Sullivan listening to past recordings as
        Hodel has been out for the entire day.
        [SKH – N.B.: Officers recap conversations on separate spools as
        follows:]

Spool #26 – 5-9 talk of trial

9-40    much talk of juggling figures.

Spool #27      13-15 – talk about deducting some money as repay-
ment of loans to father and son.

        18-22 – wire bad Skip – listen from 40 on to 46 to 48 – very
        interesting (cut this spool off at 50 the end is loose).

Spool #37

3-5     Conversation regarding tax case and Dahlia

5-17    Conversation regarding code and mailing — have to be care-
        ful — income tax starts at 15 on Spool #25

3-25 (Spool #38)

8:00P   Meyer, LAPD, on duty. . . .

11:10P  Hodel and Baron (man with accent) came in talking low –
        can't hear (recording) . . . Sounded like Hodel said some-
        thing about Black Daliah. Baron said something about F.B.I.
        Then talked about Tibet – sounded like Hodel wants to get
        out of the country. mentioned passport – Hodel giving Baron
        dope on how to write to Tibet. Hodel talking about Mexico . . .
        Hodel seems afraid about something. Hodel says his Sanatar-
        ium – if he got it started in Mexico – would be "Safe".

Mar 26, 1950 (Spool #39)

12:00A  Spool ran out – changing – talking about women.

12:07A  Not much talk – still recording. Hodel says he wants money
        and power – talking about China – talking about selling some
        of Hodel's paintings or something. Hodel talking about pic-
        ture police have of him and some girl – thought he had
        destroyed them all – wire quit at 50 – new one going on –
        not much talk.

Spool 40

1:50A    Sounds like Baron left – don't know if there is anything on
         these records or not.
         [SKH note – Final entry to HODEL FILE is as follows:]
3-27     1:00A Everyone left.
2:00A    All quiet. Good nite.

The L.A. County District Attorney's massive "Hodel File" ends
on this date. It is believed that George Hodel fled the country in the
days immediately following this last entry.

It is obvious from the officers' log entries that these are only the
most general of summaries of George Hodel's recorded conversations. However, even without benefit of the detailed information
contained on the "41 spools," we find in these transcripts hard evidence, including statements and admissions, implicating him in the
murder of Elizabeth Short, as well as the poisoning death of his own
(unnamed) secretary.

In addition, George Hodel provides us in these transcripts with
direct statements confirming his connection, influence, and payoffs
to law enforcement. ("This is the best pay off I've seen between Law
Enforcement Agencies. You do not have the right connection made
in the D.A.'s office. Two men in the D.A.'s office were transferred
and demoted because of my trial.")

In these forty days before Father flees the country we hear him
becoming more and more desperate and fearful. Clearly the DA net,
with Lieutenant Jemison in charge, is closing. We also learn that during this period my mother, Dorothy Hodel, had been interviewed by
DA investigators, and that her verbatim questions were provided to
George Hodel. He too was questioned, by both the DA's investigators
and the FBI. (No info is in the files on those interviews.) He voices his
suspicion to callers that his "phone lines are tapped" and arranges to
continue conversations from a safe line, or meet them in person.
George Hodel talks of opening a sanatorium in Mexico (most likely
for the triple purpose of running a whorehouse, treating venereal disease, and performing abortions). He informs friends that he is leaving
the country by the end of March, saying, "I am in trouble." On the
last day and in the last hours of the electronic surveillance he makes
additional damning statements to his German friend, Baron Her-

ringer,* that include mention of "the Black Dahlia," pictures the police have of him and some girl (likely Elizabeth Short), which he thought he had destroyed, and more talk of the FBI.

In addition to the electronic surveillance and transcripts, my review of the DA files provided further dramatic evidence of Father's connections to other victims. The files, through both crime reports and photographs, reveal that DA investigators were looking at George Hodel in connection with not just the Black Dahlia murder but also other crimes, including the murders of: Jeanne French, real estate agent Gladys Kern, and actress Jean Spangler, all of which I linked to my father in this book — well before I gained access to the DA files.

## Unkefer-Short-Hodel-Lenorak Connections

On January 16, 1947, the day "Jane Doe Number 1" was identified by the FBI as Elizabeth Short, Santa Barbara policewoman Mary Unkefer was one of the first important witnesses contacted by LAPD in the Black Dahlia investigation. Why? Because Officer Unkefer had direct and extended contact with Elizabeth Short after Elizabeth's September 1943 arrest for "minor possession." The *L.A. Daily News* of January 17, 1947, under the headline: "Identify Victim as Hollywood Resident," detailed Officer Unkefer's connections:

> She (Elizabeth Short) had been a clerk at the Camp Cooke post exchange near Santa Barbara and was picked up for drinking with soldiers in a cafe there.
>
> Policewoman Mary Unkefer of the Santa Barbara police department took the girl to her own home to live with her for nine days. . . .
>
> "We put her on the train for her home, and several times later she wrote to me from there" Miss Unkefer recalled. One of her letters said: "I'll never forget you thank God you picked me up when you did!"

---

*Baron Herringer was obviously a close friend and confidant to my father; however, to date I have been unable to locate any further information as to his identity or relationship to my family.

Incredibly, from information contained in these DA documents, we only now discover that Mary Unkefer — who in 1943 had been directly responsible for rescuing Elizabeth Short from a dangerous environment — in January 1950 drove from Santa Barbara to Dr. Hodel's Franklin Avenue residence and there removed another young female victim from harm's way. Unkefer, after safely returning the victim, whose name was Lillian Lenorak,* to Santa Barbara, typed a letter to Los Angeles DA investigators, describing Dr. Hodel's suspected involvement in multiple crimes, including subornation of perjury and felony assault. Here for the first time is that remarkable letter, published in its entirety, exactly as it was typed:

                                    Jan.   30-50

Dist. Attorney's Office                 209 W. Valerio St.
Los Angeles, Calif.                     Santa Barbara, Calif.

Dear Sir:
    I am sorry I missed the Gentleman from your Office on Wednesday. I work at odd hours & I arrived at home about ten minutes after your Man left for work Los Angeles.

I had expected to come to Los Angeles early this week as I had business to attend to there but find it is not necessary for me to make the trip except to give you what information I can regarding the Woman whom I brought to Santa Barbara from the home of Dr. Hodel on Franklin Ave.

Mrs. Hamilton (Mother of the young Woman) asked me to go to Los Angeles to get her & her Baby. I called Dr. Hodel before I left Santa Barbara to make sure the Patient was at his home & there would be no chance of me running into a snag when I got there as it was night & I was not prepared to have to look for her. Dr. Hodel told me that it was very

---

*Through other DA documents, we know that Lenorak was a 1949 defense witness who testified at the Hodel incest trial, was an acquaintance of George Hodel's, and when shown photographs of Elizabeth Short by DA investigators identified her as Hodel's girlfriend.

necessary for her to be removed from his home that same evening as he intended to put her in an Institution in Los Angeles if she was not immediately taken back to Santa Barbara. He informed me that two of her Friends were there & that they would return to Santa Barbara with Lillian to keep her from becoming too much of a problem on the way.

When I arrived at the Franklin address (I took a young Woman with me) I sensed something wrong as soon as I entered the building. The Dr. seemed very anxious to tell me that the Girl was in a bad mental condition & that she had attempted suicide. I asked where the parties were who were going to ride to Santa Barbara with me & he said he could not get in touch with them at that time, but when I assured him that I would not take the Girl with me unless her Friends would go along, he then called the Woman (Karoun Tootikian) who came to his home & said she would go with me. Two young men volunteered to drive another car & follow me to see that I got the Girl safely home. Joseph Barrett, who lives at the same address on Franklin & another young man Friend who was not interested in the case, except that he offered to drive Barrett up here & then take the Woman & the other man (Joe Barrett) back to Los Angeles.

When I asked to see Lillian Dr. Hodel explained that I had no need to worry about her giving me trouble on the way to Santa Barbara. He stated that he had given her a large enough dose to keep her asleep for three hours. With the aid of the Mexican maid* (who looks like a half-wit or a hop-head), we packed Lillians clothes & it was about ten P.M. before we got away from his home. Dr. Hodel & Joe Barrett took Lillian to my car, holding her up on both arms. That wakened her & she began to tell us about the Dr. She talked a great deal about her relations with him & she stated that she was very much afraid of him. She said she

*N.B.: This reference is to our housemaid, Ellen. — SKH

had witnessed an abortion performed on his own little Girl
& then she stated that he had threatened to have her Child
taken from her if she did not testify in his favor in Court. She
said he knew of some of her foolishness in connection with
a Man called Charles, & that he (the Dr.) was holding that
over her. She said that she had never attempted suicide &
that she had never cut her wrists or her hands. She stated
that the Dr. constantly gave her drugs & that when she wakened the cutting had been done. While I was in the Dr's sit-
tingroom waiting for the Woman who was to drive with us,
I asked the Dr. what had caused the Girl to go haywire so
suddenly. He said it was a great deal to do with some case
she had in Court. It was not until Lillian wakened & told us
how she had perjured herself in Court for the Dr. that I realized what case it was that had caused her so much worry.
There were scratches & bruises on her forehead & arms.
Her (three-year old) baby said the Dr. knocked his Mommie
down & made Mommie cry hard.

On the way north, the car with the young men in, drove behind us & it was after I left Lillian at the Phyco. Ward at the
Gen. Hospital that I had a chance to talk to Joe Barrett. He
stated emphatically that there was nothing wrong with Lillian except what had been brought on by the cruel treatment received from Dr. Hodel. He stated that he knew Lillian
had perjured herself at the trial because the Dr. had her under his influence. He stated that the relations between the
Dr. & his Child were terrible & were worse than I had any
idea. He stated that the Dr. boasted that the $15,000.00 he
paid Jerry Geisler was used to influence the Dist. Attorney
& that was how the Dr. was cleared of the charge against
him. He stated that Lillian had fallen in love with Charles &
that Charles was an assistant to another Dr. a Friend of
Hodel. When I asked Barrett where this Charles was now
living, he stated that he had 'taken off' after the Dr's trial &
was in San Francisco. Lillian stated that she had a very
guilty mind after the trial & told Hodel that she was going
to tell the Dist. Attorney that she had lied on the witness

stand, & that Dr. Hodel told her if she squealed that he
would name Charles & the other Dr. as being the ones who
performed the operation. Joe Barrett spoke of Dr. Hodel as
being a real 'NO GOOD GUY'.

I visited Lillian at the Hospital on Sunday (yesterday). She
seemed glad to see me & stated that she would like to tell me
all about the true facts concerning the Dr's activities & the trial
but she stated she knew he would have her done away with
as well as her Baby. She said she would like to have told the
men from your office all about it but she said she was not sure
if you were her Friends & she was just PLUMB SCARED to tell
for fear he would carry out his threat to have her Boy taken
from her & to have her committed to an insane Institution.

This morning I went to the hearing at the Phycho. Ward &
it was determined that she is mentally upset. The Dr. said a
deal of the condition was brought about from the strain of
the trial. Both Drs. Stated that they felt she should have
medical care. So she is to be taken to Camarillo State Hospital for treatment.

My personal opinion is that if the feeling between her & her
Mother was not so strained, she might have been given a
chance to go home & be taken care of by her Mother. There
seems to have never been love between those two. The
Mother takes the attitude that she is going to MAKE Lillian
do things the way she (Mother) wants them & the Girl
seems just as determined that she is not going to be always
treated as a Child. Hence there is fireworks between them.

Joe Barrett & Karoun Tootikian were here from Los Angeles
to attend the hearing. Joe has had a good chance to talk to
Dr. Hodel & he knows the Dist. Attorney's Office is interested in the case. He seems to be afraid he might be questioned about the trial because his whole attitude was
changed. He now speaks of the Dr. as 'not a bad fellow,
with plenty of worries of his own'. He spoke & acted as

though he is sorry he opened his mouth the night I brought
Lillian home from Los Angeles. Karoun Tootikian's address
is 2211 S. Highland, Dancing Teacher.

I do not know that this information will be of any help to
you. It is about all I could tell you if I came down personally.
But if there is anything I can do to help in anything that is
good & sincere, I am at your service.

Very Sincerely Yours,
Mary H. Unkefer

## George Hodel and Charles Smith, the Abortionist

Additional documents found in the DA Dahlia file include a typewritten
memo prepared by Walter Morgan and sent to his superior, Lieutenant
Frank B. Jemison. On page 5 of these notes, additional independent confirmation of Lillian Lenorak's allegations was found. Morgan's notes
summarize an interview he and Lieutenant Jemison had with witness
Mildred Bray Colby, during which she provided information that supported the charge that George Hodel's friend and colleague Charles
Smith was directly involved in the abortion of my half-sister Tamar and
that a "payoff" had been made by my father. The memo reads as follows:

### OFFICE MEMORANDUM

TO:       LIEUTENANT FRANK B. JEMISON
IN RE:    NOTES TAKEN ON JEANNE FRENCH AND
          BLACK DAHLIA MURDERS
FROM:     INVESTIGATOR WALTER MORGAN
DATE:     AUGUST 30, 1950

Page 5

3/20/50, #30-1268, Field with Lt. Jemison to
4629 Vista Del Monte (Midred Bray Colby) —

7X6316 at Doc's on Ventura Blvd. (Lincoln Con-
tinental, green) — 42R966 (woman waived at party
in 7X6316).


Jemison (to Colby): Did you know that Charlie Smith was a friend of Dr. Hodel's?

Answer:     Yes. Smith made frequent trips to
            San Francisco for tea.
Jemison:    Did you know that he has been op-
            erating girls from San Francisco
            for abortions?
Answer:     No. But I wouldn't put it past him.
Jemison:    Is this a picture of him?
Answer:     Yes. That's him all right. Smith
            said that some day he was going to
            fix Tamar. He was going to cut a
            chunk out of the calf of her leg
            and fry it and eat it in front of
            her eyes and then puke it up in
            front of her face.
Jemison:    Did you ever hear Smith mention
            the Black Dahlia?
Answer:     No.
Jemison:    Did you ever hear Hodel mention
            the Black Dahlia?
Answer:     No. The last night I was with
            Charlie Smith we went to a show.
            We got into Hollywood about 2:00
            o'clock, somewhere on Franklin
            near Normandie. [N.B.: Our Franklin
            House residence, was 100 feet west of the cor-
            ner of Franklin and Normandie-SKH] He
            went in a house somewhere on
            Franklin. After he came out we
            stopped by a place to eat and dur-
            ing the time we were eating he

|            | pulled out an envelope that con- |
|------------|-----------------------------------|
|            | tained at least $1,000 in money. |
|            | Before he went in I know he didn't |
|            | have any money. |
| Jemison:   | What date was that? |
| Answer:    | December 29, 1949. [N.B.: This was only |

December 29, 1949. [N.B.: This was only
five days after the jury acquitted Dr. Hodel of
his incest charges — SKH] His birthday
was December 28. That's how I know.
He didn't know how much he had in
the envelope. When he came out he
asked if there were any cars
cruising around and I said that
there were, and he sure got nervous
and said, "Let's get out of here."
There was another time when Smith
parked on Wilshire and he came out
with over $100.00 in new bills. The
last time I was with him he got mad
and threatened to hit me and said
that the only reason why he
wouldn't is that it would kill me
if he hit me — State 4526

## DA Investigator's Telegram Re: Charles Smith

This Western Union telegram was sent to L.A. County DA investigator Bill Snyder on March 14, 1950, by then San Francisco district
attorney Edmund G. Brown (who would be elected governor of California eight years later). The handwritten notation on it reads:

In regards to friend of Hodel, Smith abortionist.

The text of Brown's telegram reads:

REGARDING CHARLES W SMITH HAVE YOU CHECKED
WITH SACRAMENTO FOR REGISTRATION AND DRI-
VERS LICENSE IF SO WHAT DO THEY DISCLOSE RE-
GARDING AGE COLOR ETC=
     EDMUND G BROWN DISTRICT ATTORNEY=

*Exhibit 69*

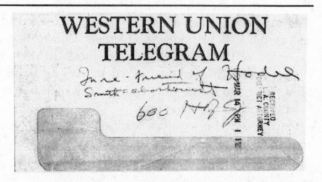

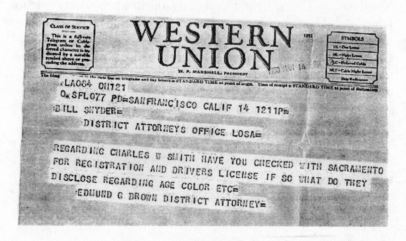

This telegram demonstrates that just thirteen days before
George Hodel fled the country, the DA investigators were attempting to identify and locate his "friend and known abortionist

connection," Charles Smith. It is doubtful that they were successful in their search, since no subsequent interview with Smith was
found in the DA file.


## DA Investigator Lieutenant Frank Jemison and the Elizabeth Short and Jeanne French Murder Investigations

I learned from the DA Dahlia files that Lieutenant Jemison was officially assigned the duty of reinvestigating the Short and French murders by the 1949 grand jury on October 13, 1949 — one week after
the arrest of Dr. George Hodel for incest. LAPD chief of police
W. A. Worton assigned homicide detectives Ed Barrett and Finis A.
Brown to assist Lieutenant Jemison, as well as Officer Jack Smyre
from Internal Affairs Division.*

Lieutenant Jemison's investigation into the Short/French murders was massive and his documentation of the facts extremely detailed. The early months of his investigation (October 1949 through
January 1950) show him familiarizing himself with the "old" LAPD
investigation (1947–49) and many investigative hours were spent by
Jemison and his subordinates in an effort to rule in or out one Leslie
Dillon, who had been investigated, named, and arrested by the LAPD
Gangster Squad as the "prime Dahlia suspect." Ultimately, Jemison
(despite ongoing protestations from the Gangster Squad detectives)
would be successful in establishing that Dillon was in San Francisco
at the time of the Elizabeth Short murder, and he was eliminated as
a suspect.

In February and March of 1950, as shown in the transcripts of
the electronic surveillance on the Franklin House, Lieutenant Jemison was totally focused on Dr. George Hodel as *the prime suspect* in
the murder of Elizabeth Short. These newly released documents
confirm what my book alleges, namely that Dr. Hodel was in fact the

---

*It is highly unusual to assign an IAD officer to a homicide investigation, and this
underscores the likelihood that some LAPD brass, possibly Deputy Chief William
Parker, then commander of IAD, suspected wrongdoing by officers. In addition, it
would also keep Deputy Chief Parker up to date and "in the loop" on the DA's ongoing
investigation.

"wealthy Hollywood man" initially described in the December 7, 1949, *Los Angeles Examiner* article "Dahlia Motel Angle Probed by Grand Jury." (That article has him checking into the East Washington Boulevard Hotel with Elizabeth Short days before her murder, as well as connecting him to the bloody clothing seen at the Franklin House.) His identity is further confirmed by the later article "Murder Cases Reopened by District Attorney" (*Los Angeles Times*, April 1, 1950) and a companion article in the *Los Angeles Daily News* of March 31, 1950, which was headlined: "DA Stalks Mutilation Killers." These articles, as discussed in previous chapters, show Lieutenant Jemison describing the suspect as a "wealthy Hollywood man" and link the suspect to the Jeanne French murder and the 1947 disappearance of the bloody clothing from the LAPD evidence lockers. Rebutting Lieutenant Jemison, LAPD deputy chief Thad Brown informed the press that "the clothing belonged to a short-lived suspect in the case, never was recorded as evidence because its owner was absolved of any connection with the crime two weeks after it occurred."

Given the sudden and unexpected termination of the electronic surveillance at the Franklin House on March 27, 1950, plus Father's recorded statement on that date to a visitor that he "is in trouble" and further mentions of "the Black Dahlia," "the FBI," and his "passport," we can assume that George Hodel on that date fled, or was about to flee, the country.

Four days later, on April 1, 1950, the *Times* article appears to confirm Father's sudden disappearance. That article opens with the sentence: "District Attorney's investigators *are now searching* [italics mine] for a man they believe to be a "hot suspect" in the three-year-old murder of Mrs. Jeanne French."

### Lieutenant Frank Jemison's Interview with Dorothy Hodel

The DA files also contain a transcribed interview between Lieutenant Jemison and my mother, Dorothy Harvey Hodel, which took place at her residence on the Santa Monica pier on March 22, 1950, just five days before her ex-husband is believed to have fled the country. At the time of this interview, Mother was unemployed, was in the

## Exhibit 70

STATEMENT OF DOROTHY HARVEY HODEL TAKEN AT 410 SANTA MONICA
PIER, SANTA MONICA BY LT. FRANK B. JEMISON AT 12:15 P. M.
ON MARCH 22, 1950.

File No.
Charge: Murder
Title:
Deputy:

Present:
Questions by: Lt. Jemison
Reported by:  Dora A. Parisho

Q  What is your full name?
A  Dorothy Harvey Hodel.

Q  What is your residence address at the present time?
A  410 Santa Monica Pier.

Q  What is your phone number here?
A  I don't have a phone. There is a fishing renting place
downstairs, SM 42421.

Q  What is your present occupation?
A  Housewife. I do a little writing, but I'm not working
at the present time.

Q  Were you formerly married to Dr. George Hodel?
A  Yes.

Q  Are you now divorced from him?
A  Yes.

Q  How long have you been divorced from him?
A  The interlocutory decree was in 1944 and the final was
in 1945.

Q  Do you have any children from him?
A  Yes, I have three boys.

*DA transcript of Dorothy Hodel interview*

process of being evicted for owing $300 in back rent, and was solely
dependent upon Father for her court-ordered alimony, amounting
to $200 a month. As can be seen in the interview, she remained to-
tally uncooperative and stonewalled all of Jemison's efforts to impli-
cate Father. The importance of this interview lies not in what we
learn from my mother but what we learn from Lieutenant Jemison's
questions, namely that George Hodel and Elizabeth Short were indeed acquainted and had been seen together at the Franklin House

before her murder, and that George Hodel, in a drunken state "on or about the time of the murder," stated, "They will never be able to prove I did that murder."*

Here are excerpted portions of that transcript:

Lt. Jemison:     I will show you a photograph of Beth Short, Santa Barbara No. 11419 and ask you whether or not you have ever seen that young lady in your life?

Dorothy Hodel:   No, I never have.

Lt. Jemison:     Did you have a conversation with Dr. Hodel about the murder of Beth Short?

Dorothy Hodel:   No, unless we mentioned it when it was in the papers, but I don't like to read about things like that. I can't say for sure that I have never mentioned her name to him, but it may have been in passing.

Lt. Jemison:     Did he ever tell you, "They can't pin that murder on me"

Dorothy Hodel:   No, to the best of my knowledge he didn't and doesn't know her.

Lt. Jemison:     On or about the date of her murder, January 15, 1947 do you remember being out until 4:00 in the morning with George Hodel and coming in slightly intoxicated? Now, that's three years ago.

Dorothy Hodel:   Well, I think I explained before we never went on drinking parties because I don't drink because of certain tendencies to drink too much and particularly if I were near him I would not drink because from a med-

---

*Lieutenant Jemison in this interview paraphrases George Hodel's statement as "They can't pin that murder on me." However, in Jemison's typed investigative summary he gives the actual quote as, "They will never be able to prove I did that murder."

ical point of view he does not approve of my drinking and I don't know that I understood the question.

Lt. Jemison: Well, the information that I have is that he was quite intoxicated himself and at that time on that occasion stated that they couldn't pin the Black Dahlia murder on him.

Dorothy Hodel: No. No, that isn't true.

Lt. Jemison: Do you remember ever telling Tamar that?

Dorothy Hodel: No.

Lt. Jemison: Did you ever tell Tamar that Dr. George Hodel was out the night before the murder with Beth Short at a party?

Dorothy Hodel: No, I was living at my brother's house at the time. We were not living at the same house. I wouldn't know what he was doing.

Lt. Jemison: What was your brother's address at that time?

Dorothy Hodel: 2121 Loma Vista Place.

Lt. Jemison: Has anybody ever told you that Dr. George Hodel had Beth Short over to his home?

Dorothy Hodel: No.

Lt. Jemison: Nobody has ever told you that?

Dorothy Hodel: No. No one has ever told me that.

Lt. Jemison: For your information her photograph has been identified by certain persons as resembling the young lady that was over to his house prior to the murder. You never heard anything about that?

Dorothy Hodel: I never did.

Lt. Jemison:      As a matter of fact you are on quite a
                  friendly relation aren't you, with Dr. George
                  Hodel?

Dorothy Hodel: We are friends.

. . .

Lt. Jemison:      I show you Sheriff's Photograph B 119364
                  and will ask you if you recognize that?

*Exhibit 71*

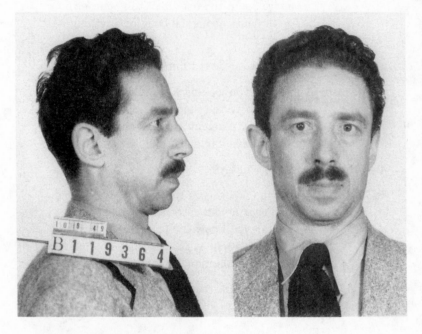

Dorothy Hodel: Yes.

Lt. Jemison:      Who is that?

Dorothy Hodel: Dr. George Hodel.

Lt. Jemison:      Now in view of the fact that the District At-
                  torney's office is interested in contacting all
                  persons that might know something about
                  whether or not Dr. Hodel had anything to do

with this murder, I now show you a photograph of a nude girl and ask you if you recognize who that girl is. In other words, we
want to know her name and where we can
contact her?

Dorothy Hodel: There is something familiar about her face.
I think she may have been some model or
something.

Lt. Jemison: Did you ever hear Dr. Hodel say anything
more about the details of this murder of
Beth Short about the body or anything
about it?

Dorothy Hodel: No, I never heard him discuss it at all.

Lt. Jemison: Well, if you look back on the events that took
place about the time of the murder, did you
have any reason to suspect that Dr. Hodel
might have had something to do with it?

Dorothy Hodel: None whatever.

Lt. Jemison: Let me advise you that we do have information that he did associate with Beth Short,
and as you know the last place she was
seen alive was at the Biltmore Hotel in the
evening of January 9, 1947.

Dorothy Hodel: I didn't know that.

## Suspect Vehicle

In our review of the serial crimes, including the kidnappings, rapes,
and murders that occurred in the years before George Hodel fled the
country in late March 1950, we know that in numerous crimes, witnesses repeatedly describe the suspect vehicle as being a "black
sedan."

On January 16, 1947, the *Los Angeles Examiner* printed the map below showing the location where Elizabeth Short's body had been posed, along with the information that witnesses had seen a black sedan parked near the body for approximately four minutes.

*Exhibit 72*

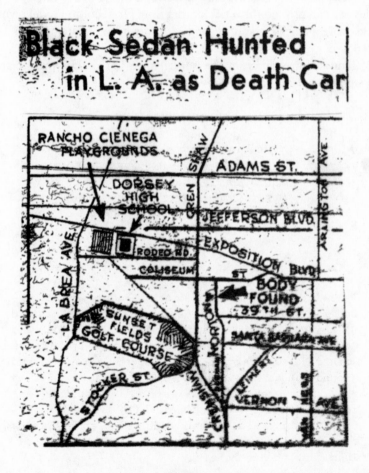

Earlier in this book I described riding around in my father's Army jeep as an eight-year-old boy in 1949, accompanying him on his "house calls." Even after all these years, that is a strong and certain memory. As a boy, and from later family conversations, I knew that my father owned and drove another car, which he called "Tar Baby," because it was black. However, since I did not know or remember its year, make, or model, I decided to exclude this fact from my book, feeling the information would detract from my objectivity as an investigator.

Thanks to the detailed documentation in the newly released DA files, we can now confirm that at that time Dr. George Hodel owned and drove a black Packard sedan California license plate number 3W 49 38.

I quote directly from the surveillance log of DA investigator Walter Morgan:

### OFFICE MEMORANDUM

```
TO:       LIEUTENANT FRANK B. JEMISON
IN RE:    NOTES TAKEN ON JEANNE FRENCH AND BLACK
          DAHLIA MURDERS
FROM:     INVESTIGATOR WALTER MORGAN

. . .


                        (page 3)


2-23-50, #30-1268, Stakeout on Hodel — 3W 49 38 —
Hodel's black Packard sedan. Tailed to Western and
Wilshire, Glendale and Temple, Hollywood and
Gower, Hollywood and Sycamore. Picked up wife on
corner, looked over old pierced arrow — parked
around the corner. Tailed to 8482 Wilshire, Art of
the Orient Auction Gallories [sic] where Hodel en-
tered at 4:55 p.m. Tailed to Wilshire and Hamil-
ton, Wilshire and Camden; Hodel stopped on Camden
for a few minutes. Tailed to Warner and Wilshire.
Then back to his home.


3-3-50, #30-1268, 3W 49 38 in Hodel's garage.
```

This vehicle, registered to George Hodel, matched not only the car seen leaving the Elizabeth Short crime scene the morning of January

15, 1947,* but also the one frequently described by witnesses and surviving victims in many of the other crimes summarized earlier in the book. To cite just a few: the kidnap/rape of Sylvia Horan by a "suave stranger, driving a black vehicle"; the car described by friends of Jean Spangler, who saw her just hours before her disappearance "with a clean-cut man in his thirties in a black sedan" in the parking lot of the Hollywood Ranch Market (directly across the street from Man Ray's residence); downtown L.A. murder victim Rosenda Mondragon, who had been seen getting into a stranger's "dark-colored" vehicle at 2:00 A.M. at Mission and Main Streets, just hours before her vicious murder.

## The Gladys Kern Homicide

District attorney's documents and logs reveal that investigators, along with the Short and French murders, were also actively attempting to link a suspect to the murders of Gladys Kern (1948) and Jean Spangler (1949).

On the following page is a copy of one of those documents, the handwritten note found in connection with the Hollywood murder of Gladys Kern.

## Kern Murder Note, February 17, 1948

This handprinted note was mailed to the police and press by the murderer of Gladys Kern, who as noted in chapter 31 was found stabbed to death in Hollywood.

This note, written before her body was discovered on February 17, 1948, was left in the *same downtown mailbox* as a note sent by the "Black

---

*The original 1947 witness informed detectives that on January 15, 1947, at approximately 6:30 A.M., he observed, as noted, the black sedan stop for a four-minute duration, at the exact location where the body was later found. My recent review of DA autopsy information further tends to establish that Elizabeth Short was slain just a few hours earlier (4:00 A.M.). This is based on the coroner's notation that rigor mortis *had not yet set in* when officers arrived at the scene (10:50 A.M.).

## *Exhibit 73*

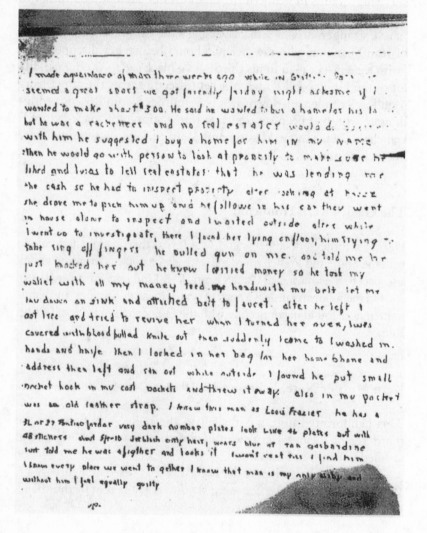

Dahlia Avenger" on January 24, 1947. (The mailbox location was two
blocks from Dr. Hodel's medical office at 7th and Flower Streets.)

I here identify the handwriting on this note as that of my father.
Forensic handwriting expert Hannah McFarland has independently

examined the writing and compared it to known samples, and it is her opinion that it is "highly probable" that the note was written by Dr. George Hill Hodel. (This is the highest level of determination, absent comparison of the original document.) This evidence, added to the already overwhelming circumstantial case previously compiled in the Kern investigation (composite, murder weapon ID, witness statements, etc.) should leave no doubt that George Hodel did in fact commit that murder as well.

## "Close It!"

In the days immediately preceding the publication of *Black Dahlia Avenger* I met and had lunch with former DA investigator Walter Morgan, the partner in 1950 of Lieutenant Frank Jemison. I gave him a copy of the book and thanked him for coming to me with the information on the "bugging" of our Franklin House. During that lunch, he clarified a misunderstanding on my part. From our previous interview, I was under the impression that Lieutenant Jemison had gone to the press with the information that LAPD had destroyed the bloody clothing belonging to the "wealthy Hollywood man" (Dr. Hodel). In reality, a reporter present at the DA's office overheard Jemison talking angrily and loudly to his fellow DA investigators about the LAPD's destruction of the suspect's bloody clothing, which as discussed earlier was related to the Jeanne French murder. This reporter broke the story the following day. Here is how Morgan put it to me:

> There was this guy, Emerson was his name. He was a newspaperman. We were at the office. Jemison was talking and raising his voice, and Frank got too vocal. This Emerson guy had big ears and overheard Frank's conversation, and it got into the newspapers. I tried to hold Frank back, but he was the excited type.

After this leak to the press, Jemison's boss, Captain H. Leo Stanley, was quoted in the same article expressing full support for his lieutenant, stating, "His investigators remain unconvinced that a bloody shirt and trousers found in the home of an acquaintance of Mrs. French have been fully eliminated as a clue to the murder."

In my original interview with Walter Morgan, prior to the publication of *Black Dahlia Avenger*, he unequivocally stated that this leak was the reason Jemison was taken off the case. In Morgan's words:

On the Jeanne French murder, Jemison accused the LAPD of hiding some bloody clothes, or getting rid of some bloody clothes from a locker. They called that the Black Dahlia number two. The accusation made headlines the next day, so the DA just took him right off the case.* The DA didn't give a damn if we knew who murdered Jeanne French at that point. We thought we were making some progress, and Jemison thought he had a good suspect, but when he said that about LAPD, that was it.

Clearly, the orders came down from "on high": close the Dahlia and Red Lipstick murders and return the cases to LAPD! Lieutenant Jemison, armed with more than enough "reasonable cause" to arrest Dr. George Hodel, and about to do so, was now ordered by his superiors to close it out. How is that done? How does the investigating officer, with reasonable cause to arrest the suspect for the two murders, go overnight from imminent arrest to case closed? By simply ignoring and omitting the investigative facts and evidence and, in his final report, writing four paragraphs on the prime suspect — George Hodel — with an exculpatory spin, and returning the case to LAPD, after inserting a disclaimer, attempting to wash clean his and his fellow officers' hands of any investigative responsibility.

Here in his own typewritten words from the DA files are excerpts from Jemison's twelve-page closing report. Though it deals with twenty-two separate suspects, we have established that by February 1950 his office was totally focused on "Suspect No. 10," Dr. George Hill Hodel. Despite the fact that he has solved the Dahlia and Red Lipstick murders, with proof that LAPD detectives destroyed con-

*This would be District Attorney William E. Simpson, the same DA that was in office at the time of George Hodel's incest trial and who it was alleged (per George Hodel's boasting) was paid $15,000 through defense attorney Jerry Giesler to influence and assure Hodel's acquittal.

necting physical evidence (bloody clothing), Lieutenant Jemison nevertheless "follows orders." As he knows in his own mind and heart that Dr. Hodel is the actual killer, Jemison's conscience will not allow him to commit an outright lie to paper (i.e., exonerating Hodel), so the best he can do as a good soldier is to include a statement "tending to eliminate Hodel." Reading between the lines, especially in Lieutenant Jemison's last paragraph, one can detect his frustration and disgust.

> Suspect 10. Doctor George Hodel, M.D., 5121 Fountain Avenue,[*] at the time of this murder had a clinic at East First Street near Alameda. Lillian La Norak, [sic] who lived with this doctor said he spent some time around the Biltmore Hotel and identified the photo of victim Short as a photo of one of the doctor's girl friends. Tamara Hodel, fifteen year old daughter stated that her mother, Dorothy Hodel, had told her that her father had been out all night on a party the night of this murder and said, "They'll never be able to prove I did that murder." Two microphones were placed in this suspect's home (see the logs and recordings made over approximately three weeks' time which tend to prove his innocence. See statement of Dorothy Hodel, former wife.) Informant Lillian LeNorak has been committed to the State Mental Institution at Camarillo. Joe Barratt [sic], a roomer at the Hodel residence cooperated as an informant. A photograph of the suspect in the nude with a nude identified colored model was secured from his personal effects. Undersigned identified this model as Mattie Comfort,[†] 3423-1/2 South Arlington, Republic 4953. She said that she was with Doctor Hodel sometime prior to the murder and that she knew [N.B.: The handwritten word "nothing" was inserted by unknown writer *after* typed report prepared, which totally reverses meaning of the sentence. See insert. — SKH] about his being associated with victim. Rudolph Walthers, known to have been acquainted with victim and also with suspect Hodel, claimed that he

---

*Jemison typo: should be 5121 Franklin Avenue.

†In approximately 1966 I accompanied my mother to an apartment on Sunset Boulevard, where she introduced me to "her good friend Mattie," a beautiful black "actress/model" who at that time appeared to be about 50. It was clear from our short visit that she and Mother had known each other from the Franklin House years.

had not seen victim in the presence of Hodel and did not believe that the doctor had ever met the victim. The following acquaintances of Hodel were questioned and none were able to connect this suspect with this murder: Fred Sexton, 1020 White Knoll Drive; Nita Moladoro, 1617-1/2 North Normandy; Ellen Taylor, 5121 Franklin Ave; Finley Thomas, 616-1/2 South Normandy; Mildred B. Colby, 4629 Vista Del Monte Street, Sherman Oaks, this witness was a girl friend of Charles Smith, abortionist friend of Hodel; Tarin Gilkey, 1025 North Wilcox; Irene Summerset, 1236-1/4 North Edgement; Norman Beckett, 1025 North Wilcox; Ethel Kane, 1033 North Wilcox; Annette Chase, 1039 North Wilcox; Dorothy Royer, 1636 North Beverly Glen. See supplemental reports, long sheets and hear recordings, all of which tend to eliminate this suspect.

### Exhibit 74

Camarillo. Joe Barratt, a roomer at the Hodel residence cooperated as an informant. A photograph of the suspect in the nude with a nude identified colored model was secured from his personal effects. Undersigned identified this model as Mattie Comfort, 3423-1/2 South Arlington, Republic 4953. She said that she was with Doctor Hodel sometime prior toz the murder and that she knew about his being associated with victim. Rudolph Walthers, known to have been acquainted with victim and also with suspect Hodel, claimed that he had not seen victim in the presence of Hodel and did not believe that the doctor had ever met the victim.

*1950 Jemison typed summary as it currently appears in DA file*

[Final paragraph]

The Beth Short murder has been at all times the responsibility of the Los Angeles Police Department Homicide Division. After the undersigned testified before the 1949 Grand Jury hearings, this Grand Jury requested the 1950 Grand Jury to continue their investigation into this murder along with that of Jeanne French. Deputy District Attorney Fred Henderson, advisor to the 1950 Grand Jury, advised the undersigned that a progress report on the investigation of these murders would be required from time to time. The undersigned advised Deputy Chief Thad Brown of this and it was *agreed that the case would never be assumed by the District Attorney's Office* [italics mine], that all of the files and evidence would remain with the Los Angeles Police Department Homicide Division and that temporarily undersigned would assist in this investigation. Chief of Police Worton, when interviewed, approved this plan. *Copies of all statements and reports were given the Los Angeles Police Department for their files* [italics mine]. See reports and statements for names of various officers working with undersigned. On October 3, 1950, the Grand Jury apparently had lost interest in these murders as they had not summoned undersigned for progress reports and Chief of the Bureau of Investigation H. Leo Stanley advised the closing of the investigation.

CLOSED

LT. FRANK B. JEMISON, Investigator

The closing paragraph leaves no further doubt: it is the "smoking gun" that proves that all references showing that Dr. George Hill Hodel was the *prime suspect* in the Elizabeth Short and Jeanne French murders have been "sanitized" and removed from LAPD files.

Through this document, Lieutenant Jemison was creating his own CYA (Cover Your Ass), making it abundantly clear that he was ordered to close the case by his superior, H. Leo Stanley, and turn over *all reports and interviews* to LAPD chiefs Thad Brown and W. A. Worton.

Lieutenant Jemison's legacy to Los Angeles was to lock and secure a copy of the "Hodel File" in the DA's vault, which the fair-minded, fair-handed district attorney Steve Cooley would, some fifty-three years later, unlock and make public.

## Elizabeth Short/George Hodel Photographs

Since this book was published, most readers found the circumstantial evidence against Dr. George Hodel exceptionally compelling *before* the discovery of the DA Dahlia files, which confirm that Dr. Hodel was indeed the prime suspect.

A vocal few (mostly Dahlia "theorists" who have either written their own book or have gone public with accusations naming other suspects) have attacked my investigation based on the fact that they do not believe the photographs taken by Father, and found in his album of "loved ones," are in fact of Elizabeth Short.

I decided from the start that I would not and will not get into any "pissing contest" with these theorists. The top photograph from Dr. Hodel's family album is compared to her Santa Barbara booking photo. The bottom right photo is from the crime-scene DA files and the only modification I have made is to airbrush over the facial lacerations in order to spare the victim's family members and readers that horrific sight. Incredibly, the pose, with the angle of the head and face and the outstretched left arm, is nearly identical in position to my father's photograph.

### *Exhibit 75*

Dr. George Hodel
photo album

Elizabeth Short
booking photo, 1943
age 19

Dr. George Hodel
photo album

Elizabeth Short
crime scene, 1947
(lacerations airbrushed)

Are the above photos and those in my fathers' album of the same young woman? In my view, absolutely. I leave it to my readers to make their own judgment.

With the release of the DA files in April 2003, we now have independent corroboration that George Hodel and Elizabeth Short were lovers. From the documents we have learned that separate witnesses placed Elizabeth Short and George Hodel as checking into the East Washington Boulevard Hotel, and meeting at the Franklin House and the Biltmore Hotel on separate occasions.

## The Public Comes to Me

My motive in writing *Black Dahlia Avenger* has always been to get the truth out before the public. My goal was — and remains — to inform. As a result of the media exposure the book has received, the public has responded generously through e-mails to my website (Blackdahliaavenger.com), letters to my publisher, and at my personal appearances and book signings. Approximately 95 percent of these responses have been overwhelmingly positive, not only about my findings but about me and my family members, especially my half-sister, Tamar. My hope was that once the public became informed some new and important information would surface. Of the many instances in which that did happen, I present here six separate incidents involving seven individuals. Each of these seven people came forward, unsolicited, with new and compelling information. They spoke out because they care about the truth.

I suspect that in the coming months more people will surface with further evidence. The simple fact is, the "riddle wrapped in a mystery, inside an enigma" has been unwrapped and will forever remain open for all to see.

-1-

We know from LAPD reports, joint tissue studies by Dr. Lemoyne Snyder and LAPD criminalist Ray Pinker, and from the FBI dossier, that all experts were united in the belief that the murder of Elizabeth Short was committed by a skilled surgeon. However, in the past, these statements have been presented as broad generalizations, lacking medical specifics. In July 2003, professor and surgeon Dr. Michael Keller, after reading my book, and examining crime-scene photographs, contacted me and provided his own far more specific and detailed insights. Here is his professional opinion, to be added to the weight of evidence that a surgeon committed the crime.

24 July, 2003
Steve —

From the information in your book, I feel in fact that Ms. Short's murderer did in fact have medical training and not just knowledge. Several reasons:

1 — To remain calm enough to completely transect a human torso with its inevitable spillages of blood, stool, gastrointestinal content and urine would have required (I think) someone who had seen it all before. This person knew where he was going.

2 — The photos of the scene and the morgue which I looked up on the Net appear to show a very clean procedure. Surgeons make bold clean incisions thru each layer of tissue with the correct amount of pressure to divide only the tissues they are attending to. The uninitiated — laypersons — usually underestimate the amount of pressure it takes just to divide skin, let alone an intervertebral disc. Their procedures often result in cuts that are serrated at the ends from going over the tissue repeatedly. We derogatorily call these "Staging Laparotomies — going thru the skin in stages." Additionally, amateurs often skive the incisions. Their cuts go thru skin at an angle to the horizontal plane so that one edge is "feathered" and the other appears peeled.

3 — The killer here was educated enough not to attempt going thru the bones of the lumbar spine. He was savvy enough to locate and divide at the disc space. Even at that, it takes tremendous will and a very sharp instrument to divide the spinous ligaments and the thick paravertebral muscles. An amateur would probably have left hack marks on the vertebral bodies as he "casted about" for the interspace.

4 — There appeared to be a willful attempt to perform or simulate the performance of a hysterectomy which at that time would have been done through a lower vertical midline as the photos appear to show. That was a medical decision.

5 — We have no reason to doubt the police medical examiner as his report precedes the cover-up and actually indicts a medical person.

6 — I believe medical knowledge would have been necessary to prolong the torture phase without killing the victim prematurely, but then again Dahmer apparently was able to trephine some of his victims and keep them alive. Still, in all, the Dahlia case seemed as though it may have been a prolonged "dance" — more skill needed.

7 — Finally I think a surgeon's hand would have been required to recontour the body in just such a way that it reproduced Man Ray's The *Minotaur* — knowing where and how much to cut. This is less of a point but I feel that there is still credence here.

Overall I feel no reason to doubt your case and in fact, taken together, if the killer was not Dr. Hodel then it must certainly have been another such professional.

Besides, as a teacher of students and both surgery and family practice residents, I am aware that their initial attempts at incisions end up as stated in #2 above. It requires about one to two years of steady practice to develop the feel of scalpel against various tissue. Persons with innate surgical ability are rare. Most of us must repeatedly experience the tactile sensations to develop the right "feel".

What I have stated is based on 20 years of surgical practice and education of young doctors. In my personal opinion, however, I am comfortable with your assertions and do believe the Dahlia was a professional work.

Sincerely,

Michael Keller, M.D.

*Exhibit 76*

**1942 diploma wherein President Franklin D. Roosevelt certified
Dr. George Hill Hodel as a Public Health surgeon**

-2-

During a book signing at a bookstore in Torrance, California, a woman asked me, "Do you think that Fred Sexton was involved in these crimes?" My answer to her was a qualified "yes." I explained that while the circumstantial evidence connecting him to some of the crimes was insufficient for the DA to state that he would charge him along with George Hodel, I was nonetheless convinced of his participation based on various crime scene signatures, composite drawings, and witness descriptions. The woman's response shocked and silenced the room. "So do I," she replied. "Fred Sexton was my stepfather, and he molested me when I was eleven years old."

Since that night, I have met with this woman and her mother (names withheld to protect their privacy), who was married to Fred Sexton during the mid- to late 1960s. They lived in Mexico and in Los Angeles, and the mother, a beautiful soul and highly successful artist, detailed for me her life with Sexton. After the molestation of her daughter, Sexton fled to Mexico, where he emptied their joint bank accounts (a very substantial amount of money, in fact a lifetime of savings earned solely by her). This woman, his second wife, obtained a divorce in the United States, while Sexton remained safe and untouchable in Mexico. At age sixty, Fred Sexton would marry a girl still in her teens, and live in comfort and security from his ex-wife's funds, while this extraordinary woman would remain in the United States, try to pick up her life, provide love and comfort to her traumatized daughter, and attempt as best she could to move forward and away from the darkness that was Fred Sexton. These disclosures, coming as they do from two highly reliable and closely related victims of Fred Sexton, further expose and corroborate his criminal nature, both as a violent abuser of women and as a child molester.

-3-

After a book signing at an Orange County, California, bookstore, I was approached by a man who identified himself (and showed me his credentials) as a retired commander (and thirty-eight-year veteran) with the Los Angeles Sheriff's Department, Commander Thomas M. Vetter. He had read my book, complimented me on my investigation, and told me that in 1962 he was personally present during a conversation between then undersheriff James Downey and famed LASD captain of detectives J. Gordon Bowers, the subject of which was the Black Dahlia murder. In the course of their discussion Downey informed Bowers that the "Black Dahlia case was solved. The suspect was a medical doctor in Hollywood involved in abortions."

-4-

Immediately after completing an interview at a well-known Los Angeles–based radio station, KNX, I was approached by engineer and production supervisor Raul Moreno. Mr. Moreno told me he had read my book, was convinced of its accuracy, and had been anxious to meet me, because he had some important information to offer that would confirm my own findings. To establish his credibility, he told me he was an LAPD reserve officer, a Los Angeles historian, and had helped research and put together some of LAPD's historical writings. He went on to say that he was a personal friend of actor Jack Webb, who performed for decades as Sergeant Joe Friday on *Dragnet*. As a child he had acted in several *Dragnet* episodes, and as an adult he had remained friends with Webb. As proof of this, he removed from his wallet an LAPD police ID card with Webb's picture on it, including his famous "Badge 714," which he informed me had been given to him by Webb. Then came the shocker:

> In 1982 I had a conversation with my longtime friend, Jack Webb.*
> We somehow got on the subject of the Black Dahlia murder. Webb told me, "You know, the Black Dahlia murder was solved." I asked him what he was talking about, and he told me that his good friend LAPD Chief Thad Brown had told him the case had been solved. Thad Brown told Webb that "the suspect was a doctor in Hollywood who lived on Franklin Ave."

"Are you sure Jack Webb told you that Thad Brown said, 'on Franklin Avenue'?" I asked. "Absolutely," he replied. "That is why I know your information is correct. Jack Webb said that Chief Brown told him, 'the Dahlia suspect was a doctor on Franklin Ave.'"

-5-

LAPD Sergeant Harry Hansen, initially assigned to the 1947 Dahlia crime-scene investigation as partner to Finis Brown (brother of Deputy Chief Thad Brown), would eventually become the Dahlia's most famous detective after Efrem Zimbalist Jr. played him in the 1975 NBC-TV dramatization *Who Is the Black Dahlia?*

After the publication of *Black Dahlia Avenger*, I was contacted by Harry Hansen's granddaughter, Judy May, who informed me that she had read my book. After some correspondence back and forth, we decided to meet. She and her husband invited me to lunch at their San Fernando Valley home, a short distance from Los Angeles. After lunch, Hansen's granddaughter brought out a box full of papers and

---

*Webb died in December of that year, at the relatively young age of sixty-two.

*Exhibit* 77

*Efrem Zimbalist Jr. & Lieutenant Harry Hansen (ret.) during*
*NBC-TV production. Inscription reads:*
*"Harry —*
*It is great being you, and being with you.*
*Fondest and best wishes to you both.*
*Always — Efrem"*

files belonging to her grandfather, and allowed me to look through them to see if they contained any important additional information about the case. As a result, I made two important discoveries. First, I learned that Harry Hansen had been with LAPD much longer than I had realized. He attended the police academy in 1926, making him definitely one of the "old guard." Hansen retired in 1968 after forty-two years of service. Second, and most important, was the discovery that among his personal effects, Hansen had preserved a packet of photographs. Mixed *together* in this single packet were crime-scene and autopsy photographs from the following three homicides: Elizabeth Short, Jeanne French, and Louise Springer. As we know, my own investigation had produced extensive evidence that my father was the perpetrator of all three crimes. Do these fifty-four-year-old photographs, secreted in Harry Hansen's attic for these many decades, inform us from beyond the grave that he also believed these crimes were the work of one man?

-6-

## Geographical Profiling

In August 2003, I was contacted by Dr. Evan R. Harrington, professor of psychology, at John Jay College of Criminal Justice in New York. Dr. Harrington advised me he was conducting research into the geographic profile of the unsolved murders as outlined in *Black Dahlia Avenger*, using "Dragnet," a geo-profile program originated by Dr. David Canter.*

Here is a partial description from Dr. Harrington on how the program functions:

> Dragnet uses a relatively simple geometric formula to locate the likely residence of an offender based on the observation from numerous published studies that most crimes (including homicide and rape) oc-

---

*Dr. Canter is the originator of geo-profiling and director of the Institute of Investigative Psychology at the University of Liverpool. His most recent book, *Mapping Murder: Secrets of Geographical Profiling*, was published in the U.S. in November 2003.

THE AFTERMATH

513

cur close to an offender's home. Dragnet uses a distance-decay function which locates an area closest to multiple crime locations entered as data in the program and describes this area as the highest probability for the home of the offender. Dragnet provides a color coded set of concentric bands around this center area, illustrating the relative probabilities for the location of the offender's home.

The data used in his analysis consisted of both my Category I (definite) and Category II (probable) crime locations. As of this writing (mid-October 2003) Dr. Harrington has presented his results to the faculty at John Jay College of Criminal Justice, and is preparing his findings for publication.

Here are his preliminary conclusions:

1) Geographic-profile analysis using only the *Category I crimes* (7 murder drop-sites; Murray, Bauerdorf, Short, French, Kern, Boomhower, Spangler-purse, and Armand Robles assault/robbery) places *the Franklin House, 5121 Franklin Avenue in the high probability zone.*

2) Geographic profile analysis using the Category I and Category II crime scenes (4 murder drop-sites; Winters, Trelstad, Mondragon, and Springer, plus the Norton, M'Grew & Horan abductions) the Dragnet profile then switches the highest profile zone away from the Franklin House; *and places the high probability zone, in an area of downtown Los Angeles, which encompasses Dr. Hodel's medical office at 727 W. 7th St.* (Data excluded from this analysis were the San Diego (Newton) and El Monte murders (Ellroy and Long) as well as the Jane Doe (George Hodel secretary poisoning, due to lack of information as to where that crime occurred.)

Dr. Harrington in his preliminary report to me states:

In conclusion, Dragnet successfully identified both the Hodel residence and the Hodel medical practice as being in areas considered highest probability for the base of the killer(s).

## Elizabeth Short — More Photographs

In February 2003, four original photographs of Elizabeth Short came up for auction on the Internet. The photographs were part of Elizabeth's personal effects, which as noted were found by *Examiner* reporters in the luggage that she checked at the downtown bus station on January 9, just before Robert Manley drove her to the Biltmore Hotel. By mutual agreement between LAPD captain Jack Donahoe and city editor James Richardson, the luggage was opened at the newspaper's office.

These recently discovered photographs appear to suggest that the police and the press split the bounty, the *Examiner* retaining these four photographs. Several of these photographs were printed in biographical articles about Elizabeth in the weeks following her murder. The historical importance of the prints, and even the fact they were of Elizabeth Short, were forgotten over the decades, and the four photographs were sold as part of a larger collection when the newspaper closed its doors in the 1970s.

These four photographs, along with hundreds of other unrelated *Examiner* morgue photos, were purchased by a retail collector of old photographs and remained lost until they were ultimately reidentified and purchased by a private buyer in the early 1990s.

Recognizing the photographs' historical and forensic importance, along with my strong personal interest, I set out to obtain them. The bidding was fierce, but fate was on my side, and in the final second I won out. My forensic examination of these photographs is pending further tests. In the meantime, however, I want to share these rare photographs with my readers. They are candid pictures of Elizabeth taken in happier times, mostly with boyfriends.

Not visible in these photographs are the handprinted names and a location written in blue ink, prior to 1947,* that are at the bottom of each photograph. The notations read as follows:

a. "Beth Short — Tim"
b. "Jax. Fla."
c. "Beth Short — Paul Morris"

*This has been established by the author's viewing archival photographs at the UCLA research center. The photographs show identical pictures before they were removed from Elizabeth Short's original photo album.

## Exhibit 78

d.  Shows reverse of photo number c, which still contains remnants
    of glue and black paper where reporters removed it from Eliza-
    beth's scrapbook. (Photos a, b, and e contain similar markings.)
e.  "Beth Short"

During my review of the DA's files, I discovered a brief interview
conducted by DA investigators with a young man who claimed to
have met Elizabeth Short in Hollywood in late October 1946. The
report indicated that he had told her he was a photographer, and
suggested he take some pictures of her. She agreed and they drove
to the east side of Hollywood, where he shot the following pictures
on the steps of John Marshall High School. (Note — Only two
poor-quality copies of the six photographs he took of Elizabeth
were found in the DA files.)

*Exhibit 79*

*Elizabeth Short, October 1946, Hollywood, California*

These six photographs, all appearing to be originals, were discovered during a follow-up visit with Harry Hansen's granddaughter, Judy, in late September 2003. (As previously mentioned, this box of Dahlia-related photographs came into her possession after the death

*Exhibit 80*

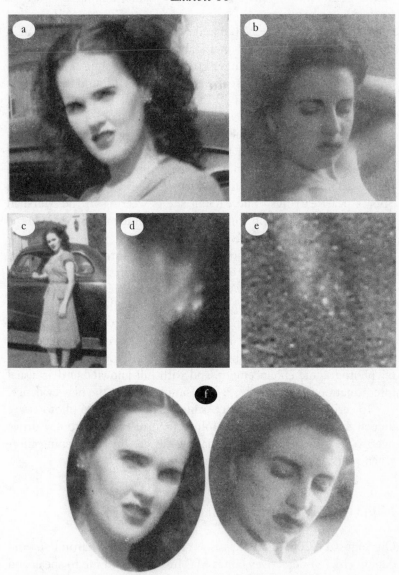

*Photographs a, c, and d, Elizabeth Short, October 1946, Hollywood, California*
*Photographs b and e taken by George Hodel, circa 1945–46*
*Photograph f, Elizabeth Short, 1946, photograph mirrored*
*and angled in comparison with Dr. George Hodel photograph*

of her grandfather.) Judy showed them to me, hoping they would further buttress my case.

Earlier in this chapter I pointed out that Detective Hansen had in this same box (his own personal Dahlia collection) grouped *together* the Short, French, and Springer homicide photographs. On this second visit and review of Hansen's personal effects, I found these never-before-seen photographs of Elizabeth Short. They contain what I firmly believe is additional connecting evidence, a thoughtprint, one I had been searching for ever since I began my investigation!

In every photograph of Elizabeth Short I viewed, I had sought this linkage but never found it. Finally, it appears Detective Hansen has reluctantly at long last provided it. The evidence? Elizabeth Short's pearl earrings. The earring she is wearing in the Marshall High School photograph appears to be the same one she wore in the photograph taken by George Hodel!

Granted, the quality is poor, and due to the variables of angle and position as well as view (right ear versus left), lighting, distance, and soft-focus, one cannot be *absolutely* positive. However, it is my professional opinion that they are one and the same. In both photographs we can clearly see small pearls, set in a circular motif. They appear to be clip-on, and we recall one of the unusual physical descriptions included in police reports was that Elizabeth Short "had no earlobes." Absent better photographic enhancement, and with full knowledge that visual interpretations are subjective, I here simply present the new evidence.

To verify (as stated in the DA's files) that these 1946 photos were indeed taken in Hollywood at John Marshall High School, I drove over to examine the site. Fortunately, despite the intervening fifty-seven years, little had changed there.


**LAPD Crime Summary Briefing**

On August 13, 2003, LAPD assistant chief of police Sharon Papa and deputy chief of detectives James McMurray invited me to speak and make an intelligence briefing before them and veteran detectives from the Robbery-Homicide Division, which included Detective Brian Carr, keeper of the Elizabeth Short "Black Dahlia" case file. The LAPD personnel present at the briefing consisted of one assis-

## Exhibit 81

*Photographs a and b — According to witness statements in the DA's
file, these photographs of Elizabeth Short were taken by him at
John Marshall High School in October 1946.
Photographs c and d — Taken by the author in October 2003 at
John Marshall High School. In photograph c we see the same number
of bricks, as well as the small brass seal on the first step.
In photograph d we are able to match the unusual window motif.*

tant chief, one deputy chief, one commander, two captains, three detectives from Robbery-Homicide Division (Carr, assigned to Major Crimes, and two detectives from the specialized unsolved Cold Case Unit), and one unidentified civilian consultant. Head Deputy DA Stephen Kay was also asked to attend, and he provided valuable legal insights and opinions as well as confirming before the department brass that, based on my evidence, were Dr. Hodel still alive, he would file two counts of murder (Elizabeth Short and Jeanne French). This two-hour presentation included an overall summary of my three-year investigation, along with the postpublication discoveries from the DA Dahlia/Hodel files. At the conclusion, I provided LAPD with the following list of thirty-one unsolved crimes. It is my professional opinion, based on my investigative findings, that George Hodel and Fred Sexton are the likely perpetrators of many if not most of these crimes. Most of the post-1950 crimes listed are likely attributable to Fred Sexton; however, as indicated in the individual crime summaries, George Hodel cannot be totally excluded, given his occasional short business trips from Asia to the Los Angeles area over the years. I have prioritized them into three categories, followed by a chronological list of all the crimes:

## CRIME CATEGORIES

I.   Definite or extremely strong evidence
II.  Probably connected, need to review crime files
III. Possibly connected, need to review crime files

### Category I

| 1. | Ora Murray         | 7/27/43  | (LASD) |
|----|--------------------|----------|--------|
| 2. | Georgette Bauerdorf| 10/12/44 | (LASD) |
| 3. | Armand Robles      | 1/10/47  | (LAPD) |
| 4. | Elizabeth Short    | 1/15/47  | (LAPD) |
| 5. | Jeanne French      | 2/10/47  | (LAPD) |
| 6. | Gladys Kern        | 2/14/48  | (LAPD) |
| 7. | Mimi Boomhower     | 8/18/49  | (LAPD) |
| 8. | Jean Spangler      | 10/7/49  | (LAPD) |

## Category II

| | | | |
|---|---|---|---|
| 1. | Sylvia Horan | 2/3/47 | (LAPD) |
| 2. | Ica M'Grew | 2/12/47 | (LAPD) |
| 3. | Evelyn Winters | 3/11/47 | (LAPD) |
| 4. | Laura Trelstad | 5/11/47 | (Long Beach PD) |
| 5. | Rosenda Mondragon | 7/8/47 | (LAPD) |
| 6. | Marian Newton | 7/17/47 | (San Diego PD) |
| 7. | Viola Norton | 2/14/48 | (Alhambra PD) |
| 8. | Louise Springer | 6/13/49 | (LAPD) |
| 9. | Jane Doe (Hodel Secretary) | 1947–49 | (LAPD) |
| 10. | Geneva Ellroy | 6/22/58 | (LASD) |
| 11. | Bobbie Long | 1/22/59 | (LASD) |

## Category III

| | | | |
|---|---|---|---|
| 1. | Loretta Robinson | 8/5/43 | (LAPD) |
| 2. | Diane Sparkes (LAPD wife) | 1/29/46 | (LAPD) |
| 3. | Irene Weeks | 6/17/46 | (San Bernardino SO) |
| 4. | Gertrude Landon | 7/10/46 | (LASD) |
| 5. | Naomi Cook | 12/11/46 | (LAPD) |
| 6. | Mary Tate | 1/18/47 | (LAPD) |
| 7. | Dorothy Montgomery | 5/2/47 | (LASD) |
| 8. | Anna Diresio | 5/12/47 | (LAPD) |
| 9. | Helene Jerome | 8/27/58 | (LAPD) |
| 10–11. | William Dorr & Ellen Criss | 11/19/63 | (LAPD) |
| 12. | Karyn Kupcinet | 11/28/63 | (LASD) |

### Law Enforcement Agency Investigating:

| | |
|---|---|
| LAPD | 20 |
| LASD | 7 |
| Long Beach | 1 |
| San Bernardino SD | 1 |
| San Diego PD | 1 |
| Alhambra PD | 1 |
| | |
| Total Crimes | 31 |

## Crimes Chronological

| | | |
|---|---|---|
| 1. Ora Murray | 7/27/43 | (LASD) |
| 2. Loretta Robinson | 8/5/43 | (LAPD) |
| 3. Georgette Bauerdorf | 10/12/44 | (LASD) |
| 4. Diane Sparks | 1/29/46 | (LAPD) |
| 5. Irene Weeks | 6/17/46 | (SBSO) |
| 6. Gertrude Landon | 7/10/46 | (LASD) |
| 7. Naomi Cook | 12/11/46 | (LAPD) |
| 8. Armand Robles | 1/10/47 | (LAPD) |
| 9. Elizabeth Short | 1/14/47 | (LAPD) |
| 10. Mary Tate | 1/18/47 | (LAPD) |
| 11. Sylvia Horan | 2/3/47 | (LAPD) |
| 12. Jeanne French | 2/10/47 | (LAPD) |
| 13. Ica M'Grew | 2/12/47 | (LAPD) |
| 14. Evelyn Winters | 3/11/47 | (LAPD) |
| 15. Dorothy Montgomery | 5/2/47 | (LASD) |
| 16. Laura Trelstad | 5/11/47 | (LONG BEACH PD) |
| 17. Anna Diresio | 5/12/47 | (LAPD) |
| 18. Rosenda Mondragon | 7/8/47 | (LAPD) |
| 19. Marian Newton | 7/17/47 | (SAN DIEGO PD) |
| 20. Viola Norton | 2/14/48 | (ALHAMBRA PD) |
| 21. Gladys Kern | 2/14/48 | (LAPD) |
| 22. Louise Springer | 6/13/49 | (LAPD) |
| 23. Mimi Boomhower | 8/18/49 | (LAPD) |
| 24. Jean Spangler | 10/7/49 | (LAPD) |
| 25. Jane Doe | 1947–1949 | (LAPD) |
| 26. Geneva Ellroy | 6/22/58 | (LASD) |
| 27. Helene Jerome | 8/27/58 | (LAPD) |
| 28. Bobbie Long | 1/22/59 | (LASD) |
| 29–30. Ellen Criss/Wm Dorr | 11/19/63 | (LAPD) |
| 31. Karyn Kupcinet | 11/28/63 | (LASD) |

During my meeting with LAPD, it was all give and no take. By that I mean that no "inside information" relating to the Dahlia or any of the other crimes was provided me. Detectives would not even confirm the existence (or absence) of evidence in any of the murder investigations.

I gave LAPD detectives a list of potential connecting evidence on many of the murders, specifically detailing potential DNA linkage of hair follicles and stamps (saliva) known to be retained as evidence in the Short, French, and Kern homicides. I advised detectives of the existence, in my possession, of "proof sheet papers" (my original 1949 Chinese Chicken drawing) that likely came from the same stock of proof sheet paper — owned by my father — as the notes that were mailed to the police and press by the "Black Dahlia Avenger." This and several other samples, I advised, were available for spectrographic analysis and comparison. I further informed those present of the newly discovered Kern note in my father's handwriting, and I provided them with a color drawing of the Kern one-of-a-kind "jungle knife." The new information summarized in this chapter, including photographic exhibits, was also provided each LAPD officer (except for the "new" photographs of Elizabeth Short and the earring comparisons, which did not come into my possession until October 2003).

The only information I learned from that LAPD meeting was that, as of that date, Detective Brian Carr had not read my book (he did acknowledge "skimming through it"), nor had he made any effort to review the DA's Dahlia/Hodel files, some four months after their existence was revealed. At the end of my two-hour summary, assisted by Head Deputy DA Stephen Kay, it was clear that most of the command staff and officers present had been won over and were anxious for a department investigation to follow up on my findings. From my own observations, the only two dissenters—who appeared on the defensive throughout my presentation—were the commander of Robbery-Homicide Division, Captain Michelena, and his own detective, Brian Carr.

Now, months later, I have it on good authority that neither Carr nor any other LAPD detective has yet reviewed any of the DA files. This willful refusal on the part of Robbery-Homicide detectives to conduct any follow-up investigation, despite the fact that Detective Carr at the August briefing, in my presence, was directed by an assistant chief of police to "get over and inspect the DA files forthwith" is perplexing, almost incomprehensible. Why would

Robbery-Homicide Division detectives choose to ignore compelling evidence presented to them by a respected veteran homicide detective and one of the DA's most respected prosecutors, in
essence sitting on their hands?

The answer to these disturbing questions may prove to be as
troubling as the questions themselves. I have heard from very reliable sources that most if not all of the Black Dahlia physical evidence
is missing from the locked evidence storage room. This would include the original Mark Hansen address book, the dozen or more
notes and stamped envelopes, the hair follicles, the victim's purse and
shoes, and her identification papers originally mailed to the *Examiner* by the Black Dahlia Avenger. In addition, the status of the physical evidence on the Jeanne French and Gladys Kern homicides is
not known.

The same sources have indicated to me that all fingerprint cards
on Dr. George Hodel are also missing. Apparently, LAPD, LASD,
FBI, and State Medical Board records — all of which should have his
prints on file — do not have them!

If true, this could explain why today's detectives are refusing to
conduct any follow-up investigation. Action would bring answers,
and those answers would force the department to shed light on a
dark past.*

## LAPD Crime Clearance—Case Solved

As a former LAPD homicide detective supervisor, I am fully aware of
what the department policy requires to clear a crime. There are two
ways: (1) a crime can be cleared by arrest, or (2) in the event of the
death of the perpetrator, it can be cleared "other." How is this done?

*LAPD detective Brian Carr, in a November 15, 2003, television interview on
*Court TV,* confirmed that he was unable to locate any fingerprints on Dr. George Hodel,
and further informed the interviewer that the Black Dahlia evidence, which could be used
for DNA comparison, "has disappeared." While attending an LAPD book-signing event
on November 22, 2003, I was informed by LAPD criminalist Ms. Elma Duke that two
years earlier she had personally handled and reviewed all the Black Dahlia evidence, including the original letters and the mailings. So either Carr is mistaken and the evidence
does exist, or it has "disappeared" sometime between 2001 and today.

In the first example, the investigating detective, after filing his case with the DA, writes a follow-up report summarizing his investigation, closing with the fact that a felony count of murder was filed, and labels the report "Crime Cleared by Arrest." (As a statistical reality, no verdict is required. So even if the defendant is found "not guilty," the crime remains cleared or "solved.") In the instance where the perpetrator is deceased, LAPD policy dictates that the crime be "Cleared Other." This type of crime clearance does not require that a DA specify that he or she would file the case. It is a judgment call on the part of the investigating detective, who must establish the evidence supporting a clearance in his follow-up. The follow-up report and clearance is reviewed by his supervisor, who approves or rejects the clearance. Either method of clearance results in the crime becoming formally classified as SOLVED.

Based on the investigation presented in this book, there are three separate crimes that by all LAPD recognized standards and policies can be cleared and classified as SOLVED. They are: the 1947 murders of Elizabeth Short (Black Dahlia), Jeanne French (Red Lipstick), and the 1948 murder of Hollywood real-estate agent Gladys Kern.

Based on LAPD's demonstrated inactivity over the past several months, and fearing that the powers that be at Robbery-Homicide Division may prevail and no further investigation will ever be conducted, I am forced into a highly irregular action.

Guided by my conscience and supported by my proven experience, training, and qualifications as a former LAPD homicide detective-supervisor, with full recognition that all the necessary objective criteria have been met, and after considering all of the evidence, forensics, and exhibits presented pre- and postpublication of this investigation, I here reclassify the murders of Elizabeth Short, Jeanne French, and Gladys Kern — CLEARED OTHER, CASES SOLVED.

LAPD Detective III Steve Hodel 11394 (ret.)
November 2003

# New Investigation:
# Hard Evidence and Forensics

*All truth passes through three stages. First, it is ridiculed. Second, it is violently opposed. Third, it is accepted as being self-evident.*
—Arthur Schopenhauer

TODAY IS JANUARY 15, 2005. It marks the fifty-eighth anniversary of the sadistic murder of Elizabeth Short. How ironic yet appropriate that on this day I find myself fitting into place the final proofs of my father's crime, which, found in the closing months of 2004, offer both "hard physical evidence" and additional confirmation of his unique surreal signature.

## Los Angeles Biltmore Hotel, January 9, 1947

My 2005 review of the secret DA files confirmed the fact that Elizabeth Short left the Biltmore Hotel on January 9, 1947, shortly after 10:00 P.M. Those files document an interview with Mr. Harold Studholme, the Biltmore bell captain, where he informed the police that he saw a figure (no further description) motion to Elizabeth from outside the Olive Street entrance. Elizabeth, who had apparently been waiting and expecting someone to arrive, then exited the hotel, and he last saw her walking south on Olive Street.

The photo on the next page shows a woman exiting the Olive Street entrance, just as Elizabeth Short did in 1947. The location remains unchanged from that time period.

Likewise, the photo showing the exterior and interior lobby of the Roosevelt Building, 727 W. 7th Street, remains unchanged from 1947. On January 9, 1947, Dr. Hodel's office was located on the twelfth floor at the top of this building.

The below aerial photograph shows the close proximity of the Biltmore Hotel to Dr. George Hodel's medical office. The "R" marks the hotel's Olive Street entrance. As supported by the bell captain's statements, Elizabeth turned right and headed south toward the Roosevelt building, possibly in the company of another. As can be seen, George Hodel's office is a short five-minute walk from the Biltmore.

*Roosevelt Building, 727 W. 7th Street*
*(Dr. Hodel's top-floor office)*

*The Biltmore Hotel's*
*Olive Street entrance*

*Roosevelt Building, 727 W. 7th Street (Dr. Hodel's top-floor office)*

*Exhibit 82*

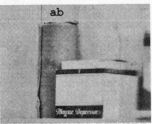

## Georgette Bauerdorf Murder Weapon

One of the Category I murders in this book offered compelling evidence that my father, George Hodel, was the killer of twenty-year-old Georgette Bauerdorf. In October 1944, the attractive young woman, a volunteer "junior hostess" at the Hollywood Canteen, had been followed home and slain in her West Hollywood apartment.

In my original 2001 investigative summary, I made specific note of the highly unusual murder weapon the killer had brought with him, a rolled nine-inch elastic knit Ace bandage. After beating the woman, he forced the bandage into her mouth, resulting in asphyxiation.

During the autopsy inquest held on October 20, 1944, the sheriff's detectives handling the case informed the inquest jurors that they had determined that "the material of this nine-inch bandage had not been sold in this city for 22 years."*

In chapter 23, I asked the question "Who, other than a medical professional, would be carrying such a 'weapon'?" I further reasoned that my father had perhaps possessed such a "weapon" in his own medical black bag, and had not purchased it in Los Angeles but placed it inside the bag when he was a young doctor on the Indian reservations, or even earlier, during his 1936 internship at San Francisco General Hospital.

In December 2004, I received the above photograph from my sister Tamar. It shows Father at work at a small clinic, possibly in

* In 2001 I attempted to locate this size, but was unable to find it ready made, so I re-created and photographed it as exhibit 55, page 304.

Santa Fe, New Mexico, circa 1937. Incredibly, we see in plain view, resting on the shelf (ab), *a rolled elastic knit nine-inch Ace bandage*. We need speculate no further whether Dr. George Hodel may have had access to such a rare and unusual weapon. Clearly he did!

## "A Doctor Did It"

In previous chapters I presented evidence from a number of authoritative sources (including LAPD's own respected criminalist Ray Pinker, who conducted tissue studies in conjunction with Dr. Lemoyne Snyder) confirming that the bisection was performed by a medical doctor.

In October, 2004, CBS's *48 Hours* television producers, in preparation for an hour-long special, decided to test the theory independently. The network went to Dr. Mark Wallack, chief of surgery at St. Vincent's Hospital in New York, and asked him to examine the crime scene photos, as well as a summary of the Short autopsy, and render an opinion. Dr. Wallack confirmed my, and LAPD's, previous findings. Here is his on-air statement from the special, *Black Dahlia Confidential:*

| | |
|---|---|
| Dr. Wallack: | You don't get this kind of training where you can invade a human body unless you've had some sort of medical training. |
| Investigative reporter Erin Moriarty: | So you're saying you think it must have been a doctor? |
| Dr. Wallack: | In my opinion—yes! |

In early 2005, I was contacted by the son of a prominent Los Angeles physician, whom I shall refer to as Dr. G. The son, a surgeon and professor of anatomy,˙ informed me that his father had been the

---

* The professor identified the medical bisection performed on Elizabeth Short as a "hemicorpectomy." He informed me that the procedure was taught in medical school during my father's years (1930s), and in his opinion, could be performed by any skilled and anatomically trained M.D.

personal physician to legendary LAPD chief William H. Parker. He stated that I had incorrectly attributed Chief Parker's death in 1966 to a heart attack, and went on to inform me that "Parker died of an abdominal aortic aneurysm that ruptured as he was preparing to give a dinner speech." According to the son, Dr. G. had previously referred Chief Parker to the Mayo Clinic for treatment, but the clinic's doctors felt repair was too risky, though they did provide him with a pacemaker.

The son went on to say that sometime after Chief Parker's death, he and his father were watching a television show about the Black Dahlia. During the show, Dr. G. told his son that LAPD had identified the Black Dahlia killer and that he was a doctor. I find this information, coming from Chief Parker's personal physician, to be highly authoritative and reliable.

I have no reason to doubt this witness's veracity. Like his father, he is a respected physician. His information is consistent with the known facts, and independently corroborates what we have heard from other high-ranking law-enforcement officers. As I close the investigation, I find it personally rewarding that Chief William H. Parker, a man I worshipped as a rookie, a man who reversed the direction of LAPD from corruption to professionalism, has here transcended time and space to add his voice in confirmation.

## Identification of the "Jane Doe" Secretary

In April 2003, *Los Angeles Times* columnist Steve Lopez wrote two articles independently confirming my own investigative findings, namely that LAPD reports showed that Dr. George Hodel was (1) named as a suspect in the Black Dahlia murder and (2) named as a suspect in the possible overdosing of his private secretary.

LAPD detective Brian Carr, unaware that the name George Hodel had ever been connected to the Dahlia investigation, immediately conducted a name search through the LAPD Dahlia files, where he indeed found a file on Dr. Hodel. He publicly acknowledged this, but was quick to point out that in the review of all of the Black Dahlia files, "*only a single-page memo was found that mentioned*

*the name George Hodel."* He added that as a result of this discovery,
LAPD would "check out his fingerprints against unidentified lifts
from the evidence." At the same time, LAPD refused to identify Dr.
Hodel's secretary, known only as "Jane Doe," either by name or by
date of death.

In the summer of 2004, a woman contacted me and asked that I call
her regarding the death of my father's secretary. To preserve her privacy, I will call her Florence X. Florence, it turns out, had worked for
my father in 1942-1943. An epidemiologist, she was employed by the
Los Angeles County Health Department and reported directly to
Dr. Hodel. They shared an office downtown, at 8th and Broadway.
Florence X was close to both of my father's secretaries at the Health
Department. She identified one as Ruth Spaulding, and indicated she
had died just at the close of World War II. Florence named my father's second secretary as Marion Herwood Keyes[†] and said that
Ruth and Marion, whom she described as "exceptionally beautiful,"
were very close. Florence worked for Dr. Hodel for eighteen
months, and recalls him throwing her a generous "going-away party"
when she left in 1943. During those years, Florence attended Dr.
Hodel's parties with both Ruth and Marion, but found that she and
her husband "did not fit in." She remembered meeting my mother at
several of the parties, and recalls seeing my brothers and me on a few
occasions. She had been told by other staff members that Dr. Hodel
had an apartment downtown, somewhere near the office, where it
was believed he would take his girlfriends. Florence recalls hearing

* Detective Carr's seemingly innocuous public statement in 2003 becomes important to the 2004 investigation because it underscores the fact that today's LAPD detectives *had no knowledge that George Hodel's name ever appeared in the files.* Like his
predecessor, Detective Kirk Mellecker, Carr was unfamiliar with the Hodel connection.
For me this was key, since it verified my suspicion that the DA's Hodel files, consisting
of hundreds of transcript pages, along with the wire recordings, which were known to
have been turned over to LAPD, were not there—confirmation that the critical files and
witness interviews naming George Hodel had been "sanitized" long ago. A full year
would pass (spring 2004) before Detective Carr would go to the DA's office, copy the
hundreds of documents, and begin to realize George Hodel's connection to the murders.
† At the time she worked for GHH, Marion Herwood Keyes was also a renowned
costume designer for the film studios, and was credited for her work in many well-
known films of the day such as *Gaslight, The Picture of Dorian Gray, The Clock,* and *The
Postman Always Rings Twice.*

George Hodel tell both Ruth and Marion that he would "like to father a child of every nationality."

Upon learning of Ruth Spaulding's death in 1945, Florence contacted George Hodel to ask him what had happened and how she had died. She was placed on hold for forty-five minutes, but Dr. Hodel never came back to the phone. Later, she had a meeting in San Francisco with Ruth's sister, who refused to talk about the death or provide any details. Ruth's sister did, however, query Florence about Dr. Hodel, saying, "What was going on there?" Florence had been unaware of Ruth's affair with Father, but believes it could have started after she left the office, sometime in 1943. April 1944 was the last time she saw Ruth Spaulding, who visited her on a trip to San Francisco. She described Ruth as "tall and slender, a kind person with an understanding nature, who had a burning desire to become a writer." At the end of our conversation, Florence told me what a special friend Ruth had been to her, and how much she "missed and loved her."

In a *Los Angeles Evening Herald Express* article dated May 10, 1945, Ruth Spaulding's name appeared, identified as one of no fewer than ten Los Angeles suicides that had occurred over a three-day period. Below is an excerpt from that article:

## 3 MORE SUICIDES

### L.A. POLICE STARTLED BY WAVE

Three more persons today had ended their own lives in the Los Angeles area, pressing police into an investigation of motives behind the unusual number of suicides which has swept the city since V.E. Day. . . .

Ruth Spaulding, 25, of 1206 West Second street, died last night in Georgia Street Receiving Hospital from an overdose of sleeping tablets, police said.

Now, finally in possession of my father's secretary's name and date of death, I conducted an immediate follow-up at the L.A. County Hall of Records and the L.A. Coroner's Office, where I was able to obtain Ruth Spaulding's death certificate and the coroner's cover sheet. All other coroner's reports, including the autopsy, were missing. However, the surviving documents provided enough information to make the link. Here is the information gleaned from the official reports:

## Coroner's Register No. 21234

In 1945 Ruth Spaulding, age 27 and single, lived at 1206 W. 2nd Street in downtown Los Angeles. [This was within easy walking distance of both Dr. Hodel's 7th Street medical office and his office at the L.A. County Health Department.] The reports, while not giving the name of her employer, list her job as "Secretary at a clinic." On May 9, 1945, at 11:45 P.M., she was brought into Georgia Street Receiving Hospital by an unidentified person(s). Unconscious and in a deep coma, she died in less than an hour. Preliminary diagnosis was "suspected ingestion of a lethal dose of barbital poisoning." No exact time of death was listed but the Coroner's report indicated that their office was notified by Georgia Street Medical staff of the death on May 10, 1945, at "12:45 A.M." LAPD was called to the hospital and took a preliminary death report under DR# 72-408.*

In "The Aftermath" chapter, I suggested that the bugged/transcribed conversation of February 18, 1950, between George Hodel and Baron Herringer, in which my father talked about the murder of his secretary, may have referred to another date, time, and location. (See footnote page 471.) Based on what we now know, clearly it did.

Let us reexamine those statements in the light of the 1945 Spaulding death investigation.

Wire recordings, Franklin House, 5121 Franklin Avenue. (Notes, punctuation, and spellings reproduced as they originally appeared.)

2/18/50 Hodel speaking to Baron Herringer
7:35P     "Supposin' I did kill the Black Dahliah. They couldn't prove

---

* I made a formal request to LAPD for information and a copy of the Spaulding death report and the related investigation involving my father. Their search for reports proved negative: "nothing in file." They advised that most "nonhomicide" reports from that time period have been disposed of as a matter of routine policy.

it now. They can't talk to my Secretary anymore because she's dead."

7:45P     (Hodel continues conversation with Baron Herringer) "Realize there was nothing I could do put a pillow over her head, and cover her with a blanket. Get a taxi. Call Georgia Street Receiving Hospital right away. Expired at 12:39. They thought there was something fishy. Anyway, now they may have figured it out. Killed her. Maybe I did kill my Secretary. . . ."

Compared to the now-known facts, my father's statements leave no doubt. George Hodel was not, as some critics have speculated, just toying and taunting the police. His 1950 recorded conversation clearly refers to the 1945 overdose of Ruth Spaulding. They are very real admissions to a very real crime. With these missing pieces, we can now easily piece together the scenario.

In 1944–45, George Hodel, divorced from my mother, was dating and romancing his L.A. County Health Department secretary, Ruth Spaulding, as well as other women, including Elizabeth Short.[*] We know that during this period George Hodel broke off his relationship with Ruth. Then, in May 1945, she threatened to reveal damning information about her ex-lover through documents she possessed. George Hodel went to her downtown apartment, drugged her, called Dorero to the apartment, gave her the incriminating documents, and ordered her to "burn them." My mother did as she was told, leaving her ex-husband with the unconscious but "still breathing" victim.[†] Once Ruth became comatose, Father called for a taxi and took her to the Georgia

---

[*] Based on newly discovered documents found in the DA file relating to Elizabeth Short's autopsy, we now know she had a Bartholin's gland cyst. The Bartholin's gland is a tiny organ on each of the labia (vaginal lips) near the opening of the vagina. If the cysts become infected they are usually very tender. Infected cysts can be caused by sexually transmitted germs. Several (not all) of her intimate boyfriends stated to detectives that she did not seem to enjoy sexual intercourse with them. This diagnosis could well explain why. It also introduces the very real possibility that Elizabeth Short could have originally met Dr. Hodel at his VD clinic, where she may have sought treatment for this problem.

[†] This single act would make her vulnerable to being considered an accessory or accomplice to murder, and I am sure my father used it to his full advantage. It was his leverage to keep her silent about whom and what she knew. The threat of "If I go to prison, you go with me" was enough to compel her silence and have her stonewall DA investigators.

Street Receiving Hospital. She was dead in less than an hour. In the transcripts, with his perfect photographic memory, he even recalls the exact time of death: "Expired at 12:39." Rules required the hospital staff to call the coroner's office as soon as practical after death. Georgia Street Receiving staff called the coroner at *12:45 A.M., only six minutes after her death.*

In his 1950 confession to his crime, my father not only admits his guilt in overdosing* Ruth Spaulding, but also connects himself to the murder of Elizabeth Short. The meaning of "Supposin' I did kill the Black Dahliah. They couldn't prove it now. They can't talk to my Secretary anymore because she's dead" now becomes clear. Had he not overdosed Ruth Spaulding, she would have been alive some twenty months later, and available as someone the police *would talk to:* a living witness (and as a woman scorned, very willing) who would not only reveal that George Hodel and Elizabeth Short were dating, but possibly also reveal their patient-doctor relationship.

## Washington Boulevard Hotel and "Mr. Barnes"

In an earlier chapter,[†] I identified two key witnesses and a specific location as playing an important role in the Black Dahlia murder in the critical first days of the investigation: Mr. and Mrs. Johnson, the owners of a downtown Los Angeles hotel at 300 East Washington Boulevard. As noted, on January 12, 1947 (three days before Elizabeth Short's body was found), they positively identified Elizabeth as checking into their hotel with a man claiming to be her husband. Using the name "Mr. Barnes," he informed the Johnsons that "he and his wife were from Hollywood." Check-in was the only time they saw Elizabeth. However, "Mr. Barnes" returned three days later, January 15, the morning that her body was discovered. Mr. Johnson made a joking remark to "Mr.

---

* This 1945 suspected overdosing of Ruth Spaulding by George Hodel is the first of three to be identified and documented in this investigation. The second was also a police-reported drugging of his girlfriend Lillian Lenorak in 1950. The third was the knockout drug given to his fourteen-year-old granddaughter Deborah at a Beverly Hills hotel in 1969, where he took her to his room to "recover" and then undressed the unconscious girl and took salacious nude photographs while she slept.

† Chapter 12, pages 158–159.

Barnes" that "he hadn't seen him in several days, and he thought he must be dead," whereupon the man immediately became agitated and nervous and fled. The Johnsons were shown photographs taken from the victim's luggage and positively identified both the victim and a *separate* male photo as being "Mr. Barnes." (The Johnsons would later inform the press that the man they had identified "was connected to a foreign government.")

In their competitive rush for a scoop, the L.A. newspapers initially created some confusion over the Johnsons' photo identifications.

In exhibit 83 we see the *Los Angeles Examiner* headlining the story on January 22, 1947. Page 2 shows the Johnsons holding and viewing

## Exhibit 83

a strip photograph (seen at the right), which was enlarged by the newspaper. The caption reads, "Mr. and Mrs. William Johnson who identified photos of Beth Short and a man as the couple who registered in their hotel Jan. 12." In fact, the Johnsons' only identification was of Elizabeth Short. "Mr. Barnes" was identified from a separate photo found in her luggage. Because of the potential for confusion, the following day the *Examiner* reprinted the photograph with a caption clarifying that the ID related solely to Elizabeth Short. It read, "CLEW-*The Los Angeles Examiner* used this picture to enable owners of an East Washington Boulevard hotel to identify Elizabeth Short as having registered at hotel. Man is unidentified." The article went on to inform readers that police were continuing their search for "Mr. Barnes."

It is obvious that from the outset the Johnsons never identified, nor did the police and press believe, that the young man in the strip photo was "Mr. Barnes." Had the Johnsons actually identified the young man in the photo, he would have become Public Enemy No. 1. I believe the separate photograph the Johnsons identified was my exhibit 10,* the photograph of Dr. George Hodel most likely mailed to Elizabeth from China in 1946 and subsequently found in her luggage. It shows my father in civilian clothes standing among the Chinese generals, which would explain the couple's "connecting him to a foreign government."†

## The "Unidentified Man"

Because the identity of the young man with Elizabeth Short in the strip photo has been kept secret by LAPD for almost sixty years, it has become part of the mysterious Dahlia lore. Some say he was Mr.

* Page 76.
† The Johnsons' reference to the "man being connected to a foreign government" most likely came from their identification of him in the photograph. LAPD detectives would not volunteer this information to civilian witnesses, so they had to have *seen* the connection. Exhibit 10 shows that connection. It is also interesting to note that in the DA transcripts, in the days immediately before he fled the country, George Hodel makes statements to Baron Herringer about the Black Dahlia and a picture the police have of him and a girl, though he "thought he had destroyed all of them" (page 477). Is this a reference to exhibit 10, a picture in police custody, he had sent to Elizabeth Short?

Barnes, the actual killer; others believe he was the guilt-ridden writer of a suicide note left on the beach next to a pair of men's trousers and shoes, who in March 1947 allegedly walked out into the ocean and drowned himself. Others believe he was Elizabeth's secret lover. Actually, he was none of the above. My latest investigation has revealed his true identity. In mid-November 2004, I tracked him down and interviewed him. He is a midwesterner, a good and decent man who spoke with me openly. Here for the first time is his story, which tells of his brief encounter with Elizabeth Short as she passed through his city on her way to California. For the sake of his privacy, let us call him "Gerald Moss." He is now eighty-three years old. Gerald met Elizabeth in Indianapolis, Indiana, in 1945, at the end of World War II.[*] He was twenty-four, she twenty-two. Attracted by her striking beauty, Gerald struck up a conversation with her:

> I met Elizabeth Short in the Circle, which is in the downtown part of town. She was beautiful, and we started talking and sort of hit it off. Everybody was celebrating the end of the war. We went to one of those booths and had our picture taken together. You know the kind, where you put in fifteen cents and out it pops. Elizabeth was wearing a black dress and I had on a light tan sport coat, but no tie. I gave her the picture of us.

From downtown, the couple took a bus to a popular local eatery. As Gerald recalls it:

> We stopped and got a bite to eat and were together maybe all of two hours before she went on by herself. I gave her my telephone number and asked her to call me when she got to California, but she never did. I was never in the military service. I had hay fever so bad that it kept me out. They were afraid if they let me in, I'd wake up the enemy. Back then I was working at General Motors as a machinist.

Gerald went on to say that a friend happened to see his picture in the newspaper with Elizabeth Short, read the story about her murder,

---

[*] His memory may be faulty on this, as my source information indicated they met in 1946.

and called him. Gerald immediately telephoned the L.A. police. As he tells it:

> After my best friend Tracy told me about my picture being found in her billfold, I called the police right away and told them that the person the newspapers called "the unidentified man" was me, but I had never been to Los Angeles. I told them how Elizabeth and I had just met those few hours in Indianapolis, and that was it.

Gerald Moss doesn't remember being recontacted by the police since he spoke with them back in 1947. The nearly sixty-year myth and mystery surrounding the "unidentified man" is here reduced to its simple truth: a chance two-hour meeting, accompanied by some friendly talk and "a bite to eat," as Elizabeth Short passed through a midwestern town.

## LAPD—the Sound of Silence

> Hodel's hardcover book was pretty compelling. Then, when all the transcripts and stuff came out from the D.A.'s office, that took it over the top for me. That would have been enough for me to bring a case against Dr. Hodel.
>
> —LAPD deputy chief James S. McMurray
> (ret.) Chief of Detectives
> *Los Angeles Times Magazine*, November 21, 2004

October 2004 was a high-water-mark month for the Dahlia investigation. The rising crescendo of media pressure finally took its toll on LAPD. For fifty-seven years the department had been hiding behind a wall of silence. The mantra was: "The Black Dahlia murder remains unsolved and is an active case. Because it is still 'open' we cannot release any information." Absolute silence prevailed.

As a direct result of two major stories about to appear on CBS and in the *Los Angeles Times*, LAPD chief William Bratton ordered his Robbery-Homicide detectives to prepare for questions and meet the press. On October 28, 2004, this historic meeting was held at Parker Center, the police administrative building. LAPD Robbery-

Homicide detectives Brian Carr and David Lambkin (detective III in charge of the Cold Case Unit) did not agree to appear on camera, but would take questions from journalists. LAPD questioned-document examiner Karen Chiarodit was also present. The three journalists present were Paul Teetor, from the *Los Angeles Times Magazine*, and Erin Moriarty and David Browning, representing CBS's *48 Hours*. The interview lasted two hours.

Here is a summary of what was learned.[†] LAPD confirmed that all of the physical evidence in the 1947 Elizabeth Short "Black Dahlia" murder had, in their words, "disappeared." Further, the physical evidence in the 1947 Jeanne French and 1948 Gladys Kern murders has also "disappeared." Detectives advised that since all the evidence is missing, no DNA comparison could be made to Dr. George Hodel.

The missing evidence in the Elizabeth Short "Black Dahlia" investigation would include:

- Original address book belonging to the victim mailed to press by the suspect
- Victim's identification and personal photographs sent in by the Avenger
- Purse and shoes belonging to Elizabeth Short
- Original twelve hand-printed notes mailed to police by "Black Dahlia Avenger" (potential DNA)
- Black hair follicles found on her body believed to belong to the suspect (victim's hair had been eliminated) (potential DNA)
- Man's "Croton military watch" found near victim's body at the crime scene
- "Promise is a promise" telegram and follow-up investigation of identity of sender

Missing evidence in the 1948 Gladys Kern stabbing murder would include:

* Ms. Chiarodit, while questioning the methodology of handwriting expert Hannah McFarland and stating that in her opinion McFarland's analysis had "lots of holes in it," nevertheless offered *no opinion* of her own. When asked if she could eliminate Dr. Hodel as the writer of the notes, she answered simply "No."

† Through reinterviews of me by both Erin Moriarty and Paul Teetor, in their follow-up preparation for the television and print articles that would appear the following month.

BLACK DAHLIA AVENGER

- Unique one-of-a-kind jungle knife (*tentatively* identified by Joe Barrett, taken from Hodel residence)
- White handkerchief left at crime scene by suspect (potential DNA)
- Original handwritten note mailed by suspect to press from same mailbox as 1947 Dahlia note (potential DNA)
- Photograph of unidentified male found in victim's desk

Missing evidence in the 1947 Jeanne French "Red Lipstick" murder would include:

- Black hair follicles belonging to the suspect (found under victim's fingernails) (potential DNA)
- White handkerchief left at crime scene by suspect (potential DNA)
- Purse, shoes, and clothing belonging to victim

When asked by reporters to explain how critical physical evidence in L.A.'s most notorious unsolved murder could "just disappear," the detectives explained that "sometimes these things happen." Speaking as a former LAPD homicide supervisor, I would, under normal conditions, have to agree with them. Physical evidence does inadvertently get signed off and disposed of when it shouldn't. However, there is nothing routine about this case, and only a *select few* detectives had access to the Dahlia evidence *and files*. Disposing of this evidence was not simply a snafu. But, for the sake of argument, let us assume for a moment that all the physical evidence in *all three murder cases* was inadvertently lost. The detectives' interview goes on to reveal a much more serious problem. Through the question-and-answer process, Carr also confirmed that LAPD is not in possession of critical documents relating to Dr. George Hodel. All of the below *Hodel-related interviews*, identified in the DA files and turned over to LAPD, have also "disappeared" from the Dahlia files. They include:

- Wire surveillance recordings of statements by Dr. George Hodel and admissions of Dr. Hodel to crimes
- Formal written interview/statements made by Dr. Hodel to DA/LAPD detectives in February 1950

- Formal written interview by witness Lillian Lenorak, identifying Dr. Hodel as boyfriend of Elizabeth Short
- Photograph and complete interview of Mr. and Mrs. Johnson wherein they identify "Mr. Barnes" as checking into hotel with victim, Elizabeth Short, two days before the murder
- Formal interview of Mattie Comfort, along with nude photographs of her and Dr. Hodel
- Formal interview of Tamar and statements made to her by my mother, Dorero, connecting George to Elizabeth
- Additional interviews of George Hodel associates known to be interviewed: Fred Sexton, Nita Moladoro, Ellen Taylor, Tarin Gilkey, Ethel Kane, Dorothy Royer, and Rudolph Walthers
- Fingerprint cards on Dr. George Hodel from his felony arrest for incest
- Fingerprint cards on Dr. George Hodel taken for his state medical licensing

To my mind, all this is key in proving my assertion that the LAPD files were sanitized long ago. With the exception of the "single memo" referred to by Carr, there was nothing in the LAPD files mentioning George Hodel *before Carr obtained the DA Hodel files in the spring of 2004.* Carr also said that while the LAPD Dahlia files did contain scientific tests conducted on other suspects (i.e., fingerprint comparisons, handwriting analysis, shoe-size comparison, polygraph examination, photograph or live lineups by witnesses, etc.), none was found on Dr. George Hodel. How then, after becoming the "prime suspect," could he have been eliminated without any further testing? Reporters followed up with a key question. "What cleared Hodel?" Detective Carr replied that he didn't know specifically and that Hodel was cleared by Lieutenant Jemison and the DA's office after they had interviewed various witnesses and associates. Detective Carr and LAPD had no additional information about how he was cleared.*

* This was a critical response by Carr. Prior to this acknowledgment, Carr had always maintained that *"LAPD cleared Dr. Hodel* as being a Dahlia suspect," but would make no further comment. He now informs us that not only do they not have any separate reports on Hodel, but further, LAPD did not participate in any of the Hodel interviews or contacts with his associates, and they have no idea why or how Lieutenant Jemison cleared him. In fact, Jemison did not "clear" Dr. Hodel. His careful wording was "tend to eliminate him."

When the reporters observed that the DA files create more questions than answers, Detective Carr responded, "I somewhat have to agree with you. We're talking about 1950. Things were done a lot different back then than they are now."

At the close of the interview, detectives indicated that since all the physical evidence is missing from the evidence lockers, there is no way to confirm DNA on Dr. Hodel, and therefore the crime cannot be cleared. Several weeks after Detectives Carr and Lambkin met with reporters, LAPD chief William Bratton appeared at a book signing at the Book Soup bookstore in West Hollywood. At the end of his short talk, he took questions. Here is a brief verbatim exchange:

Audience voice: Isn't it about time we released all the information about the Black Dahlia case? [Applause]

Chief Bratton: I just told our Cold Case Squad guys to give it [the Dahlia investigation] up. I'm more concerned about the nine murders we had last week than one going back that many years. . . . I know that is problematic for some people who would like to see it solved. But what would you have to write about if it was solved? Better it go unsolved. There are more and more books being written about it all the time.
[Absolute silence from crowd for ten seconds]

## Blowup

As my Dahlia investigation comes to a close, I again find death imitating art.

Italian director Michelangelo Antonioni's thriller *Blowup*, a seminal film of the 1960s, forced us to think and question lifestyles, mores, art, and the subjectivity of perception, all focused through the lens of a photographer's camera. In the film, a whodunit or wasitdun existentialist mystery, David Hemmings plays a mod fashion photographer who, while strolling through a London park, happens upon and takes photographs of a couple embracing. In developing the photographs, he discovers that his camera has caught a possible murder in progress. Is there a hand showing a man holding a gun in the shrubbery? A dead body? He begins to enlarge small sections of his prints (hence the title), and as they grow, they enhance the mystery as distinct pieces of the puzzle.

Some forty years after seeing this fascinating film, I now find myself cast in the same role of protagonist-photographer. The only difference: we are in the year 2005, and I have traded Hemmings's 35mm Leica for a Hewlett-Packard computer and Adobe Photoshop!

What my investigation has revealed forces me to make public crime photographs that are graphically horrifying. In previous printings of my book I have been able to restrict this aspect of the investigation to verbal descriptions, which though shocking reduced significantly the violence. Hearing is a much kinder sense than sight. For the sake of truth, and the further need to prove my case, I must, I am afraid, cross the line and delve into that darker corner. I would ask that you, my readers, consider yourself a seated juror in a murder trial. Before showing you this evidence, I will do what most prosecutors do in court: apologize for having to show you scenes so violent that they will doubtless shock your senses; but this additionally compelling evidence must be added to our case.

## Blowups 1 and 2: Elizabeth Short Identification

Many readers had no problem with my identification of the two photographs in my father's album. They saw what I saw: a young, beautiful Elizabeth Short, artistically posed. Others were not sure, and a vocal few—mostly with their own agendas—were adamant that the photos were *not* Elizabeth, claiming that her picture and the photos in my father's album were not even similar. Even novelist James Ellroy took the position that my father's photographs were not Elizabeth, but that I had nonetheless solved the case, based on my subsequent findings.

As we know, Elizabeth had many faces. She looks somewhat different in almost every known photograph. In the November 28, 2004, CBS program *Black Dahlia Confidential*, the network aired a photograph of Elizabeth Short that I had never seen. It looked as if it had been taken professionally. In it, she was wearing a blue tam. The day following the broadcast, I asked the CBS producers if they could send me a copy, which they did. Like the *Blowup* photographer, I created high-resolution scans of Elizabeth's face.

One such blowup showed a unique and unusually placed small freckle or mole, clearly visible just over her left eyebrow. Similar examination of the George Hodel photograph showed the same-sized freckle, in the same location. This anatomical anomaly is as distinct as a tattoo, and proves beyond *any* doubt that they are one and the same woman.

*Exhibit 84*

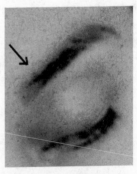
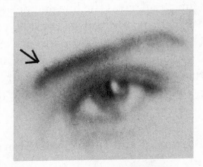

This detail caused me to search my father's second nude photograph, which showed a pronounced freckle centered midforehead, just above the eyebrows. In most of Elizabeth's photographs, this freckle was covered by makeup. However, in the crime-scene photo,

*Exhibit 85*

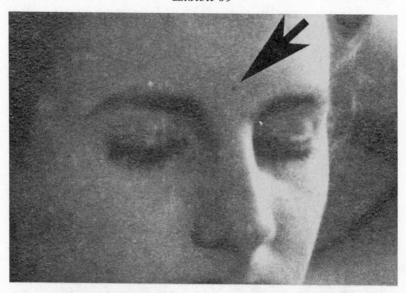

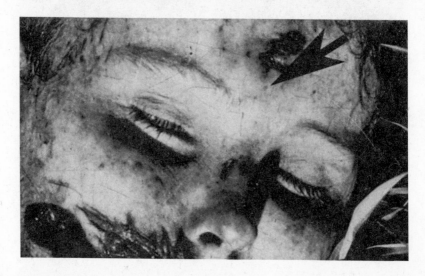

we know, the body had been washed clean. Was the freckle there? Yes. Same size, shape, and location. This is our link to the second photograph.

Exhibit 85a shows a comparison of physical features (nose and mouth) of George Hodel's photograph to Elizabeth Short's police booking photograph, taken some three years earlier. (We recall that at that time she was arrested as an underage minor for being present in a bar where alcohol was being served.) Despite the poor quality of the police photograph, incredibly, yet a third small identifying freckle can be seen on the tip of her nose.

## Blowup 3: Autopsy Photographs—Burn Marks

From the beginning of my investigation, one troubling fact has continued to gnaw at me. The actual coroner's protocol has never been

*Exhibit 85a*

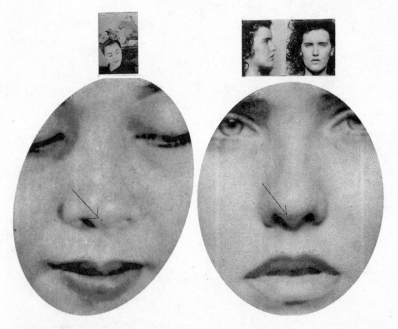

*George Hodel photo, circa 1946, Santa Barbara (angled to match position) (age nineteen)*

*Elizabeth Short booking photo, 1943*

released. Bits and pieces have appeared here and there, but never the complete report. Detective Carr made a public statement that he has never seen it "because it remains locked in the Coroner's Office." Very strange! In all of my homicide cases, I have never *not* possessed a copy of the coroner's protocol in my homicide book. It is basic to any murder investigation. Even in the DA files, it was only referred to—in part. Why? Thanks to the newly discovered crime-scene and autopsy photographs (referred to in "The Aftermath" chapter as being provided to me by Harry Hansen's granddaughter, Judy May) and the miracle of computer technology, I can now present four additional links that further connect my father to the Dahlia murder.

## Burn Marks

When Dr. Paul de River, the LAPD criminal psychiatrist, volunteered to testify before the 1949 grand jury regarding his own investigation into the Dahlia murder, the police department was not happy. He went ahead anyway. He informed the grand jury that he suspected wrongdoing and a possible cover-up, * and was aware of an ongoing turf battle between the Gangster Squad and Homicide detectives. In his secret testimony, he also informed the jurors that Elizabeth Short had been sadistically tortured in many ways, including being burned with a cigarette or cigar.

On the following page are two photocopied excerpts from Lieutenant Jemison's official report, submitted to the 1949 grand jury. On two separate pages, he categorically informs the jury that "there were no cigarette burns on Elizabeth Short's body."[†]

---

* This did not relate to Dr. George Hodel, but rather to Dr. de River's favorite suspect, Leslie Dillon, arrested almost a year earlier (January 1949). Dillon would later be cleared, after it was established that he was in San Francisco at the time of the Dahlia murder.

† We also learn that Dr. de River informed the grand jury the body had been "shaved." In fact, some pubic hair was cut or "shaved" from her body, so this could have been a semantic problem. Further note that no drug tests were performed, as "vital organs had been misplaced or accidentally thrown out."

*Exhibit 86*

page 7

There were no cigarette burns and no tattoo marks
on the body.

Mr. Ray Pinker  of the Crime Laboratory was only able
to acquire a few drops of blood from this body and
typed it as  "A B", which is a rare type of blood
appearing in less than six per cent of the human
bodies.

The officers requested that the Coroner and the County
Chemist analyze the vital organs chemically to determine for one thing whether or not her body contained
narcotics.  At a later date when the officers requested
the results they were informed that these vital organs
had been misplaced and had probably been thrown out
at the time they were cleaning up the laboratory
and further that they had made no analysis.

page 13

On January 12th at 11:30 a.m. Leslie Dillon was released.

Upon examination of the reports of the officers in Homicide
it was found that the body of  Elizabeth Short had not been shaved
as maintained by Dr. DeRiver.

It was found that there were no cigarette burns or other
burns on her body as he had maintained.

That statement is false. Lieutenant Jemison either knowingly
lied or was kept in the dark by LAPD detectives as to the actual condition of the body.

In fact there were by my count eight or nine large cigar or cigarette burn marks‘ clearly visible on the body. Exhibit 87 on the next
page is a never-before-shown autopsy photograph of Elizabeth Short.
The burn marks are clearly visible on the lower back.[†]

Also included in the DA file was an early LAPD investigative
summary written immediately following the discovery of the body.
Elizabeth was still a "Jane Doe," and therefore a detailed description

* At my request, D. P. Lyle, M.D., examined the autopsy photographs and provided
the following opinion: "The lesions high on her back appear to be moles and the lesions
on her mid-back are most likely traumatic in nature. They appear to be cigarette burns,
which are partially healed. They could be only hours old but more likely are 1 to 3 days
old, since they seem to display some degree of healing in the central portion of each."
Dr. Lyle is a practicing cardiologist, as well as a nationally respected forensics expert and
a mystery writer. A consultant for *CSI*, he has written numerous books on forensics, his
latest being *Forensics for Dummies* (2004).

† The numbers relate to identifying mole marks, and *are not* cigarette burns.

*Exhibit 87*

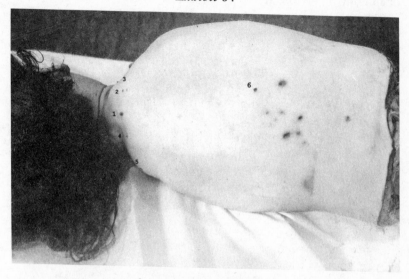

*burn marks enlarged below*

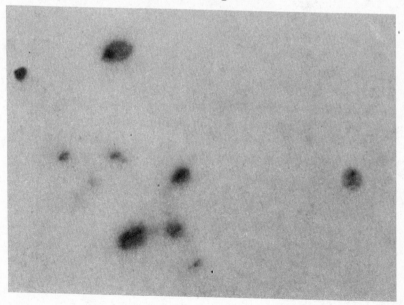

of all body marks and scars was provided. I quote directly from page 2 of that document, exactly as it was typed:*

> At 7:25PM, January 15, 1947, a description was circulated seeking identity of this girl, description being as follows: age indeterminable, young; ht 5'3"; weight 118#; all fingernails down to the quick; no bunions on feet; hair shaved on legs below the knees; hair shaved under arms; grayish green eyes; narrow, small nose, uptipped slightly; small upper lip; vaccination scar left leg between knee and thigh; small scar above left knee; 1" in length scar about 1 ½ inches to right of navel; brown hair, indication of being hennaed; extremely high forehead or hair line; no ear lobes, ears not pierced; 1 large wart center of back of neck about even with shoulder line [1]; 2 small warts to the right of the above about 1" [2 and 3]; 1 small wart on back, center of shoulder [4]; 1 large mole on left shoulder [5]; 1 wart on back, center of back, about 1" to right of medial line [6]; 1 operational scar 3 ½" in length, right side of back about 4th rib from bottom such as made for deflating a lung in T.B.

This careful documentation prohibits any possibility of interpreting the burn marks as preexisting birthmarks, and further establishes that their existence was intentionally left out of all reports.

On page 3 of his report, Lieutenant Jemison makes the following recommendation to the grand jury:

On the date of this report there are one hundred and seven remaining possible suspects after a definite elimination of two hundred and nine suspects. There have been nineteen suspects who have confessed to the murder of Elizabeth Short.

After examination of the files and evidence it appears that the investigative effort should be continued and concentrated on the following suspects:

* Bracketed numbers (1–6) in text and those in the photograph were inserted by me to identify wart and mole locations.

Leslie Dillon—Mark Hanson [sic]—Carl Balsiger—Glen Wolfe—Henry Hubert Hoffman—*Dr. George Hodel* [emphasis mine].

Also the victim's doctor, as he is a suspect and he is unknown. (Victim has stated to several persons that she was taking treatments from a Los Angeles Doctor for female trouble and asthma just prior to her death.)*

At the close of his report to the 1949 grand jury, Jemison makes the following remarkably candid observations:

These records and reports which were obtained from the officers of the police department and the Chief of Police indicated to the undersigned that the present administrators of the police department are of the opinion that there was an error made on the part of the preceding administrators when they assigned the Gangster Squad and Dr. Paul De River [sic] as psychiatrist to investigate the Short murder. They appear to be of the opinion that the Homicide Division officers should have had control over it at all times.

The LAPD records and reports indicate some stupidity and carelessness on the part of some of the more inexperienced officers who were working on the case from time to time, but as of this report dated October 28, 1949[†] there has not been found any indication of payoff, misconduct or concealment of facts on the part of any officers.

It is the consensus of Officers Ed Barrett, Jack Smyre, F.A. Brown and the undersigned that there is insufficient evidence as of

---

* As indicated earlier, it is my opinion that Elizabeth Short's "unidentified downtown doctor" and my father were one and the same. We know that Lieutenant Jemison's euphemistic term "female trouble" refers to her Bartholin's gland cysts. This could have originated as a sexually transmitted disease. The logical location for her to seek treatment? My father's First Street VD clinic. Further, note that of Lieutenant Jemison's five named suspects, Dr. George Hodel is the *only one* possessing the prerequisite medical skill and knowledge to commit the crime.

† Three weeks before the submission of this report, my father was arrested by LAPD for incest and "held to answer" in a preliminary hearing; his superior court trial would begin in two weeks. In the next three-month period, Lieutenant Jemison would identify George Hodel as the prime suspect in the Dahlia murder, initiate surveillance, and install the microphones for the bugging of our residence. With the microphones and bugging still in place, George Hodel would flee the United States.

this date, October 28, 1949, upon which any suspect could now be
brought to trial for the murder of Elizabeth Short.

> Respectfully submitted,
> Frank B. Jemison

## Blowup 4: Crime-Scene Trace Evidence

We know from 1947 reports that black hair follicles were found *on Elizabeth Short's nude body at the crime scene* and that LAPD criminalist Ray
Pinker made a microscopic comparison to the victim's hair and found
it to be different. Detectives theorized that it came from her killer. We
have also been informed by detectives that the hair follicles have "disappeared" from the evidence locker and no DNA is available. Actually,
they are only partially correct. Again, I performed high-resolution

*Exhibit 88*

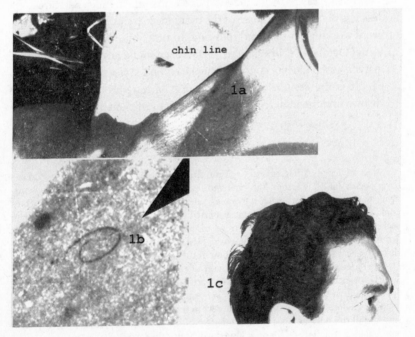

scans of the Harry Hansen/Judy May crime-scene photographs and was able to locate one of the original samples.

Exhibit 88 (1a) shows the original hair follicle on Elizabeth Short's upper chest just below the chin line. Photo 1b is an enlargement of that same hair follicle, showing it to be curly and black in color. 1c depicts George Hodel's hair as it appeared in his October 1949 booking photo for incest. Even though LAPD has "lost" this original trace evidence, preventing DNA analysis, we can still observe that the follicle found on her body matches and is consistent with my father's hair.

## Blowup 5: The Watch

Encouraged by my discoveries, I continued my macabre search, using twenty-first-century software to pixelate myself into the past. My screen monitor whisked me back. I was there: 1947 Los Angeles, 3800 block South Norton Avenue. The Black Dahlia crime scene. I could view it better, closer and cleaner, than even any of the on-scene detectives had seen it. I moved slowly from the sidewalk to the grass, then through the grass, to the paper cement sack. South to the body. Starting with the head I moved downward. Quadrant by quadrant, inch by inch. I reached the cleanly bisected upper torso. Something shined in my monitor. Sunlight reflecting off exposed bone? No, I think not. I zoomed in closer. It was an object, but blurred. I would have to rescan the original photograph at a higher resolution. That done, I zoomed in for a second look. Yes, definitely an object. It appeared mechanical. Not bone, not tissue, what was it? Closer. The object was perfectly round, approximately one inch in diameter. Dark faced with a lighter edging around the circumference. A small strip or band could be seen just to the right, angling off in a four o'clock position. It was a watch. A man's wristwatch, carefully placed *inside the body cavity*. More of my father's "art." Daddy the Dadaist. More of his surrealist's juxtaposition to shock the viewer.

But why no mention in the reports? Was this another LAPD secret? Perhaps not. We recall that a man's Croton military watch was found at the crime scene. Was this the Croton watch found by police

*Exhibit 89*

*Top photo—crime scene shows object that appears to be a man's wristwatch*
*Bottom photo—taken at coroner's office—shows object missing*

recruits who canvassed the crime scene a week after the body's removal? Had the watch gone unnoticed and fallen into the grass when
the body was moved to the coroner's wagon for transportation? I
went to the coroner's photographs. Amazingly, they showed the view
I needed to make the comparison. My blowup showed it was gone.
The object was no longer in the cavity. There are only two possibilities. The Croton was a separate watch, unrelated to the murder and
coincidentally found in the vacant lot, or it was the same watch. I find

it difficult to believe that the on-scene detectives did not see the watch. I recall photographs showing them looking directly inside the body. They must have seen it.

My father's placing a watch inside the body cavity was no casual afterthought. It was his surreal signature, and yet another imitation of and homage to Man Ray. It represented a third crime-scene clue, connecting his "work" to Man Ray's photograph *The Minotaur* and painting *The Lovers*. The complete original title to *The Lovers* is actually *A l'heure de l'Observatoire—Les amoureux (Observatory Time— The Lovers)*. The woman's lips suspended across the horizon in Man Ray's painting are of his former lover, Lee Miller, who left him in 1932 after a three-year affair. In the painting, in part, he has created a painful reminder of his own lost love. "Its title exemplifies Gertrude Stein's insistence upon embodying 'time in the composition.'"* Man Ray embodies time in his painting by including the Paris Observatory, through which the Paris meridian passed. In a second famous work, Man Ray again fragmented Lee Miller's body parts and attached a photograph of her eye to a metronome (again the representation of time) and titled it *Object of Destruction*. In George Hodel's "painting" we now discover that time has *literally been embodied* by the shocking juxtaposition of a man's watch placed inside the cadaver of his own fragmented lost love, his *object destroyed*. How ironic that one of his most dramatic touches would go unnoticed and be held back from the general public. This must have been a painful loss for the publicity-hungry artist-avenger.


## Blowup 6: The Earring

I had found the trace-evidence hair follicle on the body from the crime-scene photographs. Was I missing anything? To make sure, I decided to recheck the remaining few photographs taken at the coroner's office. More scans, this time from foot to head. I moved slowly upward, forced to endure *in magnification* the many visible horrors of my father's sadism. I finished with the head. I had seen enough. I reached to turn

* Baldwin, Neil, *Man Ray: American Artist*, p. 172. New York, Clarkson N. Potter Inc., 1988.

*Exhibit 90*

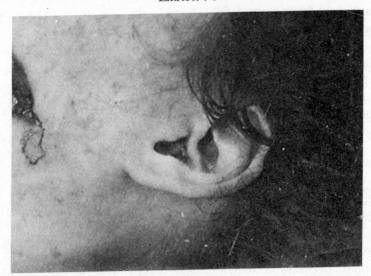

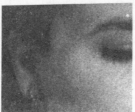
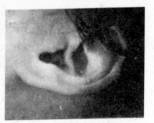

| *autopsy 90-degree* | *George Hodel photo 1* | *Short autopsy photo* |
| *rotation* | | |

off my screen, and again an object caught my eye. Perhaps it was just a small white mark on the nearly sixty-year-old print? I zoomed in on it. Something was there. Inside her left ear. Too blurred to see. Again, I rescanned with higher resolution. Another blowup. Now I could make it out. An earring. But not just any earring. It was hers. *The same earring Elizabeth Short wore in my father's nude photograph.* Small circular pearls. An additional link to the second photograph!*

* Because some of the clarity and definition seen on a computer monitor are lost through the print reproduction, I will make some of these exhibits available for better viewing through my Web site at blackdahliaavenger.com.

This link closes the circle. We now have *both photographs* in my father's album connecting him to Elizabeth, through physical identification and physical evidence. We have viewed and compared the actual hair follicle, photographically preserved and found on Elizabeth's nude body, identical to George Hodel's curly black hair. We have seen my father's sardonic and surreal placement of a watch and Elizabeth's earring, the same earring worn in my father's photograph, inside the body. And we have documentation of law enforcement's deliberate misstatement and falsification of evidentiary facts ("no burn marks on the victim's body") formally presented to a seated grand jury.

We are left with one final question: the coroner's report, locked and never released to the public. What more can it reveal? Does it contain the evidence as shown in the photographs? Do the watch, and Elizabeth's earring, still exist? Or has the full and complete report, along with the physical evidence, also simply "disappeared"?

LAPD's Chief Bratton has told us his department is off the case. "I just told our Cold Case Squad guys to give it [the Black Dahlia investigation] up." All the LAPD evidence has disappeared. There is no "ongoing investigation" and there are no more secrets. The shadows are gone and the silence is broken. That should effectively remove any objection to a public viewing of this final document. The coroner's protocol is not held within any LAPD (city) file, but is locked within the purview of the county. Two years ago, District Attorney Steve Cooley opened his county vault and let me and the public read the "Hodel File." Perhaps he will now take a second step and order the coroner's vault open as well. We shall see.*

Steve Hodel
Los Angeles, California
August 2005

---

* On July 13, 2005, I conducted an interview with UK television journalist Sam Kiley for a documentary on the Dahlia story, to air in Great Britain in December 2005. During that interview, I was advised by Kiley that he had contacted personnel from the L.A. Coroner's Office who had agreed to provide him with a copy of the complete Protocol. However, a subsequent search for the records revealed that all the files "have disappeared." Coroner's officials added that they had no idea how or when the Elizabeth Short file became "lost."

# Acknowledgments

THE PREPARATION OF THIS BOOK has been most difficult, not only because of the obvious personal conflicts that arose from the discovery of each new murder, which like distress beacons kept rising to the surface in a sea of crimes, but also because of my new and unexpected role as narrator, and the *sub rosa* nature of the investigation, which required the strictest secrecy.

A number of people need to be recognized for their help in telling the story. Most were unaware of their assistance, but all should now know that their individual contribution, small or large, aided me in piecing together the many scattered thoughtprints.

First is Roberta McCreary, who as friend/confidante/researcher was at my side and in the loop from the very beginning. Roberta shared my shocks and sorrows, and her diligence and careful review of hundreds of microfilm articles at UCLA and other Los Angeles libraries unquestionably resulted in many murders being found that would otherwise have gone unnoticed. No crime investigator could ask for a better "partner."

In Sydney, Australia, my deep gratitude goes to the constant and true friendship of Murray and Jodi Rose, who sent their strength and love from Down Under.

In Bellingham, Washington, a special thanks to my good friends: Dennis, Dave, Debra, Ruth, Barbara, and Joanie at the law firm of Anderson, Connell, and Murphy, for their mutual support. Dennis's dual role as personal friend and objective counselor provided much necessary balance. A big hug and thank you to attorney Jill Bernstein for her further support and encouragement along the bumpy road. To my ex-wife, Marsha, the mother of my children, who kept her word and respected my need for confidentiality, my heartfelt thanks. To longtime friend and mystery writer Mark Schorr in Portland, many thanks for the jump-starts. Professional kudos to my forensic expert Hannah McFarland in Seattle, who, along with her handwriting analysis, provided me with new insights into her specialized field.

In Los Angeles, to Head Deputy District Attorney Stephen Kay, whom I have known and respected as a professional colleague for thirty years, I say: Stephen, your contributions to the case have been inestimable. Thank you for your time, objectivity, ethics, and decades of dedicated public service to our city.

To my ex-ex-wife, Carole Hodel, and Ron Wong, thank you both for your help and encouragement. Gracias to my ex-partner Bill Everheart and his wife Judy for providing me with some "retreat time" in their beautiful Big Bear home.

To my literary agent, Bill Birnes, and his wife, Nancy, a special thanks for their early recognition of the importance of the story, at a time when not all the evidence was in, and for Bill's persistence in helping find the right publisher.

Special thanks to my editors/publishers, Dick and Jeannette Seaver, at Arcade Publishing. Dick's Herculean labors, experienced editing, reorganization, substitution of happier words and cleaner structure, and translation of "cop report writing" into a more palatable language have been invaluable. Arcade editor Greg Comer also deserves thanks for his diligence and dedication throughout the long editing process.

My deep gratitude to those who contributed so much without knowing: "Mary Moe," "Bill Buck," Kirk Mellecker, Myrl McBride, and my mother's old and my newfound friend, Joe Barrett.

Thank you, sister Tamar. Know that my heart is filled with joy now that *your* truth has at long last been told. Duncan, I know these revelations will bring you and the rest of our extended family much sorrow. Try to find solace in knowing that light dispels darkness. To Kelvin, I can now say, understand, dear brother, that it wasn't *you:* our father was incapable of loving anyone. To my two sons and to all future generations of our family, I say: Wear the Hodel name with courage and pride. Trust in *your own* inner guidance, and know that right motive, followed by right action, is the key to finding happiness and understanding life's mysteries. To my Filipino brother and sisters, Teresa, Diane, Mark, and their mother, Hortensia: while our contacts have been few, and our estrangements many, yet we are united through a common destiny.

To the wronged dead, and the many heroes and heroines in our story, my posthumous gratitude to you all. To LAPD Sergeant Charles Stoker: Thank you, Officer. Though it cost you everything — your name, your profession, and your peace — you single-handedly stood up and spoke out against the many abuses and corruptions of your day. Thanks too to the 1949 renegade grand jury and its foreman, Harry Lawson, for their brave stand against the corrupt politics of the time. Like Stoker, they saw and knew the truth, but were also branded and silenced.

Also to be acknowledged is the Fourth Estate, with its many voices, such as city editors James Richardson and Agness Underwood, whose bold editorials fought for the truth in hopes of protecting the public interest. Thanks too to the press's many unnamed reporters, whose relentless investigative prying and searching would eventually assist in the ultimate solutions, by documenting many of the connecting links to the serial killings. History has many such unsung heroes, men and women who were never, and never will be, recognized for the important roles they played in serving as guides to future truths.

Every now and then, something does come forward and present itself as a *curiosity*. It may be something as simple and unsuspecting as a fifty-year-old photograph. A two-by-three photo in a private family album. A never-seen or long-forgotten picture of an attractive young woman with raven hair and a natural innocence, waiting for some mental dust to fall upon the silver plate that hides her face, which then raises the picture's latent, dormant potential and reveals it to be a thoughtprint. A thoughtprint, containing the answer to a riddle wrapped in a mystery inside an enigma.

In addition to those already acknowledged in the "Aftermath" chapter, I feel I must thank a few people who contributed greatly to my investigative findings detailed therein.

To Los Angeles County District Attorney Steve Cooley and his public information officer, Sandi Gibbons, thank you both for your many courtesies and for sharing critical documents.

To Los Angeles Police Department Assistant Chief Sharon Papa, Chief of Detectives James McMurray, and Commander Jim Tatreau, thank you for allowing me to present the facts, and for listening with open minds.

To television producer and investigative journalist David Browning and his wife, Suzanne, thank you for sharing your minds and opening your hearts to assist in the pursuit of truth.

My respect and gratitude go to the modern-day representatives of the Fourth Estate—people like Steve Lopez of the *Los Angeles Times*, Andy Murr of *Newsweek*, Linda Deutsch of the Associated Press, Emily Weiner of the *Bellingham Herald*, and Josh Mankiewicz of *Dateline NBC*, who through their reportage in print and on television helped bring my story before the public.

Finally, a heartfelt "well done" to all the production and support staff at HarperCollins Publishers, with special thanks to editor David Semanki, who, in his best "hold the press" voice, kept stretching deadlines to allow for incorporation of my last-minute "Aftermath" findings.

# Bibliography

Anger, Kenneth. *Hollywood Babylon*. San Francisco: Stonehill Publishing, 1975.

———. *Hollywood Babylon II*. New York: NAL Penguin, 1984.

Bonelli, William G. *Billion Dollar Blackjack*. Beverly Hills: Civic Research Press, 1954.

Blanche, Tony, and Brad Schreiber. *Death in Paradise: An Illustrated History of the Los Angeles County Department of Coroner*. Los Angeles: General Publishing Group, 1998.

Breton, André. *Manifestoes of Surrealism*. Ann Arbor: University of Michigan Press, Ann Arbor Paperbacks, 1972.

Bruccoli, Matthew J., and Richard Layman. *A Matter of Crime*. Vol. I. San Diego: Harcourt Brace Jovanovich, 1987.

Carter, Vincent A. *LAPD's Rogue Cops*. Lucerne Valley, Calif.: Desert View Books, 1993.

Chandler, Raymond. *The Blue Dahlia: A Screenplay*. Chicago: Southern Illinois University Press, 1976.

Cohen, Mickey. *In My Own Words*. Englewood Cliffs, N.J.: Prentice-Hall, 1975.

Demaris, Ovid. *The Last Mafioso*. New York: Times Books, 1981.

De Rivers, J. Paul, M.D. *The Sexual Criminal: A Psychoanalytical Study*. Burbank, Calif.: Bloat, 1949; rev. ed. 2000.

Domanick, Joe. *To Protect and to Serve: The L.A.P.D.'s Century of War in the City of Dreams*. New York: Pocket Books, 1994.

Douglas, John, and Mark Olshaker. *The Cases That Haunt Us*. New York: Lisa Drew Books/Scribner, 2000.

———. *Mind Hunter*. New York: Lisa Drew Books/Scribner, 1995.

Ellroy, James. *The Black Dahlia*. New York: Mysterious Press, 1987.

———. *My Dark Places*. New York: Alfred A. Knopf, 1996.

————. *Crime Wave*. New York: Vintage Crime/Black Lizard Vintage Books, 1999.

Fetherling, Doug. *The Five Lives of Ben Hecht*. Toronto: Lester & Orpen, 1977.

Finney, Guy W. *Angel City in Turmoil*. Los Angeles: Amer Press, 1945.

Fowler, Will. *The Young Man from Denver*. Garden City, N.Y.: Doubleday & Company, 1962.

————. *Reporters: Memoirs of a Young Newspaperman*. Malibu, Calif.: Roundtable, 1991.

Giesler, Jerry, and Pete Martin. *The Jerry Giesler Story*. New York: Simon & Schuster, 1960.

Gilmore, John. *Severed: The True Story of the Black Dahlia Murder*. San Francisco: Zanja Press, 1994.

Goodman, Jonathan. *Acts of Murder*. New York: Lyle Stuart Books, Carol Publishing Group, 1986.

Granlund, Nils T. *Blondes, Brunettes, and Bullets*. New York: David McKay, 1957.

Gribble, Leonard. *They Had a Way with Women*. London: Arrow Books, 1967.

Grobel, Lawrence. *The Hustons*. New York: Charles Scribners's Sons, 1989.

Halberstam, David. *The Powers That Be*. New York: Alfred A. Knopf, 1979.

Hall, Angus, ed. *Crimes of Horror*. New York: Phoebus, 1976.

Halleck, Seymour L., M.D. *Psychiatry and the Dilemmas of Crime*. New York: Harper & Row, 1967.

Harris, Martha. *Angelica Huston: The Lady and the Legacy*. New York: St. Martin's Press, 1989.

Hecht, Ben. *Fantazius Mallare: A Mysterious Oath*. Chicago: Pascal Covici, 1922.

————. *The Kingdom of Evil: A Continuation of the Journal of Fantazius Mallare*. Chicago: Pascal Covici, 1924.

Heimann, Jim. *Sins of the City: The Real L.A. Noir*. San Francisco: Chronicle Books, 1999.

Henderson, Bruce, and Sam Summerlin. *The Super Sleuths*. New York: Macmillan, 1976.

Hodel, George Hill. *The New Far East: Seven Nations of Asia*. Hong Kong: Reader's Digest Far East, 1966.

Huston, John. *An Open Book.* New York: Alfred A. Knopf, 1980.

———. *Frankie and Johnny.* New York: Albert and Charles Boni, 1930.

Jeffers, Robinson. *Roan Stallion, Tamar, and Other Poems.* New York: Boni & Liveright, 1925.

Jennings, Dean. *We Only Kill Each Other: The Life and Bad Times of Bugsy Siegel.* Englewood Cliffs, N.J.: Prentice-Hall, 1967.

Kennedy, Ludovic. *The Airman and the Carpenter.* New York: Viking Penguin, 1985.

Keppel, Robert D. *Signature Killers.* New York: Pocket Books, 1997.

Klein, Norman M., and Martin J. Schiesl. *20th Century Los Angeles: Power, Promotion, and Social Conflict.* Claremont, Calif.: Regina Books, 1990.

Knowlton, Janice, and Michael Newton. *Daddy Was the Black Dahlia Killer.* New York: Pocket Books, 1995.

Lane, Brian, and Wilfred Gregg. *The Encyclopedia of Serial Killers.* New York: Diamond Books, 1992.

Martinez, Al. *Jigsaw John.* Los Angeles: J. P. Tarcher, 1975.

Morton, James. *Gangland International: An Informal History of the Mafia and Other Mobs in the Twentieth Century.* London: Little, Brown & Company, 1998.

Nickel, Steven. *Torso: The Story of Eliot Ness and the Search for a Psychopathic Killer.* Winston-Salem, N.C.: John F. Blair, 1989.

Pacios, Mary. *Childhood Shadows: The Hidden Story of the Black Dahlia Murder.* Downloaded and printed via electronic distribution from the World Wide Web. ISBN 1-58500-484-7, 1999.

Parrish, Michael. *For the People.* Los Angeles: Angel City Press, 2001.

Phillips, Michelle. *California Dreamin': The True Story of the Mamas and Papas.* New York: Warner, 1986.

Rappleye, Charles, and Ed Becker. *All American Mafioso: The Johnny Rosselli Story.* New York: Doubleday, 1991.

Reid, David. *Sex, Death and God in L.A.* New York: Random House, 1992.

Reid, Ed. *The Grim Reapers: The Anatomy of Organized Crime in America.* Chicago: Henry Regnery, 1969.

Richardson, James H. *For the Life of Me: Memoirs of a City Editor.* New York: G. P. Putnam's Sons, 1954.

Roeburt, John. *Get Me Giesler.* New York: Belmont Books, 1962.

Rothmiller, Mike, and Ivan G. Goldman. *L.A. Secret Police: Inside the L.A.P.D. Elite Spy Network*. New York: Pocket Books, 1992.

Rowan, David. *Famous American Crimes*. London: Frederick Muller, 1957.

Sade, Donatien-Alphonse-François de. *Selected Writings of de Sade*. New York: British Book Centre, 1954.

———. *The Complete Justine, Philosophy in the Bedroom and Other Writings*. New York: Grove Press, 1965.

———. *The 120 Days of Sodom and Other Writings*. New York: Grove Press, 1966.

———. *120 Days of Sodom, or the School for Libertinage*. New York: Falstaff Press, 1934.

Sakol, Jeannie. *The Birth of Marilyn: The Lost Photographs of Norma Jean by Joseph Jasgur*. New York: St. Martin's Press, 1991.

Seaver, Richard, Terry Southern, and Alexander Trocchi, eds. *Writers in Revolt: An Anthology*. New York: Frederick Fell, 1963.

Sjoquist, Arthur W. *Captain: Los Angeles Police Department 1869–1984*. Dallas: Taylor, 1984.

Smith, Jack. *Jack Smith's L.A.* New York: McGraw-Hill, 1980.

Starr, Kevin. *Inventing the Dream: California through the Progressive Era*. New York: Oxford University Press, 1985.

———. *The Dream Endures: California Enters the 1940s*. New York: Oxford University Press, 1997.

Sterling, Hank. *Ten Perfect Crimes*. New York: Stravon, 1954.

Stevenson, Robert Louis. *The Strange Case of Dr. Jekyll and Mr. Hyde and Other Stories*. New York: Barnes & Noble, 1995.

Stoker, Charles. *Thicker'n Thieves*. Santa Monica: Sidereal, 1951.

Tejaratchi, Sean, ed. *Death Scenes: A Homicide Detective's Scrapbook*. Portland: Feral House, 1996.

Terman, Lewis M. *Genetic Studies of Genius*. Vol. 1. Stanford: Stanford University Press, 1925.

Terman, Lewis M., and Melita H. Oden. *The Gifted Group at Mid-Life: Thirty-Five Years' Follow-Up of the Superior Child*. Stanford: Stanford University Press, 1959.

*True Crime—Unsolved Crimes*. Alexandria, Va.: Time-Life Books, 1993.

Tygiel, Jules. *The Great Los Angeles Swindle*. New York: Oxford University Press, 1994.

Viertel, Peter. *Dangerous Friends: At Large with Huston and Hemingway in the Fifties*. New York: Nan A. Talese/Bantam Doubleday Dell, 1992.

Underwood, Agness. *Newspaperwoman*. New York: Harper & Brothers, 1949.

Waldberg, Patrick. *Surrealism*. New York: Thames & Hudson, 1997.

Walker, Clifford James. *One Eye Closed the Other Red: The California Bootlegging Years*. Barstow, Calif.: Back Door Publishing, 1999.

Webb, Jack. *The Badge*. Greenwich, Conn.: Fawcett, 1958.

Weintraub, Alan. *Lloyd Wright: The Architecture of Frank Lloyd Wright Jr.* New York: Harry N. Abrams, 1998.

White, Leslie T. *Me, Detective*. New York: Harcourt, Brace & Company, 1936.

Wilson, Colin. *Murder in the 1940s*. New York: Carroll & Graf, 1993.

Wolf, Marvin J., and Katherine Mader. *Fallen Angels: Chronicles of L.A. Crime and Mystery*. New York: Facts on File, 1986.

## MAN RAY RESEARCH–RELATED BOOKS

Butterfield and Dunning. *Fine Photographs*. Catalog, November 17, 1999.

———. *Fine Photographs*. Catalog, May 27, 1999.

Foresta, Merry. *Perpetual Motif: The Art of Man Ray*. New York: Abbeville Press and the National Museum of American Art, 1988.

Man Ray. *Self Portrait*. Boston: Little, Brown & Company, 1963.

———. *Man Ray Photographs*. New York: Thames & Hudson, 1991.

Penrose, Roland. *Man Ray*. New York: Thames & Hudson, 1975.

Robert Berman Gallery. *Man Ray: Paris–L.A.* New York: Smart Art Press Art Catalog, 1996.

## MAGAZINE ARTICLES

Woodward, James. "Murder Casebook, Investigations into the Ultimate Crimes, 'Death for the Dahlia.'" *Marshall Cavendish Weekly*, vol. 1, part 15, Graphological insert analysis. London, 1990.

## NEWSPAPER/FOIA/INTERNET SOURCES

### Newspapers

#### Los Angeles Daily News

_____. "Woman Beaten to Death in Trip to 'See Hollywood.'" July 28, 1943.

_____. "Hot New Suspect in Murder of Girl." January 17, 1947.

_____. "Jail One in L.A. Murder, Hunt Another Man." January 18, 1947.

_____. "Vivid Women in Girl's Life." January 21, 1947.

_____. "All Citizens Urged to Aid in Dahlia Case." January 22, 1947.

_____. "Clues Break Fast in Dahlia Murder Case." January 23, 1947.

_____. "Black Purse, Shoes, Hot Dahlia Leads." January 24, 1947.

_____. "Shoe Clue, Black Book Aid Hunt." January 25, 1947.

_____. "New Note Taunts Police." January 27, 1947.

_____. "Police Ask Meeting with Dahlia Killer." January 27, 1947.

_____. "4th Dahlia Case Note." January 28, 1947.

_____. "Afraid to Surrender Slayer Writes Police." January 29, 1947.

_____. "Woman Slain in New L.A. 'Dahlia Murder.'" February 10, 1947.

_____. "Note Found." February 11, 1947.

_____. "Lie Test Demanded by Mate of Slain Nurse." February 11, 1947.

_____. "Body of Sixth Horror Murder Victim Found." May 12, 1947.

_____. "Girl Accused of Trying to Pin Dahlia Murder on Dad." February 17, 1949.

_____. "Tamar's Ma Calls Her an Awful Liar." February 22, 1949.

_____. "Jury Resumes Deliberation in Hodel Sex Trial." February 23, 1949.

_____. "Gambler Tired of Jailing Whenever a Girl Vanishes." October 13, 1949.

#### Los Angeles Examiner

_____. "Dancer Sought in Death Hunt." July 28, 1943.

_____. "Gardenia Death Suspect Named." August 5, 1943.

_____. "Jury Puzzled by Slaying." August 6, 1943.

————. "U.S. Joins Hunt for Gardenia Slayer Suspect." August 8, 1943.

————. "Oil Heiress Found Dead in Tub Mystery." October 13, 1944.

————. "Heiress Slain After Attack; Seek Soldier." October 14, 1944.

————. "Wife of Police Officer Found Shot to Death." March 11, 1946.

————. "Suspect Denies Knowledge of Crime, Admits Seeing Her." March 12, 1946.

————. "Police Get New Clew in Canyon Death." March 13, 1946.

————. "Slain Woman's Mate Gets Lie Detector Test." March 14, 1946.

————. "Quiz Sparks on Death Day." March 15, 1946.

————. "Woman's Nude Body Found in 'Lovers Lane.'" July 15, 1946.

————. "Dead Woman's Identity Believed Established." July 16, 1946.

————. "Police Jail Mate in 'Lipstick' Killing of Film Actress." January 11, 1947.

————. "Girl Torture Slaying Victim Identified by Examiner, FBI." January 17, 1947.

————. "Fiend Tortures, Kills Girl; Leaves Body in L.A. Lot." January 17, 1947.

————. "Death Victim Looked Worried Says Landlady." January 18, 1947.

————. "Miss Short Sought Help in Earlier Plight, Says Taxi Stand Manager." January 18, 1947.

————. "Red and Car Described in Black Dahlia Death." January 19, 1947.

————. "Elizabeth Short's Letters Told Feelings about Love and Marriage." January 19, 1947.

————. "Letters Tell of Lost Loves." January 20, 1947.

————. "Former Air Force Musician Tells of Trip from San Diego." January 20, 1947.

————. "Dahlia Phone Call Tracked." January 20, 1947.

————. "Elizabeth Short's Letters Reveal Hopes for Service Marriage." January 21, 1947.

————. "Night Spots Yield New Clews on Slain Girl." January 22, 1947.

————. "Black Dahlia, Man Traces to Hotel: Pictures Identified." January 22, 1947.

———. "2 Women Sought in 'Dahlia' Slaying: New Clews Found." January 23, 1947.

———. "To Motel." January 24, 1947.

———. "Jealous Blonde Pal of 'Dahlia' Sought on ex-Jockey's Tip." January 24, 1947.

———. "Hot New Suspect in Murder of Girl." January 24, 1947.

———. "Dahlia Killer Mails Contents of Missing Purse to Examiner." January 25, 1947.

———. "Police Await Black Dahlia Slayer's Pledged Surrender." January 28, 1947.

———. "Ex-Employer Tells Seeing Short Girl with Blonde, Brunette Women." January 29, 1947.

———. "Werewolf May Be Musician Says Handwriting Expert." January 29, 1947.

———. "Man Confesses Black Dahlia Slaying; Surrenders to Police" January 29, 1947.

———. "Identify Mystery Picture in Black Dahlia Poison Pen Note." January 31, 1947.

———. "Photo Taken From L.A. Boy by Footpad." January 31, 1947.

———. "Police Seek Dahlia Killer's Hideaway Outside of City." February 1, 1947.

———. "Soldier Tale of 'Dahlia' Killing Falling Apart." February 10, 1947.

———. "Black Dahlia Note Studied." February 11, 1947.

———. "Lipstick Slaying Victim's Supper Companion Sought." February 13, 1947.

———. " 'Date' by Phone Revealed in Lipstick Case." February 14, 1947.

———. "Dark-Haired Man Sought As Key to Killing Mysteries." February 16, 1947.

———. "New L.A. Slaying May Yield Clew to Dahlia Killing." February 17, 1947.

———. "Women May Link Dahlia Slaying to Print Shop Killing." February 18, 1947.

———. " 'Dream Killer' to Face Women." February 18, 1947.

———. "New Clue." February 20, 1947.

———. "2 Women Brutally Slain; Bludgeon Death Follows Pattern of Dahlia Killer." March 12, 1947.

———. "New Horror Killing." May 13, 1947.

———. "Police Find Trelstad Clew." May 15, 1947.

———. "L.A. Real Estate Woman Slain in Vacant Building." February 17, 1948.

———. "Note May Be Slaying Clew." February 17, 1948.

———. "New Clew to Woman's Slayer." February 18, 1948.

———. "Jury to Quiz Seven Officers in Black Dahlia Slaying." February 7, 1949.

———. "Mother Kidnaped, Slain; Seek Curly-Haired Man in New 'Black Dahlia' Case." June 17, 1949.

———. "Rope, Other New Clews Spur Hunt for Mad Slayer." June 20, 1949.

———. "Glamour Girl Body Hunted: Parallel to 'Dahlia' Case Seen." October 12, 1949.

———. "Man in Jail Faces Quiz on Glamour Girl." October 13, 1949.

*Los Angeles Herald Examiner*

———. "Capt. Jack Donahoe Dies." June 20, 1966.

———. "Big Brawls Bump Business in Taxi Heyday." March 21, 1976.

*Los Angeles Herald Express*

———. "Find Heiress Car in Tub Death Mystery." October 13, 1944.

———. "Lover's Lane Murder." July 15, 1946.

———. "Find Car in Murder Mystery." July 18, 1946.

———. "Girl Brutally Slain by Fiend in Vacant Lot." July 20, 1946.

———. "L.A. Doctor Tells Mind of Killer." January 17, 1947.

———. "Hunt Boy Friends in Torture Killing." January 17, 1947.

———. "Girl's Friend Tells Plans for Marriage." January 17, 1947.

———. "Policewoman Tells Seeing Girl 'Scared of Boy Friend.'" January 17, 1947.

———. "Dahlia's Love Missives in Romance with Flier." January 18, 1947.

———. "Boy Friend's Love Letters to 'Black Dahlia' Bared." January 18, 1947.

———. "Taxi Manager Tells Attack Episode." January 18, 1947.

————. "Dahlia in Love, Slain Girl's Letters Found Un-mailed." January 20, 1947.

————. "Red Tells Own Story of Romance with Dahlia." January 20, 1947.

————. "Find Dahlia Trail in Night Spots." January 21, 1947.

————. "Dahlia's Letters, Bare Slain Girl's Desire to Wed." January 21, 1947.

————. "Check Women Pals in Torture Murder." January 21, 1947.

————. "Pastor Seized at 'Dahlia' Inquest; Mother Testifies." January 22, 1947.

————. "Search City Dump." January 24, 1947.

————. "Bossy Blonde Friend of 'Black Dahlia' Sought." January 24, 1947.

————. "Check Names in Dahlia Book." January 25, 1947.

————. "Red Identifies Shoes of Werewolf Victim." January 25, 1947.

————. "Dahlia Killer Offers Surrender." January 27, 1947.

————. "Convict-Artist Tells Painting 'Dahlia' As Model." January 27, 1947.

————. "Dahlia Work of Same Man, Tests Show." January 28, 1947.

————. "Poison Pen Enters 'Dahlia' Murder." January 30, 1947.

————. "Identify Mystery Picture in 'Black Dahlia' Poison Pen Note." January 31, 1947.

————. "Hunt Murder Den." February 1, 1947

————. "Dahlia Seen in Lost Week." February 1, 1947.

————. "Noted Author Sees Arrest of 'Dahlia' Killer Soon." February 3, 1947.

————. "Attacker Subdues Woman Near 'Dahlia' Murder Spot." February 3, 1947.

————. "Latin Suspect Sought in San Diego." February 4, 1947.

————. "Kills L.A. Woman, Writes B.D. on Body." February 10, 1947.

————. "Mystery Note Left in Cab Offers New 'Dahlia' Clue." February 11, 1947.

————. "Werewolf Mysteries Deepen: Killer Footprint Is Not Husband's." February 11, 1947.

————. "Quiz Mystery Man Sharing P.O. Box of 'Lipstick' Victim." February 12, 1947.

————. "Attack Victim—Woman Threatened with 'Dahlia' Fate." February 12, 1947.

———. "Man in Print Shop Killing Tells 'Murder in a Dream.'" February 17, 1947.

———. "New Dahlia Clue." February 20, 1947.

———. "Body Found on Lot, Strangled with Pajamas." May 12, 1947.

———. "Hunt Suspect in So. Cal. Divorcee Murder." July 18, 1947.

———. "Police Missed Mad Killer, in Auto with Slain Victim, Parked Near Squad Car." June 18, 1949.

———. "Doctor Nabbed on Hollywood Incest Charge." October 7, 1949.

———. "Cryptic Note Clue to Missing Actress Mystery." October 10, 1949.

———. "Spangler Mystery Deepens." October 11, 1949.

———. "Probe Dancer's 'Secret Date' with Death." October 12, 1949.

———. "Spangler Mystery Recalls Grim List of Atrocities." October 12, 1949.

———. "Sift Old Romances of Missing Dancer." October 13, 1949.

———. "Weird L.A. Mystery in 5 Missing Persons." October 14, 1949.

———. "Unsolved L.A. Crimes Ripped by Grand Jury." January 12, 1950.

*Los Angeles Mirror*

———. "Murder Victims' Bodies Found at These Spots." June 12, 1949.

———. "Sex Death Quiz Turns to Husband." June 29, 1949.

———. "Bel-Air Socialite Missing in Mystery." August 24, 1949.

———. "Purse Clouds Widow's Fate." August 25, 1949.

———. "Public Aid Asked in Missing Widow Hunt." August 27, 1949.

———. "Wife of L.A. Abortionist in Hiding." September 17, 1949.

———. "L.A.'s Missing Mimi Ruled Legally Dead." September 30, 1949.

———. "TV Actress Feared Sex Murder Victim." October 12, 1949.

———. "Grandma Calls Tamar Hodel 'Untruthful.'" December 22, 1949.

*Los Angeles Times*

———. "Body of Beaten Woman Found on Golf Course." July 28, 1943.

———. "Woman Gives Clue to Killing on Golf Course." August 5, 1943.

———. "Sister's 'Hunch' Failed to Deter Murder Victim." August 6, 1943.

———. "Sex Fiend Slaying." January 17, 1947.

————. "Father Located Here." January 18, 1947.

————. "Actress Questioned." January 18, 1947.

————. "Airline Pilot Found in South Denies Betrothal." January 18, 1947.

————. "Girlfriends Questioned." January 18, 1947.

————. "Lived in Hollywood." January 18, 1947.

————. "Daughter Just Quiet, Home Girl, Mother Asserts." January 19, 1947.

————. "Woman Slain in Hollywood Mystery; Police Seek Anonymous Note Writer." February 17, 1948.

————. "Mystery Man Aids Hunt for Slayer of Mrs. Kern." February 19, 1948.

————. "Doctor Faces Accusation in Morals Case." October 7, 1949.

————. "Lost Actress Jovial as She Left Home." October 12, 1949.

————. "A Slaying Cloaked in Mystery and Myths." January 6, 1997.

*New York Times*

————. "President Truman's UNRRA Message to Congress." November 13, 1945.

*The San Diego Union*

————. "Divorcee Victim of Mystery Slaying." July 18, 1947.

————. "One Man Cleared in Murder Case." July 20, 1947.

————. "Woman Quizzed Again in Divorcee's Slaying." July 23, 1947.

*Washington News*

————. "Cops Seeking Female Sadist." January 21, 1947.

**Miscellaneous References**

FBI File. Elizabeth Ann Short. FOIA.

FBI File. George Hill Hodel. FOIA.

FBI Office Memorandum from Elizabeth Short file, 8 typed pages, March 27, 1947. FOIA.

Los Angeles Library Photo Database information printed on JPEG No. 73 of 84.

Los Angeles County Certificate of Death, No. 7097-029628 in name of John Arthur Donahoe.

## Internet References

Please note that Internet references are by nature unpredictable, and that Web sites listed in this section may not be current.

www.bethshort.com. Site editorial, Pamela Hazelton, LAPD interview with Detective Brian Carr.

http://www.apbnews.com/. Valerie Kalfrin, "Writer Reopens Black Dahlia Murder Case."

http://www.Larryharnisch. Black Dahlia and Dr. Walter Bayley references.

http://www.latimes.com. *Los Angeles Times* archives.

http://www.lapl.com. Los Angeles Public Library.

# Index

(SH refers to Steven Hodel; GH refers to George Hodel.)

Hodel, George Hill: arrest of, 90–93, 553*n*; art
collection of, 79, 212, 243–44, 258–59,
262, 430, 472, 476, 477; artistic aspirations
of, 88, 555, 557; birth of, 30, 57; as child
prodigy, 30, 57–58, 459, 460; childhood
and youth of, 30, 57–59, 459, 460; children
of, 31, 32–33, 34, 35, 41–42, 110, 112;
cover story of, 79; death of, 22–23, 29, 30,
31–33, 34, 436, 449; as doctor/surgeon,
30–31, 71–73, 74–78, 82–83, 254, 529–30;
early jobs of, 59–65, 66–67, 68, 71, 72–73,
182; education of, 30, 57, 58–59, 71, 460;
as father, 23, 31, 74, 80, 82–83, 84–85, 103,
109, 204–5, 250, 327; flees U.S., 538*n*,
553*n*; friends of, 34, 70, 85; funeral/burial
of, 33, 44, 229; "genius mentality" of, 30,
58, 460, 462; health of, 26–27, 28, 44, 54,
78, 98, 258–59, 261, 262, 429; intended
suicide of, 54, 275; Le Berthon's article
about, 66–68, 272; marriages of, 31, 47,
101, 110; notes of, 44, 45–46, 52–54, 275,
348; office of, 528, 534; personal
background of, 30–31, 56–57; personal
effects of, 54, 348; personality of, 23,
24–25, 31, 47, 59, 67, 87, 112, 113, 224,
253–54, 292, 445–46, 459–60, 535, 535*n*;
photographs of, 37, 78, 92, 223, 224, 253,
265–66, 267, 275, 312, 426, 428, 493,
529–530, 538, 538*n*; photography interests
of, 70, 92, 209, 275, 348, 424*n*; physical
appearance of, 75, 82, 112, 224; physical
violence by, 204–5; professional
background of, 24, 30–31, 34–35, 75, 110,
182, 529–30; sexual fantasies of, 61; as
sexually precocious, 460; SH compared
with, 24–25; and SH's application to
LAPD, 119–20; SH's letters to and from,
26–29, 246–50, 256, 307–8; SH's personal
feelings about, 455–62; SH's relationship
with, 23–26, 28–29, 31, 45, 107–8, 109,
110–14, 246–50, 448, 456–57, 461; SH's
strategy for investigating, 47–49; will of,
35, 229. *See also specific person or topic*
Hodel, George Hill Sr., 30, 38, 41–42, 56–58,
59, 73
Hodel, Hortensia, 31, 40, 47, 110, 112–13,
112*n*, 113, 214
Hodel, John Dion, 32–33, 74, 219
Hodel, June: and GH's death/burial, 22, 29,
30, 32, 33, 34, 35, 44–45, 48; GH's
marriage to, 47; GH's note to, 52–54,
275, 348; GH's proposed talk with, 44, 54;
GH's relationship with, 25, 27, 29, 30, 47,
52–53, 54; and GH's will, 35; knowledge
of GH of, 35–36, 47–48; personal and
professional background of, 29–30; and
photo album, 36, 41; SH's relationship
with, 26, 31
Hodel, Kelvin, 121, 250, 266, 351; Barrett's

relationship with, 210; childhood and
youth of, 31, 37, 74, 75, 80, 82, 83, 84,
85, 90, 101, 102, 103–9, 204–5, 327; and
GH's death, 33; and SH's personal
feelings about GH, 457; SH's relationship
with, 116
Hodel, Mark, 33
Hodel, Michael, 116, 121, 250, 351; and
Barrett's knife, 313, 316; childhood and
youth of, 31, 37, 73, 75, 80, 82, 83, 84,
85, 90, 101, 102, 103–9, 114, 204–5, 327;
and GH's death, 32; Huston as father of,
73; professional career of, 114; and SH's
personal feelings about GH, 457
Hodel, Ramon, 33
Hodel, Steven: Bellingham home of, 22, 26,
48, 128–29, 455, 457–59; birth of, 74,
219; childhood and youth of, 37, 75, 80,
82–85, 90, 101–2, 103–9, 204–5, 327,
495–96; GH's letters to and from, 26–29,
246–50, 256, 307–8; GH's relationship
with, 23–26, 28–29, 31, 45, 107–8, 109,
110–14, 246–50, 448, 456–57, 461; Kiyo's
marriage to, 115–27; Los Angeles home
of, 216, 262; naming of, 351–52, 456;
Navy service of, 103, 109, 110–14, 116;
personal feelings about GH of, 455–62;
personal heroes of, 456; professional
background of, 1–2, 23, 24, 51, 246, 257,
367, 391, 440, 449, 461
Hodel, Tamar: abortion/pregnancy of, 93,
202–3, 205–6, 208, 212, 343–44, 345,
482, 484, 485; and Barrett, 95, 96; birth
of, 71; childhood and youth of, 72, 73,
75, 84, 85, 202, 264; children of, 209,
424, 424*n*, 449; and DA's investigation,
501, 543; and Dorero's accusations
against GH, 207, 492, 501; Dorero's
relationship with, 203, 204, 207, 492,
501; Duncan's memories of, 214;
"Elizabeth Anne" doll of, 203–4; in films,
90; at Franklin Street House, 84, 85, 90;
and GH as suspect in Black Dahlia case,
95–96, 206, 207, 215, 529; and GH's
death, 32; and Huston, 204; image of,
200, 201; and incest trial, 90–102, 120,
201, 205, 206–7, 208, 210–12, 213,
214–15, 543, 553*n*, 555; and "Jane Doe"
murder, 414; Man Ray's photographs of,
204, 211, 264; Moe's memories about,
221; and Morgan connection, 449;
photographs of, 95, 204, 211, 218, 264;
public support for, 505; as runaway,
90–91, 203, 205–6, 207; Sexton's rape of,
90, 94, 96, 97, 98–100, 216, 221; SH's
conversations/interviews with, 202–15,
230, 529; and SH's personal feelings
about GH, 457; SH's relationship with,
84, 201, 264; and Spangler murder, 331